SKILLS for Success
Premium Media Site

Improve your grade with hands-on tools and resources!

- Master *Key Terms* to expand your vocabulary.
- Prepare for exams by taking practice quizzes in the *Online Chapter Review*.
- Download *Student Data Files* for the application projects in each chapter.

And for even more tools, you can access the following Premium Resources using your Access Code. Register now to get the most out of *Skills for Success!*

- *Student Training Videos* are instructor-led videos that walk through each skill in a chapter.*
- *BizSkills Videos* cover the important business skills students need to be successful—Interviewing, Communication, Dressing for Success, and more.*

*Access code required for these premium resources

Your Access Code is:

Note: If there is no silver foil covering the access code, it may already have been redeemed, and therefore may no longer be valid. In that case, you can purchase online access using a major credit card or PayPal account. To do so, go to **www.pearsonhighered.com/skills**, select your book cover, click on "Buy Access" and follow the on-screen instructions.

To Register:

- To start you will need a valid email address and this access code.
- Go to **www.pearsonhighered.com/skills** and scroll to find your text book.
- Once you've selected your text, on the Home Page for the book, click the link to access the Student Premium Content.
- Click the Register button and follow the on-screen instructions.
- After you register, you can sign in any time via the log-in area on the same screen.

System Requirements

Windows 7 Ultimate Edition; IE 8
Windows Vista Ultimate Edition SP1; IE 8
Windows XP Professional SP3; IE 7
Windows XP Professional SP3; Firefox 3.6.4
Mac OS 10.5.7; Firefox 3.6.4
Mac OS 10.6; Safari 5

Technical Support

http://247pearsoned.custhelp.com

SKILLS
For SUCCESS

with Microsoft®
Office 2013

TOWNSEND | **HAIN** | **MURRE WOLF**

PEARSON

Boston Columbus Indianapolis New York San Francisco Upper Saddle River
Amsterdam Cape Town Dubai London Madrid Milan Munich Paris Montréal Toronto
Delhi Mexico City São Paulo Sydney Hong Kong Seoul Singapore Taipei Tokyo

Library of Congress Cataloging-in-Publication Data

Townsend, Kris.

  Skills for success with Microsoft Office 2013 / Kris Townsend, Catherine Hain, Stephanie Murre Wolf. — 1st edition.
    pages cm
  ISBN-13: 978-0-13-314268-6
  ISBN-10: 0-13-314268-X
  1. Microsoft Office.   2. Business—Computer programs.   I. Hain, Catherine.   II. Wolf, Stephanie Murre.   III. Title.
  HF5548.4.M525T688 2013
  005.5—dc23

                                                                              2013002494

Editor in Chief: *Michael Payne*
Executive Editor: *Jenifer Niles*
Product Development Manager: *Laura Burgess*
Editorial Project Manager: *Carly Prakapas*
Editorial Assistant: *Andra Skaalrud*
Development Editor: *Nancy Lamm*
Director of Business & Technology Marketing: *Maggie Leen*
Marketing Manager: *Brad Forrester*
Marketing Coordinator: *Susan Osterlitz*
Marketing Assistant: *Darshika Vyas*
Managing Editor: *Camille Trentacoste*
Senior Operation Manager/Site Lead: *Nick Sklitsis*

Operations Specialist: *Maura Zaldivar-Garcia*
Senior Art Director: *Jonathan Boylan*
Text and Cover Designer: *Jonathan Boylan*
Director of Media Development: *Taylor Ragan*
Media Project Manager, Production: *John Cassar*
Full-Service Project Management: *Jouve North America*
Full-Service Project Manager: *Kevin Bradley*
Composition: *Jouve*
Printer/Binder: *Quad Graphics/Eusey Press Inc.*
Cover Printer: *Lehigh-Phoenix Color/Hagerstown*
Typeface: *Palatino LT Std Roman 10/12*

Credits and acknowledgments borrowed from other sources and reproduced, with permission, in this textbook appear on appropriate page within text.

10 9 8 7 6 5 4 3 2
ISBN-10: 0-13-351211-8
ISBN-13: 978-0-13-351211-3

Contents in Brief

Table of Contents

Part 3 | Microsoft Office
Microsoft Word

Microsoft Excel

Microsoft Access

Contributors

We'd like to thank the following people for their work on Skills for Success:

Focus Group Participants

Rose Volynskiy	*Howard Community College*
Fernando Paniagua	*The Community College of Baltimore County*
Jeff Roth	*Heald College*
William Bodine	*Mesa Community College*
Lex Mulder	*College of Western Idaho*
Kristy McAuliffe	*San Jacinto College South*
Jan Hime	*University of Nebraska, Lincoln*
Deb Fells	*Mesa Community College*

Reviewers

Barbara Anderson	*Lake Washington Institute of Technology*
Janet Anderson	*Lake Washington Institute of Technology*
Ralph Argiento	*Guilford Technical Community College*
Tanisha Arnett	*Pima County Community College*
Greg Ballinger	*Miami Dade College*
Autumn Becker	*Allegany College of Maryland*
Bob Benavides	*Collin College*
Howard Blauser	*North GA Technical College*
William Bodine	*Mesa Community College*
Nancy Bogage	*The Community College of Baltimore County*
Maria Bright	*San Jacinto College*
Adell Brooks	*Hinds Community College*
Judy Brown	*Western Illinois University*
Maria Brownlow	*Chaminade*
Jennifer Buchholz	*UW Washington County*
Kathea Buck	*Gateway Technical College*
LeAnn Cady	*Minnesota State College—Southeast Technical*
John Cameron	*Rio Hondo College*
Tammy Campbell	*Eastern Arizona College*
Patricia Christian	*Southwest Georgia Technical College*
Tina Cipriano	*Gateway Technical College*
Paulette Comet	*The Community College of Baltimore County*
Jean Condon	*Mid-Plains Community College*
Joy DePover	*Minneapolis. Com. & Tech College*
Gina Donovan	*County College of Morris*
Alina Dragne	*Flagler College*
Russ Dulaney	*Rasmussen College*
Mimi Duncan	*University of Missouri St. Louis*
Paula Jo Elson	*Sierra College*
Bernice Eng	*Brookdale Community College*
Jill Fall	*Gateway Technical College*
Deb Fells	*Mesa Community College*
Tushnelda C Fernandez	*Miami Dade College*
Jean Finley	*Asheville-Buncombe Technical Community College*
Jim Flannery	*Central Carolina Community College*
Alyssa Foskey	*Wiregrass Georgia Technical College*
David Freer	*Miami Dade College*
Marvin Ganote	*University of Dayton*
David Grant	*Paradise Valley Community College*
Clara Groeper	*Illinois Central College*
Carol Heeter	*Ivy Tech Community College*
Jan Hime	*University of Nebraska*
Marilyn Holden	*Gateway Technical College*
Ralph Hunsberger	*Bucks County Community College*
Juan Iglesias	*University of Texas at Brownsville*
Carl Eric Johnson	*Great Bay Community College*
Joan Johnson	*Lake Sumter Community College*
Mech Johnson	*UW Washington County*
Deborah Jones	*Southwest Georgia Technical College*
Hazel Kates	*Miami-Dade College, Kendall Campus*
Jane Klotzle	*Lake Sumter Community College*
Kurt Kominek	*Northeast State Community College*
Vivian Krenzke	*Gateway Technical College*
Renuka Kumar	*Community College of Baltimore County*
Lisa LaCaria	*Central Piedmont Community College*
Sue Lannen	*Brazosport College*
Freda Leonard	*Delgado Community College*
Susan Mahon	*Collin College*
Nicki Maines	*Mesa Community College*
Pam Manning	*Gateway Technical College*
Juan Marquez	*Mesa Community College*

Alysia Martinez	*Gateway Technical College*	Jeff Roth	*Heald College*
Kristy McAuliffe	*San Jacinto College*	Diane Ruscito	*Brazosport College*
Robert McCloud	*Sacred Heart University*	June Scott	*County College of Morris*
Susan Miner	*Lehigh Carbon Community College*	Vicky Seehusen	*MSU Denver*
Namdar Mogharreban	*Southern Illinois University*	Emily Shepard	*Central Carolina Community College*
Daniel Moix	*College of the Ouachitas*	Pamela Silvers	*A-B Tech*
Lindsey Moore	*Wiregrass Georgia Technical College*	Martha Soderholm	*York College*
Lex Mulder	*College of Western Idaho*	Yaacov Sragovich	*Queensborough Community College*
Patricia Newman	*Cuyamaca College*	Jody Sterr	*Blackhawk Technical College*
Melinda Norris	*Coker College*	Julia Sweitzer	*Lake-Sumter Community College*
Karen Nunan	*Northeast State Community College*	Laree Thomas	*Okefenokee Technical College*
Fernando Paniagua	*The Community College of Baltimore County*	Joyce Thompson	*Lehigh Carbon Community College*
Christine Parrish	*Southwest Georgia Technical College*	Barbara Tietsort	*University of Cincinnati, Blue Ash College*
Linda Pennachio	*Mount Saint Mary College*	Rose Volynskiy	*Howard Community College*
Amy Pezzimenti	*Ocean County College*	Sandra Weber	*Gateway Technical College*
Leah Ramalingam	*Riversity City College*	Steven Weitz	*Lehigh Carbon Community College*
Mary Rasley	*Lehigh Carbon Community College*	Berthenia Williams	*Savannah Technical College*
Cheryl Reuss	*Estrella Mountain Community College*	David Wilson	*Parkland College*
Wendy Revolinski	*Gateway Technical College*	Allan Wood	*Great Bay Community College*
Kenneth Rogers	*Cecil College*	Roger Yaeger	*Estrella Mountain Community College*

What's New For Office 2013

With Office 2013, Microsoft is taking the office to the cloud. The Skills for Success series shows students how to get the most out of Office 2013 no matter what device they are using—a traditional desktop or tablet.

Whether you are tapping and sliding with your finger or clicking and dragging with the mouse, Skills for Success shows you the way with the hallmark visual, two-page, easy-to-follow design. It covers the essential skills students need to know to get up and running with Office quickly, and it addresses Web Apps, touch screens, and the collaborative approach of Office 365. Once students complete the Instructional Skills, they put their knowledge to work with a progression of review, problem-solving, and challenging, end-of-chapter projects.

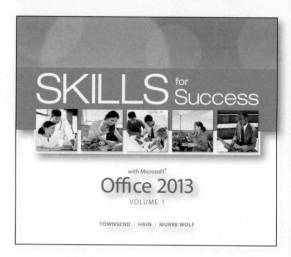

What's New for Office 2013

3 new chapters—Intro to Computer Concepts, Windows 8, and Internet Explorer 10 give you all the content you need to teach your course!

Coverage of new features of Office 2013 in an approach that is easy and effective for teaching students the skills they need to get started with Microsoft Office.

Skills Summary—new summary chart of all the Skills and Procedures covered in the chapter makes remembering what was covered easier!

Application Introductions—provide a brief overview of each application and put the chapters in context for students.

Student Training Videos—new, author-created training videos for each Skill in the chapters!

Application Capstone Projects—each application will conclude with a capstone project to help students and instructors ensure that students are ready to move onto the next application. These will also be grader projects in MyITLab.

Integrated Projects—integrated projects follow each application so that as students learn a new application, they also learn how to use it with other applications.

Office Online / Web App Projects (formerly Collaboration Project)—use a variety of the web apps available at the end of each application. Also includes an "On Your Own" project to let students try an additional project.

Additional Grader Projects—two new grader projects based on the Skills Review provide a broader variety of homework and assessment options; written by the book authors.

New Training and Assessment Simulations—written by the book authors to provide enhanced one-to-one content match in MyITlab.

OneDrive (formerly SkyDrive) Coverage included in the Common Features chapter.

Office 365 Coverage included in the Concepts chapter.

MOS mapping—located on the Instructor Resource Site provides a guide to where the MOS Core exam objectives are covered in the book, on the Companion website, and in MyITLab to help students prepare to ace the exam!

Skills for Success

with Microsoft® Office 2013 Volume 1

- **10 × 8.5 Format**—Easy for students to read and type at the same time by simply propping the book up on the desk in front of their monitor

- **Clearly Outlined Skills**—Each skill is presented in a single two-page spread so that students can easily follow along

- **Numbered Steps and Bulleted Text**—Students don't read long paragraphs of text, instead they get a step-by-step, concise presentation

- **Broad Coverage of Skills**—Gives students the knowledge needed to get up and running quickly

NEW Application Introductions provide students with a concise overview of each application to put the chapters in context

Two Page Chapter Introduction—Briefs students on what is important and sets the stage for the project they will create

File Summary—A quick summary of the files the students need to open and the names of the files they will turn in

Outcome—Shows students up front what their completed project will look like

Clock—Tells how much time students need to complete the chapter

Student Training Videos for each Skill in the chapter provide a personal, instructor-led walk through

Sequential Pagination—Saves you and your students time in locating topics and assignments

Skills List—A visual snapshot of what skills they will complete in the chapter

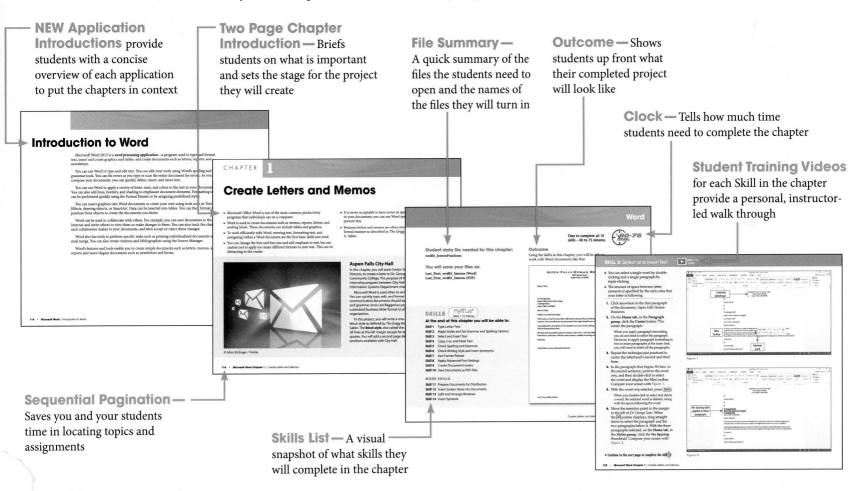

Skills for Success

Written for Today's Students — Skills are taught with numbered steps and bulleted text so students are less likely to skip valuable information

Two-Page Spreads — Each skill is presented in a concise, two-page spread to give students the visual illustration right with the steps—no flipping pages

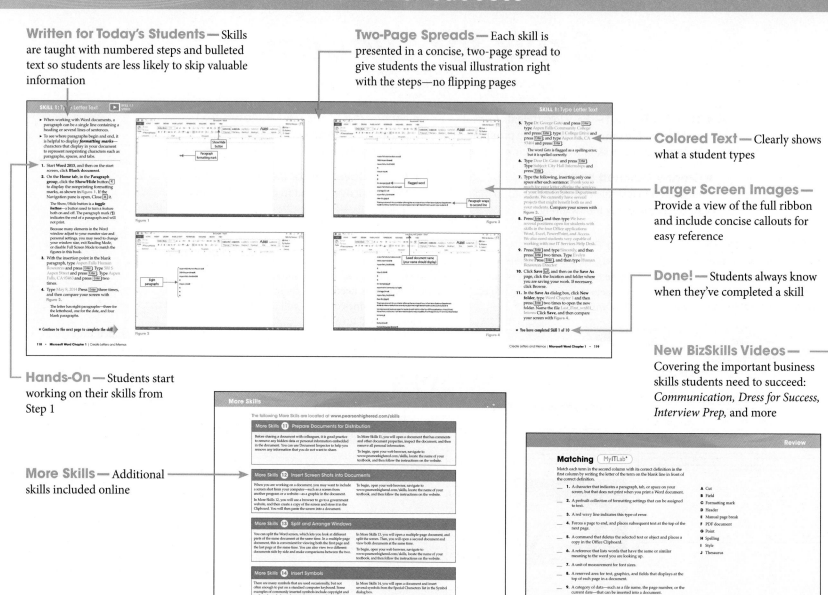

Colored Text — Clearly shows what a student types

Larger Screen Images — Provide a view of the full ribbon and include concise callouts for easy reference

Done! — Students always know when they've completed a skill

Hands-On — Students start working on their skills from Step 1

More Skills — Additional skills included online

New BizSkills Videos — Covering the important business skills students need to succeed: *Communication, Dress for Success, Interview Prep,* and more

End-of-Chapter Material—Several levels of review and assessment so you can assign the material that best fits your students' needs

NEW Skills and Procedures Summary Chart—Provides a quick review of the skills and tasks covered in each chapter

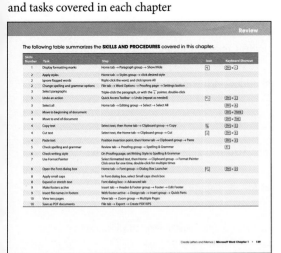

A stronger progression from point and click to practice, and to critical thinking.

From Point and Click to Critical Thinking

Skills 1–10 Guided learning	Annotated linear steps that tell 'where to click' and why.
Skills Review Guided practice	Linear steps that tell them 'where to click' one more time.
2 Skills Assessments Independent practice	Linear steps that tell them 'what to click' but not necessarily where.
Visual Skills Assessment Non-linear problem-solving	Students determine their own steps to create the document shown in the figure and described in the directions.
My Skills Transfer of skills	Students transfer their skills to a different scenario—a personal document, instead of business document.
Skills Challenge 1 Apply skills to fix problems	Typically a document that needs 'fixed' by apply the skills in the chapter. The problems are described in a way that the *challenge* is deciding how to fix the problems, not figuring out what the directions mean or how it will be graded.
Skills Challenge 2 Conduct research to solve a problem	Typically a project that requires some research to determine the content of the document. Directions are written in a way that the *challenge* is deciding what to say and how best to format the document, not figuring out what the directions mean or how it will be graded.

NEW MyITLab grader project covering all 10 skills (homework and assessment versions)

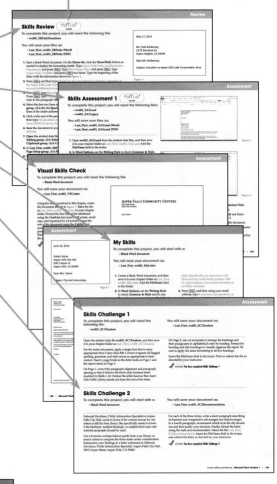

Integrated Projects—Follow each application so they are easier to manage and provide practice immediately after students work with each new application.

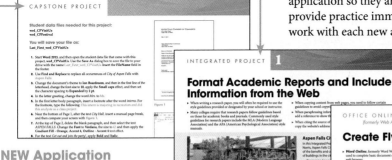

NEW Application Capstone—

For each application we provide a comprehensive project covering all of the Skills. Also available as a Grader project in MyITLab.

Office Online (formerly Web App) Projects—Students use Cloud computing to save files; create, edit, and share Office documents using Office Online; and create Windows Live groups.

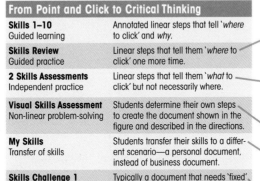

Skills for Success

MyITLab (MyITLab®)

Skills for Success combined with MyITLab gives you a completely integrated solution: Instruction, Training, & Assessment

- eText
- Training & Assessment Simulations
- Grader Projects

Student Videos!

Student Training Videos — Each skill within a chapter comes with an instructor-led video that walks students through each skill.

 (BizSkills Video) Cover the important business skills students need to be successful—*Interviewing, Communication, Dressing for Success,* and more.

Student Data — Files are all available on the Companion Website using the access code included with your book.
pearsonhighered.com/skills

Instructor Materials

NEW Application Capstone Projects — Covering all of the Skills for each application. Also available as MyITLab grader projects

NEW MOS map — Guides you and your students to coverage of the MOS Exam objectives for each application

Instructor's Manual — Teaching tips and additional resources for each chapter

Student Assignment Tracker — Lists all the assignments for the chapter; you just add in the course information, due dates and points. Providing these to students ensures they will know what is due and when

Scripted Lectures — Classroom lectures prepared for you

Annotated Solution Files — Coupled with the scoring rubrics, these create a grading and scoring system that makes grading so much easier for you

PowerPoint Lectures — PowerPoint presentations for each chapter

Audio PPTs — Provide an audio version of the PowerPoint presentations for each chapter

Prepared Exams — Exams for each chapter and for each application

NEW Detailed Scoring Rubrics — Can be used either by students to check their work or by you as a quick check-off for the items that need to be corrected

Syllabus Templates — For 8-week, 12-week, and 16-week courses

Test Bank — Includes a variety of test questions for each chapter

Companion Website — Online content such as the More Skills Projects, Online Chapter Review, Glossary, and Student Data Files are all at www.pearsonhighered.com/skills

All Student and Instructor Materials available at our Companion Websites ... pearsonhighered.com/skills

About the Authors

Kris Townsend is an Information Systems instructor at Spokane Falls Community College in Spokane, Washington. Kris earned a bachelor's degree in both Education and Business, and a master's degree in Education. He has also worked as a public school teacher and as a systems analyst. Kris enjoys working with wood, geocaching, and photography. He commutes to work by bike and also is a Lewis and Clark historical reenactor.

Catherine Hain is an instructor at Central New Mexico Community College in Albuquerque, New Mexico. She teaches computer applications classes in the Business and Information Technology School, both in the classroom and through the distance learning office. Catherine holds a bachelor's degree in Management and Marketing and a master's degree in Business Administration.

Stephanie Murre Wolf is a Technology and Computer Applications instructor at Moraine Park Technical College in Wisconsin. She is a graduate of Alverno College and enjoys teaching, writing curriculum, and authoring textbooks. In addition to classroom instruction, Stephanie actively performs corporate training in technology. She is married and has two sons; together, the family enjoys the outdoors.

A Special Thank You

Pearson Prentice Hall gratefully acknowledges the contribution made by Shelley Gaskin to the first edition publication of this series—*Skills for Success with Office 2007*. The series has truly benefited from her dedication toward developing a textbook that aims to help students and instructors. We thank her for her continued support of this series.

CHAPTER 1

Getting Started with Computer Concepts

▶ The computer is a system with many parts that perform specific functions. Understanding how these functions work helps you to become more effective when using computers to accomplish tasks.

▶ There are many types of computers, but they all work in a similar manner.

▶ Understanding how a computer works requires an understanding of the main purpose of the hardware and software on that computer.

▶ Networks, the Internet, and The Cloud have become integral parts of most computer systems.

▶ Understanding computers as systems also helps you to make informed decisions when solving problems, upgrading, or purchasing a computer.

© violetkaipa

Introduction

Computers are an integral part of daily life. You interact with them when banking, checking out books from the library, shopping, registering for classes, or having your car assessed by a repair shop.

Because you interact with computers on a daily basis, it is important to become knowledgeable about computers: how they work, how to troubleshoot problems, and how to make an informed decision when purchasing a computer system. Solid working knowledge about computers enhances your career possibilities and also makes your daily life easier.

This chapter will familiarize you with some of the fundamentals of a computer system, such as computer hardware and software, different types of computers, basics of computer networks, an overview of saving and storage, and an understanding of Cloud computing as well as an introduction to Office 365. All of these concepts can help you understand how to work with computers and how to make informed decisions when purchasing computer systems.

Time to complete all 10 concepts – 60 to 90 minutes

60-90 min.

Student data files needed for this chapter:

No documents are needed or created in this chapter.

Outcome

Using the concepts in this chapter, you will be able to answer questions like these:

- ▶ What is the difference between a reader, tablet, ultrabook, notebook, and desktop computer?
- ▶ How do keyboards, mice, and touch screens work?
- ▶ What is random access memory (RAM)?
- ▶ What is the difference between a hard disk drive and a solid-state disk drive?
- ▶ What is the difference between desktop applications and Windows 8 Store apps?
- ▶ What is a web app?
- ▶ How is each type of productivity software used?
- ▶ What do I need to set up a home network and connect to the Internet?
- ▶ What is The Cloud, and how is it used?
- ▶ How can I share my files, photos, songs, and videos?
- ▶ What is Office 365, and how is it different than the desktop Office?
- ▶ What is the first step in purchasing a computer system?
- ▶ What specifications do I need to know when purchasing a computer?

CONCEPTS

At the end of this chapter, you will better understand the following concepts:

Concept 1   The Computer Is a System
Concept 2   Common Operating Systems
Concept 3   Input Devices
Concept 4   Storage Devices
Concept 5   Apps and Applications
Concept 6   Networks
Concept 7   Cloud Computing
Concept 8   Share Files with Others
Concept 9   Office 365
Concept 10 Buying a Computer

▸ A computer is not a single component. Rather, it is a system of smaller components working together to perform four basic functions: input, processing, output, and storage.

▸ Because you interact with computers on a daily basis, it is important to have an understanding of how they work.

1. **What is a computer?** Computers can be classified and defined in several ways. A **computer** is commonly defined as a programmable electronic device that can input, process, output, and store data. For example, to create a letter on a computer, you type on a keyboard (input) using software that converts the input into a document (process) that displays on a screen (output). The characters you type and the formatting choices you make are stored in the computer's temporary or permanent memory. In this way, the four computer functions work as a system, as shown in **Figure 1**.

2. **How do the four basic computer functions work together?** The four basic computer functions work together in a cycle called the **information processing cycle**. The four functions are summarized in the table shown in **Figure 2**.

3. **What is software? Software** is a set of instructions stored on your computer. The central processing unit (CPU) processes data according to these instructions. **Operating system software** controls the way the computer works while it is running. You use **application software** to accomplish specific tasks, such as word processing and surfing the Internet.

▪ **Continue to the next page to complete the concept**

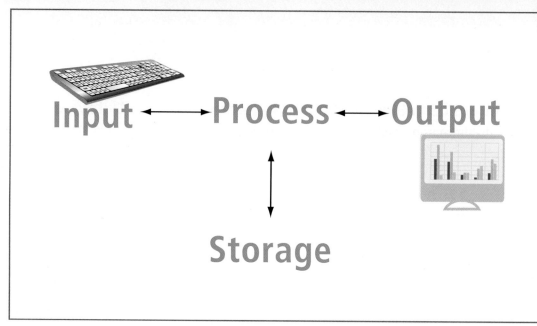

Figure 1

Information Processing Cycle	
Basic Function	**Description**
Input	The process of gathering information from the user through an **input device**—hardware that provides information to the computer, such as keyboards, mice, touch displays, and microphones.
Processing	The process of transforming, managing, and making decisions about the data and information. Most processing occurs in the **central processing unit** (**CPU**)—the hardware responsible for controlling the computer commands and operations.
Output	The display of information through an **output device**—hardware that provides information to the user, such as monitors, speakers, and printers.
Storage	The location where data resides on a computer. **Random access memory** (**RAM**) is an electronic chip that provides temporary storage. Long-term data is written to a **storage device**—hardware that stores information after a computer is powered off. Storage devices include hard drives and USB flash drives.

Figure 2

Figure 3

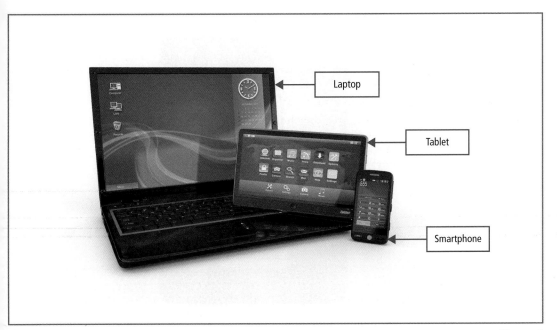

Figure 4

4. ***What types of computers are there?***

Desktop computer: A computer designed to be placed permanently on a desk or at a work station. Desktop computers typically have larger monitors and more computing power than other personal devices. A desktop computer is shown in **Figure 3**.

Laptop: A portable computer with a built-in screen, keyboard, and touchpad. Laptops range from 13 to 20 inches in width and weigh 3 pounds or more. Ultrabooks weigh less than 3 pounds.

Tablet: A portable computer built around a single touch screen. Tablets typically range from 7 to 13 inches in width and weigh between 1 and 2 pounds.

Reader: A tablet-like computer designed around entertainment features, such as books and movies. The other types of tasks that can be performed on a reader are very limited.

Smartphone: A cellular phone with an operating system. Smartphones have touch screens like a tablet and are small enough to be carried in a pocket.

5. ***What is a personal computing device?*** Portable computers are often referred to as ***devices***. The relative sizes of common devices are shown in **Figure 4**.

6. ***What other types of computers are there?*** There are many other types of computers, such as the following:

Server: A computer dedicated to providing services to other computers on a network.

Embedded computer: A small, specialized computer built into a larger component, such as an automobile and an appliance.

■ **You have completed Concept 1 of 10**

▶ The operating system is the gateway between the computer hardware and the application software you have installed on the computer.

▶ Soon after you turn on a computer, control is given to the operating system. The operating system continues running until you turn the computer off.

1. **What is a graphical user interface?** Operating systems provide a **graphical user interface** (**GUI**)—a visual system used to interact with the computer. GUI elements include icons, buttons, tiles, windows, dialog boxes, menus, and ribbons. It is through these graphical elements that you instruct the computer to perform tasks.

2. **What is a desktop?** Many, but not all, operating systems provide a **desktop**—a GUI element that simulates a real desktop in which files are placed. Both files and programs can be opened in windows, each representing a paper document placed on a desktop. The Windows 8 desktop is shown in **Figure 1**.

3. **Do all operating systems have desktops?** Several operating systems do not provide a desktop. Instead, you interact with icons or tiles on a screen. **Figure 2** shows a tablet operating system without a desktop.

4. **What is a file system?** Operating systems provide a **file system**—an organized method to save and retrieve files. Desktop computer operating systems provide a way for you to manage your files directly, while many mobile device operating systems limit the files you can see.

■ Continue to the next page to complete the concept

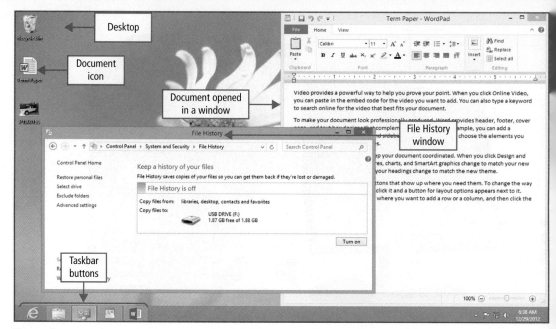

Figure 1

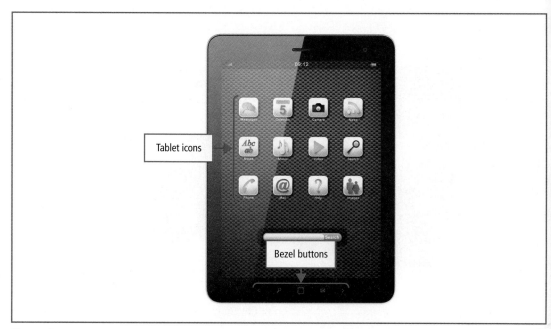

Figure 2

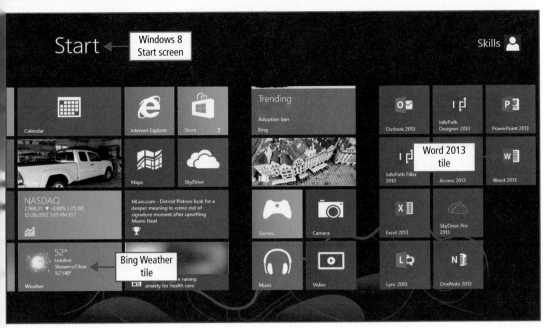

Figure 3

5. **Does Windows 8 provide a desktop?**
Windows 8 does provide a desktop, but it is no longer the screen you see after logging in to your computer. Instead, the Windows 8 Start screen displays as shown in Figure 3.

The Windows 8 Start screen displays tiles. When you click or tap a tile that is a running program, a larger view of the program fills the screen. For example, the Bing weather tile always displays current weather information in its tile. In full screen mode, it displays far more information. When you click or tap a tile that represents a file, web page, or a program that is not currently running, that file, web page, or program opens.

By providing a Start screen and a desktop, the Windows 8 operating system can perform similarly on a desktop computer, laptop, tablet, or smartphone.

6. **What are the common operating systems?** Several operating systems are available depending on the type of computer or device. However, not all computers will run with an operating system other than the one it was designed for. The common operating systems are summarized in the table shown in Figure 4.

7. **What are utility programs?** Operating systems provide **utility programs**— small programs designed to perform routine tasks or computer housekeeping tasks. Other utility programs can be purchased and installed by the computer user.

■ **You have completed Concept 2 of 10**

Common Operating Systems	
Name	**Description**
Apple iOS	A mobile operating system (OS) designed for iPhones, iPads, and other Apple devices.
Apple Mac OS X	A Unix-based OS designed for Macintosh notebooks and computers.
Google Android	A Linux-based OS designed for smartphones and tablets.
Linux	A Unix-based OS built as **open source software**—software that can be sold or given away as long as the source code is provided for free.
Microsoft Windows 8	An OS designed for computers, laptops, and tablets with Intel-based processors.
Microsoft Windows 8 RT	An OS designed for tablets with an ARM processor.
Windows Phone 8	An OS designed for smartphones that works similar to Windows 8.

Figure 4

▶ The methods you use to work with a computer depend on the types of input devices that your computer, operating system, and application software support.

1. ***How do keyboards work? Keyboards*** are input devices used to type characters and perform common commands. In addition to typing, you can perform common tasks using ***keyboard shortcuts***—combinations of Ctrl, Alt, ⊞, and character keys that perform commands when pressed. Other keys, such as the function or "F" keys, PageUp, and PrintScreen, also perform commands. Keyboards vary by manufacturer, but common keyboard areas are shown in **Figure 1**.

2. ***How do mice work? Mice*** are input devices use to point to and click screen elements. The mouse controls the position of a pointer on the screen, and commands are performed when the left or right mouse button is clicked. Typically, ***click*** means to click the left mouse button, and ***right-click*** means to click the right mouse button. Most mice also have a scroll wheel, which can be used to move up or down within windows. A typical mouse is shown in **Figure 2**.

3. ***How do keyboards and mice connect to computers?*** External input devices may connect to your computer using a wire or wirelessly using ***Bluetooth***—a technology that connects devices using radio waves over short distances. Some keyboards are ***onscreen keyboards***—virtual keyboards that display on a touch screen—and others connect to or are part of the computer itself.

■ **Continue to the next page to complete the concept**

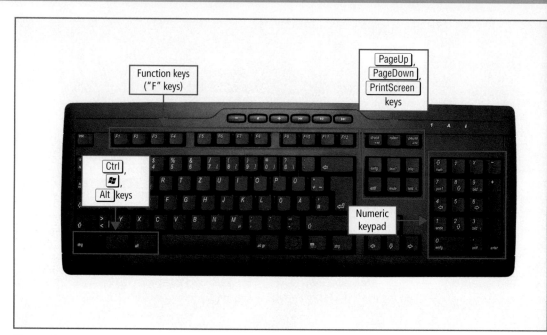

Figure 1

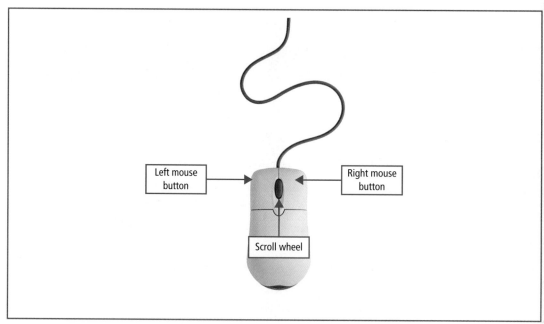

Figure 2

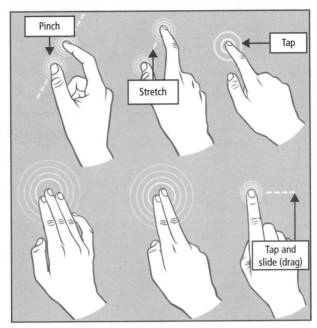

Figure 3

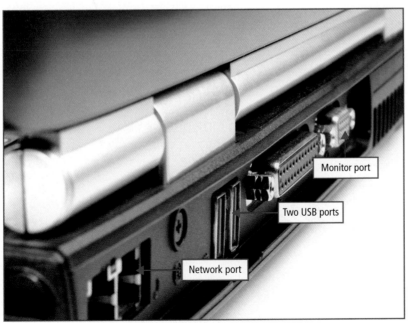

Figure 4

4. **How do touchpads work?** Some computers have a built-in **touchpad**—a flat area on which you can move the finger to position the pointer. Many touchpads can be pressed similar to pressing the left and right buttons on a mouse.

5. **How do touch screens work?** Touch screens can accept input when you touch them with your finger or a **stylus**—a pen-like pointing device used with touch screens. Touch screens use **gestures**—bodily motions that are interpreted as commands. Common gestures are described in Figure 3.

6. **Are there other input devices?** There are many ways a computer can accept input from users. **Speech recognition** technology performs commands or types text based on words spoken into a microphone. Cameras can be attached to a computer to record video or transmit video in video conferences and phone calls. **Scanners** can convert paper images into a digital image and **fingerprint scanners** read fingerprints to authorize computer users.

7. **What are ports? Ports** are the connectors on the outside of the computer to which you connect external devices. Ports are designed so that only the right type of connector can be used. For example, USB ports can accept connections from USB keyboards, mice, and flash drives. An external monitor has ports for each video standard it can accept. Common ports are shown in Figure 4.

■ **You have completed Concept 3 of 10**

- ▶ Data is stored in the computer's short-term and long-term memory.
- ▶ Storage devices include random access memory (RAM), hard drives, USB flash drives, and DVD-RW drives.

1. ***How does RAM work? RAM*** acts as the computer's short-term memory. RAM is stored in chips similar to those shown in **Figure 1**. These chips maintain the data storage by the flow of electricity, and the data disappears when the power to the computer is turned off. You need to save documents to a long-term storage location if you want to use them in the future.

2. ***What is a hard disk drive?*** A ***hard disk drive (HDD)*** is a common storage device in desktop computers. Traditional hard disk drives write and read data stored as magnetic traces on platters inside a drive similar to those shown in **Figure 2**.

3. ***What is the difference between a solid-state disk drive and a magnetic disk drive?*** A ***solid-state disk drive (SDD)*** maintains data using electricity and retains the data when the power is turned off. Internal solid-state drives are faster than magnetic drives, but magnetic drives can typically store more data. When a solid-state hard drive attaches to the computer via a USB port, it is often called an ***external drive***.

4. ***What is a USB flash drive?*** A ***USB flash drive*** is a small, portable, solid-state drive about the size of the human thumb. For this reason, they are sometimes referred to as ***thumb drives***.

■ **Continue to the next page to complete the concept** ➤

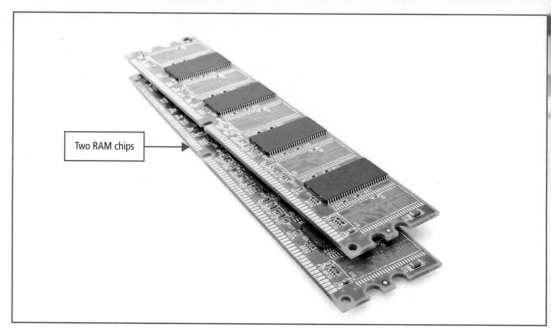

Two RAM chips

Figure 1

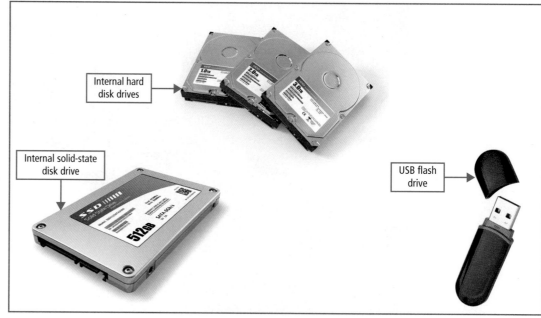

Internal hard disk drives

Internal solid-state disk drive

USB flash drive

Figure 2

Common Storage Sizes	
Unit	**Description**
Kilobyte (KB)	One thousand bytes (1 page of text)
Megabyte (MB)	One million bytes (1000 pages of text)
Gigabyte (GB)	One billion bytes (100,000 pages of text)
Terabyte (TB)	One trillion bytes (100,000,000 pages of text)
Relative Storage Capacities	
Typical Range	**Drive Type**
4–9 GB	DVD drives
8–64 GB	USB flash drives
4–128 GB	Flash memory cards
128–512 GB	Internal solid-state drives
500–3,000 GB (0.5–3 TB)	Internal hard disk dives External solid-state drives

Figure 3

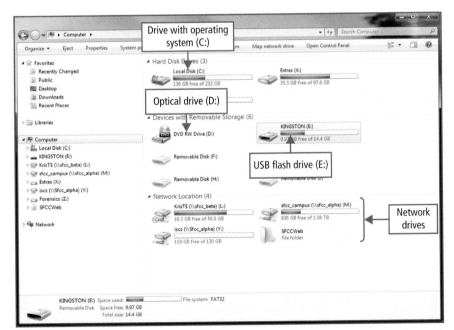

Figure 4

5. *What are other common storage devices?* A *DVD* uses optical laser technology to read and write data. *Flash-based memory cards* are solid-state drives designed for devices such as digital cameras and video recorders. Many computers have *card readers*—ports designed to accept flash-based memory cards.

6. *How is storage capacity measured?* Most common storage devices measure their capacity in either gigabytes or terabytes. Each *gigabyte* (*GB*) can store about 1,000 digital photos. A *terabyte* (*TB*) is approximately 1,000 gigabytes. A one terabyte hard drive can store approximately 1,000,000 digital photos. Relative capacities are summarized in Figure 3.

7. *What is a network drive?* Large organizations often have *network drives*—hard drives that are accessed through a network. Your school or organization may ask you to save your work to a network drive. In the Windows operating system, these drives often display in the Computer window similar to the ones shown in Figure 4.

8. *How can I identify drives?* In a Windows file system, each drive is assigned a unique volume letter. The internal drive that stores the operating system is commonly assigned the letter "C" and is often called the *C drive*. Optical drives often are assigned the letter "D" or "E," and USB flash drives are assigned the next available letter. Network drives are often assigned the highest letters, as shown in Figure 4.

■ **You have completed Concept 4 of 10**

- Most businesses, schools, and home users purchase and install applications on their computers.
- Applications are also referred to as *programs*.

1. **Can I just use the software that comes with my operating system?** Most operating systems do include software to complete common tasks. However, most computer users desire or need additional features beyond the capabilities of these types of programs. Applications that come with Windows 8 as well as some that can be purchased separately are shown in **Figure 1**.

2. **What is the difference between Microsoft Office and Microsoft Windows? Microsoft Office** is a suite of productivity programs that is purchased separately from Microsoft Windows. The most common Office programs are Word, Excel, PowerPoint, and Outlook. Many new Windows computers provide a trial version of Office, which you can then pay for after the trial period has expired. Others have Office preinstalled for an extra fee.

3. **Are there free programs that I can use?** Most of the features provided by commercial software can also be found in free software. Extra caution is needed when installing free software to ensure that the source can be trusted.

4. **What is productivity software? Productivity software** is used to accomplish tasks such as reading and composing e-mail, writing documents, and managing tasks. Common productivity application types are summarized in the table shown in **Figure 2**.

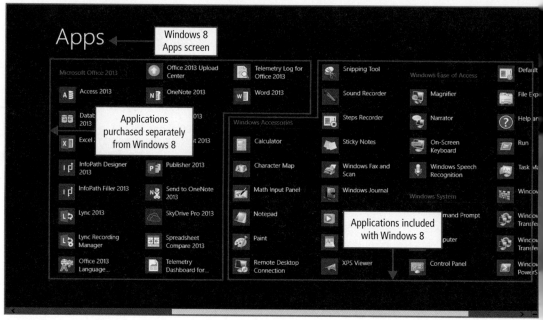

Figure 1

■ Continue to the next page to complete the concept

Common Productivity Application Types	
Application Type	**Purpose**
Word processing	To create, edit, format, and print documents containing primarily text and graphics.
Spreadsheets	To organize information in a tabular structure with numeric data, labels, formulas, and charts.
Presentation	To arrange information in slides that can be projected on a large screen in front of an audience.
Database	To store large amounts of data and retrieve that data in useful and meaningful ways.
E-mail	To receive and send e-mail. Many e-mail programs also include tools for managing appointments, contacts, and tasks.
Browser	To view web pages on the World Wide Web.

Figure 2

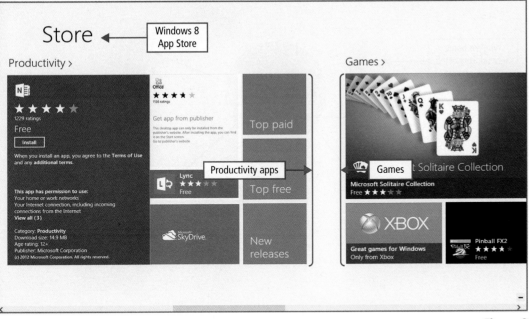

Figure 3

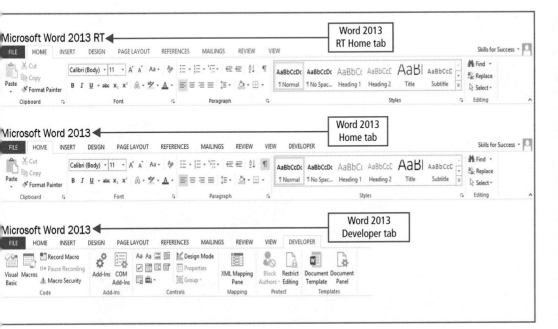

Figure 4

5. ***What is the difference between an app and an application?*** Increasingly, the term ***app*** refers to a program purchased through the computer's or device's store. These programs tend to be smaller and less expensive than traditional applications. Some devices, such as smartphones and tablets, limit you to installing only apps from their store service.

Windows 8 Store apps are downloaded and installed from the Windows 8 Store, and they run in the Start screen. They usually have less features and a different interface than ***desktop applications***—programs that run in a desktop window. The Windows 8 Store is shown in Figure 3.

6. ***Why does some software seem to work on only one or two types of computers?*** The instructions stored in a program are designed to work with specific operating systems and hardware. Smartphone apps are typically written separately for iOS, Android, or Windows 8 Phone. Desktop applications are often written for Windows, System X, or Linux.

Microsoft Office has several versions. When you use Word on a Mac (Apple System X), the program will be similar, but not identical, to the version running on a Windows computer. ***Office RT*** is an app version of Office designed to work on tablets. Word 2013 and Word 2013 RT are nearly identical. As shown in Figure 4, the Home tabs are identical, but Word 2013 RT lacks the Developer tab.

■ **You have completed Concept 5 of 10**

▶ To share files, print, and connect to the Internet, homes and businesses with 20 or less computers typically use a ***peer-to-peer network***—a small network that connects computers and devices without the need for a server.

1. ***What are the differences between a wired and a wireless network?*** Networks are either wired or wireless. ***Wired networks*** transmit signals through wires, and ***wireless networks*** transmit signals via radio waves. Without the need to run wires to every computer, wireless networks can be less expensive to install. Wired networks can transmit data faster and are more secure than wireless networks. A wireless network diagram is shown in Figure 1.

2. ***What do I need to connect my computers and devices to my network?*** Each device needs a ***network interface card*** (**NIC**). A wired NIC has a port for an RJ-45 connector. Wireless NICs have antennae for sending and receiving radio signals. All NICs need to connect to a ***router***—a network device through which computers on a network communicate. The network ports on a wired router are shown in Figure 2.

3. ***Is the Internet a network?*** The ***Internet*** is a collection of networks distributed throughout the world. The Internet has services such as e-mail, on-demand video, telephony, and the World Wide Web.

■ Continue to the next page to complete the concept ➡

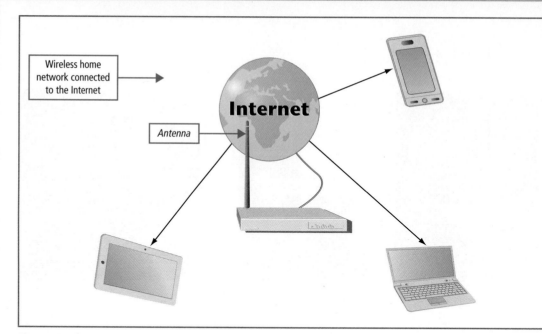

Figure 1

Figure 2

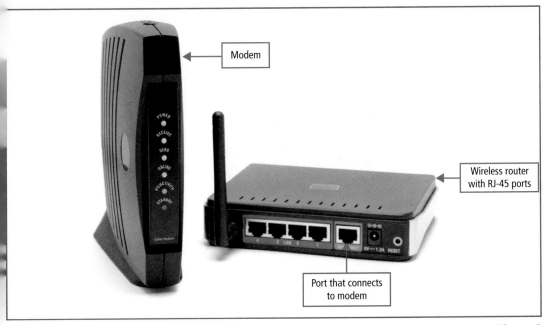

Modem

Wireless router
with RJ-45 ports

Port that connects
to modem

Figure 3

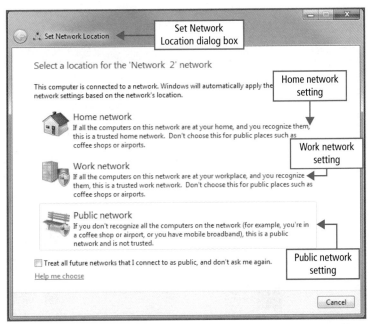

Set Network
Location dialog box

Set Network Location

Select a location for the 'Network 2' network

This computer is connected to a network. Windows will automatically apply the
network settings based on the network's location.

Home network
If all the computers on this network are at your home, and you recognize them,
this is a trusted home network. Don't choose this for public places such as
coffee shops or airports.

Home network
setting

Work network
If all the computers on this network are at your workplace, and you recognize
them, this is a trusted work network. Don't choose this for public places such as
coffee shops or airports.

Work network
setting

Public network
If you don't recognize all the computers on the network (for example, you're in
a coffee shop or airport, or you have mobile broadband), this is a public
network and is not trusted.

Public network
setting

☐ Treat all future networks that I connect to as public, and don't ask me again.

Help me choose

Cancel

Figure 4

4. **What do I need to connect my home network to the Internet?** To connect to the Internet, you need to subscribe to an **Internet service provider** (**ISP**)—an organization that provides Internet connections, typically for a fee.

Most routers are also a **gateway**—a network device through which different networks communicate. The router needs to be connected to a **modem**—a device that translates signals between a router and an ISP. A cable modem and a wireless router are shown in **Figure** 3.

5. **What types of connections do ISP's provide?** ISP connections vary depending on location. If you have cable TV, it is likely you can connect to an ISP via cable. DSL phone lines provide Internet connections via phone lines in most areas. ISP connections are also available using radio waves transmitted from satellites and line-of-sight radio towers.

6. **What is an unsecured network?** An **unsecured network** is a network that does not require a password to connect to it. When you transmit data on a local network, any device that is a member of that network can also receive that data. Malicious persons sometimes connect to unsecured networks to obtain sensitive data, such as user names and passwords of others using the network.

Figure 4 shows the Set Network Location dialog box. In Windows, selecting the Public Network option limits the type of information you send over the network. You should secure your own wireless network with a strong password.

■ **You have completed Concept 6 of 10**

▶ ***Cloud computing*** is a service such as file storage or an application provided via the Internet. Collectively, these services are referred to as ***The Cloud***.

1. ***How does The Cloud work?*** The Cloud works by storing your files, settings, and applications on servers connected to the Internet. Instead of opening files and applications stored on your internal hard drive, you open them by connecting to Cloud servers. The data is downloaded to your computer as you need it. When you save a document to The Cloud, it is uploaded to a server.

2. ***What are the benefits of Cloud computing?*** The main benefit of Cloud computing is that you can access your files and programs from any device, as diagrammed in **Figure 1**. For example, you can access your e-mail and work with documents from your desktop computer, your tablet, or your phone.

   Using The Cloud provides a layer of security. For example, if your computer or device fails or is lost, you can recover your data from The Cloud after you fix or replace the device.

3. ***What are the disadvantages of Cloud computing?*** Your device must be connected to the Internet, which is not always possible. Some services can provide limited functionality by storing copies of your files on your computer.

4. ***How does Cloud storage work?*** You can save and open files stored on The Cloud instead of your local drives. **Figure 2** shows Microsoft OneDrive.

■ Continue to the next page to complete the concept

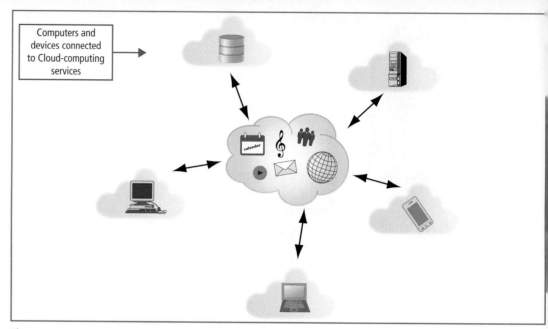

Figure 1

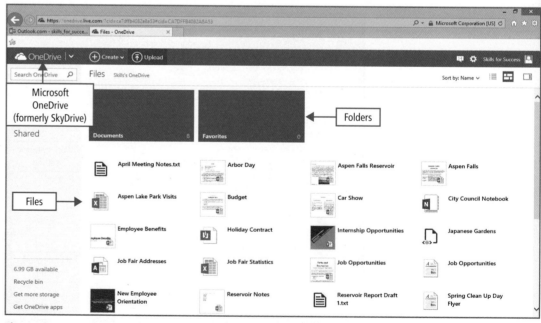

Figure 2

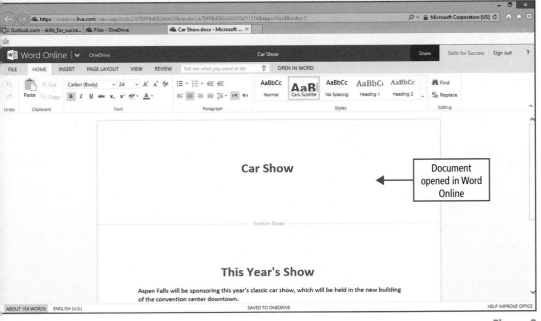

Car Show

Document opened in Word Online

Figure 3

Web album at Flickr

Flickr. Yahoo!, 2013.

Figure 4

5. ***How do web apps work? Web apps*** are programs that run in a web browser. Web apps are useful when you need to read, edit, and apply basic formatting from a computer that does not have the desktop application that made the document. For example, Word Online shown in **Figure 3** can be used to open and modify Word documents on computers that do not have Word installed.

Common web apps include applications for word processing, spreadsheets, presentations, e-mail, and calendars.

6. ***What is streaming media? Streaming media*** is a Cloud-based service that provides video and music as you watch or listen to it. The media is stored on The Cloud so that you can play them from multiple devices. Many televisions and DVD players can also play streaming media.

7. ***What are Cloud backups?*** A ***Cloud backup*** is a service that copies your files to a server so that you can recover them if needed. If you upgrade to a new device or computer, you can use these backups to move your data to the new device.

8. ***What is a web album? Web albums*** are Cloud-based services that you use to store, organize, and share photos and video. You create albums by uploading them to a Cloud-based service such a Flickr, as shown in **Figure 4**. You can then make the album available to others. Some services provide applications to edit your photos.

■ **You have completed Concept 7 of 10**

▶ You can use your network, the Internet, and Cloud computing to share with others.

1. What is sharing, and how is sharing used? One way to share is to provide access to files using a network. The Windows Create a Homegroup dialog box can be used to share your files with others on your network and is shown in **Figure 1**. *Homegroup* is a Windows networking tool that makes it easy to share pictures, videos, music, documents, and devices such as printers.

When you share a file, you set a *permission level*—the privilege to read, rename, delete, or change a file. Those with the *read privilege* can open the document, but they cannot save any changes they might make. Those without the read privilege will not be able to view the document at all.

You can *password protect* shared files so that the correct password must be entered before the file can be opened. If no password is required, the shared file is considered to be *public*.

2. How can I use e-mail to share with others? Electronic mail, or e-mail, can be used to share text, pictures, and files. You can attach files to e-mail messages or embed pictures into the messages. **Figure 2** shows an e-mail message with a file attached. In Outlook, the file can be previewed in the Reading pane or opened in the application that created it.

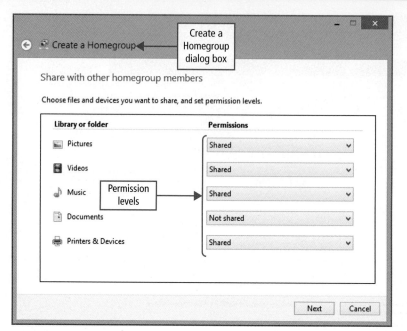

Figure 1

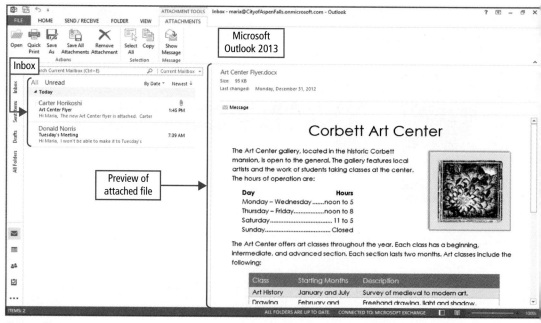

Figure 2

■ **Continue to the next page to complete the concept**

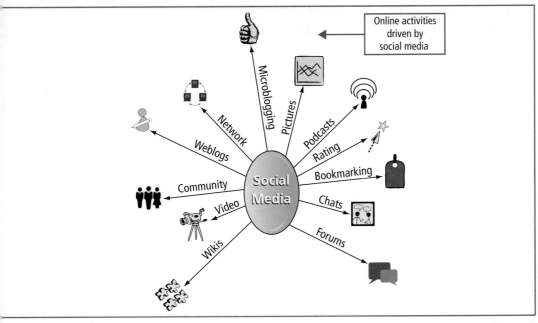

Figure 3

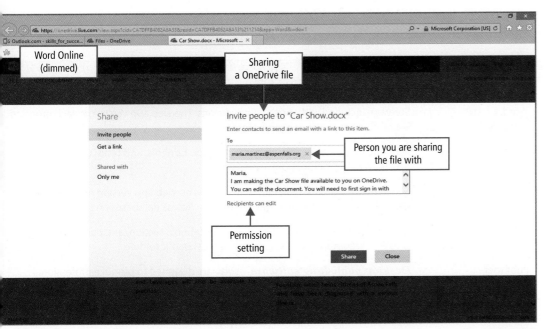

Figure 4

3. *How can I use social media to share files? Social media* is a Cloud service in which content is shared through the interactions of people connected through social networks. The comments, photos, and videos that you share may only be seen by a few of your friends. However, because of the interconnectivity of social networking, interesting content may also be viewed by millions. The online content driven by social media is diagrammed in Figure 3.

4. *How do you share files on The Cloud?* Saving files on The Cloud makes it easy to share files. Figure 4 shows a Word file stored at OneDrive and opened in Word Online. The dialog box is used to send an e-mail inviting others to share the document. They can then click a hyperlink provided in the e-mail message to open the file. If they make changes to the file, you will see those changes when you open the file.

You can also share OneDrive files by posting a link to your social media account, such as Facebook and Twitter. Those who can see your posts can follow the link to open the document. The check boxes in the lower left corner are used to set the permission level for the document that will be shared.

■ **You have completed Concept 8 of 10**

▶ **Office 365** is a Cloud-based service built around the Office suite of programs. It combines traditional Office desktop applications with Cloud services.

1. **Is Office 365 an application?** Office 365 is a collection of services, most of which can be purchased separately. When you purchase a subscription to Office 365, you can install the latest versions of Office programs on several computers from a Web page, as shown in **Figure 1**. These programs are the same desktop programs that are purchased separately from an Office 365 subscription.

2. **How do you buy Office 365?** With Office 365, you pay a monthly fee to maintain a license to use its software and services. The cost of a subscription depends on the number of users and the types of Office 365 services they require. Some subscription levels are designed for homes, and others are designed for businesses of different sizes and needs.

3. **What Office applications are provided by Office 365?** When you subscribe to Office 365, you receive additional Office applications that are not included in many home and small business editions of Office. These applications are described in the table shown in **Figure 2**.

4. **What other Cloud-based services come with Office 365?** All plans include additional OneDrive storage. The amount of additional storage depends on the subscription level. Most plans also include Office for Mac.

Figure 1

Office Applications	
Application Type	**Description**
Word, Excel, PowerPoint	Software included with most Office versions. The web app version of each program is available to the general public for free.
Outlook	Software for managing e-mail, contacts, appointments, and tasks. Outlook Web App is available for most Office 365 plans.
Access	Software for database management. There is no web app version of Access. Some Office 365 plans provide a service to publish Access databases on the Web.
OneNote	Software used to organize ideas using a notebook, section, and page metaphor. OneNote Web App is available to the general public for free.
Publisher	**Desktop publishing software**—software designed to produce professional publications, such as newsletters, letterheads, business cards, and brochures.
Lync	Video conferencing software designed primarily for businesses.

Figure 2

■ **Continue to the next page to complete the concept**

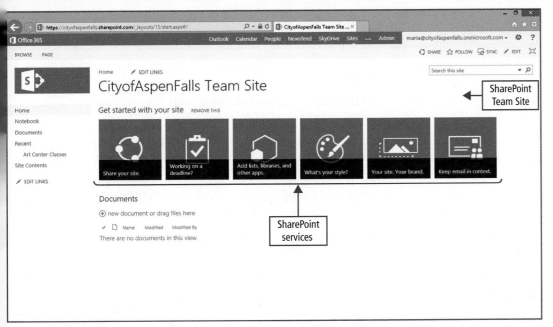

SharePoint Team Site

SharePoint services

Figure 3

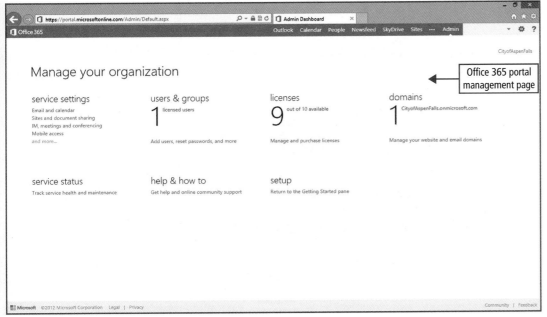

Office 365 portal management page

Figure 4

Office on Demand is a streaming version of Office that you can work with using a computer that does not have Office installed.

5. ***What business-oriented services come with Office 365?*** Office 365 provides access to several popular business services. These services can be managed from the Office 365 portal and eliminate the need for a business to purchase, install, and configure their own servers. Most business plans include ***hosted e-mail***—a service used to provide e-mail addresses and related resources.

Other servers include ***SharePoint***—a web application server designed for organizations to develop an intranet. An ***intranet*** is a website that is accessed by only individuals within the organization. A SharePoint site is shown in Figure 3. Office 365 also provides a server that can host a ***public website***—a website designed for public access.

6. ***What are the advantages of Office 365?*** Office 365 makes it easy to install and use Office on multiple devices with multiple users in multiple locations. One of the pages used to manage Office 365 users, applications, and services is shown in Figure 4.

When you save your files to OneDrive you will have access to your files and settings from any computer connected to the Internet. When you log on, you can use the desktop application, web apps, or Office on Demand to work with your documents.

■ **You have completed Concept 9 of 10**

▶ The better one understands how computer systems work, the better the ability to make an informed decision when purchasing a computer.

1. ***What is the first step in deciding what computer to buy?*** The first step in purchasing a computer is to decide how you will use it. You need to decide what types of things you want to do. It is a good idea to make a list of the software you plan to buy and determine on what operating systems that software can be installed.

2. ***Do I need a desktop or a mobile device?*** You need to decide if you need a computer that you can carry around with you. If you plan to work only when sitting at your desk, then a desktop computer will provide the most power for the least amount of money. Other factors to consider are summarized in the table shown in **Figure 1**.

3. ***Can I use a mobile device as my desktop computer?*** Many choose to use their laptop or tablet as their only computer. Although they may not be as powerful or easy to use as a desktop computer, they do perform most tasks very well. If you plan to use your computer for e-mail, browsing, word processing, or simple gaming, then this option may work well.

Because of their small screens, working with Office documents on smartphones has very limited functionality. Tablet and monitor sizes are compared in **Figure 2**.

■ **Continue to the next page to complete the concept** ➤

Common Computer Specifications	
Component	**Description**
CPU speed	***CPU speed*** is measured in calculations per second. Clock speeds do not make good comparisons.
CPU cache	***CPU caches*** are storage areas dedicated to the processor. The larger the cache, the better the performance.
Number of processors	The more processors a CPU has, the better the performance.
Graphics card	***Integrated graphics cards*** are built into the computer's main board and are sufficient for most computer users. Gamers and video developers may attach one or two ***graphics processing units*** (***GPUs***) to the computer's main board to boost performance.
RAM	The amount of RAM is measured in gigabytes. Not having enough RAM can slow computer performance.
Disk drives	Faster computers include a solid-state drive (SSD) to store the operating system and a hard disk drive to store other files.

Figure 1

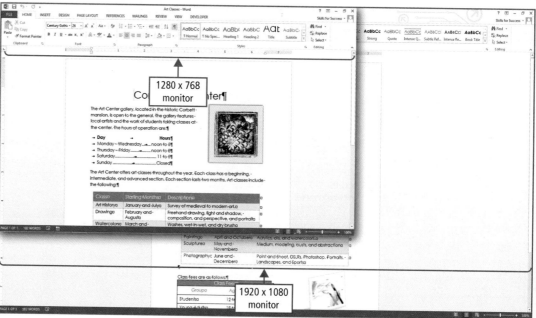

Figure 2

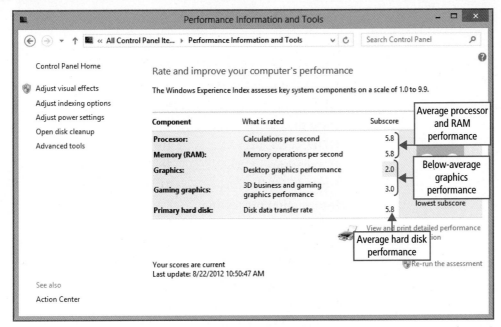

Figure 3

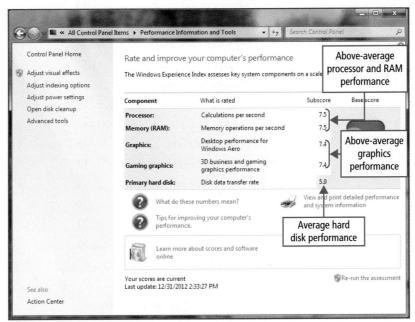

Figure 4

4. *What operating system should I pick?* Your list of planned software will determine your options for picking an operating system. For example, if you know that you will need Microsoft Word, your choices will be a Windows or a Macintosh computer. As of this writing, Office is not available on readers, iOS, or Android devices.

If you know that you will need Microsoft Office, an Office 365 subscription may be a good choice. You can use the subscription to install Office on multiple devices running Windows 7 or Windows 8, including tablets running Windows 8 RT. Macintosh desktop and laptop computers are also supported.

If you plan to use web apps instead of Office, iOS and Android tablets may be a good option.

5. *How much storage will I need?* Those who mainly browse, e-mail, and work with Office need relatively little storage space. If you plan to store music, videos, or digital photos, then you will likely need models with larger storage capacities.

6. *How much computing power will I need?* Generally, those who play high-end games need far more computing power than others. If you do not plan to play games with 3D graphics, you likely do not need the computers with faster CPUs or higher graphics capabilities. Figure 3 shows the performance rating of such a computer, and Figure 4 shows the performance rating of a computer more suitable for gaming.

DONE! You have completed Concept 10 of 10, and your presentation is complete!

Key Terms

Online Practice

The following IT simulations provide additional practice in applying the concepts learned in this chapter. To begin, open your web browser, navigate to http://media.pearsoncmg.com/ph/bp/bp_mylabs/simulations/2012/IT/index.html, and then follow the links on the web page.

What Is a Computer?

1. List the various types and characteristics of personal computers.
2. Give examples of computing devices.

Application Software

1. Identify the features and benefits of business productivity software.
2. Assess a computer system for software compatibility.

Hardware

1. Select hardware components appropriate to your needs.
2. Evaluate the advantages offered by technological components.

System Software

1. Identify basic features of the most common stand-alone operating systems.
2. Configure and modify basic features of the most common stand-alone operating systems.

Communicating and Sharing on the Web

1. Compose and respond to e-mail by following e-mail etiquette guidelines.

Networks

1. Configure your computer's software to connect to a network.
2. Secure your network connection to minimize risks of online communication.

Security and Privacy

1. Manage e-mail effectively.
2. Demonstrate safe computing practices.
3. Differentiate between legitimate and potentially harmful e-mail.

Matching

Match each term in the second column with its correct definition in the first column by writing the letter of the term on the blank line in front of the correct definition.

___ **1.** The four basic computer functions that work together in a computer system: input, processing, output, and storage.

___ **2.** The hardware responsible for controlling the computer commands and operations.

___ **3.** Computer hardware that stores information after a computer is powered off.

___ **4.** Software that controls the way the computer works while it is running.

___ **5.** Software used to accomplish specific tasks, such as word processing and surfing the Internet.

___ **6.** A collection of ports designed to accept flash-based memory cards.

___ **7.** Software that is downloaded and installed from the Windows 8 Store and run in the Start screen.

___ **8.** A card that connects a computer to a network.

___ **9.** A small network that connects computers and devices without the need for a server.

___ **10.** A collection of networks distributed throughout the world.

___ **11.** A device that translates signals between a router and an ISP.

___ **12.** Services such as file storage or an application provided via the Internet.

___ **13.** A Cloud-based service where content is shared through the interactions of people connected through social networks.

___ **14.** A Cloud-based service built around the Office suite of programs.

___ **15.** A card attached to the computer's main board to improve computer performance.

A Application

B Card reader

C Cloud computing

D Central processing unit (CPU)

E Graphics processing unit (GPU)

F Information processing cycle

G Internet

H Modem

I NIC

J Office 365

K Operating system

L Peer-to-peer networking

M Social media

N Storage device

O Windows 8 Store app

Multiple Choice

Choose the correct answer.

1. Computer hardware such as keyboards, mice, touch displays, and microphones.
   A. Input devices
   B. Output devices
   C. Storage devices

2. An electronic chip that provides temporary storage.
   A. CPU
   B. RAM
   C. Utility program

3. A bodily motion that is interpreted as a command.
   A. Gesture
   B. Speech recognition
   C. Thumb drive

4. A computer dedicated to providing services to other computers on a network.
   A. Desktop computer
   B. Reader
   C. Server

5. A drive that that stores data using electricity and retains the data when the power turned off.
   A. DVD
   B. Hard disk drive (HDD)
   C. Solid-state disk drive (SDD)

6. A unit of measure for devices that can store about 1,000 digital photos.
   A. Gigabyte
   B. Megabyte
   C. Terabyte

7. Software used to create, edit, format, and print documents containing primarily text and graphics.
   A. Presentation
   B. Spreadsheet
   C. Word processing

8. Software used to organize information in a tabular structure with numeric data, labels, formulas, and charts.
   A. Presentation
   B. Spreadsheet
   C. Word processing

9. A network that transmits signals via radio waves.
   A. Bluetooth network
   B. Wired network
   C. Wireless network

10. A network device through which different networks communicate.
    A. Router
    B. Tablet
    C. USB flash drive

11. An organization that provides Internet connections, typically for a fee.
    A. ISP
    B. Hosted e-mail
    C. Social media

12. A Windows networking tool that makes it easy to share pictures, videos, music, documents, and devices such as printers.
    A. The Cloud
    B. Homegroup
    C. Web album

13. A permission level that allows you to open, but not change, a document.
    A. Password protected
    B. Read
    C. Share

14. A website that is accessed only by individuals within the organization.
- **A.** Internet
- **B.** Intranet
- **C.** Public web site

15. A storage area dedicated to the processor.
- **A.** Cache
- **B.** DVD
- **C.** USB external drive

Topics for Discussion

1. If you needed a computer for e-mail and word processing but could only buy a tablet or a desktop computer, which one would you buy and why?

2. Given web apps such as Word Online and open source desktop applications such as openoffice.org, do you think it is necessary to purchase Microsoft Office? Why, or why not?

CHAPTER 2

Getting Started with Windows 8

- When you sign in to Windows 8, you use the Start screen to view updated information from the Internet and to launch your favorite programs.
- The Start screen adapts to whatever device you are using so that you access the same information on your desktop computer, smartphone, or tablet.
- You can perform tasks by touching the screen or wedge mouse or by clicking with a traditional mouse. For example, you can switch between open apps by swiping from the screen's left edge or by clicking the upper left or lower left corner with a mouse.

- You can use charms to perform tasks such as opening desktop applications and changing your computer settings.
- File Explorer is used to organize your files so that you can find them easily.
- You can use the Personalization window to change the appearance and behavior of the desktop.

© Maksym Dykha / Fotolia

Aspen Falls City Hall

In this chapter, you will assist Maria Martinez, City Manager, to prepare for a meeting in a nearby city. You will need to find driving directions, look at a weather forecast, and organize the files that will be needed at the meeting.

Typically, you begin working with Windows by signing in to the computer. When you sign in, your personalized changes to the Start screen and desktop will display, and you will be able to access your files. In this way, you use Windows to personalize your computer experience.

In this project, you will sign in to Windows, and then work with several programs that are part of Windows 8. You will search for files, copy them to new locations, and then organize those files into folders. You will also customize the desktop and then return the computer to its original settings. You will document your work by creating screen shots and pasting them into a WordPad document.

Time to complete all 10 skills – 60 to 90 minutes

Student data files needed for this chapter:

win02_student_data_files (a folder containing several files)

You will save your document as:

Last_First_win02_Map

Outcome

Using the skills in this chapter, you will be able to customize the desktop, manage files, and create screen shots such as this:

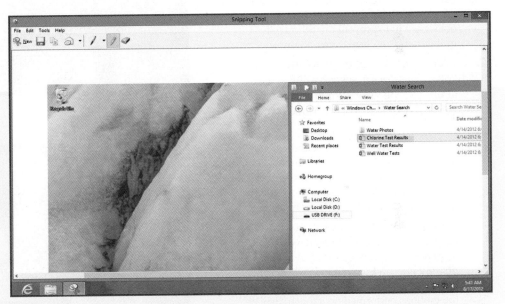

SKILLS

At the end of this chapter you will be able to:

Skill 1   Sign In to Windows 8

Skill 2   Work with Store Apps

Skill 3   Create and Save Documents

Skill 4   Search for Applications, Files, and Settings

Skill 5   Download and Unzip Student Data Files

Skill 6   View Files in File Explorer

Skill 7   Search for and Copy Files

Skill 8   Move, Rename, and Delete Files

Skill 9   Personalize the Desktop and Create Snips

Skill 10   Print, Restore Settings, and Sign Out

MORE SKILLS

Skill 11   Customize the Start Screen

Skill 12   Modify the Desktop

Skill 13   Switch to a Microsoft Account

Skill 14   Use the OneDrive App

▶ Before you work with Windows 8, you need to **sign in**—the process of connecting to a computer.

▶ Windows 8 typically asks for a user name or ID and password. If you do not have those, you may need to obtain them from your computer or network administrator.

1. If necessary, turn on your computer and monitor, and wait a few moments for the Windows 8 lock screen to display. Compare your screen with **Figure 1**.

   The **lock screen** displays shortly after you turn on a computer or device running Windows 8. It also displays when you are not signed in to prevent unauthorized individuals from using your account.

2. Click the lock screen or press any key to display the **sign-in screen**—the screen you use to type your sign in information. Compare your screen with **Figure 2**.

   Depending on your computer settings, your sign-in screen may look and behave differently than the one shown in the figure. Your password, for example, may be a picture that has areas that need to be touched or clicked in a certain order.

   You can navigate Windows 8 using the keyboard, a mouse, or if you have a touch display or mouse, by gestures. A **touch display** interprets commands when you touch it with your finger, and **gestures** are the motions performed on a touch display that are interpreted as commands. Some mice have an area for inputting gestures.

■ **Continue to the next page to complete the skill**

Lock screen (yours may be different)

9:31

Thursday, August 16

Figure 1

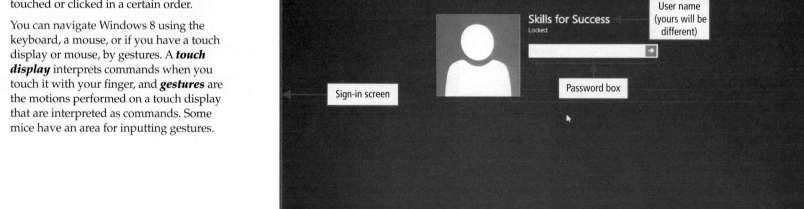

Skills for Success
Locked

User name (yours will be different)

Sign-in screen

Password box

Figure 2

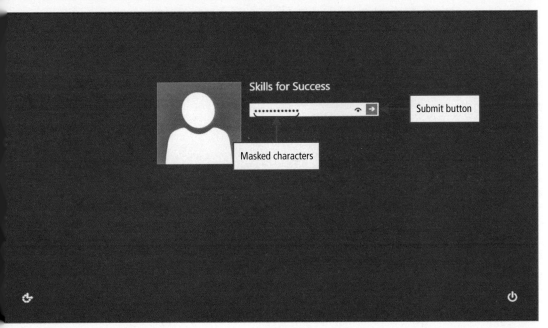

Skills for Success

Submit button

Masked characters

Figure 3

3. If necessary, select your user name. If a blank User Name box displays, type your ID in the box. In the **Password** box, type your password, and then compare your screen with Figure 3.

   To prevent unauthorized access to your data and computer settings, you should always keep your password confidential. For this reason, the password text characters are *masked characters*—text hidden by displaying characters such as bullets.

4. Press Enter or click the **Submit** button → to complete the sign in, and then compare your screen with Figure 4.

   The Start screen displays *tiles*—small windows that run applications that present live, updated information. Because the tiles are dynamic, your Start screen will rarely appear the same as the figures in this chapter.

   You can add tiles to view current information such as local weather, personalized news feeds, photo galleries, or posts on your social media accounts. Tiles can also link to your favorite programs. In the figure, tiles that open Office 2013 programs display on the right edge.

   The Start screen works the same on desktop computers, smartphones, and tablets but will adjust its layout to work best on that device.

■ **You have completed Skill 1 of 10**

Start screen
(your tiles and background may be different)

Skills for Success

Office 2013 tiles
(yours may not display)

Tiles (yours will be different)

Figure 4

▶ A **Windows 8 Store app** is a program used to perform a similar set of tasks that runs on the Start screen. For example, Calendar is used to make appointments, and Bing Weather is used to track weather.

▶ **Applications** and **programs** refer to programs that run from the desktop.

1. On the Start screen, click the **Weather** tile to open the app. If you have a touch display, you can open an app by **tapping**—touching once with the finger. If a message displays, click Block.

   Bing Weather is an app that runs in the Start screen. When you click its tile, it expands to fill the entire screen.

   Sharing your location with an app provides more personalized results. You will not need to share your location to complete the activities in this chapter.

2. If the **Enter Location** pane displays on your screen, skip to Step 5.

3. **Right-click**—click one time with the right mouse button—anywhere in the **Bing Weather** app, and then compare your screen with **Figure 1**.

   App commands are buttons and commands in an application that remain hidden until you need them. If you have a touch display, you can display app commands by **swiping**—moving across the screen with the finger—from the screen's edge.

4. In the app commands, click **Places**, and then click the **Add** tile ⊕.

5. Below **Enter Location**, click in the **Search for a city** box, and then type Cuyama, CA Compare your screen with **Figure 2**.

■ Continue to the next page to complete the skill

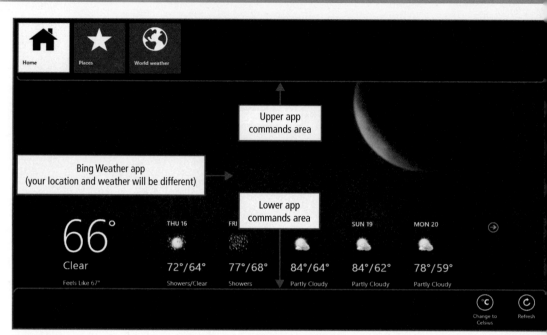

Figure 1

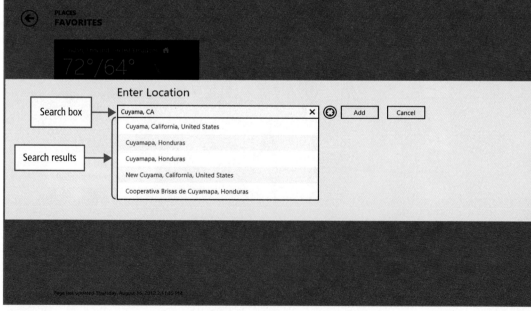

Figure 2

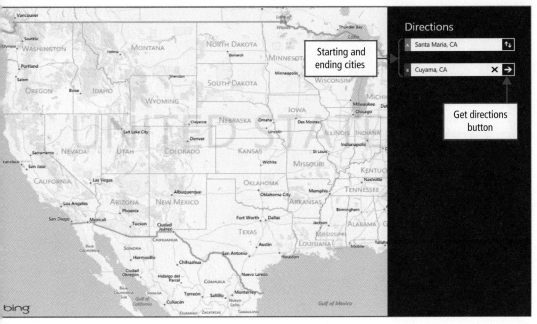

Starting and ending cities

Get directions button

Figure 3

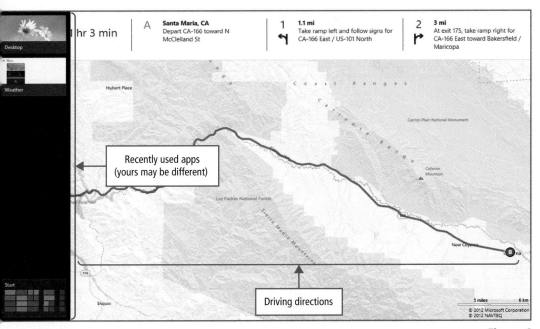

Recently used apps (yours may be different)

Driving directions

Figure 4

6. Click **Cuyama**, **California**, **United States**, and then if necessary, click **Add**.

7. Under **Favorites**, right-click the tile for **Cuyama**, **CA** and then in the lower app area, click **Set as default**.

8. Point to the lower left corner of the screen, and then click the **Start** tile to return to the Start screen. Notice the **Weather** tile displays updated weather information for Cuyama.

9. On the Start screen, click the **Maps** tile to open Bing Maps. If a message displays, click **Block**.

10. Right-click the screen to display the app commands, and then click **Directions**.

11. In the **Directions** pane **From** box, type Santa Maria, CA

12. In the **Directions** pane **To** box, type Cuyama, CA

13. Compare your screen with **Figure 3**, and then click the **Get directions** button to display the driving directions between the two cities.

14. Point to the upper left corner, and then move the mouse straight down to display all the recently used apps as shown in **Figure 4**.

   If you have a touch display, you can swipe from the left edge to display the recently used apps and then tap the app you want to use next.

15. In the recently used area, click the **Weather** button.

16. Press ⊞ to return to the Start screen, and then continue to the next skill.

   Pressing the ⊞ key is an alternate method to switch to the Start screen.

■ **You have completed Skill 2 of 10**

▶ Documents are saved as *files*—collections of data that are saved, opened, and changed by applications.

1. Watch the Start screen as you type WordPad and then compare your screen with **Figure 1**.

   On the Start screen, a search is started whenever you start typing.

2. With **WordPad** selected, press Enter to start the application. Alternately, you can click or tap WordPad.

3. If the WordPad window is not *maximized*—sized to fill the entire screen, click the Maximize ☐ button. Take a few moments to understand the WordPad window by comparing your screen with **Figure 2**.

   The WordPad window has a Quick Access Toolbar, Ribbon, and window controls. The *Quick Access Toolbar* or *QAT* is a small toolbar that contains buttons for commonly used commands such as Save and Undo.

   Ribbons contain commands placed in groups that are organized by tabs so that you can quickly find the tools you need. For example, the WordPad Ribbon has three tabs: File, Home, and View. The Home tab has five groups.

   The upper right corners of most windows have icons that you use to maximize, minimize, or close the window. Here, the WordPad window includes a button that opens its Help pages.

   Below the WordPad window, the *taskbar* displays buttons along the bottom of the desktop that represent applications and windows. Here, the WordPad window is represented by a button.

4. In the **WordPad** window, type Driving directions to Cuyama and then press Enter.

■ Continue to the next page to complete the skill

Figure 1

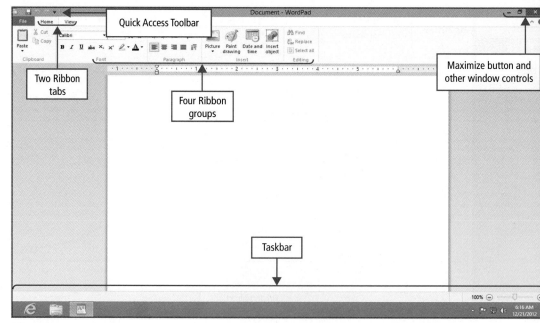

Figure 2

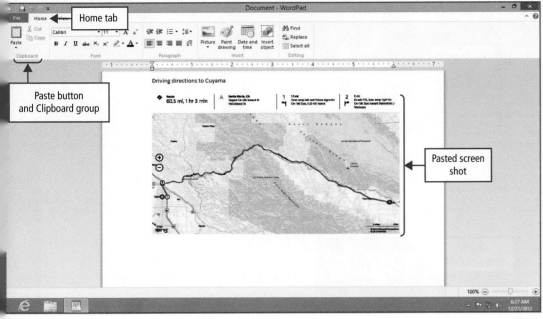

Home tab

Paste button and Clipboard group

Pasted screen shot

Figure 3

5. Point to the upper left corner of the screen, move the pointer down to display the recent apps, and then click the **Maps** thumbnail.

6. On your keyboard, above the [Home] button, press the [PrintScreen] button. The actual location and text on the button may differ slightly on your keyboard.

   When you press [PrintScreen], Windows 8 creates a **screen shot**—a picture of the current screen that can be saved as a file or inserted into documents.

7. Return to the **Start** screen, and click the **Desktop** tile to return to WordPad.

   The **desktop** is a screen you use to organize and work with your files and applications. The WordPad app runs on the desktop. The Map app runs within the Start screen.

8. On the **Home tab**, in the **Clipboard group**, click **Paste**, and then compare your screen with **Figure 3**.

9. Click the **File tab**, point to **Save as**, then click **Office Open XML document**.

10. In the **Save As** dialog box **Navigation pane**, under **Favorites**, click **Desktop**.

11. Click in the **File name** box, and then using your own name, name the file Last_First_win02_Map Compare your screen with **Figure 4**, and then click the **Save** button to save the file and close the dialog box.

    After you save a file, the file name displays in the title bar at the top of the window.

■ **You have completed Skill 3 of 10**

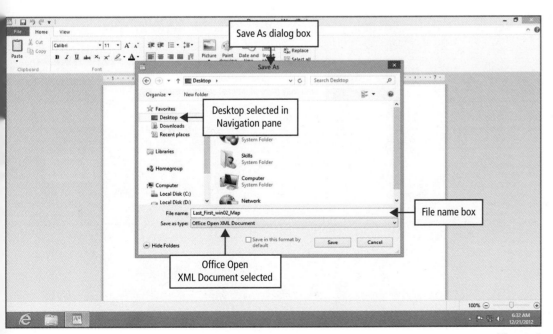

Save As dialog box

Desktop selected in Navigation pane

File name box

Office Open XML Document selected

▶ You can use the Search pane to find your applications, files, and computer settings or to search the Internet.

1. In the upper right corner of the WordPad window, click the **Minimize** button ⊟.

   When you *minimize* a window, the application is still open, but the window is closed and its button displays on the taskbar.

2. On the desktop, click the **Last_First_ win02_Map** icon one time to select it and to display the entire file name.

   On the desktop, files are represented by *icons*—small buttons used to represent files, folders, or commands. A *folder* is a container in which you store your files, and a *command* is an action used to complete a task.

3. Point to the upper right corner of the screen to display the *charms*—buttons accessed from the right edge of the screen that can be used to quickly perform common tasks. Point to the **Search** charm, and then compare your screen with **Figure 1**.

4. Click the **Search** charm to display the Apps screen. In the Search pane, type map to display the applications that match the search criteria.

5. In the **Search** pane, click **Settings**, and then compare your screen with **Figure 2**.

   Settings are saved preferences that change the way Windows or a program behaves or displays. In the figure, a link to Color Management displays because that setting provides information about mapping profiles.

■ **Continue to the next page to complete the skill** ➡

WordPad file

WordPad button on taskbar

Search button in the Charms area

Search

Share

Start

Devices

Settings

Friday December 21

Figure 1

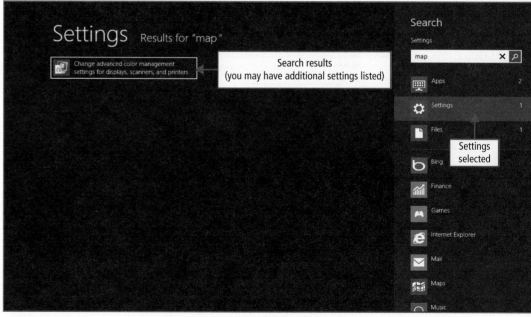

Settings   Results for "map"

Change advanced color management settings for displays, scanners, and printers

Search results (you may have additional settings listed)

Search

Settings

map ✕

Apps   2

Settings   1

Files   1

Settings selected

Bing

Finance

Games

Internet Explorer

Mail

Maps

Music

Figure 2

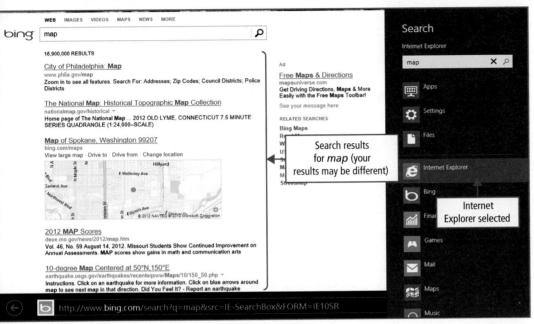

Figure 3

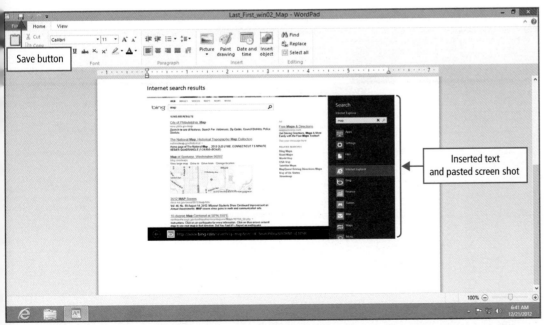

Figure 4

6. In the **Search** pane, click **Files** to display the files on your computer containing the text map. Notice that the file you saved previously is listed in the results.

7. Click **Internet Explorer** to search the Internet using the search term *map*, and then compare your screen with **Figure 3**.

   Because search engines continually update and customize their results, your list of results will look different than the one shown in the figure.

8. Press PrintScreen to create a screen shot of the search results.

9. Point to the upper right corner to display the charms, move the mouse down, and then click **Start**.

10. Click the **Desktop** tile, and then on the taskbar, click the **WordPad** button to restore the WordPad window.

11. With the insertion point to the right of the map screen shot, press Enter to create a new line, and then type Internet search results Press Enter, and then on the **Home tab**, in the **Clipboard group**, click the **Paste** button.

12. Compare your screen with **Figure 4**, and then on the Quick Access Toolbar, click **Save** . Leave WordPad open for the next skill.

- **You have completed Skill 4 of 10**

WIN 2-5 VIDEO

▶ Textbooks often provide files that you need to be able to complete projects. These files are known as *student data files*.

▶ A *compressed folder* is a file or group of files compressed into a single file. They are also referred to as *zipped folders* and the process of uncompressing them is called *unzipping*.

1. If your instructor has provided directions for obtaining the student data files for this chapter, follow those directions, and then skip to the next skill.

2. On the taskbar, click the **Internet Explorer** button to open the web browser, and if necessary, Maximize □ the window.

3. In the address bar, replace the text with pearsonhighered.com/skills and then click the **Go to** button →. Compare your screen with **Figure 1**.

4. On the web page, locate and click the link to the edition of the book you are currently using. Continue following the hyperlinks that lead to the student data files. When you find the link to the student data files, click it, and then compare your screen with **Figure 2**.

Browser settings determine what displays when you click a link that downloads files. Here, you are asked if you want to open the file, save the file to your computer's Downloads folder, or use the Save as command to save it to a different location.

■ **Continue to the next page to complete the skill**

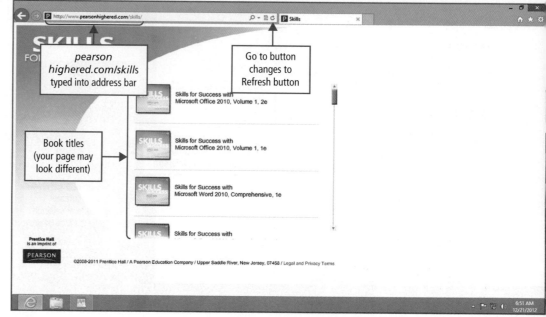

Figure 1

Screenshot from Skills for Success website. Copyright © 2012 by Pearson Education, Inc. Reprinted with permission.

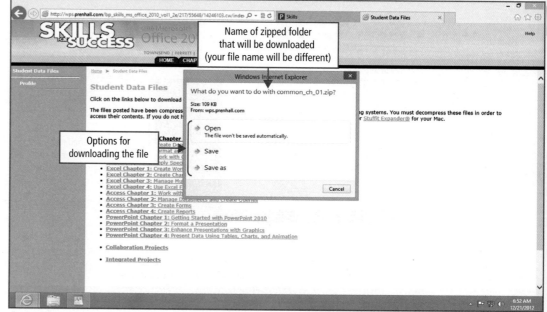

Figure 2

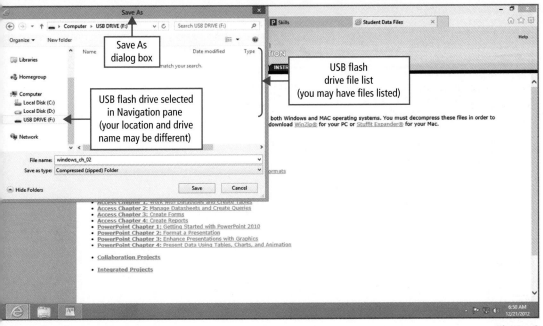

Figure 3

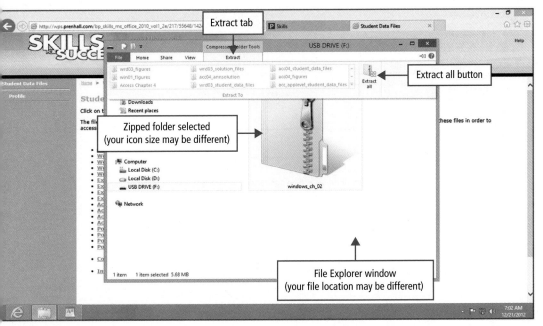

Figure 4

5. If you will be saving your work to a USB flash drive, insert it into the computer now.

6. In the **Windows Internet Explorer** dialog box, click **Save as**. In the **Navigation pane** of the **Save As** dialog box, select the location where you want to save the student data files. Compare your screen with **Figure 3**.

   In this chapter, all figures show work saved on a USB flash drive. If you are saving your work in an alternate location, use that location instead.

7. With your USB flash drive—or alternate location—selected in the **Save As** dialog box **Navigation pane**, click the **Save** button.

8. In the message that displays at the bottom of the **Internet Explorer** window, click the **Open folder** button to open File Explorer, and select the zipped folder that you downloaded in the previous step.

9. With the downloaded file still selected, click the **Extract tab**. Compare your screen with **Figure 4**, and then click the **Extract all** button.

10. In the **Extract Compressed (Zipped) Folders** dialog box, click the **Extract** button. Wait a few moments for the folder containing the files you need to open in a new window.

11. On the taskbar, right-click the **File Explorer** button , and then click **Close all windows**.

12. In **Windows Internet Explorer**, click the **Close** button . If a message displays, click the **Close all tabs** button.

■ **You have completed Skill 5 of 10**

▶ **File Explorer** is an application that is used to view, find, and organize files and folders.

▶ File Explorer displays **folder windows**—windows that show files and folders.

▶ Folder windows typically have a Navigation pane on the left and a file list on the right.

1. On the taskbar, click the **File Explorer** button ▦, and then **Maximize** □ the window. Compare your screen with Figure 1.

   When you open File Explorer from the taskbar, the Libraries folder window displays by default. **Libraries** are collections of folders and files assembled from various locations.

2. In the **Navigation pane**, click **Computer** one time to display the Computer window, and then compare your screen with Figure 2.

   The **Computer window** is used to access the drives on your computer.

3. In the list of drives, under **Devices with Removable Storage**, double-click the icon for your USB flash drive. If you are storing your work in a different location, navigate to that location instead.

4. In your location's file list, double-click the **windows_ch_02** folder—the one without the zipper in the icon—that you downloaded and extracted previously. If another folder labeled as student data files displays, double-click to open that folder.

5. Double-click the **Historic Locations** folder to open the folder and display its file list.

■ **Continue to the next page to complete the skill**

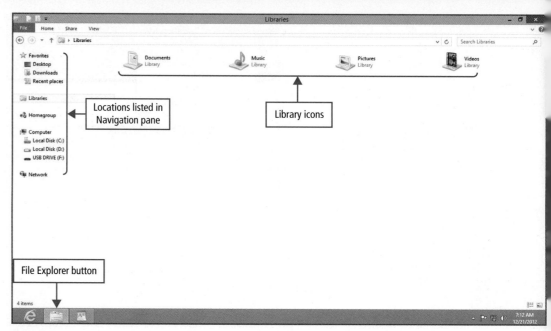

Figure 1

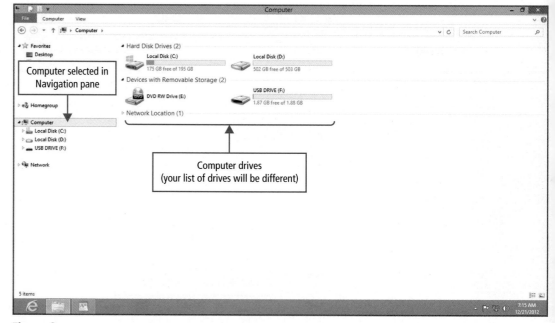

Figure 2

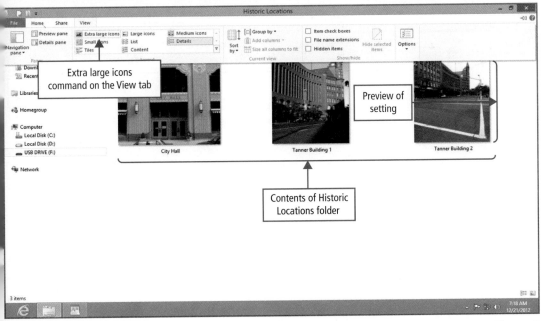

Extra large icons command on the View tab

Preview of setting

Contents of Historic Locations folder

Figure 3

6. Click **View** to display the **View tab**, and then in the **Layout group**, point to—do not click—each of the commands to preview each setting. Point to **Extra large icons**, and then compare your screen with **Figure 3**.

7. On the **View tab**, in the **Layout group**, click **Extra large icons**.

8. Click **City Hall** one time to select the file. On the **View tab**, in the **Panes group**, click **Details pane** to display details about the photo. Compare your screen with **Figure 4**, and then press PrintScreen to create a screen shot.

9. On the toolbar, click the **Up** button ↑ one time to navigate to the parent folder—the folder with all the student data files.

10. Click **Aspen Falls** one time to select the file. On the **View tab**, in the **Panes group**, click **Preview pane** to display a preview of the document.

    The Preview pane displays a preview only when an application is installed that can view and open the file. Here, Aspen Falls is a Word document, and the preview will display only if Microsoft Word is installed on your computer.

11. On the taskbar, click the **WordPad** button. With the insertion point at the end of the document, press Enter to create a new line, and then type Historic buildings

12. Press Enter, and then **Paste** the screen shot you made previously. **Save** the document. Leave WordPad and File Explorer open for the next skill.

■ **You have completed Skill 6 of 10**

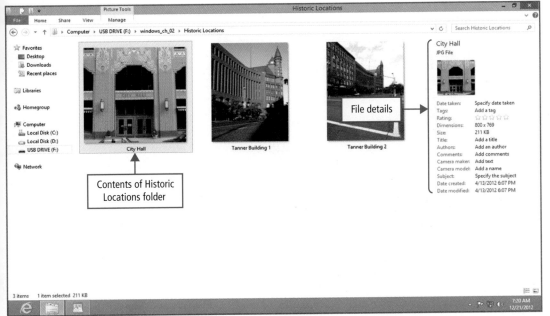

Contents of Historic Locations folder

File details

Figure 4

▶ You can find files using the folder window search box and use the Copy command to duplicate files.

1. On the taskbar, click the **File Explorer** button ⬛ to switch to the window. On the **View tab**, in the **Panes group**, click so that **Preview pane** is no longer selected.

2. If necessary, click in the file list to hide the Ribbon. Verify that the folder with all the student data files is the current folder. In the upper right corner of the window, click in the **Search** box, and then type water to display one folder and three files.

> In this manner, you can search file and folder names. From here you can expand your search to other locations or search for the word or phrase in the files, contents.

3. On the **Home tab**, in the **Select group**, click **Select all**, and then compare your screen with **Figure 1**.

> Alternately, you can select a group of files by *dragging*—pressing and holding the left mouse button while moving the mouse.

4. On the **Home tab**, in the **Clipboard group**, click **Copy**.

> The Copy command places the selected items in the *clipboard*—a memory location maintained by the operating system used to copy or move text, objects, files, or folders.

5. In the search box, click the **Close** button ⊠ to display all the files in the folder.

6. Click the **Up** button ↑ one time to return to the location where you stored the student data files folder, and then change the view to **Extra large icons**.

7. On the **Home tab**, in the **New group**, click **New folder**. Compare your screen with **Figure 2**.

■ **Continue to the next page to complete the skill** ▶

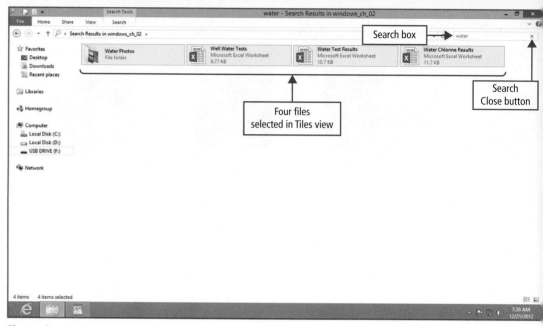

Figure 1

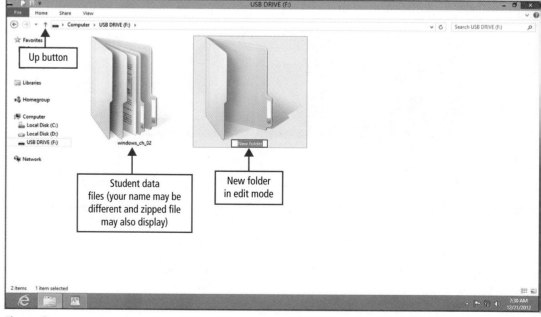

Figure 2

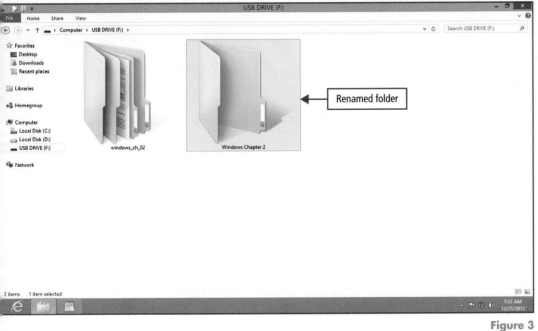

Renamed folder

Figure 3

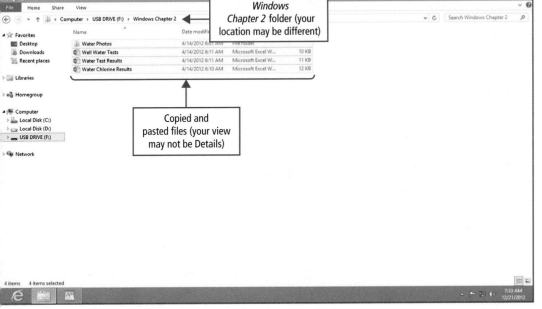

Windows Chapter 2 folder (your location may be different)

Copied and pasted files (your view may not be Details)

Figure 4

8. With **New folder** still in edit mode, type Windows Chapter 2 Press Enter to accept the name and exit edit mode. If you accidentally left edit mode before typing the folder name, right-click the folder, click Rename, and then repeat this step. Compare your screen with **Figure 3**.

    It is a good practice to store files for a project in a single folder. All the files you will work with in this chapter will be stored in the *Windows Chapter 2* folder.

9. Double-click the **Windows Chapter 2** icon to open the folder. From the **Home tab**, in the **Clipboard group**, click **Paste** to copy the folder and three files that you previously copied to the clipboard.

10. Switch the **View** to **Details**, and then compare your screen with **Figure 4**.

    When you copy and paste a folder, all the files in that folder are also pasted. The clipboard will continue to store the copied folder and files until a new object is copied or you sign out of the computer.

11. Leave the **Windows Chapter 2** folder window open for the next skill.

■ **You have completed Skill 7 of 10**

▶ You can quickly *snap* a window to either half of the screen by dragging its title bar and the pointer to the screen's edge.

▶ When you delete a file, it is moved to the **Recycle Bin**—an area on your drive that stores files you no longer need.

1. Switch to the **WordPad** window. Click the **File tab**, and then click **Exit**.

2. Point to the title bar of the **Windows Chapter 2** folder window, and then drag to the right. When the [⇩] pointer is on the right edge of the screen and a transparent outline displays as shown in **Figure 1**, release the left mouse button to snap the window to the right half of the screen.

3. Drag the **Last_First_win02_Map** icon from the desktop to a blank area in the folder window file list. When the *Copy to Windows Chapter 2* message displays, release the left mouse button, and then compare your screen with **Figure 2**.

   When you drag a file from one disk to another, a *copy* of the file is created. Here, the file on the desktop is on the computer's hard drive, and a copy is on a USB flash drive. Your file may have *moved,* as explained in the next step.

4. If you are saving your work to My Documents, the file copied in the previous step was moved, not copied, and you should read, but not perform, Steps 5 through 7.

5. Drag the **Last_First_win02_Map** icon from the desktop to the **Recycle Bin**. When the *Move to Recycle Bin* message displays, release the left mouse button.

■ **Continue to the next page to complete the skill**

Transparent outline of snapped window position

Pointer in title bar and aligned with right edge

Figure 1

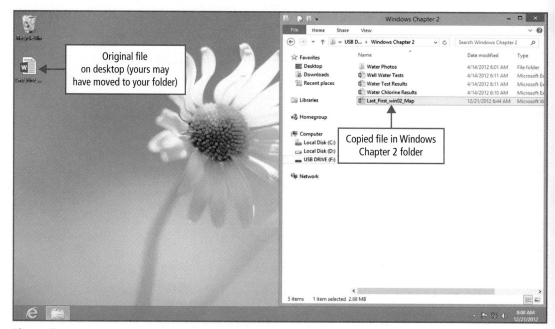

Original file on desktop (yours may have moved to your folder)

Copied file in Windows Chapter 2 folder

Figure 2

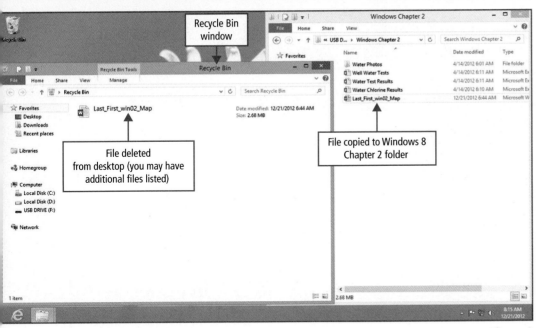

Figure 3

Figure 4

6. On the desktop, double-click the **Recycle Bin** icon to open its folder window. Compare your screen with **Figure 3**.

   When the Recycle Bin becomes full, it permanently deletes the oldest files.

7. **Close** the **Recycle Bin** folder window. In the **Windows Chapter 2** window, use the technique practiced previously to create a new folder named Water Search

8. Drag the **Water Photos** folder to the **Water Search** folder, and when the *Move to Water Search* message displays, release the left mouse button.

   When you drag a file or folder to a new location on the same disk, the file is moved, and a copy is not created. Here, the folder and all the files in it have been moved to the Water Search folder.

9. Click **Well Water Tests** to select the file. While pressing and holding [Shift], click **Water Chlorine Results**, and then release [Shift].

   Clicking a file while holding down [Shift] is called ***Shift-clicking***. Shift-clicking is often used to select a continuous range of files.

10. With the three files selected, drag one of the files to the **Water Search** folder to move all three files into the folder.

11. Open the **Water Search** folder. Click **Water Chlorine Results**, and then on the **Home tab**, in the **Organize group**, click **Rename**. Type Chlorine Test Results and then press [Enter] to rename the file. Compare your screen with **Figure 4**.

■ **You have completed Skill 8 of 10**

▶ You can customize the look of the desktop by applying a *theme*—a group of pre-built settings, including desktop background, window border color, screen saver, and system sounds.

▶ The *Snipping Tool* is an application that creates screen shots called *snips*.

1. **Minimize** ─ File Explorer so that the entire desktop displays.

2. Point to the lower right corner of the screen, and then click the **Settings** charm. In the **Settings** pane, click **Personalization**. Alternately, right-click a blank area on the desktop, and then from the shortcut menu, click Personalize.

3. Note the name of the selected theme so that you can return to it later.

4. In the **Personalization** window, under **Windows Default Themes**, click **Earth**. Compare your screen with **Figure 1**.

    The Earth theme rotates through a series of desktop backgrounds. For this reason, your desktop background may be different than the one shown in the figures.

5. **Close** × the Personalization window. On the taskbar, click the **File Explorer** button 📁 to open its window.

6. Press ⊞ to switch to the Start screen. Type Snip to search for and select the **Snipping Tool** app, and then press Enter to start Snipping Tool. Compare your screen with **Figure 2**.

7. In the **Snipping Tool** window, click the **New arrow**. In the list of snip types, click **Full-screen Snip**.

■ Continue to the next page to complete the skill ➤

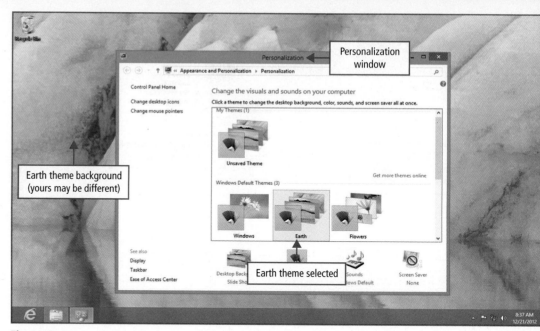

Figure 1

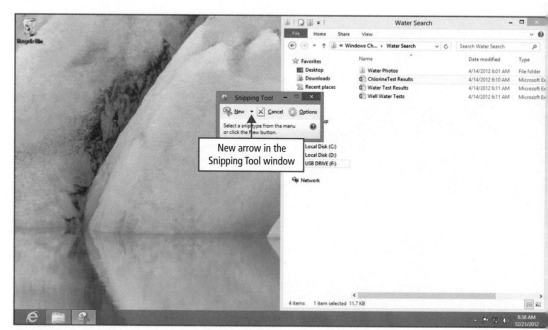

Figure 2

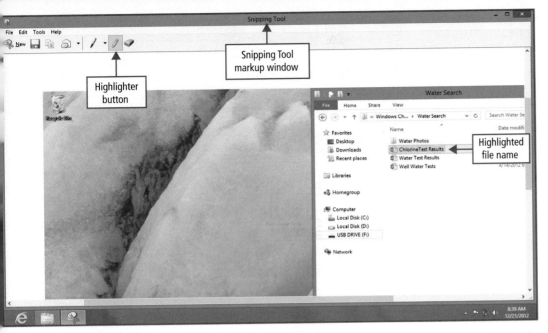

Figure 3

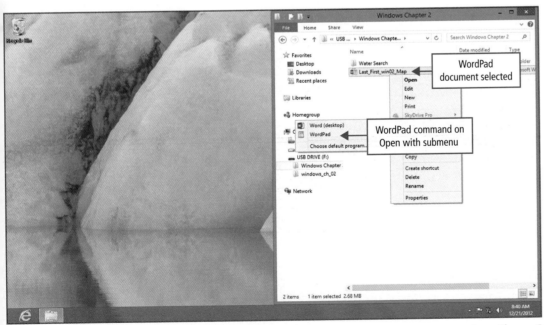

Figure 4

8. On the **Snipping Tool** toolbar, click the **Highlighter** button. Drag through the file name, *Chlorine Test Results*. Compare your screen with **Figure 3**.

9. **Close** the Snipping Tool mark-up window. When a message displays asking if you want to save the snip, click **No**.

   When you create a snip, the screen shot is placed in the clipboard. You can then paste the snip into another file or e-mail message. This technique is often helpful when you send a message to a technician about a problem you may be experiencing with your computer.

10. In the folder window, click the **Up** button one time. Right-click **Last_First_ win02_Map**, point to **Open with**, and then compare your screen with **Figure 4**.

    If Word is installed on your computer, the *Open with* submenu displays at least two applications that can open the document—Word (desktop) and WordPad. Your computer may display additional applications.

11. From the **Open with** submenu, click **WordPad** to open the document. If your computer does not display the Open with submenu, double-click the file to open it in WordPad.

12. Press and hold Ctrl, press End, and then release both keys—Ctrl + End—to position the insertion point at the end of the document.

13. On a blank line below the picture, type Snip Press Enter, click the **Paste** button, and then **Save** the document.

■ **You have completed Skill 9 of 10**

▶ Any computer settings that are changed in a *Skills for Success* project should be reset at the end of the project.

▶ If you are working at your own computer, you can use the skills practiced to customize your computer after completing that project.

1. With the document still open in WordPad, click **File**, and then click **Print**. Compare your screen with **Figure 1**.

2. If your instructor has asked you to print this project, note the name of the selected printer, and then click the Print button. Otherwise, click **Cancel**.

3. Click **File**, and then click **Exit** to close the WordPad application.

4. On the taskbar, right-click the **File Explorer** button 📁, and then click **Close window**.

5. If you are working with a USB flash drive, on the right side of the taskbar, in the notification area, click the **Show hidden icons arrow** ▴, point to the **Safely Remove Hardware and Eject Media** icon 🔌, and then compare your screen with **Figure 2**.

> The Safely Remove Hardware and Eject Media command checks to see that no applications are currently working with any files on the device. Before removing a USB flash drive, you should first save and then close those files so that any temporary files associated with them are deleted.

6. If you are working with a USB flash drive, click the icon, then click the command to eject your USB flash disk, and then remove the USB flash drive from the computer.

■ **Continue to the next page to complete the skill** ▶

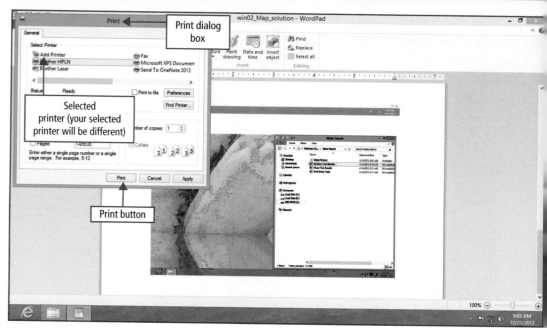

Figure 1

Figure 2

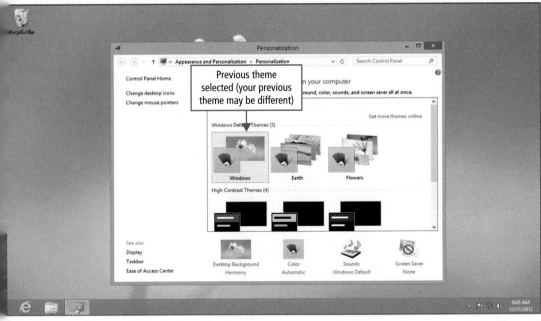

Figure 3

Figure 4

7. Right-click a blank area on the desktop, and then from the shortcut menu, click **Personalize**.

8. In the **Personalization** window, under **My Themes**, click the theme that your computer was set to before this project. Compare your screen with Figure 3, and then **Close** ☒ the Personalization window.

9. Return to the **Start** screen, and then click the **Weather** tile. Right-click in the app, and then in the app command area, click **Places**.

10. On the **Places** screen, right-click the second tile—the default location prior to this project. In the app commands, click **Set as default**. Right-click the **Cuyama, CA** tile, and then click **Remove**.

11. Press ⊞. In the upper right corner of the Start screen, click your sign in name, and then compare your screen with Figure 4.

12. From the displayed menu, click **Sign out**.

When you sign out, all applications are closed, and you cannot access your files until you sign in again. If you have any open documents that have not been saved, you will be asked if you want to save them before signing out.

13. Submit your work as directed by your instructor.

Methods for submitting work vary. Some instructors prefer to grade printouts of the documents that are created. Others may ask you to upload documents to a website such as Blackboard, MyITLab, or OneDrive. Others may ask you to attach the file to an e-mail message.

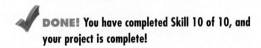 **DONE! You have completed Skill 10 of 10, and your project is complete!**

The following More Skills are located at **www.pearsonhighered.com/skills**

More Skills Customize the Start Screen

You can pin any application to the Start screen so that you can open it quickly.

In More Skills 11, you will add application tiles to the Start screen. You will create a screen shot of the modified Start screen

and then paste it into the Paint program. When you are done, you will return the Start screen to its original setting.

To begin, open your web browser, navigate to www.pearsonhighered.com/skills, locate the name of your textbook, and follow the instructions on the website.

More Skills Modify the Desktop

You can modify the desktop by adding icons and enabling a screen saver. You can also pin applications to the taskbar so that you can start them from the desktop.

In More Skills 12, you will enable a screen saver and add icons to the desktop and taskbar. You will create a file using the Snipping Tool and then change the desktop back to its previous settings.

To begin, open your web browser, navigate to www.pearsonhighered.com/skills, locate the name of your textbook, and follow the instructions on the website.

More Skills Switch to a Microsoft Account

A Microsoft account gives you access to your Windows 8 settings and Cloud-based services such as OneDrive. In this manner, you can sign in from any computer, smartphone, or tablet and have your settings and files available on that device.

In More Skills 13, you will switch a computer with a local account to one that asks you to sign in using your Microsoft

account. If you do not already have a Microsoft account, you will create one.

To begin, open your web browser, navigate to www.pearsonhighered.com/skills, locate the name of your textbook, and follow the instructions on the website.

More Skills Use the OneDrive App

You can use the OneDrive app to upload and download files to your Windows OneDrive. To connect using this app, you need to sign in using a Microsoft account.

In More Skills 14, you will use the OneDrive app to save four student data files to your OneDrive Documents folder. You will

create a screen shot of the uploaded files and then delete them from your OneDrive Documents folder.

To begin, open your web browser, navigate to www.pearsonhighered.com/skills, locate the name of your textbook, and follow the instructions on the website.

Please note that there are no additional projects to accompany the More Skills Projects, and they are not covered in the End-of-Chapter projects.

The following table summarizes the **SKILLS AND PROCEDURES** covered in this chapter.

Skills Number	Task	Steps	Icon	Keyboard Shortcut
1	Sign in	Click the lock screen. On the sign-in screen, select your user name, type your password, and then click Submit		
2	Display app commands	Right-click the app or swipe in from the bezel		
2	Switch the Start screen	Click the lower left corner, and then click the Start button	⊞	
2	Switch apps	Click the upper left corner and drag down to display the Recent tiles or swipe from the left bezel		Alt + Tab
3	Search for a Desktop app	On the Start screen, type the name of the app		
3	Start a Desktop application from the Start screen	Type the application's name		
3	Save an existing file	On the Quick Access Toolbar, click the Save button	💾	Ctrl + S
3	Create a screen shot	Press PrintScreen, and then paste the screen shot		PrintScreen Ctrl + V
4	Search for a file	Display the Charms, click Search, and in File Explorer, type the search term in the search box		
5	Download a file	Navigate to the website, and click the link to download the file(s)		
5	Unzip a folder	Extract tab → Extract All		
6	Change a file list view	View tab → Layout group		
6	Display Preview pane	View tab → Panes group → Preview pane		
6	Display Details pane	View tab → Panes group → Details pane		
7	Copy a file	With file selected, Home tab → Clipboard group → Copy		Ctrl + C
7	Paste a file	Home tab → Clipboard group → Paste		Ctrl + V
7	Create a new folder	Home tab → New group → New folder		
8	Rename a file or folder	Home tab → Organize group → Rename		
8	Move a file or folder	Drag the file or folder, or cut and paste		Ctrl + X
8	Snap a window	Drag the window's title bar to the edge of the screen		
9	Personalize the desktop	Right-click a blank area of the desktop, and then click Personalize		
9	Create a snip	From the Start screen, type Snip, press Enter, select the type of area to capture, and then save the file or paste it		
10	Print a file	File tab → Print		Ctrl + P
10	Sign out	In upper right corner, click user name, and then click Sign out		
10	Eject a USB drive	In the notification area, click Safely Remove Hardware and Eject Media, and then click the name of your USB drive	🔌	

Key Terms

Matching

Match each term in the second column with its correct definition in the first column by writing the letter of the term on the blank line in front of the correct definition.

___ **1.** To press and hold the left mouse button while moving the mouse.

___ **2.** A small rectangle or square on the Start screen that presents live, updated information.

___ **3.** Another word for app.

___ **4.** To move across the screen with the finger.

___ **5.** To size a window to fill the entire screen.

___ **6.** A screen that you use to organize and work with your files and applications.

___ **7.** A small button used to represent a file, folder, or command.

___ **8.** A container in which you store your files.

___ **9.** A group of pre-built settings, including desktop background, window border color, screen saver, and system sounds.

___ **10.** An application that creates screen shots.

A Desktop

B Drag

C Folder

D Icon

E Maximize

F Program

G Snipping Tool

H Swipe

I Theme

J Tile

Multiple Choice (MyITLab®)

Choose the correct answer.

1. To touch once with the finger.
   - A. Drag
   - B. Swipe
   - C. Tap

2. A small toolbar that contains buttons for commonly used commands such as Save and Undo.
   - A. QAT
   - B. Ribbon
   - C. Taskbar

3. An action used to complete a task.
   - A. Button
   - B. Command
   - C. Icon

4. A button accessed from the right edge of the screen that can be used to quickly perform common tasks.
   - A. Charm
   - B. Library
   - C. Tile

5. A file or group of files compressed into a single file.
   - A. App
   - B. Student data file
   - C. Zipped folder

6. An application that is used to view, find, and organize your files and folders.
   - A. Internet Explorer
   - B. Tile
   - C. File Explorer

7. A collection of folders and files assembled from various locations.
   - A. Theme
   - B. Library
   - C. Tile

8. A File Explorer folder window used to access the drives available on your computer.
   - A. Clipboard window
   - B. Computer window
   - C. Hard Drive window

9. To quickly position a window to either half of the screen by dragging the title bar and the pointer to the screen's edge.
   - A. Lock Screen
   - B. Snip
   - C. Snap

10. An area on your drive that stores files you no longer need.
    - A. Recycle Bin
    - B. Trash
    - C. Windows clipboard

Topics for Discussion

1. Start the Store app, and view the apps that are available. Which apps would you like to add, and how do you think you might use them?

2. If your desktop computer had a touchscreen, do you think you would primarily use gestures like swipe and tap to navigate between apps and windows or use the mouse? Why?

Skills Review

To complete this project, you will need the following files:

- win02_student_data_files (a folder containing several files)

You will save your file as:

- Last_First_win02_SRMeeting

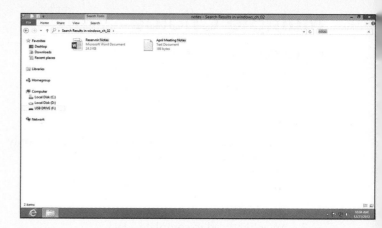

Figure 1

1. If necessary, turn on your computer and sign in.

2. On the Start screen, click the **Desktop** tile. Point to the upper right corner to display the charms, click the **Settings** charm, and then click **Personalization**.

3. In the **Personalize** window, change the theme to **Flowers**, and then **Close** the window.

4. On the taskbar, click the **File Explorer** button, and if necessary, maximize the window.

5. In the **Navigation pane**, navigate to the student data files folder that you unzipped in the previous project.

6. In the **Search** box, type notes and then compare your screen with **Figure 1**.

7. Select the two files that display in the search results, and then on the **Home tab**, in the **Clipboard group**, click **Copy**.

8. In the **Navigation pane**, display the contents of your **Windows Chapter 2** folder.

Figure 2

9. On the **Home tab**, in the **New group**, click **New Folder**, type win02_Review and then press [Enter] two times to accept the change and open the folder.

10. On the **Home tab**, in the **Clipboard group**, click the **Paste** button to copy the two files.

11. On the **View tab**, in the **Panes group**, click **Preview pane**. Select **April Meeting Notes** to preview the file. Press [Delete], read the message that displays, and then click **Yes** to delete the file.

12. Select **Reservoir Notes**, and then on the **Home tab**, in the **Organize group**, click **Rename**. Type Reservoir Recreational Activities and then press [Enter] to accept the new name. Compare your screen with **Figure 2**, and then press [PrintScreen] to create a screen shot.

- Continue to the next page to complete this Skills Review ▶

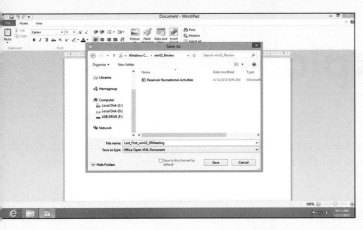

Figure 3

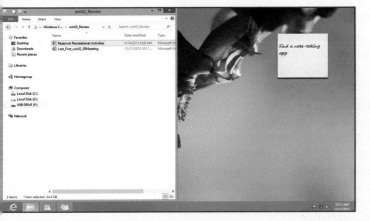

Figure 4

13. Press ⊞ to return to the Start screen, type wordpad and then press Enter to start the application.

14. In **WordPad**, type Meeting notes Press Enter , and then on the **Home tab**, in the **Clipboard group**, click **Paste** to insert the screen shot.

15. Click **File**, point to **Save as**, and then click **Office Open XML document**. In the **Save As** dialog box **Navigation pane**, navigate to your **Windows Chapter 2** folder, and then open the **win02_Review** folder.

16. In the **File name** box, replace the text with Last_First_win02_SRMeeting Compare your screen with **Figure 3**, and then click **Save**.

17. Display the charms, and then click the **Search** charm. Type notes and then click **Sticky Notes** to start the application. In the sticky note that opens, type Find a note-taking app

18. Return to the Start screen, and then click the **Store** tile. Scroll or swipe to the right to display the apps in the **Productivity** category, and then press PrintScreen .

19. Return to the **WordPad** window, press Enter , and then type Productivity apps Press Enter , **Paste** the screen shot, and then click **Save**.

20. **Minimize** the WordPad window, and then snap the **win02_Review** folder window to the left half of the screen. Compare your screen with **Figure 4**.

21. Display and click the **Search** charm, type snip and then press Enter to start Snipping Tool. In the **Snipping Tool** window, click the **New arrow**, and then click **Full-screen Snip**. **Close** the Snipping Tool mark-up window without saving the snip file.

22. On the taskbar, click **WordPad**. Press Enter , type Desktop Press Enter , **Paste** the snip, and then click **Save**.

23. If you are printing your work, click File, click Print, and then in the Print dialog box click the Print button. Click **File**, click **Print**, and then click **Exit**.

24. **Maximize** the **File Explorer** window, and then on the **View tab**, in the **Panes group**, click **Preview pane** to close the pane. **Close** the File Explorer window.

25. In the **Sticky Notes** window, click the **Delete Note** button, and then click **Yes**.

26. Right-click a blank area on the desktop, and then click **Personalize**. Click the theme that you were using prior to this project, and then **Close** the window.

27. Submit your printout or files as directed by your instructor.

 DONE! You have completed this Skills Review

CHAPTER 3

Browse with Internet Explorer

- ▶ You can use Internet Explorer to visit the millions of web pages on the World Wide Web.

- ▶ When you run Internet Explorer from the Start screen, it is optimized for mobile devices such as smart phones and tablets.

- ▶ Most websites provide navigation aids that help you find specific information at the site.

- ▶ When you are not sure where to find information, you can use special services that search the web for you.

- ▶ You can keep a list of your favorite sites and return to them with a single click. You can also revisit sites by viewing them in a list of recently visited sites.

- ▶ When you need to print a web page, you can often find a version of the page that is optimized for printing. You can also select part of the page and then print just that selection.

- ▶ Internet Explorer has several features that protect your online safety and privacy. These features can be adjusted to better meet your personal needs.

© HaywireMedia

Aspen Falls City Hall

In this chapter, you will use Internet Explorer to conduct research for Aspen Falls City Hall, which provides essential services for the citizens and visitors of Aspen Falls, California. You will assist Todd Austin, Tourism Director, to locate information about National Parks that are a short drive from the city.

The **Internet** is a global collection of networks that facilitate electronic communication such as e-mail, file sharing, and the World Wide Web. **Internet Explorer** is a program used to browse the **World Wide Web**. Also known as the **WWW**, or the **web**, the web is a collection of linked pages designed to be viewed from any computer connected to the Internet. Because so many websites and pages are available on the Internet, you may need to use the web's tools and search aids to locate, filter, and organize the information you need.

Internet Explorer provides two experiences, and each is optimized for the type of device you are using. When you are using a mobile device, you can start Internet Explorer from the Start screen, and when you are sitting at a desktop computer, you can open it from the desktop when you want to see all of its features.

In this project, you will search and navigate several websites, open sites in multiple tabs, and organize a list of favorite sites. You will practice printing web pages and saving them as files on your local drive. You will also use Internet Explorer to protect your online privacy and security while you browse the web.

Time to complete all 10 skills – 60 to 75 minutes

Student data files needed for this project:

None

You will save your files as:

Last_First_ie03_Parks (1 through 6)
Last_First_ie03_ParksMHT

Outcome

Using the skills in this chapter, you will be able to locate and view websites like this:

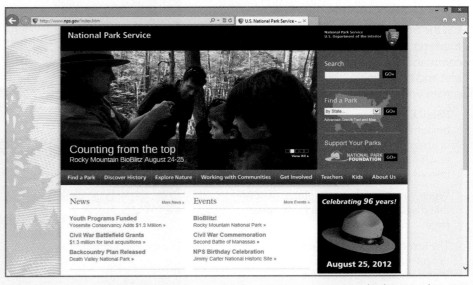

National Park Service website, 2012.

SKILLS

At the end of this chapter you will be able to:

Skill 1 Browse from the Start Screen
Skill 2 Browse from the Desktop and Add Favorites
Skill 3 Navigate and Search Websites
Skill 4 Use Accelerators and Search Providers
Skill 5 Manage Browser Tabs
Skill 6 Organize Favorites
Skill 7 Print and Save Web Pages
Skill 8 View and Delete Browsing History
Skill 9 Protect Online Privacy
Skill 10 Manage Pop-ups and Check Website Safety

MORE SKILLS

Skill 11 Change Your Home Page
Skill 12 Add Navigation Tiles to the Start Screen
Skill 13 Add Tracking Protection
Skill 14 Change Internet Security Settings

▶ Programs used to navigate the World Wide Web are called **web browsers**.

▶ To maximize the area devoted to the web page when viewed on mobile devices, Internet Explorer displays buttons and commands only when you need them. For example, you can access multiple pages and other tools in the app commands area.

1. Display the Windows 8 Start screen, and then compare your screen with **Figure 1**. If you do not have Windows 8 installed on your computer or the Start screen does not have the Internet Explorer icon, read but do not perform this skill.

2. On the **Start** screen, click the **Internet Explorer** tile. In the Internet Explorer app commands, click the text in the address bar, and then type usa.gov Compare your screen with **Figure 2**.

   Recall that you can display app commands by right-clicking or tapping the bottom area of an application window. If you have a touch screen, you can tap the address bar instead of clicking.

   When you start Internet Explorer, the page that displays is called the **default home page**.

   The text *usa.gov* is a **domain name**—a unique name assigned to a website on the World Wide Web. The text *http://* will be inserted automatically before the domain name after you navigate to the page.

3. Press Enter to display the USA.gov **home page**—the starting point for the remainder of the pages at a website. Alternately, click or tap the Go button .

■ **Continue to the next page to complete the skill**

Figure 1

Figure 2

USA.gov, 2012.

Figure 3

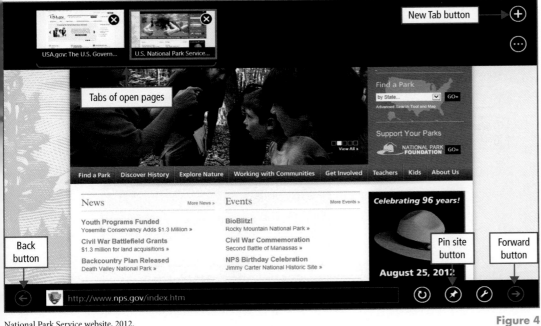

National Park Service website, 2012.

Figure 4

4. Take a few moments to familiarize yourself with the features of the USA.gov page, as described in Figure 3.

   Because the web is dynamic, the page on your computer may be different than the version shown in the figure. Here, the page displays *hyperlinks*—any text or pictures that can be clicked to move to a new page or location.

   Most web pages have a *navigation bar*—a vertical or horizontal bar with hyperlinks to the main pages of the site. Here, the page has a horizontal navigation bar that spans across the page.

5. Right-click a blank area to display the Tab and App areas. At the top of the window, click the **New Tab** button ⊕. In the address bar, type www.nps.gov and then press Enter to navigate to the National Park Service home page. Right-click a blank area of the page, and then compare your screen with Figure 4.

   The Apps command area has *Back* and *Forward* buttons to move backward or forward through your recently browsed pages. The *Pin site* button adds the page as a live tile on the Start page.

6. In the Tab area, on the **National Park Service** thumbnail, click the **Close Tab** button ⊗. **Close** ⊗ the **USA.gov** tab, and then return to the Start screen.

■ **You have completed Skill 1 of 10**

► When started from the desktop, Internet Explorer provides more functionality and displays **chrome**—the area of a web browser devoted to toolbars, Address boxes, tabs, and menus.

► A **favorite** is a stored web address that can be clicked to navigate to that page quickly.

1. From the Start screen, click the **Desktop** tile. On the taskbar, click the **Internet Explorer** button ⓔ. Take a few moments to familiarize yourself with the Internet Explorer window as described in **Figure 1**.

   If the Internet Explorer button is not on your taskbar, you can open Internet Explorer from the Start screen and navigate to the page. Then, in the app commands, click Page tools and View on the desktop.

2. At the top of the window, in the address bar, click the URL to select the text.

   A **Uniform Resource Locator**, also known as a **URL**, is a unique address of a page on the Internet.

3. Replace the selected text by typing the letters np Compare your screen with **Figure 2**.

   When you type in the address bar, the address bar Autocomplete list displays a list of recently visited websites. You can navigate to these sites by clicking them. Here, URLs http://nps.gov and http://npr.org have been typed previously. Your list will be different.

■ **Continue to the next page to complete the skill**

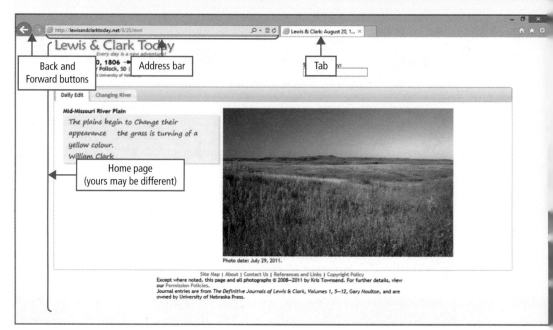

Figure 1 Lewis and Clark Today website. Copyright © 2008–2011 by Kris Townsend. Reprinted with permission.

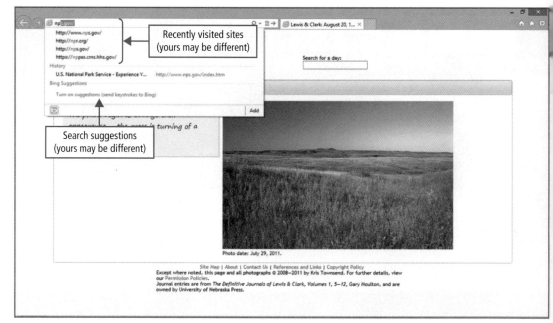

Figure 2

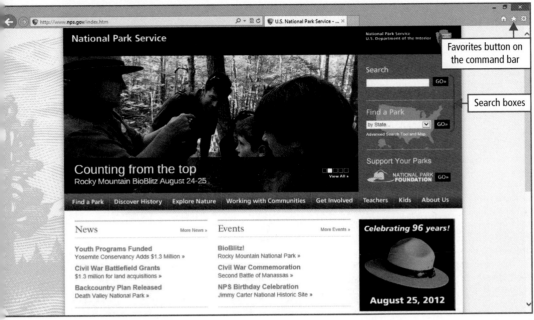

Favorites button on the command bar

Search boxes

Figure 3

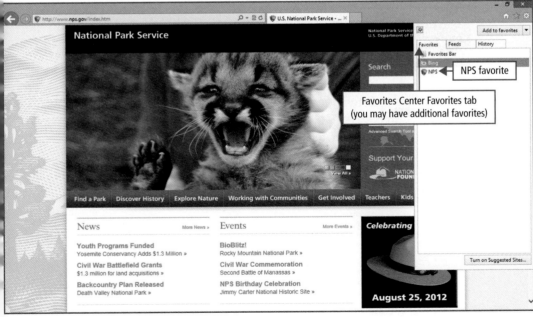

NPS favorite

Favorites Center Favorites tab (you may have additional favorites)

Figure 4

4. Finish typing nps.gov and then press [Enter]. Alternately, click the URL in the Autocomplete list. Compare your screen with **Figure 3**.

The National Park Service is a very large **website**—a collection of connected pages located at a single domain name. Large websites can consist of hundreds, or even thousands, of individual pages. The home page has search boxes and navigation bars to help you find the information you need.

5. On the command bar, click the **Favorites** button ★, and then in the **Favorites Center** that displays, click the **Add to favorites** button. In the **Add a Favorite** dialog box, in the **Name** box, replace the text with NPS and then click the **Add** button.

6. Click the **Favorites** button ★, and then compare your screen with **Figure 4**.

7. On the home page, click any hyperlink, and then on the page that displays, click any hyperlink.

8. Click the **Favorites** button ★, and then on the **Favorites tab**, click the **NPS** favorite to return to the NPS home page.

In this manner, you can return to your favorite pages quickly.

9. Leave Internet Explorer open for the next skill.

■ **You have completed Skill 2 of 10**

▶ Large websites provide navigation bars, hyperlinks, and their own search boxes, all of which you can use to find the pages you need.

1. Scroll to the bottom of the page to view the page footer, and then compare your screen with **Figure 1**.

   Web page footers typically provide links to a site index, copyright information, and a link to contact the organization.

2. In the page footer, click the **Site Index** hyperlink to display a page that outlines the site. Compare your screen with **Figure 2**.

   A *site index*—sometimes called a *site map*—is a page of hyperlinks that outline a website.

3. On the **Site Index** page, click the **About Us** hyperlink. If that link is no longer available, click a different link.

   Because most websites are updated frequently, the pages displayed in this chapter may be different. When appropriate, substitute similar links to perform each skill.

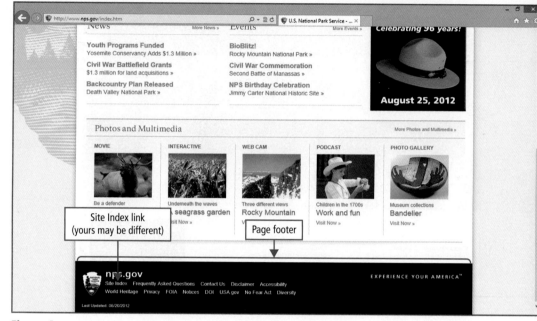

Figure 1

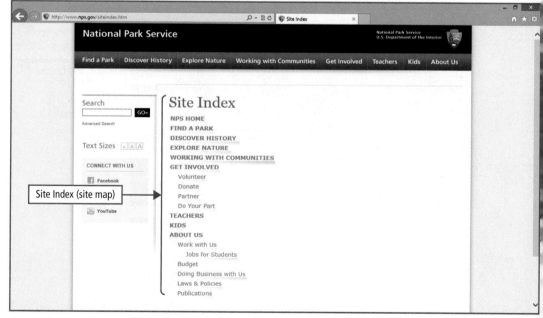

Figure 2

■ **Continue to the next page to complete the skill**

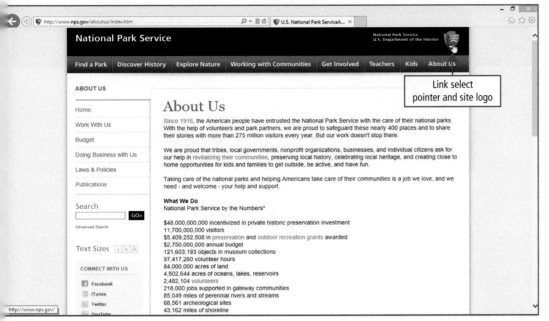

Link select pointer and site logo

Figure 3

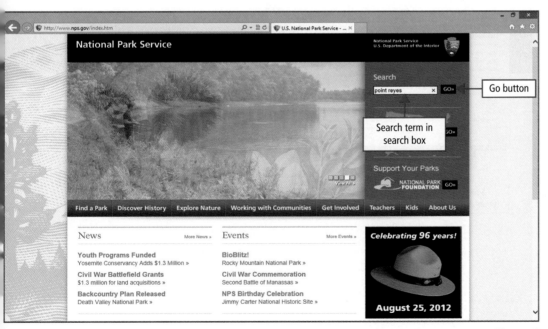

Go button

Search term in search box

Figure 4

4. In the upper-right corner of the page header, point to the **National Park Service** logo to display the link select pointer, as shown in **Figure 3**.

   The 🖑 pointer displays whenever you point to a hyperlink. Clicking a site logo typically takes you to the site's home page.

5. With the 🖑 pointer displayed, click the logo to return to the site's home page.

6. On the home page, click in the upper search box, and then type point reyes Compare your screen with **Figure 4**, and then click the **Go** button.

7. In the page of search results, click the first **Point Reyes National Seashore** hyperlink. Alternately, in the address bar, type www.nps.gov/pore and then press Enter .

8. Click the **Favorites** button ⭐, and then click **Add to Favorites**. In the **Add a Favorite** dialog box, replace the text with Point Reyes and then click the **Add** button.

9. Click the site logo to return to the home page, and leave Internet Explorer open for the next skill.

■ **You have completed Skill 3 of 10**

▶ An ***Accelerator*** is a feature that searches the web for information related to the text that you select.

▶ A ***search provider*** is a website that provides a way for you to search for information on the World Wide Web.

1. Click the **Favorites** button ⭐, and then in the **Favorites Center**, click **Point Reyes**.

2. In the opening paragraph, drag through the words *Point Reyes* to select the text. Click the **Accelerator** button ↗ that displays, and then compare your screen with **Figure 1**.

3. In the **Accelerators** list, click **Map with Bing** to display a map of Point Reyes in a new tab. If the Map with Bing accelerator does not display, in the Accelerator menu, point to All Accelerators, and then click Map with Bing.

   When you click an Accelerator, the page typically opens in a new tab. ***Tabbed browsing*** is a feature that you use to open multiple web pages in the same browser window. Each page can be viewed by clicking its tab.

4. Click the first tab starting *Point Reyes National*. In the address bar, click the Address bar arrow, and then compare your screen with **Figure 2**.

   The bottom row of the address bar Autocomplete list displays icons for the search providers that have been added to Internet Explorer on your computer. Internet Explorer's default search provider is ***Bing***.

■ Continue to the next page to complete the skill ▶

Figure 1

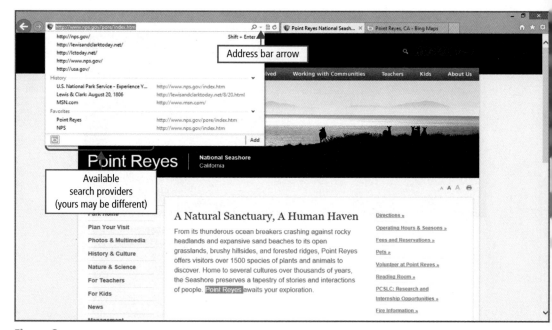

Figure 2

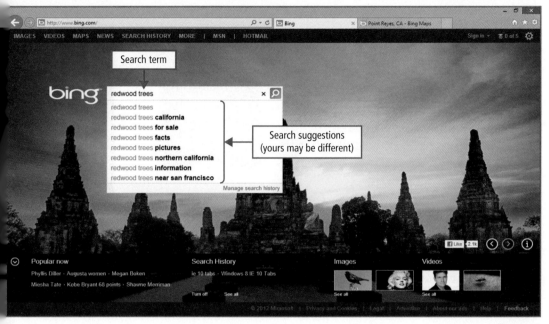

Figure 3

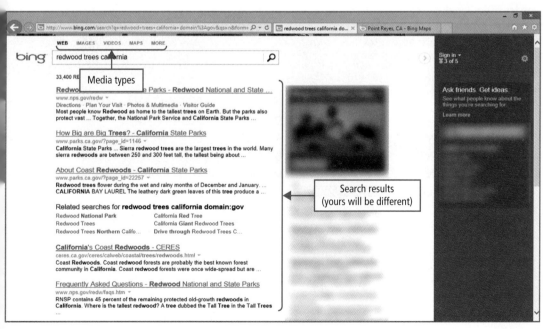

Figure 4

5. Using the techniques practiced previously, navigate to http://bing.com

6. In the **Bing** search box, type redwood trees and then compare your screen with **Figure 3**.

   Search suggestions are the words or phrases that display as you type in a search box.

7. In the list of search suggestions, click **redwood trees california**.

8. Scroll to the bottom of the search results, and then click the **Next** hyperlink to display a second page of results. Compare your screen with **Figure 4**.

   The top of the Bing search page displays links that filter your search by media type. The default media type is web pages, but you can display results for other media such as video and images.

9. In the navigation bar at the top of the page, click the **Images** link to display images related to the current search.

10. In the navigation bar at the top of the page, click the **Videos** link to display videos related to the current search.

    In this manner, you can filter your search results to specific media such as web pages, images, or video.

11. In the navigation bar at the top of the page, click the **Web** link to return to the original Bing search results.

12. Leave Internet Explorer open for the next skill.

■ **You have completed Skill 4 of 10**

▶ You can use a keyboard shortcut when clicking a hyperlink so that the page opens in a new tab.

▶ When you have multiple tabs open, you can rearrange the tabs in the tab row by dragging them. You can also view thumbnails of each open tab using the taskbar.

1. At the end of the tabs row, click the **New Tab** button [▢], and then in the new tab, navigate to bing.com

2. In the **Bing** search box, type sequoia trees domain:gov Be sure to include a space after *trees* and a colon after *domain*.

   The search will be limited to sites with the *gov* top-level domain. ***Top-level domains*** specify the organization type that sponsors a website and follow the period—often pronounced as *dot*—after a website's domain name. For example, federal and state government agencies use *.gov*, educational institutions use *.edu*, commercial entities use *.com*, and nonprofit organizations use *.org*. Most countries have their own top-level domain. A site from France, for example, may end with *.fr*.

3. Press [Enter] to complete the search, and then compare your screen with **Figure 1**.

4. In your list of search results, click the hyperlink to **Sequoia & Kings Canyon National Park** at *www.nps.gov/seki*.

5. Drag the current tab—starting *Sequoia & Kings*—to the left of the first tab. All of the other tabs shift to the right, as shown in **Figure 2**.

■ **Continue to the next page to complete the skill** ➤

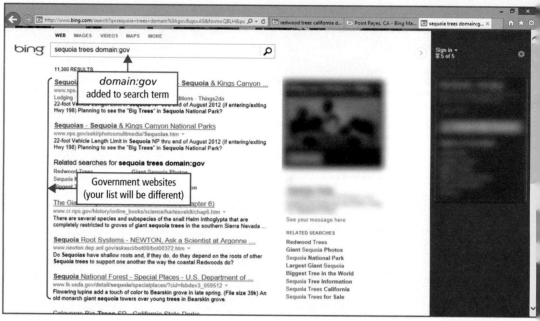

Figure 1

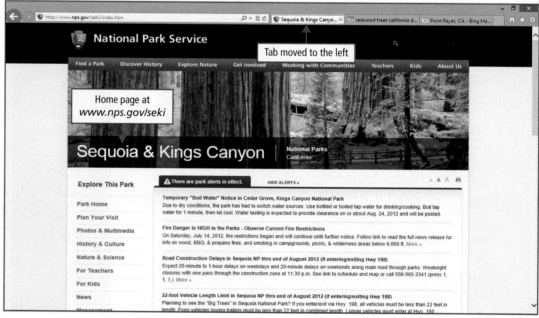

Figure 2

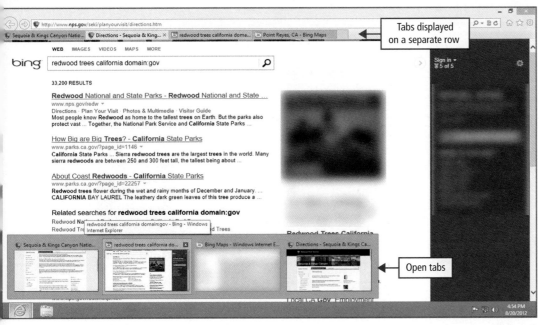

Figure 3

Figure 4

6. On the page, locate the **Directions** hyperlink. While holding [Shift] and [Ctrl] down, click **Directions** to open the page in a new tab.

7. Right-click any tab, and then from the shortcut menu, click so that the **Show tabs on a separate row** is selected (checked).

8. On the taskbar, point to the **Internet Explorer** button 🌐 to display thumbnails of each page. Point to the **redwood trees california** thumbnail, and then compare your screen with **Figure 3**.

9. On the tabs row, click the **New Tab** button 🔲 to open a new tab.

10. Click the **Favorites** button, and then click **Point Reyes**. Alternately, if the Point Reyes thumbnail displays the Frequent page, you can click the thumbnail to open the page.

11. On the web page, click **Operating Hours & Seasons**. Click the **Favorites** button ⭐, and then click the **Add to favorites arrow**. In the **Add to favorites** list, click **Add current tabs to favorites**.

12. In the **Add Tabs to Favorites** dialog box, in the **Folder Name** box, type Redwoods Research Compare your screen with **Figure 4**, and then click the **Add** button.

13. In the upper-right corner of the **Internet Explorer** window, click the **Close** button ❌.

14. In the **Internet Explorer** message, click the **Close all tabs** button to exit Internet Explorer.

   When closing the browser with multiple tabs open, a message box will ask if you want to close the current tab or all of the open tabs.

■ **You have completed Skill 5 of 10**

▶ Over time, your list of favorites may become quite long and need to be organized.

1. From the desktop, open **Internet Explorer**.

2. Click the **Favorites** button ⭐, click the **Add to favorites arrow**, and then at the bottom of the list, click **Organize favorites**. Click the **Point Reyes** favorite to select it, and then compare your screen with **Figure 1**.

3. With **Point Reyes** selected, click the **Delete** button to remove the favorite.

4. Click the **NPS** favorite, and then click the **Rename** button. With the favorite in edit mode, type NPS Home Page and then press Enter to accept the change.

5. Drag the **NPS Home Page** favorite to the **Redwoods Research** folder. When the **Redwoods Research** folder is highlighted and the *Move to Redwoods Research* message displays, as shown in **Figure 2**, release the mouse button.

6. If necessary, click the Redwoods Research folder to select it. Click the **Move** button. In the **Browse For Folder** dialog box, click the **Favorites Bar** folder, and then click **OK**.

■ **Continue to the next page to complete the skill** ▶

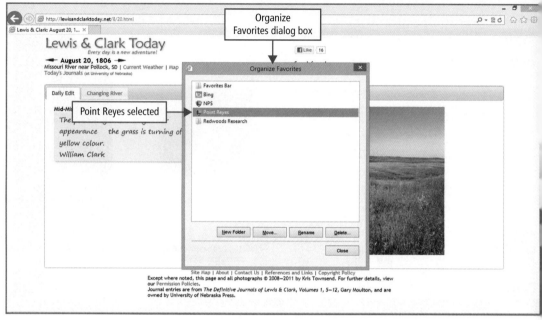

Figure 1

THE DEFINITIVE JOURNALS OF LEWIS AND CLARK by Meriwether Lewis and William Clark, edited by Gary E. Moulton. University of Nebraska Press, 1999.

Figure 2

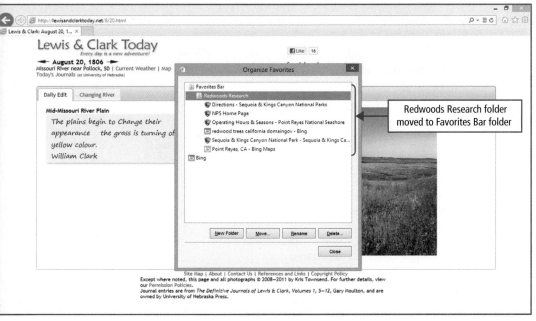

Redwoods Research folder moved to Favorites Bar folder

Figure 3

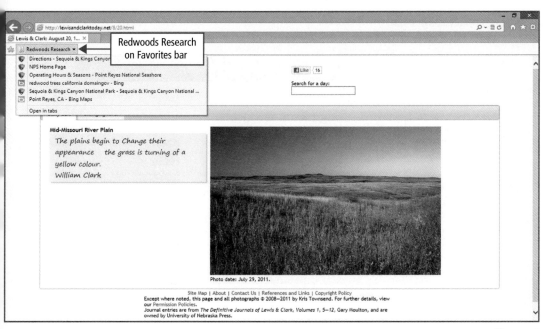

Redwoods Research on Favorites bar

Figure 4

7. In the **Organize Favorites** dialog box, click the **Favorites Bar** folder, and then click the **Redwoods Research** folder as needed to display its list. Compare your screen with **Figure 3**.

8. Press [⊞], type snip and then press [Enter] to open the Snipping Tool.

9. In the **Snipping Tool** window, click the **New arrow**, and then click **Full-screen Snip**. In the **Snipping Tool** markup window, click **Save Snip** [💾].

10. In the **Save As** dialog box, navigate to the location where you will be saving your work for this project. On the **Save As** toolbar, click **New folder**, and then type Internet Explorer Chapter 3 Press [Enter] two times to accept the new folder name and open the folder.

11. In the **Name** box, replace the text with Last_First_ie03_Parks1 Be sure the **Save as type** button displays **JPEG file**, and then click **Save**. **Close** [×] the Snipping Tool markup window.

12. **Close** [×] the Organize Favorites dialog box.

13. Right-click a blank area in the tabs row, and then click so that **Favorites bar** is selected.

14. On the Favorites bar, click the **Redwoods Research** button, and then compare your screen with **Figure 4**.

   When you add a folder to the Favorites bar, it displays as a menu. You can click an individual favorite or open all of them by clicking the Open in tabs command.

15. From the **Redwoods Research** list, click the favorite beginning *Operating Hours*.

■ **You have completed Skill 6 of 10**

▶ When you need to store information on a web page, you can print the page, print a selection on the page, or save the page to your drive.

1. On the **Operating Hours & Seasons** page, under the *Bear Valley Visitor Center* heading, drag through the paragraphs beginning *The Bear Valley* and ending with *Fridays and Saturdays*. Compare your screen with **Figure 1**.

2. Right-click the text selected in the previous step, and then from the shortcut menu, click **Print**. In the **Print** dialog box, under **Page Range**, select the **Selection** option button. Compare your screen with **Figure 2**.

   With the Selection option, only the selected information will be printed. In this manner, you can print only the information you need.

3. Start the **Snipping Tool**, and then create a **Full-screen Snip**. Save 🖫 the snip in your **Internet Explorer Chapter 3** folder with the name Last_First_ie03_Parks2

4. **Close** ❌ the Snipping Tool markup window. In the **Print** dialog box, click **Cancel**.

Figure 1

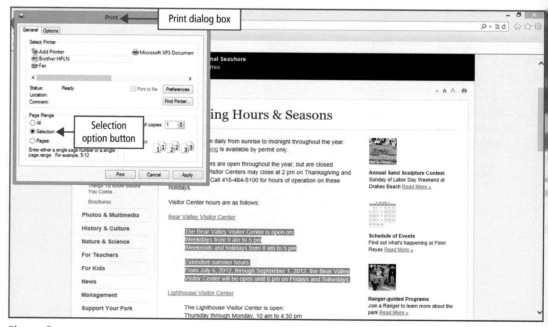

Figure 2

■ **Continue to the next page to complete the skill** ➡

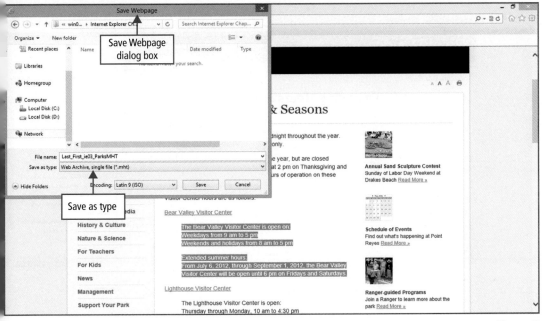

Figure 3

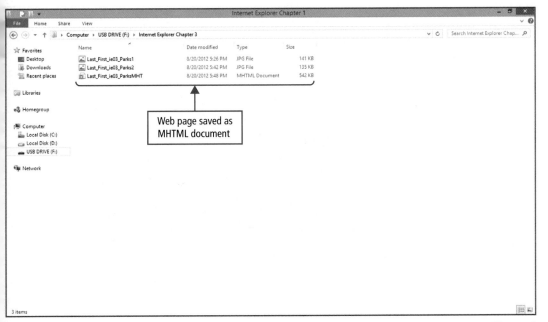

Figure 4

5. On the command bar, click the **Tools** button ⚙, point to **File**, and then click **Save as**.

6. In the **Save Webpage** dialog box, navigate to your **Internet Explorer Chapter 3** file list. In the **File name** box, replace the text with Last_First_ie03_ParksMHT

7. Click the **Save as type** button, and then click **Web Archive**, **single file (*.mht)**. Compare your screen with **Figure 3**, and then click **Save**.

> A **web archive** is a file that saves the web page text and its pictures in a single file. These files are typically assigned the *.mht* file extension. Web archives are also known as **MHTML files**.

8. On the taskbar, click the **File Explorer** button 📁. In the **Navigation** pane, navigate to and open your **Internet Explorer Chapter 3** folder. Compare your screen with **Figure 4**.

9. **Close** ⊠ the File Explorer window, and then click a blank area in the Internet Explorer window.

10. On the Favorites Bar, right-click the **Redwood Research** folder, and then from the shortcut menu, click **Delete** to remove the six favorites.

11. Right-click the Favorites bar, and then from the shortcut menu, click **Favorites bar** to hide the bar.

■ **You have completed Skill 7 of 10**

▶ As you browse the web, Internet Explorer stores information that helps you browse more efficiently. This information is called your **browsing history**.

1. In **Internet Explorer**, click the **Favorites** button ⭐, and then in the **Favorites Center**, click the **History tab**.

2. At the top of the **History** list, click the **View By** button, and then click **View By Site**. In the **History** list, click **bing (www.bing.com)**, and then compare your screen with **Figure 1**.

    On the History tab, you can open any page in your history list by clicking its URL.

3. Click the **View By** button, and then click **View By Date**. Click **Today**, and then click **nps (www.nps.gov)** to show the National Park Service sites that you visited today. Click **Site Index** to open the page.

4. Click in the address bar, type windows.microsoft.com and then press Enter.

5. **Close** ✕ Internet Explorer, and then open **Internet Explorer** from the desktop. In the address bar, select the URL. Watch the address bar **Autocomplete** list as you type windows Compare your screen with **Figure 2**.

    As you type in the address bar, your address bar Autocomplete list displays a list of sites matching your history list. Here, the Family Safety page displays after typing the first three characters—*win*. Depending on your history, you may need to type more of the address.

■ Continue to the next page to complete the skill ▶

Figure 1

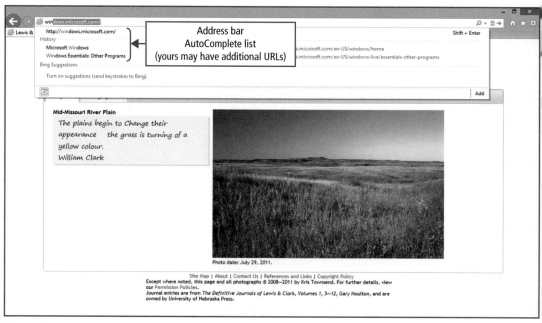

Figure 2

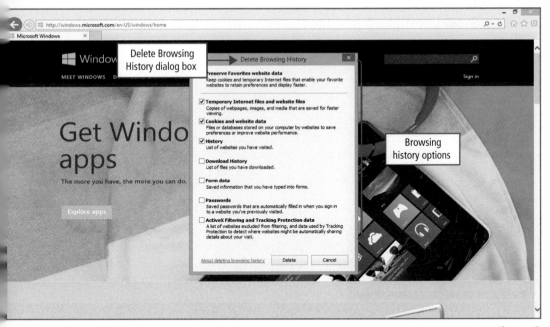

Figure 3

6. In the address bar **Autocomplete** list, click **http://windows.microsoft.com** to open the page.

   In this manner, your history list can help you navigate to websites quickly.

7. On the command bar, click the **Tools** button [⚙], point to **Safety**, and then click **Delete browsing history**. Compare your screen with **Figure 3**.

   In the Delete Browsing History dialog box, you can choose which portions of your browsing history to delete. The different options are summarized in **Figure 4**. When you want to delete all of your temporary Internet files and cookies, clear the Preserve Favorites website data check box.

8. Create a **Full-screen Snip**. **Save** [💾] the snip as a **JPEG** file in your **Internet Explorer Chapter 3** folder with the name Last_First_ie03_Parks3

9. **Close** [×] the Snipping Tool markup window.

10. If you want to delete your browsing history, in the Delete Browsing History dialog box, click the Delete button. Otherwise, click **Cancel**.

    When you are working on a **public computer**—a computer that is available to others when you are not using it—it is a good idea to delete your browsing history before logging off the computer.

11. Leave Internet Explorer open for the next skill.

■ **You have completed Skill 8 of 10**

Browsing History Settings	
Category	**Purpose**
Temporary Internet files	Copies of web pages and their images stored in your personal folder. These are used to decrease the time it takes for frequently visited pages to display.
Cookies	Small text files written by some websites as you visit them. They are used to add functionality to pages or to analyze the way you use a website.
History	A list of all the web pages you have visited.
Download History	A list of files that you have downloaded.
Form data	Information that you have typed into forms such as your logon name, e-mail address, and street address.
Passwords	Any logon passwords that you choose to save with Internet Explorer are stored here.
ActiveX Filtering and Tracking Protection Data	Data used to filter harmful sites and manage privacy.

Figure 4

▶ You can protect your privacy with **InPrivate Browsing**—an Internet Explorer window that limits the browsing history that is written.

▶ You can allow or prevent specific sites from writing cookies on your computer.

1. On the taskbar, right-click the **Internet Explorer** button 🌐, and then on the shortcut menu, under **Tasks**, click **Start InPrivate Browsing**.

2. On the **about:InPrivate** page, take a few moments to read the information about InPrivate Browsing.

3. On the taskbar, point to the **Internet Explorer** button 🌐 to display all open pages. Compare your screen with **Figure 1**.

    When you start InPrivate Browsing, a new Internet Explorer window opens. InPrivate Browsing is in effect only when that window is used.

4. On the **about:InPrivate** page, in the address bar, replace the text with nps.gov/muwo and then press Enter.

5. On the command bar, click the **Tools** button ⚙, point to **Safety**, and then click **Webpage privacy policy**. Compare your screen with **Figure 2**.

    The Privacy Report tells you if a site has written cookies. Here, the InPrivate Browsing window has accepted a cookie from the Muir Woods page. Recall that cookies typically are stored in your personal folder. InPrivate writes cookies to **RAM**—a computer's temporary electronic memory. When the window is closed, the cookie is removed from RAM.

■ Continue to the next page to complete the skill ▶

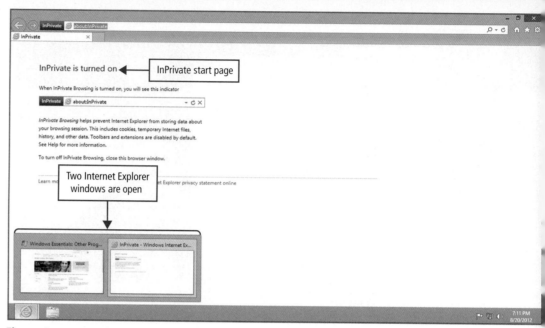

Figure 1

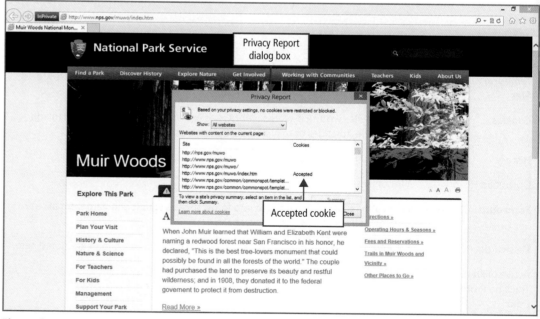

Figure 2

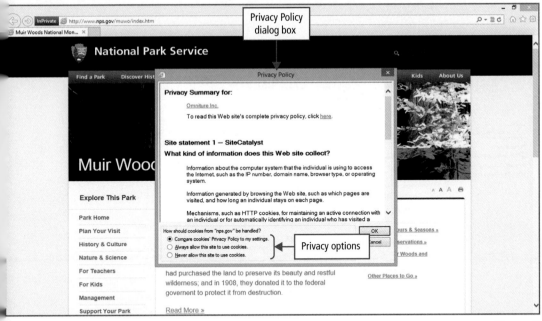

Figure 3

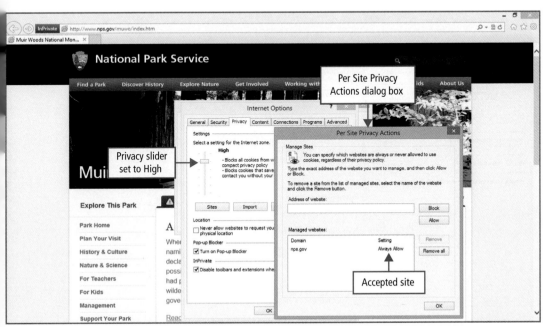

Figure 4

6. In the **Privacy Report** dialog box, scroll down, click the URL starting with *http://stats.nps.gov*, and then click the **Summary** button. Compare your screen with **Figure 3**.

   A **privacy policy** explains what types of information is collected and how it will be used.

7. At the bottom of the **Privacy Policy** dialog box, select the **Always allow this site to use cookies** option button.

8. Click **OK**, and then in the **Privacy Report** dialog box, click the **Settings** button.

9. In the **Internet Options** dialog box, drag the slider up to set the privacy level to **High**.

10. Click the **Sites** button, and then move the **Per Site Privacy Actions** dialog box to the right so that it does not cover the privacy setting slider. Compare your screen with **Figure 4**.

    With privacy set to high, only the sites you allow can write cookies. Here, only nps.gov will be allowed to write cookies.

11. Create a **Full-screen Snip**. **Save** 🔲 the snip as a **JPEG** file in your **Internet Explorer Chapter 3** folder with the name Last_First_ie03_Parks4 and then **Close** ❎ the Snipping Tool markup window.

12. In the **Per Site Privacy Actions** dialog box under **Manage sites**, click **nps.gov**, click **Remove**, and then click **OK**.

13. In the **Internet Options** dialog box, click the **Default** button to restore your original setting, and then click **OK**.

14. **Close** ❎ the **Privacy Report**, and then **Close** ❎ the InPrivate window.

■ **You have completed Skill 9 of 10**

▶ **Pop-ups** are small windows that display in addition to the web page you are viewing.

▶ **SmartScreen Filter** is a feature that helps protect you from online threats.

1. On the Internet Explorer command bar, click the **Tools** button ⚙, and then click **Internet options**. In the **Internet Options** dialog box, click the **Privacy tab**. Under **Pop-up Blocker**, click the **Settings** button, and then compare your screen with **Figure 1**.

2. In the **Pop-up Blocker Settings** dialog box, in the **Address of website to allow** box, type pearsonhighered.com and then click the **Add** button to move the site into **Allowed sites**.

3. Click the **Blocking level** button, and then click **High: Block all pop-ups**. Compare your screen with **Figure 2**.

   At many websites, pop-ups add functionality. However, some websites use pop-ups to display unwanted advertising. When you set the blocking level to high, only the sites you allow will be able to display pop-ups. Here, pages from pearsonhighered.com—such as MyITLab— are the only pages allowed to display pop-ups.

4. Create a **Full-screen Snip**. **Save** 💾 the snip as a **JPEG** file in your **Internet Explorer Chapter 3** folder with the name Last_First_ie03_Parks5 and then **Close** ✕ the Snipping Tool markup window.

5. In the **Pop-up Blocker Settings** dialog box, under **Allowed sites**, click ***.pearsonhighered.com**, and then click the **Remove** button.

■ **Continue to the next page to complete the skill** ▶

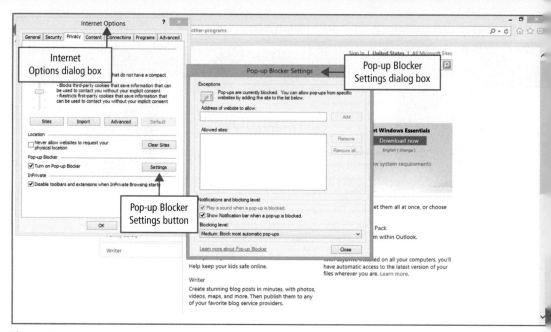

Figure 1

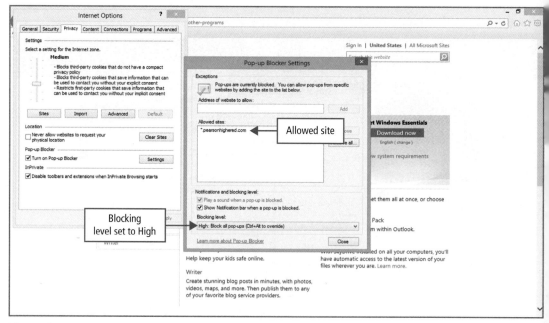

Figure 2

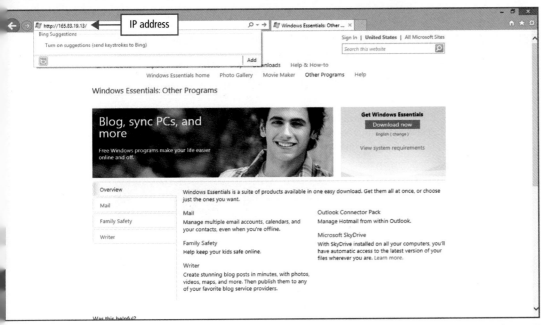

Figure 3

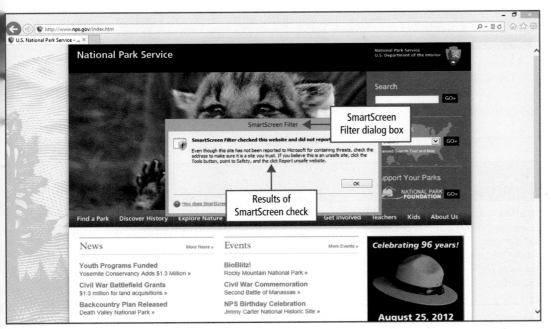

Figure 4

6. Set the **Blocking level** to **Medium: Block most automatic pop-ups**, and then close all open dialog boxes.

7. In the address bar, type the IP address http://165.83.19.13 Compare your screen with **Figure 3**.

   Be wary of websites that display an IP address instead of a domain name. An **IP address** is a unique set of numbers assigned to each computer on the Internet and are often used by **Phishing websites**—dishonest sites posing as legitimate sites to gain personal information such as your logon and bank account number.

8. Replace the IP address with nps.gov and then press Enter . On the command bar, click the **Tools** button ⚙, point to **Safety**, and then click **Check this website**. Compare your screen with **Figure 4**. If necessary, click OK to check the site.

9. Create a **Full-screen Snip**. **Save** 🖫 the snip in your **Internet Explorer Chapter 3** folder with the name Last_First_ie03_Parks6.

10. **Close** ❌ the Snipping Tool markup window, and then **Close** ❌ all open dialog boxes and windows.

✔ **DONE!** You have completed Skill 10 of 10, and your project is complete!

More Skills

The following More Skills are located at **www.pearsonhighered.com/skills**

More Skills Change Your Home Page

Recall that when you start Internet Explorer, your default home page automatically opens. You can change the default home page to any page you want.

In More Skills 11, you will change the default home page for Internet Explorer.

To begin, open your web browser, navigate to www.pearsonhighered.com/skills, locate the name of your textbook, and then follow the instructions on the website.

More Skills Add Navigation Tiles to the Start Screen

You can pin your favorite web pages to the Start screen so that you can open them with a single click. By default, pinned pages open in the version of Internet Explorer that was used to pin the page. For example, pages pinned from the Internet Explorer running from the Start screen will open in that version, and those created from the desktop will open in Desktop Internet Explorer.

In More Skills 12, you will pin pages from Internet Explorer running from the Start screen and from the desktop. You will test

each tile and then use Print Screen and Paint to create a screen shot of the Start screen. You will then remove the tiles from the Start screen.

To begin, open your web browser, navigate to www.pearsonhighered.com/skills, locate the name of your textbook, and then follow the instructions on the website.

More Skills Add Tracking Protection

You can use Internet Explorer's safety features to prevent websites from gathering information about your web browsing behaviors.

In More Skills 13, you will add a Tracking Protection service to Internet Explorer.

To begin, open your web browser, navigate to www.pearsonhighered.com/skills, locate the name of your textbook, and then follow the instructions on the website.

More Skills Change Internet Security Settings

Internet Explorer supports several web technologies that add functionality and enhance your browsing. Some sites, however, use these technologies to try to harm your computer or gain access to private information. You can customize how Internet Explorer handles these enhanced technologies. For example, you can block all of them except for the websites you specify.

In More Skills 14, you will work with the Security settings of Internet Explorer, view the four security zones, and then set a website as a trusted site.

To begin, open your web browser, navigate to www.pearsonhighered.com/skills, locate the name of your textbook, and then follow the instructions on the website.

Please note that there are no additional projects to accompany the More Skills Projects, and they are not covered in the End-of-Chapter projects.

The following table summarizes the **SKILLS AND PROCEDURES** covered in this chapter.

Skills Number	Task	Steps	Icon	Keyboard Shortcut
1	Start Internet Explorer from the Start page	From the Start screen, click the Internet Explorer tile		
1	Hide/Display app commands	Right-click a blank area of the web page		
1	Switch to Desktop Internet Explorer	Click the Page tools button	⊘	
2	Start Desktop Internet Explorer	On the taskbar, click the Internet Explorer button	e	
2	Add Favorites	Favorites → Add to Favorites button	★	Alt + C
4	Search using Accelerators	Select the desired word or words, and then click the Accelerator button	▣	
4	Search at Bing	Navigate to bing.com, and type the search terms into the search box		
4	Search for specific media	In the search results, click the link for the desired media type such as web, images, or video		
5	Limit results to top-level domains	After the search term, type domain:gov, or other top-level domain such as .org, .edu., or .com		
5	Open new tabs	On Tabs row, click New Tab	▢	Ctrl + T
5	Show tabs on a separate row	Right-click any tab		
5	Add current tabs to favorites	Click the Favorites button, and then click the Add to Favorites arrow	★	
6	Organize favorites	Click the Favorites button, and then click the Add to Favorites arrow	★	
6	Create Snips	From Start screen, type snip, and press Enter . From the New menu, click the desired Snip type, and then save		
7	Print web pages	Click Tools, point to Print, and then click Print	⚙	
7	Save web pages as MHT files	Click Tools, point to File, click Save As, and change File type to Web Archive, single file (*.mht)	⚙	
8	View browsing history	Click Favorites button, and then click History tab	★	
8	Delete browsing history	Click Tools, point to Safety, and then click Delete browsing history	⚙	Ctrl + Shift + Delete
9	Start InPrivate Browsing sessions	At the bottom of a new tab, click InPrivate Browsing		
9	View webpage privacy policies	Click Tools, point to Safety, and then click Webpage privacy policy		
9	Disable cookies	Click Tools, click Internet Options, click the Privacy tab, and then set to High or Block All Cookies		
10	Disable pop-ups	Click Tools, click Internet Options, click the Privacy tab, and then click the Pop-up Blocker Settings button		
10	Check website safety	Click Tools, point to Safety, and then click Check this website		

Key Terms

Matching

Match each term in the second column with its correct definition in the first column by writing the letter of the term on the blank line in front of the correct definition.

____ **1.** A unique name assigned to a website on the World Wide Web.

____ **2.** The starting point for the remainder of the pages at a website.

____ **3.** Any text or picture that can be clicked to move to a new page or location.

____ **4.** A feature that searches the web for information related to the text that you select.

____ **5.** A computer's temporary electronic memory.

____ **6.** A file that saves web page text and pictures in a single file. These files are typically assigned the .mht file extension.

____ **7.** An Internet Explorer window that limits the browsing history that is saved.

____ **8.** A small text file written by a website as you visit it.

____ **9.** A dishonest website posing as a legitimate site to gain personal information such as your logon and bank account number.

____ **10.** A small window that displays in addition to the web page you are viewing.

A Accelerator

B Cookie

C Domain name

D Home page

E Hyperlink

F InPrivate Browsing

G Phishing site

H Pop-up

I RAM

J Web archive

Multiple Choice

Choose the correct answer.

1. A stored web address that can be clicked to navigate to that page quickly.
   A. Favorite
   B. Quicklink
   C. Top-level domain name

2. A vertical or horizontal bar with hyperlinks to the main pages of a website.
   A. Accelerator
   B. Navigation bar
   C. Site index

3. A collection of linked pages designed to be viewed from any computer connected to the Internet.
   A. Temporary Internet files
   B. Web archive
   C. World Wide Web

4. A website that provides a way for you to search for information on the web.
   A. Accelerator
   B. Search provider
   C. Uniform Resource Locator

5. Letters after a domain name that specify the type of organization sponsoring a website—.*gov*, for example.
   A. Cookie
   B. Top-level domain
   C. URL

6. The unique address of a page on the Internet.
   A. Site index
   B. Top-level domain
   C. URL

7. The information that Internet Explorer stores as you browse the web.
   A. Browsing history
   B. Site map
   C. Wiki

8. A computer that is available to others when you are not using it.
   A. Desktop computer
   B. Mobile device
   C. Public computer

9. A browsing session that writes cookies to RAM so that they are deleted when you close the window.
   A. Accelerator
   B. Active content
   C. InPrivate Browsing

10. A unique set of numbers assigned to each computer on the Internet.
    A. Location code
    B. IP address
    C. URL

Topics for Discussion

1. Consider the websites you might visit. Which ones should be added as favorites? Of those favorites, which ones would you add to the Favorites bar?

2. In this chapter, you practiced protecting your privacy and security when you use the Internet. What websites do you think it is OK to give personal information to, and under what circumstances?

Skills Review

To complete this project, you will need the following files:

- **None**

You will save your files as:

- **Last_First_ie03_SRBLM (1 through 4)**
- **Last_First_ie03_SRBLM_MHT**

1. From the Start screen, click **Internet Explorer**. In the app commands address bar, type blm.gov and then press Enter.

2. In the app commands, click the **Page tools** button, and then click **View on the desktop** to open Desktop Internet Explorer.

3. On the **Bureau of Land Management** home page vertical navigation bar, click **Visit Us**, and then from the list that displays, click **Monuments**.

4. Navigate or scroll down to display the **California** monuments, and then click the **Carrizo Plain National Monument** hyperlink. Compare your screen with **Figure 1**.

5. Select the text *Carrizo Plain National Monument*, click the **Accelerator** that displays, and then click **Map with Bing**.

6. Click the **New Tab** button, and then navigate to *bing.com* In the search box, type carrizo plain domain:org and then click the **Search** button.

7. In the search results, Ctrl + Shift + click **The Friends of the Carrizo Plain** hyperlink to open it in a new tab.

8. Switch to the first tab. Click the **Favorites** button, and then click the **Add to favorites arrow**. In the **Add to favorites** list, click **Add current tabs to favorites**. In the **Folder Name** box, type California Monuments and then click **Add**.

9. Click the **Favorites** button, click the **Add to favorites arrow**, and then click **Organize favorites**. Click the **California Monuments** folder, and then compare your screen with **Figure 2**.

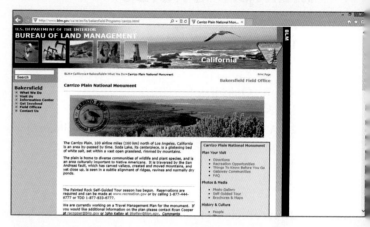

Figure 1

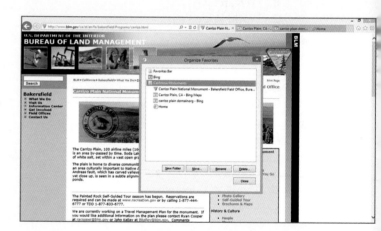

Figure 2

■ Continue to the next page to complete this Skills Review ▶

Figure 3

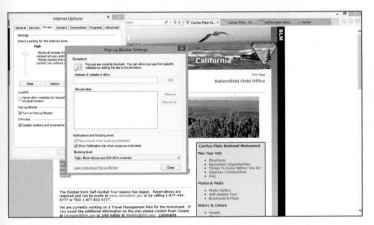

Figure 4

10. Create a **Full-screen Snip**. **Save** the snip as a **JPEG** file in your **Internet Explorer Chapter 3** folder with the name Last_First_ie03_SRBLM1 and then **Close** the Snipping Tool markup window.

11. With the **California Monuments** folder selected in the **Organize Favorites** dialog box, click the **Delete** button, and then click **Close**.

12. Open the **Favorites Center**, click the **History tab**, and then click the **Pin the Favorites Center** button. Change the view to **View By Date**. Expand **Today**, and then click **blm** (www.blm.gov). Compare your screen with **Figure 3**.

13. Create a **Full-screen Snip**. **Save** the snip as a **JPEG** file in your chapter folder with the name Last_First_ie03_SRBLM2 and then **Close** the Snipping Tool markup window. **Close** the Favorites Center pane.

14. On the **Carrizo Plain National Monument** page, select the paragraphs beginning with *The Carrizo Plain* and ending with *normally dry ponds*.

15. On the command bar, click the **Tools** button, point to **Print**, and then click **Print**. In the **Print** dialog box, under **Page Range**, select the **Selection** option button.

16. Create a **Full-screen Snip**. **Save** the snip as a **JPEG** file in your chapter folder with the name Last_First_ie03_SRBLM3 and then **Close** the Snipping Tool markup window. If you are printing this project, click **Print**. Otherwise, click Cancel.

17. On the command bar, click the **Tools** button, and then click **Internet options**. In the **Internet Options** dialog box, click the **Privacy tab**.

18. Change the **Privacy** setting to **High**, and then open the **Pop-up Blocker Settings** dialog box. Set the **Blocking level** to **High**, and then position the dialog box so that the settings in both dialog boxes display. Compare your screen with **Figure 4**.

19. Create a **Full-screen Snip**. **Save** the snip as a **JPEG** file in your chapter folder with the name Last_First_ie03_SRBLM4 and then **Close** the Snipping Tool markup window.

20. Set the **Blocking level** to **Medium**, or your previous setting, and then click the **Close** button. In the **Internet Options** dialog box, click the **Default** button, and then click **OK**.

21. Click **Tools**, point to **File**, and then click **Save As**. In the **Save Webpage** dialog box, navigate to your chapter folder. Name the file Last_First_ie03_SRBLM_MHT Change the file type to **Web Archive, single file (*.mht)**, and then click **Save**.

22. **Close** Internet Explorer. Submit your printout or files as directed by your instructor.

 DONE! You have completed this Skills Review

Common Features of Office 2013

- ▶ Microsoft Office is a suite of several programs—Word, PowerPoint, Excel, Access, and others.

- ▶ Each Office program is used to create different types of personal and business documents.

- ▶ The programs in Office 2013 share common tools that you use in a consistent, easy-to-learn manner.

- ▶ Common tasks include opening and saving files, entering and formatting text, and printing your work.

- ▶ Because of the consistent design and layout of the Office applications, when you learn to use one Microsoft Office application, you can apply many of the same techniques when working in the other Microsoft Office applications.

© spaxiax / Fotolia

Aspen Falls City Hall

In this project, you will create documents for the Aspen Falls City Hall, which provides essential services for the citizens and visitors of Aspen Falls, California. You will assist Janet Neal, Finance Director, to prepare a presentation for the City Council. The presentation will explain retail sales trends in the city. The information will help the council to predict revenue from local sales taxes.

Microsoft Office is a suite of tools designed for specific tasks. In this project, the data was originally stored in an Access database. You will use Excel to create a chart from that data and then use PowerPoint to display the chart to an audience. Next, you will use Word to write a memo to update your supervisor about the project's status. In this way, each application performs a different function and creates a different type of document.

In this project, you will create a new Word document from an online template and open existing files in Excel and PowerPoint. You will write a memo, format an Excel worksheet and update chart data, and then place a copy of the chart into a PowerPoint presentation. You will also format a database report in Access. In all four applications, you will apply the same formatting to provide a consistent look and feel.

Time to complete all 10
skills – 60 to 90 minutes

Student data files needed for this chapter:

cf01_RetailChart (Excel)   cf01_RetailData (Access)
cf01_RetailSlides (PowerPoint)

You will save your files as:

Last_First_cf01_RetailMemo (Word)
Last_First_cf01_RetailChart (Excel)
Last_First_cf01_RetailSlides (PowerPoint)
Last_First_cf01_RetailData (Access)

SKILLS

At the end of this chapter you will be able to:

Skill 1 Start Office Applications

Skill 2 Create Documents from Templates

Skill 3 Type and Edit Text

Skill 4 Save Files and Create Folders

Skill 5 Apply Themes and Format Text

Skill 6 Preview and Print Documents

Skill 7 Open and Save Student Data Files

Skill 8 Format Worksheets

Skill 9 Copy and Paste Objects and Format Slides

Skill 10 Format Access Reports

MORE SKILLS

Skill 11 Store Office Files on OneDrive

Skill 12 Use Office Help

Skill 13 Send Files as E-mail Attachments

Skill 14 Optimize Office 2013 RT

Outcome

Using the skills in this chapter, you will be able to
work with Office documents like this:

Aspen Falls City Hall

Memo

To: Janet Neal

From: Your Name

cc: Maria Martinez

Date: July 1, 2014

Re: Sales Revenue

As per your request, the *Retail Sales* slides will be ready by the end of today. I will send them
to you so you can insert them into your presentation. Let me know if you have any questions.

► The way that you start an Office application depends on what operating system you are using and how your computer is configured.

► Each application's Start screen displays links to recently viewed documents and thumbnails of sample documents that you can open.

1. If necessary, turn on the computer, sign in, and navigate to the desktop. Take a few moments to familiarize yourself with the various methods for starting Office applications as summarized in **Figure 1**.

   One method that works in both Windows 7 and Windows 8 is to press ⊞—the Windows key located between Ctrl and Alt —to display the Start menu or screen. With Start displayed, type the application name, and then press Enter .

2. Use one of the methods described in the previous step to start **Word 2013**, and then take a few moments to familiarize yourself with the Word Start screen as shown in **Figure 2**.

   Your list of recent documents will vary depending on what Word documents you have worked with previously. Below the list of recent documents, the *Open Other Documents* link is used to open Word files that are not listed.

Common Methods to Start Office 2013 Applications	
Location	**Description**
Start screen tile	Click the application's tile.
Desktop	Double-click the application's desktop icon.
Taskbar	Click the application's taskbar button.
Windows 7 Start menu	Click Start, and look in the pinned or recently used programs. Or click All Programs, and locate the Office application or the Microsoft Office 2013 folder.
All locations	Press ⊞, type the application's name, and then press Enter .

Figure 1

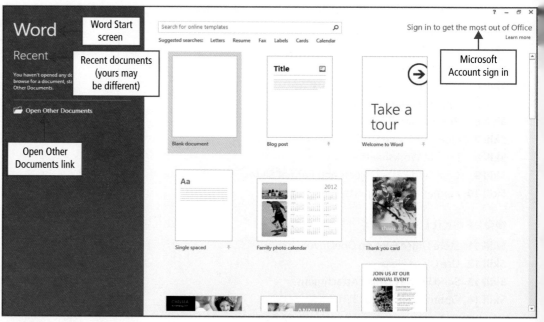

Figure 2

■ Continue to the next page to complete the skill ▶

Figure 3

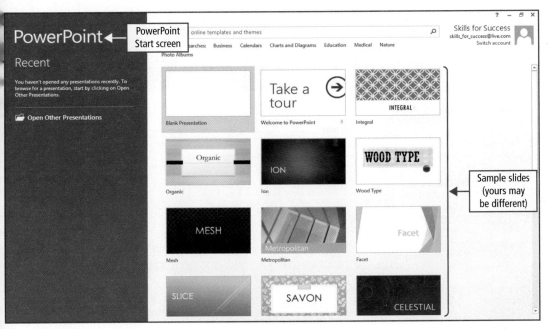

Figure 4

3. If desired, click **Sign in to get the most out of Office**, and then follow the onscreen directions to sign in using your Microsoft account.

Logging in enables you to access Microsoft Cloud services such as opening and saving files stored on your OneDrive (previously called SkyDrive). Unless otherwise directed, signing in to your Microsoft account is always optional in this book. To protect your privacy, you should sign in only if you are already signed in to Windows using a unique username, not a shared account. For example, many public computers share an account for guests.

4. Using the technique just practiced, start **Excel 2013**, and then compare your screen with **Figure 3**.

Worksheets are divided into *cells*—boxes formed by the intersection of a row and column into which text, objects, and data can be inserted. In Excel, cells can contain text, formulas, and functions. Worksheets can also display charts based on the values in the cells.

When you are logged in to your Microsoft account, your name and picture will display in the upper right corner of the window.

5. Start **PowerPoint 2013**, and then compare your screen with **Figure 4**.

PowerPoint presentations consist of *slides*—individual pages in a presentation that can contain text, pictures, or other objects. PowerPoint slides are designed to be projected as you talk in front of a group of people. The PowerPoint Start screen has thumbnails of several slides formatted in different ways.

■ **You have completed Skill 1 of 10**

▶ Office provides access to hundreds of *templates*—pre-built documents into which you insert text using the layout and formatting provided in the documents.

▶ Templates for Word documents, Excel workbooks, PowerPoint presentations, and Access databases can be opened from the start screen or the New page on each application's File tab.

1. On the taskbar, click the **Word** button 📄 to make it the active window.

2. If the Word Start screen no longer displays, on the File tab, click New.

3. Click in the **Search for online templates** box, and then type memo Click the **Start searching** button 🔍, and then compare your screen with **Figure 1**.

> The New page displays templates that are available online. These online templates are provided by Microsoft and others who submit them to microsoft.com. These online templates must be downloaded before you can work with them. Because the template list is dynamic, your search results may be different.

> On the New page, the right pane can be used to filter your search by category. You can also pin a template so that it always displays on the start screen and New page.

4. Scroll down the list of memos, and then click the **Memo (Professional design)** thumbnail. Compare your screen with **Figure 2**.

> The preview screen provides information about the template so that you can evaluate it before deciding to download it to your computer. You should download templates only from sources that you trust.

■ **Continue to the next page to complete the skill**

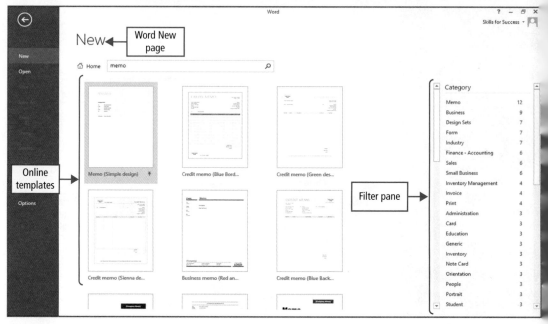

Figure 1

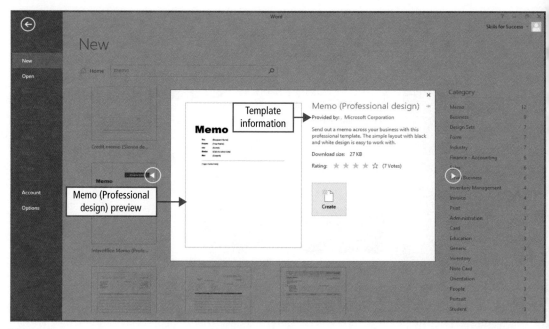

Figure 2

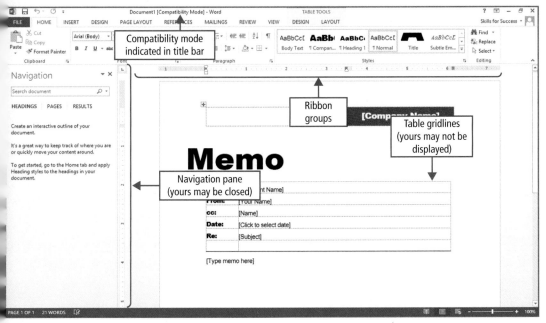

Figure 3

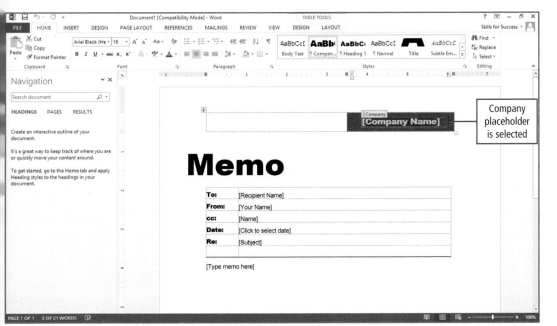

Figure 4

5. In the **Memo (Professional design)** preview, click the **Create** button. Wait a few moments for the memo to download and open. Compare your screen with **Figure 3**.

> Templates create new, unsaved documents. Here, the title bar displays the text *Document1* and ***Compatibility Mode***—a mode that limits formatting and features to ones that are supported in earlier versions of Office.

> Above the memo, the Quick Access Toolbar and Ribbon display. The Office Ribbon organizes commands into groups. Because the Ribbon adapts to the size of the document window, you may need to adjust the size of your window if you want your Ribbon to display exactly as shown in the figures in this book.

> To the left of the document, the Navigation pane is used to move through the document. Below the word *Memo*, the table gridlines may or may not display depending on your settings. These gridlines do not print, and you can work with documents with them displayed or turned off.

6. In the upper-right corner of the memo, click—or tap—the **Company** placeholder—*[Company Name]*—to select it, and then compare your screen with **Figure 4**.

> Templates often contain ***placeholders***— reserved, formatted spaces into which you enter your own text or objects. If no text is entered, the placeholder text will not print.

7. With the **Company** placeholder selected, type Aspen Falls City Hall

8. Leave the memo open for the next skill.

■ **You have completed Skill 2 of 10**

▶ To *edit* is to insert, delete, or replace text in an Office document, workbook, or presentation.

▶ To edit text, you need to position the **insertion point**—a flashing vertical line that indicates where text will be inserted—at the desired location, or select the text you want to replace.

1. Click the first **Name** placeholder—*[Recipient Name]*—and then type Janet Neal

2. Click the second **Name** placeholder—*[Your Name]*—and then type your own first and last name.

3. In the third **Name** placeholder—*[Name]*—type Maria Martinez

4. Click the **Date** placeholder—*[Click to select date]*— and then type the current date.

5. In the **Subject** placeholder, type Sales Tax Revenue Compare your screen with **Figure 1**.

6. Click *[Type memo here]*, and then type the following: As per your request, the Retail Sales slides will be ready by the end of today. I will send them to you so you can insert them into your presentation. Let me know if you have any questions. Compare your screen with **Figure 2**.

As you type, the insertion point moves to the right. To improve clarity, the figures in this book typically will not display the insertion point.

At the right margin, Word determines whether the word you are typing will fit within the established margin. If it does not fit, Word moves the entire word to the beginning of the next line. This feature is called **word wrap**. Within a paragraph, you do not need to press Enter to create new lines.

■ **Continue to the next page to complete the skill** ➤

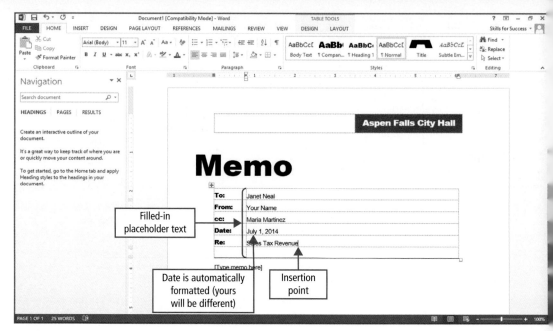

Figure 1

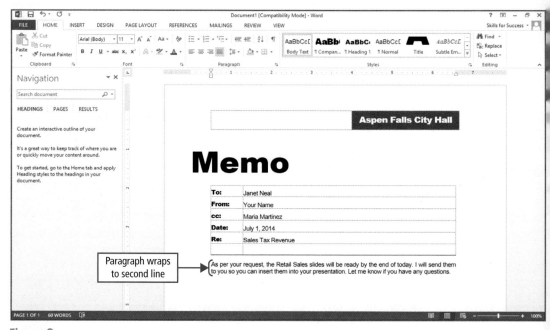

Figure 2

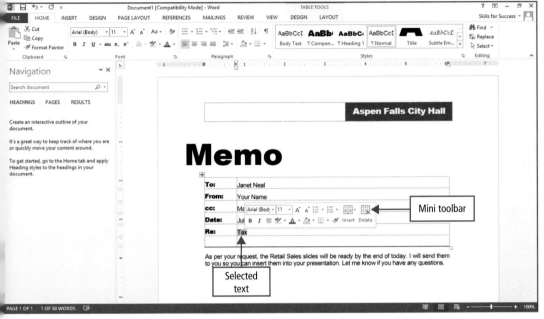

Figure 3

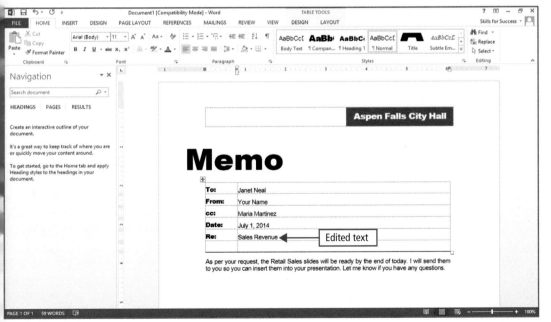

Figure 4

7. In the **Re:** line, click to the left of *Sales* to place the insertion point at the beginning of the word. Press Delete six times to delete the word *Sales* and the space that follows it.

   The Delete key deletes one letter at a time moving from left to right. The name on your keyboard may vary—for example, DEL, Del, or Delete.

8. In the **Re:** line, click to the right of *Revenue* to place the insertion point at the end of the word.

9. Press Backspace eight times to delete the word *Revenue* and the space that precedes it.

   The Backspace key deletes one letter at a time moving from right to left. The name on your keyboard may vary—for example, BACK, Backspace, or simply a left-facing arrow.

10. In the **Re:** line, double-click—or double-tap—the word *Tax* to select it, and then compare your screen with **Figure 3**.

    To **double-click** is to click the left mouse button two times quickly without moving the mouse. To **double-tap**, tap the screen in the same place two times quickly.

    After selecting text, the **Mini toolbar**—a toolbar with common formatting commands—displays near the selection.

11. Type Sales Revenue to replace the selected word, and then compare your screen with **Figure 4**.

    When a word or paragraph is selected, it is replaced by whatever you type next, and the Mini toolbar no longer displays.

■ **You have completed Skill 3 of 10**

CF 1-4
VIDEO

▶ New documents are stored in **RAM**—the computer's temporary memory—until you save them to more permanent storage such as your hard drive, USB flash drive, or online storage.

1. If you are saving your work on a USB flash drive, insert the drive into the computer. If a notice to choose what happens with removable drives displays, ignore it.

   This book assumes that your work will be saved to OneDrive or a USB flash drive. If you are saving your work to a different location, you will need to adapt these steps as necessary.

2. On the Word **Quick Access Toolbar**, click the **Save** button 🖫, and then compare your screen with **Figure 1**.

   The Save As page is used to select the location where you want to save your work. You can choose to save to your OneDrive or other locations on your computer. If you have favorite folders in which you like to save your files, you can add them to the Save As page so that you can then select them with a single click.

3. Under **Recent Folders**, click the location where you are saving your work. If your location is not displayed, click the **Browse** button, and then in the Save As dialog box, navigate to your location.

4. On the **Save As** dialog box toolbar, click the **New folder** button, and then type Common Features Chapter 1 Compare your screen with **Figure 2**.

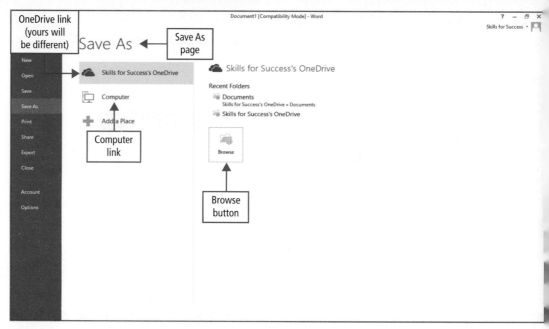

Figure 1

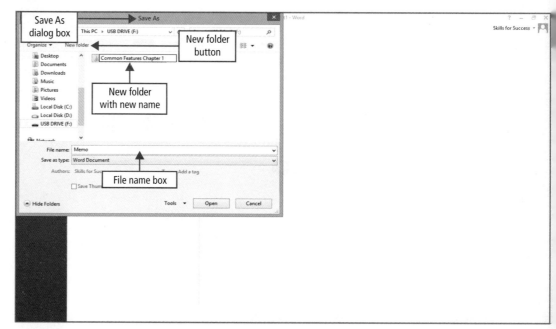

Figure 2

■ Continue to the next page to complete the skill

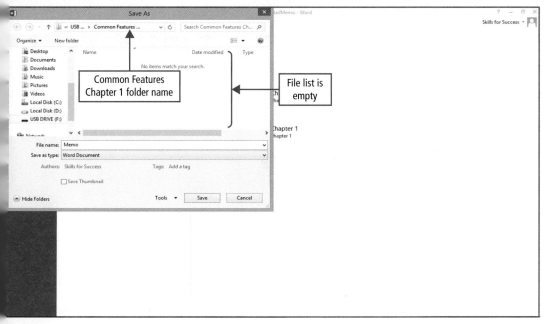

Common Features Chapter 1 folder name

File list is empty

Figure 3

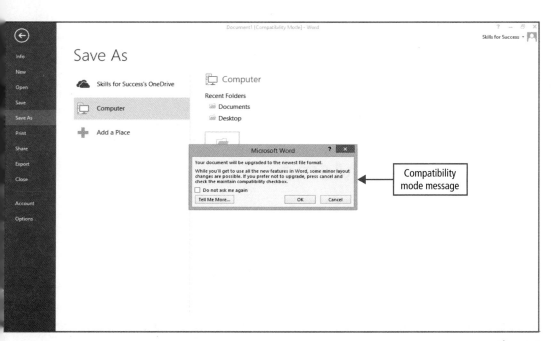

Compatibility mode message

Figure 4

5. Press Enter to accept the folder name, and then press Enter again to open the new folder as shown in **Figure 3**.

Before saving a new file, you should open the folder in which you want to store the file.

6. In the **Save As** dialog box, click in the **File name** box one time to highlight all of the existing text.

7. With the text in the **File name** box still highlighted, using your own name, type Last_First_cf01_RetailMemo

In this book, you should substitute your first and last name whenever you see the text *Last_First* or *Your Name*.

8. Click **Save**, and then compare your screen with **Figure 4**.

A message may display to inform you that the document will convert to the latest file format for Word documents.

9. Read the displayed message, and then click **OK**.

After the document is saved, the name of the file displays on the title bar at the top of the window and the text *[Compatibility Mode]* no longer displays.

10. Leave the memo open for the next skill.

▪ **You have completed Skill 4 of 10**

► To **format** is to change the appearance of the text—for example, changing the text color to red.

► Before formatting an Office document, it is a good idea to pick a **theme**—a pre-built set of unified formatting choices including colors and fonts.

1. Click the **Design tab**. In the **Themes group**, click the **Themes** button, and then compare your screen with **Figure 1**.

    Each theme displays as a thumbnail in a **gallery**—a visual display of selections from which you can choose.

2. In the **Themes** gallery, point to—but do not click—each thumbnail to preview its formatting with **Live Preview**—a feature that displays what the results of a formatting change will be if you select it.

3. In the **Themes** gallery, click the third theme in the second row—**Retrospect**.

    A **font** is a set of characters with the same design and shape. Each theme has two font categories—one for headings and one for body text.

4. Click anywhere in the text *Aspen Falls City Hall* to make it the active paragraph. With the insertion point in the paragraph, click the **Home tab**.

5. In the **Paragraph group**, click the **Shading arrow** ⬛▾. In the first row of the gallery under **Theme Colors**, click the sixth choice—**Orange, Accent 2**. Compare your screen with **Figure 2**.

    In all themes, the Accent 2 color is the sixth choice in the color gallery, but the color varies depending on the theme. Here, the Retrospect theme Accent 2 color is a shade of orange.

■ Continue to the next page to complete the skill ➤

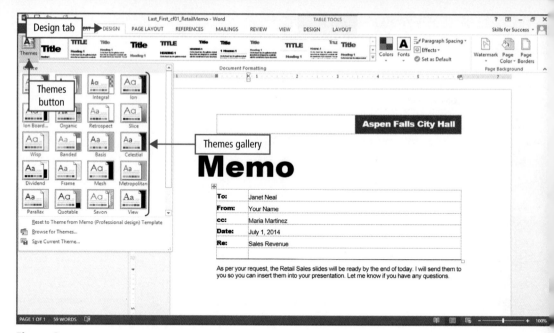

Figure 1

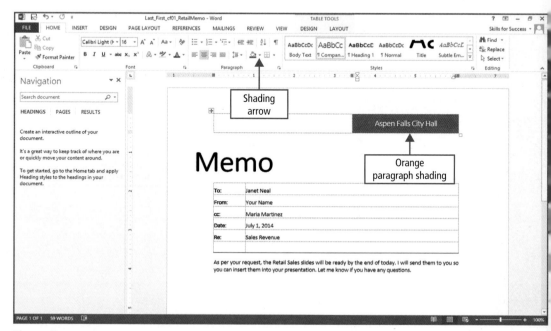

Figure 2

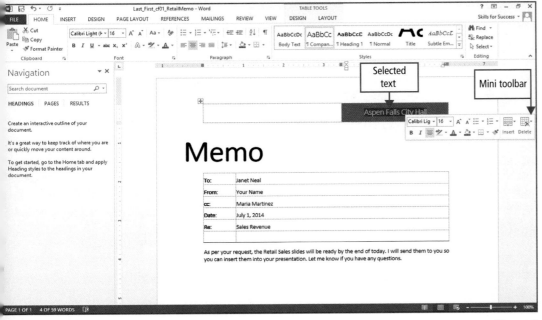

Figure 3

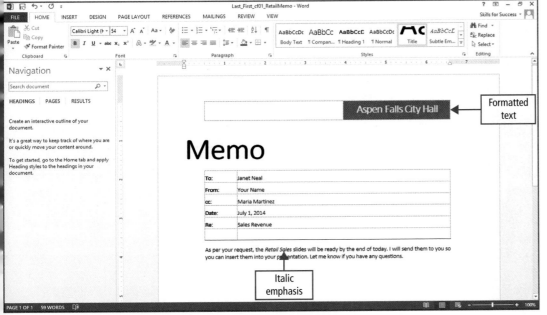

Figure 4

6. In the upper-right corner, ***drag***—press and hold the left mouse button while moving the mouse—to select the text *Aspen Falls City Hall*, and then compare your screen with **Figure 3**. To select by dragging with a touch display, tap in the text, and then drag the selection handle.

   Before formatting text, the text must be selected. If the Mini toolbar does not display, you can right-click or tap the selected text.

7. On the Mini toolbar, click the **Font Size arrow** , and then from the list, click **20** to increase the size of the selected text. On the Mini toolbar, click the **Bold** button .

8. On the Mini toolbar, click the **Font Color arrow** , and then under **Theme colors**, click the fifth color in the second row—**Orange, Accent 1, Lighter 80%**. Alternately, on the Home tab, in the Font group, click the **Font Color arrow** .

9. In the paragraph that begins *As per your*, drag to select the text *Retail Sales*. From the Mini toolbar, click the **Italic** button .

   Alternately, you can use a ***keyboard shortcut***—a combination of keys that performs a command. Here, you could press Ctrl + I .

10. Click a blank area of the document, and then compare your screen with **Figure 4**. Carefully check the memo for spelling errors. If spelling errors are found, use the techniques practiced previously to correct them.

11. Click the **Save** button .

■ **You have completed Skill 5 of 10**

▶ Before printing, it is a good idea to preview the document on the Print page.

▶ On the Print page, you can check that blank pages won't be printed by accident.

1. Click the **File tab**, and then compare your screen with **Figure 1**.

> **Backstage view** is a collection of pages on the File tab used to open, save, print, and perform other file management tasks. In Backstage view, you can return to the open document by clicking the Back button.

2. On the **File tab**, click **Print** to display the Print page. Click the **Printer** menu, and then compare your screen with **Figure 2**.

> The Printer list displays available printers for your computer along with their status. For example, a printer may be offline because it is not turned on. The **default printer** is indicated by a check mark, and is automatically selected when you do not choose a different printer.

> In a school lab or office, it is a good idea to check the list of available printers and verify that the correct printer is selected. It is also important that you know where the printer is located so that you can retrieve your printout.

3. Press Esc—located in the upper-left corner of most keyboards—to close the Printer menu without selecting a different printer.

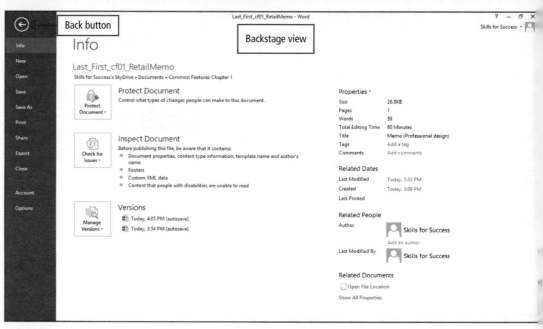

Figure 1

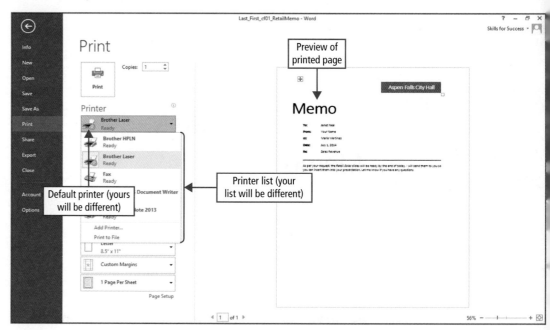

Figure 2

■ **Continue to the next page to complete the skill**

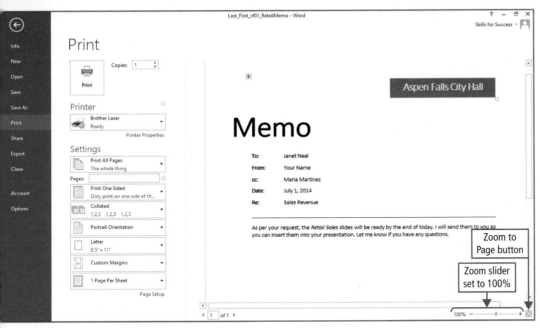

Figure 3

4. In the lower-right corner of the **Print** page, click the **Zoom In** button until the zoom level displays **100%**. Compare your screen with **Figure 3**.

   The size of the print preview depends on the size of your monitor. When previewed on smaller monitors, some documents may not display accurately. If this happens, you can zoom in to see a more accurate view.

5. To the right of the **Zoom** slider, click the **Zoom to Page** button 🔲 to return to your original zoom level.

   If you are working at a touch display, you can zoom in and out using gestures. The gestures are summarized in the table in **Figure 4**.

6. If you are printing your work for this project, note the location of the selected printer, click the **Print** button, and then retrieve your printouts from the printer.

   You should print your work only if your instructor has asked you to do so. Many instructors prefer to grade electronic versions that have been sent as e-mail attachments, copied to a network drive, or uploaded to a learning management system such as Blackboard.

7. In the upper-right corner of the window, click the **Close** button [x].

   If you have made changes to a document without saving them, you will be prompted to save those changes when you close the document.

Common Touch Screen Gestures	
Gesture	**Description**
Tap	Touch one time with the finger.
Slide	Touch an object and then move the finger across the screen.
Swipe	Slide in from a screen edge to display app commands, charms, or other temporary areas.
Pinch	Slide two fingers closer together to shrink or zoom in.
Stretch	Slide two fingers apart to enlarge or zoom out.

Figure 4

■ **You have completed Skill 6 of 10**

▶ In this book, you will frequently open student data files.

1. Before beginning this skill, the student files folder for this chapter should be downloaded and unzipped or copied similar to the one described in **Figure 1**. Follow the instructions in the book or provided by your instructor.

2. On the taskbar, click the **Excel** button to return to the Excel 2013 Start screen. If necessary, start Excel.

3. On the **Excel 2013** Start screen, click **Open Other Workbooks** to display the Open page. If you already had a blank workbook open, click the File tab instead.

4. On the **Open** page, click **Computer**, and then click the **Browse** button.

5. In the **Open** dialog box Navigation pane, navigate to the student files for this chapter, and then compare your screen with **Figure 2**.

6. In the **Open** dialog box, select **cf01_ RetailChart**, and then click the **Open** button.

7. If the Protected View message displays, click the **Enable Editing** button.

   Documents downloaded from a website typically open in **Protected View**—a view applied to documents downloaded from the Internet that allows you to decide if the content is safe before working with the document.

8. Click the **File tab**, and then click **Save As**. On the **Save As** page, click the location where you created your chapter folder, and then navigate as needed to open the **Common Features Chapter 1**. If necessary, click Browse and then navigate in the Save As dialog box.

■ **Continue to the next page to complete the skill** ▶

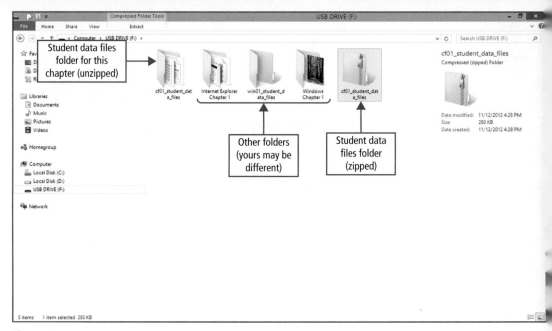

Figure 1

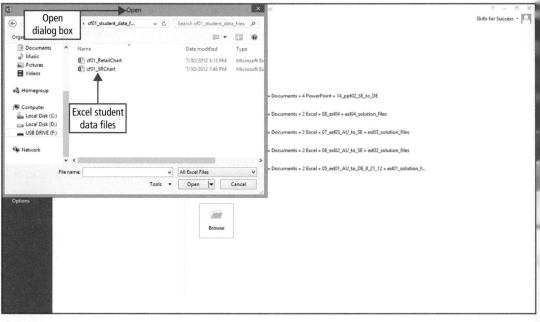

Figure 2

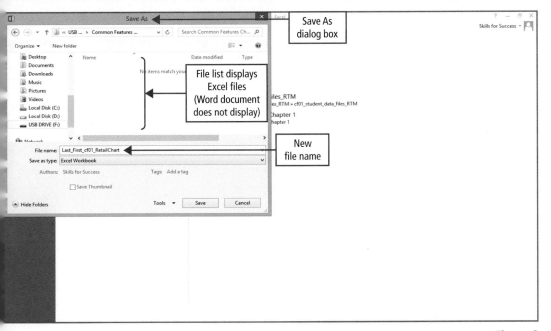

File list displays Excel files (Word document does not display)

Save As dialog box

New file name

Figure 3

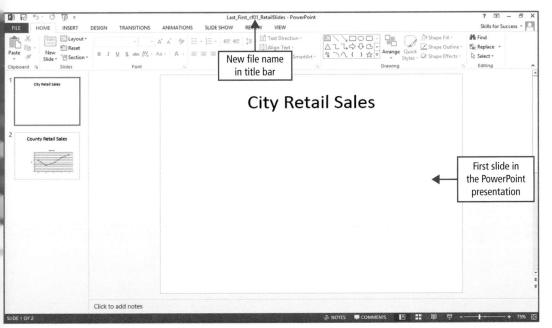

New file name in title bar

First slide in the PowerPoint presentation

City Retail Sales

Figure 4

9. In the **File Name** box, change the existing text to Last_First_cf01_RetailChart using your own name.

10. Compare your screen with **Figure 3**, and then click the **Save** button.

In this manner, you can use the Save As command to create a copy of a file with a new name. The original student data file will remain unchanged.

By default, the Save As dialog box displays only those files saved in the current application file format. Here, the Excel file is listed, but the Word file you saved previously may not display.

11. On the taskbar, click the **PowerPoint** button 🔳 to return to the PowerPoint Start screen. If necessary, start PowerPoint.

12. On the **PowerPoint 2013** Start screen, click **Open Other Presentations** to display the Open page. If you already had a blank presentation open, click the File tab instead.

13. On the **Open** page, click **Computer**, and then click the **Browse** button. In the **Open** dialog box, navigate to the student files for this chapter, and then open **cf01_RetailSlides**. If necessary, enable the content.

14. On the **File tab**, click **Save As**, and then use the Save As page to navigate as needed to open your **Common Features Chapter 1** folder in the Save As dialog box.

On most computers, your Word and Excel files will not display because the PowerPoint Save As dialog box is set to display only presentation files.

15. Name the file Last_First_cf01_ RetailSlides and then click **Save**. Compare your screen with **Figure 4**.

■ **You have completed Skill 7 of 10**

▶ To keep formatting consistent across all of your Office documents, the same themes are available in Word, Excel, PowerPoint, and Access.

▶ To format text in Excel, you typically select the cell that holds the text and then click the desired formatting command.

1. On the taskbar, click the **Excel** button 🔣 to return to the workbook.

2. Click cell **B9**—the intersection of column **B** and row **9**—to select the cell. Compare your screen with **Figure 1**.

   A selected cell is indicated by a thick, dark-green border.

3. With cell **B9** selected, type 4.37 and then press Enter to accept the change and update the chart.

   The chart is based on the data in columns A and B. When the data is changed, the chart changes to reflect the new values.

4. On the **Page Layout tab**, in the **Themes group**, click the **Themes** button, and then click the **Restrospect** thumbnail. Compare your screen with **Figure 2**.

   The Retrospect theme applies the same colors, fonts, and effects as the Retrospect theme in other Office applications. Here, the font was changed to Calibri.

5. At the top of the worksheet, right-click the title *Aspen Falls* to display the Mini toolbar. Click the **Font Size arrow** 11 ▾, and then click **14** to increase the font size.

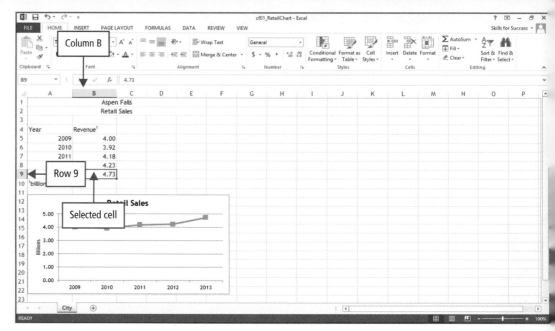

Figure 1

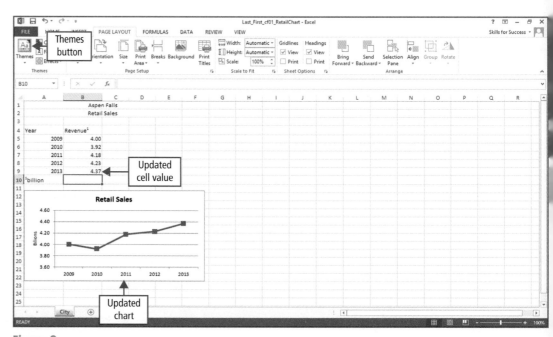

Figure 2

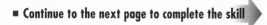
■ **Continue to the next page to complete the skill**

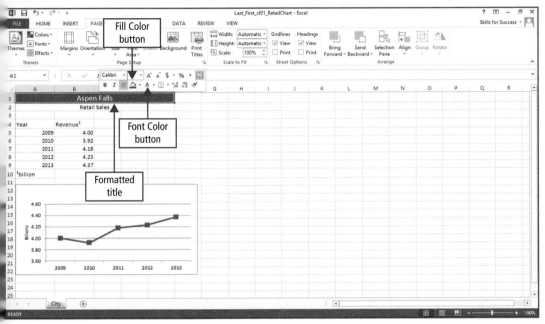

Figure 3

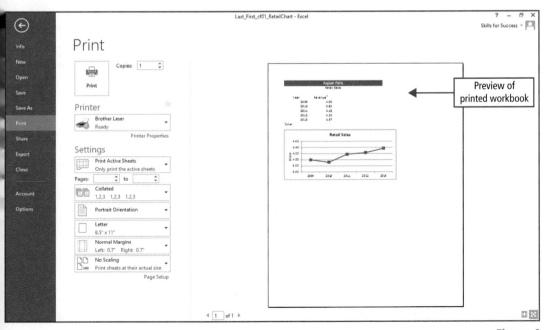

Figure 4

6. With the title cell still selected, on the Mini toolbar, click the **Fill Color arrow**, and then under **Theme Colors**, click the sixth choice—**Orange, Accent 2**.

7. In the **Font group**, click the **Font Color arrow**, and then under **Theme Colors**, click the first choice—**White, Background 1**. Compare your screen with **Figure 3**.

8. Click cell **A4**. On the **Home tab**, in the **Alignment group**, click the **Center button** to center the text. Repeat to center the text in cell **B4**.

9. Click cell **A10**, and then in the **Font group**, change the **Font Size** to **9**.

10. On the **File tab**, click **Print**, and then compare your screen with **Figure 4**.

    The Excel Print page is used in the same manner as the Word Print page. Here, you can preview the document, select your printer, and verify that the worksheet will print on a single page. By default, the gridlines do not print.

11. If you are printing your work for this project, print the worksheet. Otherwise, click the **Back** button to return to Normal view.

12. On the **Quick Access Toolbar**, click **Save**.

■ **You have completed Skill 8 of 10**

▶ In Office, the *copy* command places a copy of the selected text or object in the **Office Clipboard**—a temporary storage area that holds text or an object that has been cut or copied.

▶ The *paste* command inserts a copy of the text or object from the Office Clipboard.

1. In the Excel window, click the chart's border to select the chart, and compare your screen with **Figure 1**.

   In Office, certain graphics such as charts and SmartArt display a thick border when they are selected.

2. On the **Home tab**, in the **Clipboard group**, click the **Copy** button 🖺 to place a copy of the chart into the Office Clipboard.

3. On the taskbar, click the **PowerPoint** button 🔳 to return to **Last_First_cf01_RetailSlides**, which you saved previously.

4. With **Slide 1** as the active slide, on the **Home tab**, in the **Clipboard group**, click the **Paste** button to insert the copied Excel chart. If you accidentally clicked the Paste arrow to display the Paste Options, click the Paste button that is above it. Compare your screen with **Figure 2**.

5. Click the **Design tab**, and then in the **Themes group**, click the **More** button ▾. Point to several thumbnails to preview their formatting, and then under **Office**, click the seventh choice—**Retrospect**.

   In PowerPoint, themes are sets of colors, fonts, and effects optimized for viewing in a large room with the presentation projected onto a screen in front of the audience.

■ Continue to the next page to complete the skill

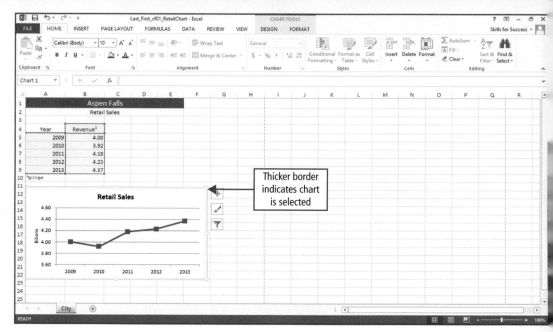

Figure 1

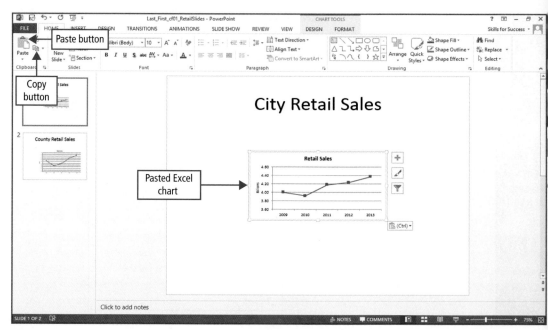

Figure 2

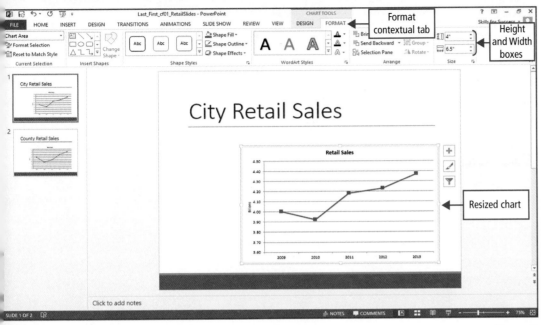

Format contextual tab

Height and Width boxes

Resized chart

Figure 3

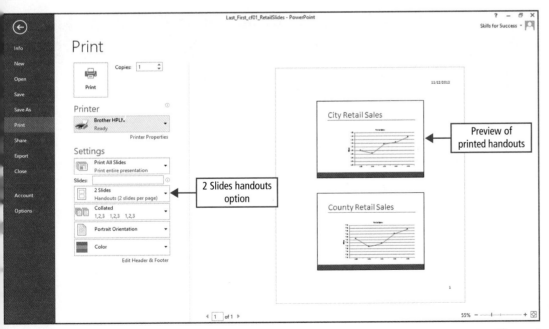

2 Slides handouts option

Preview of printed handouts

Figure 4

6. Drag through the slide title text *City Retail Sales* to select it. On the **Home tab**, in the **Font group**, click the **Font Size arrow**, and then click **60**. Alternately, right-click the selected text, and then use the Mini toolbar to change the font size.

7. Click any area in the chart, and then click the chart's border so that only the chart is selected.

8. Click the **Format tab**, and then in the **Size group**, click the **Height** spin box up arrow until the value is **4"**. Repeat this technique to change the **Width** value to **6.5"**, and then compare your screen with **Figure 3**.

   The Format tab is a ***contextual tab***—a tab that displays on the Ribbon only when a related object such as a graphic or chart is selected.

9. On the **File tab**, click **Print**. On the **Print** page, under **Settings**, click the button with the text *Full Page Slides*. In the gallery that displays, under **Handouts**, click **2 Slides**. Compare your screen with **Figure 4**.

10. If you are printing your work, click **Print** to print the handout. Otherwise, click the **Back** button to return to Normal view.

11. Click **Save**, and then **Close** the presentation window.

12. On the taskbar, click the **Excel** button to make it the active window, and then **Close** the window. If a message displays asking you to save changes, click Save.

■ **You have completed Skill 9 of 10**

CF 1-10
VIDEO

▶ Access reports present data in a way that is optimized for printing.

1. Start **Access 2013**, and then on the Start screen, click **Open Other Files**. On the **Open** page, click **Computer**, and then click **Browse**.

2. In the **Open** dialog box, navigate to the location where you are storing your student data files for this chapter. In the **Open** dialog box, select **cf01_RetailData**, and then click the **Open** button.

3. Take a few moments to familiarize yourself with the Access Window objects as described in **Figure 1**.

   Database files contain several different types of objects such as tables, queries, forms, and reports. Each object has a special purpose summarized in the table in **Figure 2**.

4. On the **File tab**, click **Save As**. With **Save Database As** selected, click the **Save As** button.

5. In the **Save As** dialog box, navigate to your **Common Features Chapter 1** folder. In the **File name** box, name the file Last_First_cf01_RetailData and then click **Save**. If a security message displays, click the Enable Content button.

   Malicious persons sometimes place objects in database files that could harm your computer. For this reason, the security message may display when you open a database that you did not create. You should click the Enable Content button only when you know the file is from a trusted source.

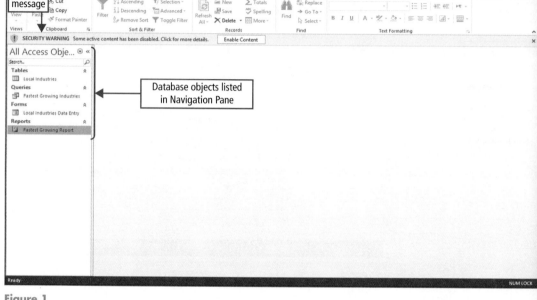

Figure 1

Common Database Objects	
Object	**Description**
Table	Stores the database data so that records are in rows and fields are in columns.
Query	Displays a subset of data in response to a question.
Form	Used to find, update, and add table records.
Report	Presents tables or query results optimized for onscreen viewing or printing.

Figure 2

▪ **Continue to the next page to complete the skill** ▶

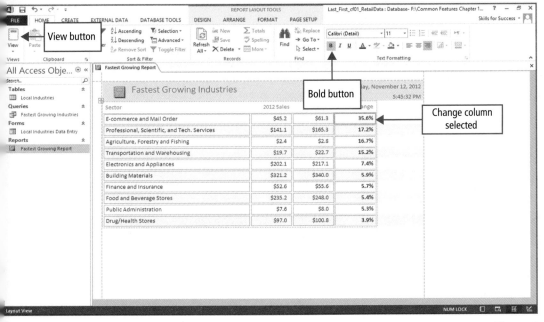

Figure 3

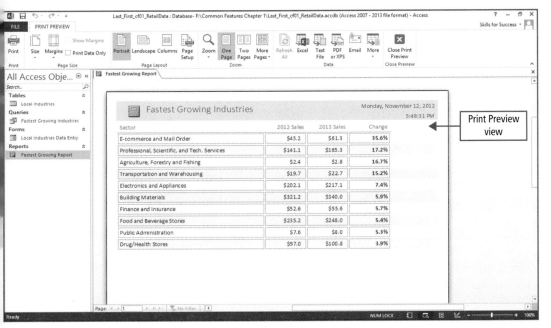

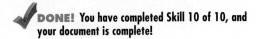

Figure 4

6. In the **Navigation pane**, under **Reports**, double-click **Fastest Growing Report**.

7. On the **Home tab**, in the **Views group**, click the **View** button one time to switch to Layout view.

8. On the **Design tab**, in the **Themes group**, click **Themes**, and then click the seventh thumbnail—**Retrospect**.

9. Near the top of the **Change** column, click the first value—*35.6%*—to select all the values in the column.

10. Click the **Home tab**, and then in the **Text Formatting group**, click the **Bold** button [B]. Compare your screen with **Figure 3**.

11. On the **Home tab**, click the **View arrow**, and then click **Print Preview**. Compare your screen with **Figure 4**. If necessary, in the Zoom group, click the One Page button to zoom to 100%.

12. If your instructor asked you to print your work, click the Print button and then print the report.

13. Click **Save** [💾] to save the formatting changes, and then **Close** [✕] the report.

   Objects such as reports are opened and closed without closing the Access application itself.

14. **Close** [x] the Access window, and then submit your printouts or files for this chapter as directed by your instructor.

✔ **DONE!** You have completed Skill 10 of 10, and your document is complete!

The following More Skills are located at **www.pearsonhighered.com/skills**

More Skills (11) Store Office Files on OneDrive

You can sign in to your Microsoft account from Word, Excel, or PowerPoint, and then open and save files from online storage services such as OneDrive. Storing files on OneDrive enables you to access your files from any computer connected to the Internet. After signing in to your account, you can open and save files stored on OneDrive using the same techniques used for files stored on local computer drives.

In More Skills 11, you will create a Microsoft account if you don't already have one. You will sign in to that account, connect your Office program to OneDrive, and then save a Word, Excel, and PowerPoint file to OneDrive. You will document your work by creating a snip of your OneDrive folder.

To begin, open your web browser, navigate to www.pearsonhighered.com/skills, locate the name of your textbook, and then follow the instructions on the website.

More Skills (12) Use Office Help

Microsoft Office 2013 has a Help system in which you can search for articles that show you how to accomplish tasks.

In More Skills 12, you will use the Office 2013 Help system to learn how to find out which version of Office you are using. You will then paste a snip of that screen into a Word document.

To begin, open your web browser, navigate to www.pearsonhighered.com/skills, locate the name of your textbook, and then follow the instructions on the website.

More Skills (13) Send Files as E-mail Attachments

You can send a document, workbook, or presentation as a file attached to an e-mail message. On the Save & Send page, you can attach the file in its native format or change it to a format that can be opened in a different program. To complete this skill, you need to have a mail program such as Outlook installed and configured to send mail using your e-mail account.

In More Skills 13, you will send a Word document as an e-mail attachment. You will document your work by creating a snip, and then either send the e-mail message and attachment or cancel without sending.

To begin, open your web browser, navigate to www.pearsonhighered.com/skills, locate the name of your textbook, and then follow the instructions on the website.

More Skills (14) Optimize Office 2013 RT

Office 2013 RT is a version of Office designed for phones and tablets. Instead of the mouse and keyboard, you can use gestures and the Touch Keyboard to perform tasks.

In More Skills 14, you will work with Excel Office RT. You will switch between Full Screen and Standard views, use gestures instead of the mouse, and type via an onscreen keyboard.

To begin, open your Internet browser, navigate to www.pearsonhighered.com/skills, locate the name of your textbook, and then follow the instructions on the website.

Please note that there are no additional projects to accompany the More Skills Projects, and they are not covered in the End-of-Chapter projects.

The following table summarizes the **SKILLS AND PROCEDURES** covered in this chapter.

Skills Number	Task	Step	Icon	Keyboard Shortcut
1	Start Office applications	Display Start menu or screen, and then type application name	⊞	
2	Open a template	Start the application; or if already started: File tab → New		
4	Create a new folder while saving	Save As dialog box toolbar → New folder		
4	Save	Quick Access toolbar → Save	💾	Ctrl + S
5	Change a font	Home tab → Font group → Font arrow	Calibri (Body) ▾	Ctrl + Shift + F
5	Apply italic	Home tab → Font group → Italic	*I*	Ctrl + I
5, 8	Change font color	Home tab → Font group → Font Color arrow	A ▾	
5, 8	Change background color	Home tab → Font group → Fill Color arrow	🎨 ▾	
5, 8, 9, 10	Apply a theme	Design tab → Themes		
5, 8, 9, 10	Change font size	Home tab → Font group → Font Size arrow	11 ▾	Ctrl + < Ctrl + >
5, 10	Apply bold	Home tab → Font group → Bold	**B**	Ctrl + B
6, 7, 9, 10	Preview the printed page	File tab → Print		Alt + Ctrl + I
7	Open a file	File tab → Open		Ctrl + O
7, 9, 10	Save a file with new name and location	File tab → Save As		F12
8	Center align text	Home tab → Paragraph group → Center	≡	Ctrl + E
9	Copy	Select text or object → Home tab → Clipboard group → Copy	📋	Ctrl + C
9	Paste	Home tab → Clipboard group → Paste	📋	Ctrl + V

Key Terms

Matching

Match each term in the second column with its correct definition in the first column by writing the letter of the term on the blank line in front of the correct definition.

____ **1.** An individual page in a presentation that can contain text, pictures, or other objects.

____ **2.** A pre-built document into which you insert text using the layout and formatting provided in that document.

____ **3.** A mode applied to documents that limits formatting and features to ones that are supported in earlier versions of Office.

____ **4.** To insert, delete, or replace text in an Office document, workbook, or presentation.

____ **5.** A pre-built set of unified formatting choices including colors, fonts, and effects.

____ **6.** To change the appearance of text.

____ **7.** A set of characters with the same design and shape.

____ **8.** A feature that displays the result of a formatting change if you select it.

____ **9.** A view applied to documents downloaded from the Internet that allows you to decide if the content is safe before working with the document.

____ **10.** A command that moves a copy of the selected text or object to the Office clipboard.

A Compatibility

B Copy

C Edit

D Font

E Format

F Live Preview

G Protected

H Slide

I Template

J Theme

Multiple Choice

Choose the correct answer.

1. The flashing vertical line that indicates where text will be inserted when you start typing.
   A. Cell reference
   B. Insertion point
   C. KeyTip

2. A reserved, formatted space into which you enter your own text or object.
   A. Gallery
   B. Placeholder
   C. Title

3. Until you save a document, the document is stored here.
   A. Office Clipboard
   B. Live Preview
   C. RAM

4. A collection of pages on the File tab used to open, save, print, and perform other file management tasks.
   A. Backstage view
   B. Page Layout view
   C. File gallery

5. A temporary storage area that holds text or an object that has been cut or copied.
   A. Office Clipboard
   B. Dialog box
   C. Live Preview

6. A toolbar with common formatting buttons that displays after you select text.
   A. Gallery toolbar
   B. Mini toolbar
   C. Taskbar toolbar

7. A command that inserts a copy of the text or object from the Office Clipboard.
   A. Copy
   B. Insert
   C. Paste

8. A visual display of choices—typically thumbnails—from which you can choose.
   A. Gallery
   B. Options menu
   C. Shortcut menu

9. A tab that displays on the Ribbon only when a related object such as a graphic or chart is selected.
   A. Contextual tab
   B. File tab
   C. Page Layout tab

10. A database object that presents tables or query results in a way that is optimized for onscreen viewing or printing.
    A. Form
    B. Report
    C. Table

Topics for Discussion

1. You have briefly worked with four Microsoft Office programs: Word, Excel, PowerPoint, and Access. Based on your experience, describe the overall purpose of each program.

2. Many believe that computers enable offices to go paperless—that is, to share files electronically instead of printing and then distributing them. What are the advantages of sharing files electronically, and in what situations is it best to print documents?

Skills Review

To complete this project, you will need the following files:

- cf01_SRData (Access)
- cf01_SRChart (Excel)
- cf01_SRSlide (PowerPoint)

You will save your files as:

- Last_First_cf01_SRData (Access)
- Last_First_cf01_SRChart (Excel)
- Last_First_cf01_SRSlide (PowerPoint)
- Last_First_cf01_SRMemo (Word)

1. Start **Access 2013**, and then click **Open Other Files**. Click **Computer**, and then click **Browse**. In the **Open** dialog box, navigate to the student data files for this chapter, click **cf01_SRData**, and then click **Open**.

2. On the **File tab**, click **Save As**, and then click the **Save As** button. In the **Save As** dialog box, navigate to your chapter folder. Name the file Last_First_cf01_SRData, and then click **Save**. If necessary, enable the content.

3. In the **Navigation** pane, double-click **Budget Report**, and then click the **View** button to switch to Layout view. On the **Design tab**, click **Themes**, and then click **Retrospect**.

4. Click the **View arrow**, click **Print Preview**, and then compare your screen with **Figure 1**. If you are printing this project, print the report.

5. Click **Save**, **Close** the report, and then **Close** Access.

6. Start **Excel 2013**, and then click **Open Other Workbooks**. Use the **Open** page to locate and open the student data file **cf01_SRChart**.

7. On the **File tab**, click **Save As**. Click **Browse**, and then navigate to your chapter folder. Name the file Last_First_cf01_SRChart and then click **Save**.

8. With the worksheet title selected, on the **Home tab**, in the **Font group**, click the **Font Size arrow**, and then click **24**.

9. Click cell **B7**, type 84.3 Press [Enter], and then click **Save**.

10. Click the border of the chart, and then compare your screen with **Figure 2**.

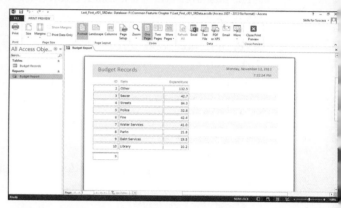

Figure 1

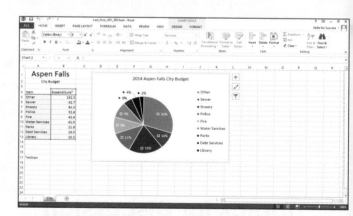

Figure 2

■ Continue to the next page to complete this Skills Review

11. On the **Home tab**, in the **Clipboard group**, click the **Copy** button.

12. Close the **Excel** window, and then start **PowerPoint 2013**. Click **Open Other Presentations**, and then open the student data file **cf01_SRSlide**.

13. On the **File tab**, click **Save As**. Click **Browse**, and then navigate to your chapter folder. Name the file Last_First_cf01_SRSlide and then click **Save**.

14. On the **Home tab**, in the **Clipboard group**, click **Paste** to insert the chart.

15. On the **Design tab**, in the **Themes group**, click the seventh choice—**Retrospect**. Compare your screen with **Figure 3**.

16. If you are printing this project, on the File tab, click Print, change the Settings to Handouts, 1 Slide, and then print the handout.

17. Click **Save**, and then **Close** PowerPoint.

18. Start **Word 2013**. On the Start screen, in the **Search for online templates** box, type memo and then click the **Start searching** button. Locate the **Memo (Elegant design)**, click its thumbnail, and then click the **Create** button to open it.

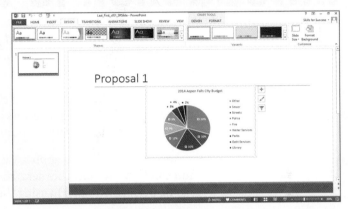

19. Click *[RECIPIENT NAME]*, and then type Janet Neal

20. Change *[YOUR NAME]* to your own name, and then change *[SUBJECT]* to City Budget

21. Change *[CLICK TO SELECT DATE]* to the current date, and then change *[NAME]* to Maria Martinez

22. Change *[Type your memo text here]* to the following: I am pleased to tell you that the city budget items that you requested are ready. I will send you the Access report and PowerPoint slide today.

23. Click to the left of *INTEROFFICE* and then press ⟨Delete⟩ several times to delete the word and the space following it.

24. On the **Design tab**, click the **Themes** button, and then click **Retrospect**.

25. Double-click the word *MEMORANDUM* to select it. On the Mini toolbar, click the **Font Color arrow**, and then click the fifth color—**Orange, Accent 1**.

26. With *MEMORANDUM* still selected, on the Mini toolbar, click the **Bold** button one time to remove the bold formatting from the selection, and then change the **Font Size** to 24.

27. Click **Save**, click **Browse**, and then navigate to your chapter folder. Name the file Last_First_cf01_SRMemo and then click **Save**. In the compatibility message, click **OK**. Click a blank area of the document, and then compare your screen with **Figure 4**.

28. If you are printing your work, print the memo.

Figure 3

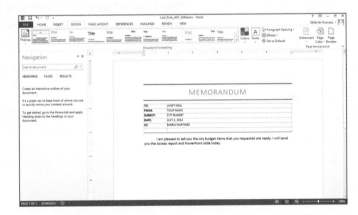

Figure 4

29. Click **Save**, and then **Close** the memo. Submit your printouts or files as directed by your instructor.

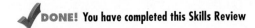
DONE! You have completed this Skills Review

Introduction to Word

Microsoft Word 2013 is a ***word processing application***—a program used to type and format text, insert and create graphics and tables, and create documents such as letters, reports, and newsletters.

You can use Word to type and edit text. You can edit your work using Word's spelling and grammar tools. You can fix errors as you type or scan the entire document for errors. As you compose your documents, you can quickly delete, insert, and move text.

You can use Word to apply a variety of fonts, sizes, and colors to the text in your documents. You can also add lines, borders, and shading to emphasize document elements. Formatting tasks can be performed quickly using the Format Painter or by assigning predefined styles.

You can insert graphics into Word documents or create your own using tools such as Text Effects, drawing objects, or SmartArt. Data can be inserted into tables. You can then format and position these objects to create the documents you desire.

Word can be used to collaborate with others. For example, you can save documents to the Internet and invite others to view them or make changes to them. You can also track the changes each collaborator makes to your documents, and then accept or reject those changes.

Word also has tools to perform specific tasks such as printing individualized documents using mail merge. You can also create citations and bibliographies using the Source Manager.

Word's features and tools enable you to create simple documents such as letters, memos, and reports and more elegant documents such as newsletters and forms.

Text Effects

Formatted text

Formatted picture

Columns of text

Tabbed list

Formatted table

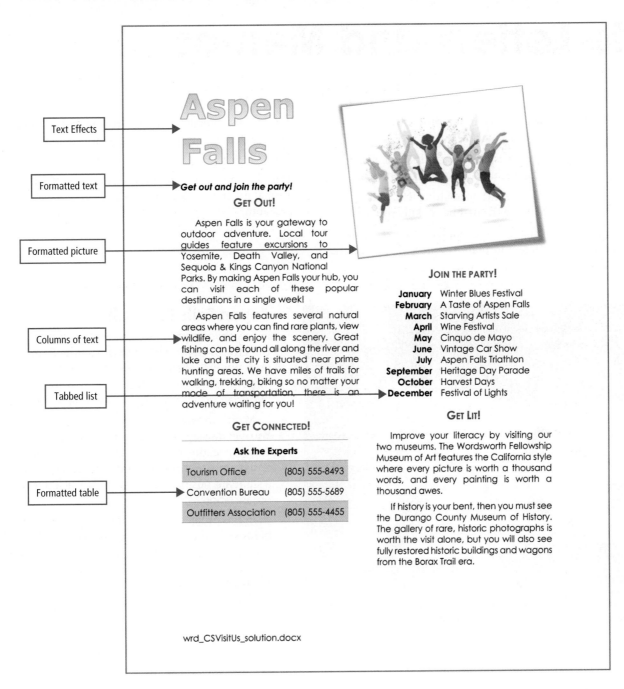

Aspen Falls

Get out and join the party!

GET OUT!

Aspen Falls is your gateway to outdoor adventure. Local tour guides feature excursions to Yosemite, Death Valley, and Sequoia & Kings Canyon National Parks. By making Aspen Falls your hub, you can visit each of these popular destinations in a single week!

Aspen Falls features several natural areas where you can find rare plants, view wildlife, and enjoy the scenery. Great fishing can be found all along the river and lake and the city is situated near prime hunting areas. We have miles of trails for walking, trekking, biking so no matter your mode of transportation, there is an adventure waiting for you!

GET CONNECTED!

Ask the Experts

Tourism Office	(805) 555-8493
Convention Bureau	(805) 555-5689
Outfitters Association	(805) 555-4455

JOIN THE PARTY!

January	Winter Blues Festival
February	A Taste of Aspen Falls
March	Starving Artists Sale
April	Wine Festival
May	Cinquo de Mayo
June	Vintage Car Show
July	Aspen Falls Triathlon
September	Heritage Day Parade
October	Harvest Days
December	Festival of Lights

GET LIT!

Improve your literacy by visiting our two museums. The Wordsworth Fellowship Museum of Art features the California style where every picture is worth a thousand words, and every painting is worth a thousand awes.

If history is your bent, then you must see the Durango County Museum of History. The gallery of rare, historic photographs is worth the visit alone, but you will also see fully restored historic buildings and wagons from the Borax Trail era.

wrd_CSVisitUs_solution.docx

Create Letters and Memos

- Microsoft Office Word is one of the most common productivity programs that individuals use on a computer.

- Word is used to create documents such as memos, reports, letters, and mailing labels. These documents can include tables and graphics.

- To work efficiently with Word, entering text, formatting text, and navigating within a Word document are the first basic skills you need.

- You can change the font and font size and add emphasis to text, but use caution not to apply too many different formats to your text. This can be distracting to the reader.

- It is never acceptable to have errors in spelling, grammar, or word usage in your documents; you can use Word spelling and grammar tools to prevent this.

- Business letters and memos are often structured and formatted in a formal manner as described in *The Gregg Reference Manual* by William A. Sabin.

© Julien Eichinger

Aspen Falls City Hall

In this chapter, you will assist Evelyn Stone, Human Resources Director, to create a letter to Dr. George Gato of Aspen Falls Community College. The purpose of the letter is to establish an internship program between City Hall and the students in the Information Systems Department chaired by Dr. Gato.

Microsoft Word is used often to write business letters and memos. You can quickly type, edit, and format text. Because business communication documents should be free of mistakes, spelling and grammar errors are flagged as you type. Most businesses apply a standard business letter format to all letters coming from the organization.

In this project, you will write a one-page business letter using the block style as defined by *The Gregg Reference Manual* by William A. Sabin. The **block style**, also called the **full-block style**, typically begins all lines at the left margin except for letterheads, tables, and block quotes. You will add a second page detailing the various internship positions available with City Hall.

Time to complete all 10
skills – 60 to 75 minutes

Student data file needed for this chapter:

wrd01_InternPositions

You will save your files as:

Last_First_wrd01_Interns (Word)
Last_First_wrd01_Interns (PDF)

Outcome

Using the skills in this chapter, you will be able to work with Word documents like this:

ASPEN FALLS HUMAN RESOURCES
500 S Aspen Street
Aspen Falls, CA 93463

May 8, 2014

Dr. George Gato
Aspen Falls Community College
1 College Drive
Aspen Falls, CA 93464

Dear Dr. Gato

Subject: City Hall Internships

Thank you so much for your letter offering the services of your Information Systems Department students. We currently have several projects that might benefit both us and your students.

I have attached a description of the positions we are currently seeking. Please call City Hall at (805) 555-1016 to discuss this further.

We have several positions open for students with skills in the four Office applications: Word, Excel, PowerPoint, and Access. We also need students capable of working with our IT Services Help Desk.

Sincerely,

Evelyn Stone, Human Resources Director

Last_First_wrd01_Interns

SKILLS

MyITLab®
Skills 1-10 Training

At the end of this chapter you will be able to:

Skill 1 Type Letter Text
Skill 2 Apply Styles and Set Grammar and Spelling Options
Skill 3 Select and Insert Text
Skill 4 Copy, Cut, and Paste Text
Skill 5 Check Spelling and Grammar
Skill 6 Check Writing Style and Insert Synonyms
Skill 7 Use Format Painter
Skill 8 Apply Advanced Font Settings
Skill 9 Create Document Footers
Skill 10 Save Documents as PDF Files

MORE SKILLS

Skill 11 Prepare Documents for Distribution
Skill 12 Insert Screen Shots into Documents
Skill 13 Split and Arrange Windows
Skill 14 Insert Symbols

► When working with Word documents, a paragraph can be a single line containing a heading or several lines of sentences.

► To see where paragraphs begin and end, it is helpful to display *formatting marks*— characters that display in your document to represent nonprinting characters such as paragraphs, spaces, and tabs.

1. Start **Word 2013**, and then on the start screen, click **Blank document**.

2. On the **Home tab**, in the **Paragraph group**, click the **Show/Hide** button ¶ to display the nonprinting formatting marks, as shown in **Figure 1**. If the Navigation pane is open, Close ✕ it.

> The Show/Hide button is a *toggle button*—a button used to turn a feature both on and off. The paragraph mark (¶) indicates the end of a paragraph and will not print.

> Because many elements in the Word window adjust to your monitor size and personal settings, you may need to change your window size, exit Reading Mode, or disable Full Screen Mode to match the figures in this book.

3. With the insertion point in the blank paragraph, type Aspen Falls Human Resources and press Enter. Type 500 S Aspen Street and press Enter. Type Aspen Falls, CA 93463 and press Enter two times.

4. Type May 8, 2014 Press Enter three times, and then compare your screen with **Figure 2**.

> The letter has eight paragraphs—three for the letterhead, one for the date, and four blank paragraphs.

■ Continue to the next page to complete the skill

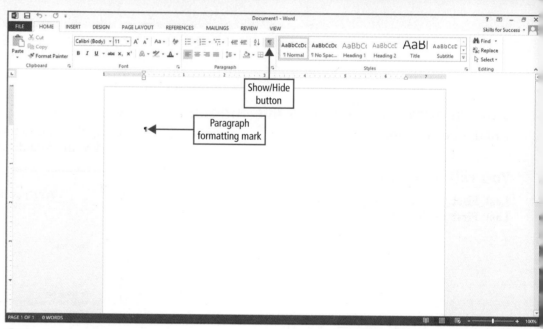

Figure 1

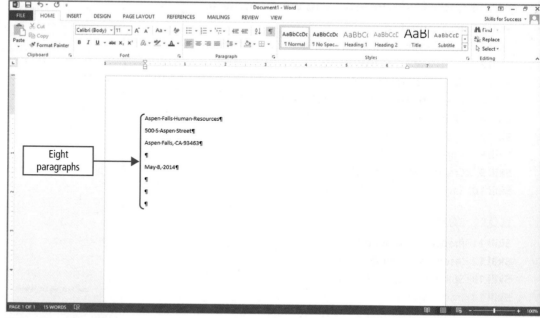

Figure 2

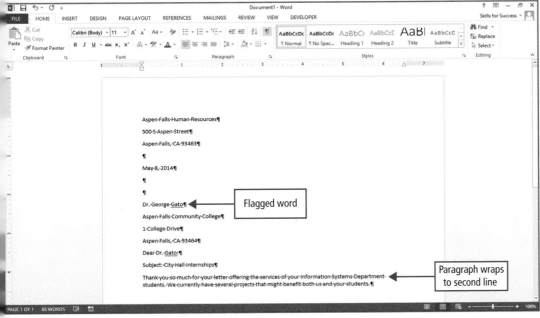

Figure 3

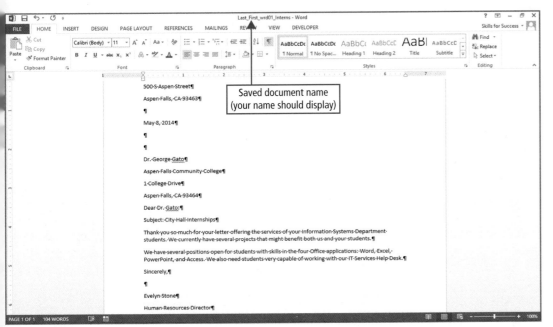

Figure 4

5. Type Dr. George Gato and press Enter; type Aspen Falls Community College and press Enter; type 1 College Drive and press Enter; and type Aspen Falls, CA 93464 and press Enter.

> The word *Gato* is flagged as a spelling error, but it is spelled correctly.

6. Type Dear Dr. Gato: and press Enter. Type Subject: City Hall Internships and press Enter.

7. Type the following, inserting only one space after each sentence: Thank you so much for your letter offering the services of your Information Systems Department students. We currently have several projects that might benefit both us and your students. Compare your screen with **Figure 3**.

8. Press Enter, and then type We have several positions open for students with skills in the four Office applications: Word, Excel, PowerPoint, and Access. We also need students very capable of working with our IT Services Help Desk.

9. Press Enter and type Sincerely, and then press Enter two times. Type Evelyn Stone Press Enter, and then type Human Resources Director

10. Click **Save** [💾], and then on the **Save As** page, click the location and folder where you are saving your work. If necessary, click Browse.

11. In the **Save As** dialog box, click **New folder**, type Word Chapter 1 and then press Enter two times to open the new folder. Name the file Last_First_wrd01_ Interns Click **Save**, and then compare your screen with **Figure 4**.

■ **You have completed Skill 1 of 10**

▶ You can format text quickly by applying *styles*—pre-built collections of formatting settings that can be assigned to text.

▶ During the writing process, it is a good idea to look for *flagged errors*—wavy lines indicating spelling or grammar errors. You can right-click these flagged errors to see a list of suggestions for fixing them.

1. In the inside address, right-click the word *Gato*, and then compare your screen with **Figure 1**.

   Red wavy lines indicate words that have been flagged as possible spelling errors, and the shortcut menu provides suggested spellings.

2. From the shortcut menu, click **Ignore All**, and verify that both instances of the word *Gato* are no longer flagged as spelling errors.

3. Hold down ⌨Ctrl, and then press ⌨Home, to move the insertion point to the beginning of the document.

4. Move the pointer to the left of the first line of the document to display the 🔾 pointer. Drag down to select the first two lines of the document. On the **Home tab**, in the **Styles group**, click the **No Spacing** thumbnail. Compare your screen with **Figure 2**.

   The Normal style has extra space after each paragraph. The No Spacing style does not apply this extra space after each paragraph, and the extra space between the lines of the letterhead have been removed.

■ **Continue to the next page to complete the skill**

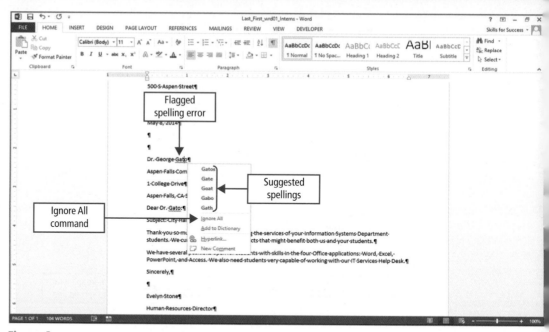

Figure 1

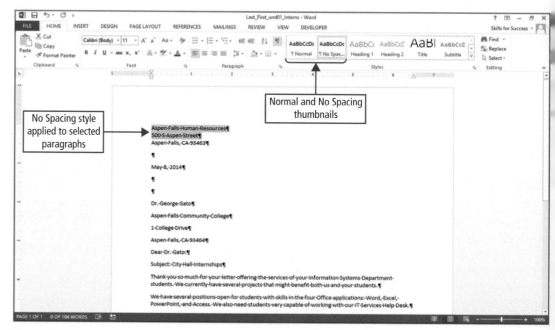

Figure 2

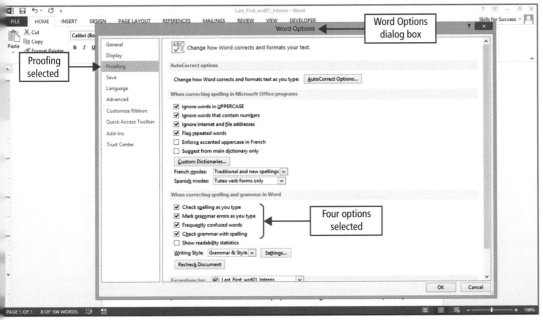

Figure 3

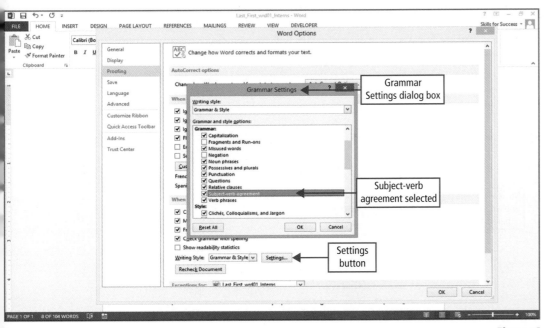

Figure 4

5. Click the **File tab**, and then click **Options**. On the left pane of the **Word Options** dialog box, click **Proofing**.

6. Under **When correcting spelling and grammar in Word**, verify that the first four check boxes are selected as shown in **Figure 3**.

7. To the right of **Writing Style**, click the **Settings** button. In the **Grammar Settings** dialog box, under **Writing style**, be sure that **Grammar Only** is selected.

8. In the **Grammar Settings** dialog box, scroll down to display all the **Grammar** options. Select the **Subject-verb agreement** check box. Compare your screen with **Figure 4**, and then click **OK**.

   In this manner you can customize the types of errors that should be flagged as you work with a document. At the end of this project, you will return the grammar and spelling options back to their original settings.

9. Click **OK** to close the **Word Options** dialog box.

10. Click the **Save** button ⊞. Alternately, press Ctrl + S.

■ **You have completed Skill 2 of 10**

► WRD 1-3
VIDEO

► You can select a single word by double-clicking and a single paragraph by triple-clicking.

► The amount of space between letter elements is specified by the style rules that your letter is following.

1. Click anywhere in the first paragraph of the document, *Aspen Falls Human Resources*.

2. On the **Home tab**, in the **Paragraph group**, click the **Center** button to center the paragraph.

    When you apply paragraph formatting, you do not need to select the paragraph. However, to apply paragraph formatting to two or more paragraphs at the same time, you will need to select all the paragraphs.

3. Repeat the technique just practiced to center the letterhead's second and third lines.

4. In the paragraph that begins *We have*, in the second sentence, point to the word *very*, and then double-click to select the word and display the Mini toolbar. Compare your screen with **Figure 1**.

5. With the word *very* selected, press Delete .

    When you double-click to select and delete a word, the selected word is deleted, along with the space following the word.

6. Move the insertion point in the margin to the left of *Dr. George Gato*. When the pointer displays, drag straight down to select the paragraph and the two paragraphs below it. With the three paragraphs selected, on the **Home tab**, in the **Styles group**, click the **No Spacing** thumbnail. Compare your screen with **Figure 2**.

■ Continue to the next page to complete the skill

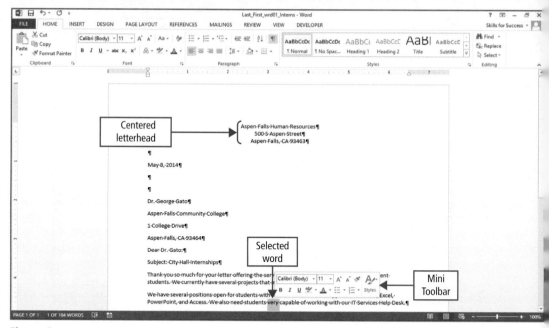

Figure 1

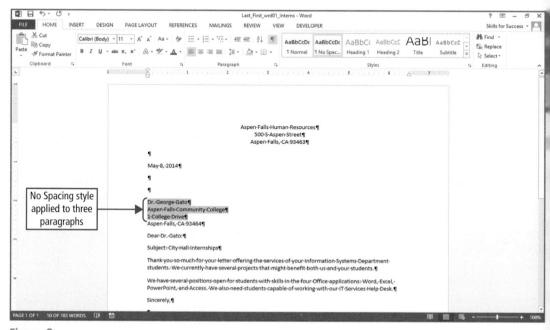

Figure 2

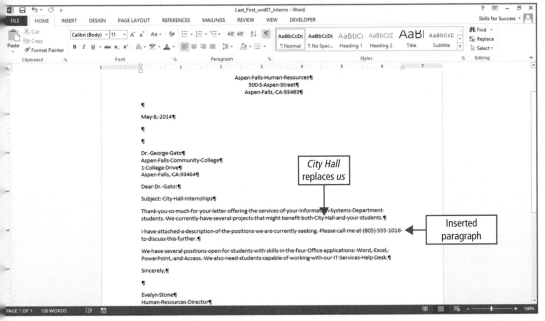

City Hall
replaces *us*

Inserted
paragraph

Figure 3

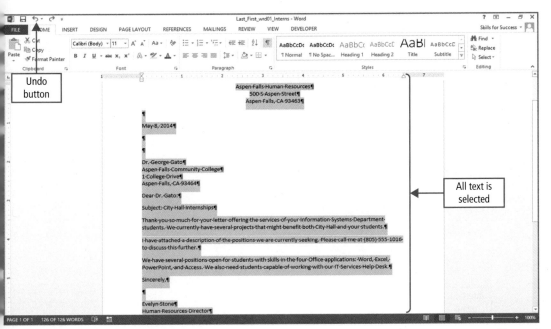

Undo
button

All text is
selected

Figure 4

7. Triple-click the signature, *Evelyn Stone*, to select the paragraph, and then apply the **No Spacing** style.

8. In the paragraph that begins *Thank you*, double-click the word *us* to select it, and then type City Hall

9. In the paragraph that begins *Thank you*, click to position the insertion point at the end of the paragraph—following the period after *students*.

10. Press Enter one time, and then type I have attached a description of the positions we are currently seeking. Please call me at (805) 555-1016 to discuss this further. Compare your screen with **Figure 3**.

11. On the **Home tab**, in the **Editing group**, click **Select**, and then click **Select All** to select all of the text in the document. Alternately, press Ctrl + A.

12. On the **Home tab**, in the **Font group**, click the **Font arrow**. Scroll down the list of fonts, and then click **Cambria**.

13. Press Ctrl + Home , and then on the Quick Access Toolbar, click the **Undo** button one time to change the font back to Calibri. Compare your screen with **Figure 4**.

    As you work with a document, you need to be aware when text is selected. For example, if you start typing when the entire document is selected, all the text will be replaced with whatever new text you type. You can use the Undo button to fix this type of mistake.

14. Click anywhere in the document to deselect the text, and then **Save** the changes.

■ **You have completed Skill 3 of 10**

▶ The copy command places a copy of the selected text or object in the ***clipboard***—a temporary storage area that holds text or an object that has been cut or copied.

1. Press `Ctrl` + `End` to move the insertion point to the end of the document.

2. Click the **Page Layout tab**. In the **Page Setup group**, click **Breaks**, and then click **Page**. Alternately, press `Ctrl` + `Enter`. Compare your screen with **Figure 1**.

   A ***manual page break***—forcing a page to end at a location you specify—is added at the end of Page 1.

3. On the **File tab**, click **Open**. On the **Open** page, click **Computer**, and then click the **Browse** button.

4. In the **Open** dialog box, navigate to the student files for this chapter. Click **wrd01_InternPositions**, and then click **Open**.

5. On the **Home tab**, in the **Editing group**, click **Select**, and then click **Select All**.

6. With the text selected, on the **Home tab**, in the **Clipboard group**, click the **Copy** button. Alternately, press `Ctrl` + `C`.

7. On the taskbar, point to the **Word** button 🔲. Click the **Last_First_wrd01_Interns** thumbnail to make it the active window.

8. With the insertion point still at the end of the document, click the **Home tab**. In the **Clipboard group**, click the **Paste arrow**, and then compare your screen with **Figure 2**.

   The Paste button has two parts—the Paste button and the Paste arrow that displays paste options.

■ **Continue to the next page to complete the skill**

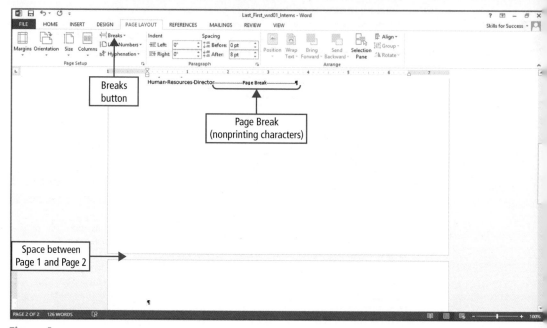

Figure 1

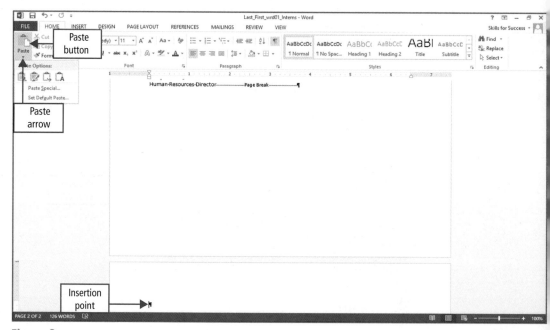

Figure 2

9. Click the **Paste** button, and then compare your screen with **Figure 3**.

> When you paste, you insert a copy of the text or object stored in the clipboard and the Paste Options button displays near the pasted text. The spelling and grammar errors in the pasted text will be corrected in the next skill.

10. Press `Esc` to hide the Paste Options button. In the bulleted text, select the paragraph *Using the Internet* including the paragraph mark.

11. On the **Home tab**, in the **Clipboard group**, click the **Cut** button. Alternately, press `Ctrl` + `X`.

> The *cut* command deletes the selected text or object and places a copy in the Office clipboard.

12. In the bulleted list, click to place the insertion point to the left of the text *Microsoft Word* and to the right of the bullet and tab formatting mark. In the **Clipboard group**, click the **Paste** button. Alternately, press `Ctrl` + `V`. Compare your screen with **Figure 4**.

> In this manner, you can move text by cutting it and then pasting it somewhere else.

13. On the taskbar, point to the **Word** button, point to the **wrd01_InternPositions** thumbnail, and then click the thumbnail's **Close** button.

14. Click in the letter document to make it the active window, and then **Save** the changes.

■ **You have completed Skill 4 of 10**

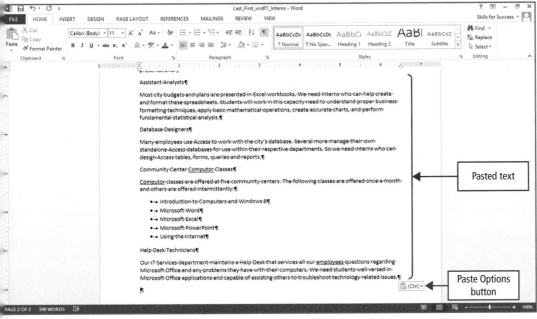

Figure 3

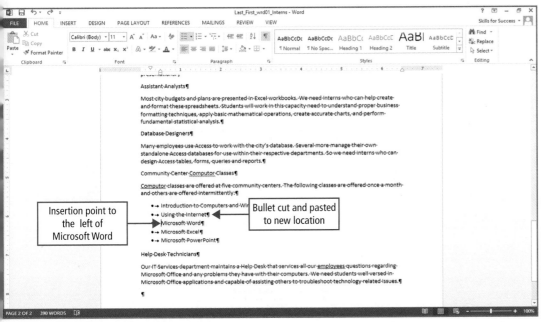

Figure 4

WRD 1-5
VIDEO

▶ When you are done typing the text of a document, it is a good idea to run the Spelling and Grammar checker to check for potential errors.

1. Press `Ctrl` + `Home` to place the insertion point at the beginning of the document.

2. Click the **Review tab**, and then in the **Proofing group**, click **Spelling & Grammar**. Alternately, press `F7`. Compare your screen with **Figure 1**.

   Spelling and grammar errors display in a task pane on the right side of the window. The first error is a grammar error indicating the verb *has* is not in the correct form. The checker suggests that the verb be changed to *have*.

3. In the **Grammar** pane, click the **Change** button to accept the suggested verb form change and move to the next error.

4. In the **Spelling** pane, click the **Delete** button to remove the repeated word *the*, and then compare your screen with **Figure 2**.

   When a misspelled word is encountered, you can replace it with one of the suggested spellings or add it to the custom dictionary. Words added to the custom dictionary will not be flagged as spelling errors. If you accidentally add a misspelled word to the dictionary, you can open the dictionary from the Options dialog box and delete the word.

   The Spelling task pane often displays definitions to help you decide if the suggested spelling is the correct choice. By signing in to your Microsoft account, you can access additional online dictionaries.

■ **Continue to the next page to complete the skill**

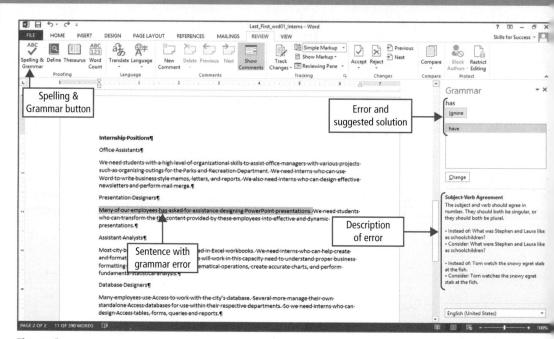

Figure 1

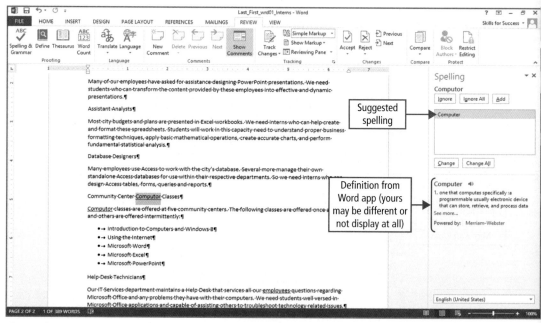

Figure 2

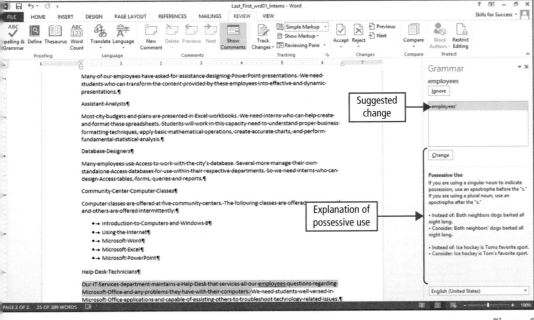

Figure 3

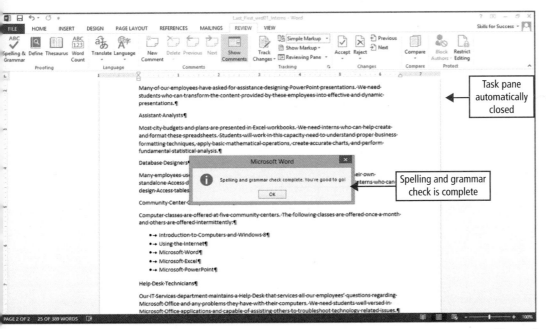

Figure 4

5. In the **Spelling** pane, click the **Change All** button to change both instances of the misspelled word, and then compare your screen with **Figure 3**.

Many grammar errors are explained in the Grammar pane so that you can make an informed decision to ignore or accept the suggested change. Here, the word *employees* should have an apostrophe to indicate possessive use.

6. In the **Grammar** pane, click the **Change** button to add the apostrophe, and then compare your screen with **Figure 4**.

When all flagged errors have been changed or ignored, a message displays indicating that the check is complete. If you did not receive this message after completing this step, you may have typing errors, and you should fix them before continuing.

7. In the message indicating that the spelling and grammar check is complete, click **OK**, and then **Save** 🖫 the document.

■ **You have completed Skill 5 of 10**

▶ To help improve your writing style, you use the Style Checker to find weaknesses in your writing style. You can also insert synonyms.

1. On the **File tab**, click **Options**. In the **Word Options** dialog box, click **Proofing** to display the spelling and grammar options.

2. Click the **Writing Style arrow**, and then click **Grammar & Style**. Compare your screen with **Figure 1**.

3. In the **Word Options** dialog box, click the **Recheck Document** button. Read the message that displays, click **Yes**, and then click **OK**.

4. Press Ctrl + Home, and then notice that *Gato* is again flagged as a potential spelling error.

   By clicking the Recheck Document button, you can run the Spelling & Grammar checker again and previously ignored errors will again be flagged.

5. Scroll as needed to display the heading *Assistant Analysts* on Page 2. Right-click the flagged words *are presented,* and then from the shortcut menu, click **Ignore Once**.

   Although passive voice is not a grammar error, too much use of passive voice weakens your writing. Some instances can be ignored.

6. Under the heading *Database Designers,* right-click the word *So,* and then compare your screen with **Figure 2**.

7. From the shortcut menu, click **Therefore**, to correct the style error.

8. Under the heading *Community Center Computer Classes,* right-click to read the first error message, and then press Esc to close the shortcut menu.

■ **Continue to the next page to complete the skill**

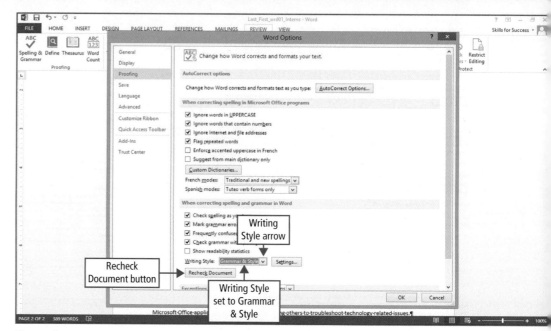

Figure 1

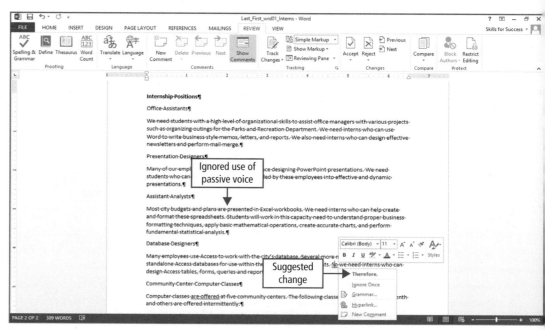

Figure 2

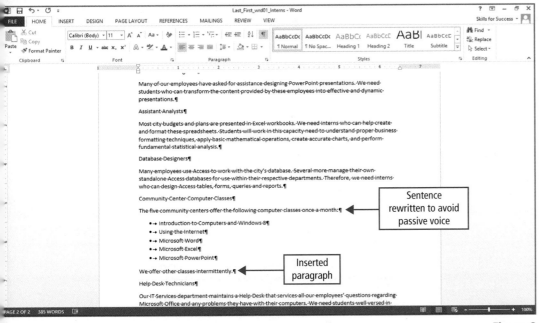

Figure 3

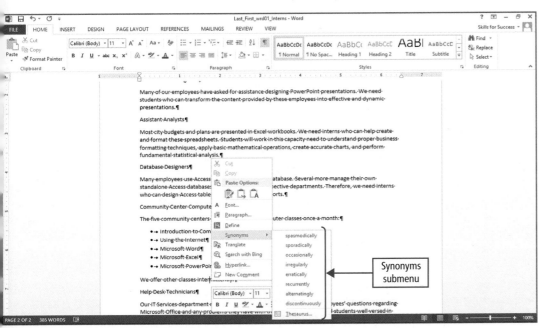

Figure 4

9. Point to the left of the paragraph starting *Computer classes are offered,* and then when the ⌐ pointer displays, double-click to select the entire paragraph.

10. With the entire paragraph selected, type the following: The five community centers offer the following computer classes once a month: to remove the two instances of passive voice.

11. In the bulleted list, click to the right of *PowerPoint,* and then press Enter. On the **Home tab**, in the **Styles group**, click **Normal** to apply the default document formatting. Type We offer other classes intermittently. and then compare your screen with **Figure 3**.

12. Right-click the word *intermittently,* and then from the shortcut menu, point to **Synonyms**. Compare your screen with **Figure 4**.

The Synonyms command displays a submenu with alternate word choices. In this manner, Word Thesaurus can be accessed quickly. A **_thesaurus_** lists words that have the same or similar meaning to the word you are looking up.

13. From the **Synonyms** submenu, click **occasionally** to replace the word *intermittently.*

14. Open the **Word Options** dialog box, display the **Proofing** options, and then change the **Writing Style** to **Grammar Only**.

15. Click the **Settings** button, and then in the **Grammar Settings** dialog box, click **Reset All**. Click **OK** two times to close all open dialog boxes.

16. **Save** 💾 your work.

■ **You have completed Skill 6 of 10**

WRD 1-7
VIDEO

▶ Formatting document text should help organize the document visually without detracting from its message.

▶ A set of formatting choices can be applied with Format Painter quickly and consistently.

1. Select the first paragraph of the letterhead, *Aspen Falls Human Resources*. On the **Home tab**, in the **Font group**, click the **Font Size arrow**, and then click **16**.

2. With the first paragraph still selected, click the **Font arrow**, click **Cambria**, and then apply **Bold** B.

3. In the letterhead, drag to select the two paragraphs beginning with *500* and ending with *93463*. In the **Font group**, click the **Italic** button I, and then compare your screen with **Figure 1**.

4. In the letterhead, click in the text *Aspen Falls Human Resources*. On the **Home tab**, in the **Clipboard group**, click the **Format Painter** button.

5. Press PageDown as needed to display the top of Page 2. With the ▲I icon, drag through the heading *Internship Positions*. Compare your screen with **Figure 2**, and then release the left mouse button.

   In this manner you can copy a collection of formatting settings to other text in the document. When you release the left mouse button, Format Painter will no longer be active.

■ **Continue to the next page to complete the skill**

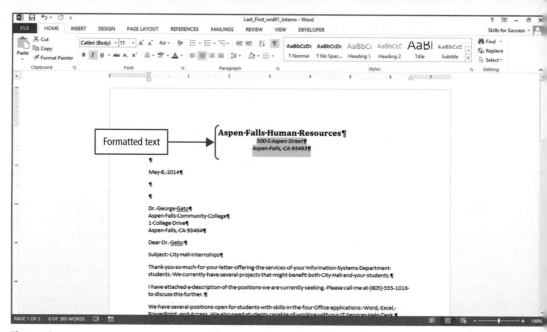

Figure 1

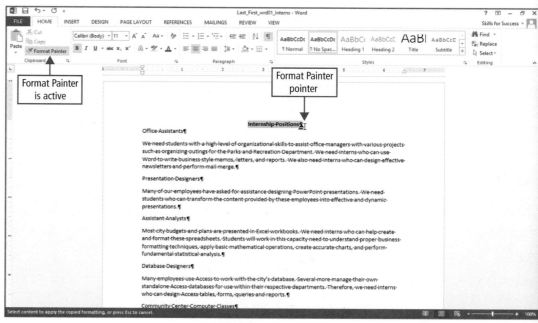

Figure 2

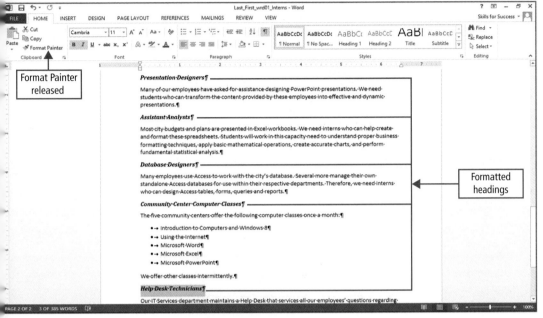

Figure 3

6. Near the top of Page 2, select the heading *Office Assistants*, and then apply the **Cambria** font, **Bold** B , and **Italic** I .

7. With the heading *Office Assistants* still selected, in the **Clipboard group**, double-click the **Format Painter** button . Drag through the *Presentation Designers* heading, and then notice that Format Painter remains active.

8. Drag through the *Assistant Analysts* heading to apply the formatting, and then repeat this technique to apply the formatting to the three remaining headings on Page 2.

9. In the **Clipboard group**, click the **Format Painter** button to release it, and then compare your screen with **Figure 3**.

   In this manner you can use Format Painter multiple times to format headings and other document elements. You can also release Format Painter by pressing Esc , clicking Undo, or pressing Ctrl + Z .

10. **Save** the document, and then take a moment to review the common formatting options as described in the table in **Figure 4**.

■ **You have completed Skill 7 of 10**

Common Formatting Options

Format	Description
Font	A set of characters with a common design.
Font size	The size of the characters typically measured in points.
Bold	Extra thickness applied to characters to emphasize text.
Italic	A slant applied to characters to emphasize text.
Underline	A line under characters used to emphasize text.
Text effects	A set of decorative formatting applied to characters.
Highlight color	Shading applied to the background of characters.
Font color	The color applied to the characters.

Figure 4

▶ Dialog boxes often contain commands that are not on the Ribbon. Many of these dialog boxes can by launched from their Ribbon group. For example, the Font dialog box can be opened by clicking the Dialog Box Launcher button in the Font group.

1. At the beginning of the letter, select the first paragraph, *Aspen Falls Human Resources*.

2. On the **Home tab**, in the **Font group**, point to—do not click—the **Font Dialog Box Launcher**, and then compare your screen with **Figure 1**.

    When you point to a Dialog Box Launcher button, the name of the dialog box and the name of the keyboard shortcut that opens it display. A thumbnail of the dialog box displays next to its description.

3. Click the **Font Dialog Box Launcher** button to open the Font dialog box.

4. In the **Font dialog** box, under **Font style**, click **Regular** to remove the Bold font style.

5. Under **Effects**, select the **Small caps** check box, and then compare your screen with **Figure 2**.

    The ***small caps*** effect displays all characters in uppercase while making any character originally typed as an uppercase letter taller than the ones typed as lowercase characters. Small caps is an alternate to using bold or italic to emphasize text. A preview of the effect displays at the bottom of the Font dialog box.

■ **Continue to the next page to complete the skill**

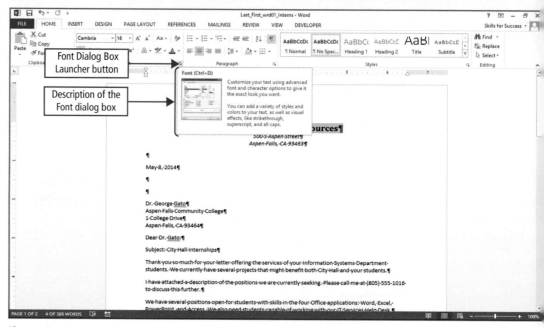

Figure 1

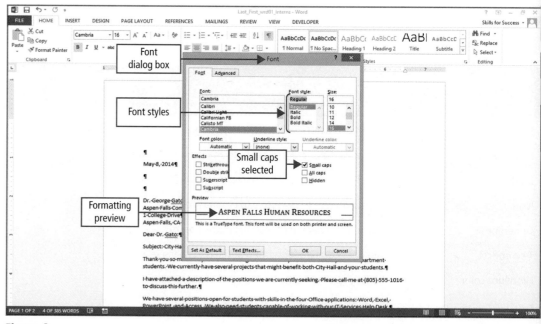

Figure 2

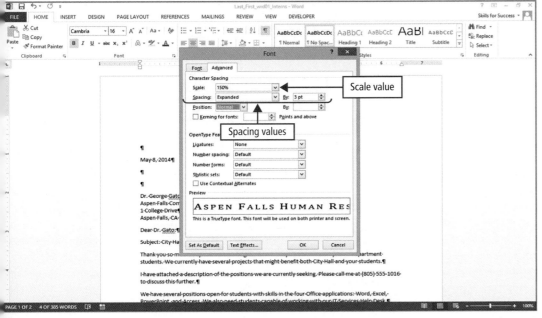

Figure 3

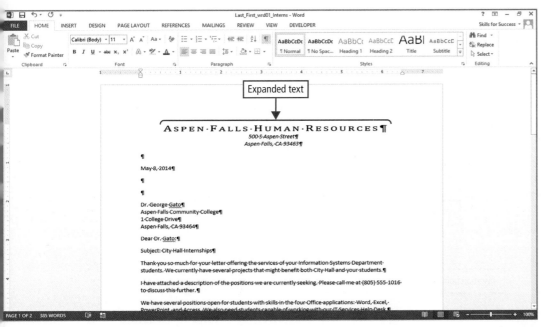

Figure 4

6. In the **Font** dialog box, click the **Advanced tab**.

7. On the **Advanced tab** of the **Font** dialog box, under **Character Spacing**, click the **Scale arrow**, and then click **150%**.

8. Under **Character Spacing**, click the **Spacing arrow**, and then click **Expanded**.

9. To the right of **Spacing**, in the **By** box, replace the value *1 pt* with *3 pt*.

10. Press Tab, and then compare your screen with **Figure 3**.

   Font sizes and the spacing between characters are measured in ***points***—a unit of measure with 72 points per inch. Here, the characters will have an additional 3 points of space between them.

11. Click **OK** to accept the changes and close the dialog box.

12. Click anywhere in the document to deselect the text, and then compare your screen with **Figure 4**.

   An organization's letterhead is typically formatted differently than the rest of the letter to make it stand out. Here, the text is centered and the department's name has been expanded and stretched.

13. **Save** the document.

■ **You have completed Skill 8 of 10**

WRD 1-9
VIDEO

▶ A *header* and *footer* are reserved areas for text, graphics, and fields that display at the top (header) or bottom (footer) of each page in a document.

▶ You can insert a built-in header or footer, or you can create your own custom header or footer.

▶ Throughout this book, you will insert the document file name in the footer of each document.

1. Press Ctrl + Home to move to the beginning of the document. On the **Insert tab**, in the **Header & Footer group**, click the **Footer** button.

2. In the **Footer** gallery, scroll down the gallery of built-in footers, and then compare your screen with **Figure 1**.

    You can quickly insert a footer by selecting a built-in from the Footer gallery.

3. Below the **Footer** gallery, click **Edit Footer**. Notice that at the bottom of Page 1, below **Footer**, the insertion point is blinking in the footer, and the **Design** contextual tab displays on the Ribbon, as shown in **Figure 2**.

    When you want to create or edit your own custom footer, you need to make the footer area active. You can do this using the Edit Footer command or by double-clicking in the footer area.

4. On the **Header & Footer Tools Design tab**, in the **Insert group**, click the **Quick Parts** button. From the displayed list, click **Field**.

    A *field* is a category of data—such as a file name, a page number, or the current date—that can be inserted into a document.

■ Continue to the next page to complete the skill ➡

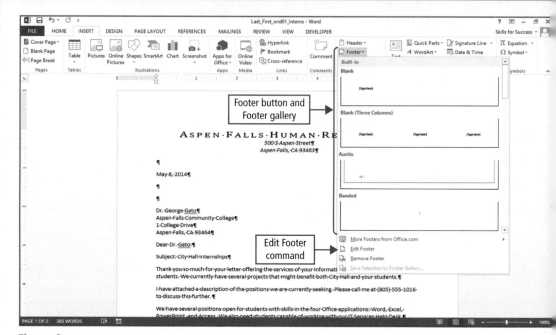

Figure 1

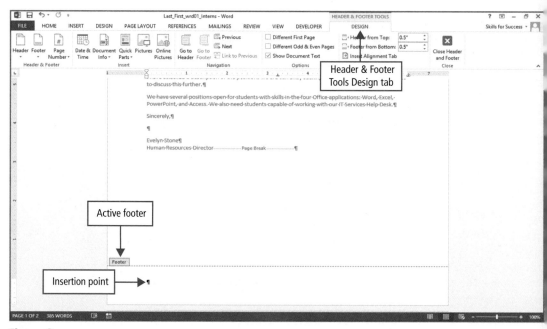

Figure 2

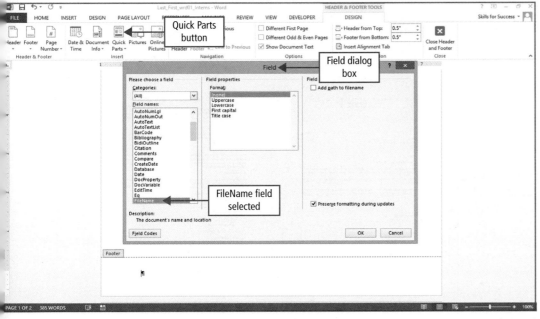

Figure 3

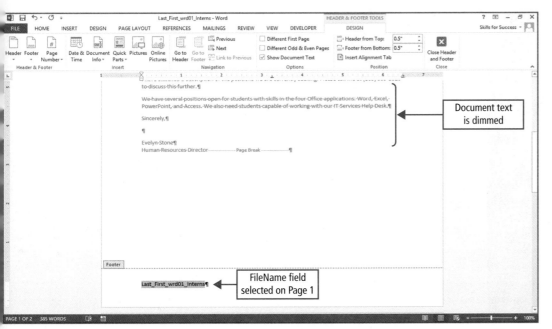

Figure 4

5. Under **Field names**, scroll down to see what types of fields are available, and then click the **FileName** field. Compare your screen with **Figure 3**.

   Spaces between multiple words in field names are removed to create a single word.

6. Under **Format**, be sure that **(none)** is selected, and then at the bottom of the **Field** dialog box, click **OK** to insert the file name in the footer.

7. Scroll to display the bottom of Page 1, click the **FileName** field one time to select it, and then compare your screen with **Figure 4**.

   By default, footers are inserted on each page of the document. When you select a field, it is shaded in gray.

8. On the **Design tab**, click the **Close Header and Footer** button. Scroll to display the bottom of Page 1 and the top of Page 2, and then notice that the header and footer areas are inactive as indicated by the dimmed file name.

   While the document text is active, the footer text cannot be edited. When the footer area is active, the footer text is black, and the document text is dimmed and cannot be edited.

9. **Save** 🖫 the document.

■ **You have completed Skill 9 of 10**

▶ Before printing, it is a good idea to set the zoom level to view one or more pages without scrolling.

▶ You can save documents in different formats so that people who do not have Word can read them.

1. Press **Ctrl** + **Home** to move to the beginning of the document. On the **Home tab**, in the **Paragraph group**, click the **Show/Hide** button ¶ so that the formatting marks do not display.

   Because formatting marks do not print, hiding them gives you a better idea of how the printed page will look.

2. On the **View tab**, in the **Zoom group**, click **Multiple Pages**, and then compare your screen with **Figure 1**.

   When you zoom to display multiple pages, a best fit is calculated based on your monitor size. Here, two pages are displayed with a zoom level of 52 percent. If you have a different-sized monitor, your zoom percentage may be different.

3. In the **Zoom group**, click the **100%** button to return to your original zoom level.

4. On the **File tab**, click **Print**. On the **Print** page, click the **Next Page** button ▶ to preview Page 2, and then compare your screen with **Figure 2**.

5. If you are printing your work for this project, print the letter. Otherwise, click the **Back** button ⊖.

6. Click **Save** 🖫. Click the **File tab**, and then click **Export**. On the **Export** page, click the **Create PDF/XPS** button.

■ **Continue to the next page to complete the skill**

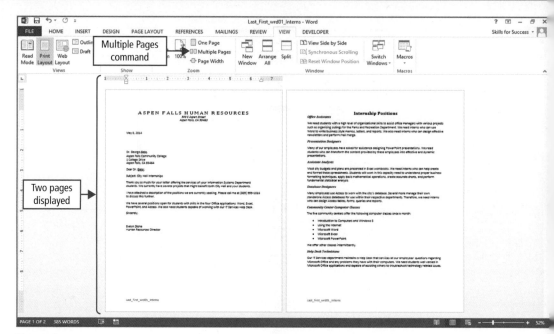

Figure 1

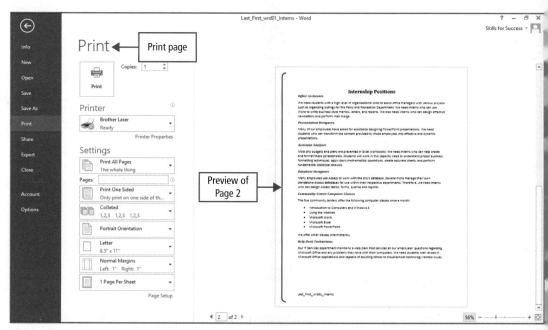

Figure 2

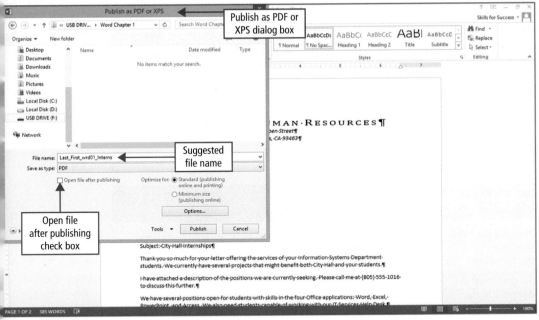

Figure 3

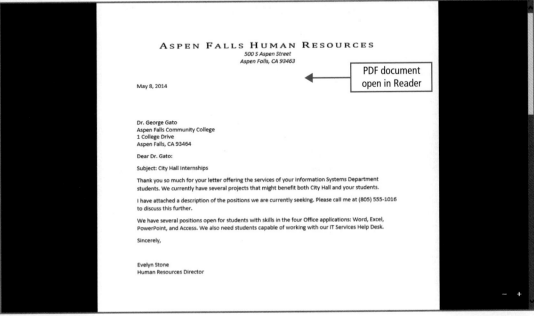

Figure 4

7. In the **Publish as PDF or XPS** dialog box, navigate to your **Word Chapter 1** folder. Notice that the Word document is not listed and the suggested file name is identical to the Word memo as shown in **Figure 3**.

A *PDF document* is an image of a document that can be viewed using a PDF reader such as Adobe Acrobat Reader or Windows 8 Reader instead of the application that created the original document.

Here, you can use the same file name as the Word document because a PDF document file extension will be *.pdf* instead of *.docx*—the file extension assigned to Word documents.

The Word file is not listed in the dialog box because only files with the extensions .pdf and .xps will be listed. The original Word file is in the folder and will not be altered.

8. Select the **Open file after publishing** check box, and then click **Publish**.

9. Wait a few moments for the document to publish and then open in your default PDF viewer. Compare your screen with **Figure 4**.

10. If your file opened in Reader, press 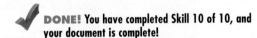, and then click the Desktop tile, and then on the taskbar, click the Word button ![Word] to return to Word. Otherwise, Close your PDF viewer application window.

11. **Close** ![X] the Word letter. If you are prompted to save changes, click Save. Submit your printout or files as directed by your instructor.

✔ **DONE!** You have completed Skill 10 of 10, and your document is complete!

More Skills

The following More Skills are located at **www.pearsonhighered.com/skills**

More Skills Prepare Documents for Distribution

Before sharing a document with colleagues, it is good practice to remove any hidden data or personal information embedded in the document. You can use Document Inspector to help you remove any information that you do not want to share.

In More Skills 11, you will open a document that has comments and other document properties, inspect the document, and then remove all personal information.

To begin, open your web browser, navigate to www.pearsonhighered.com/skills, locate the name of your textbook, and then follow the instructions on the website.

More Skills Insert Screen Shots into Documents

When you are working on a document, you may want to include a screen shot from your computer—such as a screen from another program or a website—as a graphic in the document.

In More Skills 12, you will use a browser to go to a government website, and then create a copy of the screen and store it in the Clipboard. You will then paste the screen into a document.

To begin, open your web browser, navigate to www.pearsonhighered.com/skills, locate the name of your textbook, and then follow the instructions on the website.

More Skills Split and Arrange Windows

You can split the Word screen, which lets you look at different parts of the same document at the same time. In a multiple-page document, this is convenient for viewing both the first page and the last page at the same time. You can also view two different documents side by side and make comparisons between the two.

In More Skills 13, you will open a multiple-page document, and split the screen. Then, you will open a second document and view both documents at the same time.

To begin, open your web browser, navigate to www.pearsonhighered.com/skills, locate the name of your textbook, and then follow the instructions on the website.

More Skills Insert Symbols

There are many symbols that are used occasionally, but not often enough to put on a standard computer keyboard. Some examples of commonly inserted symbols include copyright and trademark symbols, mathematical operators, and special dashes that are longer than hyphens. These symbols can be found and inserted from the Symbols group on the Insert tab.

In More Skills 14, you will open a document and insert several symbols from the Special Characters list in the Symbol dialog box.

To begin, open your web browser, navigate to www.pearsonhighered.com/skills, locate the name of your textbook, and then follow the instructions on the website.

Please note that there are no additional projects to accompany the More Skills Projects, and they are not covered in the End-of-Chapter projects.

The following table summarizes the **SKILLS AND PROCEDURES** covered in this chapter.

Skills Number	Task	Step	Icon	Keyboard Shortcut
1	Display formatting marks	Home tab → Paragraph group → Show/Hide	¶	Ctrl + *
2	Apply styles	Home tab → Styles group → click desired style		
2	Ignore flagged words	Right-click the word, and click Ignore All		
2	Change spelling and grammar options	File tab → Word Options → Proofing page → Settings button		
3	Select paragraphs	Triple-click the paragraph, or with the ⟁ pointer, double-click		
3	Undo an action	Quick Access Toolbar → Undo (repeat as needed)	↺	Ctrl + Z
3	Select all	Home tab → Editing group → Select → Select All		Ctrl + A
3	Move to beginning of document			Ctrl + Home
4	Move to end of document			Ctrl + End
4	Copy text	Select text, then Home tab → Clipboard group → Copy	📋	Ctrl + C
4	Cut text	Select text, the Home tab → Clipboard group → Cut	✂	Ctrl + X
4	Paste text	Position insertion point, then Home tab → Clipboard group → Paste		Ctrl + V
5	Check spelling and grammar	Review tab → Proofing group → Spelling & Grammar		F7
6	Check writing style	On Proofing page, set Writing Style to Spelling & Grammar		
7	Use Format Painter	Select formatted text, then Home → Clipboard group → Format Painter Click once for one time, double-click for multiple times		
8	Open the Font dialog box	Home tab → Font group → Dialog Box Launcher	🗔	Ctrl + D
8	Apply small caps	In Font dialog box, select Small caps check box		
8	Expand or stretch text	Font dialog box → Advanced tab		
9	Make footers active	Insert tab → Header & Footer group → Footer → Edit Footer		
9	Insert file names in footers	With footer active → Design tab → Insert group → Quick Parts		
10	View two pages	View tab → Zoom group → Multiple Pages		
10	Save as PDF documents	File tab → Export → Create PDF/XPS		

Key Terms

Online Help Skills

1. Start **Word 2013**, and then in the upper-right corner of the Word Start screen, click the **Help** button ⁇.

2. In the **Word Help** window **Search help** box, type screentips and then press Enter .

3. In the search result list, click **Show or hide ScreenTips**. Read the article, and then scroll to the video at the end of the article. Compare your screen with **Figure 1**.

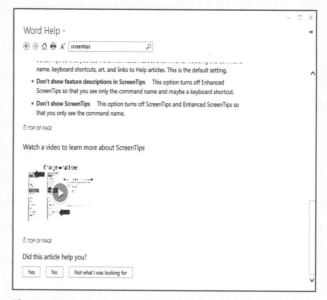

Figure 1

4. Turn on your speakers or put on headphones, and then watch the video to answer the following questions: What are the three options for viewing ScreenTips? Which option do you think you prefer, and why?

Matching

Match each term in the second column with its correct definition in the first column by writing the letter of the term on the blank line in front of the correct definition.

___ **1.** A character that indicates a paragraph, tab, or space on your screen, but that does not print when you print a Word document.

___ **2.** A pre-built collection of formatting settings that can be assigned to text.

___ **3.** A red wavy line indicates this type of error.

___ **4.** Forces a page to end, and places subsequent text at the top of the next page.

___ **5.** A command that deletes the selected text or object and places a copy in the Office Clipboard.

___ **6.** A reference that lists words that have the same or similar meaning to the word you are looking up.

___ **7.** A unit of measurement for font sizes.

___ **8.** A reserved area for text, graphics, and fields that displays at the top of each page in a document.

___ **9.** A category of data—such as a file name, the page number, or the current date—that can be inserted into a document.

___ **10.** An image of a document that can be viewed using a reader such as Adobe Acrobat Reader instead of the application that created the original document.

A Cut

B Field

C Formatting mark

D Header

E Manual page break

F PDF document

G Point

H Spelling

I Style

J Thesaurus

BizSkills Video

1. What is a professional network and how would you build one?

2. What are some of the best sources for job leads?

Multiple Choice (MyITLab®)

Choose the correct answer.

1. A button used to turn a feature both on and off.
   A. Dialog Launcher button
   B. Spin button
   C. Toggle button

2. To change Proofing settings, first display the:
   A. File tab
   B. Home tab
   C. Reference tab

3. In the Grammar Options dialog box, which is a category that can be enabled or disabled?
   A. Check spelling as you type
   B. Small caps
   C. Subject-verb agreement

4. A wavy line indicating a possible spelling, grammar, or style error.
   A. AutoComplete error
   B. Flagged error
   C. ScreenTip

5. This keyboard shortcut places the insertion point at the beginning of the document.
   A. Ctrl + A
   B. Ctrl + PageUp
   C. Ctrl + Home

6. The Spelling & Grammar group is located on this Ribbon tab.
   A. Home
   B. References
   C. Review

7. The Undo button is located here.
   A. Quick Access Toolbar
   B. Ribbon Home tab
   C. Ribbon Review tab

8. A font effect that displays all characters in uppercase while making any character originally typed as an uppercase letter taller than the ones typed as lowercase characters.
   A. CamelCase
   B. Small caps
   C. Uppercase

9. To view two pages at the same time, on the View tab, in the Zoom group, click this command.
   A. Fit Two
   B. Multiple Pages
   C. Two Pages

10. The typical file extension assigned to a Word document.
    A. .docx
    B. .pdf
    C. .xps

Topics for Discussion

1. Many organizations have professionally designed letterhead printed on sheets of paper. When writing a letter such as the one in this chapter, what would you need to do differently to accommodate stationery that already has your organization's name and address printed at the top? What might you need to do differently to print the letter?

2. When you check the spelling in a document, one of the options is to add unrecognized words to the dictionary. If you were working for a large company, what types of words do you think you would add to your dictionary?

Skills Review

MyITLab®
Grader

To complete this project, you will need the following file:

- wrd01_SRParkDonations

You will save your files as:

- **Last_First_wrd01_SRParks (Word)**
- **Last_First_wrd01_SRParks (PDF)**

1. Start a blank Word document. On the **Home tab**, click the **Show/Hide** button as needed to display the formatting marks. Type Aspen Falls Parks and Recreation Department and press Enter. Type 500 S Aspen Street and press Enter. Type Aspen Falls, CA 93463 and press Enter two times. Type the beginning of the letter with the information shown in **Figure 1**.

2. Press Enter, and then type Thank you for your interest in making a donation to the Aspen Falls Lake Conservation Area. You asked about projects for which we need additional resources, so I have attached a list of possible projects.

3. Press Enter, type Sincerely, and then press Enter two times. Type Leah Kim Press Enter, type Parks and Recreation Director and then apply the No Spacing style to the paragraph *Leah Kim*.

4. Select the first two lines of the letterhead. On the **Home tab**, in the **Styles group**, click the **No Spacing** button. Repeat this procedure with the first two lines of the inside address.

5. Click at the end of the paragraph that ends *possible projects*. Press Enter, and then type All donations made to the Friends of the Aspen Falls Conservation Areas (FAFCA) are tax deductible. Compare your screen with **Figure 2**.

6. **Save** the document in your **Word Chapter 1** folder as Last_First_wrd01_SRParks

7. **Open** the student data file, **wrd01_SRParkDonations**. On the **Home tab**, in the **Editing group**, click **Select**, and then click **Select All**. On the **Home tab**, in the **Clipboard group**, click **Copy**. **Close** the document.

8. In **Last_First_wrd01_SRParks**, press Ctrl + End. On the **Page Layout tab**, in the **Page Setup group**, click **Breaks**, and then click **Page**.

9. On the **Home tab**, in the **Clipboard group**, click **Paste**.

May 17, 2014

Mr. Fred Ashkenazy
2279 Shoreline Dr.
Aspen Heights, CA 93449

Dear Mr. Ashkenazy:

Subject: Donation to Aspen Falls Lake Conservation Area

Figure 1

Figure 2

- Continue to the next page to complete this Skills Review ▶

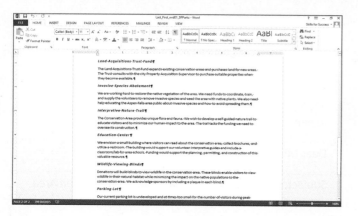

Figure 3

Figure 4

10. Select the heading *Land Acquisitions Trust Fund* and the paragraph that follows it. On the **Home tab**, in the **Clipboard group**, click **Cut** to remove the two paragraphs.

11. Click to the left of the heading *Invasive Species Abatement*, and then in the **Clipboard group**, click **Paste**.

12. On the **File tab**, click **Options**, and display the **Proofing** page. Change the **Writing Style** setting to **Grammar & Style**, and then click **OK**.

13. In the paragraph starting *The Land Acquisitions*, select the text *is used to expand*, and then type expands In the same sentence, change *purchase* to purchases

14. On the **File tab**, click **Options**, and display the **Proofing** page. Change the **Writing Style** setting to **Grammar Only**, and then click **OK**.

15. On the **Review tab**, in the **Proofing group**, click the **Spelling & Grammar** button. Use the **Spelling** and **Grammar** task panes to fix all spelling and grammar errors in the document.

16. In the paragraph below the *Wildlife Viewing Blinds* heading, right-click *inhabitants*, and then use the **Synonyms** submenu to change the word to **populations**.

17. Using the **Format Painter**, apply the formatting in the *Land Acquisitions Trust Fund* heading to the five other headings on the page. Compare your screen with **Figure 3**.

18. In the letterhead, select the paragraph starting *Aspen Falls Parks*. On the **Home tab**, in the **Font group**, click the **Font Dialog Box Launcher**.

19. In the **Font** dialog box, select **Small caps**, and then click the **Advanced tab**. Change the **Spacing** to **Expanded**, leave the **By** value at **1 pt**, and then click **OK**. Apply the **Cambria** font and font size **16**.

20. On the **Insert tab**, in the **Header & Footer group**, click the **Footer** button, and then click **Edit Footer**.

21. On the **Design tab**, in the **Insert group**, click the **Quick Parts** button, and then click **Field**. Under **Field names**, scroll down and click **FileName**. Click **OK**, and then click **Close Header and Footer**. Compare your screen with **Figure 4**.

22. On the **File tab**, click **Export**. On the **Export** page, click the **Create PDF/XPS** button.

23. In the **Publish as PDF or XPS** dialog box, navigate to your **Word Chapter 1** folder. Be sure the **Open file after publishing** check box is selected, and then click **Publish**.

24. View the document in a PDF viewer, and then **Close** the window.

25. Click **Save**, and then **Close** ☒ Word. Submit the files as directed by your instructor.

 DONE! You have completed this Skills Review

Skills Assessment 1

MyITLab®
Grader

To complete this project, you will need the following files:

- wrd01_SA1Land
- wrd01_SA1Legacy

You will save your files as:

- Last_First_wrd01_SA1Land (Word)
- Last_First_wrd01_SA1Land (PDF)

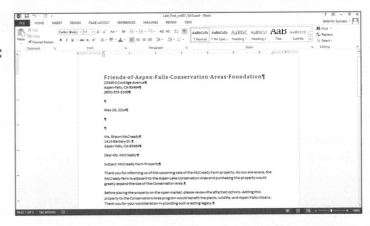

Figure 1

1. Open **wrd01_SA1Land** from the student data files, and then save it in your chapter folder as Last_First_wrd01_SA1Land Add the **FileName** field to the footer.

2. In **Word Options**, set the **Writing Style** to check **Grammar & Style**.

3. After the date, insert two blank lines and the following inside address: Ms. Shawn McCready; 1414 Barbary Dr.; Aspen Falls, CA 93464

4. For the first three lines of the letterhead, apply the **No Spacing** style. Repeat this procedure with the first two lines of the inside address.

5. For the letterhead's first line, apply the **Cambria** font, font size **16**, and then set the **Character Spacing** to **Expanded** by **1.3 pt**.

6. Below the inside address, add the salutation Dear Ms. McCready:

7. After the salutation, insert a new paragraph with the text Subject: McCready Farm Property Ignore all flagged errors for McCready, and then compare your screen with **Figure 1**.

8. Open the student data file **wrd01_SA1Legacy**. **Copy** all of the text, and then **Close** the document.

9. At the end of **Last_First_wrd01_SA1Land**, insert a manual page break, and then at the top of Page 2, paste the contents of the clipboard.

10. On Page 2, below *Gift and Estate Planning*, replace the word *various* with the suggested synonym **several**.

11. In the last bullet under *Life Estate Gift Annuity*, fix the style error using the suggestion in the flagged error's shortcut menu.

12. Use **Cut** and **Paste** to move the *Outright Gift* heading and its two bullets so that the section comes before the *Life Estate Gift Annuity* heading.

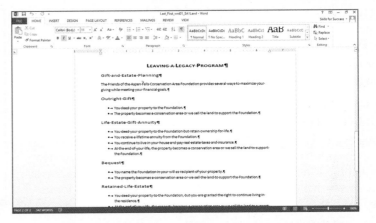

Figure 2

13. In **Word Options**, set the **Writing Style** to check **Grammar Only**.

14. Fix all spelling and grammar errors in the document.

15. Use **Format Painter** to apply the formatting in the *Gift and Estate Planning* heading to the five other headings on Page 2.

16. Compare your screen with **Figure 2**, and then **Save** the document.

17. Save the file as a PDF document in your chapter folder with the name Last_First_wrd01_SA1Land

18. **Close** all open windows, and then submit the files as directed by your instructor.

DONE! You have completed Skills Assessment 1

Skills Assessment 2

To complete this project, you will need the following files:

- wrd01_SA2Memo
- wrd01_SA2Topics

You will save your files as:

- Last_First_wrd01_SA2Memo
- Last_First_wrd01_SA2PDF

Figure 1

1. Open **wrd01_SA2Memo** from the student data files, and then save it in your chapter folder as Last_First_wrd01_SA2Memo Add the **FileName** field to the footer.

2. With the insertion point in the blank paragraph at the top of the document, apply the **No Spacing** style, and then press Enter five times. Type Memorandum

3. For the word *Memorandum*, set the **Font Size** to **36** and the **Character Spacing** to **Expanded** by **2.5 pt**.

4. In the last blank line of the document, type Jamie:

5. Press Enter, and then type the following paragraph: I have been thinking about the suggestion made at the Board of Trustees meeting the other night that we hire an outside company to design a virtual tour of the library. The virtual tour might consist of several modules featuring different topics. I have listed some of the topics on the next page.

6. At the end of the paragraph that ends *the next page,* insert a new paragraph with the text Let me know what you think. Press Enter two times, type Doug and then compare your screen with **Figure 1**.

7. At the end of the document, insert a manual page break, and then on Page 2, copy and paste all of the text from the student data file, **wrd01_SA2Topics**.

8. Cut the heading *Building Interior* and the paragraph that follows it, and then paste it before the *Building Exterior* heading.

9. In **Word Options**, set the **Writing Style** to check **Grammar & Style**. Use the **Spelling & Grammar** checker to fix all spelling, grammar, and style errors in the document.

10. In **Word Options**, set the **Writing Style** to check **Grammar Only**.

Figure 2

11. In the paragraph below *Building Exterior,* replace the word *striking* with the suggested synonym **prominent**.

12. Use **Format Painter** to apply the formatting in the *Building Interior* heading to the other four headings on Page 2.

13. Compare your screen with **Figure 2**, and then **Save** the document.

14. Save the file as a PDF document in your chapter folder with the name Last_First_wrd01_SA2PDF

15. **Close** all open windows, and then submit the files as directed by your instructor.

 DONE! You have completed Skills Assessment 2

Visual Skills Check

To complete this project, you will need the following file:

- Blank Word document

You will save your document as:

- Last_First_wrd01_VSCenter

Using the skills practiced in this chapter, create the document shown in **Figure 1**. **Save** the file as Last_First_wrd01_VSCenter in your chapter folder. Format the first line of the letterhead using the **Cambria** font sized at **24** points, small caps, and expanded by **1.5** points. Format the rest of the document using the **Calibri** font sized at **11** points. Maintain the space between paragraphs as shown in **Figure 1**. Insert the FileName field in the footer. Print or submit the file as directed by your instructor.

 DONE! You have completed Visual Skills Check

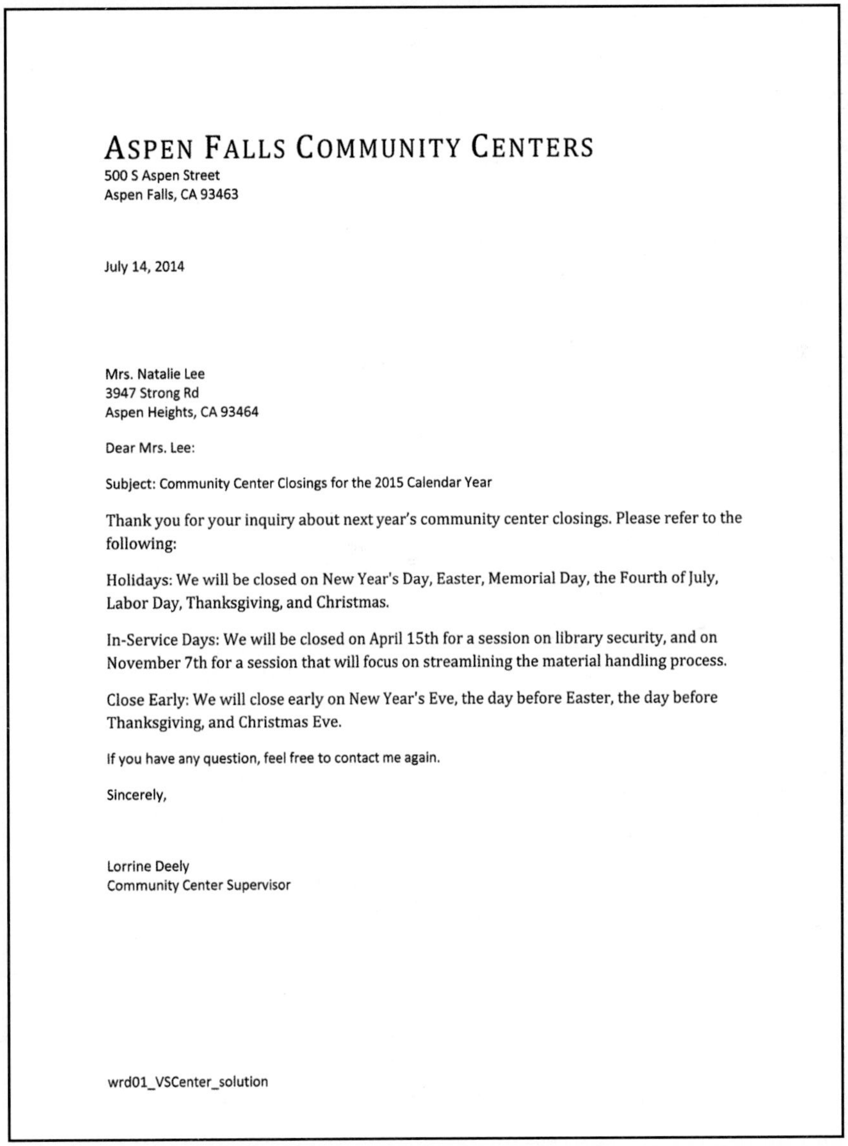

ASPEN FALLS COMMUNITY CENTERS
500 S Aspen Street
Aspen Falls, CA 93463

July 14, 2014

Mrs. Natalie Lee
3947 Strong Rd
Aspen Heights, CA 93464

Dear Mrs. Lee:

Subject: Community Center Closings for the 2015 Calendar Year

Thank you for your inquiry about next year's community center closings. Please refer to the following:

Holidays: We will be closed on New Year's Day, Easter, Memorial Day, the Fourth of July, Labor Day, Thanksgiving, and Christmas.

In-Service Days: We will be closed on April 15th for a session on library security, and on November 7th for a session that will focus on streamlining the material handling process.

Close Early: We will close early on New Year's Eve, the day before Easter, the day before Thanksgiving, and Christmas Eve.

If you have any question, feel free to contact me again.

Sincerely,

Lorrine Deely
Community Center Supervisor

wrd01_VSCenter_solution

Figure 1

June 10, 2014

Evelyn Stone
Aspen Falls City Hall
500 S Aspen St
Aspen Falls, CA 93464

Dear Mrs. Stone:

Subject: City Hall Internships

Figure 1

Your Name
1234 N Your St
Your City, State 99999

June 10, 2014

Evelyn Stone
Aspen Falls City Hall
500 S Aspen St
Aspen Falls, CA 93464

Dear Mrs. Stone:

Subject: City Hall Internships

One of my instructors at Aspen Falls Community College, Dr. Gato, suggested that I contact you regarding internships at Aspen Falls City Hall. My studies at the college qualify me for such a position starting as early as next term.

As you review the enclosed resume, please notice my training in Microsoft Office and my organizational skills. Specifically, my experience with Word and my work-study position with Dr. Gato indicate a successful internship as an Office Assistant.

If you have any questions, or if you want to schedule an interview, please contact me at (805) 555-3355 or e-mail me at youremail@address.

Sincerely,

Your Name

Last_First_wrd01_MyLetter.docx

Figure 2

My Skills

To complete this project, you will start with a:

- **Blank Word document**

You will save your document as:

- **Last_First_wrd01_MyLetter**

1. Create a blank Word document, and then save it in your chapter folder as Last_First_wrd01_MyLetter Add the **FileName** field to the footer.

2. In **Word Options**, set the **Writing Style** to check **Grammar & Style** and fix any flagged errors as you compose the letter in the next steps.

3. Type your first and last name, and then press Enter. On the next two lines of the letterhead, type your own address information. Complete the beginning of the letter as follows with the information shown in **Figure 1**.

4. Press Enter and type One of my instructors at Aspen Falls Community College, Dr. Gato, suggested that I contact you regarding internships at Aspen Falls City Hall. My studies at the college qualify me for such a position starting as early as next term.

5. Press Enter and type As you review the enclosed resume, please notice my training in Microsoft Office and my organizational skills. Specifically, my experience with Word and my work-study position with Dr. Gato indicate a successful internship as an Office Assistant.

6. Press Enter, and then using your e-mail address, type If you have any questions, or if you want to schedule an interview, please contact me at (805) 555-3355 or e-mail me at youremail@address.

7. Press Enter, and then type Sincerely, Press Enter two times, and then type your name.

8. Select the first two lines of the letterhead, and then apply the **No Spacing** style. Repeat this procedure with the first three lines of the inside address.

9. Using the techniques practiced in this chapter, format the letterhead to make it stand out slightly from the rest of the letter, and then compare your screen with **Figure 2**.

10. Print or submit the files as directed by your instructor.

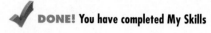 **DONE! You have completed My Skills**

Skills Challenge 1

To complete this project, you will need the following file:

- wrd01_SC1Trustees

You will save your document as:

- Last_First_wrd01_SC1Trustees

Open the student data file **wrd01_SC1Trustees**, and then save it in your chapter folder as Last_First_wrd01_SC1Trustees

For the entire document, apply a single font that is more appropriate than Comic Sans MS. Correct or ignore all flagged spelling, grammar, and style errors as appropriate to their context. Insert a page break so the letter ends on Page 1 and the report starts on Page 2.

On Page 1, correct the paragraph alignment and paragraph spacing so that it follows the block style business letter modeled in Skills 1–10. Format the letter head so that *Aspen Falls Public Library* stands out from the rest of the letter.

On Page 2, use cut and paste to arrange the headings and their paragraphs in alphabetical order by heading. Format the heading and side headings to visually organize the report. Be sure to apply the same formatting to all five headings.

Insert the FileName field in the footer. Print or submit the file as directed by your instructor.

 DONE! You have completed Skills Challenge 1

Skills Challenge 2

To complete this project, you will start with a:

- Blank Word document

You will save your document as:

- Last_First_wrd01_SC2Recommendation

Deborah Davidson, Public Information Specialist at Aspen Falls City Hall, needs to know if the current format for city letters is still the best choice. She specifically needs to know if the *blockstyle, modified-blockstyle,* or *modified-block style with indented paragraphs* should be used.

Use a business correspondence guide from your library or search online to compare the three styles under consideration. Summarize your findings in a letter addressed to Deborah Davidson, Public Information Specialist, Aspen Falls City Hall, 500 S Aspen Street, Aspen Falls, CA 93463.

For each of the three styles, write a short paragraph describing its features and comparative advantages and disadvantages. In a fourth paragraph, recommend which style the city should use and then justify your decision. Finally, format the letter using the style you recommended. Name the file Last_First_SC2Recommendation Insert the FileName field in the footer, and submit the letter as directed by your instructor.

 DONE! You have completed Skills Challenge 2

CHAPTER 2

Create Business Reports

- Informal business reports are often formatted using guidelines in *The Gregg Reference Manual* by William A. Sabin. These guidelines specify the way the text is formatted, the way notes display, and the types of citations used.

- A footnote or endnote can be inserted when you have supplemental information that does not fit well in the document.

- When you use quotations or paraphrase information created by someone else, you need to cite your sources in the document and list them at the end of the document.

- Report style guidelines specify how headings and side headings should be formatted. Your guidelines should also specify how much space should be above and below paragraphs, how the first line should be indented, and how much space should be between each line.

- Document margins are the spaces that display on the outer edges of a printed page. All four page margins can be adjusted independently.

- Lists make information easier to understand. Use numbered lists when information is displayed in a sequence and use bulleted lists when information can appear in any order.

Led vectoriel © gam16

Aspen Falls City Hall

In this chapter, you will finish a report for Richard Mack, Aspen Falls Assistant City Manager. The report provides a cost-benefit analysis regarding LED lights and makes recommendations based on that analysis. The study was conducted at the request of the city in cooperation with the Durango County Museum of History located in Aspen Falls.

If someone has requested that you write a report for them, you should ask them for guidelines regarding length, style, and format. Academic reports typically follow a set of guidelines such as MLA or Chicago, while the guidelines for business reports vary. Reports are either formal or informal. Formal reports include front matter such as a separate title page and a table of contents and back matter such as bibliographies and appendixes. Informal reports do not contain front matter, are short in length, and may have an optional bibliography.

In this project, you will edit and format an informal business report using the guidelines from *The Gregg Reference Manual* by William A. Sabin. You will edit text and then insert comments in footnotes. Following *The Chicago Manual of Style,* you will add sources to the document, cite those sources, and then insert a bibliography. Finally, you will format the document following standard guidelines for informal business reports.

Time to complete all 10
skills – 60 to 75 minutes

Student data file needed for this chapter:

wrd02_LEDs

You will save your document as:

Last_First_wrd02_LEDs

SKILLS

MyITLab®
Skills 1-10 Training

At the end of this chapter, you will be able to:

Skill 1   Find and Replace Text
Skill 2   Insert and Modify Footnotes
Skill 3   Add Sources
Skill 4   Insert Citations and Bibliographies
Skill 5   Format Bulleted and Numbered Lists
Skill 6   Set Paragraph Indents
Skill 7   Modify Line and Paragraph Spacing
Skill 8   Set Line and Page Break Options and Modify Styles
Skill 9   View Multiple Pages and Set Margins
Skill 10 Create Custom Headers and Footers

MORE SKILLS

Skill 11 Record AutoCorrect Entries
Skill 12 Use AutoFormat to Create Numbered Lists
Skill 13 Format and Customize Lists
Skill 14 Create Standard Outlines

Outcome

Using the skills in this chapter, you will be able to work with Word documents like this:

LED LIGHTS

A Museum Exhibit Case Study

By Your Name

July 21, 2014

In April 2014, the Durango County Museum of History installed a small exhibit titled *Our heritage: Pictures from the past.* The collection consists of five daguerreotypes and several silver albumen prints. A study was made to measure the benefits and costs of using LED lights instead of traditional halogen lamps.

RISKS OF LIGHTING HISTORIC PHOTOGRAPHS

All lighting harms photographs. (Lavedrine 2003) It is the task of the conservator to minimize this harm so that the photographs can be viewed for a significant span of time, typically 50 to 100 years. For these reasons, historical photographs are displayed only periodically in rooms with significantly reduced lighting. These practices minimize the visitor experience and according to Hunt, reducing light levels diminishes color saturation and contrast. (Hunt 1952, 190-199)

In all lighting systems, ultraviolet light (UV) must be eliminated as that spectrum harms photographs the most. Halogen lights must have UV filters installed which adds to their cost and effectiveness. LED lamps do not emit UV light and do not need extra filters. According to a study by the Getty Conservation Institute, fading from LED lamps does not result in any more damage than conventional halogen lamps with ultraviolet filtering. They found that it is likely using LED lamps results in less fading of photographic materials. (Druzik and Miller 2011)

METHODOLOGY

In the new exhibit, 12 watt PAR38 20° lamps were utilized. The temperature rating for these lamps was 2700 Kelvin. Although the LED light output was significantly less than traditional halogen lamps, some screening was still needed. UV filters were not installed because LED lights do not emit any significant levels of ultra-violet light. This simplified the installation process.

▶ The Navigation pane can be used to find text quickly.

▶ When you need to find and then replace several instances of the same words or phrases, you can use the Find and Replace dialog box.

1. Start **Word 2013**, and then from the student files, open **wrd02_LEDs**. If necessary, display the formatting marks.

2. On the **File tab**, click **Save As**, and then click **Browse**. In the **Save As** dialog box, navigate to the location where you are saving your files. Create a folder named Word Chapter 2 and then save the document as Last_First_wrd02_LEDs

3. On the **View tab**, in the **Show group**, verify that the **Navigation Pane** check box is selected, and then compare your screen with **Figure 1**.

4. With the insertion point at the top of the document, press Enter five times. On the **Home tab**, in the **Styles group**, click the **Heading 1** thumbnail. Type LED LIGHTS and then press Enter. Type A Museum Exhibit Case Study and then press Enter.

5. Using your own name, type By Your Name and then press Enter. Type the current date, and then press Enter.

6. Click to place the insertion point to the left of the title. Press and hold Shift while clicking to the right of the date to select the four lines.

7. In the **Paragraph group**, click the **Center** button ≡, and then compare your screen with **Figure 2**.

In an informal report, there should be 2 inches of space above the title, and the title, subtitle, writer's name, and date should be centered.

■ **Continue to the next page to complete the skill**

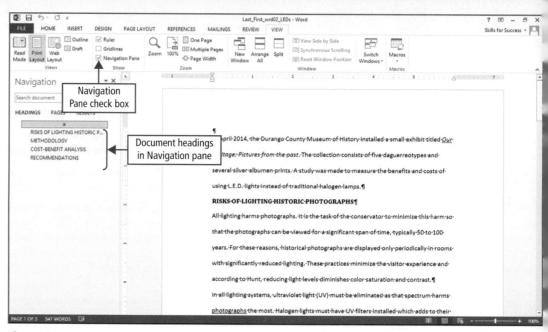

Figure 1

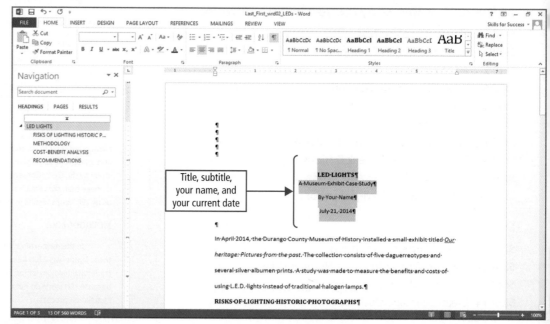

Figure 2

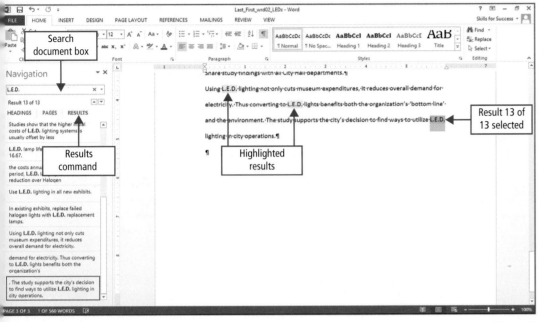

Figure 3

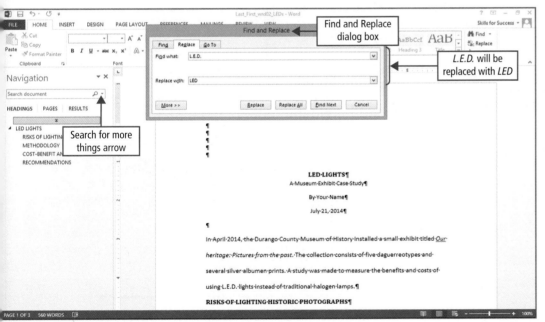

Figure 4

8. In the **Navigation** pane **Search document** box, type L.E.D. and then click **Results** to display the results.

9. Scroll to the bottom of the **Results** list, click the last search result, and then compare your screen with **Figure 3**.

In this manner, you can quickly find and navigate to a word or phrase in a document. In the document, each instance of the searched text is highlighted.

10. Click in the document, and then press Ctrl + Home to move the insertion point to the beginning of the document. In the **Navigation** pane, click the **Search for more things arrow**, and then click **Replace** to open the Find and Replace dialog box.

11. Verify that the **Find what** box has the text *L.E.D.*, and then in the **Replace with** box, type LED Compare your screen with **Figure 4**.

When you open the Find and Replace dialog box from the Navigation pane, the word or phrase you want to find is automatically entered into the *Find what* box.

12. Click the **Find Next** button to select the next occurrence of *L.E.D.* Click the **Replace** button to replace the initials and move to the next occurrence. Click **Replace** to replace another occurrence of *L.E.D.* with *LED*.

In this manner, you can replace each instance one at a time.

13. Click the **Replace All** button to replace the 11 remaining occurrences. Read the message that displays, click **OK**, and then **Close** the Find and Replace dialog box. **Save** 🖫 the document.

■ **You have completed Skill 1 of 10**

▶ A ***footnote*** is a note or comment placed at the bottom of the page. An ***endnote*** is a note or comment placed at the end of a section or a document.

1. In the **Navigation** pane, click the **Headings** command, and then click the **METHODOLOGY** heading to display that section of the report.

2. Click to the right of the period in the paragraph ending *output to the desired level.* Click the **References tab**, and then in the **Footnotes group**, click the **Insert Footnote** button.

> A footnote displays at the bottom of the page with a number *1* before the insertion point. A line is also inserted above the footnote area to separate it from the document text.

3. Type Screening is the process of installing layers of metal window screen. Compare your screen with **Figure 1**.

4. Navigate to the **COST-BENEFIT ANALYSIS** section, and then click to the right of the sentence ending *LED lamp life is longer by a factor of 16.67.*

5. Repeat the technique just practiced to insert a second footnote with the text Derived from industry standards. Compare your screen with **Figure 2**.

> Footnote numbers are inserted and formatted as ***superscript***—text that is positioned higher and smaller than the other text.

■ **Continue to the next page to complete the skill**

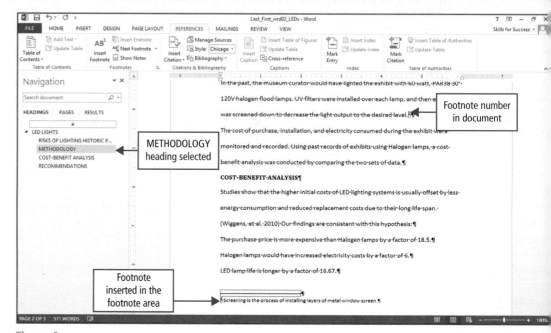

Figure 1

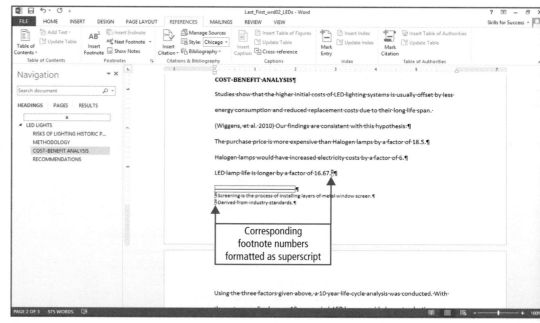

Figure 2

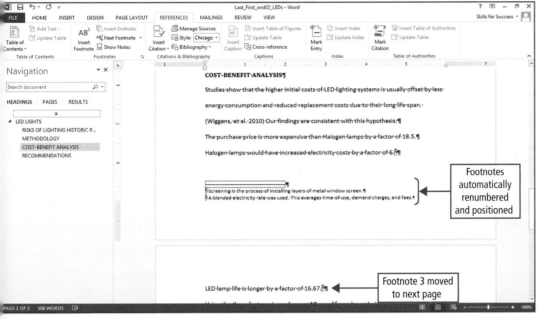

Footnotes automatically renumbered and positioned

Footnote 3 moved to next page

Figure 3

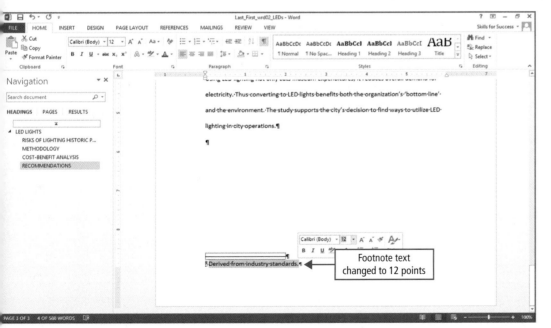

Footnote text changed to 12 points

Figure 4

6. Above the footnotes, click to the right of the sentence ending *increased electricity costs by a factor of 6.* Insert another footnote with the text A blended electricity rate was used. This averages time-of-use, demand charges, and fees. Compare your screen with **Figure 3**.

Footnotes automatically position themselves at the bottom of the correct page and adjust so that they are renumbered sequentially.

7. At the bottom of Page 2, select the text of the first footnote without selecting the footnote number. Change the font size to **12**.

Most style manuals call for the footnote text to be the same size as the document text. Footnote numbers are typically smaller than the report text.

8. Repeat the technique just practiced to change the text of footnote two to **12** points. Take care to format just the text and not the footnote number.

9. Scroll to the bottom of Page 3 to display the third footnote, and then change the footnote text to **12** points.

10. Compare your screen with **Figure 4**, and then **Save** 🖫 the document.

■ **You have completed Skill 2 of 10**

▶ A **source** is the reference used to find information or data.

1. On the **References tab**, in the **Citations & Bibliography group**, click the **Style arrow**, and then click **Chicago Sixteenth Edition**.

2. In the **Citations & Bibliography group**, click **Manage Sources**, and then under **Current List**, click the source starting *Wiggins*. Compare your screen with **Figure 1**.

> The Master List sources are available for all your documents, and the Current List sources are available only for a single document. The Preview pane displays citations and bibliography entries in the format for the selected style—here, Chicago Sixteenth Edition. The check mark indicates that the source has been cited in the document.

3. Click the **New** button, and then verify the **Type of Source** is **Book**.

4. In the **Author** box, type Bertrand Lavedrine and then in the **Title** box, type A Guide to the Preventive Conservation of Photograph Collections

5. For the **Year**, type 2003 and for the **City**, type Los Angeles For the **Publisher**, type Getty Conservation Institute and then compare your screen with **Figure 2**.

> The Create Source dialog box displays the fields required by the Chicago style for the selected source type.

6. Click **OK**, and then in **Source Manager**, preview the new source's citation and bibliography entry.

> The author's last name followed by a comma was placed before the first name when you closed the dialog box.

7. Click the **New** button, and then change the **Type of Source** to **Journal Article**.

■ **Continue to the next page to complete the skill** ➤

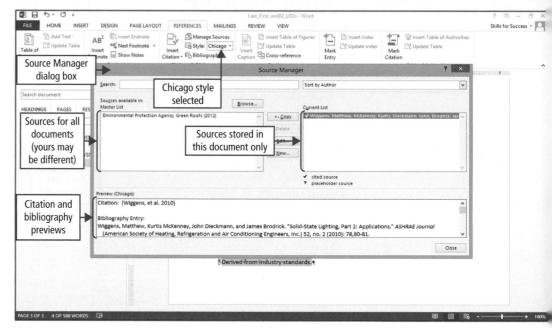

Figure 1

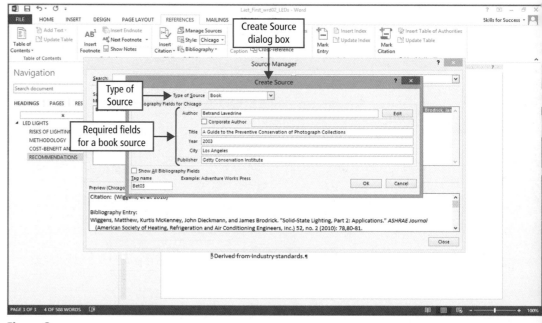

Figure 2

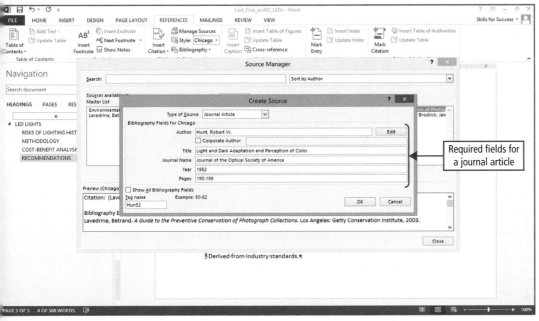

Required fields for
a journal article

Figure 3

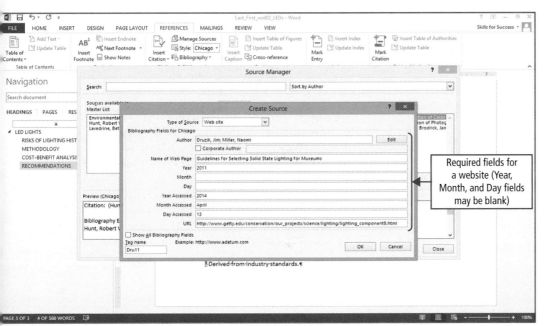

Required fields for
a website (Year,
Month, and Day fields
may be blank)

Figure 4

8. In the **Author** box, type Hunt, Robert W and then in the **Title** box, type Light and Dark Adaptation and Perception of Color

9. For the **Journal Name**, type Journal of the Optical Society of America and in the **Year** box, type 1952 In the **Pages** box, type 190-199 Compare your screen with **Figure 3**, and then click **OK**.

10. Click the **New** button, and then change the **Type of Source** to **Web site**.

11. In the **Author** box, type Druzik, Jim; Miller, Naomi and in the **Name of Web Page** box, type Guidelines for Selecting Solid State Lighting for Museums

12. In the **Year** box, type 2011 In the **Year Accessed** box, type 2014 The **Month Accessed** is April and the **Day Accessed** is 13

13. In the **URL** box, type http://www. getty.edu/conservation/our_projects/ science/lighting/lighting_component8. html Compare your screen with **Figure 4**, and then click **OK**.

14. In the **Source Manager** dialog box **Master List**, select the first source created in this skill. Verify you selected the title in the **Master List**—*not* the one in the Current List—and then click the **Delete** button. Repeat to delete the other two sources created in this skill from the **Master List**, and then click the **Close** button.

When you add a new source, it is placed in both the Master and Current Lists. If you do not plan to use a source in other documents, it can be deleted from the Master List. However, take care to leave the sources in the Current List.

■ **You have completed Skill 3 of 10**

WRD 2-4
VIDEO

▶ When you quote or refer to information from another source, you need to credit that source.

▶ A **bibliography** is a compilation of sources referenced in a report and listed on a separate page.

▶ A **citation** is a note in the document that refers the reader to a source in the bibliography.

1. Navigate to the **RISKS OF LIGHTING HISTORIC PHOTOGRAPHS** section.

2. Click to the right of the period ending the first sentence *All lighting harms photographs*. On the **References tab**, in the **Citations & Bibliography group**, click **Insert Citation**, and then compare your screen with **Figure 1**.

   When you insert a citation field, the sources stored in Source Manager display in the gallery.

3. In the **Citation** gallery, click the **Lavedrine**, **Bertand** source to insert the citation.

4. In the same paragraph, click to the right of the period of the sentence ending *saturation and contrast*. Repeat the technique just practiced to insert the citation for **Hunt**, **Robert W**.

5. Click the citation just inserted, click the field's **Citation Options arrow**, and then click **Edit Citation**. In the **Pages** box, type 192 click **OK**, and then compare your screen with **Figure 2**.

   Many business reports use the **author-date citation**, which contains the author's last name, the publication year, and the specific page number(s) if one is available.

■ Continue to the next page to complete the skill

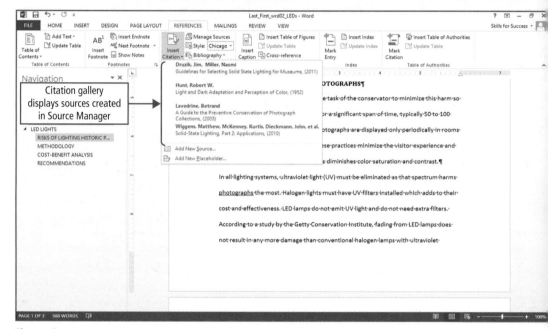

Figure 1

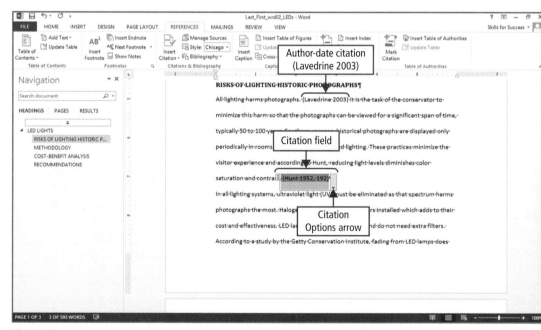

Figure 2

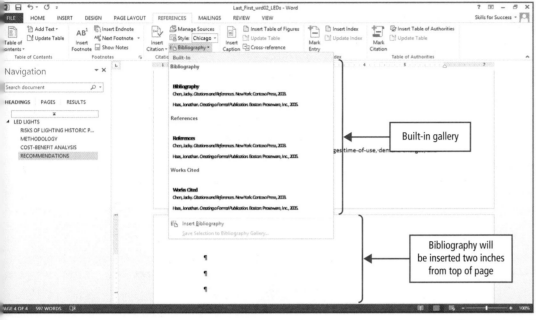

Figure 3

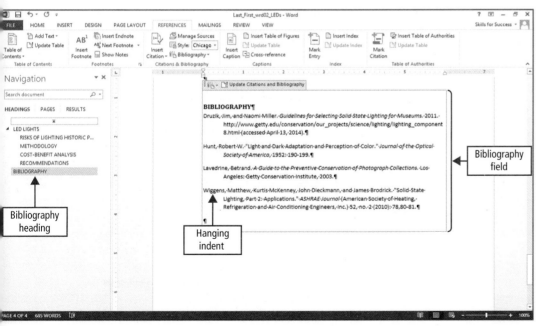

Figure 4

6. At the top of Page 2, click to the right of the period of the sentence ending *fading of photographic materials,* and then insert the citation for **Druzik**, **Jim R**, **Miller**, **Naomi**.

7. Press Ctrl + End , and then press Ctrl + Enter to insert a manual page break and start a new page. Press Enter two times to create about 2 inches of space from the top of the page.

8. On the **References tab**, in the **Citations & Bibliography group**, click the **Bibliography** button, and then compare with **Figure 3**.

9. From the gallery, click the **Bibliography** thumbnail to insert a bibliography field. If necessary, scroll up to display the inserted bibliography field.

   In the Chicago style, the Bibliography field displays each source using hanging indents. In a ***hanging indent***, the first line extends to the left of the rest of the paragraph.

10. Double-click the *Bibliography* title, and then type BIBLIOGRAPHY In the **Navigation** pane, verify that the *BIBLIOGRAPHY* title has been added as a level 1 heading. Compare your screen with **Figure 4**.

    In an informal report, the first-level headings should be uppercase and centered. You will center this title in a later skill.

11. **Save** 💾 the document.

    If you change the reference style or report sources, you can update the citation and bibliography fields by clicking the field, and then selecting its update command.

■ **You have completed Skill 4 of 10**

▶ A **bulleted list** is a list of items with each item introduced by a symbol—such as a small circle or check mark—in which the list items can be presented in any order.

1. Navigate to the **COST-BENEFIT ANALYSIS** section.

2. If necessary, scroll down to display the bottom of Page 2 and the top of Page 3.

3. Point to the left of the paragraph that starts *The purchase price is more* to display the ◢ pointer, and then drag straight down to select the three paragraphs starting *The Purchase price* and ending with *factor of 16.67* including the footnote number and paragraph marks. Compare your screen with **Figure 1**.

   When you select text with footnotes, the text in the footnotes area will not be selected.

4. If your ruler does not display, on the View tab, in the Show group, select the Ruler check box.

5. On the **Home tab**, in the **Paragraph group**, click the **Bullets arrow** ☰▾, and then in the **Bullets** gallery, click the solid circle bullet.

   The Bullets gallery displays commonly used bullet characters, and the most recently used bullet displays at the top.

6. In the **Paragraph group**, click the **Increase Indent** button ☲ one time, and then compare your screen with **Figure 2**.

   In reports, lists are typically indented 0.5 inches on the left with a hanging indent set to 0.25 inches for the first line.

■ Continue to the next page to complete the skill

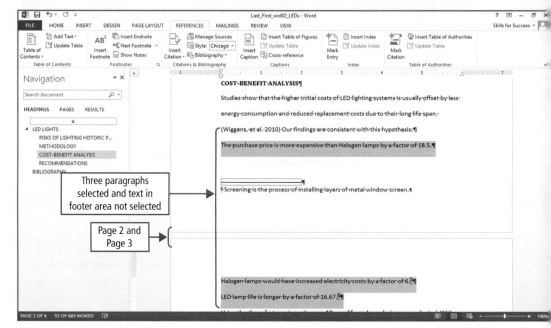

Figure 1

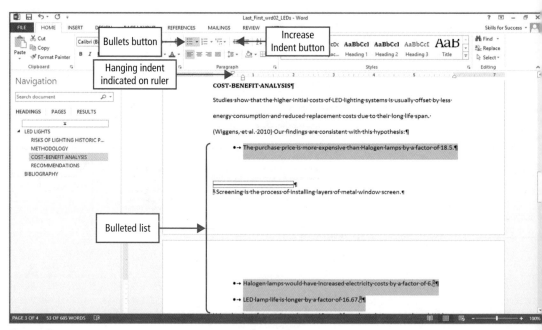

Figure 2

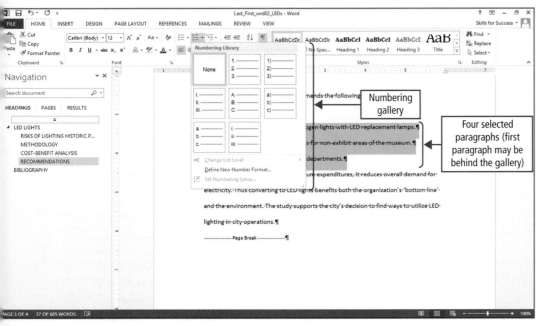

Figure 3

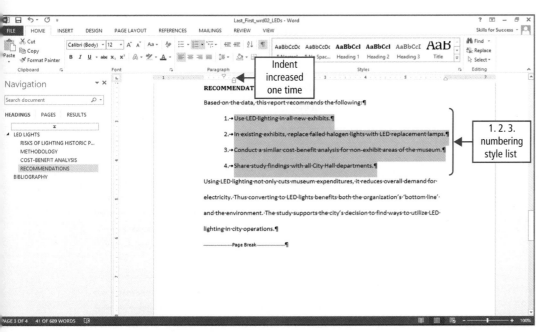

Figure 4

7. Navigate to the **RECOMMENDATIONS** section, and then select the four paragraphs beginning *Use LED lighting in all new* and ending with *City Hall departments.*

8. On the **Home tab**, in the **Paragraph group**, click the **Numbering arrow** , and then compare your screen with **Figure 3**.

> A **numbered list** is a list of items with each item introduced by a consecutive number or letter to indicate definite steps, a sequence of actions, or chronological order.
>
> The Numbering gallery displays common formats that can be used to enumerate lists. For all lists, you should refer to the style guidelines specified for your report. Certain bullet characters may be specified or a different numbering system may need to be applied.

9. In the **Numbering** gallery, click the thumbnail with the *1. 2. 3.* formatting.

10. In the **Paragraph group**, click the **Increase Indent** button one time, and then compare your screen with **Figure 4**.

11. **Save** the document.

■ **You have completed Skill 5 of 10**

▶ An ***indent*** is the position of paragraph lines in relation to a page margin.

1. Navigate to the **LED LIGHTS** heading, and then click in the body paragraph that starts *In April 2014*.

2. On the **Home tab**, in the **Paragraph group**, click the **Paragraph Dialog Box Launcher** 🔲.

   The Paragraph dialog box has commands and settings that are not available in the Paragraph group.

3. Under **Indentation**, click the **Special arrow**, and then click **First line**. Compare your screen with **Figure 1**.

   The ***first line indent*** is the location of the beginning of the first line of a paragraph in relation to the left edge of the remainder of the paragraph. In this case, the *By* box displays *0.5"*, which will indent the first line of the current paragraph one-half inch.

4. Click **OK** to indent the first line of the paragraph. On the ruler, verify that the **First Line Indent** marker is now at the **0.5 inch** mark.

5. Click in the paragraph starting *All lighting harms photographs*. Press F4 to repeat the previous task.

   The F4 keyboard shortcut repeats the last command. If you performed an additional task after setting the previous indent, you will need to set the indent using the Paragraph dialog box.

6. Click in the next paragraph starting *In all lighting systems*, press F4, and then compare your screen with **Figure 2**.

■ **Continue to the next page to complete the skill** ➤

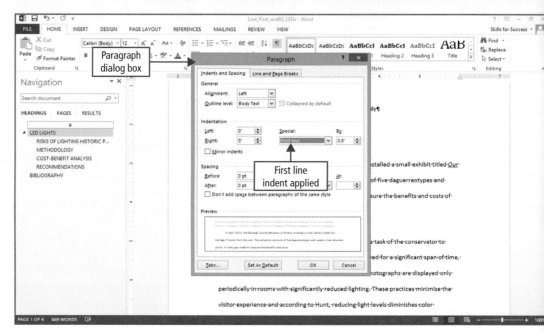

Figure 1

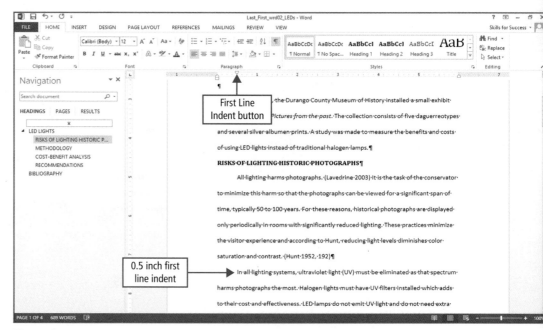

Figure 2

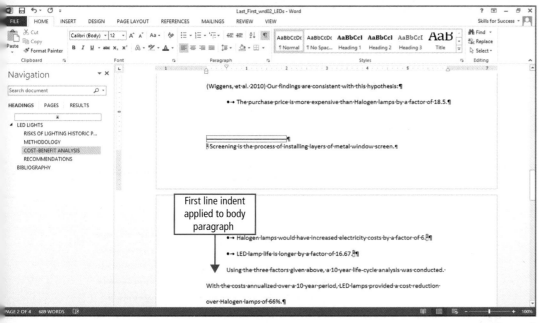

First line indent applied to body paragraph

Figure 3

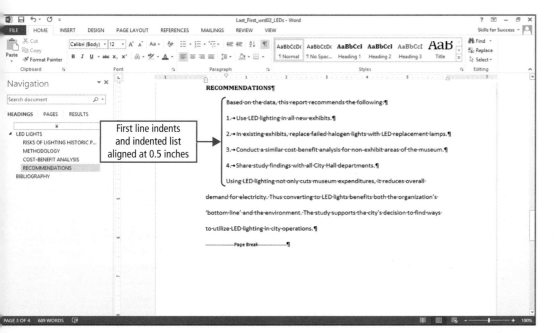

First line indents and indented list aligned at 0.5 inches

Figure 4

7. In the **METHODOLOGY** section, click in the first paragraph beginning *In the new exhibit*. On the ruler, drag the **First Line Indent** button to the **0.5 inch** mark on the ruler.

   In this manner, you can set the first line indent in the Paragraph dialog box or on the ruler.

8. Select the two paragraphs beginning *In the past* and *The cost of purchase*, and then repeat one of the techniques practiced in this skill to set a **0.5 inch** first line indent to both paragraphs.

9. Navigate to the **COST-BENEFIT ANALYSIS** section, and then apply a **0.5 inch** first line indent to the two paragraphs starting *Studies show that* and *Using the three factors*. Compare your screen with **Figure 3**.

   Recall that the bulleted list was indented to 0.5 inches in the previous skill and already has a hanging indent.

10. Navigate to the **RECOMMENDATIONS** section, and then apply a 0.5 inch first line indent to the two paragraphs starting *Based on the data* and *Using LED lighting not only cuts*. Compare your screen with **Figure 4**.

    In a report, the paragraph first line indents and the bullets or numbers in a list should all align at the 0.5 inch mark.

11. **Save** 🖫 the document.

■ **You have completed Skill 6 of 10**

▶ *Line spacing* is the vertical distance between lines of text in a paragraph, and *paragraph spacing* is the vertical distance above and below each paragraph. Both may need to be adjusted to match your report's style guide.

1. In the **Navigation** pane, click the **LED LIGHTS** heading. Select the title and the three paragraphs after it. On the **Home tab**, in the **Paragraph group**, click the **Paragraph Dialog Box Launcher** 🔲.

2. In the **Paragraph** dialog box, under **Spacing**, click the **Before up spin arrow** one time to change the value to **0 pt**, and then change the **After** value to **12 pt**.

3. Click the **Line Spacing arrow**, and then click **Single**. Compare your screen with **Figure 1**, and then click **OK**.

    Reports should have a blank line between each element. The style guide you follow should specify if this should be done by inserting a blank paragraph or by adjusting the paragraph spacing.

4. Click in the body paragraph that begins *In April 2014*. In the **Paragraph group**, click the **Line and Paragraph Spacing** button 🔲, and then compare your screen with **Figure 2**.

    To increase readability in longer reports, the default line spacing should be 2.0, which is *double-spacing*—the equivalent of a blank line of text displays between each line of text.

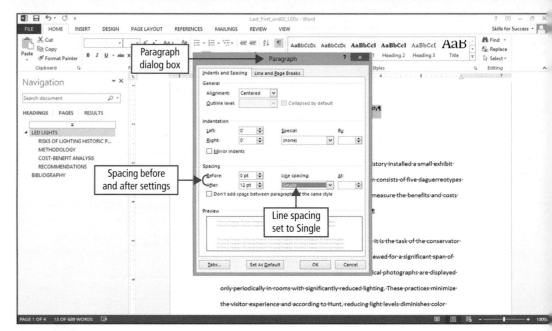
Figure 1

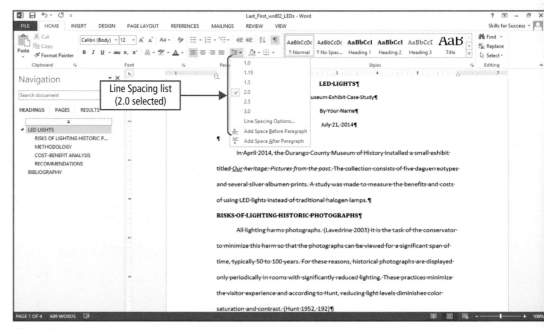
Figure 2

■ **Continue to the next page to complete the skill** ➡

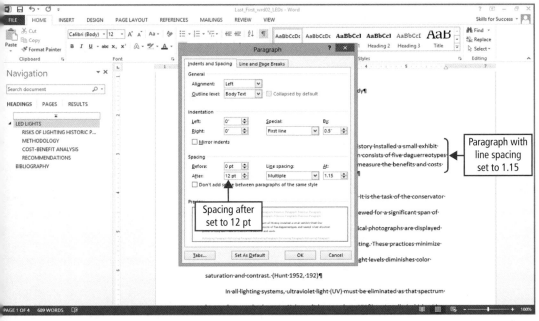

Figure 3

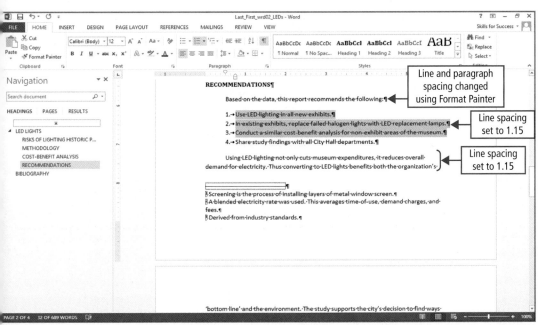

Figure 4

5. In the **Line Spacing** list, point to **1.15** to preview the setting, and then click **1.15**.

In shorter, informal reports such as this report, you can reduce the amount of line spacing so that the report fits on fewer pages. Text with a line spacing of 1.15 has been found to be easier to read than single-spaced text.

6. Open the **Paragraph** dialog box, and then change the **After** setting to **12 pt**. Compare your screen with **Figure 3**, and then click **OK**.

7. With the insertion point still in the paragraph, double-click the **Format Painter** button. With the Format Painter pointer ⬝, click one time in the nine remaining body paragraphs—do not drag—to apply the line and paragraph spacing formatting. Do not apply the formatting to the headings, bulleted list items, numbered list items, or bibliography items. When you are done, click the **Format Painter** button so it is no longer active.

8. Navigate to the **COST-BENEFIT ANALYSIS** section, and then select the first two bulleted list items. In the **Paragraph group**, click the **Line Spacing** button, and then click **1.15**.

9. In the **RECOMMENDATIONS** section, select the first three numbered list items, and then set the **Line Spacing** to **1.15**. Compare your screen with **Figure 4**.

10. Save 🖫 the document.

■ **You have completed Skill 7 of 10**

▶ You may need to adjust line and page break options to avoid problems when headings and paragraphs split across two pages.

▶ You can format elements quickly by modifying the styles assigned to them.

1. In the **Navigation** pane, click the **BIBLIOGRAPHY** header, and then compare your screen with **Figure 1**.

   The Bibliography header was assigned the Heading 1 style, but it does not have the same alignment and paragraph spacing as the document title.

2. Navigate to the document title, **LED LIGHTS**. With the insertion point in the title paragraph, on the **Home tab**, in the **Styles group**, right-click the **Heading 1** thumbnail. From the shortcut menu, click **Update Heading 1 to Match Selection**.

   Recall that for paragraph formatting, the paragraph does not actually need to be selected. Here, the Heading 1 style was updated based on the formatting of the paragraph the insertion point was in.

3. Navigate to the **BIBLIOGRAPHY** heading, and then compare your screen with **Figure 2**.

   The heading is now center aligned with 12 points of space below the paragraph. In this manner, you can format a document quickly by modifying its styles.

4. Navigate to the **METHODOLOGY** section. Click in the paragraph that begins *In the new exhibit,* and then open the **Paragraph** dialog box.

■ **Continue to the next page to complete the skill**

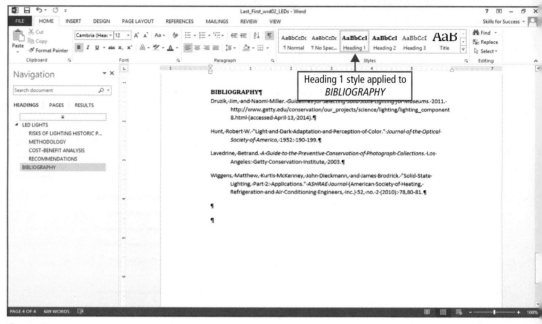

Figure 1

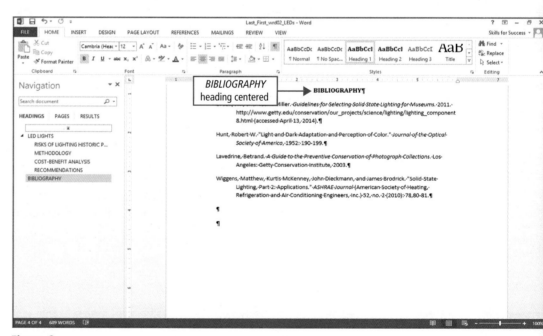

Figure 2

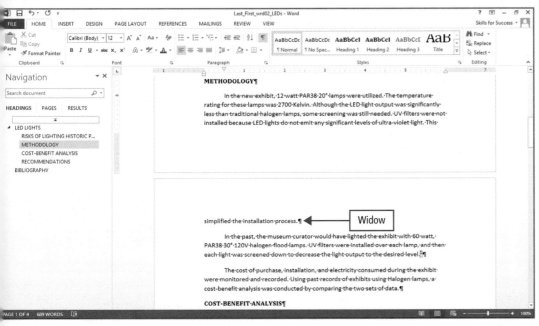

Figure 3

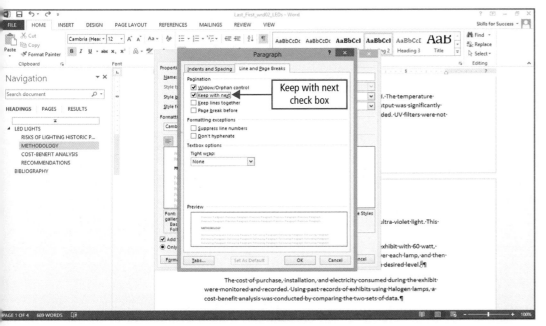

Figure 4

5. In the **Paragraph** dialog box, click the **Line and Page Breaks tab**, clear the **Widow/Orphan control** check box, and then click **OK**. Compare your screen with **Figure 3**.

The top of Page 3 displays a ***widow***—the last line of a paragraph displays as the first line of a page. An ***orphan*** is the first line of a paragraph that displays as the last line of a page. Both widows and orphans should be avoided.

6. On the **Quick Access Toolbar**, click the **Undo** button ↺ to enable widow and orphan control. Alternately, press Ctrl + Z.

7. Click to place the insertion point in the *METHODOLOGY* header. In the **Styles group**, right-click the **Heading 2** thumbnail, and then from the shortcut menu, click **Modify**.

8. In the lower corner of the **Modify Style** dialog box, click the **Format** button, and then click **Paragraph**.

9. On the **Line and Page Breaks tab** of the **Paragraph** dialog box, select the **Keep with next** check box, and then compare your screen with **Figure 4**.

10. Click **OK** two times to close the dialog boxes and update the Heading 2 style.

Headings should have the *Keep with next* option selected so that at least two lines of the paragraph that follows them always display on the same page as the heading. Here, the setting has been applied to all the document's side headings—Heading 2.

11. **Save** 🖫 the document.

■ **You have completed Skill 8 of 10**

▶ **Margins** are the spaces between the text and the top, bottom, left, and right edges of the paper.

▶ Viewing multiple pages on a single screen is useful when you need to evaluate the overall layout of a document.

1. Navigate to the **LED LIGHTS** heading. On the **View tab**, in the **Zoom group**, click **Multiple Pages**. Compare your screen with **Figure 1**.

   The number of pages that display when you view multiple pages depends on the dimensions of your monitor or window. On large monitors, your window may be large enough to display three pages and the text may be large enough to edit and format.

2. In the **Navigation** pane, click the **BIBLIOGRAPHY** heading. **Close** ☒ the Navigation pane, and then compare your screen with **Figure 2**.

   Depending on the audience, you may want to reduce the length of a report to as few pages as possible. Here, the end of the report body uses a small portion of Page 3. Reducing the size of the side margins may fit the report on three pages instead of four.

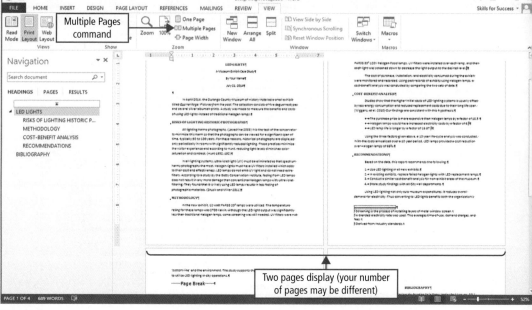

Figure 1

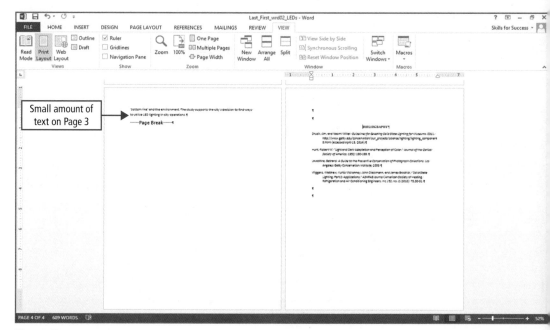

Figure 2

■ **Continue to the next page to complete the skill** ▶

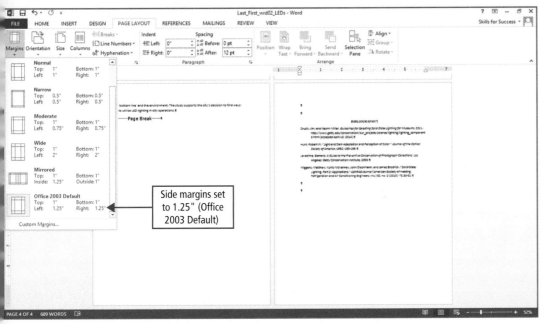

Figure 3

3. On the **Page Layout tab**, in the **Page Setup group**, click **Margins**, and then compare your screen with **Figure 3**.

The Margins gallery displays thumbnails and descriptions of common margin settings. Here, the report is set to the default margin sizes used in an older version of Word—Word 2003.

In a report, the top and bottom margins are typically 1.0 inch each, and the side margins are 1.25 inches each. In a short informal report, you can change the side margins to 1 inch each if needed.

4. In the **Margins** gallery, click the **Normal** thumbnail to set the margins to 1 inch on all four sides. Compare your screen with **Figure 4**.

With the smaller margins, the report title and body now fit on two pages, and the Bibliography is on the third page. Before setting the margins on a report, you should check the assigned style guidelines for the dimensions that you should use.

5. Scroll up to view Page 1 and Page 2, and then on the **View tab**, in the **Zoom group**, click **100%** to return to the default view.

If you are working on a large monitor, you may still see two pages displayed with the 100% zoom level. If so, you can snap the window to either half of the screen to see only one page at a time.

6. Save ⊟ the document.

■ **You have completed Skill 9 of 10**

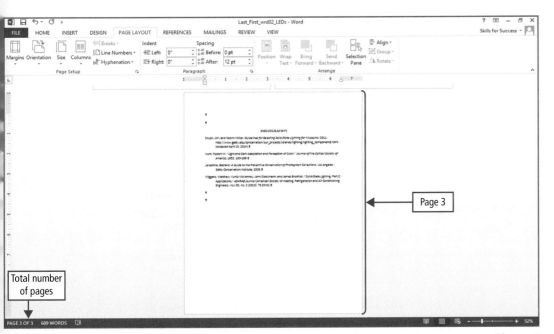

Figure 4

- Headers and footers can include text you type, fields, and graphics.
- On the first page of a document, you can set the headers and footers so that they do not display.

1. Press [Ctrl] + [Home] to move the insertion point to the beginning of the document. On the **Insert tab**, in the **Header & Footer group**, click **Page Number**. In the **Page Number** list, point to **Top of Page**, and then compare your screen with **Figure 1**.

2. In the **Page Number** gallery, use the vertical scroll bar to scroll through the page number options. When you are through, scroll to the top of the list. Under **Simple**, click **Plain Number 3** to insert the page number at the top and right margins.

   When you insert a pre-built page number in this manner, the header and footer areas are activated so that you can continue working with them.

3. Under **Header & Footer Tools**, on the **Design tab**, in the **Options group**, select the **Different First Page** check box, and notice the page number on Page 1 is removed.

4. Scroll to the top of Page 2, and verify that the page number displays, as shown in **Figure 2**.

   In reports where the body starts on the same page as the title, the page number is not included on the first page.

■ Continue to the next page to complete the skill ▶

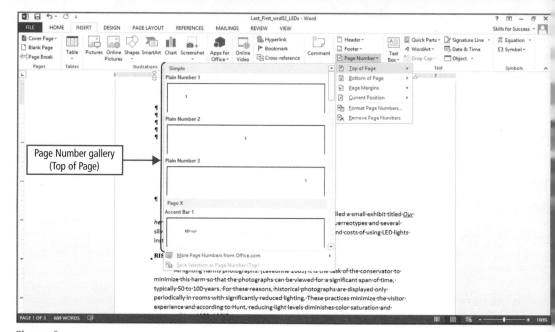

Figure 1

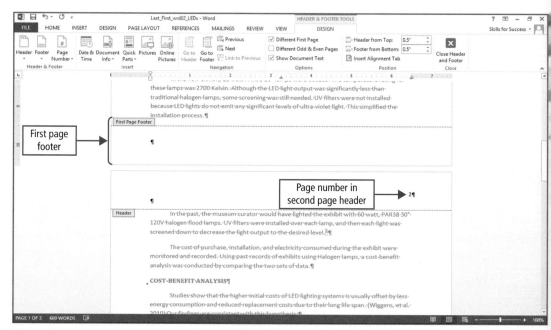

Figure 2

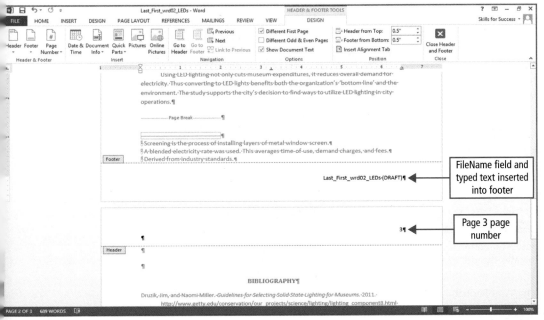

FileName field and typed text inserted into footer

Page 3 page number

Figure 3

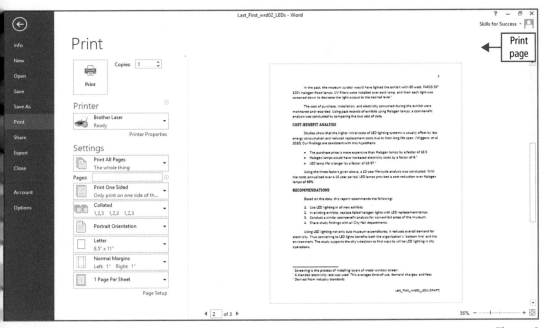

Print page

Figure 4

5. Scroll to the bottom of Page 2, and then click in the footer area. If you accidentally deactivated the header and footer areas, double-click the footer area.

6. In the **Insert group**, click the **Quick Parts** button, and then click **Field**. Under **Field names**, scroll down, click **FileName**, and then click **OK**.

7. Add a space, and then type (DRAFT) Be sure to include the parentheses.

> In this manner, headers and footers can contain both fields such as page numbers and file names and text that you type.

8. On the **Home tab**, in the **Paragraph group**, click the **Align Right** button, and then compare your screen with **Figure 3**.

> In a business setting, this footer would be removed before the report is published.

9. Double-click in the report body to deactivate the footer area. On the **File tab**, click **Print**, and then compare your screen with **Figure 4**.

10. If you are printing your work, print the report. Otherwise, click the **Back** button .

11. **Save** 🖫 the document, **Close** ☒ Word, and then submit the document as directed by your instructor.

DONE! You have completed Skill 10 of 10, and your document is complete!

The following More Skills are located at **www.pearsonhighered.com/skills**

More Skills Record AutoCorrect Entries

If you enable the AutoCorrect feature in Word, when you misspell a word that is contained in the AutoCorrect list, the misspelling is corrected automatically. You can add words that you commonly misspell as you type, or you can open a dialog box and add words or phrases that you want to have automatically corrected. This feature can also be used to create shortcuts for phrases that you type regularly.

In More Skills 11, you will open a short document and use two methods to add items to the AutoCorrect Options list.

To begin, open your web browser, navigate to www.pearsonhighered.com/skills, locate the name of your textbook, and then follow the instructions on the website.

More Skills Use AutoFormat to Create Numbered Lists

If you create numbered lists frequently, you can use AutoFormat to start typing the list, and the program will automatically add numbers and formatting to the list as you type.

In More Skills 12, you will open a document, set the AutoFormat options, and then create a numbered list that is formatted automatically.

To begin, open your web browser, navigate to www.pearsonhighered.com/skills, locate the name of your textbook, and then follow the instructions on the website.

More Skills Format and Customize Lists

There are several other formatting changes you can make to numbered and bulleted lists. You can change the numbering scheme, and you can change the character used for the bullet symbol. You can also increase or decrease the indent of both types of lists.

In More Skills 13, you will open a document and change the numbering on a numbered list. You will also increase the indent on a bulleted list.

To begin, open your web browser, navigate to www.pearsonhighered.com/skills, locate the name of your textbook, and then follow the instructions on the website.

More Skills Create Standard Outlines

Longer reports may require an outline so that you can plan and organize the report. Typically, report outlines follow style guidelines that specify formatting, paragraph spacing, indents, and numbering style.

In More Skills 14, you will create an outline for a report following the standard outline format as defined in *The Gregg Reference Manual* by William A. Sabin.

To begin, open your web browser, navigate to www.pearsonhighered.com/skills, locate the name of your textbook, and then follow the instructions on the website.

Please note that there are no additional projects to accompany the More Skills Projects, and they are not covered in the End-of-Chapter projects.

The following table summarizes the **SKILLS AND PROCEDURES** covered in this chapter.

Skill Number	Task	Step	Icon	Keyboard Shortcut
1	Find text	In the Navigation pane, use the search box and click Results		Ctrl + F
1	Find and replace text	In the Navigation pane, click the Search for more things arrow		Ctrl + H
1	Navigate by headings	In the Navigation pane, click Headings		
2	Insert footnotes	References tab → Footnotes group → Insert Footnote		
3	Add or edit sources	References tab → Citations & Bibliography group → Manage Sources		
3	Set reference styles	References tab → Citations & Bibliography group → Style		
4	Insert citations	References tab → Citations & Bibliography group → Insert Citation		
4	Insert a bibliography	References tab → Citations & Bibliography group → Bibliography	📑	
5	Apply bullet lists	Home tab → Paragraph group → Bullets arrow	☰	
5	Apply numbered lists	Home tab → Paragraph group → Numbering arrow	☰	
5	Indent lists	Home tab → Paragraph group → Increase Indent	☰	
6	Set first line indents	Paragraph group → Paragraph Dialog Box Launcher → Special → First Line		
7	Modify line and paragraph spacing	Paragraph group → Paragraph Dialog Box Launcher		
7	Repeat the last command			F4
8	Enable widow and orphan control	Paragraph group → Paragraph Dialog Box Launcher → Line and Page Breaks tab		
8	Set keep with next control	Paragraph group → Paragraph Dialog Box Launcher → Line and Page Breaks tab		
8	Modify styles	Right-click style thumbnail in Styles group, and then click Modify. Click the Format button and open desired dialog box.		
9	Update styles	Click or select text with desired style formatting. Right-click the style's thumbnail in Styles group, and then click Update command.		
9	Change margins	Page Layout tab → Margins		
10	Add page numbers	Insert tab → Header & Footer group → Page Number		
10	Apply different first page headers and footers	Header & Footer Tools → Design tab → Different first page		

Key Terms

Online Help Skills

1. Start **Word 2013**, and then in the upper right corner of the start page, click the **Help** button ?.

2. In the **Word Help** window **Search help** box, type word count and then press Enter.

3. In the search result list, click **Find the word count**. Compare your screen with **Figure 1**.

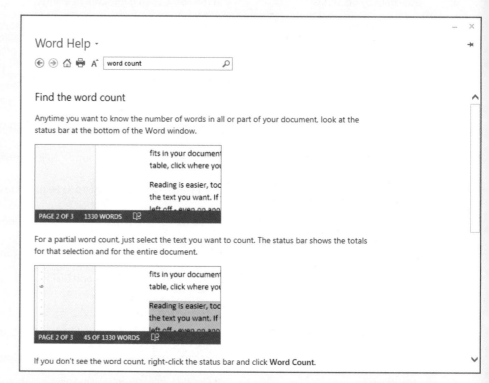

Figure 1

4. Read the article to answer to the following question: How can you find out how many words are in the document without counting the words in the footnotes?

Matching

Match each term in the second column with its correct definition in the first column by writing the letter of the term on the blank line in front of the correct definition.

____ **1.** The pane used to find document text.

____ **2.** A comment or notation added to the end of a section or document.

____ **3.** The reference used to find information or data when writing a report.

____ **4.** The citation type used for the Chicago style.

____ **5.** A list of sources displayed on a separate page at the end of a report.

____ **6.** The type of list used for items that are in chronological or sequential order.

____ **7.** The equivalent of a blank line of text displayed between each line of text in a paragraph.

____ **8.** The vertical distance above and below each paragraph in a document.

____ **9.** The position of the first line of a paragraph relative to the text in the rest of the paragraph.

____ **10.** The space between the text and the top, bottom, left, and right edges of the paper when you print the document.

A Author-date

B Bibliography

C Double-spacing

D Endnote

E First line indent

F Margin

G Navigation

H Numbered

I Paragraph spacing

J Source

BizSkills Video

1. What are some actions that you should take when attending a job fair?

2. What actions should be avoided when attending a job fair?

Multiple Choice (MyITLab®)

Choose the correct answer.

1. To place a note on the same page as the comment or notation, use which of these?
   A. Footnote
   B. Endnote
   C. Citation

2. This is placed in body paragraphs and points to an entry in the bibliography.
   A. Footnote
   B. Citation
   C. Endnote

3. The number of inches from the top edge of the paper to the beginning of the bibliography.
   A. 0.5 inches
   B. 1 inch
   C. 2 inches

4. In a Chicago style bibliography, this type of indent is used for each reference.
   A. Hanging indent
   B. First line indent
   C. Left alignment

5. Items that can be listed in any order are best presented using which of the following?
   A. Bulleted list
   B. Numbered list
   C. Outline list

6. The default line spacing in a long report.
   A. Custom
   B. Single
   C. Double

7. The vertical distance between lines in a paragraph.
   A. Spacing after
   B. Line spacing
   C. Text wrapping

8. The last line of a paragraph that displays as the first line of a page.
   A. Single
   B. Stray
   C. Widow

9. The pre-built setting that places all four margins at 1.0 inches.
   A. Narrow
   B. Normal
   C. Office 2003 Default

10. This type of alignment positions the text so that it is aligned with the right margin.
    A. Right
    B. Center
    C. Left

Topics for Discussion

1. You can build and save a list of master sources you have used in research papers and reports and display them using Manage Sources. What are the advantages of storing sources over time?

2. Paragraph text can be left aligned, centered, right aligned, or justified. Left alignment is the most commonly used. In what situations would you use centered text? Justified text? Can you think of any situations where you might want to use right alignment?

Skills Review

To complete this project, you will need the following file:

- wrd02_SRWeb

You will save your file as:

- Last_First_wrd02_Web

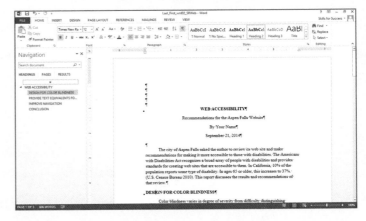

Figure 1

1. Start **Word 2013**. Open **wrd02_SRWeb**. Save the document in your chapter folder as Last_First_wrd02_SRWeb

2. Click to the right of *By*, add a space, and then type your name.

3. Click in the first body paragraph beginning *The city of Aspen Falls*. Click the **Paragraph Dialog Box Launcher**, and then in the **Paragraph** dialog box, under **Special**, select **First line**. Under **Spacing**, change the **After** value to **12 pt**, and then click **OK**. Click in the paragraph beginning *Color blindness varies*, and then press F4 to repeat the formatting.

4. Click in the side heading beginning *DESIGN FOR*. In the **Styles group**, right-click **Heading 2**, and then click **Modify**. In the **Modify Style** dialog box, click the **Format** button, and then click **Paragraph**. In the **Paragraph** dialog box, click the **Line and Page Breaks tab**, and then select the **Keep with next** check box. Click **OK** two times. Compare your screen with **Figure 1**.

5. On the **References tab**, in the **Citation & Bibliography group**, verify that **Chicago** is selected, and then click **Manage Sources**.

6. Select the source for **Bennett, Jean**, and then click the **Edit** button. Change the **Type of Source** to **Journal Article**. Add the **Journal Name** The New England Journal of Medicine and the **Pages** 2483-2484

7. Click **OK**, and then **Close** Source Manager. In the *DESIGN FOR COLOR BLINDNESS* section, click to the right of the sentence ending *degree of color blindness*. In the **Citation & Bibliography group**, click **Insert Citation**, and then click the **Bennett, Jean** source.

8. Right-click the citation just inserted, and then click **Edit Citation**. In the **Edit Citation** dialog box, type 2483 and then click **OK**. Deselect the citation, and then compare your screen with **Figure 2**.

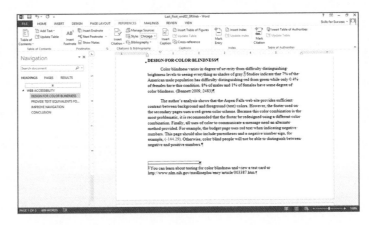

Figure 2

■ Continue to the next page to complete this Skills Review

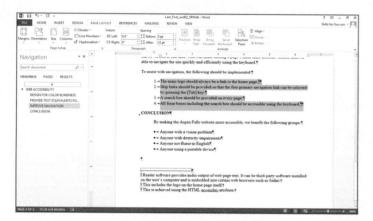

Figure 3

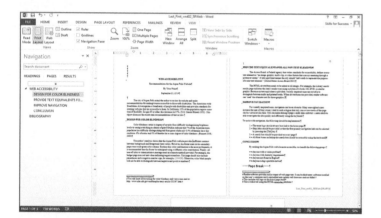

Figure 4

9. If necessary, display the Navigation pane. In the **Navigation** pane search box, type web site and then click **Results**.

10. In the **Navigation** pane, click the **Search for more things arrow**, and then click **Replace**. In the **Replace with** box, type website Click **Replace All**. Click **OK**, and then **Close** the dialog box.

11. Navigate to the *IMPROVE NAVIGATION* section, and then click to the right of the sentence ending *link to the home page*. In the **Footnotes group**, click **Insert Footnote**, and then type This includes the logo on the home page itself.

12. In the footnote just inserted, select the text but not the footnote number, and then change the font size to **12** points.

13. Select the four paragraphs beginning *The main logo* and ending with *using the keyboard*. Apply a numbered list with the *1. 2. 3.* format. In the **Paragraph group**, click the **Increase Indent** button one time.

14. In the *CONCLUSION* section, select the four paragraphs beginning *Anyone with a vision* and ending with *a portable device*. Apply a bulleted list with the solid round circle. On the **Home tab**, in the **Paragraph group**, click the **Increase Indent** button one time.

15. With the bulleted list still selected, in the **Paragraph group**, click the **Line and Spacing** button, and then click **1.15**. Repeat this formatting for the paragraphs in the numbered list.

16. On the **Page Layout tab**, in the **Page Setup group**, click the **Margins** button, and then click **Normal**. Compare your screen with **Figure 3**.

17. Move to the end of the document, and then press [Ctrl] + [Enter] to insert a page break. At the top of Page 3, press [Enter] two times.

18. On the **References tab**, in the **Citations & Bibliography group**, click **Bibliography**, and then click the **Bibliography** thumbnail. Change the *Bibliography* heading to BIBLIOGRAPHY

19. On the **Insert tab**, in the **Header & Footer group**, click **Page Number**, point to **Top of Page**, and then click **Plain Number 3**. In the **Options group**, select the **Different First Page** check box.

20. Navigate to the Page 2 footer, and then click in the footer. Insert the **FileName** field, add a space, and then type (DRAFT) In the **Paragraph group**, click the **Align Right** button, and then double-click in the document.

21. On the **View tab**, in the **Zoom group**, click **Multiple Pages**, and then compare your screen with **Figure 4**.

22. Save the document, and then submit it as directed by your instructor.

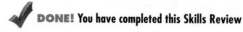 **DONE!** You have completed this Skills Review

Skills Assessment 1

To complete this project, you will need the following file:

- wrd02_SA1Tourism

You will save your document as:

- Last_First_wrd02_SA1Tourism

1. Start **Word 2013**, and then open the student data file **wrd02_SA1Tourism**. Save the document in your chapter folder as Last_First_wrd02_SA1Tourism

2. Click to the right of *By,* add a space, and then type your name.

3. Replace all occurrences of the phrase *City of Aspen Falls* with Aspen Falls

4. In the first body paragraph beginning *The Aspen Falls Tourism,* set a **0.5 inch** first line indent and the spacing after to **12 pt**. Repeat the same formatting to the paragraph beginning *The number of people visiting.*

5. Modify the **Heading 2** style so that **Keep with next** is enabled.

6. In the *DEMOGRAPHICS* section, apply a solid circle bullet to the four paragraphs beginning *Stay longer than* and ending with *drive to Aspen Falls.* Increase the list's indent to **0.5 inches** and set the line spacing to **1.15.**

7. Use **Source Manager** to edit the source for **Law, Christopher M.** Change the source type to **Journal Article**, and then add the **Journal Name** Urban Studies and the **Pages** 599-618

8. In the *DEVELOPMENT AREAS* section, after the sentence ending *is a recent practice,* insert a citation using **Law, Christopher M.** as the reference. Edit the citation field to include the pages 599-618

9. Apply a list with the *1. 2. 3.* format to the three paragraphs beginning *Agritourism* and ending with *Sports Tourism.* Increase the indent of the numbered list to **0.5 inches** and set the line spacing to **1.15.**

10. Insert a footnote after the list item *Agritourism* with the text Agritourism caters to those interested in visiting farms, ranches, and wineries. Change the footnote's text to **12** points.

11. In the blank paragraph below the *SUMMARY* section, insert a manual page break. Press [Enter] two times, and then insert the **Bibliography** built-in field. Change the bibliography's heading to BIBLIOGRAPHY

12. In the header, insert the **Plain Number 3** page number so that it displays on all pages except for Page 1.

13. In the **Page 2** footer, insert the **FileName** field, add a space, and then type (DRAFT) Align the footer paragraph with the right margin, and then close the footer.

14. Change the page margins to **Normal** (1 inch on all sides).

15. Compare your document with **Figure 1**. **Save** the document, and then submit it as directed by your instructor.

 DONE! You have completed Skills Assessment 1

Figure 1

TRAVEL AND TOURISM

Trends for the Aspen Falls Metro Area

By Your Name

September 21, 2014

The Aspen Falls Tourism Department in cooperation with the Aspen Falls Chamber of Commerce surveyed random tourists[1] about their visit to Aspen Falls. Other key indicators were assembled from public records. These include airport arrivals and departures and room tax revenues. From this analysis trends, demographics, and recommendations are provided in this report.

TRENDS

The number of people visiting Aspen Falls grew about 10% last year, and for the first time topped the 1 million mark. Over the past 10 years, spending by convention and event attendees has risen consistently. However, this past year saw a decrease in business tourist spending of 4%. This decline was offset by an increase in spending from leisure visitors. Overall, spending by business and leisure tourists increased by over 9%.

DEMOGRAPHICS

The study shows that 60% of Aspen Falls tourists are from California—resident visitors. Further, non-resident tourists:

- Stay longer than resident visitors.
- Are slightly older than resident visitors.
- Have a higher average household income than resident visitors.
- Fly in instead of drive to Aspen Falls.

Other studies have shown that on average, leisure visitors travel with larger parties and stay longer than business visitors. (Tribe 2011) These demographics suggest that marketing to

---

[1] A tourist is any person staying for one or more nights in the Aspen Falls metro area outside of their regular residence. A tourist can be classified as either a business visitor or a leisure visitor.

non-resident leisure visitors would have the gre... area.

DEVELOPMENT AREAS

Treating tourism as a growth industry is in recent years that the classifications of tourism field. Currently, specialty tourism is seeing the seeing robust potential.

Given its location and economy, the As... three specialty areas:

1. Agritourism[2]
2. Wildlife Tourism
3. Sports Tourism

According to the World Tourism Organi... of international tourism growth. (World Touris... leisure visitors from China is not mutually excl...

SUMMARY

The economic benefits from promoting... would have a significant impact on the local eco... local organizations enhance the visitor experien... conservation areas attract more visitors while p... improving venues for playing sports and organi... resident and non-resident visitors.

---

[2] Agritourism caters to those interested in visiting farms, ranches, and wineries.

wrd02_SA1Tourism_solution (DRAFT)

Skills Assessment 2

To complete this project, you will need the following file:

- wrd02_SA2Wildlife

You will save the document as:

- Last_First_wrd02_SA2Wildlife

1. Start **Word 2013**, and then open the student data file **wrd02_SA2Wildlife**. Save the document in your chapter folder as Last_First_wrd02_SA2Wildlife

2. Click to the right of *By*, add a space, and then type your name.

3. Replace all occurrences of the word *fisherman* with angler and then all occurrences of the word *fishermen* with anglers

4. In the first body paragraph beginning *This report summarizes,* set a **0.5 inch** first line indent and the spacing after to **12 pt**. Repeat the same formatting to the paragraph beginning *The 2013 survey was provided.*

5. Modify the **Heading 2** style so that **Widow/Orphan control** and **Keep with next** are enabled.

6. Use **Source Manager** to edit the source for **U.S. Fish & Wildlife Service**. Change the source type to **Document from a Web site**, and then add the **URL** http://www.census.gov/prod/www/abs/fishing.html

7. In the *FINDINGS* section, after the sentence ending *with the state trend,* insert a citation using **U.S. Fish_Wildlife Service** as the reference.

8. In the same section, apply a solid circle bullet to the two paragraphs beginning *Each angler spent* and ending with *equipment and trip expense.* Increase the list's indent to **0.5 inches** and set the line spacing to **1.15**.

9. At the end of the second bulleted list item, insert a footnote with the text Equipment includes binoculars, clothing, tents, and backpacking equipment. Change the footnote's text to **12** points.

10. In the *RECOMMENDATIONS* section, apply a list with the *1. 2. 3.* format to the six paragraphs beginning *Maintain existing natural areas* and ending with *wildlife recreation areas.* Increase the indent of the numbered list to **0.5 inches** and set the line spacing to **1.15**.

11. In the blank paragraph below the numbered list, insert a manual page break. Press Enter two times, and then insert the

Bibliography built-in field. Change the bibliography's heading to BIBLIOGRAPHY

12. In the header, insert the **Plain Number 3** page number so that it displays on all pages except for Page 1.

13. In the **Page 2** footer, insert the **FileName** field, add a space, and then type (DO NOT RELEASE YET) Align the footer paragraph with the right margin, and then close the footer.

14. Change the page margins to **Office 2003 Default** (1.25 inches on the sides).

15. Compare your document with **Figure 1**. **Save** the document, and then submit it as directed by your instructor.

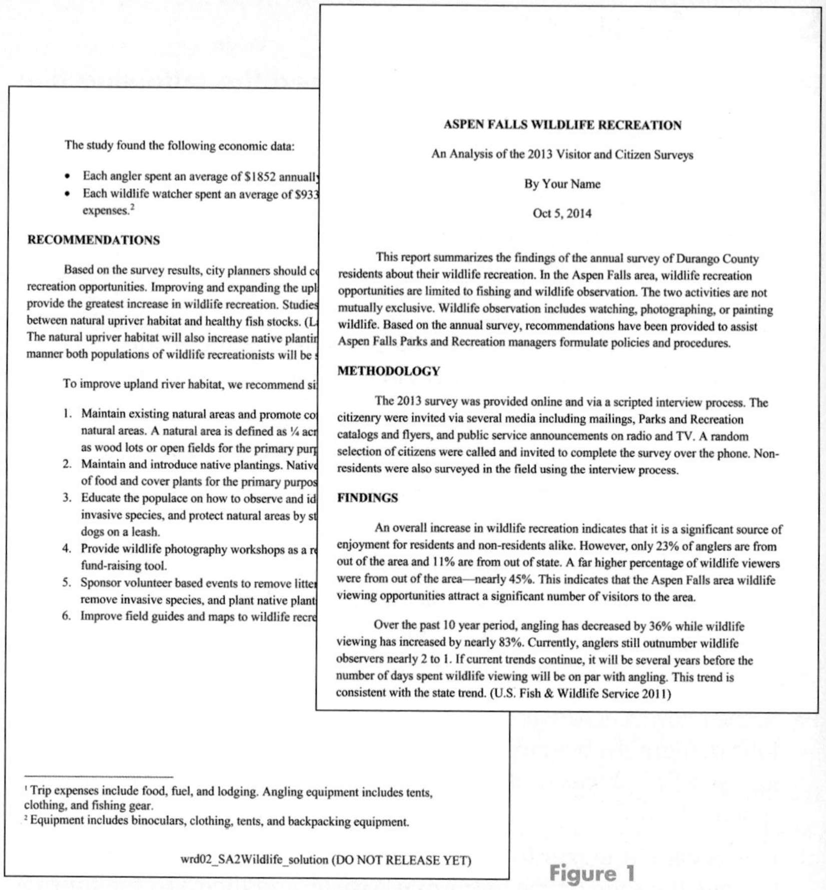

 DONE! You have completed Skills Assessment 2

The study found the following economic data:

- Each angler spent an average of $1852 annually
- Each wildlife watcher spent an average of $933 expenses.[2]

RECOMMENDATIONS

Based on the survey results, city planners should c recreation opportunities. Improving and expanding the upl provide the greatest increase in wildlife recreation. Studies between natural upriver habitat and healthy fish stocks. (L The natural upriver habitat will also increase native planti manner both populations of wildlife recreationists will be

To improve upland river habitat, we recommend si

1. Maintain existing natural areas and promote co natural areas. A natural area is defined as ¼ ac as wood lots or open fields for the primary purp
2. Maintain and introduce native plantings. Native of food and cover plants for the primary purpos
3. Educate the populace on how to observe and id invasive species, and protect natural areas by st dogs on a leash.
4. Provide wildlife photography workshops as a r fund-raising tool.
5. Sponsor volunteer based events to remove litte remove invasive species, and plant native plant
6. Improve field guides and maps to wildlife recre

[1] Trip expenses include food, fuel, and lodging. Angling equipment includes tents, clothing, and fishing gear.
[2] Equipment includes binoculars, clothing, tents, and backpacking equipment.

wrd02_SA2Wildlife_solution (DO NOT RELEASE YET)

ASPEN FALLS WILDLIFE RECREATION

An Analysis of the 2013 Visitor and Citizen Surveys

By Your Name

Oct 5, 2014

This report summarizes the findings of the annual survey of Durango County residents about their wildlife recreation. In the Aspen Falls area, wildlife recreation opportunities are limited to fishing and wildlife observation. The two activities are not mutually exclusive. Wildlife observation includes watching, photographing, or painting wildlife. Based on the annual survey, recommendations have been provided to assist Aspen Falls Parks and Recreation managers formulate policies and procedures.

METHODOLOGY

The 2013 survey was provided online and via a scripted interview process. The citizenry were invited via several media including mailings, Parks and Recreation catalogs and flyers, and public service announcements on radio and TV. A random selection of citizens were called and invited to complete the survey over the phone. Non-residents were also surveyed in the field using the interview process.

FINDINGS

An overall increase in wildlife recreation indicates that it is a significant source of enjoyment for residents and non-residents alike. However, only 23% of anglers are from out of the area and 11% are from out of state. A far higher percentage of wildlife viewers were from out of the area—nearly 45%. This indicates that the Aspen Falls area wildlife viewing opportunities attract a significant number of visitors to the area.

Over the past 10 year period, angling has decreased by 36% while wildlife viewing has increased by nearly 83%. Currently, anglers still outnumber wildlife observers nearly 2 to 1. If current trends continue, it will be several years before the number of days spent wildlife viewing will be on par with angling. This trend is consistent with the state trend. (U.S. Fish & Wildlife Service 2011)

Figure 1

Visual Skills Check

To complete this project, you will need the following file:

- wrd02_VSSecurity

You will save your document as:

- Last_First_wrd02_VSSecurity

Open the student data file **wrd02_VSSecurity**, and then save it in your chapter folder as Last_First_wrd02_VSSecurity

To complete this document, set the margins to Office 2003 Default. Format the three lists as shown in **Figure 1**. The lists have been indented to 0.5 inches, line spacing is 1.15, and the spacing after is 12 points.

The front matter is center aligned, the *By* line should display your own name, and the date should display your current date. The date paragraph's spacing after is set to 12 points.

The body paragraph has a first line indent of 0.5 inches, spacing after of 12 points, and line spacing of 1.15. At the end of the paragraph, a footnote has been inserted with the text Federal Trade Commission. Protecting Personal Information: A Guide for Business. Washington, November 2011. The footnote text is size 12, and the source title is italic.

Submit the file as directed by your instructor.

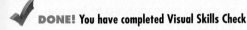

DONE! You have completed Visual Skills Check

SECURING DATA
A Summary for Aspen Falls City Government
By Your Name
October 12, 2014

Several laws require the city to keep sensitive data secure. Most notably are the Federal Trade Commission Act, Fair Credit Reporting Act, and the Gramm-Leach-Bliley Act. To comply with these laws and respect the rights of our citizens and those who do business with City Hall, the FTC recommends following these 5 key principles.[1]

1. Take stock. Know what personal information is stored on city systems.
2. Scale down. Keep only what we need to conduct city business.
3. Lock it. Prevent physical and virtual access to all information systems.
4. Pitch it. Dispose of all data that is no longer needed.
5. Plan ahead. Create an incident response plan.

PHYSICAL SECURITY

- Keep all paper documents, CDs, DVDs, and other storage medium in a locked room or locked file cabinet.
- Train employees to put away all files and log off their computer at the end of their shifts.
- Keep servers in locked rooms with access restricted only to authorized IT Department staff.
- Keep long term storage offsite and access should be limited only to those employees with a legitimate need for the data.
- Install alarms and institute a procedure for reporting unfamiliar persons on the premises.

VIRTUAL SECURITY

- Encrypt all sensitive information.
- Restrict employee privileges to install software.
- Keep anti-malware software up to date.
- Conduct periodic security audits including penetration testing.

---

[1] Federal Trade Commission. *Protecting Personal Information: A Guide for Business*. Washington, November 2011.

Figure 1

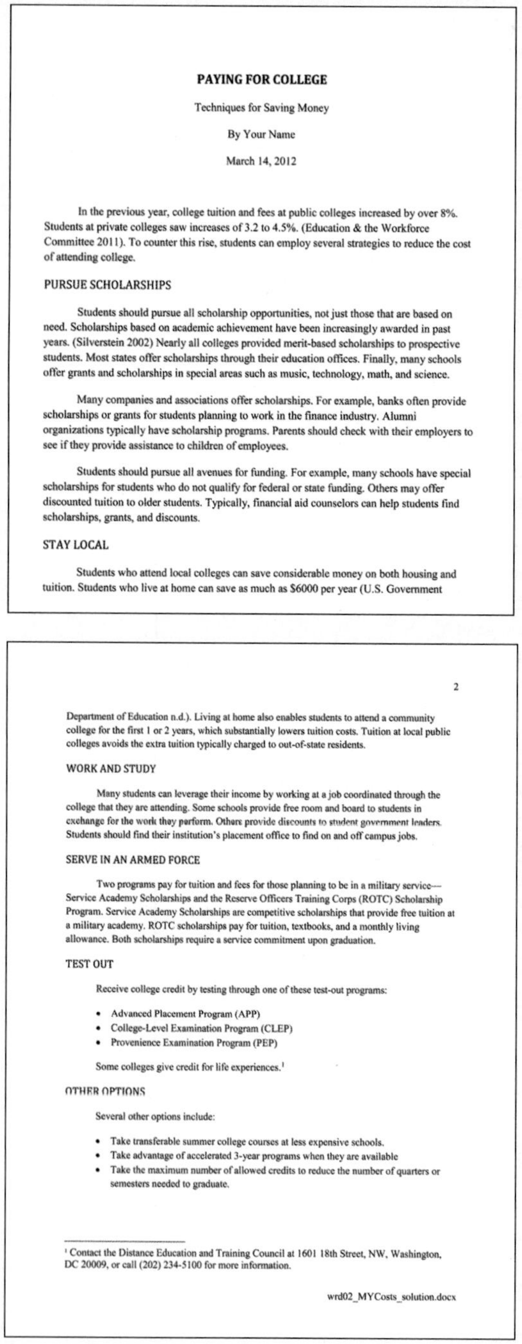

PAYING FOR COLLEGE

Techniques for Saving Money

By Your Name

March 14, 2012

In the previous year, college tuition and fees at public colleges increased by over 8%. Students at private colleges saw increases of 3.2 to 4.5%. (Education & the Workforce Committee 2011). To counter this rise, students can employ several strategies to reduce the cost of attending college.

PURSUE SCHOLARSHIPS

Students should pursue all scholarship opportunities, not just those that are based on need. Scholarships based on academic achievement have been increasingly awarded in past years. (Silverstein 2002) Nearly all colleges provided merit-based scholarships to prospective students. Most states offer scholarships through their education offices. Finally, many schools offer grants and scholarships in special areas such as music, technology, math, and science.

Many companies and associations offer scholarships. For example, banks often provide scholarships or grants for students planning to work in the finance industry. Alumni organizations typically have scholarship programs. Parents should check with their employers to see if they provide assistance to children of employees.

Students should pursue all avenues for funding. For example, many schools have special scholarships for students who do not qualify for federal or state funding. Others may offer discounted tuition to older students. Typically, financial aid counselors can help students find scholarships, grants, and discounts.

STAY LOCAL

Students who attend local colleges can save considerable money on both housing and tuition. Students who live at home can save as much as $6000 per year (U.S. Government

---

2

Department of Education n.d.). Living at home also enables students to attend a community college for the first 1 or 2 years, which substantially lowers tuition costs. Tuition at local public colleges avoids the extra tuition typically charged to out-of-state residents.

WORK AND STUDY

Many students can leverage their income by working at a job coordinated through the college that they are attending. Some schools provide free room and board to students in exchange for the work they perform. Others provide discounts to student government leaders. Students should find their institution's placement office to find on and off campus jobs.

SERVE IN AN ARMED FORCE

Two programs pay for tuition and fees for those planning to be in a military service—Service Academy Scholarships and the Reserve Officers Training Corps (ROTC) Scholarship Program. Service Academy Scholarships are competitive scholarships that provide free tuition at a military academy. ROTC scholarships pay for tuition, textbooks, and a monthly living allowance. Both scholarships require a service commitment upon graduation.

TEST OUT

Receive college credit by testing through one of these test-out programs:

- Advanced Placement Program (APP)
- College-Level Examination Program (CLEP)
- Provenience Examination Program (PEP)

Some colleges give credit for life experiences.[1]

OTHER OPTIONS

Several other options include:

- Take transferable summer college courses at less expensive schools.
- Take advantage of accelerated 3-year programs when they are available
- Take the maximum number of allowed credits to reduce the number of quarters or semesters needed to graduate.

---

[1] Contact the Distance Education and Training Council at 1601 18th Street, NW, Washington, DC 20009, or call (202) 234-5100 for more information.

wrd02_MYCosts_solution.docx

Figure 1

My Skills

To complete this project, you will need the following file:

- wrd02_MYCosts

You will save your document as:

- Last_First_wrd02_MYCosts

1. Start **Word 2013**, and then open the student data file **wrd02_MYCosts**. Save the document in your chapter folder as Last_First_wrd02_MYCosts

2. Click to the right of *By*, add a space, and then type your name.

3. Replace all occurrences of the phrase *you* with students

4. In the first body paragraph beginning *In the previous year,* set a **0.5 inch** first line indent and the spacing after to **12 pt**. Repeat the same formatting to the paragraph beginning *Students should pursue all scholarship opportunities.*

5. Update the **Heading 1** style to match the formatting of the report title.

6. Use **Source Manager** to edit the source for **U.S. Government**. Change the source type to **Web site**, and then add the **URL** https://studentaid2.ed.gov/getmoney/pay_for_college/cost_35.html

7. In the *STAY LOCAL* section, after the sentence ending *$6000 per year,* insert a citation using **U.S. Government Department of Education** as the reference.

8. In the *TEST OUT* section, after the last sentence ending *credit for life experiences,* insert a footnote with the text Contact the Distance Education and Training Council at 1601 18th Street, NW, Washington, DC 20009, or call (202) 234-5100 for more information.

9. In the footnote just inserted, change the footnote text font size to **12** points.

10. At the end of the document, apply a solid circle bullet to the three paragraphs beginning *Take transferable summer* and ending with *semesters needed to graduate.* Increase the indent of the list items to **0.5 inches** and set the line spacing to **1.15**.

11. In the blank paragraph below the last bulleted list, insert a manual page break. Press [Enter] two times, and then insert the **Bibliography** built-in field. Change the bibliography's heading to BIBLIOGRAPHY

12. In the header, insert the **Plain Number 3** page number so that it displays on all pages except for Page 1.

13. In the **Page 2** footer, insert the **FileName** field, align the footer paragraph with the right margin, and then close the footer.

14. Change the page margins to **Normal** (1 inch on all sides).

15. Compare your document with Figure 1. **Save** the document, and then submit your work as directed by your instructor.

 DONE! You have completed My Skills

Skills Challenge 1

To complete this project, you will need the following file:

- wrd02_SC1Aging

You will save your document as:

- Last_First_wrd02_SC1Aging

Open the student data file **wrd02_SC1Aging**, and then save it in your chapter folder as Last_First_wrd02_SC1Aging

Format the report following informal business report rules modeled in Skills 1–10. Take care to apply the appropriate paragraph spacing, paragraph line spacing, paragraph alignment, and indents for front matter, headings, body paragraphs, and lists. Adjust the font sizes and font colors of headings and footnotes to those used in an informal business

report. Apply one of the prebuilt margins accepted in an informal business report, making sure that the report fits within a total of three pages.

Insert your name in the By line and the FileName field in the footer. Adjust the page numbers to the correct format and placement. Submit the report as directed by your instructor.

 DONE! You have completed Skills Challenge 1

Skills Challenge 2

To complete this project, you will need the following file:

- **New blank Word document**

You will save your document as:

- Last_First_w02_SC2Parks

The Aspen Falls Planning Department is working with the Travel and Tourism Bureau to explore ways to use the city as the base of operation for tourists who want to visit important sites within a day's drive. Using the skills you practiced in this chapter, create a report on the nearby major nature attractions. These could include Yosemite National Park (250 miles), Death Valley National Park (200 miles), Sequoia National Forest (180 miles), and the Channel Islands National Park (40 miles). Research three of these sites, and write a report about the highlights of what a visitor might find at each. Include

an introduction, a section for each of the three attractions, and a conclusion. Add your sources to Source Manager, and insert them in citations and a bibliography. Format the report as an informal business report.

Save the document as Last_First_wrd02_SC2Parks Insert the FileName field and the current date in the footer, and check the entire document for grammar and spelling. Submit the report as directed by your instructor.

 DONE! You have completed Skills Challenge 2

CHAPTER 3

Create Flyers

- You can enhance the effectiveness of your message and make your document more attractive by adding graphics.
- Digital images—such as those you have scanned or taken with a digital camera or a cell phone—can be added to a document and formatted using distinctive borders and other interesting and attractive effects.
- You can organize lists in rows and columns by using tabs.

- Word tables are used to organize lists and data in columns and rows without needing to create tab settings.
- You can use tables to summarize and emphasize information in an organized arrangement of rows and columns that make complex information easy to understand at a glance.
- You can format tables manually or apply a number of different formats quickly using built-in styles.

Alexey Klementiev / Fotolia

Aspen Falls City Hall

In this chapter, you will create a flyer for Carter Horikoshi, the Parks and Recreation Art Center Supervisor. The flyer will promote the art gallery and art classes provided at the Art Center. The flyer needs to describe the gallery hours, art classes, and the class fees.

An effective flyer organizes the content visually. For example, a prominent title and a graphic need to pull the reader's attention to the flyer. Subheadings should be smaller than the title, and the least prominent text should be used for the paragraphs, lists, or tables. The overall formatting and layout need to help the reader flow through the flyer's message, typically in a top to bottom direction. Wrapping text around graphics is an important technique to provide this flow.

Before formatting, you should select a theme, and then select choices from that theme's colors and fonts. In this manner, you can select formatting that works well together and does not detract from the flyer's desired look and feel. Placing content in tables or tabbed lists helps organize the flyer's message, and it is also a good idea to provide ample white space between flyer elements.

In this project, you will insert, resize, and move pictures, and apply picture styles and artistic effects. You will set tab stops and use tabs to enter data. You will also work with tables, add rows and columns, format the tables' contents, and modify their layout and design.

Time to complete all 10 skills – 45 to 60 minutes

Student data files needed for this chapter:

wrd03_Art

wrd03_ArtPhoto1

wrd03_ArtPhoto2

wrd03_ArtClasses

You will save your file as:

Last_First_wrd03_Art

Outcome

Using the skills in this chapter, you will be able to work with Word documents like this:

Corbett Art Center

The Art Center gallery, located in the historic Corbett mansion, is open to the general. The gallery features local artists and the work of students taking classes at the center. The hours of operation are:

Day	Hours
Monday – Wednesday	noon to 5
Thursday – Friday	noon to 8
Saturday	11 to 5
Sunday	Closed

The Art Center offers art classes throughout the year. Each class has a beginning, intermediate, and advanced section. Each section lasts two months. Art classes include the following:

Class	Starting Months	Description
Art History	January and July	Survey of medieval to modern art.
Drawing	February and August	Freehand drawing, light and shadow, composition, and perspective, and portrait
Watercolors	March and September	Washes, wet-in-wet, and dry brush
Painting	April and October	Acrylics, oils, and watercolors.
Sculpture	May and November	Medium, modeling, busts, and abstraction
Photography	June and December	Point and Shoot, DSLRs, Photoshop, Portraits, Landscapes, and Sports

Class fees are as follows:

Class Fees		
Group	Ages	Cost
Students	12 to 17	$ 64.00
Young Adults	18 to 24	78.00
Adults	25 to 59	125.00
Seniors	60+	38.00

wrd03_Art_soluton.docx

SKILLS

Skills 1-10 Training

At the end of this chapter, you will be able to:

Skill 1 Insert Text and Pictures from Files

Skill 2 Resize and Align Pictures

Skill 3 Apply Picture Styles and Artistic Effects

Skill 4 Set Tab Stops

Skill 5 Type Tabbed Lists

Skill 6 Apply Table Styles

Skill 7 Create Tables

Skill 8 Delete and Add Table Rows and Columns

Skill 9 Format Text in Table Cells

Skill 10 Format Tables

MORE SKILLS

Skill 11 Insert Text Boxes

Skill 12 Format with WordArt

Skill 13 Convert Text into Tables

Skill 14 Insert Drop Caps

▶ You can insert text and pictures from other files into the document you are working on.

▶ By inserting pictures from files, you can include pictures taken with digital cameras, tablets, or cell phones. You can also include files created by scanners or downloaded from the Web.

1. Start **Word 2013**, and then from the student files, open **wrd03_Art**. If your rulers do not display, on the View tab, in the Show group, select the Ruler check box.

2. On the **File tab**, click **Save As**, and then click **Browse**. In the **Save As** dialog box, navigate to the location where you are saving your files, create and open a folder named Word Chapter 3 and then **Save** the document as Last_First_wrd03_Art

3. On the **Design tab**, in the **Document Formatting group**, click the **Themes** button, and then click the **Wisp** thumbnail.

4. Select the document title *Corbett Art Center*, change the **Font Size** to **26**, and then **Center** the title. Compare your screen with **Figure 1**.

5. Position the insertion point to the left of *The Art Center gallery*. On the **Insert tab**, in the **Illustrations group**, click the **Pictures** button.

6. In the **Insert Picture** dialog box, navigate to your student files, select **wrd03_ArtPhoto1**, and then click **Insert**. Compare your screen with **Figure 2**.

   When you insert a picture, it is inserted as part of the paragraph the insertion point was in, and the Layout Options button displays to the right of the picture.

■ **Continue to the next page to complete the skill**

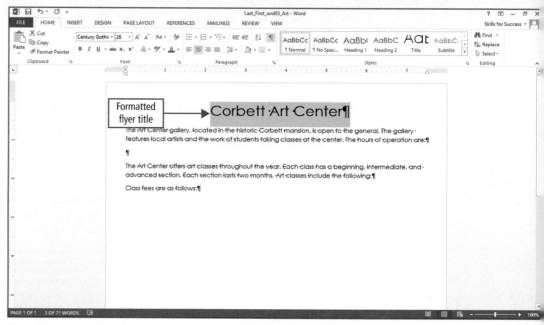

Figure 1

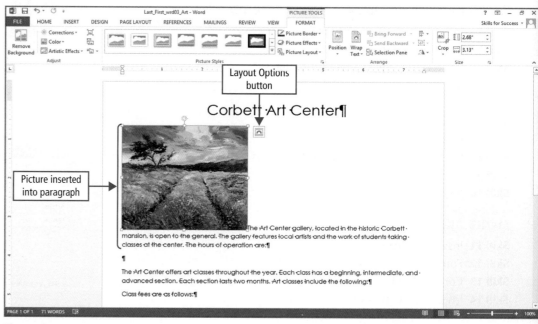

Figure 2

Boyan Dimitrov / Fotolia

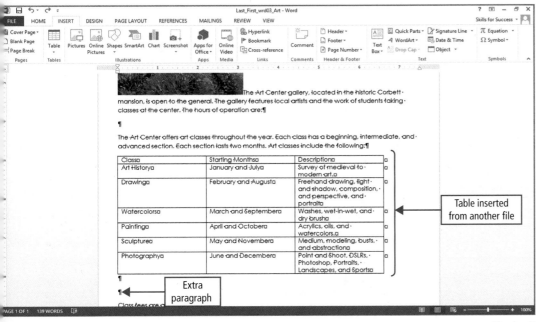

Figure 3

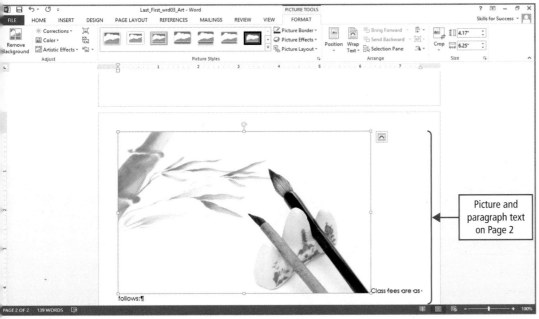

ulián Rovagnati / Fotolia

Figure 4

7. At the end of the paragraph that begins *The Art Center offers art classes*, click to position the insertion point to the right of the colon, and then press Enter .

8. On the **Insert tab**, in the **Text group**, click the **Object arrow**, and then click **Text from File**.

9. In the **Insert File** dialog box, navigate to your student files, select **wrd03_ ArtClasses**, and then click **Insert** to insert the table. Compare your screen with **Figure 3**.

10. With the insertion point in the second blank paragraph below the inserted table, press Backspace to remove the extra blank paragraph that is created when you insert text from a file.

11. Position the insertion point to the left of *Class fees are as follows* and then use the technique practiced previously to insert the **wrd03_ArtPhoto2** picture from the student data files for this chapter. Compare your screen with **Figure 4**.

Because the picture is too large to fit in the available space at the bottom of the first page, a new page was added containing just the picture and the paragraph. You will move the figure in the next skill.

12. Save ⊞ the document.

■ **You have completed Skill 1 of 10**

▶ When you select a graphic, *sizing handles*—small squares or circles on an object's border—display and the Format contextual tab is added to the Ribbon.

▶ You can move graphics precisely using *Alignment Guides*—lines that display when an object is aligned with document objects such as margins and headings.

1. On Page 2, be sure the **wrd03_ArtPhoto2** paint brushes picture is selected.

2. On the right border of the picture, locate the middle—square—sizing handle. Point to the sizing handle to display the ⟷ pointer, and then drag to the left to approximately **2 inches** on the horizontal ruler, as shown in **Figure 1**, and then release the left mouse button.

   When you size an image using the middle sizing handles, the picture does not resize proportionally.

3. On the **Format tab**, in the **Adjust group**, click the **Reset Picture arrow** 🖼, and then click **Reset Picture & Size**.

4. Point to the sizing handle in the lower right corner of the picture. When the ⬉ pointer displays, drag up and to the left until the right border of the picture aligns at approximately **2 inches** on the horizontal ruler. Release the left mouse button, and then compare your screen with **Figure 2**.

   When you size an image using the corner sizing handles, the picture resizes proportionally.

■ Continue to the next page to complete the skill ➤

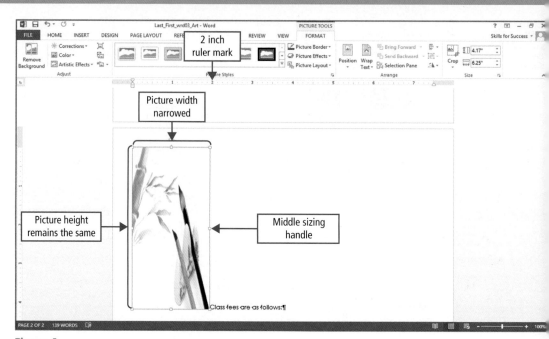

Figure 1

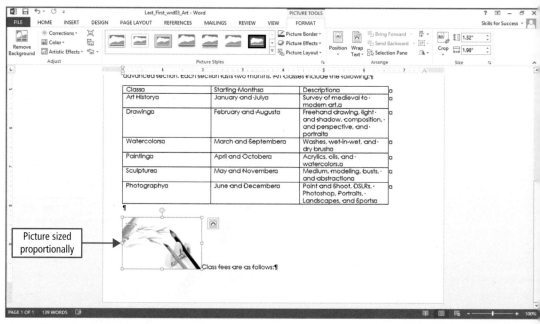

Figure 2

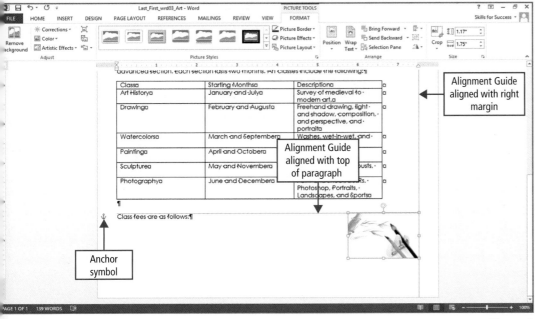

Figure 3

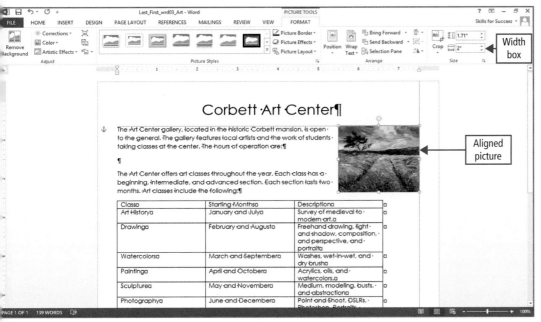

Figure 4

5. With the second picture still selected, on the **Format tab**, in the **Size group**, select the value in the **Width** box. Type 1.75 and then press Enter to change the size of the picture to 1.75 inches wide and approximately 1.17 inches in height.

6. With the second picture still selected, click its **Layout Options** button, and then under **With Text Wrapping**, click the first thumbnail—**Square**.

   The Square text wrapping option changes the picture to a ***floating object***, which you can move independently of the surrounding text. An ***anchor*** symbol displays to the left of a paragraph to indicate which paragraph is associated with the picture.

7. Point to the picture to display the pointer. Drag the picture so that the Alignment Guides align with the right margin and the top of the paragraph that begins *Class fees*. Compare your screen with **Figure 3**, and then release the left mouse button.

   If your Alignment Guides do not display, on the Page Layout group, in the Arrange group, click Align, and then click Use Alignment Guides.

8. Press Ctrl + Home, and then select the flower field picture. On the **Format tab**, in the **Size group**, change the **Width** to 2".

9. Repeat the technique practiced previously to change the picture's layout to **Square**.

10. Repeat the technique just practiced to position the picture as shown in **Figure 4**.

11. **Save** the document.

■ **You have completed Skill 2 of 10**

▸ You can add special effects to graphics to make them look like drawings or paintings.

▸ You can also apply built-in picture styles and then format that style's borders, effects, or layouts.

1. Press Ctrl + End, and then click the picture with the paint brushes.

2. On the **Format tab**, in the **Picture Styles group**, click the **More** button ⏷, and then point to several thumbnails to view them using Live Preview.

3. In the gallery, use ScreenTips text to locate and click the eighteenth thumbnail—**Perspective Shadow, White**—and then compare your screen with **Figure 1**.

4. In the **Picture Styles group**, click the **Picture Effects** button, point to **Bevel**, and then click the first effect in the second row—**Angle**.

   In this manner you can adjust the Picture Style settings applied in the Quick Style gallery. Here, the bevel setting assigned by the picture style was changed from Round to Angle.

5. Click the **Picture Effects** button, point to **3-D Rotation**, and then under **Perspective**, click the first effect in the third row—**Perspective Contrasting Right**. Click in a paragraph to deselect the picture, and then compare your screen with **Figure 2**.

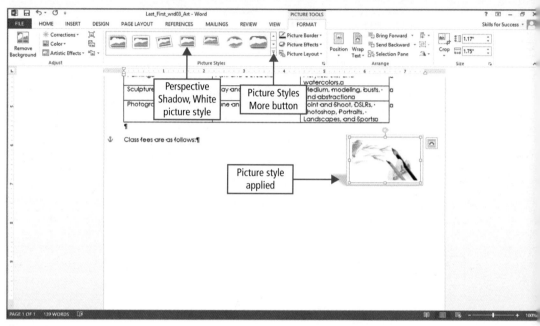

Figure 1

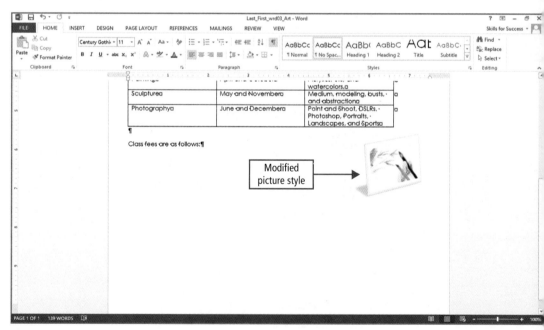

Figure 2

■ Continue to the next page to complete the skill

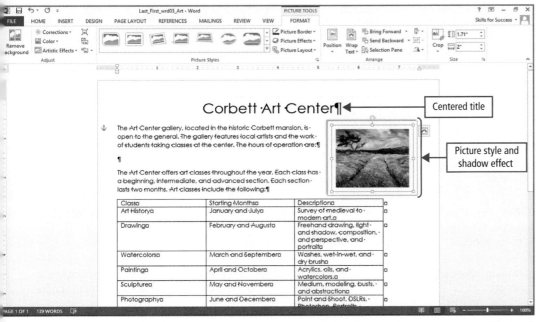

Figure 3

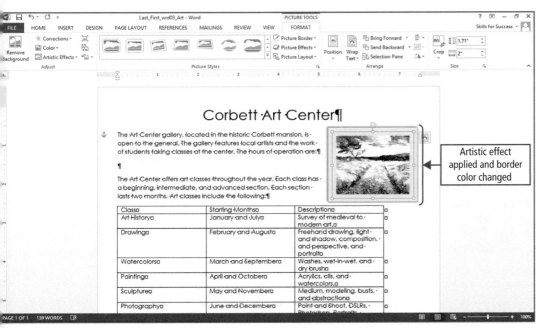

Figure 4

6. Press `Ctrl` + `Home` to move to the top of the document, select the flower field picture, and then apply the sixteenth picture style—**Moderate Frame, White**.

7. Click the **Picture Effects** button, point to **Shadow**, and then click the last thumbnail under **Outer—Offset Diagonal Top Left**.

When applying shadow effects, all the shadows should be on the same side(s) of each graphic. Because the new style increased the size of the picture, the title has wrapped to the left and is no longer centered.

8. With the picture still selected, press ↓ approximately two times until the document title is centered. Compare your screen with **Figure 3**.

To move objects in small precise increments, you can *nudge* them in this manner by selecting the object and then pressing one of the arrow keys.

9. In the **Adjust group**, click the **Artistic Effects** button. Point to several thumbnails in the gallery to preview available effects, and then click the fourth effect—**Pencil Sketch**.

10. With the picture still selected, in the **Picture Styles group**, click the **Picture Border** button. In the second row under **Theme Colors**, click the seventh color—**Brown, Accent 3, Lighter 80%**. Compare your screen with **Figure 4**.

11. Save 🖫 the document.

■ **You have completed Skill 3 of 10**

▶ A ***tab stop*** is a specific location on a line of text and marked on the Word ruler to which you can move the insertion point by pressing ⎇Tab⎇. Tabs are used to align and indent text.

▶ Tab stops can be set and modified using the ruler or in the Tabs dialog box.

1. Click in the blank paragraph below the paragraph starting *The Art Center gallery.*

2. On the left end of the horizontal ruler, notice the **Tab Selector** button ⌊L⌋—the icon displayed in your button area may be different.

3. Click the button several times to view the various tab styles and paragraph alignment options available. Pause at each tab stop type, and then view the information in the table in **Figure 1** to see how each of the tab types is used.

4. With the insertion point still in the blank paragraph, click the **Tab Selector** button until the **Left Tab** icon ⌊L⌋ displays.

5. On the horizontal ruler, point to the mark that indicates **0.25 inches**, and then click one time to insert a left tab stop. Compare your screen with **Figure 2**.

> The default tab stops are every half inch. When you add your own tab stop, it replaces the default tab stops up to that place on the ruler. To the right of that tab, the next half inch mark will be the next default tab stop.

■ **Continue to the next page to complete the skill**

Tab and Paragraph Alignment Options		
Type	**Button**	**Description**
Left	⌊L⌋	The left edge of the text is aligned at the tab stop and extends to the right.
Center	⊥	Text is centered around the tab stop.
Right	⌐	The right edge of the text is aligned at the tab stop and extends to the left.
Decimal	⊥·	The decimal point aligns at the tab stops.
Bar	⌐	A vertical bar is inserted in the document at the tab stop.
First Line Indent	▽	The first line of a paragraph is indented.
Hanging Indent/Left Indent	△	The top half of the button indents all lines except the first line in a paragraph. The bottom half moves the left indent of the entire paragraph.

Figure 1

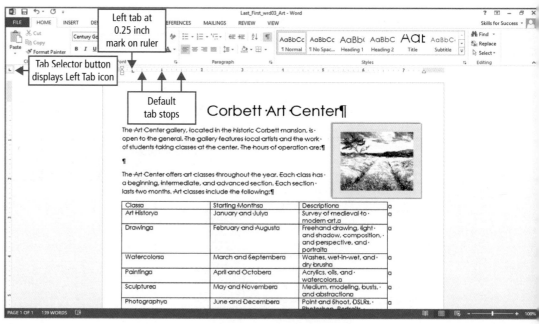

Figure 2

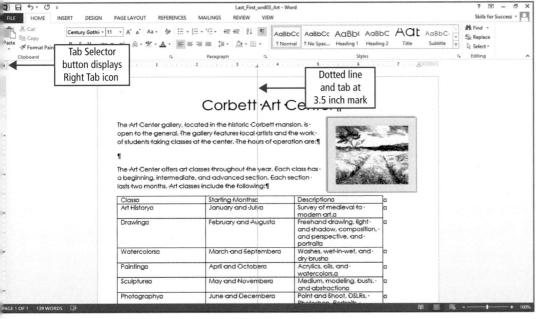

Figure 3

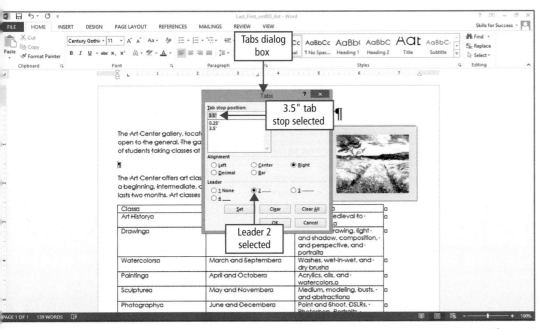

Figure 4

6. Click the **Tab Selector** button two times to display the **Right Tab** icon 　.

7. On the ruler, point to the mark that indicates **3.5 inches**. Click and hold down the mouse button. Notice that a dotted line indicates the tab location in the document, as shown in **Figure 3**. In this manner, you can determine whether the tab stop is exactly where you want it.

8. Release the mouse button to insert the right tab stop.

9. On the **Home tab**, click the **Paragraph Dialog Box Launcher** 　. At the bottom of the **Paragraph** dialog box, click the **Tabs** button. Alternately, double-click a tab stop on the ruler.

10. In the **Tabs** dialog box, under **Tab stop position**, select the tab stop at **3.5"**. Under **Leader**, select the **2** option button to add a dot leader to the selected tab stop. Near the bottom of the dialog box, click the **Set** button, and then compare your screen with **Figure 4**.

   A *leader* is a series of characters that form a solid, dashed, or dotted line to fill the space preceding a tab stop; a *leader character* is the symbol used to fill the space. A *dot leader* is a series of evenly spaced dots that precede a tab stop.

11. In the **Tabs** dialog box, click **OK**, and then **Save** 　 the document.

■ **You have completed Skill 4 of 10**

▶ The Tab key is used to move to the next tab stop in a line of text.

▶ When you want to relocate a tab stop, you can drag the tab stop marker to a new location on the ruler.

1. Be sure your insertion point is still in the blank paragraph and the tab stops you entered display on the horizontal ruler.

2. Press Tab to move the insertion point to the first tab stop you placed on the ruler. Type Day and then press Tab to move to the right tab with the dot leader that you created.

3. Type Hours and then press Enter. Compare your screen with **Figure 1**.

   When your insertion point is positioned at a right tab stop and you begin to type, the text moves to the left. When you press Enter, the new paragraph displays the same tab stop markers on the ruler as the previous paragraph.

4. Press Tab, type Monday - Wednesday and then press Tab. Type noon to 5 and then press Enter.

5. Press Tab, type Thursday - Friday and then press Tab. Type noon to 8 and then press Enter.

6. Press Tab, type Saturday and then press Tab. Type 11 to 5 and then press Enter.

7. Press Tab, type Sunday and then press Tab. Type Closed and compare your screen with **Figure 2**.

■ **Continue to the next page to complete the skill**

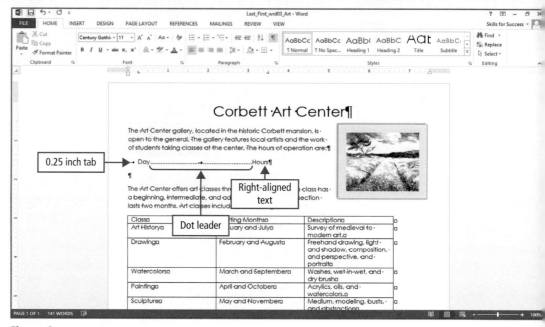

Figure 1

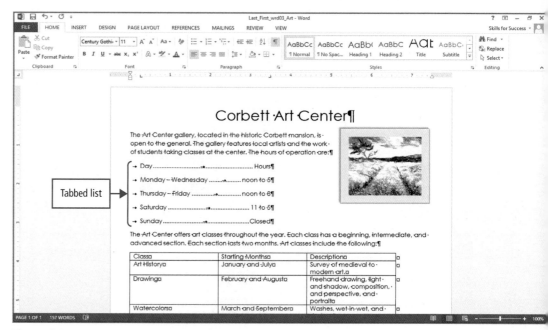

Figure 2

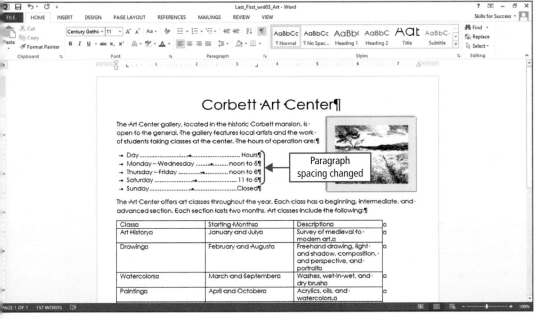

Corbett Art Center¶

The Art Center gallery, located in the historic Corbett mansion, is open to the general. The gallery features local artists and the work of students taking classes at the center. The hours of operation are:¶

→ Day..Hours¶
→ Monday – Wednesday ....noon to 6¶
→ Thursday – Friday ....noon to 8¶
→ Saturday.....................................11 to 6¶
→ Sunday.......................................Closed¶

Paragraph spacing changed

The Art Center offers art classes throughout the year. Each class has a beginning, intermediate, and advanced section. Each section lasts two months. Art classes include the following:¶

Classa	Starting Monthsa	Descriptiona	a
Art Historya	January and Julya	Survey of medieval to modern art.a	a
Drawinga	February and Augusta	Freehand drawing, light and shadow, composition, and perspective, and portraita	
Watercolorsa	March and Septembera	Washes, wet-in-wet, and dry brusha	a
Paintinga	April and Octobera	Acrylics, oils, and watercolors.a	

Figure 3

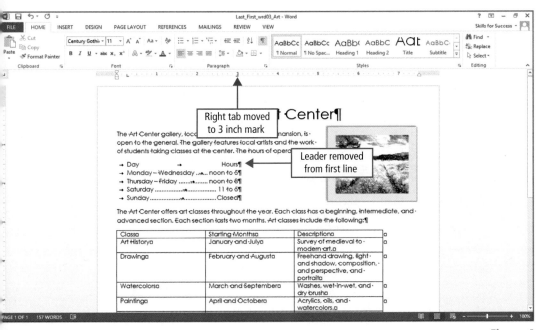

t Center¶

The Art Center gallery, loc... mansion, is open to the general. The gallery features local artists and the work of students taking classes at the center. The hours of opera...

Right tab moved to 3 inch mark

→ Day   Hours¶
→ Monday – Wednesday ...... noon to 6¶
→ Thursday – Friday .... noon to 8¶
→ Saturday...................... 11 to 6¶
→ Sunday........................Closed¶

Leader removed from first line

The Art Center offers art classes throughout the year. Each class has a beginning, intermediate, and advanced section. Each section lasts two months. Art classes include the following:¶

Classa	Starting Monthsa	Descriptiona	a
Art Historya	January and Julya	Survey of medieval to modern art.a	a
Drawinga	February and Augusta	Freehand drawing, light and shadow, composition, and perspective, and portraita	
Watercolorsa	March and Septembera	Washes, wet-in-wet, and dry brusha	a
Paintinga	April and Octobera	Acrylics, oils, and watercolors.a	

Figure 4

8. Select the first four lines of the tabbed list starting with *Day* and ending with *11 to 5*. Do not select the paragraph that begins *Sunday*.

9. On the **Home tab**, in the **Paragraph group**, click the **Line Spacing** button, and then click **Remove Space After Paragraph**. Click anywhere in the document to deselect the text, and then compare your screen with **Figure 3**.

10. Select all five lines in the tabbed list. On the horizontal ruler, place the tip of the pointer over the right tab mark at **3.5 inches** on the horizontal ruler. When the ScreenTip *Right Tab* displays, drag left to move the tab mark to **3 inches**.

11. Click in the first line of the tabbed list. On the horizontal ruler, point to the right tab mark again. When the ScreenTip *Right Tab* displays, double-click to open the **Tabs** dialog box.

12. In the **Tabs** dialog box, select the **3"** tab stop, and then under **Leader**, click the **None** option button. Click **OK**, and then compare your screen with **Figure 4**.

Tabs are added or changed only for the selected paragraphs. Here, the leader is removed only from the first line in the tabbed list.

13. **Save** the document.

■ **You have completed Skill 5 of 10**

▶ Because tables can hold text, numbers, or graphics, they are often used to lay out and summarize data.

▶ You can format each table element individually, or you can apply table styles to the entire table.

1. Scroll as needed to display the entire table.

    A table consists of cells arranged in rows and columns. Here, the table contains seven rows and three columns.

2. Click in any cell in the table to display the Table Tools contextual tabs—Design and Layout. Below Table Tools, click the **Design tab**, and then in the **Table Styles group**, notice that a number of predesigned table styles are available.

3. Point to the fourth style—**Plain Table 3**—to preview style, as shown in **Figure 1**.

4. In the **Table Styles group**, click the **More** button ⤓.

5. In the **Table Styles** gallery, use the vertical scroll bar to scroll to the bottom of the gallery. Under **List Tables**, locate the **List Table 4 - Accent 4** thumbnail, and then point to it, as shown in **Figure 2**.

    Because the width of the Table Styles gallery changes depending on the size of your window, the position of your thumbnails may be different than in the figure.

6. Click one time to apply the **List Table 4 - Accent 4** table style.

    You need only to click in a table to apply a table style. You do not need to select the table first.

■ **Continue to the next page to complete the skill**

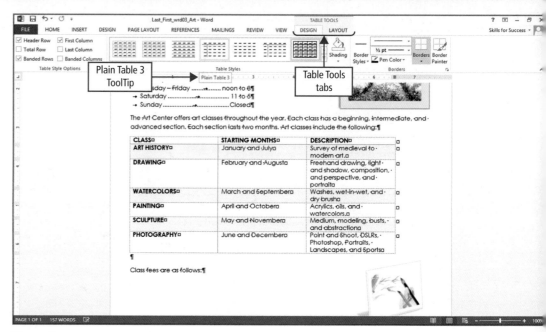

Figure 1

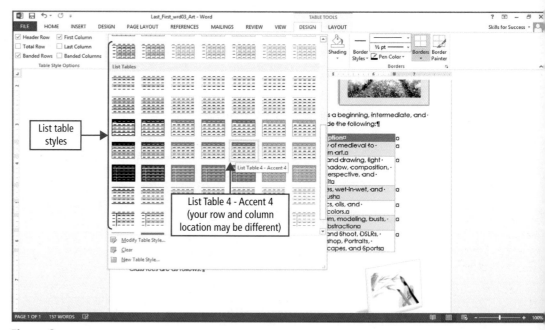

Figure 2

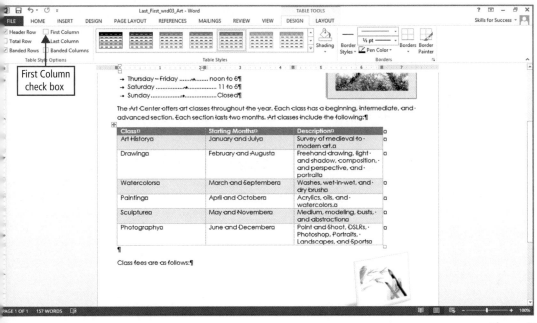

First Column check box

Figure 3

7. In the **Table Style Options group**, clear the **First Column** check box to remove the bold from the first column, as shown in **Figure 3**.

   In this manner you can customize how a pre-built table style is applied to a table. Here, the formatting assigned to the first column was disabled.

8. Click the **Layout tab**. In the **Cell Size group**, click the **AutoFit** button, and then click **AutoFit Contents**.

   The columns, which were all the same width, adjust to the best fit based on the content in the cells.

9. In the **Table group**, click the **Properties** button. In the **Table Properties** dialog box, be sure the **Table tab** is selected. Under **Size**, select the **Preferred width** check box. In the **Preferred width** box, change the existing value to **6"**.

10. In the **Table Properties** dialog box, under **Alignment**, click **Center**. Compare your screen with **Figure 4**, and then click **OK** to set the table width and to center the table between the left and right margins.

11. Save ⊞ the document.

■ **You have completed Skill 6 of 10**

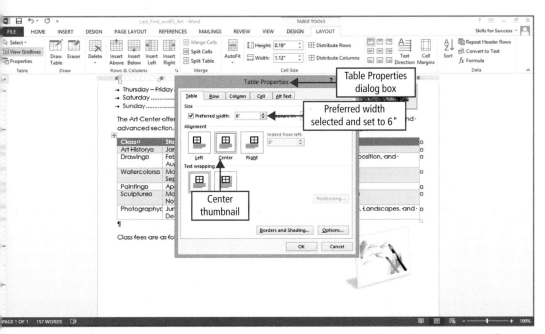

Table Properties dialog box

Preferred width selected and set to 6"

Center thumbnail

Figure 4

▶ To create a table using the Insert Table command, you need to specify the number of rows and columns you want to start with.

▶ A table created with the Insert Table command retains the formatting of the paragraph above the table and the columns are of equal width.

1. Press Ctrl + End, and then press Enter to create a new blank paragraph at the bottom of the document.

2. Click the **Insert tab**, and then in the **Tables group**, click the **Table** button. In the fifth row, point to the second box, and then compare your screen with **Figure 1**.

The top of the Table gallery displays the dimensions of the table, with the number of columns first, followed by the number of rows—in this instance, you are creating a 2x5 table.

3. Click one time to insert a **2x5 Table**. Scroll as needed to view the table just inserted, and then compare your screen with **Figure 2**.

Like a graphic, a table is associated with a paragraph. Here, the table's paragraph formatting mark displays below the table.

When no objects are in the way, an inserted table will extend from the left margin to the right margin. Here, the table wraps below the floating image that is attached to the paragraph above the table.

■ Continue to the next page to complete the skill

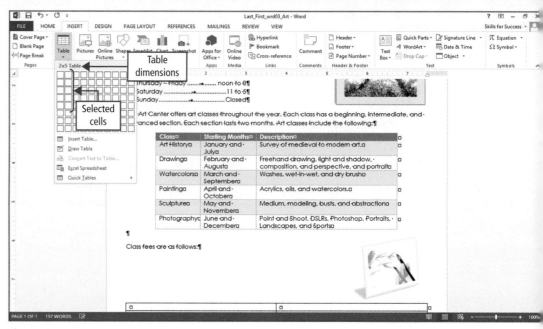

Figure 1

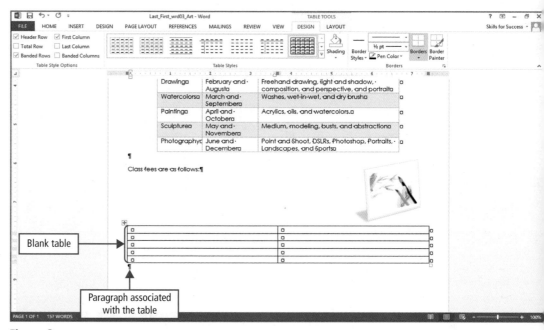

Figure 2

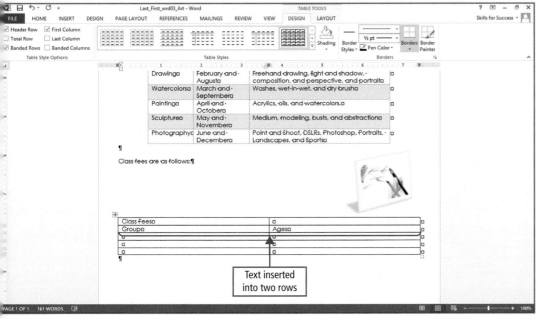

Figure 3

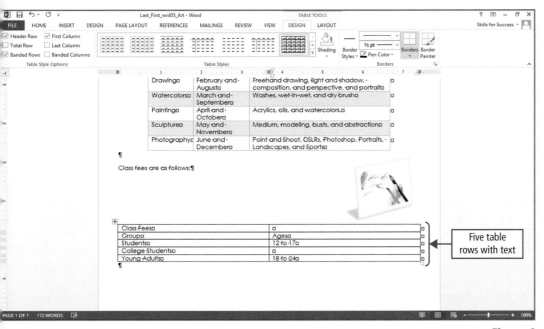

Figure 4

4. Be sure the insertion point is located in the upper left cell of the new table. Type Class Fees and then press Tab.

You can use Tab or the arrow keys to move among cells in a table. When you press Enter, a second line in the same cell is created. If this happens, you can press Backspace to remove the inserted paragraph.

5. Press Tab again to move to the first cell in the second row. Type Group and then press Tab.

6. Type Ages and then press Tab. Compare your screen with **Figure 3**.

7. With the insertion point in the first cell of the third row, type Students and then press Tab. Type 12 to 17 and then press Tab.

8. In the first cell of the fourth row, type College Students and then press ↓.

9. In the first cell of the last row, type Young Adults and then press Tab. Type 18 to 24 and then compare your screen with **Figure 4**.

10. Save the document.

■ **You have completed Skill 7 of 10**

▶ You can add rows to the beginning, middle, or end of a table, and you can delete one or more rows, if necessary.

▶ You can add columns to the left or right of the column that contains the insertion point.

1. In the fourth row of the table, click anywhere in the *College Students* cell.

   To delete a row, you need only position the insertion point anywhere in the row.

2. On the **Layout tab**, in the **Rows & Columns group**, click the **Delete** button, and then click **Delete Rows**. If you accidentally click Delete Columns, on the Quick Access Toolbar, click the Undo button ↶ and try again.

3. Right-click the *Young Adults* cell. On the Mini toolbar, click the **Insert** button, and then click **Insert Below** to add a row.

4. Type *Adults* and then notice that although the entire row was selected when you started typing, the text was entered into the row's first cell. Press [Tab], and then type *25 to 59* Press [Tab] to add a new row, and then compare your screen with **Figure 1**.

   When the insertion point is in the last cell, you can add another row by pressing [Tab].

5. In the first cell of the new row, type *Seniors* and then press [Tab]. Type *60+* and then compare your screen with **Figure 2**.

■ **Continue to the next page to complete the skill**

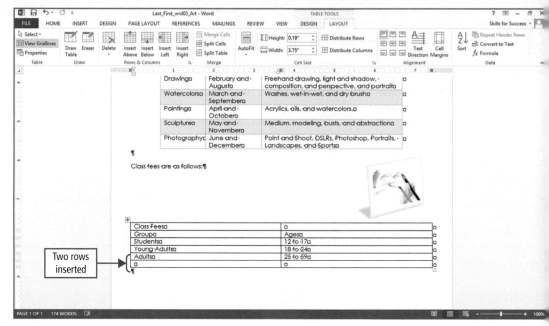

Figure 1

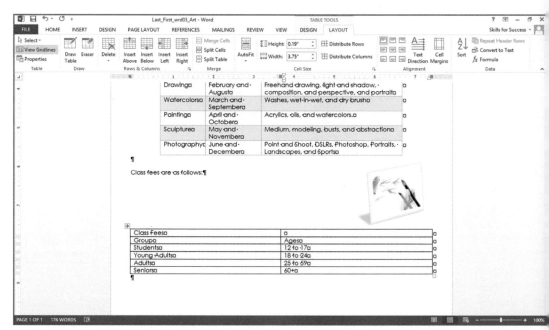

Figure 2

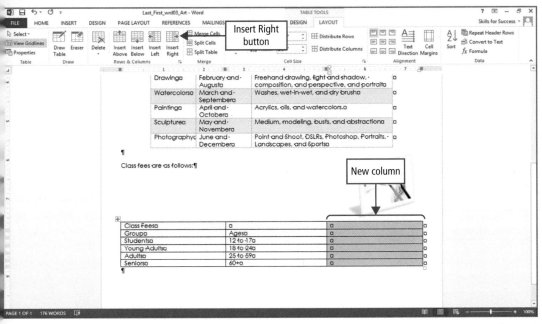

Figure 3

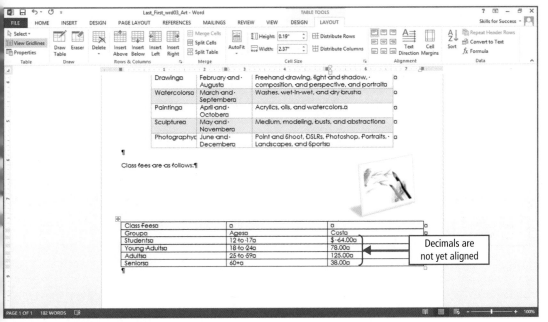

Figure 4

6. Be sure the insertion point is positioned in a cell in the second column of the table.

7. On the **Layout tab**, in the **Rows & Columns group**, click the **Insert Right** button to insert a new column to the right of the column that contained the insertion point, as shown in **Figure 3**.

   An alternate method to insert rows and columns is to point to a table border, and then click the Insert button that displays at the top of the column or beginning of the row. When you insert a new column, the existing columns are resized to fit within the width of the table.

8. In the new column, click in the second row, and then type Cost

9. Press ↓ to move to the next cell in the column, and then type 64.00

10. Press ↓, and then type 78.00 In the next cell down, type 125.00 and in the last cell of the table, type 38.00

11. In the third row, click to position the insertion point to the left of *64.00*. If the entire cell is selected, point closer to the *64.00* and click again. Type $ and then press SpaceBar two times. Compare your screen with **Figure 4**.

    A dollar sign is typically added only to the first row in a column of numbers and to the *Totals* row, if there is one. You will align the decimal points in this column in the next skill.

12. **Save** 🔲 the document.

■ **You have completed Skill 8 of 10**

▶ Text in a table is formatted using the same techniques as text in paragraphs.

▶ When you apply paragraph formatting to text in a table, it is applied only to the cell the text is in.

1. Position the pointer in the left margin to the left of the first row of the lower table to display the 🔊 pointer, and then click one time to select the row.

2. Under **Table Tools**, on the **Design tab**, in the **Table Styles group**, click the **Shading arrow** 🎨▾, and then in the first row, click the seventh color—**Brown**, **Accent 3**.

3. With the entire row still selected, change the font size to **12**, and then change the font color to the first color in the first row—**White**, **Background 1**. Compare your screen with **Figure 1**.

4. Repeat the technique just practiced to select the second row of the table, and then apply the **Center** ≡ paragraph alignment.

5. With the second row still selected, change the font color to the eighth choice in the first row—**Olive Green**, **Accent 4**.

6. Click in the third cell in the third row—*$ 64.00*. Drag down to select the remaining cells in the column, and then apply the **Align Right** ≡ paragraph alignment. Compare your screen with **Figure 2**.

   Numbers are typically aligned to the right in table cells.

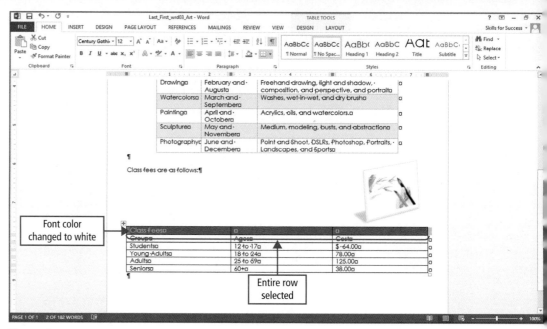

Figure 1

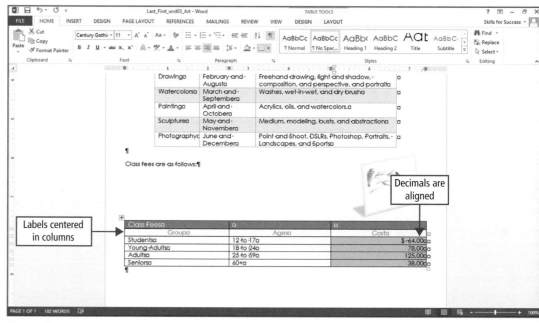

Figure 2

■ Continue to the next page to complete the skill ▶

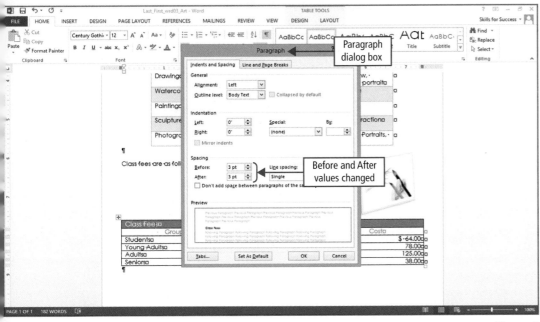

Figure 3

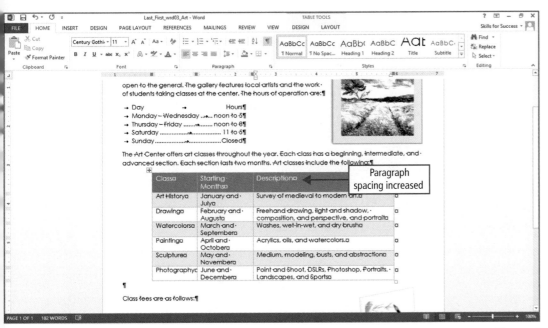

Figure 4

7. Click in the first cell—*Class Fees*. Click the **Paragraph Dialog Box Launcher** button. In the **Paragraph** dialog box, under **Spacing**, select the text in the **Before** box, and then type 3 pt Change the **After** value to 3 pt and then compare your screen with **Figure 3**.

   When you type numbers into the Before and After boxes without providing a unit of measure, the points unit will automatically be applied.

8. Click **OK** to accept the change and close the dialog box.

9. Scroll up to view the first table, select the first row, and then change the font size to **12**. Click the **Bold** button B to remove the bold, and then set the paragraph spacing **Before** and **After** to 3 pt

10. Click in another cell to deselect the row, and then compare your screen with **Figure 4**.

11. **Save** the document.

■ **You have completed Skill 9 of 10**

▶ To improve a table's readability, you can merge cells, change column widths, remove borders, and align text vertically.

▶ In a table, ***vertical alignment*** determines the space above and below a text or object in relation to the top and bottom of the cell.

1. In the upper table, click in any cell in the middle column. On the **Layout tab**, in the **Cell Size group**, click the **Width up spin arrow** as needed to widen the middle column to **1.6"**.

2. In the lower table, repeat the technique just practiced to change the first column's width to **1.5"**, the second column's width to **1.2"**, and the third column's width to **0.8"**.

3. In the lower table, select the first row. On the **Layout tab**, in the **Merge group**, click the **Merge Cells** button.

4. On the **Layout tab**, in the **Alignment group**, click the **Align Top Center** button. Click to deselect the row, and then compare your screen with **Figure 1**.

5. In the lower table, point to the second row, and then with the ⟋ pointer, drag down to select rows two through six. In the **Cell Size group**, change the **Height** value to **0.3"**.

6. Select the second row, and then in the **Alignment group**, click the **Align Center** button. Compare your screen with **Figure 2**.

7. In the first column of the lower table, select the four cells starting with *Students* and ending with *Seniors*. In the **Alignment group**, click the **Align Center Left** button.

■ Continue to the next page to complete the skill ▶

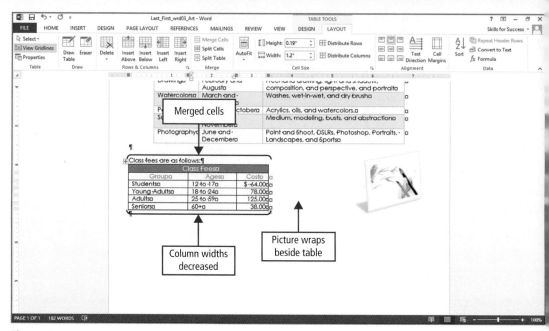

Figure 1

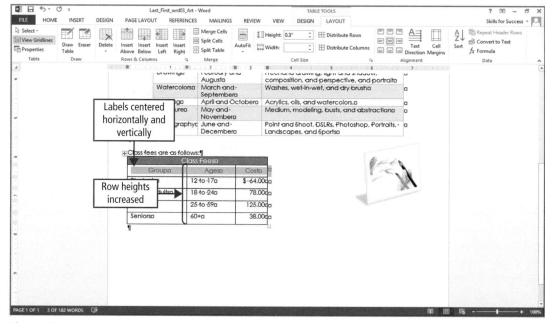

Figure 2

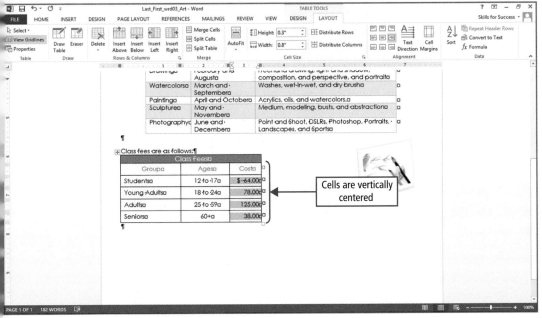

Figure 3

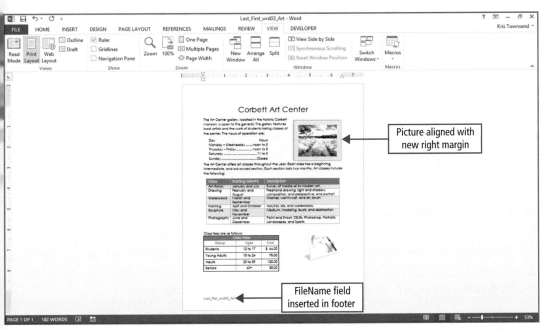

Figure 4

8. In the second column, select the cells starting with *12 to 17* and ending with *60+*. In the **Alignment group**, click the **Align Center** button ▤.

9. In the third column, select the cells starting with *$ 64.00* and ending with *38.00*. In the **Alignment group**, click the **Align Center Right** button ▤. Compare your screen with **Figure 3**.

10. Above and to the left of the lower table, click the **Table Selector** button ⊞ to select the table.

11. On the **Table Tools Design tab**, in the **Borders group**, click the **Borders arrow**, and then notice that several types of borders are selected in the gallery.

12. In the **Border** gallery, click **Inside Vertical Border** to remove the border from the table. Click a cell to deselect the table, and then click the **Show/Hide** button ¶ to hide the formatting marks.

13. On the **View tab**, in the **Zoom group**, click **One Page**.

14. On the **Page Layout tab**, in the **Page Setup group**, click **Margins**, and then click **Normal** to increase the margin widths. Using the Alignment Guides, align the first picture with the right margin and the top of the first body paragraph.

15. Add the **FileName** field to the footer, deactivate the footer area, and then compare your screen with **Figure 4**.

16. **Save** ▤ the document, **Close** ✕ Word, and then submit your work as directed by your instructor.

✔ **DONE! You have completed Skill 10 of 10, and your document is complete!**

The following More Skills are located at **www.pearsonhighered.com/skills**

More Skills Insert Text Boxes

Text boxes are floating objects that can be placed anywhere in a document. They are useful when you want to present text in a different orientation from other text. Text boxes function as a document within a document, and they can be resized or moved. Text in a text box wraps in the same manner it wraps in any document.

In More Skills 11, you will open a document and create a text box. You will also resize and format the text box.

To begin, open your web browser, navigate to www.pearsonhighered.com/skills, locate the name of your textbook, and then follow the instructions on the website.

More Skills Format with WordArt

When you create a flyer or a newsletter, you might want to use a distinctive and decorative title. Word provides a feature called WordArt that you can use to change text into a decorative title.

In More Skills 12, you will open a document and create a title that uses WordArt.

To begin, open your web browser, navigate to www.pearsonhighered.com/skills, locate the name of your textbook, and then follow the instructions on the website.

More Skills Convert Text into Tables

You can create a new table by using the Table button on the Insert tab. You can also use the Table button to convert a tabbed list into a table.

In More Skills 13, you will open a document and convert a tabbed list into a table. You will also format the table.

To begin, open your web browser, navigate to www.pearsonhighered.com/skills, locate the name of your textbook, and then follow the instructions on the website.

More Skills 14 Insert Drop Caps

Word provides a number of methods to format text distinctively. To give text the professional look you often see in books and magazines, you can use a large first letter to begin the first paragraph of the document.

In More Skills 14, you will open a document and create a drop cap for the first character of the first paragraph.

To begin, open your web browser, navigate to www.pearsonhighered.com/skills, locate the name of your textbook, and then follow the instructions on the website.

Please note that there are no additional projects to accompany the More Skills Projects, and they are not covered in the End-of-Chapter projects.

The following table summarizes the **SKILLS AND PROCEDURES** covered in this chapter.

Skills Number	Task	Step	Icon
1	Insert pictures	Insert tab → Illustrations group → Pictures	
1	Insert text from files	Insert tab → Text group → Object arrow, and click Text from File	
2	Resize pictures	Drag the corner resizing handles, or Format tab → Size group commands	
2	Reset pictures	Format tab → Adjust group → Reset Picture	
2	Float pictures	Select picture → Layout options button → Square	
3	Set Picture Styles	Format tab → Picture Styles group commands	
3	Set Artistic Effects	Format tab → Adjust group → Artistic Effects	
4	Set tab stops	Click the Tab Selector to pick the desired tab, and then click the ruler at the desired location.	
4	Add leaders	Home → Paragraph → Paragraph Dialog Box Launcher → Tab button In the Tabs dialog box, select the desired tab, and then select the desired leader option	
6	Apply table styles	Design tab → Table Styles group commands	
6	Modify table style options	Design tab → select or clear Table Style Options group check boxes	
6	AutoFit cells	Layout tab → Cell Size group → AutoFit	
7	Insert tables	Insert tab → Tables group → Table button → Select the desired dimensions	
8	Add or delete rows and columns	Click in the desired cell → Mini Toolbar Insert button	
9	Apply cell shading	Design tab → Table Styles group → Shading	
9	Adjust row and column sizes	Layout tab → Cell Size group commands	
10	Merge cells	Select the cells to be merged, and then Layout tab → Merge Cells	
10	Align cells vertically	Layout tab → Alignment group commands	
10	Edit table borders	Home tab → Paragraph group → Borders	

Key Terms

Online Help Skills

1. Start **Word 2013**, and then in the upper right corner of the start page, click the **Help** button ⟦?⟧.

2. In the **Word Help** window **Search help** box, type banded rows and then press ⟦Enter⟧.

3. In the search result list, click **"Banded Rows" is under "Table Tools/Table Style Options"**. Compare your screen with **Figure 1**.

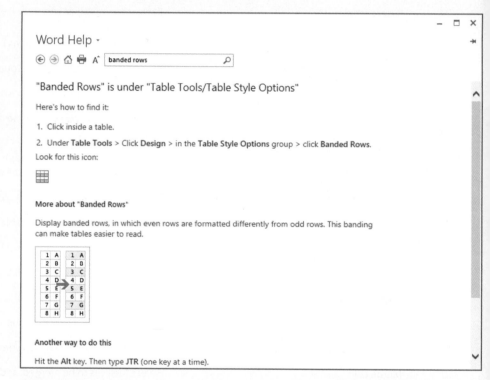

Figure 1

4. Read the article to answer the following questions: What are banded rows and how can you insert or remove them from tables? How might they be useful?

Matching

Match each term in the second column with its correct definition in the first column by writing the letter of the term on the blank line in front of the correct definition.

___ **1.** When you select a picture, this button displays next to the image so that you can change text wrapping settings quickly.

___ **2.** A layout option that sets a picture to "float" so that it can be moved independently of the paragraph.

___ **3.** The type of sizing handle used to resize a picture proportionally.

___ **4.** A line that displays when an object is aligned with a document object such as a margin or heading.

___ **5.** A prebuilt set of formatting options that can be applied to a graphic with a single click.

___ **6.** A specific location in the document, marked on the Word ruler, to which you can move using the Tab key.

___ **7.** A series of characters that form a solid, dashed, or dotted line that fills the space preceding a tab stop.

___ **8.** Information presented in rows and columns to summarize and present data effectively and efficiently.

___ **9.** A pre-built set of formatting options that can be applied to a table with a single click.

___ **10.** The command used to make the size of the table columns reflect the data in the columns.

A Alignment Guide

B AutoFit Contents

C Corner

D Layout Options

E Leader

F Picture Style

G Square

H Tab Stop

I Table

J Table Style

BizSkills Video

1. What types of questions should you have prepared for the interviewer?

2. What is the most important thing you can convey during an interview?

Multiple Choice MyITLab®

Choose the correct answer.

1. When you select a picture, you can use these to change the picture's size.
   A. Arrow keys
   B. Sizing handles
   C. Layout Options

2. The symbol that indicates which paragraph a picture is associated with.
   A. Anchor
   B. Paragraph mark
   C. Em dash

3. To move a selected picture small distances using an arrow key.
   A. Drag
   B. Bump
   C. Nudge

4. A series of evenly spaced dots that precede a tab.
   A. Ellipsis
   B. Tab stop position
   C. Dot leader

5. When you make a change to a tab stop in the Tabs dialog box, click this button to apply the changes.
   A. Set
   B. Clear
   C. Apply

6. The intersection of a row and column in a table.
   A. Banded row
   B. Cell
   C. Banded column

7. This command can be used to make a picture look more like a drawing or a painting.
   A. Artistic Effects
   B. Change Picture
   C. Compress Pictures

8. Use this key to move from one part of a table to another.
   A. Alt
   B. Tab
   C. Ctrl

9. How many columns are in a 3x7 table?
   A. 3
   B. 7
   C. 21

10. Numbers in a table are typically aligned this way.
    A. Left
    B. Center
    C. Right

Topics for Discussion

1. Tables have largely taken the place of tabs in most documents. Can you think of any situations where you might want to use tabs instead of tables? What would you have to do to a table to make it look like a tabbed list?

2. Pictures add interest to your documents when used in moderation. What guidelines would you recommend for using pictures—or any other type of graphics—in a document?

Skills Review

To complete this project, you will need the following files:

- wrd03_SRAdventures
- wrd03_SRGeo
- wrd03_SRHikes

You will save your file as:

- Last_First_wrd03_SRAdventures

1. Start **Word 2013**, and then open the student data file **wrd03_SRAdventures**. **Save** the file in your chapter folder as Last_First_wrd03_SRAdventures

2. Click to position the insertion point in the blank paragraph below *year's line-up includes:*. On the **Insert tab**, in the **Text group**, click the **Object button arrow**, and then click **Text from File**. Locate and insert **wrd03_SRHikes**, and then press ⌴Backspace⌴ one time to remove the extra paragraph.

3. Right-click in the first row of the table. On the Mini toolbar, click the **Insert** button, and then click **Insert Above**.

4. In the first cell of the new row, type Hike and then press ⌴Tab⌴. In the second cell, type Length and then press ⌴Tab⌴. In the third cell, type Difficulty and then press ⌴Tab⌴. In the last cell, type Description

5. With the insertion point in the table, click the **Design tab**. In the **Table Styles group**, click the **More** button, and then under **Grid Tables**, click **Grid Table 7 Colorful - Accent 6**.

6. On the **Layout tab**, in the **Cell Size group**, click the **AutoFit** button, and then click **AutoFit Contents**.

7. Click the **Table Selector** button to select the entire table. On the **Layout tab**, in the **Alignment group**, click the **Align Center Left** button.

8. Click in a cell in the second column, and then in the **Cell Size group**, click the **Width up spin arrow** to set the width to column **0.9"**. Compare your screen with **Figure 1**.

9. Click in the blank paragraph below the paragraph that ends *Climbing Center*. On the **Insert tab**, in the **Tables group**, click the **Table** button, and then insert a **2x4** table.

10. In the table just inserted, add the text as shown in **Figure 2**.

Figure 1

Class	Date
Intro to Rock Climbing	March 22
Fitness through Climbing	March 29
Family Vertical Climbing	April 5

Figure 2

■ Continue to the next page to complete this Skills Review ➤

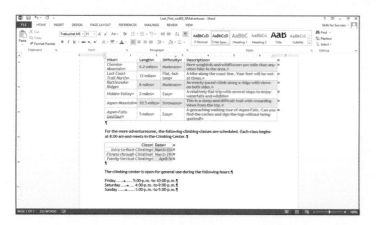

Figure 3

Figure 4

11. On the **Design tab**, apply the same table style you applied to the upper table—**Grid Table 7 Colorful - Accent 6**. On the **Layout tab**, in the **Cell Size group**, click the **AutoFit** button, and then click **AutoFit Contents**.

12. Select the three cells that contain dates. On the **Home tab**, in the **Paragraph group**, click the **Align Right** button.

13. Press Ctrl + End to position the insertion point at the end of the document. On the left side of the horizontal ruler, click the **Tab Selector** button to display the Right Tab icon. Insert a right tab at **2.75 inches** on the horizontal ruler.

14. Double-click the tab mark. In the **Tabs** dialog box, under **Leader**, select **2**, click **Set**, and then click **OK**. Type the following tabbed list, pressing Tab before typing the text in the second column:

Friday	5:00 p.m. to 10:00 p.m.
Saturday	4:00 p.m. to 9:00 p.m.
Sunday	1:00 p.m. to 5:00 p.m.

15. Compare your screen with **Figure 3**.

16. Click to the left of the paragraph that begins *For the more adventuresome*. On the **Insert tab**, in the **Illustrations group**, click the **Pictures** button, and then locate and insert **wrd03_SRGeo**.

17. On the **Format tab**, in the **Size group**, select the number in the **Width** box, type **2.5** and then press Enter.

18. Scroll up to display the bottom of Page 1. Click the picture's **Layout Options** button, and then under **With Text Wrapping**, click **Square**.

19. Drag the picture to the right and slightly up. When the Alignment Guides display and align with the top of the paragraph beginning *For the more adventuresome* and the right page margin, release the left mouse button.

20. On the **Format tab**, in the **Picture Styles group**, click the sixth thumbnail—**Soft Edge Rectangle**.

21. In the **Picture Styles group**, click the **Picture Effects** button, point to **3-D Rotation**, and then under **Perspective**, click the second to last choice—**Perspective Heroic Extreme Left**.

22. Add the **FileName** field to the footer, and then deactivate the footer. Hide the formatting marks, set the zoom level to **One Page**, and then compare your document with **Figure 4**.

23. **Save** the document, **Close** Word, and then submit the file as directed by your instructor.

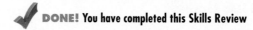 **DONE! You have completed this Skills Review**

Skills Assessment 1

To complete this document, you will need the following files:

- wrd03_SA1Festival
- wrd03_SA1Photo
- wrd03_SA1Bands

You will save your document as:

- Last_First_wrd03_SA1Festival

1. Start **Word 2013**, and then open the student data file **wrd03_SA1Festival**. Save the file in your chapter folder as Last_First_wrd03_SA1Festival

2. With the insertion point to the left of the flyer title, insert the picture from the student file **wrd03_SA1Photo**. Apply the **Square** layout, change the **Width** to 3.5", and then align the picture with the top of the title paragraph and the document's right margin. Apply the **Bevel Rectangle** picture style (the twenty-first choice), and then apply the **Preset** picture effect—**Preset 5**.

3. In the blank paragraph below *line-up includes the following:*, insert the text from the student file **wrd03_SA1Bands**. Add a fourth column, and then in cells two to seven, add the following times:

   4:00 p.m.
   7:00 p.m.
   12:00 p.m.
   4:00 p.m.
   7:00 p.m.
   2:00 p.m.

4. Add a new row below the table's last row, and then enter the following: Obia, Afro-Latin Groove, Sunday, 5:00 p.m.

5. Select the table, and then apply the **Grid Table 1 Light - Accent 2** table style. Change the font size to **14** points and the row height to **0.3"**. Set the first row to **Align Center**, and rows two to eight to **Align Center Left**.

6. In the first row, merge cells three and four, and then **AutoFit** the columns to their contents. Change the table's **Alignment** property to **Center** the table between the side margins.

A Taste of Aspen Falls

A Taste of Aspen Falls is an annual food and music event held in Aspen Falls City Park. This year features more than 50 food vendors and over 75 free concerts on 4 different stages. All concerts are free and no food item is over $7.95.

This year's artist line-up includes the following:

Band	Genre	Day and Time	
Noseeums	Eclectic Mix	Friday	4:00 p.m.
Fork in the Road	Electric Blues	Friday	7:00 p.m.
Hungary Creek	Folk-Americana	Saturday	12:00 p.m.
Green Sword	Mexi-Cali	Saturday	4:00 p.m.
Pete's Fork	Rock	Saturday	7:00 p.m.
Wendover	Acoustic Rock	Sunday	2:00 p.m.
Obia	Afro-Latin Groove	Sunday	5:00 p.m.

Plan your good times now!

Friday..................... 4:00 to 10:00
Saturday .... 10:00 to 10:00
Sunday................... 10:00 to 8:00

Last_First_wrd03_SA1Festival.docx

Luchshen / Fotolia

Figure 1

7. In the blank paragraph at the end of the document, set a left tab stop at **0.25 inches** and a right tab stop at **2.5 inches**. Add a dot leader to the right tab stop, and then enter the following text to create a tabbed list:

Friday	4:00 to 10:00
Saturday	10:00 to 10:00
Sunday	10:00 to 8:00

8. Add the file name to the footer. **Save** the document, and then print or submit the file as directed by your instructor. Compare your completed document with **Figure 1**.

 DONE! You have completed Skills Assessment 1

Skills Assessment 2

To complete this document, you will need the following files:

- wrd03_SA2College
- wrd03_SA2Photo
- wrd03_SA2Prices

You will save your document as:

- Last_First_wrd03_SA2College

1. Start **Word 2013**, and then open the student data file **wrd03_SA2College**. Save the file in your chapter folder as Last_First_wrd03_SA2College

2. In the blank paragraph below *Several health care providers*, insert a 2x6 table, and then add the following text:

Provider	Plan(s)
Ultra Shield	PPO
Sunshine Health Cooperative	PPO, HMO
HealthWise Choice	PPO
United Southwest Health	HMO
Morgan Association Health Plan of CA	PPO

3. In the blank paragraph after *prices are as follows:*, insert the text from the student file **wrd03_SA2Prices**, and then remove the second blank paragraph below the table.

4. In the second table, add a new first row, and then enter the following column headings: Unit Type, Average Rate, and Vacancy Rate

5. For both document tables, apply the **Grid Table 4 - Accent 5** table style. **AutoFit** the columns to their contents, and then change the table's **Alignment** property to **Center** the table between the side margins.

6. In the second table, change the currency and percent values in the cells below *Average Rate* and *Vacancy Rate* to the **Align Right** paragraph alignment.

7. In the blank paragraph at the end of the document, click the **Tab Selector** to display the **Decimal Tab** icon, and then click the

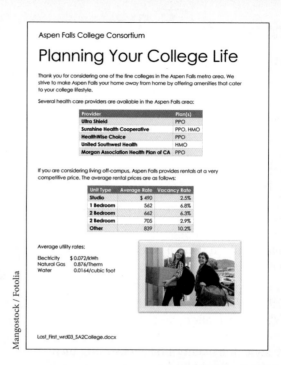

Mangostock / Fotolia

Figure 1

1.25 inch mark on the ruler. Enter the following text using the tab to align the decimal points in the second column:

Electricity	$ 0.072/kWh
Natural Gas	0.876/Therm
Water	0.0164/cubic foot

8. With the insertion point to the left of the paragraph *Average utility rates*, insert the picture from the student file **wrd03_SA2Photo**. Apply the **Square** layout, change the **Width** to 3", and then align the picture with the top of the *Average utility rates* paragraph and the document's right margin.

9. Apply the **Beveled Matte**, **White** picture style (the second choice), and then change the **Picture Border** color to the ninth choice in the second row—**Lavender, Accent 5, Lighter 80%**.

10. Add the file name to the footer. **Save** the document, and then print or submit the file as directed by your instructor. Compare your completed document with **Figure 1**.

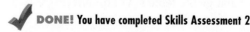

DONE! You have completed Skills Assessment 2

Visual Skills Check

To complete this document, you will need the following files:

- wrd03_VSConservation
- wrd03_VSPhoto
- wrd03_VSWildlife

You will save your document as:

- Last_First_wrd03_VSConservation

Open the student file **wrd03_VSConservation**, and then save it in your chapter folder as Last_First_wrd03_VSConservation **Create the document shown in Figure 1.**

The picture is the student data file **wrd03_VSPhoto**, has the **Soft Edge Rectangle** picture style, and is 3 inches wide. The table can be inserted from the student data file **wrd03_VSWildlife**, but you will need to add the last row and its text. The table is formatted with the **Grid Table 4 - Accent 5** table style, and the table style options have been changed. The cell sizes have been changed to AutoFit Contents, and the row headings are vertically centered in each cell. Insert the FileName field in the footer, and then print or submit the file as directed by your instructor.

 DONE! You have completed Visual Skills Check

Durango County
Conservation Futures Program

Aspen Falls Conservation Area

In 1994, the Durango County Commissioners created the Conservation Futures Program to preserve county natural areas in perpetuity. The program expands existing natural areas and creates new areas by acquiring properties nominated by county citizens. The Aspen Falls Conservation Area has returned the Aspen River to its natural meandering course benefiting wildlife, natural vegetation, and citizens alike.

The Aspen Falls Conservation Area features the following wildlife and plants:

Songbirds	Spring is an especially good time to observe songbirds during the breeding season. Over 100 species of birds have been spotted in the area.
Raptors	Attracted by the abundant forage fish found in the restored river, two nesting Bald eagle pairs live here year-round and several more nest each winter. Other raptors include osprey, red-tailed hawk, kestrel, and the long-eared owl.
Tule Elk	Approximately 25 elk visit the area to feed and can often be seen from the area's wildlife viewing blinds.
Beaver	Beaver are returning to the area. Their dams, diversions, and ponds attract birds, fish, and native plants which attract a wide array of wildlife to the area.
Sensitive Plants	Rare or endangered plants include Snow Mountain buckwheat, Drymaria-like western flax, Adobe lily, and Hall's madia.

Last_First_wrd03_VSConservation.docx

VL@D / Fotolia

Figure 1

TUTORING

A+

Math, English, and Computer Literacy

Reasonable Rates

Contact Your Name at (555) 555-5555.

Flexible Hours

Your Name (555) 555-5555	Your Name (555) 555-5555	Your Name (555) 555-5555	Your Name (555) 555-5555	Your Name (555) 555-5555	Your Name (555) 555-5555	Your Name (555) 555-5555	Your Name (555) 555-5555	Your Name (555) 555-5555

Matthew Benoit / Fotolia

Figure 1

My Skills

To complete this document, you will need the following files:

- wrd03_MYFlyer
- wrd03_MYPhoto

You will save your document as:

- Last_First_wrd03_MYFlyer

1. Start **Word 2013**, and then open the student data file **wrd03_MYFlyer**. Save the file in your chapter folder as Last_First_wrd03_MYFlyer

2. Apply the **Organic** theme. Select all of the document text, and then change the font color to the ninth choice in the first row— **Orange**, **Accent 5**.

3. Select the flyer title, *Tutoring*, and then in the **Font Size** box, replace the existing value with 84 and then press Enter.

4. In the blank paragraph after the title, insert the picture from the student file **wrd03_MYPhoto**. Resize the picture proportionally by changing the width to **3.5"**.

5. For the picture, apply the nineteenth picture style—**Relaxed Perspective**, **White**.

6. In the first paragraph below the picture, change the font size to **26**. For the last three document paragraphs, change the font size to **18**.

7. Click the **Insert tab**. In the **Header & Footer group**, click the **Footer** button, and then click **Edit Footer**.

8. In the footer, insert a **9x1** table. In the first cell, type your first and last name. Press Enter, and then type the phone number (555) 555-5555

9. Drag through the text taking care not to select the entire cell, and then on the **Home tab**, click the **Copy** button. Paste the text into the table's eight remaining cells. If you accidentally copied the cell, undo and select just the text before clicking Copy.

10. Select the entire table, and then click the **Layout tab**. In the **Alignment group**, click the **Text Direction** button one time to rotate the text from top to bottom as indicated by the arrows in the Text Direction button.

11. Set the **Table Row Height** to **1.6"**, and then with the entire table selected, change the alignment to **Align Center** so that the text is centered both vertically and horizontally in the cells.

12. On the **Layout tab**, in the **Table group**, click **Properties**. In the **Table Properties** dialog box, under **Alignment**, click **Center**. Under **Text wrapping**, click the **Around** button, and then click **OK**.

13. Double-click in the body to deactivate the footer area, and then click the **Page Layout tab**. In the **Page Setup group**, click the **Margins** button, and then click **Narrow**.

14. **Save** the document, and then compare your completed document with **Figure 1**. Submit the file as directed by your instructor.

 DONE! You have completed My Skills

Skills Challenge 1

To complete this document, you will need the following file:

- wrd03_SC1Softball

You will save your document as:

- Last_First_wrd03_SC1Softball

The Aspen Falls Parks and Recreation Department has a Spring Softball flyer that needs updating. To update the flyer, open the student data file **wrd03_SC1Softball**, and then save it in your chapter folder as Last_First_wrd03_SC1Softball Add the FileName field to the footer.

Improve the flyer by applying the skills practiced in this chapter. Assign a suitable theme, and then use the theme's fonts and colors to format the title in a manner demonstrated in this chapter's project. Create and format headings for each section. Use Online Pictures to insert a picture that complements the flyer's message. Size, position, and format

the picture using picture styles or artistic effects so that the picture attracts the reader's eye to the flyer.

Organize the content using at least one table, a tabbed list, and a bulleted list. Format the table(s) in a manner that is consistent with the title formatting. In the tabbed list(s), assign a leader and alignment as appropriate to the content. Assign paragraph spacing to provide white space between flyer elements and adjust the margins if needed so that the flyer displays on a single page. Submit your flyer as directed by your instructor.

 DONE! You have completed Skills Challenge 1

Skills Challenge 2

To complete this document, you will need the following file:

- New blank Word document

You will save your document as:

- Last_First_wrd03_SC2Resume

On the Word start page or Open page, search for and select the Basic Resume template provided by Microsoft Corporation. If that template is no longer available, pick a different résumé template. Download the template, and then save it in your chapter folder as Last_First_wrd03_SC2Resume Insert the FileName field into the footer.

Create your own résumé by filling in the template. Using the skills you have practiced in this chapter, add or remove

sections as appropriate and position the section featuring your strongest area (for example, experience, education, or skills) immediately below the objective. Be sure the résumé fits on a single page, and reformat table cells and text as needed.

Check the entire document for grammar and spelling, and then submit the file as directed by your instructor.

 DONE! You have completed Skills Challenge 2

CHAPTER 4

Create Newsletters and Mail Merge Documents

- ▶ Newsletters often display articles in two or three columns and have a title that spans across the columns. Text is typically easier to read when it is in columns.
- ▶ Clip art can be downloaded from Office.com and then inserted and formatted in much the same way as a picture.
- ▶ SmartArt graphics display information visually and can add a professional look to a document.

- ▶ To draw attention to a small amount of text, you can add a border and shading to the paragraph.
- ▶ You can use the mail merge feature in Word to create mailing labels to distribute flyers or brochures.
- ▶ In a mail merge, you can take an existing list of names and addresses from other Office applications and insert them into a mailing labels document.

© Kratuanoiy / Fotolia

Aspen Falls City Hall

In this chapter, you will assist Todd Austin, the Aspen Falls Tourism Director, to create a newsletter about the Aspen Falls Farmers' Market. The newsletter will be mailed to local farmers promoting their participation in the market. The newsletter will be mailed, so you will also create mailing labels with the addresses of local farms.

An effective newsletter uses large, attractive text and graphics to invite readers to read the articles. Subtitles, graphics, and other formatting can help those who only scan the newsletter to gain the information they desire. Word's library of SmartArt graphics can help you create graphics that communicate a message with very little text. You can save time by formatting as desired and then creating your own Quick Style based on that formatting. After the style is created, you apply that formatting with a single click.

In this project, you will create a one-page flyer with an artistic title and a two-column format. You will add text effects to the newsletter title, and add page and paragraph borders and shading. You will insert a clip art graphic and create a SmartArt graphic. Finally, you will create mailing labels by merging data from one file to a label template.

Time to complete all 10
skills – 60 to 90 minutes

Student data files needed for this chapter:

wrd04_Farmers
wrd04_FarmerAddresses

You will save your files as:

Last_First_wrd04_Farmers
Last_First_wrd04_FarmerAddresses (not submitted)
Last_First_wrd04_FarmerLabels (not submitted)
Last_First_wrd04_FarmerMerged

Outcome

Using the skills in this chapter, you will be able to create a Word document like this:

SKILLS

MyITLab®
Skills 1-10 Training

At the end of this chapter you will be able to:

Skill 1 Modify Themes and Create Columns
Skill 2 Modify Margins and Columns
Skill 3 Apply Text Effects
Skill 4 Create Styles
Skill 5 Add Borders and Shading to Paragraphs and Pages
Skill 6 Insert and Adjust Online Pictures
Skill 7 Insert SmartArt
Skill 8 Format SmartArt
Skill 9 Create Labels Using Mail Merge
Skill 10 Preview and Print Mail Merge Documents

MORE SKILLS

Skill 11 Optimize Documents for Read Mode
Skill 12 Work in Outline View
Skill 13 Manage Document Properties
Skill 14 Save Documents as Web Pages

- You can modify a theme by selecting a different set of colors, fonts, or effects.
- In a newsletter, multiple columns make text easier to read.

1. Start **Word 2013**, and then open the student data file **wrd04_Farmers**. Use **Save As** to create a folder named Word Chapter 4 and then **Save** the document as Last_First_wrd04_Farmers

2. Display the formatting marks, and then add the **FileName** field to the footer.

3. Click the **View tab**, and then in the **Zoom group**, click **One Page**. Compare your screen with Figure 1.

   Because you are not editing text, it is typically best to view the entire page when working with the overall look and feel of a page.

4. On the **Design tab**, in the **Document Formatting group**, click **Themes**, and then click **Wisp**.

5. In the **Document Formatting group**, click the **Fonts** button. Scroll down the list of font sets, and then click **Century Gothic-Palatino Linotype**. Compare your screen with Figure 2.

   To improve readability in printed newsletters, body text is often given a *serif font*—a font where the letters have extra details or hooks at the end of each stroke. Article titles are often given a *sans serif font*—a font where the letters do not have *serifs*—the extra details or hooks at the end of each stroke.

   Here, the colors and effects of the Wisp theme have been applied, but the default fonts have been changed to Century Gothic for headings and Palatino Linotype for body text.

■ **Continue to the next page to complete the skill**

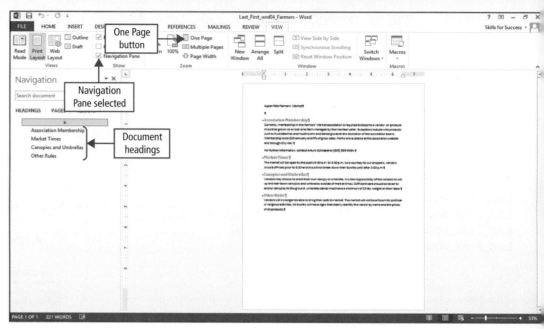

Figure 1

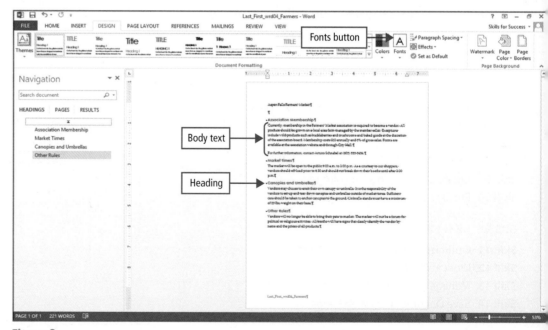

Figure 2

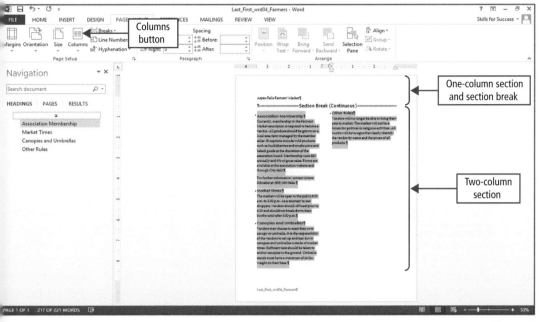

Figure 3

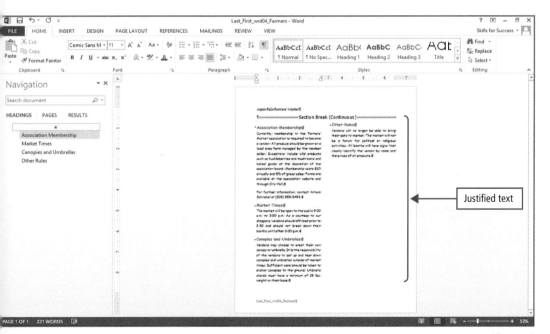

Figure 4

6. Locate the subtitle *Association Membership*, and then position the pointer to the left of the first word in the paragraph. Drag down to the end of the document—including the paragraph mark in the last paragraph.

7. Click the **Page Layout tab**. In the **Page Setup group**, click the **Columns** button, click **Two**, and then compare your screen with **Figure 3**.

   A section break displays above the two-column text. A ***section*** is a portion of a document that can be formatted differently from the rest of the document. A ***section break*** marks the end of one section and the beginning of another section.

8. With the two columns of text still selected, change the font to **Comic Sans MS**.

   Because this newsletter is only one page long, a serif font is not needed for the body text. The new font has wider characters than the previous selection, so some of the text moved from the first column into the second column.

9. With the text still selected, on the **Home tab**, in the **Paragraph group**, click the **Justify** button ⊟.

10. Click anywhere in the two-column text to deselect the text, and then compare your screen with **Figure 4**.

    Justified text aligns the text with both the left and right margins. Justified text is often used in documents with multiple columns, although some wide gaps can occur in the text.

11. **Save** ⊟ the document.

■ **You have completed Skill 1 of 10**

▶ You can increase or decrease the space between the columns and apply custom margins to adjust the document layout.

▶ A *column break* forces the text following the break to flow into the next column.

1. On the **Page Layout tab**, in the **Page Setup group**, click **Margins**, and then below the **Margins gallery**, click **Custom Margins** to open the Page Setup dialog box.

2. In the **Page Setup** dialog box, under **Margins**, use the **down spin arrows** to change the **Top** and **Bottom** margins to **0.8"**.

3. Under **Preview**, click the **Apply to arrow**, and then click **Whole document**. Compare your screen with **Figure 1**, and then click **OK** to close the dialog box.

   Unless you specify otherwise, when documents have multiple sections, the Page Setup dialog box applies the changes only to the current section.

4. With the insertion point in the two columns of text, on the **Page Layout tab**, in the **Page Setup group**, click the **Columns** button. Below the **Columns gallery**, click **More Columns** to display the Columns dialog box. Compare your screen with **Figure 2**.

   When you set column options, you only need to place the insertion point in the section that the columns are applied to.

   The Columns dialog box can be used to set the number of columns and the distance between them. By default, the columns are of equal width with 0.5 inches of space between them.

■ **Continue to the next page to complete the skill** ➤

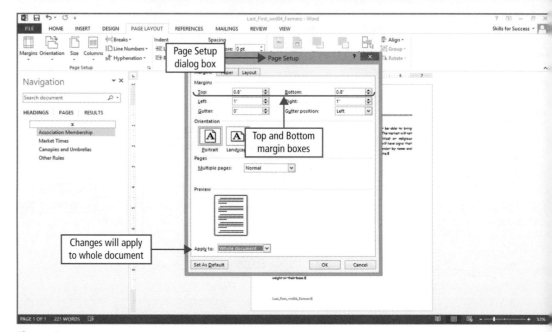

Figure 1

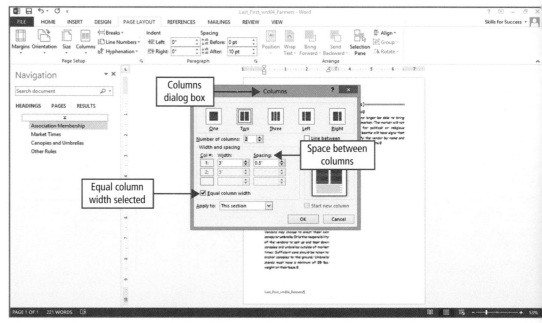

Figure 2

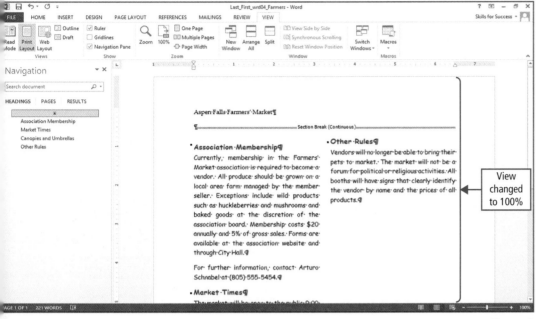

Figure 3

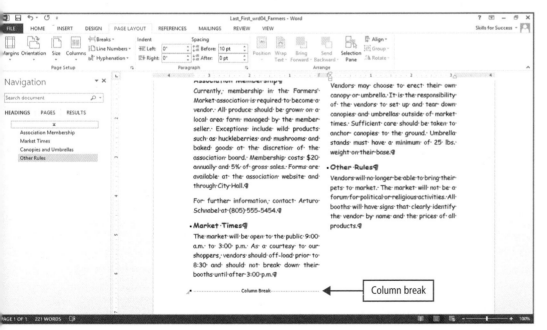

Figure 4

5. In the **Columns** dialog box, under **Width and spacing**, click the first **Spacing down spin arrow** two times to change the spacing between the columns to **0.3"**. Click **OK** to accept the changes and close the dialog box.

> Both columns will remain of equal width because the *Equal column width* check box is selected. When you decrease the spacing between columns, the width of each column is increased, in this case from 3.0 to 3.1 inches.

6. On the **View tab**, in the **Zoom group**, click **100%**. Press `Ctrl` + `Home`, and then compare your screen with **Figure 3**.

> If you are working with a larger monitor, you may prefer to work with the document in One Page view instead of at 100%.

7. In the left column, click to position the insertion point to the left of the subtitle *Canopies and Umbrellas*.

8. On the **Page Layout tab**, in the **Page Setup group**, click the **Breaks** button. In the **Breaks gallery**, under **Page Breaks**, click **Column**.

9. Scroll to display the column break at the bottom of column 1, and then compare your screen with **Figure 4**.

> Column breaks display as nonprinting characters, and after the break, the remaining text flows into the second column.

10. Save the document.

■ **You have completed Skill 2 of 10**

► **Text effects** are decorative formats, such as outlines, shadows, text glow, and colors, that make text stand out in a document.

► You should use text effects sparingly, at most just for titles or subtitles.

1. At the top of the document, select the title *Aspen Falls Farmers' Market* including the paragraph mark.

2. With the title text still selected, on the **Home tab**, in the **Font group**, click the **Font arrow** `Calibri (Body)`, and then under **Theme Fonts**, click **Century Gothic**.

3. In the **Font group**, click in the **Font Size** box `11` to select the existing value. Type **30** and then press `Enter`.

   By typing the desired size, you can assign a font size that is not included in the Font Size list.

4. On the **Home tab**, in the **Paragraph group**, click the **Center** button, and then compare your screen with **Figure 1**.

5. On the **Home tab**, in the **Font group**, click the **Text Effects and Typography** button `A`. Compare your screen with **Figure 2**.

   The Text Effects gallery displays thumbnails of pre-built text effects and commands for applying individual text effects settings.

Figure 1

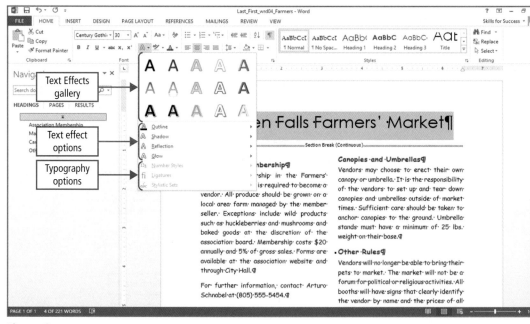

Figure 2

■ **Continue to the next page to complete the skill**

Figure 3

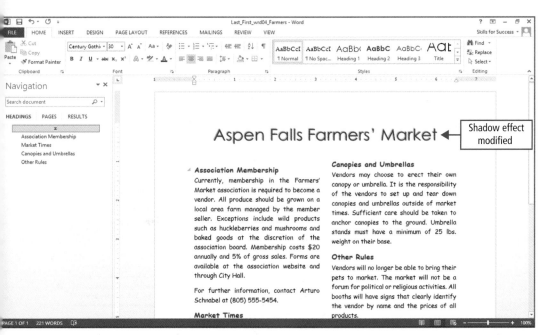

Figure 4

6. In the **Text Effects gallery**, in the first row, click the second thumbnail—**Fill - Dark Red**, **Accent 1**, **Shadow**.

7. On the **Home tab**, in the **Paragraph group**, click the **Show/Hide** button so that it is no longer selected.

> At times, it is helpful to format text with the nonprinting formatting marks hidden.

8. Click the **Home tab**, and then click the **Paragraph Dialog Box Launcher**. In the **Paragraph** dialog box, change the **Spacing After** to **0 pt**, change the **Line spacing** to **Single**, and then click **OK**. Click to deselect the text, and then compare your screen with **Figure 3**.

9. Select the newsletter title paragraph. In the **Fonts group**, click the **Text Effects and Typography** button. In the **Text Effects gallery**, point to **Outline**, and then point to several colors to preview the outline effects.

10. Repeat the technique just practiced to preview the shadow, reflection, and glow effects.

11. In the **Text Effects gallery**, point to **Shadow**, and then under **Outer**, click the last thumbnail—**Offset Diagonal Top Left**. Deselect the text, and then compare your screen with **Figure 4**.

> In this manner, you can modify the text effect settings. Here, the shadow's position and distance from the text were changed.

12. Save the document.

■ **You have completed Skill 3 of 10**

▶ A **Quick Style** is a style that can be accessed from a Ribbon gallery of thumbnails.

▶ You can create and name your own styles, and then add them to the Style gallery so that you can apply them with a single click.

1. Display the formatting marks, and then at the top of the left column, click to place the insertion point in the subtitle *Association Membership*. Compare your screen with **Figure 1**.

> The subtitles in this newsletter have been assigned the Heading 2 style. The black square to the left of the subtitle indicates that it will always stay with the next paragraph. Recall that text assigned a Heading style can also be collapsed and expanded.

2. Select the subtitle *Association Membership* including the paragraph mark. On the **Home tab**, in the **Font group**, click the **Font Dialog Box Launcher** 🔲.

3. In the **Font** dialog box, change the font to **Century Gothic** and the **Size** to **16**.

4. Click the **Font color arrow**, and then under **Theme Colors**, click the last color in the last row—**Green, Accent 6, Darker 50%**.

5. Under **Effects**, select the **Small caps** check box. Compare your screen with **Figure 2**, and then click **OK**.

6. With the text still selected, open the **Paragraph** dialog box. Under **General**, change the **Alignment** to **Centered**. Change the **Spacing Before** to **0 pt**, and the **Spacing After** to **6 pt**. Change the **Line spacing** to **Single**, and then click **OK**.

■ **Continue to the next page to complete the skill** ▶

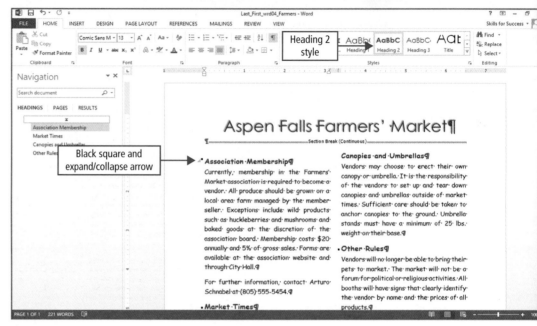

Figure 1

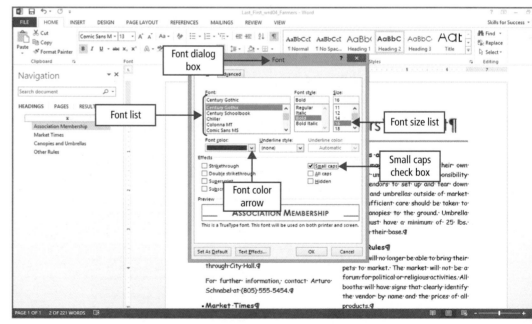

Figure 2

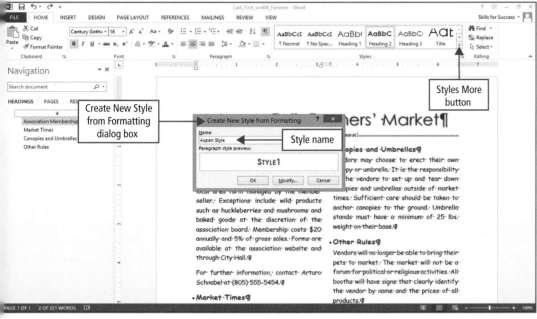

Create New Style from Formatting dialog box

Style name

Styles More button

Figure 3

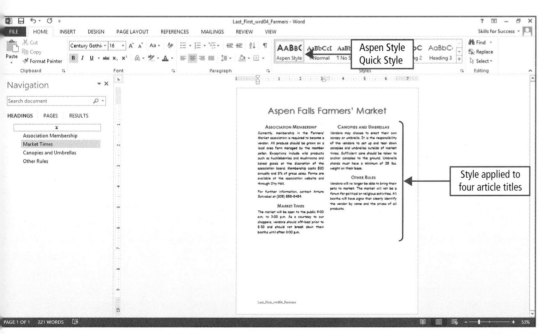

Aspen Style Quick Style

Style applied to four article titles

Figure 4

7. With the subtitle text still selected, on the **Home tab**, in the **Styles group**, click the **More arrow** ⬇, and then below the **Styles gallery**, click **Create a Style**.

8. In the **Create New Style from Formatting** dialog box, under **Name**, type Aspen Style Compare your screen with **Figure 3**, and then click **OK** to add the style to the Styles gallery.

When you create a style in this manner, the style is available only in the same document. In other documents, the style will not display in the Styles gallery.

9. Click to place the insertion point in the subtitle *Canopies and Umbrellas*. On the **Home tab**, in the **Styles group**, click the **Aspen Style** thumbnail to apply the style.

10. Repeat the technique just practiced to apply the **Aspen Style** style to the *Market Times* and *Other Rules* subtitles.

11. On the **View tab**, in the **Zoom group**, click **One Page**. Hide the formatting marks, and then compare your screen with **Figure 4**.

The styles that you create can be modified and updated in the same manner that pre-built styles are updated.

12. Save 🖫 the document.

■ **You have completed Skill 4 of 10**

▶ To make a paragraph stand out in a document, you can add a paragraph border or paragraph shading.

▶ You can use page borders to frame flyers or posters, giving the document a more professional look.

1. On the **Design tab**, in the **Page Background group**, click the **Page Borders** button.

2. On the **Page Border tab** of the **Borders and Shading** dialog box, under **Setting**, click **Box**.

3. Click the **Color arrow**, and then in the first row under **Theme Colors**, click the last color—**Green**, **Accent 6**. Click the **Width arrow**, and then click **1½ pt**. Compare your screen with **Figure 1**, and then click **OK** to add the page border.

4. Change the **Zoom** to **100%**, and then display the formatting marks.

5. At the end of the first article, click in the paragraph starting *For further information*.

6. On the **Home tab**, in the **Paragraph group**, click the **Borders arrow**, and then at the bottom of the gallery, click **Borders and Shading**.

7. In the **Borders and Shading** dialog box, click the **Shading tab**. Click the **Fill arrow**, and then under **Theme Colors**, click the last color in the third row—**Green**, **Accent 6**, **Lighter 60%**. Compare your screen with **Figure 2**.

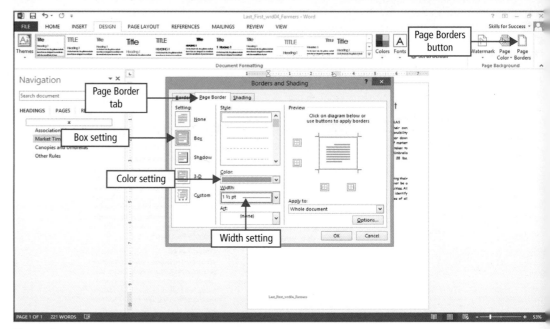

Figure 1

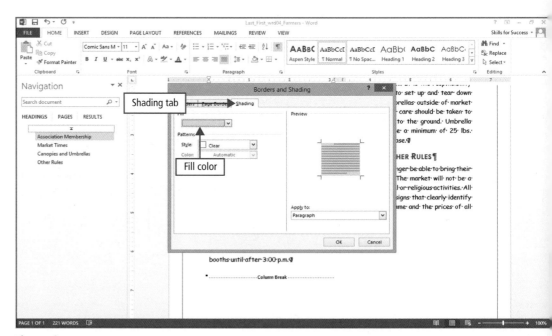

Figure 2

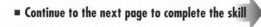 **Continue to the next page to complete the skill**

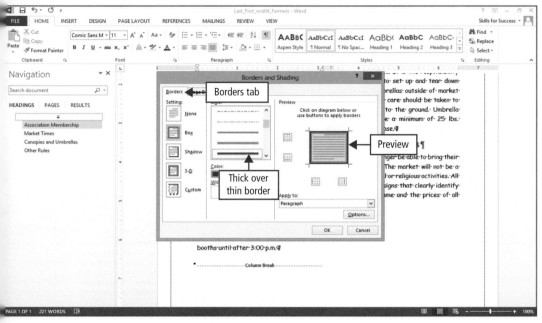

Figure 3

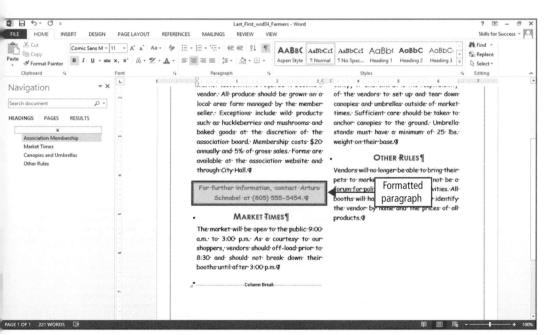

Figure 4

8. In the **Borders and Shading** dialog box, click the **Borders tab**.

9. On the **Borders tab**, under **Setting**, click **Box**. Under **Style**, scroll down and select the first line style with a thick upper line and a thin bottom line.

10. Click the **Color arrow**, and then under **Theme Colors**, click the last color in the last row—**Green**, **Accent 6**, **Darker 50%**. Notice that a preview of the box displays in the Preview area, as shown in **Figure 3**.

11. Click **OK** to apply the changes and close the dialog box. **Center** ☰ the paragraph, select the text, and then apply **Bold** ⓑ.

12. In the **Font group**, click the **Font Color arrow** Ⓐ ▾, and then under **Theme Colors**, in the last row, click the first color—**White**, **Background 1**, **Darker 50%**. Deselect the text, and then compare your screen with **Figure 4**.

13. **Save** 🖫 the document.

■ **You have completed Skill 5 of 10**

▶ ***Clip art*** is an image, drawing, or photograph accessed from Microsoft Office Online and other online providers.

▶ You search for and select graphics in the Insert Pictures dialog box.

1. In the first article, click to position the insertion point to the left of *Currently, membership in*.

2. On the **Insert tab**, in the **Illustrations group**, click the **Online Pictures** button to display the Insert Pictures dialog box.

   The Insert Pictures dialog box is used to connect with online services such as Office.com Clip Art and your SkyDrive. You may have additional providers listed, and if you are not signed in, your SkyDrive may not display.

3. In the **Insert Pictures** dialog box, in the Office.com **Clip Art** box, type grape farmer and then click the **Search** button. Point to the figure shown in **Figure 1**.

   Because the clip art available at Office.com can change, your search results may be different. If the image is no longer available, choose another image for this project and adjust the steps as necessary.

4. Click the clip to select it, and then click the **Insert** button to insert it into the document. Compare your screen with **Figure 2**.

■ **Continue to the next page to complete the skill**

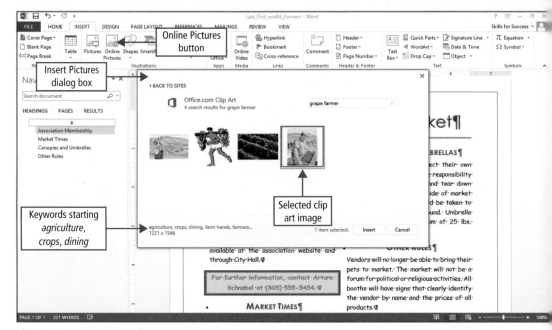

Figure 1

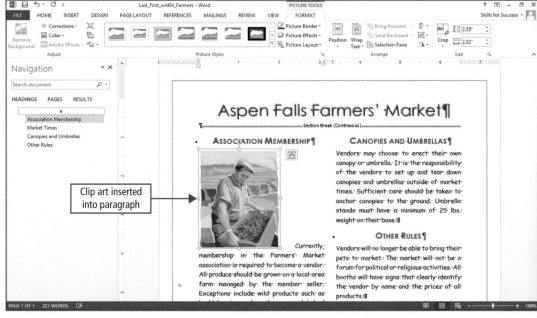

Figure 2

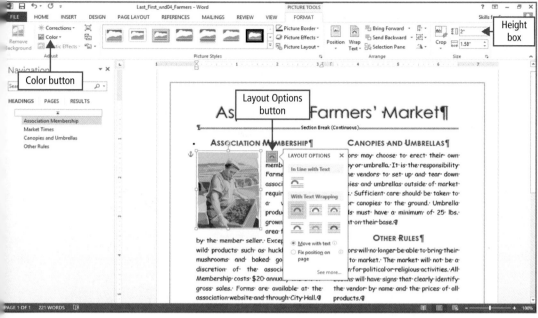

Color button

Layout Options button

Height box

Figure 3

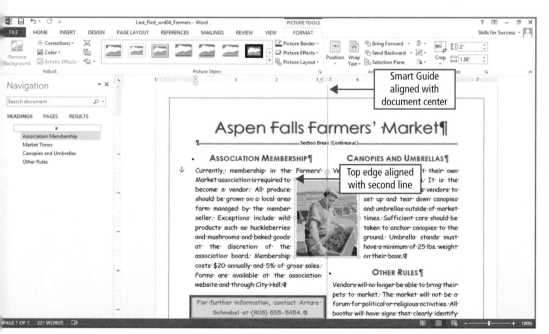

Smart Guide aligned with document center

Top edge aligned with second line

Figure 4

5. With the image selected, on the **Format tab**, in the **Adjust group**, click **Color**, and then point to several thumbnails to preview their effects.

6. In the **Recolor gallery**, in the second row, click the last choice—**Green, Accent color 6 Dark**.

   You can change picture adjustments and styles to clip art in the same manner you modify photographs. Here, the look and feel of the clip has been changed from a painting to a historic photograph using the same color tones as in the titles and subtitles.

7. With the image selected, click the **Layout Options** button, and then under **With Text Wrapping**, click the first thumbnail—**Square**.

8. On the **Format tab**, in the **Size group**, change the **Height** value to **2"**. Compare your screen with **Figure 3**.

9. Point to the image to display the pointer. Drag the image to position it as shown in **Figure 4**.

10. **Save** the document.

■ **You have completed Skill 6 of 10**

► A ***SmartArt graphic*** is a pre-built visual representation of information.

► You can choose from many different SmartArt layouts to communicate your message or ideas.

1. Press Ctrl + End to move the insertion point to the end of the document. On the **Insert tab**, in the **Illustrations group**, click the **SmartArt** button.

2. In the **Choose a SmartArt Graphic** dialog box, scroll down and look at the various types of layouts that are available.

3. On the left side of the dialog box, click **Cycle**. Click the first layout—**Basic Cycle**, and then compare your screen with **Figure 1**.

4. In the **Choose a SmartArt Graphic** dialog box, read the description of the selected layout, and then click **OK**. Compare your screen with **Figure 2**. If the Text pane displays to the left of the graphic, click the Text Pane button on the left border to close it.

   When SmartArt is selected, two SmartArt Tools contextual tabs display—Design and Format. Inside the graphic, each shape has a text placeholder.

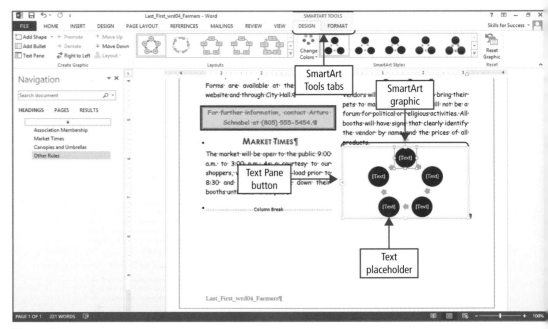

Figure 1

Figure 2

■ **Continue to the next page to complete the skill**

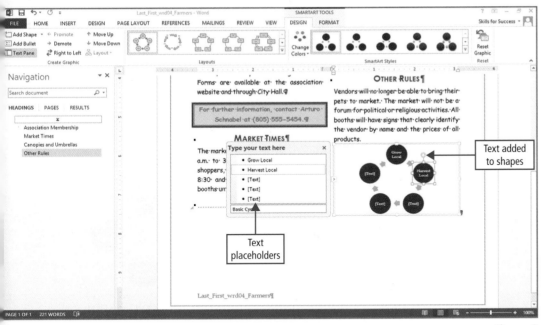

Figure 3

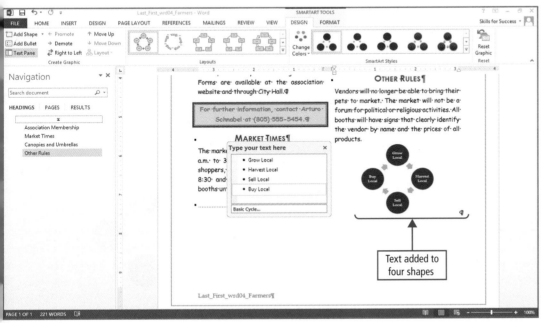

Figure 4

5. In the upper shape, click the **[Text]** placeholder, and then type Grow Local

6. In the middle-right shape, click the **[Text]** placeholder, and then type Harvest Local

   As you work with SmartArt, the shape and font sizes automatically adjust to the contents.

7. On the left border, click the **Text Pane** button, and then compare your screen with **Figure 3**.

   The Text pane displays text as bullets and provides an alternate method of entering text. In the pane, you can remove or add shapes by removing or adding bullets, and you can insert subordinate shapes by indenting bullets.

8. In the **Text** pane, click the first **[Text]** placeholder—the third bullet, and then type Sell Local Notice that while you type in the bulleted list, the text also displays in the third SmartArt shape.

   To move to the next [Text] shape in the Text pane, you can also press Enter.

9. Press ↓ to move to the next bullet, and then type Buy Local

10. With the insertion point to the right of the text *Buy Local*, press Delete to remove the fifth shape, and then compare your screen with **Figure 4**.

11. **Close** ✕ the Text pane, and then **Save** 🖫 the document.

■ **You have completed Skill 7 of 10**

▶ You can resize an entire SmartArt graphic, or you can resize its individual shapes.

1. Click the border of the SmartArt graphic to select the graphic without selecting any of its shapes.

2. Click the **Format tab**, and then click the **Arrange group** button. Click **Position**, and then under **With Text Wrapping**, click the last thumbnail—**Position in Bottom Right with Square Text Wrapping**.

> On smaller monitors, some groups collapse and are accessed only by clicking a button. If you are working with a larger monitor, your Arrange and Size groups may not be collapsed.

3. Scroll to display the SmartArt graphic. On the **Format tab**, click the **Size group** button, change **Height** value to **2.7"**, and then compare your screen with **Figure 1**.

> When you change the height or width of a SmartArt graphic, the graphic width is not resized proportionally.

4. In the SmartArt graphic, click the first shape, and then click its border so that the border is a solid line. Press and hold **Ctrl** while clicking the other three shapes. Compare your screen with **Figure 2**.

■ **Continue to the next page to complete the skill**

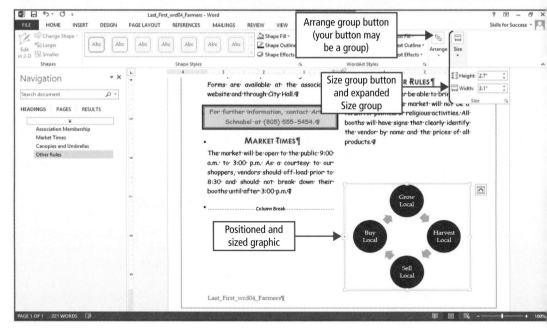

Figure 1

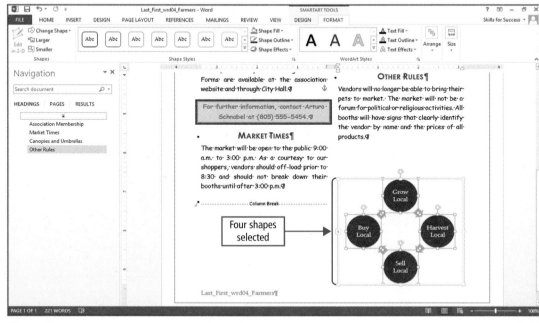

Figure 2

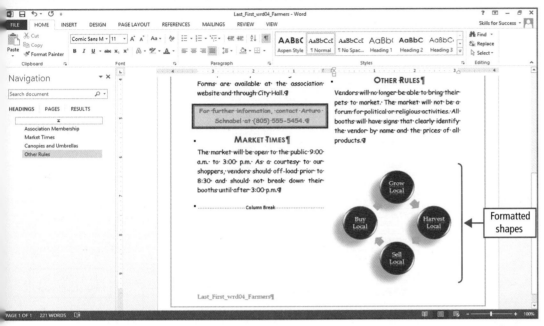

Figure 3

Figure 4

5. With all four shapes selected, on the **Format tab**, in the **Shape Styles group**, click the **Shape Fill** button. Under **Theme Colors**, click the last color in the last row—**Green, Accent 6, Darker 50%**.

6. In the **Shape Styles group**, click the **Shape Effects** button. Point to **Preset**, and then under **Presets**, click the first effect in the second row—**Preset 5**.

7. With all four shapes still selected, in the **WordArt Styles group**, click the **Text Effects** button. Point to **Reflection**, and then under **Reflection Variations**, click the first effect—**Tight Reflection, touching**.

8. Click in the text to deselect the SmartArt graphic, and then compare your screen with **Figure 3**.

9. On the **View tab**, in the **Zoom group**, click the **One Page** button. Hide the formatting marks, and then compare your screen with **Figure 4**.

10. In the **Zoom group**, click the **100%** button, and then **Save** 🖫 the document.

11. **Close** ⊠ the document window.

■ **You have completed Skill 8 of 10**

▶ The *mail merge* feature is used to customize letters or labels by combining a main document with a data source.

▶ The *main document* contains the text that remains constant; the *data source* contains the information—such as names and addresses—that changes with each letter or label.

1. Start **Word 2013**, and then open the student data file **wrd04_FarmerAddresses**. Save the document in your **Word Chapter 4** folder as Last_First_wrd04_FarmerAddresses Add the **FileName** field to the footer.

2. Take a moment to examine the table of names and addresses.

> This table will be the data source for the mailing labels you will create to mail the farmers' market newsletter.

3. Point to the table's lower left corner, and then click the **Insert** button ⊕ to add a new row.

4. In the new row, enter the information for Sweet Honey Farm, 173 Valley View Rd, Aspen Falls, CA, 93464, (805) 555-1821 and then compare your screen with **Figure 1**.

5. **Save** 🖫, and then **Close** ✕ the document.

6. Start **Word 2013**, and then on the start page, click **Blank document**. Save the file in your chapter folder as Last_First_wrd04_FarmerLabels

7. Click the **Mailings tab**. In the **Start Mail Merge group**, click the **Start Mail Merge** button, and then click **Labels** to open the Label Options dialog box, as shown in **Figure 2**.

■ Continue to the next page to complete the skill

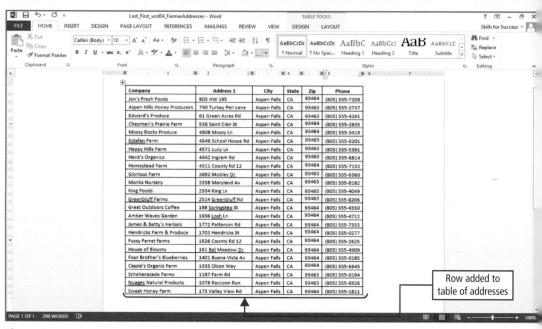

Figure 1

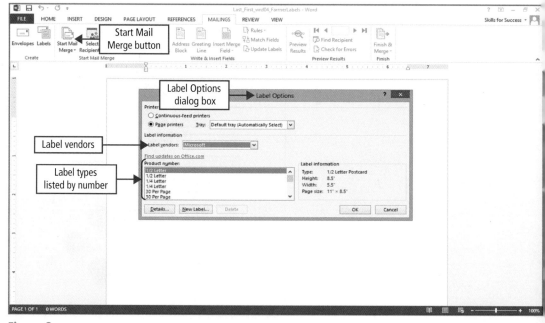

Figure 2

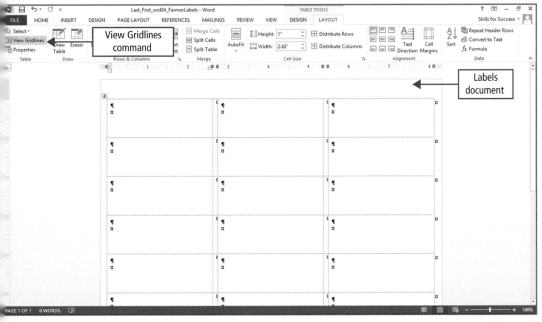

Figure 3

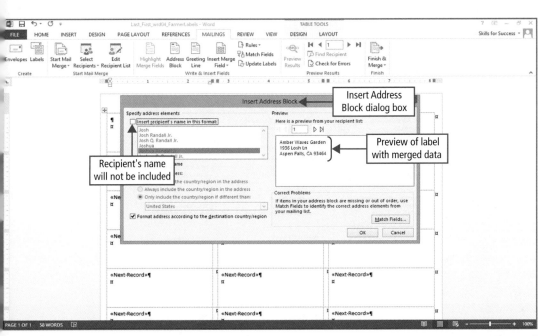

Figure 4

8. Under **Label information**, click the **Label vendors arrow**, scroll down, and then click **Avery US Letter**. Under **Product number**, click a label, and then press 5. Scroll down and click **5160 Easy Peel Address Labels**, and then click **OK**.

9. Compare your screen with **Figure 3**. If necessary, on the Layout tab, in the Table group, select View Gridlines and display the formatting marks.

> The Avery 5160 address label has precut sheets with three columns of 10 labels each.

10. On the **Mailings tab**, in the **Start Mail Merge group**, click the **Select Recipients** button, and then click **Use an Existing List**.

11. In the **Select Data Source** dialog box, navigate to your **Word Chapter 4** folder, click **Last_First_wrd04_ FarmerAddresses**, and then click **Open**.

12. In the **Start Mail Merge group**, click the **Edit Recipient List** button. In the row of column headings, click the **Company** heading one time to sort the list by company names, and then click **OK**.

13. In the **Write & Insert Fields group**, click the **Address Block** button. In the **Insert Address Block** dialog box, under **Specify address elements**, clear the **Insert recipient's name in this format** check box. Compare your screen with **Figure 4**, and then click **OK**.

> **Merge fields** merge and display data from specific columns in the data source. They are surrounded by nonprinting characters—for example, «AddressBlock» and «Next Record».

14. **Save** ⊞, and then **Close** ✕ the document.

■ **You have completed Skill 9 of 10**

► When you open a merge document, you need to confirm that you want to open the document. Confirmation runs an **SQL Select Query**—a command that selects data from a data source based on the criteria you specify.

1. Start **Word 2013**, and then open **Last_First_wrd04FarmerLabels**. Compare your screen with **Figure 1**.

   The message informs you that data from the data source will be placed in the document. If you have moved to a different computer or are saving to a network drive, you may also be asked to locate the data source file—*Last_First_wrd04_FarmersAddresses*.

2. Read the message, and then click **Yes** to open the labels document.

   If you encounter a similar message when opening a document that you did not expect to contain merged data, you should click No to protect your privacy.

3. On the **Mailings tab**, in the **Preview Results group**, click the **Preview Results** button. In the **Write & Insert Fields group**, click **Update Labels**.

   The Update Labels command is used to fill in the data for the remaining rows in the data source.

4. Click the **Table Selector** button ⊞ to select all the labels. Open the **Paragraph** dialog box, change the **Spacing Before** to **0 pt**, and then click **OK**.

5. With the text still selected, click the **Layout tab**, and then in the **Alignment group**, click the **Align Center Left** button 🗏 to vertically center the label text. Deselect the table, and then compare your screen with **Figure 2**.

■ **Continue to the next page to complete the skill** ➤

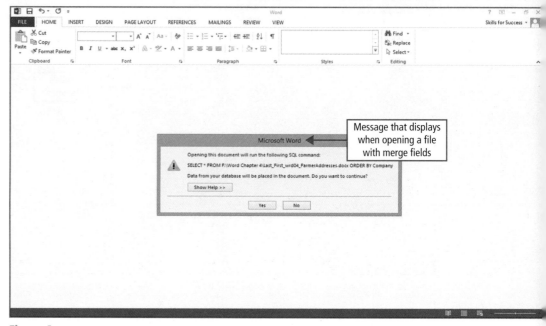

Figure 1

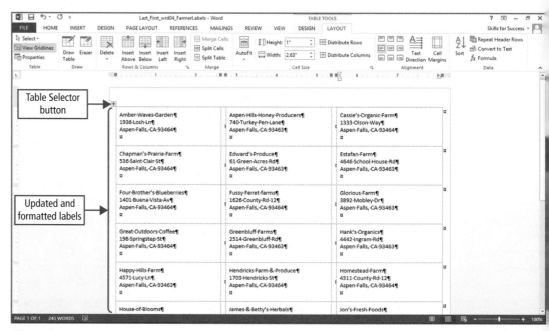

Figure 2

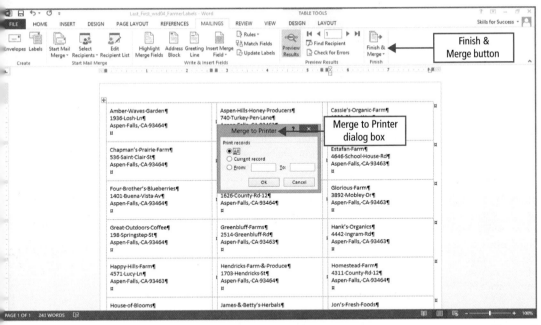

Figure 3

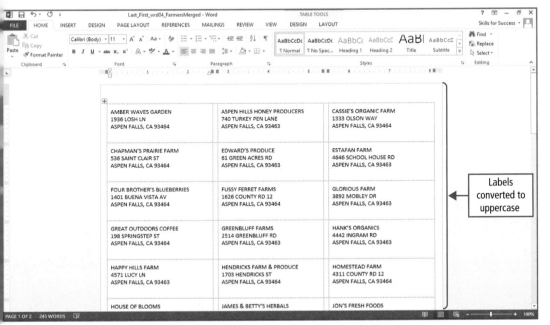

Figure 4

6. Click the **Mailings tab**. In the **Finish group**, click the **Finish & Merge** button, and then click **Print Documents**. Compare your screen with **Figure 3**.

> Typically a merge is complete by sending the document with its merged data to a printer with the label sheet(s) inserted into the appropriate printer tray.

7. In the **Merge to Printer** dialog box, click **Cancel**. In the **Finish group**, click the **Finish & Merge** button, and then click **Edit Individual Documents**. In the **Merge to New Document** dialog box, click **OK** to create a new document named *Labels1*.

> When you merge to a new document, the merge fields are replaced with the corresponding data from each row in the data source and the new document does not contain any merge fields.

8. Save 🖫 the document in your **Word Chapter 4** folder as Last_First_wrd04_FarmersMerged Add the **FileName** field to the footer.

9. Select the table, and then click the **Home tab**. In the **Font group**, click the **Change Case arrow** Aa▾, and then click **UPPERCASE**.

10. Click to deselect the table, and then hide the formatting marks. Press Ctrl + Home , and then compare your screen with **Figure 4**.

11. Save 🖫, and then **Close** ✕ all open documents. Submit the files as directed by your instructor.

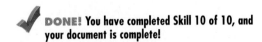
DONE! You have completed Skill 10 of 10, and your document is complete!

More Skills

The following More Skills are located at **www.pearsonhighered.com/skills**

More Skills Optimize Documents for Read Mode

Read Mode is a view used to view, but not edit, a Word document. If you plan to share a document with others using Read Mode, you can optimize the headings and graphics for Read Mode and set the document to always open in Read Mode.

In More Skills 11, you will format headings and graphics to work in Read Mode, adjust Read Mode options, and protect a document so that it always opens in Read Mode.

To begin, open your web browser, navigate to www.pearsonhighered.com/skills, locate the name of your textbook, and then follow the instructions on the website.

More Skills Work in Outline View

When you work with a document, assigning outline levels to various parts of the text can be helpful. When you use outline levels, you can move blocks of text around in a document just by moving an outline item—all associated text moves with the outline item.

In More Skills 12, you will open a document, switch to Outline view, create outline levels, and move outline text.

To begin, open your web browser, navigate to www.pearsonhighered.com/skills, locate the name of your textbook, and then follow the instructions on the website.

More Skills Manage Document Properties

Document properties are the detailed information about your document that can help you identify or organize your files, including the name of the author, the title, and keywords. Some document properties are added to a document when you first create it. You can add others as necessary.

In More Skills 13, you will open a document, view its properties, and add additional properties.

To begin, open your web browser, navigate to www.pearsonhighered.com/skills, locate the name of your textbook, and then follow the instructions on the website.

More Skills Save Documents as Web Pages

When you plan to save a Word document as a web page, you can work in Web Layout view to preview the document as a web page. When you have the document formatted the way you want, you can save the document in a format as a web page, and then view in a web browser.

In More Skills 14, you will work with a document in Web Layout view and then save it as a web page. You will then open the file in Internet Explorer.

To begin, open your web browser, navigate to www.pearsonhighered.com/skills, locate the name of your textbook, and then follow the instructions on the website.

Please note that there are no additional projects to accompany the More Skills Projects, and they are not covered in the End-of-Chapter projects.

The following table summarizes the **SKILLS AND PROCEDURES** covered in this chapter.

Skills Number	Task	Step	Icon
1	Change the Fonts theme	Design tab → Document Formatting group → Fonts	
1	Justify text	Home tab → Paragraph group → Justify	☰
1	Create columns	Page Layout tab → Page Setup group → Columns	
2	Modify margins	Page Layout tab → Page Setup group → Margins → Custom Margins	
2	Modify columns	Layout tab → Page Setup group → Columns → More Columns	
2	Insert column breaks	Page Layout tab → Page Setup group → Breaks → Column Break	
3	Apply text effects	Home tab → Font group → Text Effects	A ▾
4	Create styles	Home tab → Styles group → More → Create a Style	
5	Add page borders	Design tab → Page Background group → Page Border	
5	Apply paragraph borders and shading	Home tab → Paragraph group → Border → Borders and Shading	⊞ ▾
6	Insert Online Pictures	Insert tab → Illustrations group → Online Pictures	
6	Color graphics	Format tab → Adjust group → Color	
7	Create SmartArt	Insert tab → Illustrations group → SmartArt	
7	Edit SmartArt text	Type directly in each shape or type in the Text pane	
8	Format SmartArt	Use the commands in the Design and Format contextual tabs	
9	Create mail merge labels	Mailings tab → Start Mail Merge → Labels	
9	Connect to a data source	Mailings tab → Start Mail Merge group → Select Recipients	
9	Insert merge fields	Mailings tab → use the commands in the Write & Insert Fields group	
10	Preview mail merge	Mailings tab → Preview Results	
10	Fill in all labels	Mailings tab → Write & Insert Fields → Update Labels	
10	Finish mail merges	Mailings tab → Finish group → Finish & Merge → Print documents or Edit Individual Documents	

Key Terms

Online Help Skills

1. Start **Word 2013**, and then in the upper right corner of the start page, click the **Help** button ?.

2. In the **Word Help** window **Search help** box, type mail merge list and then press Enter.

3. In the search result list, click **Set up a mail merge list with Word or Outlook**. Compare your screen with **Figure 1**.

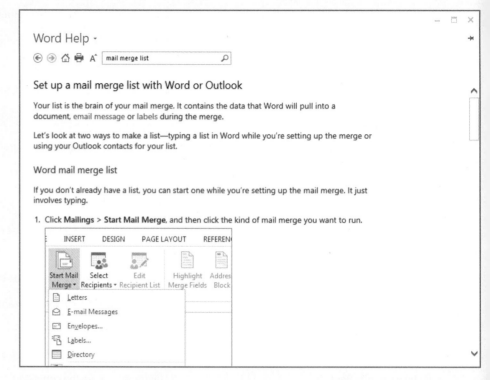

Figure 1

4. Read the article to answer the following questions: How do mail merge lists differ from external data sources? How are they the same? When might you want to use a mail merge list instead of an external data source?

Matching

Match each term in the second column with its correct definition in the first column by writing the letter of the term on the blank line in front of the correct definition.

___ **1.** You can change the font set that a theme uses by clicking the Fonts button on this tab.

___ **2.** A portion of a document that can be formatted differently from the rest of the document.

___ **3.** In the Columns gallery, the command that displays the Columns dialog box.

___ **4.** Any style that displays in a Ribbon gallery.

___ **5.** A pre-built set of decorative formats that make text stand out in a document.

___ **6.** An image, drawing, or photograph accessed from Microsoft Office Online and other online providers.

___ **7.** An extra detail or hook at the end of a character stroke.

___ **8.** A field that reserves space in a SmartArt shape but does not print until you insert your own text.

___ **9.** A feature that combines a main document and a data source to create customized letters or tables.

___ **10.** In mail merge, the command used to modify all labels based on changes made to the original label.

A Clip art

B Design

C Mail merge

D More Columns

E Placeholder

F Quick Style

G Section

H Serif

I Text effects

J Update Labels

BizSkills Video

1. What is the purpose of a cover letter and what steps can you take to make them more effective?

2. Consider the various ways to organize resume information. Which layout do you think would be best for your particular education, skills, and experience?

Multiple Choice

Choose the correct answer.

1. A font where the letters do not have serifs.
   A. Non serif
   B. Plain print
   C. Sans serif

2. The default width assigned to columns.
   A. Proportional
   B. Equal
   C. Unbalanced

3. A paragraph alignment that aligns the text with both the left and right margins.
   A. Center
   B. Justified
   C. Left/Right

4. This moves the text that follows it to the top of the next column.
   A. Page break
   B. Column break
   C. Continuous break

5. A type of break that is used to create a new section that can be formatted differently from the rest of the document.
   A. Page
   B. Column
   C. Section

6. To change the color of the background in a paragraph, add this to the text background.
   A. Shading
   B. A border
   C. Text emphasis

7. A pre-built visual representation of information in which you can enter your own text.
   A. Mail merge
   B. Online picture
   C. SmartArt

8. Used by a mail merge document, this file contains information such as names and addresses.
   A. Data source
   B. Main document
   C. Merge document

9. In a mail merge document, this document contains the text that remains constant.
   A. Data source
   B. Main document
   C. Merge document

10. When you open a mail merge document, a message displays informing that this will be run.
    A. Insert records query
    B. SQL Select Query
    C. Update fields query

Topics for Discussion

1. In this chapter, you practiced inserting a clip art image in a document. When do you think clip art images are most appropriate, and in what kind of documents might clip art images be inappropriate? If you had to create a set of rules for using clip art in a document, what would the top three rules be?

2. In this chapter, you used the mail merge feature in Word to create mailing labels. With mail merge, you can also insert one field at a time—and the fields do not have to be just names and addresses. Can you think of any situations where you might want to insert fields in a letter or another document?

Skills Review

MyITLab® Grader

To complete this project, you will need the following files:

- wrd04_SRUtilities
- wrd04_SRAddresses

You will save your files as:

- Last_First_wrd04_SRUtilities
- Last_First_wrd04_SRLabels

1. Start **Word 2013**, and then open the student data file **wrd04_SRUtilities**. Save the file in your chapter folder as Last_First_wrd04_SRUtilities Add the **FileName** field to the footer.

2. Locate the subtitle *Take the Lead with LEDs*, and then select the document text from that point to the end of the document. On the **Page Layout tab**, in the **Page Setup group**, click the **Columns** button, and then click **Two**.

3. Position the insertion point at the beginning of the subtitle *Free Energy Audits*. On the **Page Layout tab**, in the **Page Setup group**, click the **Breaks** button, and then click **Column**. Compare your screen with **Figure 1**.

4. Select the title *Utility News*. On the **Home tab**, in the **Font group**, click the **Text Effects and Typography** button. Point to **Shadow**, and then click the first choice under **Outer—Offset Diagonal Bottom Right**.

5. Select the subtitle *Take the Lead with LEDs*, and then click the **Font Dialog Box Launcher**. Under **Effects**, select the **Small caps** check box, and then click **OK**. In the **Paragraph group**, click the **Center** button.

6. With the subtitle still selected, in the **Styles group**, click the **More** button, and then click **Create a Style**. In the **Create New Style from Formatting** dialog box, name the style Utility Subtitle and then press Enter.

7. Click in the second subtitle—*Free Energy Audits*. On the **Home tab**, in the **Styles group**, click the **Utility Subtitle** thumbnail. Compare your screen with **Figure 2**.

8. On the **Insert tab**, in the **Illustrations group**, click the **Online Pictures** button. In the **Insert Pictures** dialog box, in the **Search Office.com** box, type female architects and then click **Search**.

9. Click the image shown in **Figure 3** (or a similar image if this one is not available), and then click the **Insert** button.

- Continue to the next page to complete this Skills Review

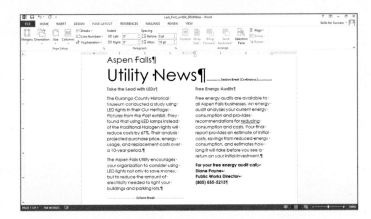

Figure 1

Figure 2

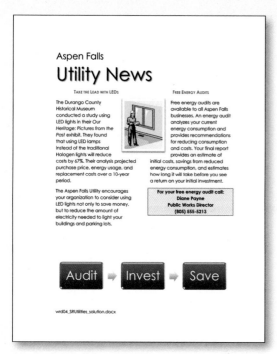

Figure 3

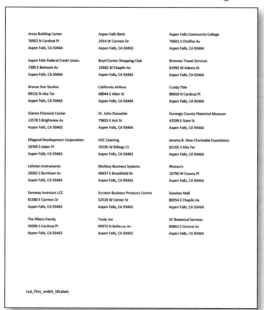

Figure 4

10. Click the picture's **Layout Options** button, and then click **Square**. On the **Format tab**, in the **Size group**, change the **Width** to **1.5"**. Use the alignment guides to center the image between the side margins and align the top with the paragraph that begins, *The Durango County*.

11. With the clip art graphic still selected, click the **Format tab**, and then apply the first picture style—**Simple Frame, White**.

12. Click in the last paragraph in the document. In the **Paragraph group**, click the **Borders arrow**, and then click **Borders and Shading**. In the **Borders and Shading** dialog box, click **Box**, and then click the **Shading tab**. Click the **Fill arrow**, and then click the ninth color in the second row—**Orange, Accent 5, Lighter 80%**. Click **OK**, and then apply the **Center** paragraph alignment.

13. On the **Insert tab**, in the **Illustrations group**, click the **SmartArt** button. Click **Process**, click the first layout—**Basic Process**, and then click **OK**.

14. Click the SmartArt's border, and then click the **Format tab**. Click the **Arrange group** button, click **Position**, and then click the **Position in Bottom Center with Square Text Wrapping** thumbnail. Set the **Height** to **1.75"** and **Width** to **6.2"**.

15. On the **Design tab**, in the **SmartArt Styles group**, click the **More** button, and then click the first style under **3-D—Polished**.

16. For the three bullets, type Audit, Invest, and Save Compare your document with Figure 3, and then **Save** and **Close** the document.

17. Start **Word 2013**, and then create a blank document. On the **Mailings tab**, click the **Start Mail Merge** button, and then click **Labels**. In the **Label Options** dialog box, verify that **Avery US Letter** is selected. Under **Product number**, click **5160**, and then click **OK**. In the **Start Mail Merge group**, click **Select Recipients**, click **Use an Existing List**, and then locate and open **wrd04_SRAddresses**.

18. In the **Write & Insert Fields group**, click the **Address Block** button, clear the **Insert recipient's name in this format** check box, and then click **OK**. In the **Write & Insert Fields group**, click the **Update Labels** button.

19. In the **Finish group**, click the **Finish & Merge** button, click **Edit Individual Documents**, and then click **OK**. **Save** the document in your chapter folder as Last_First_wrd04_SRLabels and then add the **FileName** field to the footer. Compare your document with Figure 4.

20. Click **Save**, and then **Close** all other Word documents without saving changes.

✔ **DONE! You have completed this Skills Review**

Skills Assessment 1 MyITLab® Grader

To complete this document, you will need the following files:

- wrd04_SA1Racers
- wrd04_SA1Addresses

You will save your documents as:

- Last_First_wrd04_SA1Racers
- Last_First_wrd04_SA1Merged

Figure 1

1. Start **Word 2013**, and then open the student data file **wrd04_SA1Racers**. Save the file to your chapter folder as Last_First_wrd04_SA1Racers and then add the **FileName** field to the footer.

2. Apply the **Slice** theme, and then change the fonts theme to **Candara**. For the title *Aspen Falls Triathlon,* apply the last text effect—**Fill - Light Turquoise, Background 2, Inner Shadow**.

3. Use Online Pictures and the search term triathlon to insert the clip art shown in **Figure 1**. If that clip art image is not available, find a similar image. Set the graphic's height to **1.6"**, and its position to **Position in Top Left with Square Text Wrapping**. Color the picture to **Light Turquoise, Background color 2 Light** (first column, third row).

4. Starting with the subtitle *This Year's Race* and ending with the phone number, apply the two-column layout and change column spacing to **0.3"**. Insert a column break at the beginning of the *This Year's Sponsors* subtitle.

5. Create a new Quick Style named Racers Subtitle based on the *This Year's Race* subtitle, and then apply the style to the other subtitle—*This Year's Sponsors*.

6. For the paragraph starting *Consider becoming a sponsor,* apply a box border with a **1½ pt** wide line, and a border color of **Orange, Accent 5** (ninth column, first row). For the same paragraph, set the shading to **Orange, Accent 5, Lighter 80%** (ninth column, second row).

7. Insert a SmartArt graphic with the **Basic Timeline** layout (second column, fourth row under **Process**). Set the SmartArt's position to **Position in Bottom Center with Square Text Wrapping**. Change the height to **2"** and width to **5.6"**.

8. Change the SmartArt text to Swim, Bike, and then Run as shown in Figure 1. **Save**, and then **Close** the document.

Figure 2

9. Create a blank document, and then start a **Labels** mail merge using **Avery US Letter** label 5160. Use **wrd04_SA1Addresses** as the data source. Insert an **Address Block** clearing the option to include the recipient names, and then update the labels.

10. Merge the labels to a new document, and then edit that document by converting all the text to uppercase. Save the document in your chapter folder as Last_First_wrd04_SA1Merged and then insert the **FileName** field into the footer. Compare with Figure 2, and then **Save** and **Close** the document. **Close** the original mail merge document without saving changes.

 DONE! You have completed Skills Assessment 1

Skills Assessment 2

To complete this document, you will need the following files:

- wrd04_SA2Center
- wrd04_SA2Addresses

You will save your documents as:

- Last_First_wrd04_SA2Center
- Last_First_wrd04_SA2Merged

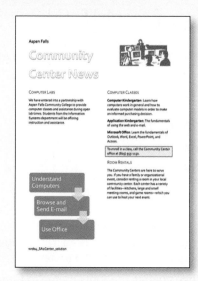

Figure 1

1. Start **Word 2013**, and then open the student data file **wrd04_SA2Center**. Save the file in your chapter folder as Last_First_wrd04_SA2Center and then add the **FileName** field to the footer.

2. Apply the **Retrospect** theme, and then change the fonts theme to **Corbel**. For the title *Community Center News*, apply the **Fill - White Outline**, **Accent 1**, **Shadow** text effect (fourth column, first row).

3. Use Online Pictures and the search term computer class to insert the clip art shown in **Figure 1**. If that clip art image is not available, find a similar image. Set the graphic's height to **1.2"**, and its position to **Position in Top Right with Square Text Wrapping**. Color the picture to **Green**, **Accent color 6 Light** (last column, last row).

4. Starting with the subtitle *Computer Labs* and ending with the last paragraph, apply the two-column layout and change column spacing to **0.7"**. Insert a column break at the beginning of the *Computer Classes* subtitle.

5. Create a new **Quick Style** named Center Subtitle based on the *Computer Labs* subtitle, and then apply the style to the other two subtitles— *Computer Classes* and *Room Rentals*.

6. For the paragraph starting *To enroll in a class*, apply a box border with a 1½ pt wide line, and a border color of **Brown**, **Accent 3** (seventh column, first row). For the same paragraph, set the shading to **Green**, **Accent 6**, **Lighter 80%** (last column, second row).

7. Insert a SmartArt graphic with the **Staggered Process** layout (third column, sixth row under **Process**). Set the SmartArt's position to **Position in Bottom Left with Square Text Wrapping**, and then change the shape's width and height to **3.0"**.

8. In the SmartArt shapes, change the text to Understand Computers, Browse and Send E-mail, and then Use Office as shown in **Figure 1**. **Save**, and then **Close** the document.

9. Create a blank document, and then start a **Labels** mail merge using **Avery US Letter** label 5160. Use **wrd04_SA2Addresses** as the data

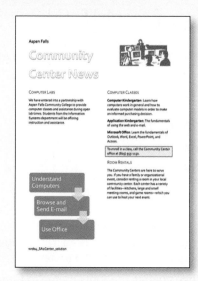

Figure 2

source. Insert an **Address Block** accepting the default settings, and then update the labels.

10. Merge the labels to a new document and then edit that document by converting all the text to uppercase. Save the document in your chapter folder as Last_First_wrd04_SA2Merged and then add the **FileName** field to the footer. Compare with **Figure 2**, and then **Save** and **Close** the document. **Close** the original mail merge document without saving changes.

 DONE! You have completed Skills Assessment 2

Visual Skills Check

To complete this document, you will need the following file:

- wrd04_VSRecycle

You will save your document as:

- Last_First_wrd04_VSRecycle

Start **Word 2013**, and then open the student data file **wrd04_VSRecycle**. Save the file in your chapter folder as Last_First_w04_VSRecycle Add the **FileName** field in the footer.

To complete this project, format the file as shown in **Figure 1**. The theme is **Ion Boardroom** with the **Tw Cen MT** fonts theme. The title is **48** points, the text effect is **Gradient Fill - Lavender**, **Accent 1**, **Reflection**, and the font color has been changed to **Dark Purple**, **Text 2**, **Lighter 40%**. The graphic can be located and inserted from microsoft.com Clip Art—use a substitute if this image is not available. The clip art height has been set to **1"**.

Apply the two-column layout with **0.7"** between columns, and then add a column break as shown in **Figure 1**. Use the formatting in the first subtitle to create a Quick Style named Recycle Subtitle and then apply that style to the second subtitle. The shaded paragraph uses the default **Shadow** border, and the fill color is **Lavender**, **Accent 5**, **Lighter 80%**.

Insert and format the SmartArt as shown in **Figure 1**. The layout is **Text Cycle**, the height is **4"**, and the width is **6.5"**. The SmartArt style has been changed to **Powder**. Submit the project as directed by your instructor.

 DONE! You have completed Visual Skills Check

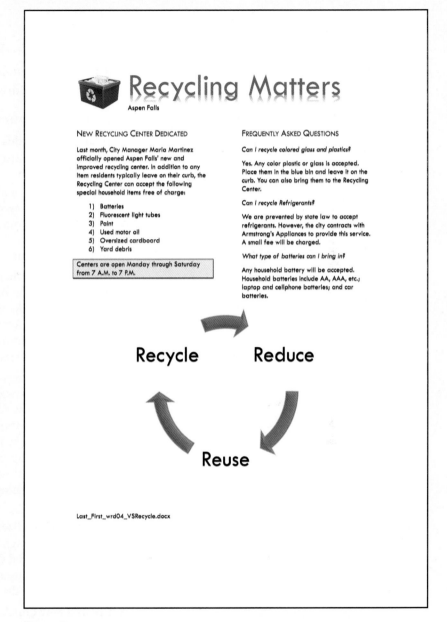

Figure 1

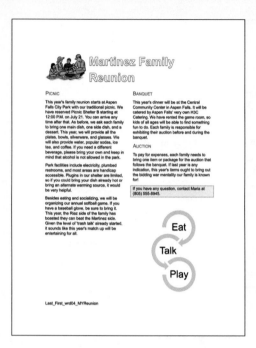

Figure 1

Figure 2

My Skills

To complete this document, you will need the following files:

- wrd04_MYReunion
- wrd04_MYAddresses

You will save your documents as:

- Last_First_wrd04_MYReunion
- Last_First_wrd04_MYLabels

1. Start **Word 2013**, and then open the student data file **wrd04_MYReunion**. Save the file to your chapter folder as Last_First_wrd04_MYReunion and then add the **FileName** field to the footer.

2. Apply the **Facet** theme, and then change the fonts theme to **Arial**. For the title *Martinez Family Reunion,* apply the **Fill - White Outline**, **Accent 1**, **Shadow** text effect (fourth column, first row), and then change the **Font size** to **32**.

3. Use Online Pictures and the search term family picnic to insert the clip art shown in **Figure 1**. If that clip art image is not available, find a similar image. Set the graphic's height to **1"**, and its position to **Position in Top Left with Square Text Wrapping**. Color the picture to **Brown**, **Accent color 6 Dark** (last column, second row).

4. Starting with the subtitle *Picnic* and ending with the last paragraph, apply the two-column layout and change the column spacing to **0.3"**. Insert a column break at the beginning of the *Banquet* subtitle.

5. Create a new **Quick Style** named Reunion Subtitle based on the *Picnic* subtitle, and then apply the style to the other two subtitles—*Banquet* and *Auction.*

6. For the paragraph starting *If you have any questions,* apply a box border with a 1½ **pt**

wide line, and a border color of **Dark Green**, **Accent 2** (sixth column, first row). For the same paragraph, set the shading to **Dark Green**, **Accent 2**, **Lighter 80%** (sixth column, second row).

7. Insert a SmartArt graphic with the **Circle Arrow Process** layout. Set the SmartArt's position to **Position in Bottom Right with Square Text Wrapping**, and then change the graphic's height to **3.2"** and width to **3"**.

8. In the SmartArt shapes, change the text to Eat, Talk, and then Play as shown in **Figure 1**. **Save**, and then **Close** the document.

9. Create a blank document, and then start a **Labels** mail merge using **Avery US Letter** label **5160**. Use **wrd04_MYAddresses** as the data source. Insert an **Address Block** accepting the default settings, and then update the labels.

10. Merge the labels to a new document, and then edit that document by converting all the text to uppercase. Save the document in your chapter folder as Last_First_wrd04_MYLabels and then add the **FileName** field to the footer. Compare with **Figure 2**, and then **Save** and **Close** the document. **Close** the original mail merge document without saving changes.

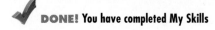 **DONE! You have completed My Skills**

Skills Challenge 1

To complete this document, you will need the following file:

- wrd04_SC1Fire

You will save your document as:

- Last_First_wrd04_SC1Fire

Open the student data file, **wrd04_SC1Fire**, and then save it in your chapter folder as Last_First_wrd04_SC1Fire Add the **FileName** field to the footer.

Using the techniques practiced in this chapter, format and layout the document as a two-column newsletter. Apply text effects to the title so that it stands out from the rest of the text. Locate and insert a clip art graphic from microsoft.com that works well with the newsletter theme of fire protection. Size, format, and position the clip art to pull the reader's eye from

the title to the newsletter text. Format the subtitles so they stand out from the articles, and then create a style for that format. Apply the style to both subtitles. Replace the text *Air → Fuel → Heat* with a SmartArt graphic that illustrates this relationship as a triangle. Format, size, and position the graphic to fill the bottom of the newsletter.

Submit the completed newsletter as directed by your instructor.

 DONE! You have completed Skills Challenge 1

Skills Challenge 2

To complete this document, you will need the following file:

- wrd04_SC2Addresses

You will save your document as:

- Last_First_wrd04_SC2Merged

Create a blank Word document, and then start the merge process to create Avery 5160 mailing labels. For the recipient's list, use **wrd04_SC2Addresses**. To complete the labels document, you will need to click the **Match Fields** button in the **Insert Address Block** dialog box and then use the **Match Fields** dialog box to match the columns in the data source. When you have inserted the Address Block with all the fields

matched, update all the labels, and then merge the labels to a new document. Save the merged document as Last_First_wrd04_SC2Merged Close the merged document, and then close the original document without saving it. Submit the merged document as directed by your instructor.

 DONE! You have completed Skills Challenge 2

CAPSTONE PROJECT

Student data files needed for this project:
wrd_CPVisitUs
wrd_CPFestival

You will save your file as:
Last_First_wrd_CPVisitUs

1. Start **Word 2013**, and then open the student data file that came with this project, **wrd_CPVisitUs**. Use the **Save As** dialog box to save the file to your drive with the name Last_First_wrd_CPVisitUs Insert the **FileName** field in the footer.

2. Use **Find and Replace** to replace all occurrences of *City of Aspen Falls* with Aspen Falls

3. Change the document's theme to **Ion Boardroom**, and then in the first line of the letterhead, change the font size to **18**, apply the **Small caps** effect, and then set the character spacing to **Expanded** by **2 pt**.

4. In the letter greeting, change the word *Mrs.* to Ms.

5. In the first letter body paragraph, insert a footnote after the word *interns*. For the footnote, type the following: This intern is majoring in recreation and did this analysis as a class project.

6. Near the bottom of Page 1, after the text *City Hall*, insert a manual page break, and then compare your screen with **Figure 1**.

7. At the top of Page 2, delete the blank paragraph, and then select the text *ASPEN FALLS*. Change the **Font** to **Verdana**, the size to 42 and then apply the **Gradient Fill - Orange**, **Accent 4**, **Outline - Accent 4** text effect.

8. For the text *Get out and join the party!*, apply **Bold** and **Italic**.

9. For the newsletter articles, starting with *Get Out!* and ending with *Borax Trail era*, apply two columns of equal width with **0.3** spacing between them.

10. For the article title, *Get Out!*, apply the **Small caps** effect, and then change the font color to the fifth theme color—**Plum**, **Accent 1**. **Center** align the paragraph, change the **Spacing Before** to **12 pt**, and then compare your screen with **Figure 2**.

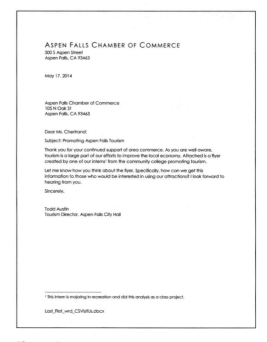

Figure 1

Figure 2

■ **Continue to the next page to complete the skill**

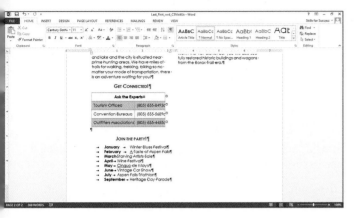

Figure 3

Figure 4

11. Create a new style named Article Title based on the formatting applied to the *Get Out!* title in the previous step. Apply the **Article Title** style to the other three article titles.

12. In the first article, apply a first line indent of 0.25 inches to the paragraph beginning *Aspen Falls is your gateway*. In the same paragraph, set the line spacing to **Single** (1.0), and the **Spacing Before** and **Spacing After** the paragraph to **6 pt** each. Set the paragraph's alignment to **Justified**.

13. Use **Format Painter** to apply the formatting of the paragraph formatted in the previous step to the article paragraphs beginning *Aspen Falls features, Improve your literacy*, and *If history is your bent*.

14. In the *Get Connected!* article, delete the text *Phone numbers* but not the paragraph mark, and then in the blank paragraph, insert a **2x3** table. In the table, add the following:

Tourism Office	(805) 555-8493
Convention Bureau	(805) 555-5689
Outfitters Association	(805) 555-4455

15. Add a new row above the table, and then merge the new row's cells into one cell. In the new row, type Ask the Experts

16. For the table, apply the **List Table 2 - Accent 1** table style, and then clear the **First Column** table style option. Set the cell sizes to **AutoFit to Contents**.

17. Select the table, and then on the **Layout tab**, in the **Cell Size group**, set the **Height** to 0.3". Set the alignment of the first row to **Center** and the alignment of the cells in rows 2 to 4 to **Center Left**. Compare your screen with **Figure 3**.

18. On Page 2, insert the picture from the student data file **wrd_CSFestival**. Set the picture's position to **Top Right with Square Text Wrapping**, and then set the **Width** to **3.0"**. Apply the **Rotated**, **White** picture style.

19. Insert a column break before the *Join the Party!* article title.

20. In the *Join the Party!* article, select the tabbed list, and use the **Tab** dialog box to add a **Right** tab at **1"** and a **Left** tab at **1.15"**.

21. After the last item in the tabbed list, add the following event:

December   Festival of Lights

22. In the tabbed list, **Bold** the word *December*, and then compare your screen with **Figure 4**.

23. **Save** and then **Close** Word. Submit the project as directed by your instructor.

 DONE! You have completed Word Capstone Project

Format Academic Reports and Include Information from the Web

▶ When writing a research paper, you will often be required to use the style guidelines provided or designated by your school or instructor.

▶ Many colleges require that research papers follow guidelines based on those for academic books and journals. Commonly used style guidelines for research papers include the MLA (Modern Language Association) and the APA (American Psychological Association) style manuals.

▶ When copying content from web pages, you need to follow certain guidelines to avoid copyright infringement.

▶ When paraphrasing information written by someone else, you need to add a reference to show the source of the information.

▶ When citing the source of content copied from a web page, you can copy the website's address and paste it into your citation.

© alisonhancock / Fotolia

Aspen Falls City Hall

In this Integrated Project, you will write an academic report for Donald Norris, Aspen Falls City Engineer. The report provides a brief overview of the benefits and costs of rooftop gardens—gardens placed on top of buildings in the city.

If someone has requested that you write a report for them, you should ask them for guidelines regarding length, style, and format. Many college instructors prefer the MLA style because of its simplicity, readability, and flexibility. If you are writing an academic research paper, your instructor or college will likely have specified which style and edition of that particular style you should follow. They will also likely provide the resources you need to research, organize, write, and format the paper.

In this project, you will format a research paper following the MLA style manual, seventh edition. You will research a topic on the Web, paraphrase the information, and then cite the source. Finally, you will add a Works Cited section to the report.

Time to complete this
project – 30 to 60 minutes

Student data file needed for this project:

wrd_IP01Rooftops

You will save your file as:

Last_First_wrd_IP01Rooftops

Outcome

Using the skills in this project, you will be able to
format a research paper that looks like this:

Lastname 1

Your Name

Donald Norris

Engineering

March 23, 2014

Rooftop Garden Benefits and Costs

   Rooftop gardens are growing popular as people realize the benefits they offer. People
living in urban areas, apartments, or residences with small gardening spaces now build gardens
transforming the city scape into a beautiful and relaxing environment. In addition to these
benefits, rooftop gardens can create savings that offset the cost of their initial investment and
maintenance.

   The main benefit and cost savings of roof gardens come from their insulating properties.
Roof gardens are barriers between the outside and the building environment which reduces the
energy need to cool and heat the building. Additionally, roof gardens reduce greenhouse gas
emissions and reduce air pollution. (Environmental Protection Agency)

   There are many options for the placement of a rooftop garden including wood-frame
structures. However, the primary guiding principal is that roof gardens should be built on
structures that are strong enough to support them. According to Osmundson, rooftop gardens
work best with either steel-framed buildings or buildings built from reinforced concrete. (18)

   Weaker structures or structures that require additional support be added can be
transformed into a rooftop garden. However, these can cost significantly more to build
depending on the initial weight-bearing capability of that structure.

   The main consideration when designing a rooftop garden is to consider whether the
structure can withstand not only the weight of the garden but also the water needed to maintain

At the end of this project you will be able to:

► Format academic reports in the MLA style
► Search for information on the Web
► Paraphrase information found on the Web
► Avoid copyright infringement and plagiarism
► Copy URLs and add them to a list of references
► Insert and format bibliographies in the MLA style

1. Start **Word 2013**, and then open the student data file that came with this project, **wrd_IP01Rooftops**. Use the **Save As** dialog box to save the file to your drive with the name Last_First_wrd_IP01Rooftops

2. With the insertion point at the beginning of the document and using your own name, type Your Name and then press ⎷Enter⎸.

3. Type Donald Norris and press ⎷Enter⎸. Type Engineering and press ⎷Enter⎸. Type March 23, 2014 and press ⎷Enter⎸.

4. Type Rooftop Garden Benefits and Costs and then press ⎷Enter⎸. Compare your screen with **Figure 1**.

   This paper follows the MLA guidelines. In an MLA research paper, the first four lines consist of your name, the person for whom the report was prepared, the name of the class or business, and the date. There is typically no cover page.

5. At the top of the document, double-click the header area. Type your last name, and then press ⎷SpaceBar⎸. On the **Insert tab**, in the **Header & Footer group**, click the **Page Number** button, point to **Current Position**, and then click **Plain Number**.

6. On the **Home tab**, in the **Paragraph group**, click the **Align Right** button ☰. Double-click below the header, and then compare your screen with **Figure 2**.

7. Press ⎷Ctrl⎸ + ⎷A⎸, and then change the **Font Size** to **12** and the **Font** to **Times New Roman**.

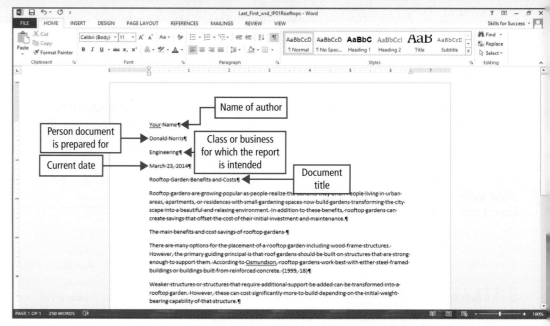

Figure 1

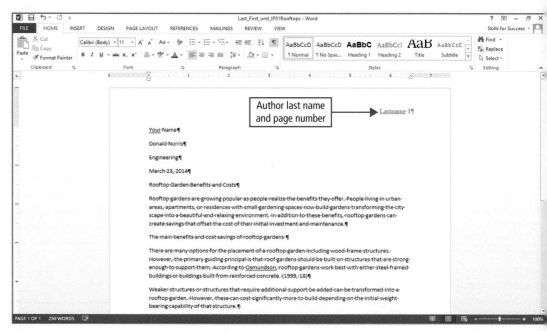

Figure 2

■ Continue to the next page to complete the skill

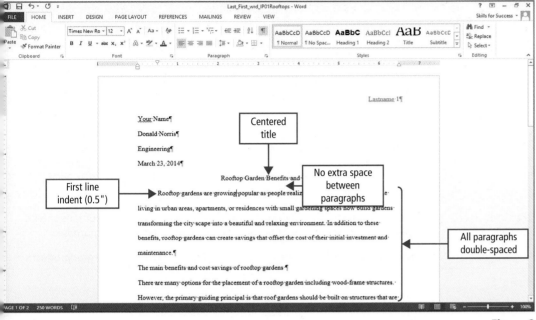

Figure 3

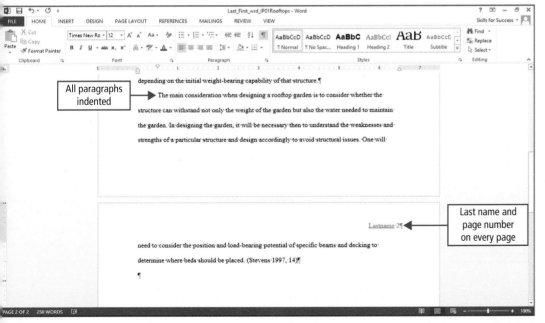

Figure 4

8. With the entire document still selected, click the **Line and Paragraph Spacing** button, and then click **2.0**. Click the **Line and Paragraph Spacing** button again, and then click **Remove Space After Paragraph**.

In an MLA research paper, the margins are all set to 1 inch—the default for a new Word document. The rest of the text—including the title, any footnotes, and the references at the end of the document—is double-spaced, with no extra space between paragraphs.

9. Press Ctrl + Home. Click in the title that begins *Rooftop Garden Benefits,* and then **Center** the paragraph.

The title and the Works Cited page headings are the only elements of the paper that are centered.

10. Click in the first paragraph below the title, and then click the **Paragraph Dialog Box Launcher**. In the **Paragraph** dialog box, under **Indentation**, click the **Special arrow**, click **First line**, and then click **OK**. Compare your screen with **Figure 3**.

In MLA style, the first line of all body text paragraphs and notes are indented 0.5".

11. Click to the left of the paragraph that begins *The main benefits and cost savings,* scroll to the end of the document, hold down Shift, and then click to the right of the citation *(Stevens 1997 14)*. Press F4 to repeat the First Line Indent command.

12. **Save** the document, deselect the text, scroll up to display the break between Pages 1 and 2, and then compare your screen with **Figure 4**.

■ **Continue to the next page to complete the skill**

13. Open your web browser and navigate to www.epa.gov In the page's search box, type green roofs and then press [Enter]. Locate and read an article about the benefits of rooftop gardens.

14. Return to **Word**. Near the beginning of the document, locate the paragraph that begins *The main benefits and cost savings*. In your own words, complete the paragraph with two or three sentences that paraphrase the information you found on the main benefits and cost savings of rooftop gardens.

15. Take a moment to read the information in the table in **Figure 5**.

16. Return to the browser. In the **Address bar**, select and **Copy** the web address—the URL.

17. In the Word document, click the **References tab**. In the **Citations & Bibliography group**, click the **Style arrow**, and then click **MLA**.

18. Be sure the insertion point is at the end of the paragraph you wrote previously, and then add a space.

19. In the **Citations & Bibliography group**, click **Insert Citation**, and then click **Add New Source**.

20. Click the **Type of Source arrow**, and then click **Web site**. Select the **Corporate Author** check box, and then in the **Corporate Author** box, type Environmental Protection Agency

21. Select the **Show All Bibliography Fields** check box, scroll down the list, and then in the **URL** box, paste the URL that you copied. Compare your screen with **Figure 6**.

With MLA, the URL field is an optional field when citing sources for web pages.

■ **Continue to the next page to complete the skill**

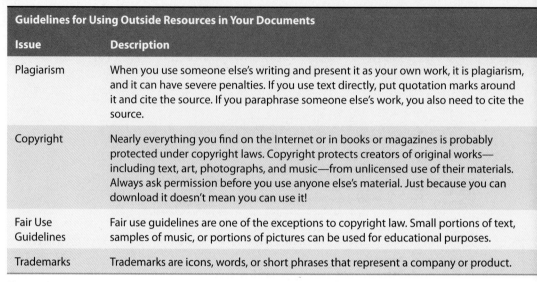

Guidelines for Using Outside Resources in Your Documents	
Issue	**Description**
Plagiarism	When you use someone else's writing and present it as your own work, it is plagiarism, and it can have severe penalties. If you use text directly, put quotation marks around it and cite the source. If you paraphrase someone else's work, you also need to cite the source.
Copyright	Nearly everything you find on the Internet or in books or magazines is probably protected under copyright laws. Copyright protects creators of original works—including text, art, photographs, and music—from unlicensed use of their materials. Always ask permission before you use anyone else's material. Just because you can download it doesn't mean you can use it!
Fair Use Guidelines	Fair use guidelines are one of the exceptions to copyright law. Small portions of text, samples of music, or portions of pictures can be used for educational purposes.
Trademarks	Trademarks are icons, words, or short phrases that represent a company or product.

Figure 5

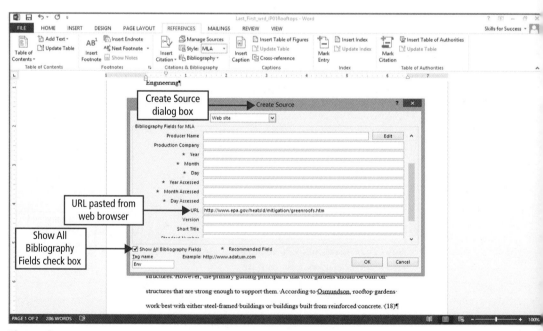

Figure 6

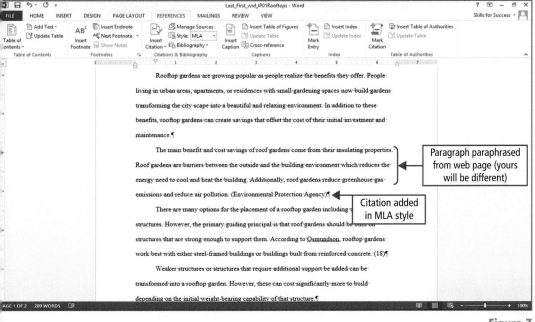

Figure 7

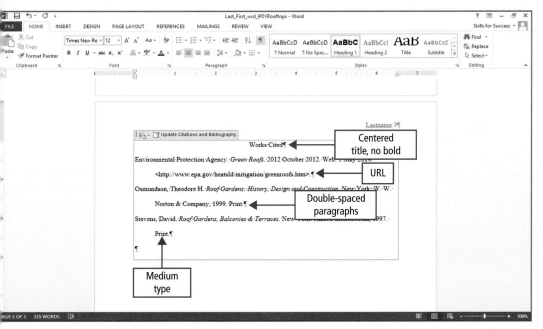

Figure 8

22. Clear the **Show All Bibliography Fields** check box, and then fill out the rest of the information if it is provided on the web page you selected. In the **Medium** box, type Web When you are done, click **OK**, and then compare your screen with **Figure 7**.

  The MLA seventh edition citation style recommends that the medium be included. For example, a book may be in print, an eBook, or accessed from a website. Instructors often specify which mediums they will accept.

23. Press Ctrl + End, and then press Ctrl + Enter to create a new page.

24. On the **References tab**, in the **Citations & Bibliography group**, click the **Bibliography** button, and then click **Works Cited**. Press Backspace.

25. Select all of the text on the *Works Cited* page including the title. On the **Home tab**, change the **Font Size** to **12** and the **Font** to **Times New Roman**. Change the **Line Spacing** to **2.0**. Click the **Line Spacing** button again, and then click **Remove Space After Paragraph**.

26. Select the *Works Cited* title, and then click the **Bold** button one time to remove the bold. **Center** the paragraph, and then compare your screen with **Figure 8**.

27. **Save** and then **Close** Word. **Close** 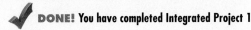 the browser window. Submit the project as directed by your instructor.

✔ **DONE! You have completed Integrated Project 1**

Use Excel Data in Word Mail Merge

► Mail merge enables you to select data from various sources. The data source could include an Excel workbook, an Outlook Contacts list, a Word table, an Access database, or a text file.

► Excel tables typically store data in the same manner as a Word table that has been set up as a data source in a mail merge.

► When fields are arranged in columns and records in rows, you can use the Excel worksheet as a data source in a Word mail merge.

► The mail merge data can be filtered before being merged into a Word document.

© alisonhancock / Fotolia

Aspen Falls City Hall

Aspen Falls City Hall has started a new program that uses interns from the local community college to teach computer classes at the city's community centers. Lorrine Deely, Community Center Supervisor, needs to mail a letter to each of the new interns thanking them for their service and asking them to attend an orientation. In order to personalize the letters, she would like to write a letter with data merged from an Excel file to complete information such as the intern's address, name, and the class each is teaching.

Addresses and other data are often created in programs other than Word. When that data is organized into tables, it can usually be used as a source for Word Mail Merge documents. In a table of addresses, each person's data is in a unique row. The data is then organized by column. For example, the street address would be one column, and the state would be another column. Excel spreadsheets are a common file format that makes it easy to organize data into rows and columns.

In this project, you will import data from an Excel workbook to create letters in Word. You will insert an address block, a name block, and an individual field to create the mail merge letter. After completing the letter, you will merge one of the letters into a new document to provide a document for your instructor to grade.

Time to complete this
project – 30 to 60 minutes

Student data files needed for this project:

wrd_IP02Instructors (Excel)
wrd_IP02Letter (Word)

You will save your files as:

Last_First_wrd_IP02Letter
Last_First_wrd_IP02Merged

Outcome

Using the skills in this project, you will be able to work with Office documents like this:

SKILLS

At the end of this project you will be able to:

▶ Create letters using mail merge
▶ Use Excel worksheets as mail merge data sources
▶ Insert Address Block, Greeting Line, and individual merge fields
▶ Finish and merge letters into individual documents

Aspen Falls Parks and Recreation

500 S Street
Aspen Falls, CA 93463

June 17, 2014

84560 S Florida Dr
Aspen Falls, CA 93464

Dear Jeffery Tebow:

Thank you so much for agreeing to volunteer for the upcoming City Parks Volunteer Day. You will be working to provide Trail Maintenance. Please dress appropriately for the job you will be working on.

To minimize our impact at local parks and wildlife conservation areas, we will be meeting at the North Community Center at 8:00 this coming Saturday. Transportation to your assigned area will be provided from there. Please bring water, snacks, and a lunch. Coolers are OK and can be left on the van while you work.

Thank you for your service to Aspen Falls, and I hope you have a wonderful time!

Sincerely,

Leah Kim
Parks and Recreation Director

1. Start **Word 2013**, and then open the student data file **wrd_IP02Letter**. **Save** the file in your chapter folder as Last_First_wrd_IP02Letter

2. Click the **Mailings tab**. In the **Start Mail Merge group**, click the **Start Mail Merge** button, and then click **Letters**.

3. In the **Start Mail Merge group**, click the **Select Recipients** button, and then click **Use an Existing List**.

4. In the **Select Data Source** dialog box, navigate to the student data files for this project, click **wrd_IP02Instructors**, and then click **Open**. Compare your screen with **Figure 1**.

   Because Excel workbooks can contain multiple worksheets in a single workbook, the Select Table box is used to select the desired worksheet. Here, the Art_Instructors worksheet contains the data that needs to be merged.

5. In the **Select Table** dialog box, be sure that **Art_Instructors** is selected, and then click **OK**.

6. In the letter, click to the left of the word *ADDRESS*. In the **Write & Insert Fields group**, click **Address Block**. In the **Insert Address Block** dialog box, clear the **Insert recipient's name in this format** check box, and then click **OK**. To the right of the merge field, delete the word *ADDRESS*.

7. In the **Preview Results group**, click **Preview Results**, and then compare your screen with **Figure 2**.

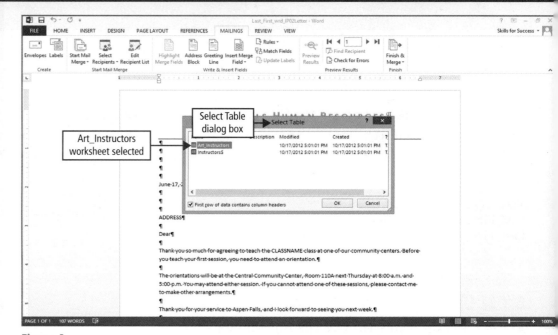

Figure 1

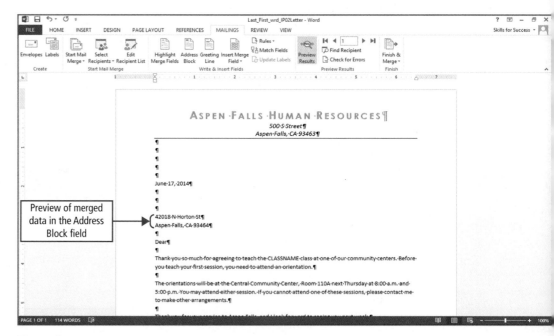

Figure 2

■ **Continue to the next page to complete the skill**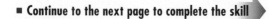

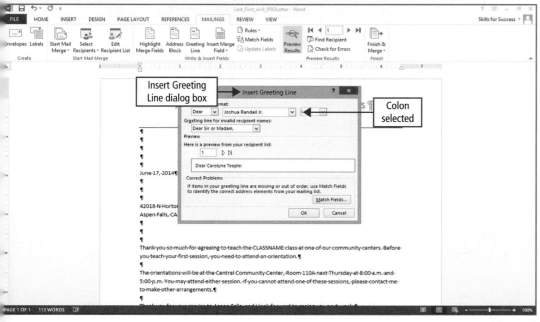

Figure 3

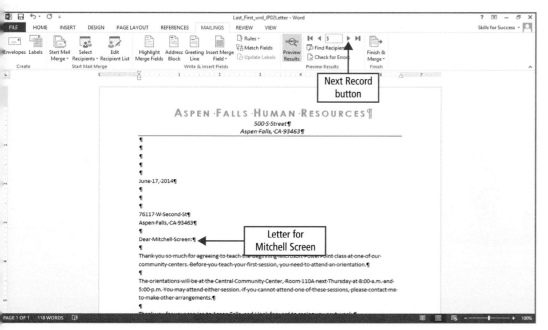

Figure 4

8. Click to the left of the word *Dear*, and then press Delete four times to delete the word. In the **Write & Insert Fields group**, click the **Greeting Line** button.

9. In the **Insert Greeting Line** dialog box, under **Greeting line format**, click the third **arrow**, and then click the colon (**:**). Compare your screen with **Figure 3**, and then click **OK**.

10. In the first body paragraph, double-click the word *CLASSNAME* to select it. In the **Write & Insert Fields group**, click the **Insert Merge Field button arrow**, and then click **Classes**. After the field just inserted, add a space.

11. In the **Preview Results group**, click the **Next Record** button four times to display the fifth letter—the letter for *Mitchell Screen*. Compare your screen with **Figure 4**.

12. In the **Finish group**, click the **Finish & Merge** button, and then click **Edit Individual Documents**. In the **Merge to New Document** dialog box, select the **Current record** option button, and then click **OK**.

13. Save 🖫 the new merged document in your chapter folder as Last_First_wrd_ IP02Merged and then **Close** ✕ the document.

14. Save Last_First_wrd_IP02Letter and then **Close** ✕ the document. Submit the project as directed by your instructor.

✔ **DONE! You have completed Integrated Project 2**

Create Flyers Using Word Online

▶ **Word Online**, formerly Word Web App, is a cloud-based application used to complete basic document editing and formatting tasks using a web browser.

▶ Word Online can be used to create or edit documents using a web browser instead of the Word program—Word 2013 does not need to be installed on your computer.

▶ When you create a document using Word Online, it is saved on your OneDrive so that you can work with it from any computer connected to the Internet.

▶ You can share your document with colleagues or groups, either giving them read-only access or allowing them to edit the document.

▶ You can use Word Online to perform basic editing and formatting tasks including inserting tables and images.

▶ If you need a feature not available in Word Online, you can edit your document in Microsoft Word and save it on your OneDrive.

© Maridav / Fotolia

Aspen Falls City Hall

This project assumes that you are working at a computer that does not have the desktop version of Microsoft Word installed. Instead, you will create, edit, and format a flyer using Word Online. You will create a document for Leah Kim, Parks and Recreation Supervisor. The flyer needs to outline the city's policy for photography in city parks.

Word Online is used to create or open Word documents from any computer or device connected to the Internet. When needed, you can edit text, format the document, or insert objects such as pictures and tables. You can save these documents on your OneDrive and continue working with them later when you are at a computer that has Word 2013 available. In Word Online, you edit your document in **Editing View** and view the document as it will print in **Reading View**.

In this project, you will use Word Online to create a short flyer. You will type and edit text, apply styles, and create a bulleted list. You will insert a picture from a file, size and position it, and then insert a table. Finally, you will open the document in Word 2013 to format the table.

Time to complete this project – 30 to 60 minutes

Student data file needed for this project:

wrd_WAPark

You will save your file as:

Last_First_wrd_WAPhotos

SKILLS MyITLab®

At the end of this project you will be able to use Word Online to:

▶ Create new Word documents from OneDrive

▶ Type text in Editing View

▶ Apply styles

▶ Add emphasis to text

▶ Change text alignment

▶ Insert pictures from files

▶ Create tables

▶ Switch to desktop Word to complete editing

▶ View documents in Reading View

Outcome

Using the skills in this project, you will be able to create and edit a Word Online document like this:

City of Aspen Falls Parks and Recreation

Photography Policy

We encourage photography in city parks and conservation areas. If you are taking pictures as a recreational activity and will not earn more than $3,000 total revenue from the sale of the photographs, no fees or permits are needed. If you are not a hobby photographer, the following requirements must be met:

- Complete a photography permit application form.
- Provide proof of liability insurance.
- Pay a refundable damage deposit.
- Pay the permit fee as specified in the table below.
- Commercial photography in conservation areas is not allowed.

Photography fees:

Hobby Photography	**No Fee**
Commercial Photography	$200 per day
Motion Pictures or Feature Films	$625 per four hours

1. Start **Internet Explorer** 🔵, navigate to live.com and log on to your Microsoft account. If you do not have an account, follow the links and directions on the page to create one.

2. After logging in, navigate as needed to display your **OneDrive** page, and then compare your screen with **Figure 1**.

   OneDrive and Web App technologies are accessed through web pages that can change often, and the formatting and layout of some pages may often be different than the figures in this book. Also, steps may be different if you have not signed Word 2013 into your Microsoft account. You may need to adapt the steps to complete the actions they describe.

3. On the toolbar, click **Create**, and then click **Word document**.

4. Above the Ribbon, point to the text *Document1*, click one time, type Last_First_wrd_WAPhotos and then click a blank area in the document.

5. On the **Home tab**, in the **Styles group**, click the **Heading 2** style, and then type City of Aspen Falls Parks and Recreation

6. Press `Enter`. In the **Styles group**, click the **Heading 1** style, and then type Photography Policy

7. Select the first two title lines, and then in the **Paragraph group**, click the **Center** button 🔳.

8. Select the text *Photography Policy*, and then in the **Font group**, click the **Font Size arrow** 11 ▾, and then click **24**. Compare your screen with **Figure 2**.

■ Continue to the next page to complete the skill ▶

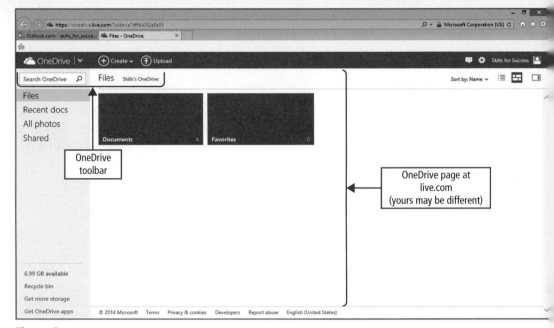

Figure 1

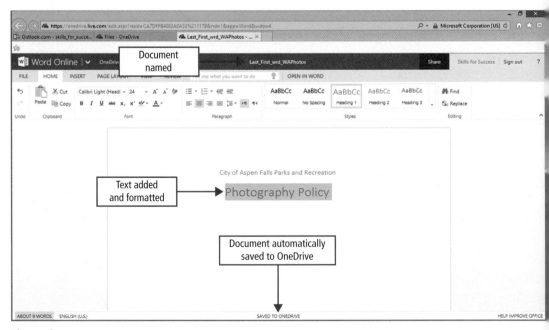

Figure 2

- Complete a photography permit application form.

- Provide proof of liability insurance.

- Pay a refundable damage deposit.

- Pay the permit fee as specified in the table below.

- Commercial photography in conservation areas is not allowed.

Figure 3

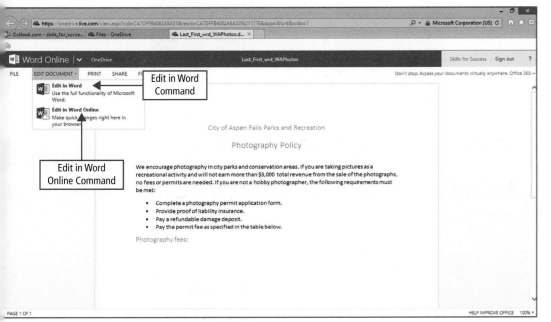

Figure 4

9. Position the insertion point to the right of *Policy*, and then press [Enter] two times. In the **Styles group**, click the **Normal** style to reapply the style's formatting to the blank paragraph.

10. Type the following text: We encourage photography in city parks and conservation areas. If you are taking pictures as a recreational activity and will not earn more than $3,000 total revenue from the sale of the photographs, no fees or permits are needed. If you are not a hobby photographer, the following requirements must be met:

11. Press [Enter], and then in the **Paragraph group**, click the **Bullets** button ⊟ ▾. Create a bulleted list using the text found in the table in **Figure 3**.

12. After typing the list, press [Enter] two times, and then type Photography fees:

13. With the insertion point in the *Photography fees* paragraph, apply the **Heading 2** style.

14. Click the **View tab**. In the **Document Views group**, click the **Reading View** button.

    Reading View displays the document as it will print, but you cannot edit in this view. You must save the document before switching to Reading View.

15. Click **Edit Document**, compare your screen with **Figure 4**, and then click **Edit in Word Online**.

▪ **Continue to the next page to complete the skill**

16. In the first bullet, position the insertion point to the right of the line that ends *permit application form*. Click the **Insert tab**, and then in the **Pictures group**, click the **Picture** button. In the **Choose File to Upload** dialog box, navigate to the student files for this project, and then open **wrd_WAPark**.

17. Click the picture to select it, and then click the **Format tab**. In the **Image Size group**, click in the **Scale** box, and then type 75 and press Enter to change the size of the picture to 75 percent of its original size. Compare your screen with **Figure 5**.

> When a picture is selected, the Format tab displays and the picture has a washed-out effect.

18. Click in the document, and then click Ctrl + End to move to the end of the document. Press Enter, and then click the **Normal** style to reapply the style's formatting.

19. Click the **Insert tab**, and then in the **Tables group**, click the **Table** button. In the third row, click the second square to create a **2x3** table.

20. In the first table cell, type Hobby Photography and then press Tab. Type No Fee and then press Tab.

21. Type Commercial Photography and then press Tab. Type $200 per day and then press Tab.

22. Type Motion Pictures or Feature Films and then press Tab. Type $625 per four hours and then compare your screen with **Figure 6**.

■ **Continue to the next page to complete the skill**

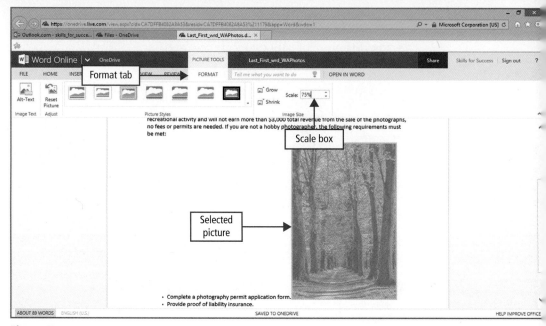

Figure 5

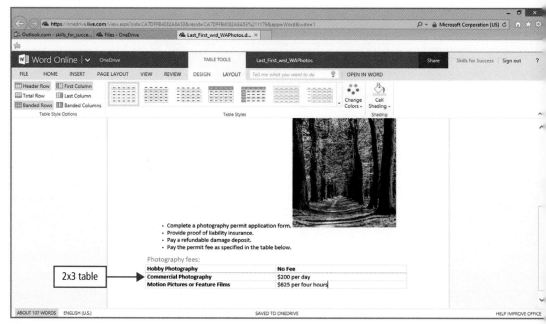

Figure 6

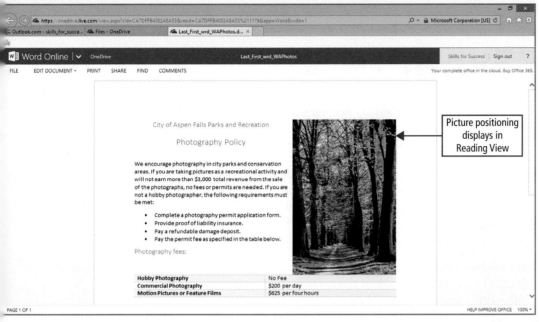

Figure 7

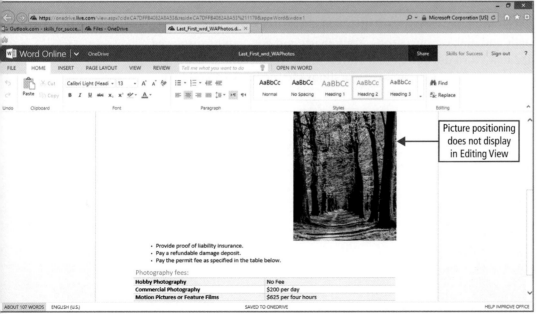

Figure 8

23. To the right of the **Layout tab**, click **OPEN IN WORD**. Read all messages that display, and then click **Allow** or **Yes** as needed to open the document in Word 2013.

24. If necessary, switch to Print Layout view. Click the picture to select it, and then click the **Format tab**. In the **Arrange group**, click the **Position** button, and then click the third thumbnail—**Position in Top Right with Square Text Wrapping**.

25. Click in the table, and then click the **Design tab**. Click the **Table Styles More** button ⬇, and then under **Grid Tables**, click the fourth style in the second row— **Grid Table 2 - Accent 3**. In the **Table Style Options** group, clear the **Header Row** check box.

26. **Save** 🖫 the document, and then **Close** ☒ Word 2013.

27. Press F5 to refresh to web page. On the **View tab**, click **Reading View**, and then compare your screen with **Figure 7**.

28. Click **Edit Document**, and then click **Edit in Word Online**. Compare your screen with **Figure 8**.

> Features not supported by Word Online will not be available in Edit View. Here, the picture layout does not display. This feature however, does display in Reading View and when opened in Word 2013.

29. Click the **View tab**, and then click **Reading View**. **Print**, **Download** and submit, or **Share** the document as directed by your instructor.

30. In the top left corner of the **Internet Explorer** window, click the **Sign out** link, and then **Close** ☒ the browser window.

 DONE! You have completed the Word Online Project!

Introduction to Excel

Microsoft Excel 2013 is a ***spreadsheet application***—a program used to store information and to perform numerical analysis of data that is arranged in a grid of cells. This grid is organized in rows identified by numbers and columns identified by letters.

A business spreadsheet can be used for many purposes including tracking budgets and summarizing results. You can create formulas using mathematical operations such as addition, subtraction, multiplication, and division. Formulas can refer to the value stored in a cell and when you change the value of the cell, the formula will recalculate the results. Because the results are immediately displayed, Excel is frequently used by businesses to help make decisions.

Once you have entered your data and formulas into Excel, you can format the text and values, or wrap text in a cell and merge cells to improve the look of the spreadsheet. You can change the row height and the column width, and insert or delete rows and columns.

You can sort and filter data, or apply conditional formatting to data to help you find the information you are looking for more quickly. You can also use cell styles, borders, or font colors and shading to highlight important data.

You can present your Excel data in a wide variety of charts, including pie charts, line charts, or bar charts. Charts show trends and make comparisons. Your charts and data can be displayed in an Excel workbook or copied to a Word document or a PowerPoint presentation. Excel can be used to collaborate with others. For example, you can save workbooks to the Internet and then invite others to view or make changes to your workbooks.

Cell styles applied

Merged cells

Formatted values

Column chart

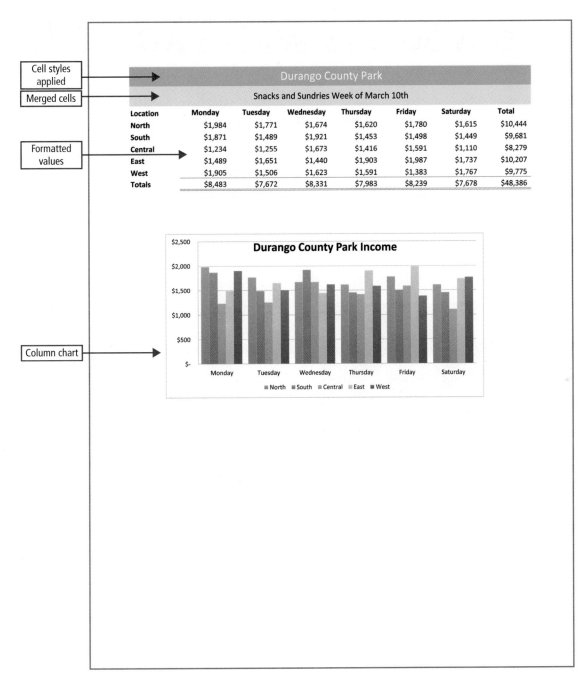

Location	Monday	Tuesday	Wednesday	Thursday	Friday	Saturday	Total
North	$1,984	$1,771	$1,674	$1,620	$1,780	$1,615	$10,444
South	$1,871	$1,489	$1,921	$1,453	$1,498	$1,449	$9,681
Central	$1,234	$1,255	$1,673	$1,416	$1,591	$1,110	$8,279
East	$1,489	$1,651	$1,440	$1,903	$1,987	$1,737	$10,207
West	$1,905	$1,506	$1,623	$1,591	$1,383	$1,767	$9,775
Totals	$8,483	$7,672	$8,331	$7,983	$8,239	$7,678	$48,386

Create Workbooks with Excel 2013

- ▶ Microsoft Office Excel 2013 is used worldwide to create workbooks and to analyze data that is organized into columns and rows.

- ▶ After data is entered into Excel, you can perform calculations on the numerical data and analyze the data to make informed decisions.

- ▶ When you make changes to one or more number values, you can immediately see the effect of those changes in totals and charts that rely on those values.

- ▶ An Excel workbook can contain a large amount of data—up to 16,384 columns and 1,048,576 rows.

- ▶ The basic skills you need to work efficiently with Excel include entering and formatting data and navigating within Excel.

- ▶ When planning your worksheet, think about what information will form the rows and what information will form the columns. Generally, rows are used to list the items and columns to group or describe the items in the list.

© Elenathewise / Fotolia

Aspen Falls Outdoor Recreation

In this chapter, you will create a workbook for Amado Pettinelli, the Outdoor Recreation Supervisor. Mr. Pettinelli wants to know the attendance at each city attraction and the revenue each venue generates for the city. He plans to recommend to the Aspen Falls City Council that the busiest attractions receive more city funding in the next fiscal year.

A business spreadsheet can be used for many purposes including tracking budgets, manufacture measurements, or employees. The spreadsheet data can be manipulated using arithmetic and mathematical formulas commonly used in the modern-day business world. If you are asked to create a spreadsheet, you need to know if the results of the data manipulation will be presented in numerical or in graphical format.

In this project, you will create a new Excel workbook and enter data which displays the total number of visitors at the various city attractions in Aspen Falls. You will format the data, construct formulas, and insert functions. You will calculate the percent of weekday visitors at each of the locations and insert a footer. Finally, you will check the spelling in the workbook.

Time to complete all 10 skills – 60 to 90 minutes

Student data file needed for this chapter:

Blank Excel workbook

You will save your workbook as:

Last_First_exl01_Visitors

Outcome

Using the skills in this chapter, you will be able to work with Excel worksheets like this:

Aspen Falls Outdoor Recreation						
Visitors to City Attractions						
Location	Weekends	Weekdays	All Visitors	Difference	Entrance Fee	Total Fees
Zoo	3,169	1,739	4,908	1,430	$ 10	$ 49,080
Pool	5,338	3,352	8,690	1,986	$ 10	$ 86,900
Aquarium	9,027	3,868	12,895	5,159	$ 12	$ 154,740
Garden	4,738	2,788	7,526	1,950	$ 4	$ 30,104
Museum	3,876	913	4,789	2,963	$ 11	$ 52,679
Total	26,148	12,660	38,808			$ 373,503

Percent of Weekday Visitors	
Zoo	35.4%
Pool	38.6%
Aquarium	30.0%
Garden	37.0%
Museum	19.1%

SKILLS

Skills 1-10 Training

At the end of this chapter you will be able to:

Skill 1 Create and Save Workbooks

Skill 2 Enter Data and Merge and Center Titles

Skill 3 Construct Addition and Subtraction Formulas

Skill 4 Construct Multiplication and Division Formulas

Skill 5 Adjust Column Widths and Apply Cell Styles

Skill 6 Insert the SUM Function

Skill 7 AutoFill Formulas and Data

Skill 8 Format, Edit, and Check Spelling

Skill 9 Insert Footers and Adjust Page Settings

Skill 10 Display Formulas and Print Worksheets

MORE SKILLS

Skill 11 Create Workbooks from Templates

Skill 12 Insert Names into Formulas

Skill 13 Create Templates

Skill 14 Manage Document Properties

► An Excel **workbook** is a file that you can use to organize various kinds of related information. A workbook contains **worksheets**, also called **spreadsheets**—the primary documents that you use in Excel to store and work with data.

► The worksheet forms a grid of vertical columns and horizontal rows. The small box where one column and one row meet is a cell.

1. Start **Excel 2013**, and then click **Blank workbook**. In the lower right, notice the zoom—magnification level.

   Your zoom level should be 100%, but most figures in this chapter are zoomed to 120%.

2. Verify the cell in the upper left corner is the **active cell**—the cell outlined in green in which data is entered when you begin typing—as shown in **Figure 1**.

   In a worksheet, columns have alphabetical headings across the top, and rows have numerical headings down the left side. When a cell is active, the headings for the column and row in which the cell is located are shaded. The column letter and row number that identify a cell is the **cell address**, also called the **cell reference**.

3. In cell **A1**, type Aspen Falls Outdoor Recreation and then press Enter to accept the entry.

4. In cell **A2**, type Visitors and then press Enter two times. Compare your screen with **Figure 2**.

5. In cell **A4**, type Location and press Tab to make the cell to the right—**B4**—active.

■ **Continue to the next page to complete the skill**

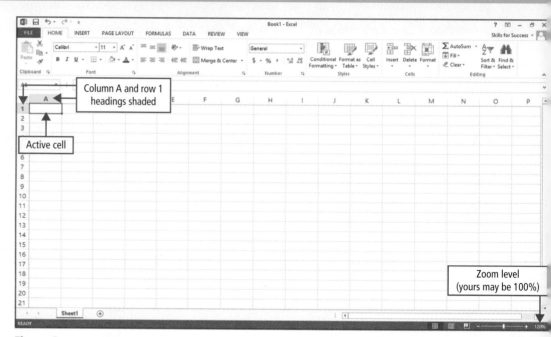

Column A and row 1 headings shaded

Active cell

Zoom level (yours may be 100%)

Figure 1

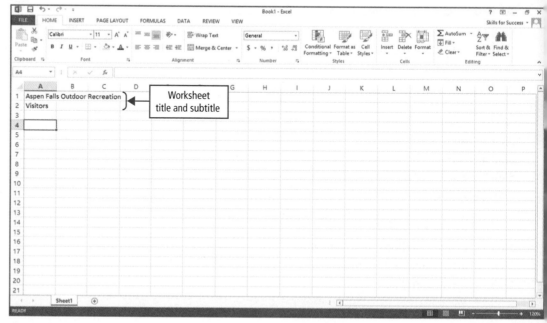

Worksheet title and subtitle

Figure 2

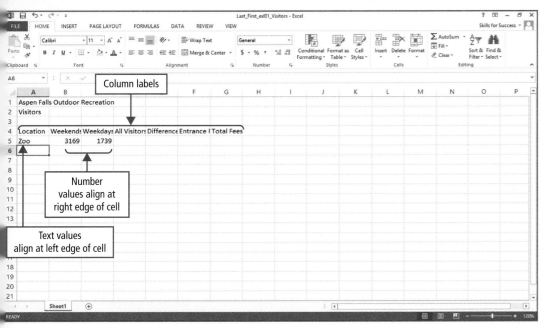

Figure 3

Common Ways to Move or Scroll Through a Worksheet

Key	Description
Enter	Move down one row.
Tab	Move one column to the right.
Shift + Tab	Move one column to the left.
↓ ↑ → ←	Move one cell in the direction of the arrow.
Ctrl + Home	Move to cell A1.
Ctrl + End	Move to the lowest row and the column farthest to the right that contains data.

Figure 4

6. With cell **B4** the active cell, type the following labels, pressing Tab between each label:
   Weekends
   Weekdays
   All Visitors
   Difference
   Entrance Fee
   Total Fees

   Labels at the beginning of columns or rows help readers understand the data.

   To correct typing errors, click a cell and retype the data. The new typing will replace the existing data.

7. Click cell **A5**, type Zoo and then press Tab. Type 3169 and press Tab. Type 1739 and then press Enter. Compare your screen with **Figure 3**.

   Data in a cell is called a *value*. You can have a *text value*—character data in a cell that labels number values, or a *number value*—numeric data in a cell. A text value is also referred to as a *label*. Text values align at the left cell edge, and number values align at the right cell edge.

8. Click **Save** 🖫. On the **Save As** page, click **Computer**, and then click the **Browse** button. In the **Save As** dialog box, navigate to the location where you are saving your files. Click **New folder**, type Excel Chapter 1 and then press Enter two times. In the **File name** box, name the workbook Last_First_exl01_Visitors and then press Enter.

9. Take a few moments to familiarize yourself with common methods to move between cells as summarized in the table in **Figure 4**.

■ **You have completed Skill 1 of 10**

▶ To create an effective worksheet, you enter titles and subtitles and add labels for each row and column of data. It is a good idea to have the worksheet title and subtitle span across all the columns containing data.

1. In cell **A6**, type Aquarium and press [Tab].

2. In cell **B6**, type 9027 and press [Tab]. In cell **C6**, type 3868 and press [Enter].

3. In row **7** and row **8**, type the following data:

   | Garden | 5738 | 2877 |
   | Museum | 3876 | 913 |

4. In cell **A9**, type Total and press [Enter]. Compare your screen with **Figure 1**.

5. Click cell **B1**, type Worksheet and press [Enter]. Click cell **A1**, and then compare your screen with **Figure 2**.

   When text is too long to fit in a cell and the cell to the right of it contains data, the text will be ***truncated***—cut off. Here, the text in cell A1 is truncated.

   The ***formula bar***—a bar below the Ribbon that displays the value contained in the active cell and is used to enter or edit values or formulas.

   Data displayed in a cell is the ***displayed value***. Data displayed in the formula bar is the ***underlying value***. Displayed values often do not match their underlying values.

6. On the Quick Access Toolbar, click the **Undo** button ⟲ to remove the text in cell **B1**.

   Long text in cells overlaps into other columns only when those cells are empty. Here, A1 text now overlaps B1 because that cell is empty.

■ **Continue to the next page to complete the skill**

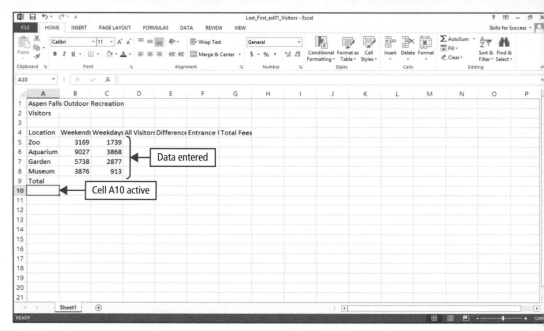

Figure 1

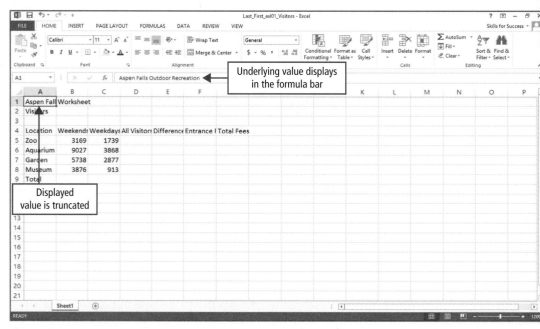

Figure 2

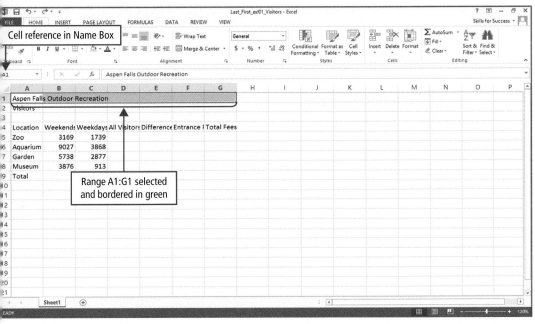

Figure 3

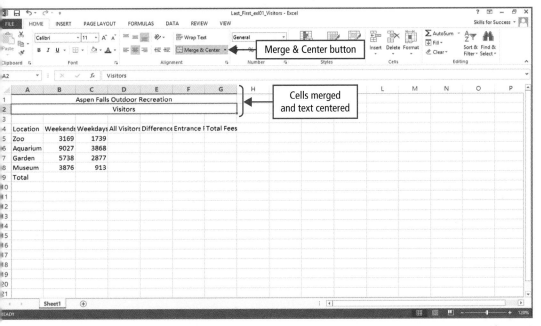

Figure 4

7. Point to the middle of cell **A1** to display the ⊕ pointer. Hold down the left mouse button, and then drag to the right to select cells **A1** through **G1**. Compare your screen with **Figure 3**. To select a range on a touch screen, tap the cell, and then drag the selection handle.

> The selected range is referred to as *A1:G1* (A1 through G1) A **range** is two or more cells in a worksheet that are adjacent (next to each other). A colon (:) between two cell references indicates that the range includes the two cell references and all the cells between them.

> When you select a range, a thick green line surrounds the range, and all but the first cell in the range are shaded. The first cell reference will be displayed in the **Name Box**—an area by the formula bar that displays the active cell reference.

8. On the **Home tab**, in the **Alignment group**, click the **Merge & Center** button.

> The selected range, A1:G1, merges into one larger cell, and the data is centered in the new cell. The cells in B1 through G1 can no longer be selected individually because they are merged into cell A1.

9. Using the technique just practiced, merge and center the range **A2:G2**.

10. **Save** 🖫 the workbook, and then compare your screen with **Figure 4**.

■ **You have completed Skill 2 of 10**

EXL 1-3
VIDEO

▶ A cell's underlying value can be a text value, a number value, or a *formula*—an equation that performs mathematical calculations on number values in the worksheet.

▶ Formulas begin with an equal sign and often include an *arithmetic operator*—a symbol that specifies a mathematical operation such as addition or subtraction.

Symbols Used in Excel for Arithmetic Operators	
+ (plus sign)	Addition
- (minus sign)	Subtraction (also negation)
* (asterisk)	Multiplication
/ (forward slash)	Division
% (percent sign)	Percent
^ (caret)	Exponentiation

Figure 1

1. Study the symbols that Excel uses to perform mathematical operations, as summarized in the table in **Figure 1**.

2. In cell **D5**, type =B5+C5 and then press Enter.

> When you include cell references in formulas, the values in those cells are inserted. Here, the total number of visitors for the Zoo location equals the sum of the values in cells B5 and C5 (3169+ 1739 = 4908).

> When you type a formula, you might see a brief display of function names that match the first letter you type. This Excel feature, called **Formula AutoComplete**, suggests values as you type a function.

3. In cell **D6**, type the formula to add cells **B6** and **C6**, =B6+C6 and then press Enter.

4. In cell **D7**, type = and then click cell **B7** to automatically insert *B7* into the formula. Compare your screen with **Figure 2**.

> Cell **B7** is surrounded by a moving border indicating that it is part of an active formula.

5. Type + Click cell **C7**, and then press Enter to display the result *8615*.

> You can either type formulas or construct them by pointing and clicking in this manner.

■ **Continue to the next page to complete the skill**

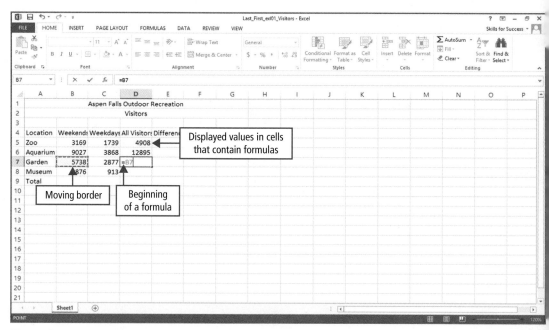

Figure 2

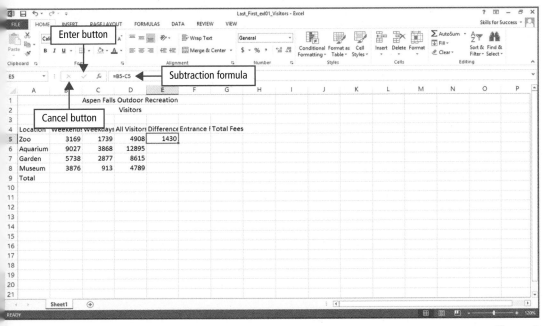

Figure 3

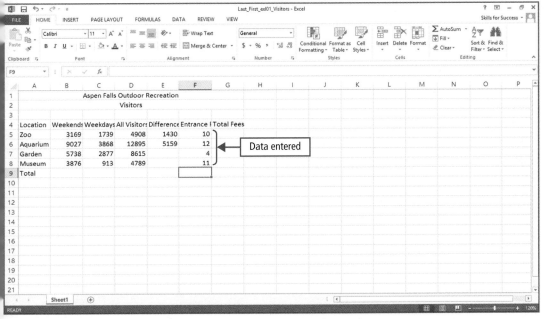

Figure 4

6. In cell **D8**, use point and click to construct a formula that adds cells **B8** and **C8**.

7. In cell **E5**, type =B5-C5 On the formula bar, click the **Enter** button ☑ to confirm the entry while keeping cell *E5* the active cell, and then compare your screen with **Figure 3**.

   Here, the underlying value for cell *E5* displays as a formula in the formula bar and the displayed value, *1430*, displays in the cell as a result of the formula.

   If you make an error entering a formula, you can click the Cancel button and then start over. Alternately, you can press the Esc key.

8. In cell **E6**, use point and click to enter the formula =B6-C6 to display the difference for the Aquarium weekend and weekday visitors. (You will complete the column E formulas in Skill 7.)

9. In column F, type the following data as listed in the table below, and then compare your screen with **Figure 4**.

Cell	Value
F5	10
F6	12
F7	4
F8	11

10. **Save** 🖫 the workbook.

■ **You have completed Skill 3 of 10**

▶ The four most common operators for addition (+), subtraction (-), multiplication (*), and division (/) can be found on the number keypad at the right side of a standard keyboard, or on the number keys at the top of a keyboard.

1. In cell **G5**, type =D5*F5—the formula that multiplies the total Zoo visitors by its entrance fee. On the formula bar, click the **Enter** button ☑, and then compare your screen with **Figure 1**.

The ***underlying formula***—the formula as displayed in the formula bar—multiplies the value in cell D5 (*4908*)—by the value in cell F5 (*10*) and displays the result in cell G5 (*49080*).

2. In the range **G6:G8**, enter the following formulas:

Cell	Formula
G6	=D6*F6
G7	=D7*F7
G8	=D8*F8

3. In cell **A11**, type Percent of Weekday Visitors and then press Enter. Compare your screen with **Figure 2**.

■ **Continue to the next page to complete the skill** ▶

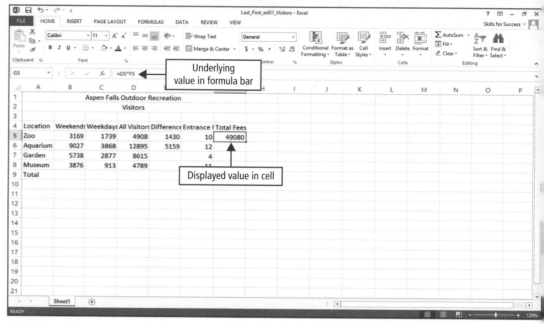

Figure 1

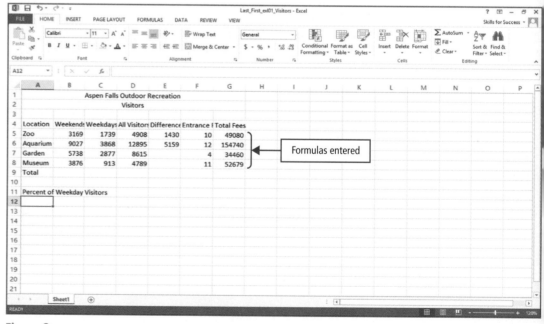

Figure 2

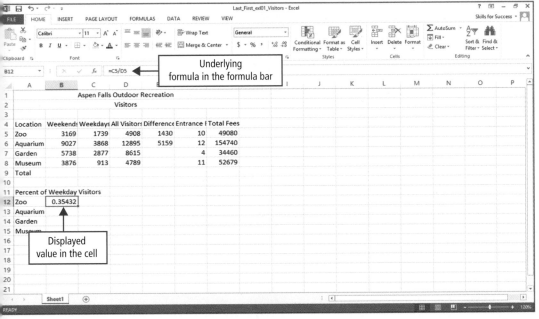

Figure 3

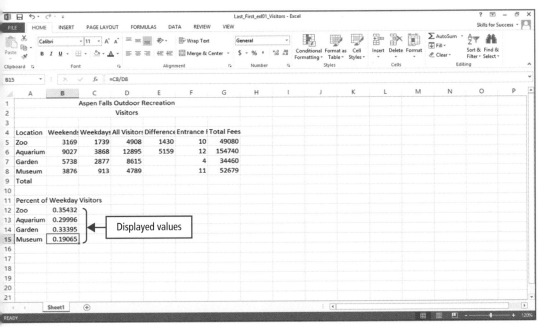

Figure 4

4. Select the range **A5:A8**, and then on the **Home tab**, in the **Clipboard group**, click the **Copy** button 📋. Click cell **A12**, and then in the **Clipboard group**, click the **Paste** button.

   The four location labels are copied to the range A12:A15.

5. Press [Esc] to remove the moving border around the copied cells.

6. In cell **B12**, construct the formula to divide the number of Weekday Zoo visitors by the Total Zoo visitors, $=C5/D5$ and then click the **Enter** button ✓. Compare your screen with **Figure 3**.

   Percentages are calculated by taking the amount divided by the total and will be displayed in decimal format. Here, the underlying formula in B12 ($=C5/D5$) divides the weekday Zoo visitors (*1739*) by the total Zoo visitors (*4908*).

7. Construct the formulas to calculate the percent of weekday visitors for each location, and then compare your screen with **Figure 4**.

Cell	Formula
B13	$=C6/D6$
B14	$=C7/D7$
B15	$=C8/D8$

8. **Save** 💾 the workbook.

■ **You have completed Skill 4 of 10**

EXL 1-5
VIDEO

▶ The letter that displays at the top of a column is the ***column heading***. The number that displays at the left of a row is the ***row heading***.

▶ ***Formatting*** is the process of specifying the appearance of cells or the overall layout of a worksheet.

1. Click cell **A4**. On the **Home tab**, in the **Cells group**, click the **Format** button, and then click **Column Width**. In the **Column Width** dialog box, type 13

2. Compare your screen with **Figure 1**, and then click **OK**.

    The default column width will display 8.43 characters when formatted in the standard font. Here, the width is increased to display more characters.

3. Select the range **B4:G4**.In the **Cells group**, click the **Format** button, and then click **Column Width**. In the **Column Width** dialog box, type 12 and then click **OK**.

4. Select cells **A11:B11**. On the **Home tab**, in the **Alignment group**, click the **Merge & Center arrow** ⊞ Merge & Center ▾, and then on the displayed list, click **Merge Across**. Compare your screen with **Figure 2**.

    Merge Across merges the selected cells without centering them.

5. Click cell **A1** to select the merged and centered range A1:G1. In the **Cells group**, click the **Format** button, and then click **Row Height**. In the **Row Height** dialog box, type 22.5 and then click **OK**.

■ **Continue to the next page to complete the skill**

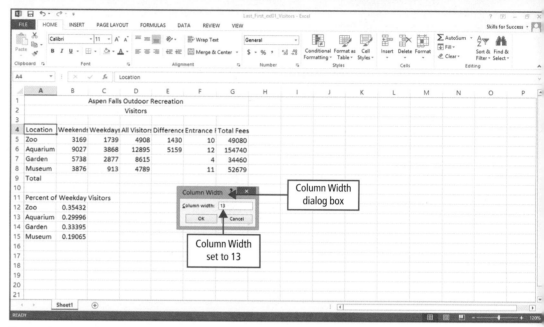

Figure 1

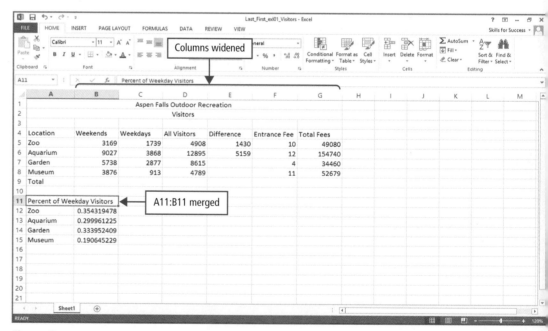

Figure 2

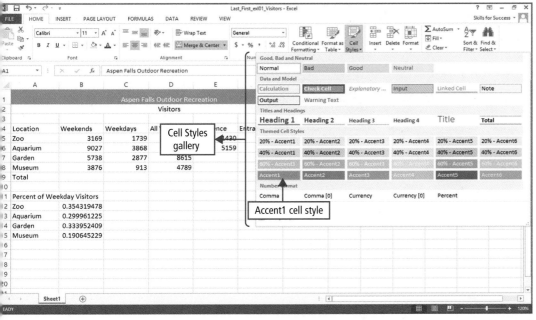

Figure 3

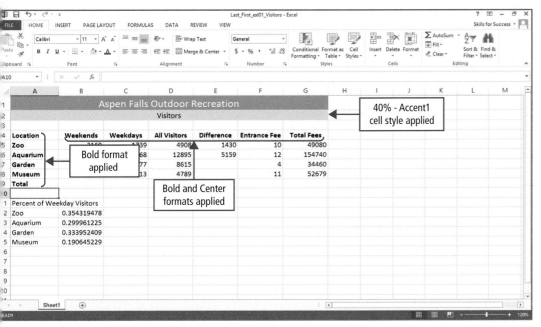

Figure 4

6. With **A1:G1** still selected, in the **Styles group**, click the **Cell Styles** button. In the **Cell Styles** gallery, under **Titles and Headings**, use Live Preview to view the title as you point to **Heading 1** and then **Heading 2**.

> A **cell style** is a prebuilt set of formatting characteristics, such as font, font size, font color, cell borders, and cell shading.

7. Under **Themed Cell Styles**, point to the **Accent1** style. Compare your screen with **Figure 3**, and then click **Accent1**.

8. In the **Font group**, click the **Font Size arrow** [11 ▾] and then click **16**.

9. Click cell **A2**, and then using the technique you just practiced, apply the **40% - Accent1** cell style. In the **Font group**, click the **Increase Font Size** button [Å] one time to change the font size to **12**.

10. Select the range **B4:G4**. Right-click the selected range to display a shortcut menu and the Mini toolbar. On the Mini toolbar, click the **Bold** button [B] and then click the **Center** button [≡] to apply bold and to center the text within each of the selected cells.

11. Select the range **A4:A9**. Display the Mini toolbar, and then apply **Bold** to the selected range. Click cell **A10**, and then compare your screen with **Figure 4**.

12. **Save** [⊟] the workbook.

- **You have completed Skill 5 of 10**

EXL 1-6
VIDEO

▶ You can create your own formulas, or you can use a *function*—a prewritten Excel formula that takes a value or values, performs an operation, and returns a value or values.

▶ The AutoSum button is used to insert common summary functions into a worksheet.

▶ When cell references are used in a formula or function, the results are automatically recalculated whenever those cells are edited.

1. Click cell **B9**. On the **Home tab**, in the **Editing group**, click the **AutoSum** button, and then compare your screen with **Figure 1**.

   SUM is an Excel function that adds all the numbers in a range of cells. The range in parentheses, *(B5:B8)*, indicates the range of cells on which the SUM function will be performed.

   When the AutoSum button is used, Excel first looks *above* the selected cell for a suitable range of cells to sum. When no suitable data is detected, Excel then looks to the *left* and proposes a range of cells to sum. Here, the range B5:B8 is surrounded by a moving border, and *=SUM(B5:B8)* displays in cell B9.

2. Press [Enter] to display the function result—*21810*.

3. Select the range **C9:D9**. In the **Editing group**, click the **AutoSum** button, and then compare your screen with **Figure 2**.

■ **Continue to the next page to complete the skill**

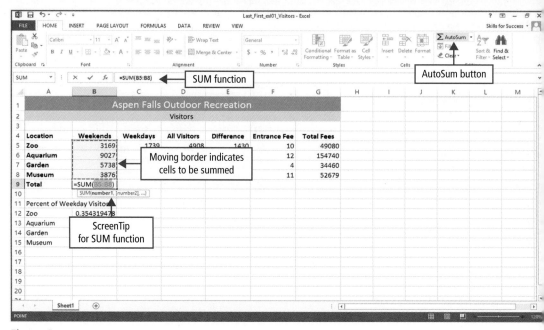

Figure 1

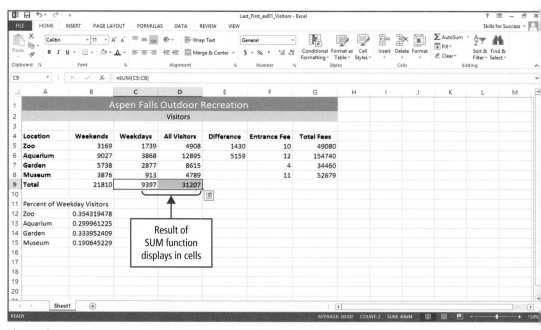

Figure 2

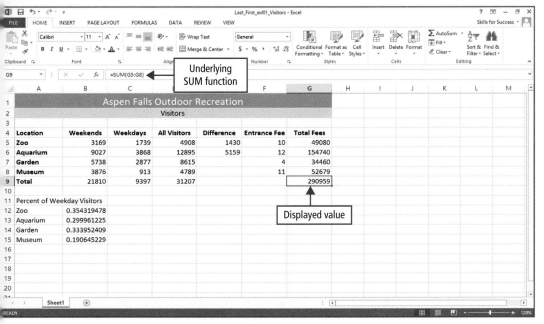

Figure 3

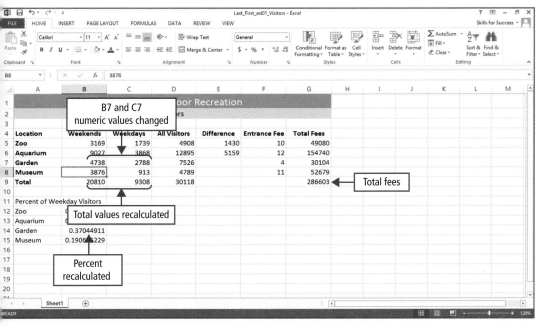

Figure 4

4. Click cell **C9**, and then in the formula bar, verify that the SUM function adds the values in the range *C5:C8*.

5. Click cell **D9**, and verify that the SUM function adds the values in the range *D5:D8*.

6. Using the technique just practiced, in cell **G9**, insert the SUM function to add the values in the range **G5:G8**. Verify cell **G9** is the active cell, and then compare your screen with **Figure 3**.

7. In cell **B7**, type 4738 Watch the totals in cells B9, G7 and G9 update as you press ⌨Tab.

> In cell B9, the displayed value changed to 20810, but the underlying formula remained the same.

8. In cell **C7**, type 2788 and then press ⌨Enter to update the totals in cells C9, G7 and G9. Compare your screen with **Figure 4**.

9. **Save** 💾 the workbook.

■ **You have completed Skill 6 of 10**

▶ Text, numbers, formulas, and functions can be copied down rows and also across columns to insert formulas and functions quickly.

▶ When a formula is copied to another cell, Excel adjusts the cell references relative to the new location of the formula.

---

1. Click cell **E6**. With cell **E6** selected, point to the ***fill handle***—the small green square in the lower right corner of the selection—until the ⊞ pointer displays as shown in **Figure 1**.

> To use the fill handle, first select the cell that contains the content you want to copy—here the formula =*B6-C6*.

2. Drag the ⊞ pointer down to cell **E8**, and then release the mouse button.

3. Click cell **E7**, and verify on the formula bar that the formula copied from E6 changed to=*B7-C7*. Click cell **E8**, and then compare your screen with **Figure 2**.

> In each row, the cell references in the formula adjusted *relative to* the row number—B6 changed to B7 and then to B8. This adjustment is called a ***relative cell reference*** because it refers to cells based on their position *in relation to* (relative to) the cell that contains the formula.

■ **Continue to the next page to complete the skill** ▶

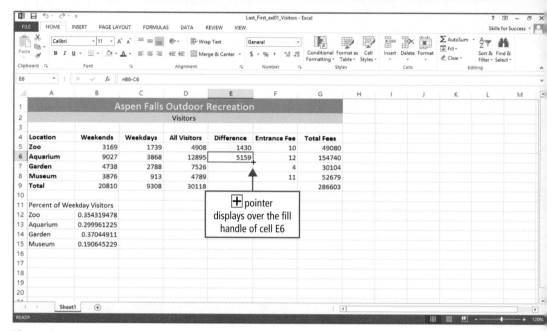

Figure 1

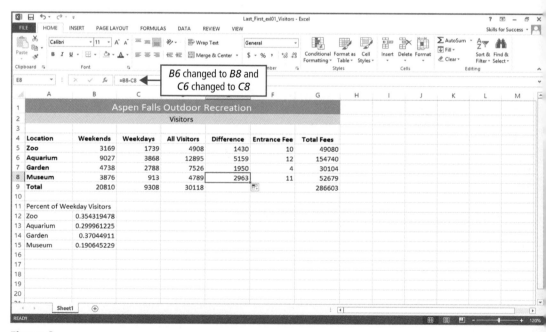

Figure 2

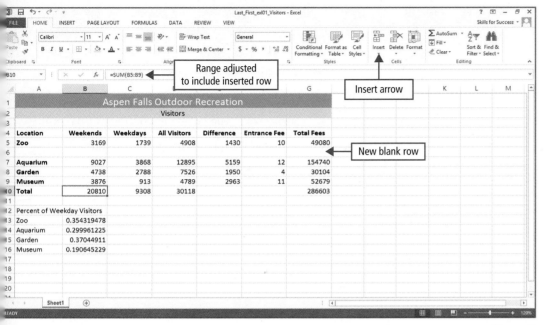

Figure 3

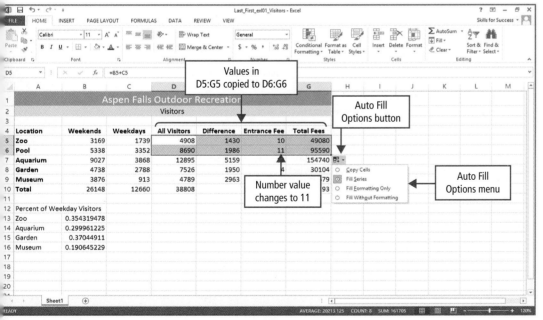

Figure 4

4. Click cell **A6**. In the **Cells group**, click the **Insert arrow**, and then click **Insert Sheet Rows**. Click cell **B10**, and then compare your screen with **Figure 3**.

> When you insert a new row or column, the cell references and the ranges in formulas or in functions adjust to include the new row or column. Here, in cell B10, the range in the function automatically updated to include the new row in the range.

5. In cell **A6**, type Pool and then press [Tab].

> By default, formatting (bold) from the row above is applied to an inserted row.

6. In cell **B6**, type 5338 and then press [Tab] to enter the value and update the column total in cell *B10* to *26148*.

7. In cell **C6**, type 3352 and press [Tab].

8. Select cells **D5:G5**. Point to the fill handle so that the ⊞ pointer displays, and then drag the ⊞ pointer down one row. Release the mouse button, and then click the **Auto Fill Options** button ⊞. Compare your screen with **Figure 4**.

> Three formulas and a number are copied. When you copy number values using the fill handle, the numbers automatically increment for each row or column. Here, the number value in cell F5 increased by one when it was copied to cell F6.

9. In the **Auto Fill Options** menu, click **Copy Cells**.

> With the Copy Cells option, number values are literally copied and do not increment. Here, the number value in cell F6 changes to *10*.

10. **Save** 🖫 the workbook.

■ **You have completed Skill 7 of 10**

EXL 1-8
VIDEO

▶ Always check spelling after you have finished formatting and editing your worksheet data.

1. Click cell **A14**, and repeat the technique used previously to insert a new row. In cell **A14**, type Pool and then press Enter.

2. Click cell **B13**, and then use the fill handle to copy the formula down to cell **B14**.

3. Double-click cell **A2** to edit the cell contents. Use the arrow keys to move to the right of the word *Visitors*. Add a space, type to City Attractions and then press Enter.

   Alternately, double-tap cell A2 to edit the cell.

4. Select the range **F5:G10**. In the **Styles group**, click the **Cell Styles** button, and then under **Number Format**, click **Currency [0]**. Take a few moments to familiarize yourself with the Number Formats as summarized in the table in **Figure 1**.

5. Select the range **B5:E10**. Click the **Cell Styles** button, and then under **Number Format**, click **Comma [0]**.

6. Select the range **B13:B17**. In the **Number group**, click the **Percent Style** button %, and then click the **Increase Decimal** button one time. Compare your screen with **Figure 2**.

   The Increase Decimal and Decrease Decimal buttons do not actually add or remove decimals, but they change how the underlying decimal values display in the cells.

■ **Continue to the next page to complete the skill**

Number Formats	
Format	**Description**
Comma	Adds commas where appropriate and displays two decimals.
Comma [0]	Adds commas where appropriate and displays no decimals.
Currency	Adds the dollar sign, commas where appropriate, and displays two decimals.
Currency [0]	Adds the dollar sign, commas where appropriate, and displays no decimals.
Percent	Adds the percent sign and multiplies the number by 100.

Figure 1

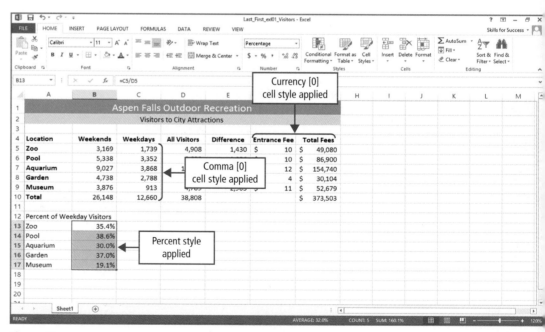

Figure 2

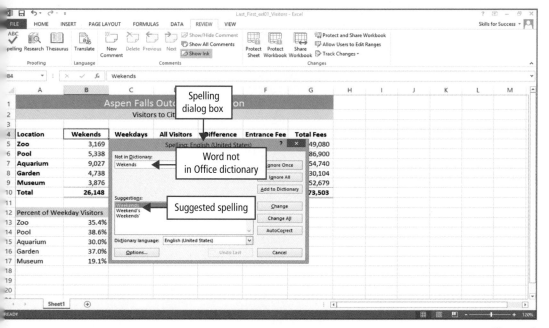

Figure 3

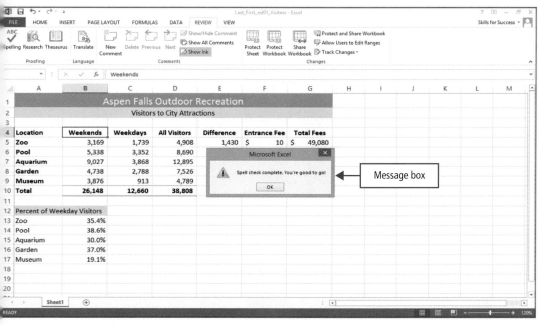

Figure 4

7. Select the range **B10:D10**. Hold down Ctrl, and then click cell **G10**. Click the **Cell Styles** button. Under **Titles and Headings**, click the **Total** style.

8. Select cell **A12**, and then click the **Cell Styles** button. Under **Themed Cell Styles**, click **40% - Accent1**.

9. Press Ctrl + Home to make cell **A1** active. On the **Review tab**, in the **Proofing group**, click the **Spelling** button.

The spelling checker starts with the active cell and moves to the right and down, so making cell A1 the active cell before beginning is useful.

10. In the **Spelling** dialog box, under **Not in Dictionary**, a misspelled word displays as shown in **Figure 3**.

This word is not in the Office dictionary; however, words not in the dictionary are not necessarily misspelled. Many proper nouns or less commonly used words are not in the Office dictionary.

To correct a misspelled word and to move to the next word not in the Office dictionary, under Suggestions, verify that the correct spelling is selected, and then click the Change button.

11. Continue to use the spelling checker to correct any remaining errors you may have made. When the message **Spell check complete. You're good to go!** displays, as shown in **Figure 4**, click **OK**.

When words you use often are not in the Office dictionary, you can click *Add to Dictionary* to add them.

12. Save 🖫 the workbook.

■ **You have completed Skill 8 of 10**

▶ In Excel, **Page Layout view** is used to adjust how a worksheet will look when it is printed.

1. Click the **Insert tab**, and then in the **Text group**, click the **Header & Footer** button to switch to **Page Layout view** and to display the **Header & Footer Tools Design** contextual tab.

2. On the **Design tab**, in the **Navigation group**, click the **Go to Footer** button to move to the Footer area. Click just above the word **Footer** to place the insertion point in the left section of the Footer area.

3. In the **Header & Footer Elements group**, click the **File Name** button. Compare your screen with **Figure 1**.

   Predefined headers and footers insert placeholders with instructions for printing. Here, the *& [File]* placeholder instructs Excel to insert the file name when the worksheet is printed.

4. In the **Header & Footer Elements group**, click in the middle section of the Footer area, and then click the **Current Date** button. Click the right section of the Footer area, and type City Attractions Click in a cell just above the footer to exit the Footer area.

5. Click the **Page Layout tab**. In the **Sheet Options group**, under **Gridlines**, select the **Print** check box.

6. In the **Page Setup group**, click the **Margins** button. Below the **Margins** gallery, click **Custom Margins**. In the **Page Setup** dialog box, under **Center on page**, select the **Horizontally** check box, and then compare your screen with **Figure 2**.

■ Continue to the next page to complete the skill

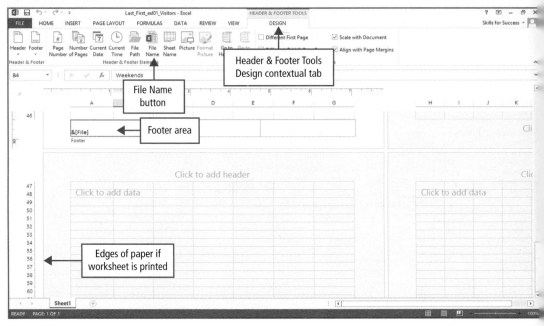

Figure 1

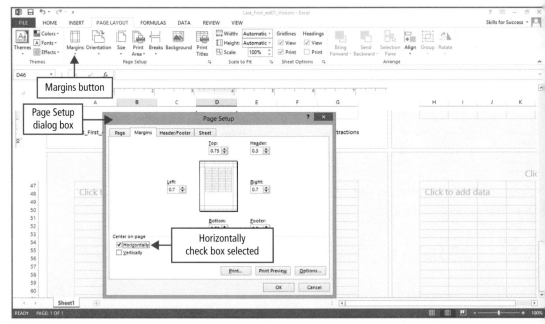

Figure 2

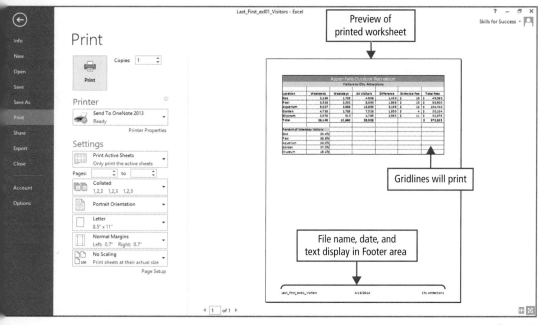

Figure 3

7. In the **Page Setup** dialog box, click **Print Preview**, and then compare your screen with **Figure 3**.

8. Click the **Back** button ⊖. On the lower right side of the status bar, click the **Normal** button 🏢 to return to Normal view, and then press ⌃Ctrl + Home to make cell **A1** active.

   > *Normal view* maximizes the number of cells visible on the screen. The page break—the dotted line between columns G and H—indicates where one page ends and a new page begins.

9. At the bottom of your worksheet, right-click the **Sheet1** worksheet tab, and then from the shortcut menu, click **Rename**. Type Attraction Visitors and then press Enter to change the worksheet tab name. Compare your screen with **Figure 4**.

10. Save 🖫 the workbook.

■ **You have completed Skill 9 of 10**

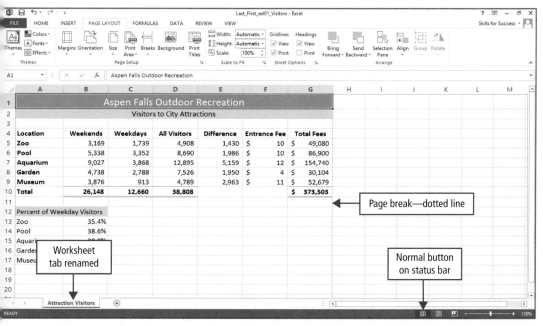

Figure 4

EXL 1-10
VIDEO

▶ Underlying formulas and functions can be displayed and printed.

▶ When formulas are displayed in cells, the orientation and worksheet scale may need to be changed so that the worksheet prints on a single page.

1. Click the **Formulas tab**. In the **Formula Auditing group**, click the **Show Formulas** button to display the underlying formulas in the cells. Compare your screen with **Figure 1**.

   Columns often become wider when formulas are displayed. Here, the printed worksheet extends to a second page.

2. Click the **File tab**, and then click **Print**.

   Below the preview of the printed page, *1 of 3* indicates that the worksheet will print on three pages.

3. In **Backstage** view, on the bottom of the **Print** page, click the **Next Page** button ▶ two times to view the second and the third pages, and then compare your screen with **Figure 2**.

4. Click the **Back** button ⬅. On the **Page Layout tab**, in the **Page Setup group**, click the **Orientation** button, and then click **Landscape** so that the page orientation will be wider than it is tall.

■ **Continue to the next page to complete the skill** ▶

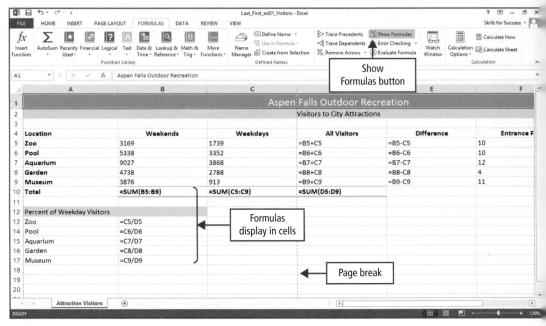

Figure 1

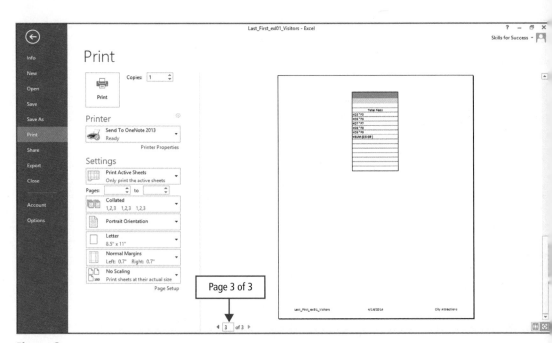

Figure 2

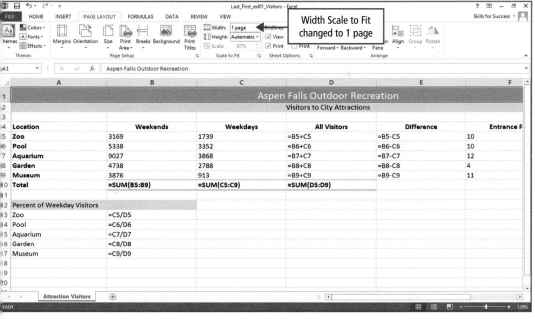

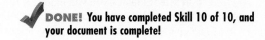

Figure 3

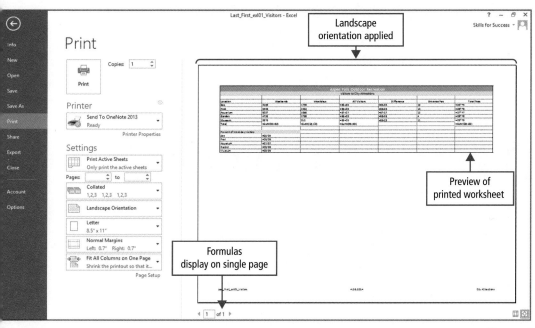

Figure 4

5. In the **Scale to Fit group**, click the **Width arrow**, and then click **1 page**. Compare your screen with **Figure 3**.

   Scaling adjusts the size of the printed worksheet to fit on the number of pages that you specify.

6. Click the **File tab**, and then click **Print**. Compare your screen with **Figure 4**.

   1 of 1 displays at the bottom of the Print page to notify you that the worksheet will now print on one page.

7. If you are directed by your instructor to submit a printout with your formulas displayed, click the Print button.

8. Click the **Back** button. On the **Formulas tab** in the **Formula Auditing group**, click the **Show Formulas** button to hide the formulas.

9. If you are printing your work, print the worksheet with the values displayed and formulas hidden.

10. **Save** the workbook, and then **Close** Excel. Submit the workbook file or printouts as directed by your instructor.

DONE! You have completed Skill 10 of 10, and your document is complete!

More Skills

The following More Skills are located at **www.pearsonhighered.com/skills**

More Skills Create Workbooks from Templates

Templates are used to build workbooks without having to start from scratch. You can save time by using one of many predefined templates from Microsoft Office Online.

In More Skills 11, you will use a Calendar template downloaded from Microsoft Office Online to create a schedule.

To begin, open your web browser, navigate to www.pearsonhighered.com/skills, locate the name of your textbook, and then follow the instructions on the website.

More Skills Insert Names into Formulas

Instead of using cell references in formulas and functions, you can assign names that refer to the same cell or range. Names can be easier to remember than cell references, and they can add meaning to formulas, making them easier for you and others to understand.

In More Skills 12, you will open a workbook and practice various ways to name cell ranges. You will then use the names in formulas.

To begin, open your web browser, navigate to www.pearsonhighered.com/skills, locate the name of your textbook, and then follow the instructions on the website.

More Skills Create Templates

You can save one of your own workbooks as a template to use again, or you can download a template from Microsoft Office Online and then customize the template.

In More Skills 13, you will modify a Time Card template downloaded from Microsoft Office Online and then use the template to create a new weekly time card.

To begin, open your web browser, navigate to www.pearsonhighered.com/skills, locate the name of your textbook, and then follow the instructions on the website.

More Skills Manage Document Properties

Document properties are the detailed information about your workbook that can help you identify or organize your files, including the name of the author, the title, and keywords. Some workbook properties are added to the workbook when you create it. You can add others as necessary.

In More Skills 14, you will open a workbook, open the Document Information Panel, and add document properties.

To begin, open your web browser, navigate to www.pearsonhighered.com/skills, locate the name of your textbook, and then follow the instructions on the website.

Please note that there are no additional projects to accompany the More Skills Projects, and they are not covered in the End-of-Chapter projects.

The following table summarizes the **SKILLS AND PROCEDURES** covered in this chapter.

Skill Number	Task	Step	Icon	Keyboard Shortcut
2	Merge cells	Home tab → Alignment group → Merge & Center	Merge & Center	
3	Accept a cell entry	Formula bar → Enter	✓	Enter
5	Adjust Column Width	Home tab → Cells group → Format → Column Width		
5	Adjust Row Height	Home tab → Cells group → Format → Row Height		
5	Apply Cell Styles	Home tab → Styles group → Cell Styles		
6	Insert SUM function	Home tab → Editing group → AutoSum	Σ AutoSum	
7	Insert a row	Home tab → Cells group → Insert → Insert Sheet Rows		
8	Check spelling	Review tab → Proofing group → Spelling		F7
8	Edit inside cells	Double-click		F2
8	Increase Decimals	Home tab → Number group → Increase Decimal	←.0 .00	
8	Decrease Decimals	Home tab → Number group → Decrease Decimal	.00 →.0	
9	Display workbook in Normal View	Status bar → Normal	⊞	
9	Move to cell A1			Ctrl + Home
9	Insert text and fields into footers	Insert tab → Text group → Header & Footer		
9	Rename a worksheet tab	Right-click worksheet tab → Rename		
10	Display formulas	Formulas tab → Formula Auditing group → Show Formulas		Ctrl + [`]
10	Scale to Print on one page	Page Layout tab → Scale to Fit group → Width		
10	Change Page Orientation	Page Layout tab → Page Setup group → Orientation		

Key Terms

Online Help Skills

1. Start **Excel 2013**, and then in the upper right corner of the start page, click the **Help** button [?].

2. In the **Excel Help** window **Search help** box, type Broken formula and then press Enter .

3. In the search result list, click **Why is my formula broken**, and then compare your screen with **Figure 1**.

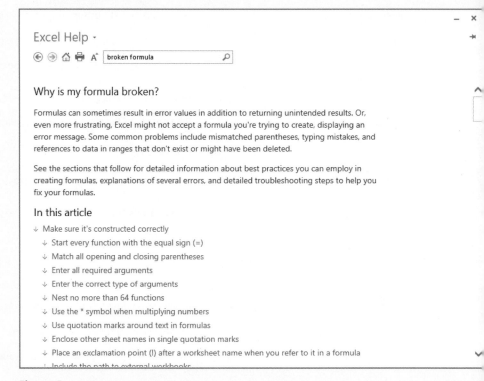

Figure 1

4. Read the article to answer the following questions: What results in a #DIV/0 error? What function can you nest with your division operation to avoid this error?

Matching

Match each term in the second column with its correct definition in the first column by writing the letter of the term on the blank line in front of the correct definition.

___ **1.** An Excel file that contains one or more worksheets.

___ **2.** The primary document that you use in Excel to store and work with data.

___ **3.** The cell, surrounded by a green border, ready to receive data or be affected by the next Excel command.

___ **4.** The identification of a specific cell by its intersecting column letter and row number.

___ **5.** Data in a cell—text or numbers.

___ **6.** Data in a cell made up of text only.

___ **7.** Data in a cell made up of numbers only.

___ **8.** Two or more cells on a worksheet.

___ **9.** The Excel window area that displays the address of a selected cell.

___ **10.** An Excel feature that suggests values as you type a function.

A Active cell

B Cell reference

C Formula AutoComplete

D Name Box

E Number value

F Range

G Text value

H Value

I Workbook

J Worksheet

BizSkills
Video

1. What are the best ways to network online?

2. What are some of the biggest pitfalls in using social media to communicate a personal brand?

Multiple Choice

Choose the correct answer.

1. An Excel window area that displays the value contained in the active cell.
   A. Formula bar
   B. Workbook
   C. Name Box

2. The column letter and row number that identify a cell.
   A. Cell window
   B. Cell address
   C. Cell file name

3. The data displayed in a cell.
   A. Viewed value
   B. Inspected value
   C. Displayed value

4. An equation that performs mathematical calculations on number values.
   A. Method
   B. Formula
   C. System

5. Page headers and footers can be changed in this view.
   A. Print preview
   B. Page Layout view
   C. Normal view

6. Symbols that specify mathematical operations such as addition or subtraction.
   A. Hyperlinks
   B. Bookmarks
   C. Arithmetic operators

7. The number that displays at the left of a row.
   A. Row heading
   B. Row name
   C. Row border

8. A prewritten Excel formula.
   A. Method
   B. Function
   C. Exponent

9. The small green square in the lower right corner of the active cell.
   A. Border
   B. Fill handle
   C. Edge

10. A view that maximizes the number of cells visible on the screen.
    A. Page Layout view
    B. Standard view
    C. Normal view

Topics for Discussion

1. What is the advantage of using cell references instead of actual number values in formulas and functions?

2. What are some things you can do to make your worksheet easier for others to read and understand?

3. According to the Introduction to this chapter, how do you decide which information to put in columns and which to put in rows?

Skills Review

MyITLab®
Grader

To complete this project, you will need the following file:

- **Blank Excel document**

You will save your file as:

- **Last_First_exl01_SRFitness**

1. Start **Excel 2013**. In cell **A1**, type Aspen Falls Fitness Events and then in cell **A2**, type Number of Participants In cell **A4**, type Department and then pressing [Tab] after each label, type Spring, Fall, Total Participants and Difference

2. In rows **5** through **9**, enter the following data starting in cell **A5**:

City Hall	185	140	Engineering	169	147
Finance	147	136	City Council	195	152
IT Services	130	117			

3. In cell **D5**, type =B5+C5 and then in cell **E5**, type =B5-C5 Select the range **D5:E5**. Point to the fill handle, and then drag down through row **9**. Compare your screen with **Figure 1**.

4. **Save** the workbook in your chapter folder with the name Last_First_exl01_SRFitness

5. On the **Insert tab**, in the **Text group**, click the **Header & Footer** button. In the **Navigation group**, click the **Go to Footer** button, and then click in the left footer. In the **Header & Footer Elements group**, click the **File Name** button. Click in a cell just above the footer. On the lower right side of the status bar, click the **Normal** button, and then press [Ctrl]+[Home].

6. In cell **A10**, type Total and then select the range **B10:D10**. On the **Home tab**, in the **Editing group**, click the **AutoSum** button.

7. Click cell **A7**. In the **Cells group**, click the **Insert arrow**, and then click **Insert Sheet Rows**. In the new row **7**, type the following data: Public Works and 95 and 87

8. Select the range **D6:E6**, and then use the fill handle to copy the formulas down one row.

9. In cell **A13**, type Fall Participants as a Percent of Total

10. Select the range **A5:A10**, and then on the **Home tab**, in the **Clipboard group**, click the **Copy** button. Click cell **A14**, and then in the **Clipboard group**, click the **Paste** button. Press [Esc] and then compare your screen with **Figure 2**.

■ Continue to the next page to complete this Skills Review ➤

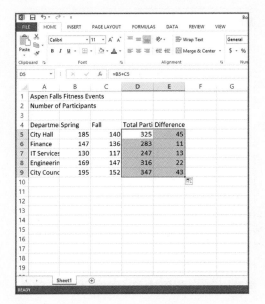

Figure 1

Figure 2

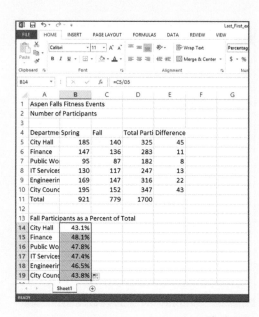

Figure 3

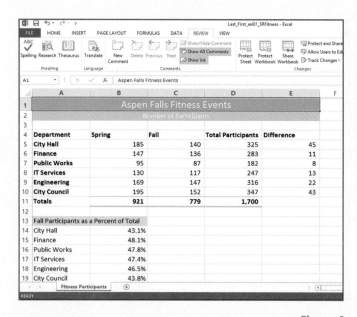

Figure 4

11. In cell **B14**, type =C5/D5 and then on the formula bar, click the **Enter** button. In the **Number group**, click the **Percent Style** button, and then click the **Increase Decimal** button one time. With cell **B14** still the active cell, use the fill handle to copy the formula down through row **19**. Compare your screen with **Figure 3**.

12. Select the range **A1:E1**, and then on the **Home tab**, in the **Alignment group**, click the **Merge & Center** button. In the **Styles group**, click the **Cell Styles** button, and then click **Accent 6**. In the **Font group**, click the **Font Size arrow**, and then click **16**. Select the range **A2:E2**, and then click the **Merge & Center** button. Click the **Cell Styles** button, and then click **60% - Accent 6**.

13. Select the range **A4:E4**. On the **Home tab**, in the **Cells group**, click the **Format** button, and then click **Column Width**. In the **Column Width** dialog box, type 16 and the click **OK**.

14. With the range **A4:E4** still selected, hold down Ctrl, and then select the range **A5:A11**. In the **Font group**, click the **Bold** button.

15. Select range **B5:E11**. In the **Styles group**, click the **Cell Styles** button, and then click **Comma [0]**. Select the range **B11:D11**. Click the **Cell Styles** button, and then click the **Total** style.

16. Select the range **A13:B13**. In the **Alignment group**, click the **Merge & Center arrow**, and then click **Merge Across**. Click the **Cell Styles** button, and then click **40% - Accent6**.

17. Press Ctrl + Home. On the **Review tab**, in the **Proofing group**, click the **Spelling** button, and then correct any spelling errors.

18. Right-click the **Sheet1** worksheet tab, and from the shortcut menu, click **Rename**. Type Fitness Participants and then press Enter. **Save**, and then compare your screen with **Figure 4**. If directed by your instructor, display and format the worksheet formulas as described in Skill 10, and then print the worksheet.

19. Submit the printouts or workbook as directed by your instructor.

DONE! You have completed this Skills Review

Skills Assessment 1

MyITLab®
Grader

To complete this project, you will need the following file:

- exl01_SA1Path

You will save your workbook as:

- Last_First_exl01_SA1Path

1. Start **Excel 2013**. From your student data files, open **exl01_SA1Path**. Save the workbook in your chapter folder as Last_First_exl01_SA1Path Add the file name to the worksheet's left footer, add the current date to the center footer, and then type Bike Path Costs in the right footer. Return to **Normal** view.

2. For the range **A1:E1**, merge and center and apply the **Accent5** cell style. Increase the font size to **18** points. For the range **A2:E2**, merge and center and apply the **40% - Accent 5** cell style. Widen column **A** to *20*. For all column and row labels, apply **Bold**.

3. For the range **E5:E13**, insert the **SUM** function to add the three costs for each row. In the range **B14:E14**, insert the **SUM** function to provide totals for each column.

4. Select the nonadjacent ranges **B5:E5** and **B14:E14**. Apply the **Currency [0]** cell style.

5. Select the range **B6:E13**, and then apply the **Comma [0]** cell style. Select the range **B14:E14**, and then apply the **Total** cell style.

6. Insert a new row above row 7. In cell **A7**, type Aspen Lakes and as the costs for the new location, type 4763 and 18846 and 1498 Use the fill handle to copy the formula in cell **E6** to cell **E7**.

7. **Copy** the location names from the range **A5:A14** to the range **A20:A29**.

8. Making sure to type the decimals, in cells **B20** and **B21**, type .03 In cells **B22** and **B23**, type .05 and in cell **B24**, type .06 Use the fill handle to copy the value in cell **B24** down through cell **B29**. Select the range **B20:B29**, and then apply the **Percent Style** number format.

9. In cell **C20**, enter a formula that calculates the cost by multiplying cell **E5** by cell **B20**. AutoFill the formula in cell **C20** down through cell **C29**.

10. Rename the **Sheet 1** worksheet tab as Path Costs

Aspen Falls				
Bike Path Construction Costs				
Location	Brush Clearing	Paving	Landscaping	Total Cost
Cornish Forest	$ 5,883	$ 15,580	$ 3,271	$ 24,734
Haack Center	6,234	18,916	1,697	26,847
Aspen Lakes	4,763	18,846	1,498	25,107
Hamilton Hills Park	4,981	17,169	1,805	23,955
Hansen Hills	4,209	14,062	2,437	20,708
Plasek Park	3,247	12,691	3,971	19,909
Price Lakes	3,648	19,387	2,927	25,962
Rodman Creek	4,515	13,120	1,934	19,569
Schroder Brook	3,862	19,166	2,036	25,064
Terry Park	2,569	17,506	1,756	21,831
Total	$ 43,911	$ 166,443	$ 23,332	$ 233,686

Location	Increase	Cost Increase		
Cornish Forest	3%	$ 742.02		
Haack Center	3%	$ 805.41		
Aspen Lakes	5%	$ 1,255.35		
Hamilton Hills Park	5%	$ 1,197.75		
Hansen Hills	6%	$ 1,242.48		
Plasek Park	6%	$ 1,194.54		
Price Lakes	6%	$ 1,557.72		
Rodman Creek	6%	$ 1,174.14		
Schroder Brook	6%	$ 1,503.84		
Terry Park	6%	$ 1,309.86		

Figure 1

11. Use **Page Setup** to center the worksheet **Horizontally**. Set the **Gridlines** to print.

12. Check and correct any spelling errors, ignoring the proper names.

13. **Save** the workbook. Submit the workbook as directed by your instructor. If you are instructed to do so, display the worksheet formulas, scale the worksheet to print on one page.

14. Compare your completed worksheet with **Figure 1**.

 DONE! You have completed Skills Assessment 1

Skills Assessment 2

To complete this project, you will need the following file:

- exl01_SA2Guests

You will save your workbook as:

- Last_First_exl01_SA2Guests

1. Start **Excel 2013**. From the student data files, open **exl01_SA2Guests**. Save the workbook in your chapter folder as Last_First_exl01_SA2Guests Add the file name to the worksheet's left footer, and then add the Current Date to the right footer. Return to **Normal** view.

2. In cell **D5**, construct a formula to add the *1st Qtr.* and *2nd Qtr.* guests who are *Over 70*. In cell **E5**, construct a formula to calculate the increase of guests of the *2nd Qtr.* over the *1st Qtr.* guests who are *Over 70*.

3. In cell **F5** for the *Over 70* row, construct a formula to divide *2nd Qtr.* guests by the *1st Half Total Guests*.

4. AutoFill the formulas in the range **D5:F5** down through row **17**.

5. In cell **A18**, type Total and then in row **18**, insert the functions to total columns **B:D**.

6. Insert a new row above row **15**, and then in the new cell, **A15**, type 20 to 25 In cell **B15**, type 17196 and in cell **C15** type 19133

7. For the range **B5:E19** apply the **Comma [0]** cell style, and for the range **F5:F18** apply the **Percent** number style and display one decimal.

8. Merge and center the range **A1:F1**, and then apply the **Accent6** cell style. Increase the font size to **18**. Merge and center the range **A2:F2**, and then apply the **40% - Accent 6** cell style. Increase the font size to **14**.

9. Widen columns **A:C** to **11.00**, and then widen columns **D:F** to **14.00**.

10. For the column and row labels, apply **Bold**. In the range **B19:D19**, apply the **Total** cell style.

11. For the range **A22:C22**, apply the **Merge Across** alignment and the **40% - Accent 6** cell style.

12. In cell **C24**, construct a formula to multiply *1st Half Total Guests* in the *Over 70* row by the*Projected Percent Increase* in cell **B24**. Apply the **Comma [0]** cell style. AutoFill the formula down through row **37**.

13. Rename the worksheet tab Aspen Lakes Guests

Aspen Lakes Recreation Area					
Number of Guests					
Ages	1st Qtr.	2nd Qtr.	1st Half Total Guests	2nd Qtr. Increase Over 1st Qtr.	2nd Qtr. as Percent of Total
Over 70	14,102	15,216	29,318	1,114	51.9%
65 to 70	15,125	17,854	32,979	2,729	54.1%
60 to 65	11,175	18,273	29,448	7,098	62.1%
55 to 60	15,110	16,572	31,682	1,462	52.3%
50 to 55	19,114	19,841	38,955	727	50.9%
45 to 50	18,475	21,418	39,893	2,943	53.7%
40 to 45	12,064	13,242	25,306	1,178	52.3%
35 to 40	14,628	16,232	30,860	1,604	52.6%
30 to 35	14,543	19,975	34,518	5,432	57.9%
25 to 30	17,933	19,724	37,657	1,791	52.4%
20 to 25	17,196	19,133	36,329	1,937	52.7%
15 to 20	30,516	32,597	63,113	2,081	51.6%
10 to 15	13,469	17,439	30,908	3,970	56.4%
Under 10	17,876	19,599	37,475	1,723	52.3%
Total	231,326	267,115	498,441		

Projected 2nd Half Guests					
Ages	Projected Percentage Increase	Projected Increase in Guests			
Over 70	2%	586			
65 to 70	8%	2,638			
60 to 65	4%	1,178			
55 to 60	1%	317			
50 to 55	5%	1,948			
45 to 50	6%	2,394			
40 to 45	9%	2,278			
35 to 40	3%	926			
30 to 35	6%	2,071			
25 to 30	15%	5,649			
20 to 25	14%	5,086			
15 to 20	18%	11,360			
10 to 15	21%	6,491			
Under 10	23%	8,619			

Figure 1

14. Check and correct any spelling errors.

15. Use Page Setup to center the page **Horizontally**. Set the **Gridlines** to print, and then **Save** the workbook.

16. If you are instructed to do so, display the worksheet formulas, scale the worksheet to print on one page, and then print with the formulas displayed.

17. Switch to **Normal** view, and then compare your completed worksheet with **Figure 1**. **Close** Excel, and then submit the workbook as directed by your instructor.

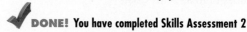 **DONE! You have completed Skills Assessment 2**

Visual Skills Check

To complete this project, you will need the following file:

- Blank Excel workbook

You will save your workbook as:

- Last_First_exl01_VSWorkers

Start **Excel 2013**. Open a new blank workbook, and then **Save** the workbook in your chapter folder as Last_First_exl01_VSWorkers Create the worksheet shown in **Figure 1**. The width of column **A** is 20 and the width of columns **B:F** is 13. Construct formulas that display the results shown in columns **D** and **F**, row **13**, and the range **B18:B25**. The title uses the **Accent4** cell style, and the font size is **20.** The subtitle uses the **40% - Accent 4** cell style, and the font size is **16.** The title and subtitle should be merged and centered. Using **Figure 1** as your guide, apply the **Currency [0]** cell style, the **Comma [0]** cell style, the **Total** cell style, the **Percent** number style, and the **Bold** format. On the range **A17:B17**, use Merge Across and apply the **40%-Accent2** cell style. Rename the *Sheet1* sheet tab as Park Workers Check and correct any spelling errors. Add the file name to the left footer. **Save** the workbook, and then submit the workbook as directed by your instructor.

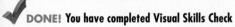 **DONE! You have completed Visual Skills Check**

Aspen Falls						
Park Workers						
	Price Park	Silkwood Park	Total Workers	Wage	Total Wages	
Ticket Sellers	75	52	127	$ 15	$	1,905
Security	92	79	171	25		4,275
Landscapers	19	11	30	20		600
Life Guards	23	23	46	15		690
Cashiers	73	58	131	15		1,965
Parking Attendants	15	11	26	15		390
Maintenance	21	28	49	20		980
Cleaning	29	17	46	18		828
Total	347	279	626		$	11,633

Price Park as Percent of Total Workers	
Ticket Sellers	59.1%
Security	53.8%
Landscapers	63.3%
Life Guards	50.0%
Cashiers	55.7%
Parking Attendants	57.7%
Maintenance	42.9%
Cleaning	63.0%

Figure 1

My College Enrollment				
Course Name	**Fall**	**Spring**	**Summer**	**Course Total**
Algebra	1,173	938	415	2,526
Intro to Computers	1,043	857	497	2,397
Biology	578	311	253	1,142
World History	688	549	372	1,609
American History	824	598	397	1,819
Management	367	228	103	698
English	1,292	1,125	573	2,990
Semester Total	5,965	4,606	2,610	13,181

Summer as a Percent of Total	
Algebra	16.4%
Intro to Computers	20.7%
Biology	22.2%
World History	23.1%
American History	21.8%
Management	14.8%
English	19.2%

Figure 1

My Skills

To complete this project, you will need the following file:

- exl01_MYCollege

You will save your workbook as:

- Last_First_exl01_MYCollege

1. Start **Excel 2013**. From the student data files, open **exl01_MYCollege**. Save the workbook in your chapter folder as Last_First_exl01_MYCollege Add the file name to the worksheet's left footer, and then return to **Normal** view.

2. For the range **A1:E1**, merge and center and apply the **Accent3** cell style.

3. Widen column **A** to 20, and then widen columns **B:E** to 12

4. For the range **B3:E3**, center the labels. For all column and row labels, apply **Bold**.

5. In cell **E4**, insert the **SUM** function to provide the total for the row. AutoFill the formula in cell **E4** down through cell **E9**.

6. For the range **B10:E10**, insert the **SUM** function to provide totals for each column. With the range **B10:E10** still selected, apply the **Total** cell style.

7. For the range **B4:E10**, apply the **Comma [0]** cell style.

8. Insert a new row above row **7**. In cell **A7**, type World History and as the enrollment for the new course, type 688 and 549 and 372 AutoFill the formula in cell **E6** to cell **E7**.

9. **Copy** the course names from the range **A4:A10** to the range **A15:A21**.

10. In cell **B15**, create a formula that calculates the summer semester as a percent of the total course enrollment by dividing cell **D4** by cell **E4**. Apply the **Percent Style** number format, and display one decimal. AutoFill the formula in cell **B15** down through cell **B21**.

11. For the range **A14:B14**, merge across and apply the **40% - Accent3** cell style.

12. Rename the **Sheet 1** worksheet tab as Enrollment

13. Use **Page Setup** to center the worksheet **Horizontally**.

14. Check and correct any spelling errors.

15. **Save** the workbook. Submit the workbook as directed by your instructor. If you are instructed to do so, display the worksheet formulas, scale the worksheet to print on one page.

16. Compare your completed worksheet with **Figure 1**.

✓ **DONE! You have completed My Skills**

Skills Challenge 1

To complete this project, you will need the following file:

- exl01_SC1Employees

You will save your workbook as:

- Last_First_exl01_SC1Employees

Start **Excel 2013**, and then open the workbook **exl01_SC1Employees**. Save the workbook in your chapter folder as Last_First_exl01_SC1Employees Duncan Chueng, the Park Operations Manager for Aspen Falls, wants to total and compare the number of employees at the city recreation areas. Using the skills you practiced in this chapter, correct the SUM function for each row and column. Format the worksheet using cell styles and number formats as practiced in this chapter. Merge and center the title across the correct columns.

Correct the number formats. No decimals should display in rows 5:11. Adjust column widths as necessary to display all data. Set the gridlines to print, and center the data horizontally on the page. Add the file name in the worksheet's left footer, and check for spelling errors. Save the workbook, and then submit the workbook as directed by your instructor.

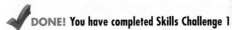 **DONE! You have completed Skills Challenge 1**

Skills Challenge 2

To complete this project, you will need the following file:

- exl01_SC2Painting

You will save your workbook as:

- Last_First_exl01_SC2Painting

Start **Excel 2013**, and then open the workbook **exl01_SC2Painting**. Save the workbook in your chapter folder as Last_First_exl01_SC2Painting The Art Center wants to total and compare the number of students enrolled in the painting classes in the different neighborhoods. Using the skills you practiced in this chapter, insert appropriate formulas and functions. Adjust column widths and row heights as necessary

to display all data. Format the worksheet as appropriate. Add the file name in the worksheet's left footer, and check for spelling errors. Save the workbook, and then submit the workbook as directed by your instructor.

DONE! You have completed Skills Challenge 2

CHAPTER 2

Insert Summary Functions and Create Charts

- ► Functions are prewritten formulas that have two parts—the name of the function and the arguments that specify the values or cells to be used by the function.

- ► Functions analyze data to answer financial, statistical, or logical questions. Summary functions are used to recap information.

- ► Excel provides various types of charts that can make your data easier to understand.

- ► Column charts show data changes over a period of time or illustrate comparisons among items.

- ► Pie charts illustrate how each part relates to the whole. Pie charts display the relative sizes of items in a single data series.

- ► Charts can be enhanced with effects such as 3-D and soft shadows to create compelling graphical summaries.

Fotolia: Zwei Frauen im Büro © Jeanette Dietl

Aspen Falls City Hall

In this chapter, you will finish a workbook for Thelma Perkins, a Risk Management Specialist in the Finance Department. The workbook displays the department expenditures for Aspen Falls. The City Council requires that the Finance Department present departmental information annually for review and approval.

Companies use formulas and statistical functions to manipulate and summarize data to make better decisions. Summary results can include the data totals or averages. Results can be displayed graphically as charts, providing a visual representation of data. Commonly used chart types include line charts to illustrate trends over time or bar charts to illustrate comparisons among individual items. Based on the type of data selected, the Quick Analysis tools provide chart type options.

In this project, you will open an existing workbook, construct formulas containing absolute cell references, and AutoFill the formulas to other cells. You will insert the statistical functions AVERAGE, MAX, and MIN. You will create and format column charts and pie charts, and insert WordArt. Finally, you will prepare the chart sheet and the worksheet to meet printing requirements.

Time to complete all 10 skills – 60 to 90 minutes

Student data file needed for this chapter:

exl02_Expenditures

You will save your workbook as:

Last_First_exl02_Expenditures

Outcome

Using the skills in this chapter, you will be able to work with Excel worksheets like this:

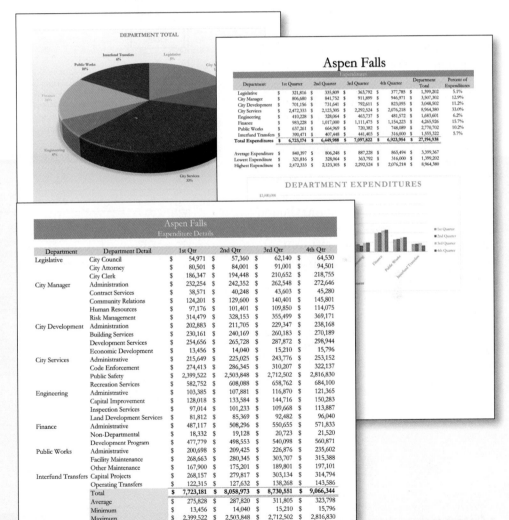

SKILLS

MyITLab®
Skills 1-10 Training

At the end of this chapter you will be able to:

Skill 1 Align and Wrap Text
Skill 2 Apply Absolute Cell References
Skill 3 Format Numbers
Skill 4 Insert the AVERAGE Function
Skill 5 Insert the MIN and MAX Functions
Skill 6 Create Column Charts
Skill 7 Format Column Charts
Skill 8 Create and Format Pie Charts
Skill 9 Update Charts and Insert WordArt
Skill 10 Preview and Print Multiple Worksheets

MORE SKILLS

Skill 11 Insert, Edit, and Delete Comments
Skill 12 Change Chart Types
Skill 13 Copy Excel Data to Word Documents
Skill 14 Fill Data with Flash Fill

▶ The **Text wrap** format displays text on multiple lines within a cell.

1. Start **Excel 2013**, open the student data file **exl02_Expenditures**, and then compare your screen with **Figure 1**.

2. On the **File tab**, click **Save As**. On the **Save As** page, click the **Browse** button. Navigate to the location where you are saving your files. Click **New folder**, type Excel Chapter 2 and then press ⏎Enter⏎ two times. In the **File name** box, name the workbook Last_First_exl02_Expenditures and then press ⏎Enter⏎.

3. Verify *Expenditures* is the active worksheet. On the **Insert tab**, in the **Text group**, click the **Header & Footer** button. In the **Navigation group**, click the **Go to Footer** button. Click just above the word **Footer**, and then in the **Header & Footer Elements group**, click the **File Name** button. Click a cell above the footer. On the status bar, click the **Normal** button 🔲, and then press ⌷Ctrl⌷ + ⌷Home⌷.

4. Click cell **B2**. Point at the fill handle to display the ✛ pointer, and drag right through cell **E2** to AutoFill the labels. Compare your screen with **Figure 2**.

> Excel's AutoFill feature can generate a series of values into adjacent cells. A **series** is a group of numbers, text, dates, or time periods that come one after another in succession. For example, the months *January, February, March* are a series. Likewise, *1st Quarter, 2nd Quarter, 3rd Quarter,* and *4th Quarter* form a series.

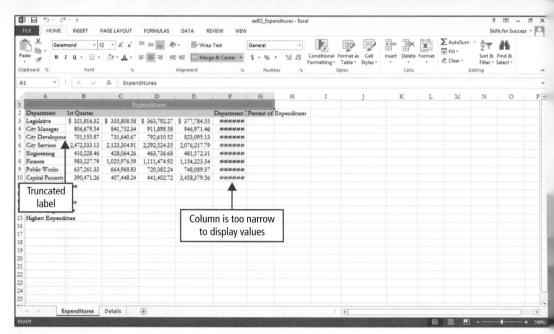

Figure 1

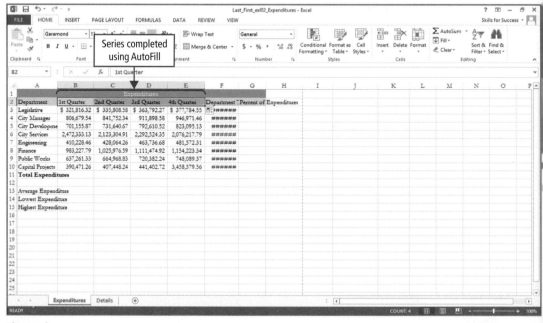

Figure 2

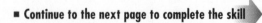
■ **Continue to the next page to complete the skill** ▶

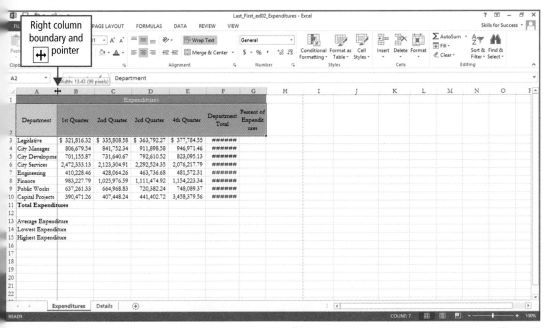

Figure 3

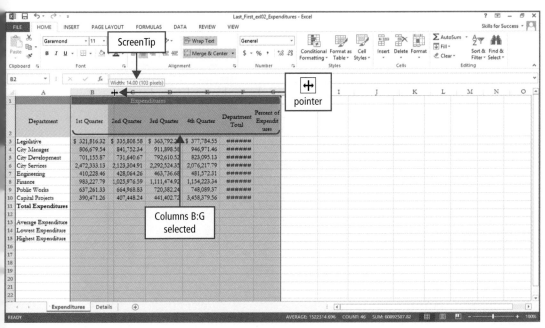

Figure 4

5. Select the range **A2:G2**. On the **Home tab**, in the **Alignment group**, click the **Wrap Text** button, the **Middle Align** button ≣, and the **Center** button ≣.

6. In the column heading area, point to the right boundary of column **A** to display the ⊞ pointer, as shown in **Figure 3**.

7. With the ⊞ pointer displayed, double-click to **AutoFit** the column—automatically change the column width to accommodate the longest entry.

8. In the column heading area, click the column **B** heading, and then drag right through column **G** to select columns **B:G**. Click the right boundary of column **B** to display the ⊞ pointer, and then drag to the right until the ScreenTip indicates *Width: 14:00 (103 pixels)* as shown in **Figure 4**. Release the mouse button.

9. Select the range **A3:A10**, and then in the **Alignment group**, click the **Increase Indent** button ≣.

10. **Save** 🖫 the workbook.

■ **You have completed Skill 1 of 10**

▶ The Quick Analysis Lens button is used to apply conditional formatting or to insert charts and totals.

▶ Excel uses rules to check for formula errors. When a formula breaks a rule, the cell displays an **error indicator**—a green triangle that indicates a possible error in a formula.

▶ An **absolute cell reference** is a cell reference that remains the same when it is copied or filled to other cells. To make a cell reference absolute, insert a dollar sign ($) before the row and column references.

1. Select **B3:F10**, click the **Quick Analysis Lens** button 📊, and then compare your screen with **Figure 1**.

2. In the **Quick Analysis** gallery, click **Totals**, and then click the first option—**SUM**—to insert column totals.

3. Click **G3**, and then type =F3/F11 On the **formula bar**, click the **Enter** button ✓. Double-click **G3** to display the range finder, and then compare your screen with **Figure 2**.

   The **range finder** outlines all of the cells referenced in a formula. It is useful for verifying which cells are used in a formula and for editing formulas.

4. Press Esc to close the range finder. Point to the **G3** fill handle, and then AutoFill the formula down through **G10** to display **error values**—messages that display whenever a formula cannot perform the calculations in a formula. The #DIV/0! error value displays in a cell whenever the underlying formula attempts to divide by zero.

■ Continue to the next page to complete the skill

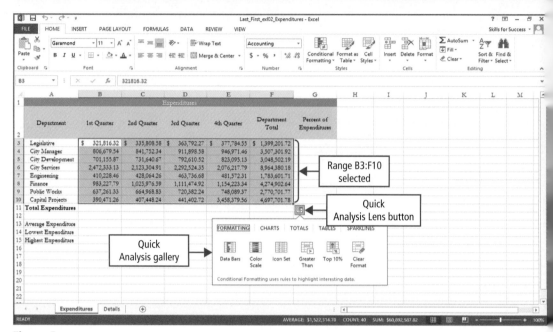

Figure 1

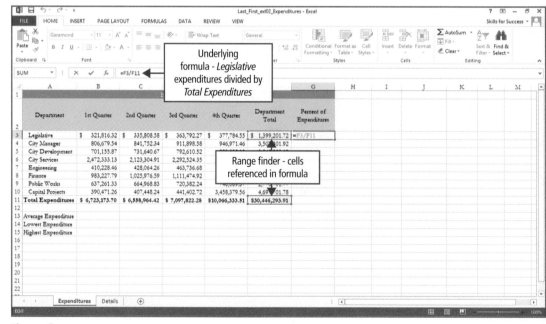

Figure 2

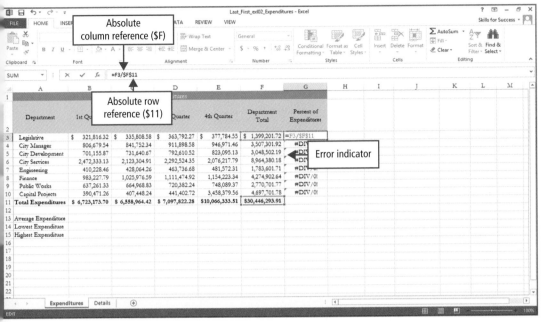

Figure 3

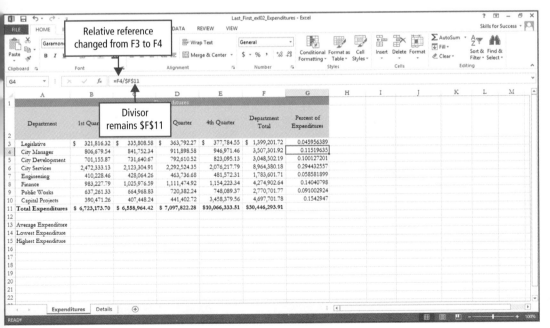

Figure 4

5. Click cell **G4**. To the left of the cell, point to the **Error Message** button [▼] to display the ScreenTip—*The formula or function used is dividing by zero or empty cells.*

6. Double-click cell **G4** to display the range finder.

   The formula was copied with a relative cell reference. In the copied formula, the cell reference to cell F4 is correct, but the formula is dividing by the value in cell F12, an empty cell. In this calculation, the divisor must be cell F11.

7. Press [Esc] and then double-click cell **G3**. In the formula, click the reference to cell **F11**, and then press [F4] to insert a dollar sign ($) before the column reference *F* and the row reference *11* as shown in **Figure 3**.

   The dollar signs are used to indicate an absolute cell reference.

8. On the **formula bar**, click the **Enter** button [✓] and then AutoFill the formula in cell **G3** down through cell **G10**.

9. Click cell **G4**, and verify that the divisor refers to cell *$F$11*, as shown in **Figure 4**.

   The cell reference for the row *City Manager Department Total* changed relative to its row; however, the value used as the divisor—*Total Expenditures* in cell F11—remains absolute.

10. Press the [↓] two times and verify that the divisor remains constant—$F$11—while the dividend changes relative to the row.

11. **Save** [💾] the workbook.

■ **You have completed Skill 2 of 10**

EXL 2-3
VIDEO

▶ A *number format* is a specific way that Excel displays numbers. For example, the number of decimals, or whether commas and special symbols such as dollar signs display.

▶ By default, Excel displays the **General** *format*—a number format that does not display commas or trailing zeros to the right of a decimal point.

1. Click cell **B2**, and then on the **Home tab**, in the **Number group**, notice that *General* displays. Compare your screen with **Figure 1**.

2. Select the range **B3:F11**. In the **Number group**, click the **Decrease Decimal** button two times to round the number and hide the decimals. Click cell **B6**, and then compare your screen with **Figure 2**.

   The Decrease Decimal button hides the displayed value decimals. The underlying value shows the decimals.

3. Select the range **G3:G10**. In the **Number group**, click the **Percent Style** button and then click the **Increase Decimal** button one time to add one decimal to the applied Percent Style. In the **Alignment group**, click the **Center** button.

■ Continue to the next page to complete the skill

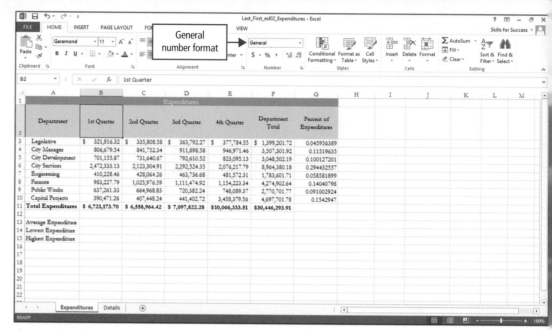

Figure 1

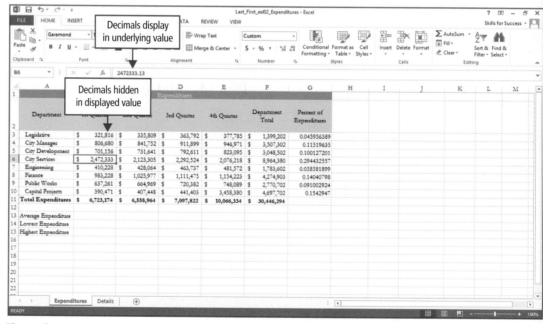

Figure 2

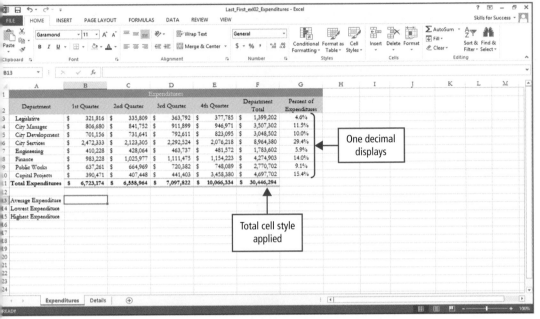

Figure 3

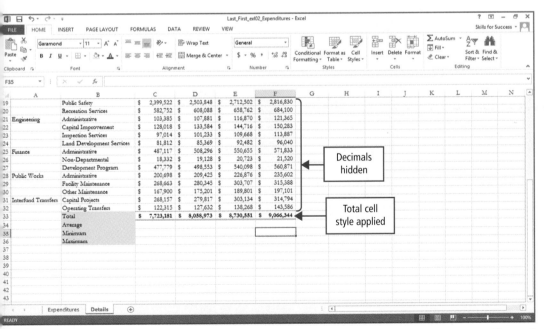

Figure 4

4. Select the range **B11:F11**. In the **Styles group**, click the **Cell Styles** button, and then under **Titles and Headings**, click **Total**. Click cell **B13**, and then compare your screen with **Figure 3**.

5. Along the bottom of the Excel window, notice the ***worksheet tabs***, the labels along the lower border of the workbook window that identify each worksheet. Click the **Details** worksheet tab to make it the active worksheet.

6. Click cell **C5**. Hold down the Ctrl + Shift keys. With both keys held down, press the ↓ one time and the → one time to select the range **C5:F32**.

7. With the range **C5:F32** selected, click the **Quick Analysis Lens** button. In the **Quick Analysis** gallery, click **Totals**, and then click the first option—**SUM**.

8. With the range **C5:F32** still selected, hold down the Shift key and press the ↓ one time to include row **33**—the range *C5:F33* is selected. In the **Number group**, click the **Decrease Decimal** button two times.

9. Select the range **C33:F33**, and then apply the **Total** cell style. Click cell **F35**, and then compare your screen with **Figure 4**.

10. **Save** the workbook.

■ **You have completed Skill 3 of 10**

EXL 2-4
VIDEO

▶ **Statistical functions** are predefined formulas that describe a collection of data—for example, averages, maximums, and minimums.

▶ The **AVERAGE function** adds a group of values and then divides the result by the number of values in the group.

1. Click the **Expenditures** worksheet tab, and then click cell **B13**. On the **Home tab**, in the **Editing group**, click the **AutoSum arrow**, and then in the list of functions, click **Average**. Look in the formula bar and in cell B13 to verify that the range B3:B12 is the suggested range of cells that will be averaged as shown in **Figure 1**.

The range in parentheses is the function *argument*—the values that a function uses to perform operations or calculations. The arguments each function uses are specific to that function. Common arguments include numbers, text, cell references, and range names.

When data is above or to the left of a selected cell, the function argument will automatically be entered. Often, you will need to edit the argument range.

2. With the insertion point in the function argument, click cell **B3**. On the range finder, click a sizing handle, and then drag down to select the argument range **B3:B10**, to exclude the *Total Expenditures* value in cell B11. On the formula bar, click the **Enter** button ☑ to display the result *$840,397*. Compare your screen with **Figure 2**.

■ **Continue to the next page to complete the skill**

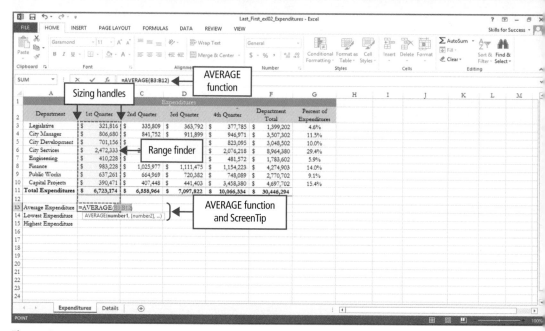

Figure 1

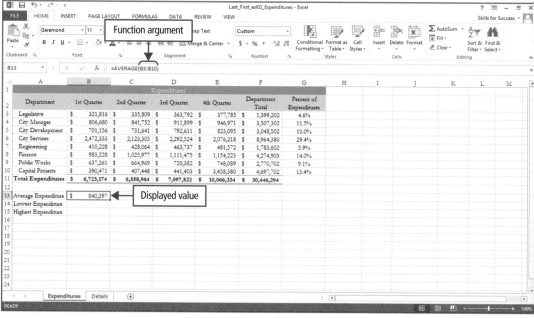

Figure 2

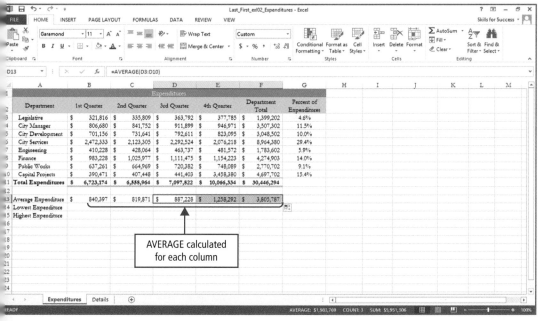

AVERAGE calculated for each column

Figure 3

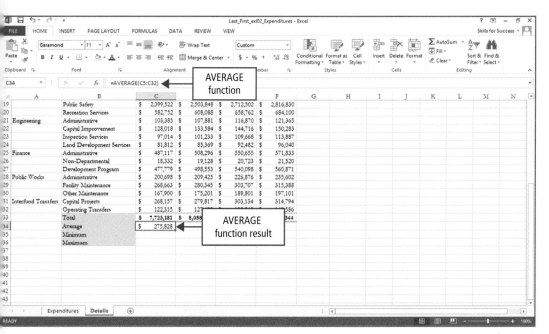

AVERAGE function

AVERAGE function result

Figure 4

3. Click cell **C13**. In the **Editing group**, click the **AutoSum arrow**, and then in the list of functions, click **Average**. In the formula bar and in the cell, notice that Excel proposes to average the value in cell *B13*, not the values in column C.

4. With cell reference B13 highlighted in the function argument, click cell **C3**, and then use the range finder sizing handle to select the range **C3:C10**. On the formula bar, click the **Enter** button ✓ to display the result *$819,871*.

5. Click cell **D13**. Using the techniques just practiced, enter the **AVERAGE** function using the argument range **D3:D10**, and then on the formula bar, click the **Enter** button ✓.

6. Verify that cell **D13** is the active cell, and then AutoFill the function to the right through cell **F13**. Compare your sheet to **Figure 3**.

7. Click the **Details** worksheet tab, and then click cell **C34**. Enter the **AVERAGE** function using the argument range **C5:C32**. Do not include the *Total* value in cell *C33* in the function argument. Compare your sheet to **Figure 4**.

8. Display the worksheet footers, click in the left footer, and then click the **File Name** button. Click in the right footer, and then click the **Sheet Name** button. Return to Normal view.

9. **Save** 🖫 the workbook.

■ **You have completed Skill 4 of 10**

▶ The **MIN function** returns the smallest value in a range of cells.

▶ The **MAX function** returns the largest value in a range of cells.

1. Click cell **C35**. Type =Mi and then in the Formula AutoComplete list, double-click **MIN**. With the insertion point blinking in the function argument, click cell **C32**, and then use the range finder sizing handles to drag up and select the range **C5:C32**. Press Enter to display the result *$13,456*.

> The MIN function evaluates the range provided in the function argument— C5:C32—and then returns the lowest value—*$13,456*. Here, the *Total* and *Average* values in cells *C33* and *C34* should not be included in the argument range.

2. Verify that **C36** is the active cell. Type =Ma and then in the Formula AutoComplete list, double-click **MAX**. Using the technique just practiced, select the range **C5:C32**, and then on the formula bar, click the **Enter** button ✔ to display the result *$2,399,522*. Compare your screen with **Figure 1**.

> The MAX function evaluates all of the values in the range C5:C32 and then returns the highest value found in the range.

3. Select the range **C34:C36**. AutoFill the formulas to the right through column **F**, and then compare your screen with **Figure 2**.

> In this manner, you can AutoFill several different functions or formulas at the same time. Here, the different functions at the beginning of each row are filled across the columns.

■ **Continue to the next page to complete the skill** ➤

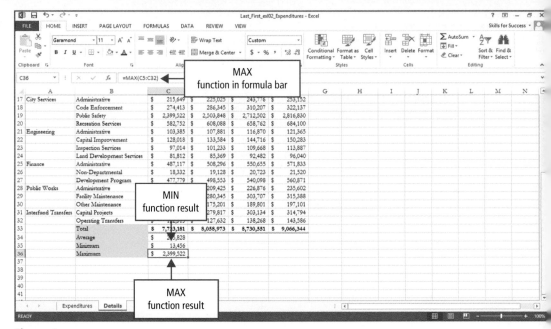

Figure 1

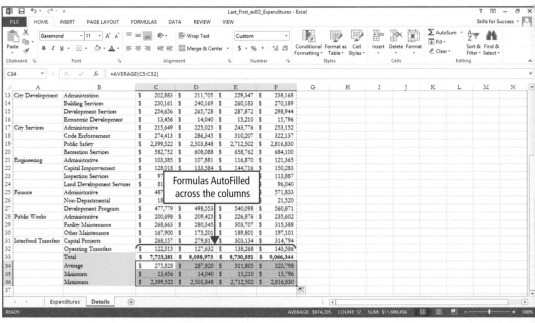

Figure 2

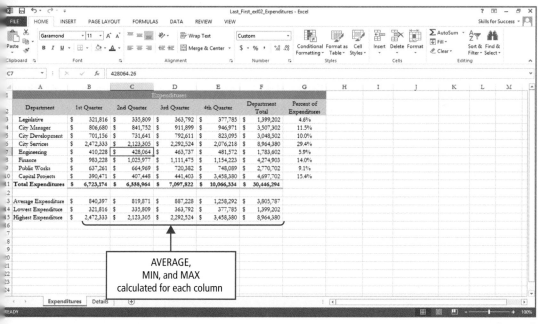

Figure 3

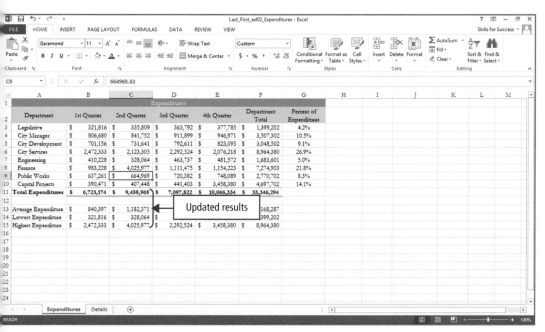

Figure 4

4. Click the **Expenditures** worksheet tab. In cell **B14**, repeat the technique just practiced to insert the **MIN** function, using the range **B3:B10** as the function argument in the parentheses. Verify that the result is *$321,816*.

5. In cell **B15**, insert the **MAX** function using the range **B3:B10** as the function argument. Verify that the result is *$2,472,333*. Take care that the argument range does not include the cells with the total expenditures or average expenditures.

6. AutoFill the formulas in **B14:B15** to the right through column **F**. Review the functions, and verify that the lowest and highest values in each column were selected from each of the ranges for the MIN and MAX functions. Click cell **C7**, and then compare your screen with **Figure 3**.

7. With cell **C7** as the active cell, type 328,064 and then press Enter. In cell **C8**, type 4,025,977 and then press Enter. Verify that the MIN and MAX values in cells **C14** and **C15**, and the SUM and AVERAGE functions were automatically updated. Compare your screen with **Figure 4**.

8. **Save** 🖫 the workbook.

■ **You have completed Skill 5 of 10**

▶ A *chart* is a graphical representation of data used to show comparisons, patterns, and trends.

▶ A *column chart* is useful for illustrating comparisons among related numbers.

1. Verify *Expenditures* is the active worksheet. Select the range **A2:E10**—do *not* include the *Department Total* column or the *Total Expenditures* row in your selection. Click the **Quick Analysis Lens** button, and then in the **Quick Analysis** gallery, click **Charts**. Compare your screen with **Figure 1**.

2. In the **Quick Analysis** gallery, click the third chart—**Clustered Column**—to insert the chart and display the *Chart Tools* contextual tabs. Compare your screen with **Figure 2**.

When you insert a chart in this manner, an *embedded chart*—a chart that is placed on the worksheet containing the data—is created. Embedded charts are beneficial when you want to view or print a chart with its source data.

An *axis* is a line bordering the chart plot area that is used as a frame of reference for measurement. The *category axis* is the axis that displays the category labels. A *category label* is nonnumeric text that identifies the categories of data. Here, the worksheet's row labels—the department names in A2:A10—are used for the category labels.

The *value axis* is the axis that displays the worksheet's numeric data.

The *y-axis* is the vertical axis of a chart, and the *x-axis* is the horizontal axis of a chart.

■ Continue to the next page to complete the skill

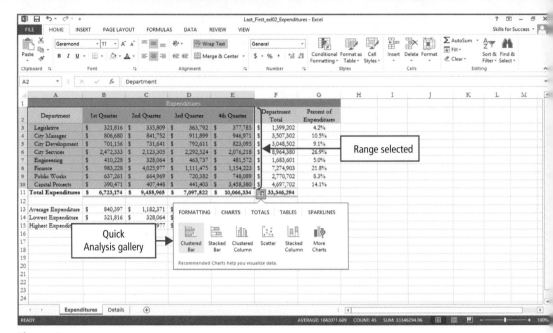

Figure 1

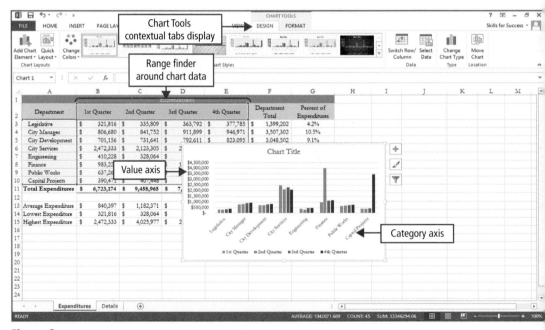

Figure 2

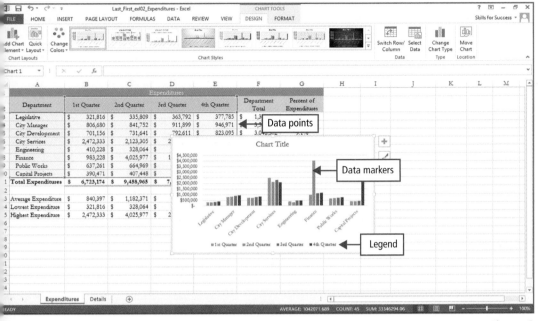

Figure 3

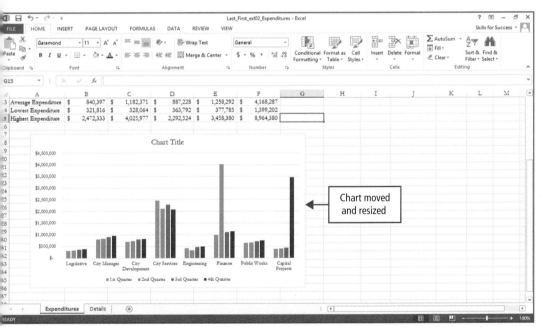

Figure 4

3. On the left side of the chart, locate the numerical scale, and then on the bottom, locate the quarters displayed in the legend. Compare your screen with **Figure 3.**

In the worksheet, each cell in the blue range finder is referred to as a **data point**—a chart value that originates in a worksheet cell. Each data point is represented in a chart by a **data marker**—a column, a bar, an area, a dot, a pie slice, or another symbol that represents a single data point.

Data points that are related to one another form a **data series**, and each data series has a unique color or pattern represented in the chart **legend**—a box that identifies the patterns or colors that are assigned to the data series or categories in the chart. Here, each quarter is a different data series, and the legend shows the color assigned to each quarter.

4. Point to the upper border of the chart to display the ⬚ pointer, and then move the chart to position its upper left corner in the middle of cell **A17**. If you are working with a touch screen, you can touch the chart and slide it to the correct position.

5. Scroll down to display row **36**. Point to the lower right corner of the chart to display the ⬚ pointer, and then drag to resize the chart to display the lower right chart corner in the middle of cell **G36**. Click cell **G15** and then compare your screen with **Figure 4**.

6. Save 🖫 the workbook.

■ **You have completed Skill 6 of 10**

EXL 2-7
VIDEO

► You can modify the overall look of a chart by applying a ***chart layout***—a pre-built set of chart elements that can include a title, a legend, or labels.

► You can modify the overall look of a chart by applying a ***chart style***—a pre-built chart format that applies an overall visual look to a chart by modifying its graphic effects, colors, and backgrounds.

1. Click the border of the chart to select the chart and display the chart buttons.

2. To the right of the chart, click the **Chart Styles** button, and then click **Style 3**. At the top of the **Chart Styles** gallery, click the **Color tab**, and then under **Colorful**, click **Color 3**. Compare your screen with **Figure 1**.

3. Click the **Chart Styles** button to close the gallery.

4. On the **Design tab**, in the **Chart Layouts group**, click the **Quick Layout** button. Point at the different layouts to preview the layouts on the chart. Point at **Layout 9**, and then compare your screen with **Figure 2**.

5. In the **Quick Layout** gallery, click **Layout 9** to add the axes titles and to move the legend to the right side of the chart.

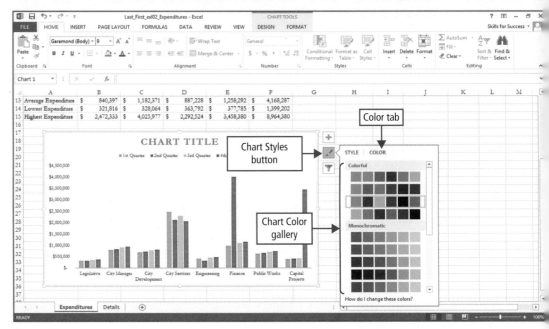

Figure 1

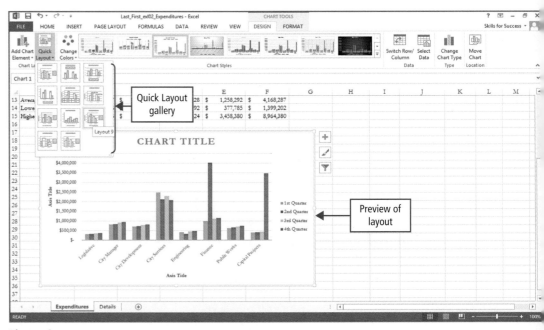

Figure 2

■ **Continue to the next page to complete the skill**

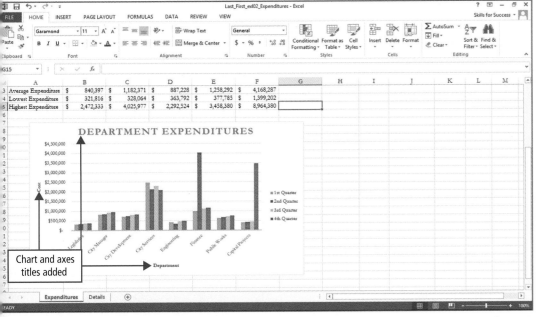

Figure 3

6. At the top of the chart, click the text *Chart Title*, and then type Department Expenditures to insert the text into the formula bar. Press `Enter` to accept the text. Verify that your text replaced any text in the chart title.

7. Below the horizontal axis, click the text *Axis Title*, type Department and then press `Enter`.

8. To the left of the vertical axis, click the text *Axis Title*, type Cost and then press `Enter`.

9. Click cell **G15** to deselect the chart. **Save** 🖫 the workbook, and then compare your screen with **Figure 3**.

10. Take a moment to examine the various types of charts available in Excel, as summarized in **Figure 4**.

■ **You have completed Skill 7 of 10**

Chart Types Commonly Used in Excel	
Chart type	**Used to**
Column	Illustrate data changes over a period of time or illustrate comparisons among items.
Line	Illustrate trends over time, with time displayed along the horizontal axis and the data point values connected by a line.
Pie	Illustrate the relationship of parts to a whole.
Bar	Illustrate comparisons among individual items.
Area	Emphasize the magnitude of change over time.

Figure 4

▶ A *pie chart* displays the relationship of parts to a whole.

▶ A *chart sheet* is a workbook sheet that contains only a chart and is useful when you want to view a chart separately from the worksheet data.

1. Verify *Expenditures* is the active sheet. Select the range **A2:A10**. Hold down `Ctrl`, and then select the nonadjacent range **F2:F10**.

2. On the **Insert tab**, in the **Charts group**, click the **Recommended Charts** button, and then compare your screen with **Figure 1**.

3. In the **Insert Chart** dialog box, click the **Pie** thumbnail, and then click **OK**.

Here, the row labels identify the slices of the pie chart, and the department totals are the data series that determine the size of each pie slice.

4. On the **Design tab**, in the **Location group**, click the **Move Chart** button. In the **Move Chart** dialog box, select the **New sheet** option button. In the **New sheet** box, replace the highlighted text *Chart1* with Expenditure Chart as shown in **Figure 2**.

5. In the **Move Chart** dialog box, click **OK** to move the pie chart to a chart sheet.

6. On the **Design tab**, in the **Type group**, click the **Change Chart Type** button. In the **Change Chart Type** dialog box, click the **3-D Pie** thumbnail and then click **OK**.

The chart is changed from a two-dimensional chart to a three-dimensional chart. **3-D**, which is short for *three-dimensional*, refers to an image that appears to have all three spatial dimensions—length, width, and depth.

■ **Continue to the next page to complete the skill** ▶

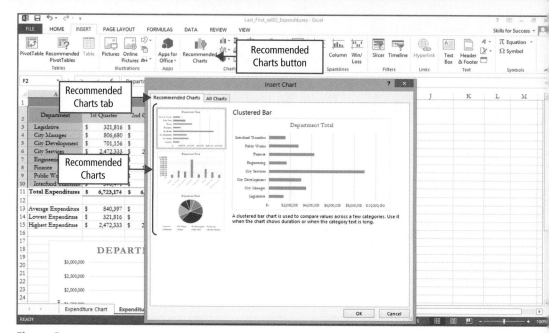

Figure 1

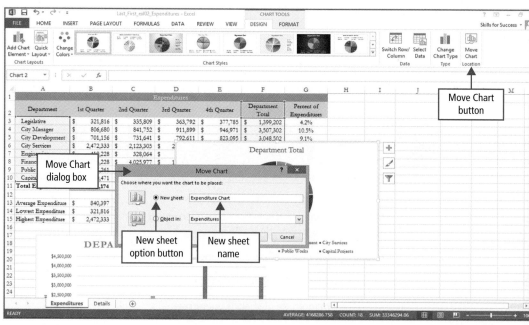

Figure 2

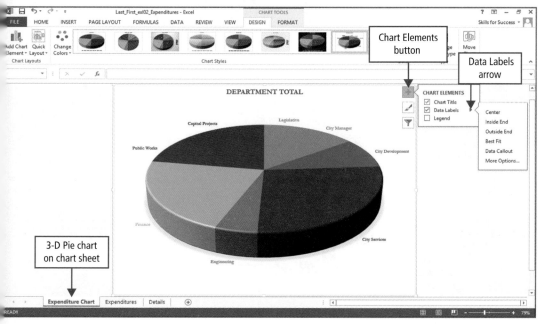

Figure 3

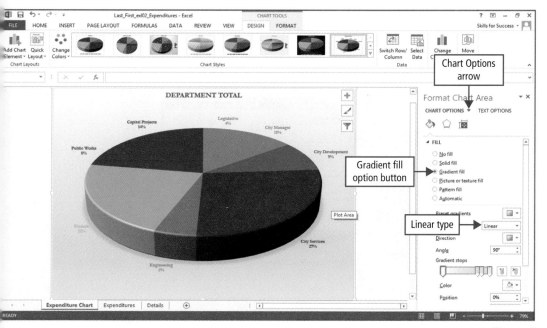

Figure 4

7. To the right of the chart, click the **Chart Styles** button. In the **Chart Styles** gallery, scroll down, and then click **Style 8**.

8. To the right of the chart, click the **Chart Elements** button. Under **Chart Elements**, point at **Data Labels**, and then click the **Data Labels arrow**. Compare your screen with **Figure 3**.

9. In the **Data Labels** list, click **More Options** to open the Format Data Labels pane.

10. In the **Format Data Labels** pane, under **Label Contains**, select the **Percentage** check box. Verify that the **Category Name** check box is selected, and then clear any other check boxes.

11. At the top of the pane, click the **Label Options arrow** and then click **Chart Area**, to open the Format Chart Area pane. In the **Format Chart Area** pane, click the **Fill & Line** button, and then click **Fill**. Click the **Gradient fill** option button, and verify that the Type is *Linear*. Compare your screen with **Figure 4**.

12. **Close** the **Format Chart Area** pane.

13. On the **Insert tab**, in the **Text group**, click the **Header & Footer** button. In the **Page Setup** dialog box, click the **Custom Footer** button. Verify that the insertion point is in the **Left section** box, and then click the **Insert File Name** button. Click in the **Right section** box, and then click the **Insert Sheet Name** button. Click **OK** two times.

14. **Save** the workbook.

- **You have completed Skill 8 of 10**

▶ A chart's data series and labels are linked to the source data in the worksheet. When worksheet values are changed, the chart is automatically updated.

1. Click the **Expenditures** worksheet tab to display the worksheet. Scroll as necessary to display row **8** at the top of the window and the chart at the bottom of the window. In the column chart, note the height of the *Finance* data marker for the 2nd Quarter and the *Capital Projects* data marker for the 4th Quarter.

2. Click cell **C8**. Type 1,017,000 and then press Enter to accept the new value. Notice the animation in the chart when changes are made to its source data. Compare your screen with **Figure 1**.

3. Click cell **E10**, type 316,000 and then press Enter.

   In cell G10, the *Capital Projects* expenditure now represents 5.7% of the projected total.

4. Click the **Expenditure Chart** worksheet tab to display the pie chart. Verify that in the pie chart, the slice for *Capital Projects* displays 6%.

   When underlying data is changed, the pie chart percentages and pie slices are automatically recalculated and resized. On the chart, 5.7% is rounded up to 6%.

5. Right-click the **Capital Projects** data label to select all of the data labels, and in the shortcut menu click **Font**. In the **Size** box, type 11 Compare your screen with **Figure 2**, and then click **OK**.

■ **Continue to the next page to complete the skill**

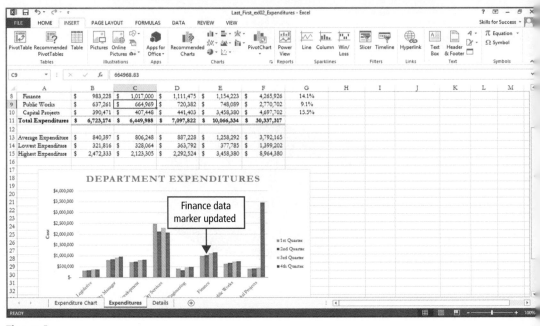

Figure 1

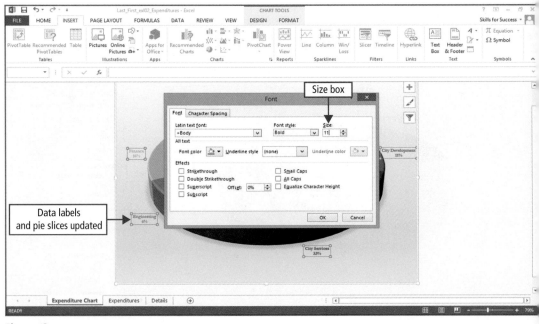

Figure 2

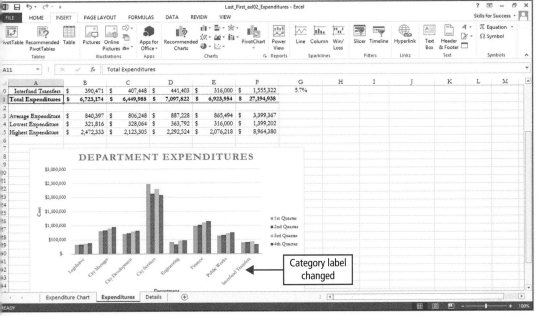

Figure 3

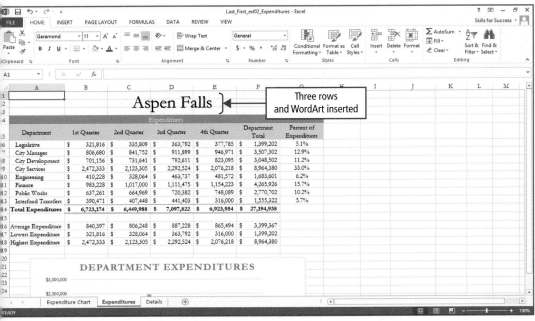

Figure 4

6. Click the **Expenditures** worksheet tab, and then in cell **A10**, change *Capital Projects* to Interfund Transfers Press [Enter] and then scroll down to verify that the column chart category label changed. Compare your screen with **Figure 3**.

7. Click the **Expenditure Chart** worksheet tab, and verify that the data label on the pie chart displays as *Interfund Transfers*.

8. Click the **Expenditures** worksheet tab. Scroll up, and then select the range **A1:G3**. On the **Home tab**, in the **Cells group**, click the **Insert arrow**, and then click **Insert Sheet Rows** to insert three blank rows.

9. On the **Insert tab**, in the **Text group**, click the **Insert WordArt** button [A]. In the **WordArt** gallery, click the first style in the first row—**Fill - Black**, **Text 1**, **Shadow**. Immediately type Aspen Falls

10. Select the WordArt text. In the mini toolbar, click the **Font Size** button [11] and then click **32**.

11. Point to the bottom border of the WordArt box, and then with the pointer, drag to position the WordArt object to approximately the range **C1:E3**. Click cell **A1** to deselect the WordArt, and then compare your screen with **Figure 4**.

12. **Save** [💾] the workbook.

- **You have completed Skill 9 of 10**

▶ Before you print an Excel worksheet, you can use Page Layout view to preview and adjust the printed document.

1. Verify *Expenditures* is the active worksheet. Scroll down, and then click the column chart to select the chart. Click the **File tab**, and then click **Print**. Compare your screen with **Figure 1**.

    When an embedded chart is selected, only the chart will print.

2. Click the **Back** button ⊕. Click cell **A19** to deselect the chart.

3. On the **View tab**, in the **Workbook Views group**, click the **Page Layout** button. On the left side of the status bar, notice that *Page: 1 of 2* displays, informing you that the data and the column chart would print on two pages.

4. On the **Page Layout tab**, in the **Scale to Fit group**, click the **Width arrow**, and then click **1 page**. Click the **File tab**, and then click **Print**. Compare your screen with **Figure 2**.

    1 of 1 displays at the bottom of the screen, indicating that the WordArt, the data, and the column chart will all print on one page.

5. Click the **Back** button ⊕. On the status bar, click the **Normal** button ▦ and then press [Ctrl] + [Home] to make cell **A1** the active cell.

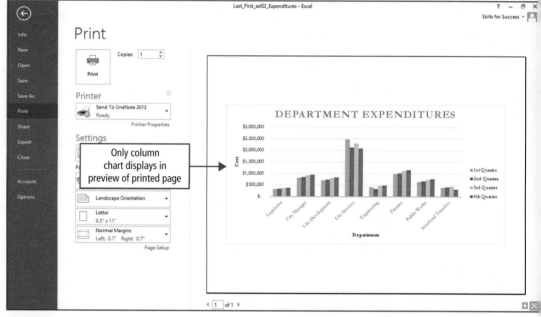

Figure 1

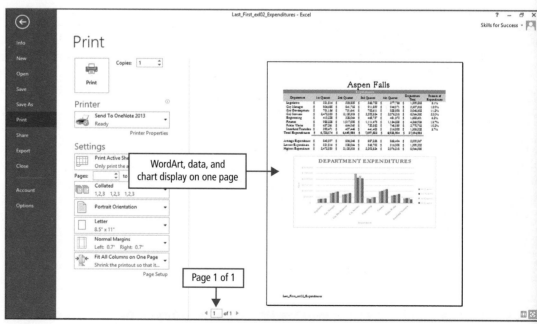

Figure 2

■ **Continue to the next page to complete the skill**

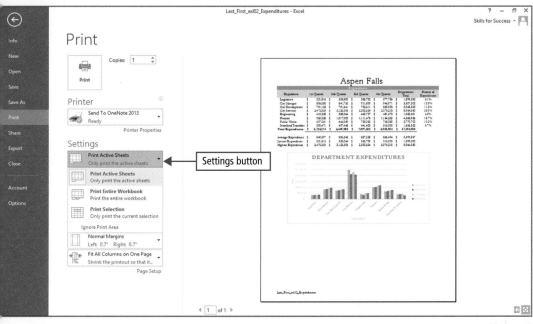

Figure 3

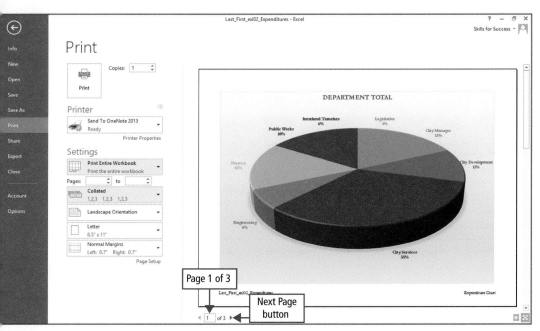

Figure 4

6. On the **Review tab**, in the **Proofing group**, click the **Spelling** button, and then check the spelling of the worksheet. When the message *Spell check complete. You're good to go!* displays, click **OK**.

7. Save 🖫 the workbook.

8. Click the **File tab**, and then click **Print**. Under **Settings**, click the first button. Compare your screen with **Figure 3**.

9. On the displayed list, click **Print Entire Workbook**. Notice at the bottom of the screen, *1 of 3* displays, and the chart sheet with the pie chart is the first page. Compare your screen with **Figure 4**.

10. At the bottom of the screen, click the **Next Page** button ▶ to preview the worksheet containing your WordArt, the data, and the column chart. Save 🖫 the workbook. Submit the workbook as directed by your instructor. If you are printing your work for this project, print the workbook. Otherwise, click the **Back** button .

11. If your instructor asked you to print formulas, display the worksheet formulas, AutoFit the column widths, and then print the formulas.

12. **Close** ☒ Excel. Submit the file or printouts as directed by your instructor.

✔ **DONE! You have completed Skill 10 of 10, and your document is complete!**

The following More Skills are located at **www.pearsonhighered.com/skills**

More Skills Insert, Edit, and Delete Comments

You can add comments to cells in a worksheet to provide reminders, to display clarifying information about data within the cells, or to document your work. When you point to a cell that contains a comment, the comment and the name of the person who created the comment display.

In More Skills 11, you will insert, edit, and delete comments.

To begin, open your web browser, navigate to www.pearsonhighered.com/skills, locate the name of your textbook, and then follow the instructions on the website.

More Skills Change Chart Types

After you create a chart, you may determine that a different chart type might be easier for the readers of your chart to understand. For example, you can change a bar chart to a column chart. The column chart and a bar chart are good choices to illustrate comparisons among items.

In More Skills 12, you will create a bar chart and then change the chart type to a column chart.

To begin, open your web browser, navigate to www.pearsonhighered.com/skills, locate the name of your textbook, and then follow the instructions on the website.

More Skills 13 Copy Excel Data to Word Documents

You can copy the data and objects created in one application to another application, saving time and ensuring accuracy because data is entered only one time.

In More Skills 13, you will create a chart in Excel and then copy the chart and paste it into a Word document.

To begin, open your web browser, navigate to www.pearsonhighered.com/skills, locate the name of your textbook, and then follow the instructions on the website.

More Skills 14 Fill Data with Flash Fill

Instead of entering data manually, you can use Flash Fill to recognize a pattern in your data and automatically enter the rest of your data. You can use the fill handle or the fill command to AutoFill data that follow a pattern or series—for example, hours, days of the week, or numeric sequences such as even numbers.

In More Skills 14, you will use Flash Fill to enter data in cells.

To begin, open your web browser, navigate to www.pearsonhighered.com/skills, locate the name of your textbook, and then follow the instructions on the website.

Please note that there are no additional projects to accompany the More Skills Projects, and they are not covered in the End-of-Chapter projects.

The following table summarizes the **SKILLS AND PROCEDURES** covered in this chapter.

Skill Number	Task	Step	Icon	Keyboard Shortcut
1	Wrap text	Home tab → Alignment group → Wrap Text		
1	Middle align text	Home tab → Alignment group → Middle Align	≡	
1	Center text	Home tab → Alignment group → Center	≡	
1	Increase indent	Home tab → Alignment group → Increase Indent		
2	Insert the SUM function	Quick Analysis Lens button → Totals → SUM		
2	Create an absolute cell reference	Select cell reference → Type $		F4
3	Apply the Percent style	Home tab → Number group → Percent Style	%	
3	Increase the number of display decimals	Home tab → Number group → Increase Decimal		
4	Calculate an average	Home tab → Editing group → Sum arrow → Average		
5	Calculate a minimum	Home tab → Editing group → Sum arrow → Min		
5	Calculate a maximum	Home tab → Editing group → Sum arrow → Max		
6	Insert a chart using the Quick Analysis Lens	Quick Analysis Lens button → Charts → select desired chart		
7	Apply a chart style	Chart Style → Style		
7	Apply a chart layout	Design tab → Chart Layouts group → Quick Layout → Layout		
8	Insert a recommended chart	Insert tab → Charts group → Recommended Charts → select desired chart		
8	Move a chart to its own worksheet	Design tab → Locations group → Move Chart → New sheet		
8	Change the chart type	Design tab → Type group → Change Chart Type → Type		
8	Change chart data labels	Chart Elements → Data labels arrow → More Options → Format Data labels pane		
9	Insert WordArt	Insert tab → Text group → WordArt	𝐴 ▾	
10	Adjust scale	Page Layout tab → Scale to Fit group → Width arrow → Page		
10	Print an entire workbook	File tab → Print → Settings → Print Entire Workbook		

Key Terms

Online Help Skills

1. Start **Excel 2013**, and then in the upper right corner of the start page, click the **Help** button ⟨?⟩.

2. In the **Excel Help** window **Search help** box, type Keyboard shortcuts and then press ⟨Enter⟩.

3. In the search result list, click **Keyboard shortcuts in Excel**, and then compare your screen with **Figure 1**.

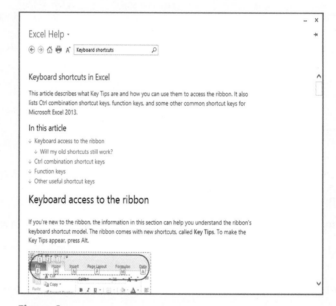

Figure 1

4. Read the article to answer the following question: How can you use Key Tips to access the ribbon?

Matching

Match each term in the second column with its correct definition in the first column by writing the letter of the term on the blank line in front of the correct definition.

___ **1.** A command with which you can display text on multiple lines within a cell.

___ **2.** A cell reference that refers to a cell by its fixed position in a worksheet and does not change when the formula is copied.

___ **3.** Rules that specify the way numbers should display.

___ **4.** The default format applied to numbers.

___ **5.** The value(s) that determine how a function should be used.

___ **6.** A graphical representation of data in a worksheet that shows comparisons, patterns, and trends.

___ **7.** A chart line that contains words as labels.

___ **8.** A chart line that contains numeric data.

___ **9.** The function that adds a group of values and then divides the result by the number of values in the group.

___ **10.** The Excel feature that outlines all of the cells referenced in a formula.

A Absolute cell reference

B Argument

C AVERAGE

D Category axis

E Chart

F General format

G Number format

H Range finder

I Text wrap

J Value axis

BizSkills Video

1. Why should you practice for an interview?

2. How should you answer a question about a missing reference?

Multiple Choice

Choose the correct answer.

1. Automatically changing the column width to accommodate the longest column entry.
   - A. Drag and drop
   - B. AutoFit
   - C. Auto adjust

2. A green triangle that indicates a possible error in a formula.
   - A. Error indicator
   - B. Message
   - C. Dialog Box Launcher

3. A chart type useful for illustrating comparisons among related numbers.
   - A. Pie chart
   - B. Area chart
   - C. Column chart

4. A chart placed on a worksheet with the source data.
   - A. Chart sheet
   - B. Column chart
   - C. Embedded chart

5. The related data points in a chart.
   - A. Column
   - B. Data series
   - C. Chart point

6. The box that identifies the patterns or colors assigned to the data series.
   - A. Legend
   - B. Dialog box
   - C. Message box

7. A predesigned combination of chart elements.
   - A. 3-D chart
   - B. Chart layout
   - C. Chart

8. A pre-built chart format that applies an overall visual look to a chart.
   - A. Data marker
   - B. Chart finder
   - C. Chart style

9. The chart type that best displays the relationship of parts to a whole.
   - A. Pie chart
   - B. Area chart
   - C. Column chart

10. A worksheet that contains only a chart.
    - A. Worksheet
    - B. Chart area
    - C. Chart sheet

Topics for Discussion

1. Search current newspapers and magazines for examples of charts. Which charts catch your eye and why? Do the charts appeal to you because of their color or format? Is something intriguing revealed to you in the chart that you have never considered before? What are some formatting changes that you think make a chart interesting and valuable to a reader?

2. Do you think 3-D pie charts distort the data in a way that is misleading? Why or why not?

Skills Review

To complete this project, you will need the following file:

- exl02_SRRevenue

You will save your file as:

- Last_First_exl02_SRRevenue

1. Start **Excel 2013**, and open the file **exl02_SRRevenue**. **Save** the file in your chapter folder as Last_First_exl02_SRRevenue Add the file name in the worksheet's left footer, and the sheet name in the right footer. Return to Normal view.

2. In the column heading area, point to the right boundary of column **A** and double-click to AutoFit the column width. Click the column **B** heading, and then drag right to select columns **B:F**. Click the right boundary of column **B**, and then drag to the right until the ScreenTip indicates *Width:13:00 (109 pixels)*.

3. Select the range **A1:F1**. On the **Home tab**, in the **Alignment group**, click the **Wrap Text**, **Middle Align**, and **Center** buttons.

4. Select the range **B2:E13**. Click the **Quick Analysis** button, click **Totals**, and then click the first option—**SUM**.

5. Select the range **B2:E14**. In the **Number group**, click the **Decrease Decimal** button two times. Select the range **B14:E14**. In the **Styles group**, click the **Cell Styles** button, and then click **Total**.

6. In cell **F2**, type =E2/$E$14 and then on the formula bar, click the **Enter** button. With cell F2 the active cell, in the **Number group**, click the **Percent Style** button, and the **Increase Decimal** button. In the **Alignment group**, click the **Center** button. AutoFill the formula in cell **F2** down through cell **F13**. Click cell **A15**, and then compare your screen with **Figure 1**.

7. Click cell **B16**. Type =Av and then in the formula AutoComplete list, double-click **AVERAGE**. For the function argument, select the range **B2:B13**, and then press [Enter]. Using the same function argument range, in cell **B17**, enter the **MAX** function. Select the range **B16:B17**, and then AutoFill the formulas to the right through column **D**. Compare your screen with **Figure 2**.

- Continue to the next page to complete this Skills Review

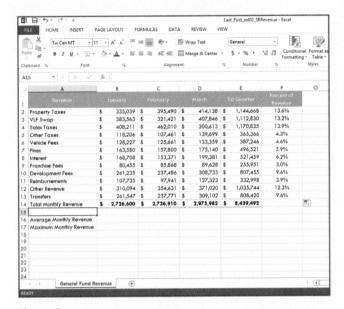

Figure 1

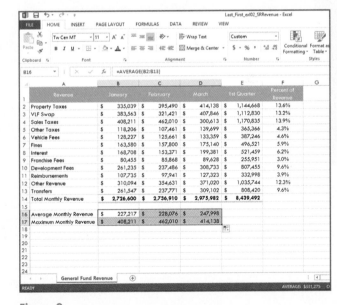

Figure 2

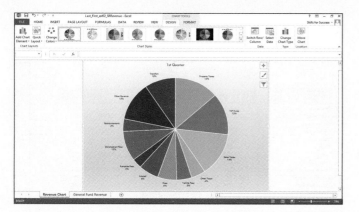

Figure 3

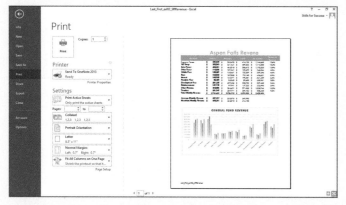

Figure 4

8. Select the range **A1:D13**. Click the **Quick Analysis Lens** button, click **Charts**, and then click the **Clustered Column** thumbnail. Move and resize the chart to display in approximately the range **A20:F40**. At the top right corner of the chart, click the **Chart Styles** button, and then click the **Style 9** thumbnail. Click the **Chart Title**, type General Fund Revenue and then press Enter.

9. Select the nonadjacent ranges **A1:A13** and **E1:E13**. On the **Insert tab**, in the **Charts group**, click the **Recommended Charts** button. On the **All Charts tab**, click **Pie**, and then click **OK**.

10. On the **Design tab**, in the **Location group**, click the **Move Chart** button. In the **Move Chart** dialog box, select the **New sheet** option button, type the sheet name Revenue Chart and then click **OK**.

11. On the **Design tab**, in the **Chart Layouts group**, click the **Quick Layout** button, and then click **Layout 1**.

12. Click the **Chart Elements** button, click the **Data Labels arrow**, and then click **More Options**. In the **Format Data Labels** pane, under **Label Position**, click **Outside End**.

13. Click the **Label Options arrow**, and then click **Chart Area**. In the **Format Chart Area** pane, click the **Fill & Line** button, and then click **Fill**. Select the **Gradient fill** option button, and then **Close** the Format Chart Area pane. Compare your screen with **Figure 3**.

14. On the **Insert tab**, in the **Text group**, click the **Header & Footer** button. In the **Page Setup** dialog box, click the **Custom Footer** button. Insert the **File Name** in the left section, and insert the **Sheet Name** in the right section.

15. Click the **General Fund Revenue** worksheet tab. Select the range **A1:A3**. On the **Home tab**, in the **Cells group**, click the **Insert arrow**, and then click **Insert Sheet Rows**. On the **Insert tab**, in the **Text group**, click the **Insert WordArt** button, and then in the first row, click the second thumbnail—**Fill - Turquoise, Accent 1 Shadow**. Immediately type Aspen Falls Revenue Select the text in the WordArt. On the mini toolbar, change the **Font Size** to **36**. Point to the bottom border of the WordArt, and then move the WordArt to approximately the range **B1:E3**.

16. Click cell **A1**. Click the **Page Layout tab**. In the **Scale to Fit group**, click the **Width** arrow, and then click **1 page** button.

17. Click the **File tab**, and then click **Print**. Compare your screen with **Figure 4**.

18. **Save** the workbook, and then submit the workbook as directed by your instructor.

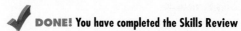

DONE! You have completed the Skills Review

Skills Assessment 1  MyITLab® Grader

To complete this project, you will need the following file:

- exl02_SA1Debt

You will save your workbook as:

- Last_First_exl02_SA1Debt

---

1. Start **Excel 2013**, and open the file **exl02_SA1Debt**. **Save** the workbook in your chapter folder as Last_First_exl02_SA1Debt Add the file name in the worksheet's left footer and the sheet name in the right footer. Return to Normal view.

2. Select the range **A2:I2**, and then apply the alignment **Wrap Text** and **Middle Align**.

3. Select the column headings **B:I**, and then AutoFit the column widths.

4. In the range **B8:H8**, insert the column totals, and apply the **Total** cell style.

5. Select the range **B3:H8**, and then display no decimals.

6. In cell **I3**, calculate the *Percent of Total Debt*. In the formula, use an absolute cell reference when referring to cell **H8**. AutoFill the formula down through cell **I7**, and then format the results as percentages with one decimal place.

7. In the range **B10:G10**, insert a function to calculate the highest monthly debt. In the range **B11:G11**, insert a function to calculate the lowest monthly debt. In the range **B12:G12**, insert a function to calculate the average monthly debt.

8. Insert a **Pie** chart based on the nonadjacent ranges **A2:A7** and **H2:H7**. Move the pie chart to a chart sheet with the sheet name Debt Chart

9. For the pie chart, apply **Layout 6**, and then apply the **Chart Style 3**. Change the data label **Font Size** to **12**. Add the file name in the chart sheet's left footer and the sheet name in the right footer.

10. On the **Debt** worksheet, insert a **Clustered Column** chart based on the range **A2:G7**. Move the chart below the data, and then resize the chart to approximately the range **A15:I38**. Apply the chart **Style 5**. Change the chart title to City Debt

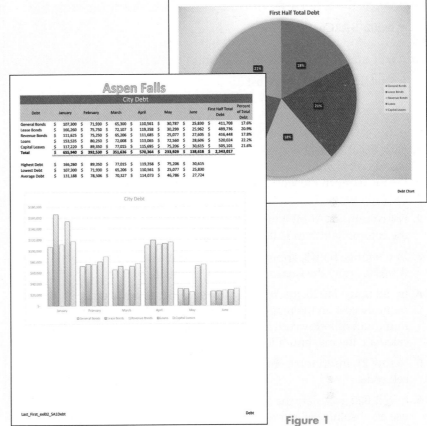

Figure 1

11. Insert three sheet rows at the top of the worksheet. Insert **WordArt**, using the style **Gradient Fill – Purple, Accent 4, Outline - Accent 4**. Change the WordArt text to Aspen Falls and then change the **Font Size** to **36**. Move the WordArt to the top of the worksheet, centering it above the data.

12. Adjust the **Scale to Fit** to fit the WordArt, data, and column chart on one page.

13. **Save** the workbook, and then compare your completed workbook with **Figure 1**.

14. **Close** Excel, and then submit the workbook as directed by your instructor.

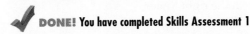 **DONE! You have completed Skills Assessment 1**

Skills Assessment 2

To complete this project, you will need the following file:

- exl02_SA2Cost

You will save your workbook as:

- Last_First_exl02_SA2Cost

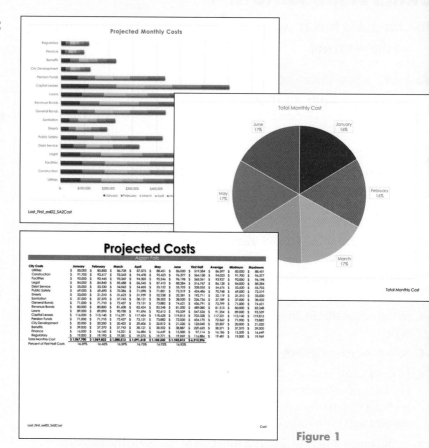

Figure 1

1. Start **Excel 2013**, and open the file **exl02_SA2Cost**. **Save** the workbook in your chapter folder as Last_First_exl02_SA2Cost Add the file name in the worksheet's left footer, and the sheet name in the right footer. Return to Normal view.

2. For column **A**, AutoFit the column width. For columns **B:K**, change the column width to **11.00 (93 pixels)**.

3. In the range **B3:K3**, apply the **Center** alignment. In the range **A4:A20**, apply the **Increase Indent** alignment.

4. In the range **I4:I20**, insert a function to calculate the average monthly cost. In the range **J4:J20**, insert a function to calculate the minimum monthly cost. In the range **K4:K20**, insert a function to calculate the maximum monthly cost.

5. In row **21**, insert totals for columns **B:H**, and then apply the **Total** cell style.

6. In cell **B22**, calculate the *Percent of First Half Costs*. In the formula, use an absolute cell reference when referring to cell **H21**. Format the result as a percent and display two decimals. AutoFill the formula to the right through column **G**.

7. Insert a **Stacked Bar** chart based on the range **A3:G20**. Move the stacked bar chart to a chart sheet named Projected Costs Chart Apply the chart **Style 11**. Change the Chart Title to Projected Monthly Costs Add the file name in the chart sheet's left footer and the sheet name in the right footer.

8. Click the **Cost** worksheet tab. Insert a **Pie** chart based on the nonadjacent ranges **A3:G3** and **A21:G21**. Move the pie chart to a chart sheet named Total Monthly Cost Apply the chart **Layout 1**. Change the data label position to **Data Callout**, and change the data label **Font Size** to **12**. Add the file name in the chart sheet's left footer and the sheet name in the right footer.

9. On the **Cost** worksheet, insert four blank lines at the top of the worksheet. Insert a WordArt with the **Fill - Black**, **Text 1**, **Outline - Background 1**, **Hard Shadow - Background 1** style. In the WordArt, type the text Projected Costs and then change the **Font Size** to **44**. Move the WordArt to the top of the worksheet, centering it above the data.

10. Scale the **Cost** worksheet to print on **1 page**.

11. **Save** the workbook, and then compare your completed workbook with **Figure 1**.

12. **Close** Excel, and then submit the workbook as directed by your instructor.

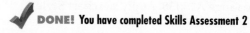 **DONE! You have completed Skills Assessment 2**

Visual Skills Check

To complete this project, you will need the following file:

- exl02_VSNetAssets

You will save your workbook as:

- Last_First_exl02_VSNetAssets

Start **Excel 2013**, and open the file **exl02_VSNetAssets**. **Save** the workbook in your chapter folder as Last_First_exl02_VSNetAssets Create the worksheet as shown in **Figure 1**. Calculate the *Percent of Total Net Assets* using an absolute cell reference. In rows **13:15**, insert the statistical functions that correspond with the row labels. Format the values and text as shown. Create the pie chart, and then move and resize the chart as shown in the figure. The chart uses the **Layout 4** chart layout, data label font size **11**, and in the chart area the **Linear Down** gradient fill. Insert the file name in the worksheet's left footer. **Save** the workbook, and then submit the workbook as directed by your instructor.

 DONE! You have completed Visual Skills Check

Aspen Falls					
Net Assets					
Business-type Activities					
Asset	July	August	September	Total	Percent of Total Net Assets
Transportation	$ 268,755	$ 275,082	$ 282,086	$ 825,923	25.9%
Port	$ 242,886	$ 245,688	$ 247,253	$ 735,827	23.1%
Water	$ 175,885	$ 180,256	$ 193,008	$ 549,149	17.2%
Power	$ 117,006	$ 108,832	$ 115,038	$ 340,876	10.7%
Hospital	$ 213,468	$ 250,865	$ 275,066	$ 739,399	23.2%
Total Net Assets	$ 1,018,000	$ 1,060,723	$ 1,112,451	$ 3,191,174	
Minimum Asset	$ 117,006	$ 108,832	$ 115,038		
Maximum Asset	$ 268,755	$ 275,082	$ 282,086		
Average Asset	$ 203,600	$ 212,145	$ 222,490		

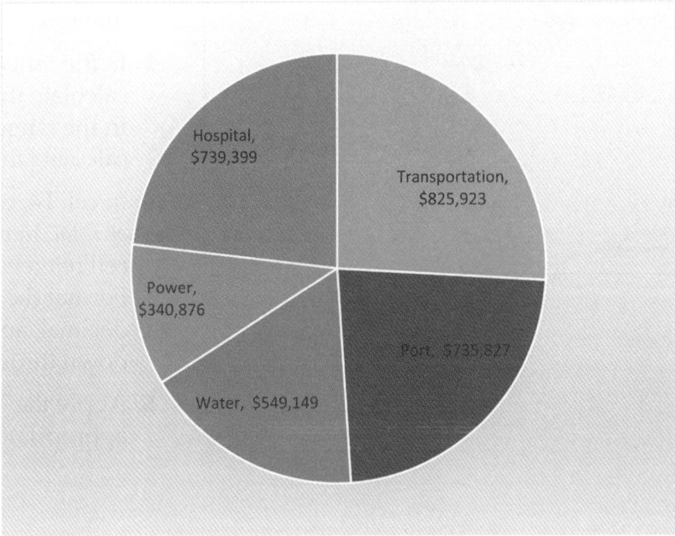

Hospital, $739,399

Transportation, $825,923

Power, $340,876

Port, $735,827

Water, $549,149

Last_First_exl02_VSNetAssets

Figure 1

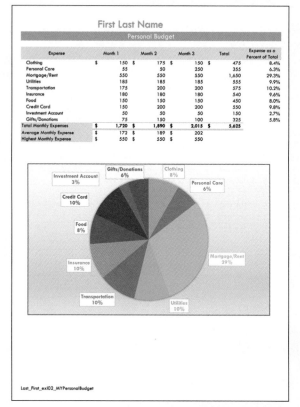

First Last Name

Personal Budget

Expense	Month 1	Month 2	Month 3	Total	Expense as a Percent of Total
Clothing	$ 150	$ 175	$ 150	$ 475	8.4%
Personal Care	55	50	250	355	6.3%
Mortgage/Rent	550	550	550	1,650	29.3%
Utilities	185	185	185	555	9.9%
Transportation	175	200	200	575	10.2%
Insurance	180	180	180	540	9.6%
Food	150	150	150	450	8.0%
Credit Card	150	200	200	550	9.8%
Investment Account	50	50	50	150	2.7%
Gifts/Donations	75	150	100	325	5.8%
Total Monthly Expenses	$ 1,720	$ 1,890	$ 2,015	$ 5,625	
Average Monthly Expense	$ 172	$ 189	$ 202		
Highest Monthly Expense	$ 550	$ 550	$ 550	550	

Last_First_exl02_MYPersonalBudget

Figure 1

My Skills

To complete this project, you will need the following file:

- exl02_MYPersonalBudget

You will save your workbook as:

- Last_First_exl02_MYPersonalBudget

1. Start **Excel 2013**, and open the file **exl02_MYPersonalBudget**. **Save** the workbook in your chapter folder as Last_First_exl02_MYPersonalBudget Add the file name in the worksheet's left footer, and then return to Normal view.

2. Change the alignments of the row **3** labels, and indent the column **A** expense labels. In the range **B14:E14**, insert the column totals.

3. In the range **B15:D15**, insert a function to calculate the average monthly expense. In the range **B16:D16**, insert a function to calculate the maximum monthly expense.

4. In cell **F4**, calculate the *Expense as a Percent of Total*. In the formula, use an absolute cell reference when referring to the total. Format the results as percentages with one decimal, and then AutoFill the formula down through cell **F13**.

5. Apply the **Total** cell style where appropriate.

6. Insert a **Pie** chart based on the nonadjacent ranges **A3:A13** and **E3:E13**.

7. Move the pie chart to an appropriate location below your data, and then resize the chart.

8. Format the pie chart with any of the chart options of your choice including layout, style, or color.

9. At the top of the worksheet, insert three blank rows. Insert a WordArt using your first and last names as the WordArt text. Move the WordArt above the data and resize to fit in the blank rows.

10. Adjust the scaling to fit the data and the pie chart on one page when printed.

11. **Save** the workbook, and then submit the workbook as directed by your instructor. Compare your completed workbook with Figure 1.

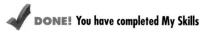 **DONE! You have completed My Skills**

Skills Challenge 1

To complete this project, you will need the following file:

- exl02_SC1Budget

You will save your workbook as:

- Last_First_exl02_SC1Budget

Start **Excel 2013.** Open the file **exl02_SC1Budget**, and then save the workbook in your chapter folder as Last_First_exl02_SC1Budget During the fourth quarter of this year, the Accounting Department developed a summary of the proposed Aspen Falls budget. Correct the errors in the statistical functions—you may want to display the formulas. Use an absolute cell reference when correcting the percent. Correct the number formats, and format the labels appropriately. Modify the WordArt and the column chart. Verify that the WordArt, data, and column chart will print on one page. Add the file name in the worksheet's left footer. Save the workbook, and then submit the workbook as directed by your instructor.

 DONE! You have completed Skills Challenge 1

Skills Challenge 2

To complete this project, you will need the following file:

- exl02_SC2Classes

You will save your workbook as:

- Last_First_exl02_SC2Classes

Start **Excel 2013**, and then open the workbook **exl02_SC2Classes**. Save the workbook in your chapter folder as Last_First_exl02_SC2Classes Carter Horikoshi, the Art Center Supervisor, created a workbook to track how many students attended Community Center classes last summer. He wants to determine if he should offer more classes this summer based on the number of students from last summer. He wants to know the total enrollment and the average enrollment for each month and for each class. He would like to view a chart that summarized the enrollment data. Using the skills you learned in this chapter, provide Mr. Horikoshi a workbook to assist him in his decision. Add the file name in the worksheet's left footer. Save the workbook, and then submit the workbook as directed by your instructor.

 **DONE! You have completed Skills Challenge 2**

CHAPTER 3

Manage Multiple Worksheets

- ▶ Organizations typically create workbooks that contain multiple worksheets. In such a workbook, the first worksheet often summarizes the detailed information in the other worksheets.

- ▶ In an Excel workbook, you can insert and move worksheets to create the detailed worksheets and summary worksheet that you need.

- ▶ By grouping worksheets, you can edit and format the data in multiple worksheets at the same time. The changes you make on the active sheet are reflected in all of the sheets included in the group.

- ▶ You can create multiple worksheets quickly by copying and pasting information from one worksheet to other worksheets.

- ▶ You can color code each worksheet tab so that detailed information can be quickly located.

- ▶ When you use multiple math operators in a single formula, you must take care to ensure the operations are carried out in the intended order.

- ▶ When building a summary worksheet, you will typically use formulas that refer to cells in the other worksheets.

© Jas

Aspen Falls City Hall

In this chapter, you will work with a spreadsheet for Diane Payne, the Public Works Director in Aspen Falls. She wants to know the revenue generated from parking meters and parking tickets in different locations throughout the city. Understanding how much revenue is generated from the meters and tickets and the costs associated with park maintenance and upgrades will help Diane decide if more meters should be added and if more personnel should be hired to enforce parking regulations.

A workbook, composed of multiple worksheets, allows Diane to collect data from different worksheets but analyze those worksheets grouped together as a whole. When you have a large amount of data to organize in a workbook, dividing the data into logical elements, such as locations or time periods, and then placing each element in a separate worksheet often makes sense. In other words, it is often better to design a system of worksheets instead of trying to fit all of the information on a single worksheet. You can then collect and input the data on an individual basis and see the summarized results with minimal effort.

In this project, you will work with grouped worksheets to enter formulas and apply formatting on all selected worksheets at the same time. You will create formulas that use multiple math operators, construct formulas that refer to cells in other worksheets, and create and format a clustered bar chart.

Time to complete all 10 skills – 60 to 90 minutes

Student data file needed for this chapter:

exl03_Parking

You will save your workbook as:

Last_First_exl03_Parking

Outcome

Using the skills in this chapter, you will be able to work with Excel worksheets like this:

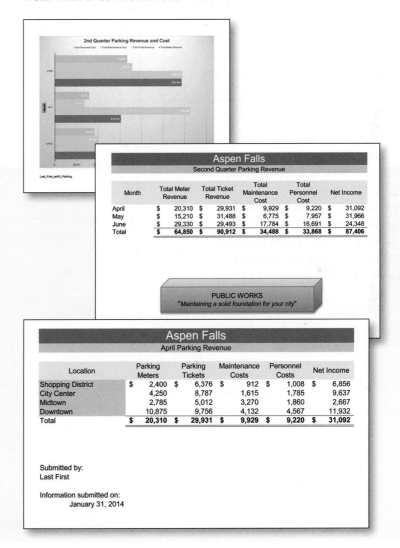

SKILLS

MyITLab®
Skills 1–10 Training

At the end of this chapter you will be able to:

Skill 1 Organize Worksheet Tabs

Skill 2 Enter and Format Dates

Skill 3 Clear Cell Contents and Formats

Skill 4 Move Cell Contents and Use Paste Options

Skill 5 Enter Data in Grouped Worksheets

Skill 6 Insert Multiple Math Operators in Formulas

Skill 7 Format Grouped Worksheets

Skill 8 Insert, Hide, Delete, and Move Worksheets

Skill 9 Create Summary Worksheets

Skill 10 Create Clustered Bar Charts

MORE SKILLS

Skill 11 Create Organization Charts

Skill 12 Create Line Charts

Skill 13 Set and Clear Print Areas

Skill 14 Create, Edit, and Delete Hyperlinks

EXL 3-1
VIDEO

▶ When a workbook contains more than one worksheet, you can move among worksheets by clicking the worksheet tabs.

▶ *Tab scrolling buttons* are buttons to the left of worksheet tabs used to display worksheet tabs that are not in view.

1. Start **Excel 2013**, and then open the student data file **exl03_Parking**. Click the **File tab**, and then click **Save As**. Click the **Browse** button, and then navigate to the location where you are saving your files. Click **New folder**, type Excel Chapter 3 and then press Enter two times. In the **File name** box, using your own name, name the workbook Last_First_exl03_Parking and then press Enter.

2. At the bottom of the Excel window, click the **Sheet2** worksheet tab to make it the active worksheet, and then compare your screen with **Figure 1**.

3. Click the **Sheet1** worksheet tab to make it the active worksheet.

4. On the **Home tab**, in the **Cells group**, click the **Format** button, and then click **Rename Sheet**. Compare your screen with **Figure 2**.

5. Verify the **Sheet1** worksheet tab name is selected, type April and then press Enter to accept the name change.

> You can use up to 31 characters in a worksheet tab name.

■ **Continue to the next page to complete the skill**

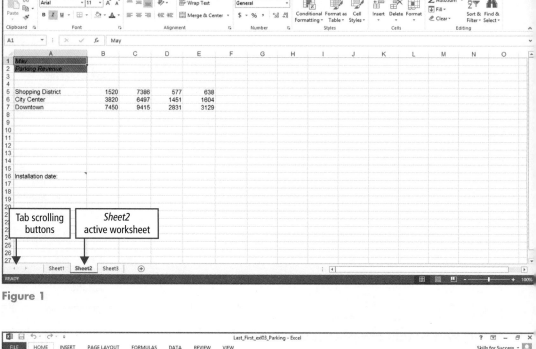

Figure 1

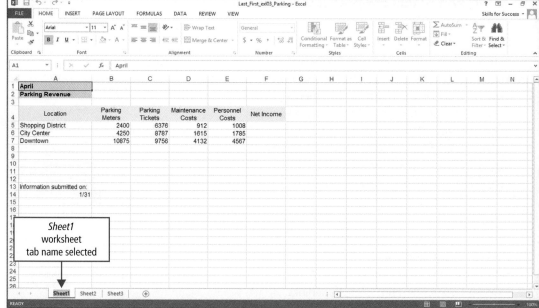

Figure 2

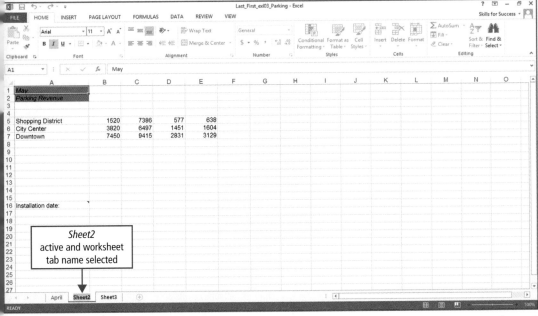

Figure 3

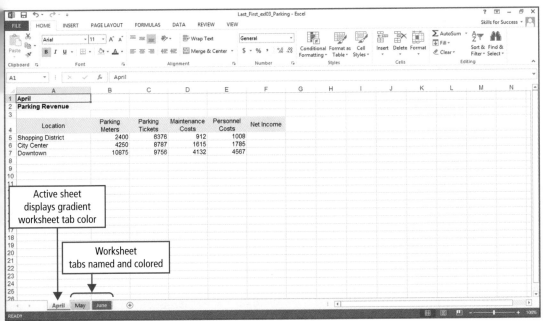

Figure 4

6. Double-click the **Sheet2** worksheet tab to make it the active sheet and to select the sheet name. Compare your screen with **Figure 3**.

7. With the **Sheet2** worksheet tab name selected, type May and then press Enter.

8. Using either of the two methods just practiced, rename the **Sheet3** worksheet tab as June and then press Enter.

9. Verify that the **June** sheet is the active worksheet. On the **Page Layout tab**, in the **Themes group**, click the **Colors** button. Scroll down, and then click **Slipstream** to change the theme colors for this workbook.

10. On the **Home tab**, in the **Cells group**, click the **Format** button, and then point to **Tab Color** to display the colors associated with the *Slipstream* theme colors. Click the fifth color in the first row—**Blue**, **Accent 1**. Alternately, right-click the worksheet tab, and then click Tab Color.

   A gradient color on a worksheet tab indicates that the worksheet is active. When a worksheet is not active, the entire worksheet tab is filled with the selected color.

11. Use the technique just practiced to change the worksheet tab color of the **May** worksheet tab to the sixth color in the first row—**Turquoise**, **Accent 2**.

12. Change the worksheet tab color of the **April** worksheet tab to the seventh color in the first row—**Green**, **Accent 3**. Compare your screen with **Figure 4**.

13. Save the workbook.

■ **You have completed Skill 1 of 10**

▶ When you enter a date, it is assigned a *serial number*—a sequential number.

▶ Dates are stored as sequential serial numbers so they can be used in calculations. By default, January 1, 1900, is serial number 1. January 1, 2014, is serial number 41640 because it is 41,640 days after January 1, 1900. Serial numbers make it possible to perform calculations on dates, for example, to find the number of days between two dates by subtracting the older date from the more recent date.

▶ When you type any of the following values into cells, Excel interprets them as dates: *7/4/10, 4-Jul, 4-Jul-10, Jul-10*. When typing in these date formats, the [-] (hyphen) key and the [/] (forward slash) key function identically.

▶ You can enter months using the entire name or first three characters. Years can be entered as two or four digits. When the year is left off, the current year will be inserted.

1. On the **April** sheet, click cell **A14** to display the underlying value *1/31/2014* in the formula bar. On the **Formulas tab**, in the **Formula Auditing group**, click the **Show Formulas** button. Compare your screen with **Figure 1**.

   The date, *January 31, 2014*, displays as 41670—the number of days since the reference date of January 1, 1900.

2. On the **Formulas tab**, in the **Formula Auditing group**, click the **Show Formulas** button to display the date.

3. On the **Home tab**, in the **Number group**, click the **Number Format arrow** (**Figure 2**).

   In the Number Format list, you can select common date, time, and number formats, or click *More Number Formats* to display additional built-in number formats.

■ **Continue to the next page to complete the skill** ▶

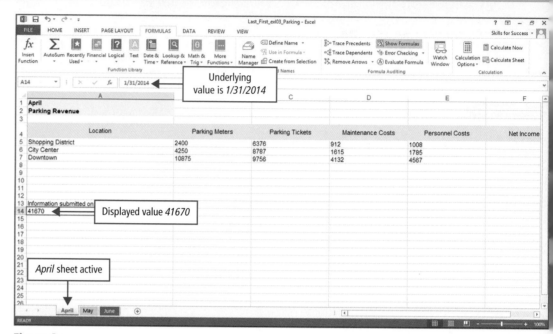

Figure 1

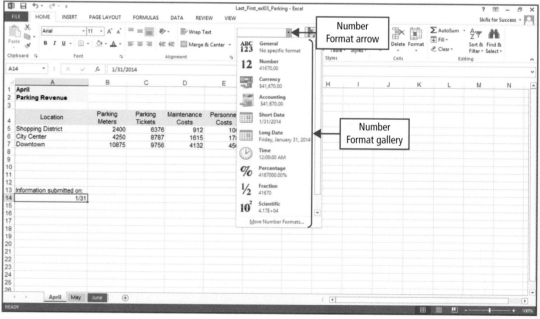

Figure 2

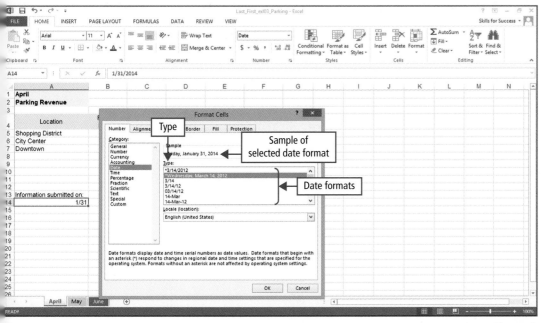

Figure 3

4. At the bottom of the **Number Format** list, click **More Number Formats**. On the **Number tab** of the **Format Cells** dialog box, notice Date is selected at the left. Under **Type**, click ***Wednesday, March 14, 2012**, to show a sample of the selected date format. Compare your screen with **Figure 3**.

   The date *Wednesday, March 14, 2012,* will not display in your worksheet. This is a sample of a format that can be applied to your current date.

5. Under **Type**, scroll down, click **March 14, 2012**, and then click **OK** to display the date in cell A14 as *January 31, 2014.*

6. Click the **May** worksheet tab to make it the active worksheet, and then click cell **A17**. Type 8/11/98 and then on the **formula bar**, click the **Enter** button ☑ to accept the entry and change the year from *98* to *1998.*

   When a two-digit year between 30 and 99 is entered, a twentieth-century date is applied to the date format—*8/11/1998.*

7. Click the **June** worksheet tab, and then click cell **A17**. Hold down Ctrl and press ⌤—the semicolon key. Press Enter to confirm the entry and to enter the current date.

   The Ctrl + ⌤ shortcut enters the current date, obtained from your computer, into the selected cell using the default date format. The table in **Figure 4** summarizes how Excel interprets various date formats.

8. **Save** 🖫 the workbook.

■ **You have completed Skill 2 of 10**

Date Format AutoComplete	
Date Typed As	**Completed by Excel As**
7/4/14	7/4/2014
7-4-98	7/4/1998
7/4 or 7-4	4-Jul (current year assumed)
July 4 or Jul 4	4-Jul (current year assumed)
Jul/4 or Jul-4	4-Jul (current year assumed)
July 4, 1998	4-Jul-98
July 2014	Jul-14
July 1998	Jul-98

Figure 4

EXL 3-3
VIDEO

▶ Cells can contain formatting, comments, hyperlinks, and **content**—underlying formulas and data.

▶ You can clear the formatting, comments, hyperlinks, or the contents of a cell.

1. Click the **April** worksheet tab, and then click cell **A1**. On the **Home tab**, in the **Editing group**, click the **Clear** button, and then compare your screen with **Figure 1**.

2. On the menu, click **Clear Contents**. Look at cell **A1**, and verify that the text has been cleared but that the fill color applied to the cell still displays.

> Alternately, to delete the contents of a cell, you can press Delete , or you can tap a cell and then on the Mini toolbar, click Clear.

3. In cell **A1**, type Parking Revenue and then on the **formula bar**, click the **Enter** button ☑.

4. With cell **A1** still selected, in the **Editing group**, click the **Clear** button, and then click **Clear Formats** to clear the formatting from the cell. Compare your screen with **Figure 2**.

5. Select cell **A2**. On the **Home tab**, in the **Editing group**, click the **Clear** button, and then click **Clear All** to clear both the cell contents and the cell formatting.

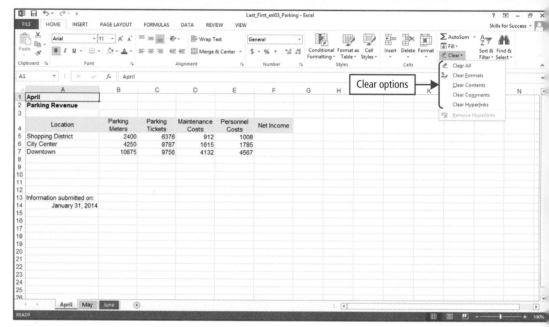

Figure 1

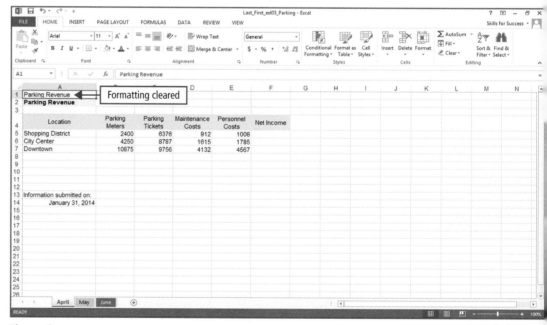

Figure 2

■ Continue to the next page to complete the skill

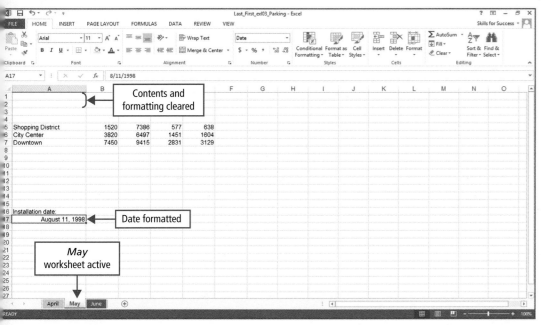

Figure 3

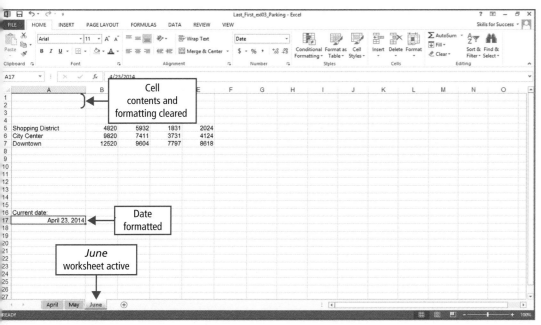

Figure 4

6. Display the **May** worksheet, and then select the range **A1:A2**. In the **Editing group**, click the **Clear** button, and then click **Clear All**.

7. Click cell **A16** to display the comment. On the **Home tab**, in the **Editing group**, click the **Clear** button, and then click **Clear Comments** to clear the comment from the cell.

8. Click cell **A17**. On the **Home tab**, in the **Number group**, click the **Number Format arrow**. At the bottom of the **Number Format** list, click **More Number Formats**. In the **Format Cells** dialog box, under **Type**, scroll down, click **March 14**, **2012**, and then click **OK** to display the date in cell **A17** as *August 11, 1998*. Compare your screen with **Figure 3**.

9. Display the **June** worksheet. Select the range **A1:A2**, and then use the technique just practiced to clear the contents and formatting from the selected range.

10. Click cell **A17**, and then use the technique just practiced to apply the date format *March 14, 2012*, to the current date. Compare your screen with **Figure 4**.

11. Make **April** the active sheet, and then **Save** 🖫 the workbook.

■ **You have completed Skill 3 of 10**

▶ Data from cells and ranges can be copied and then pasted to other cells in the same worksheet, to other worksheets, or to worksheets in another workbook.

▶ The *Clipboard* is a temporary storage area for text and graphics. When you use either the Copy command or the Cut command, the selected data is placed in the Clipboard, from which the data is available to paste.

1. On the **April** sheet, select the range **A13:A14**. Point to the lower edge of the green border surrounding the selected range until the pointer displays. Drag downward until the ScreenTip displays *A16:A17*, as shown in **Figure 1**, and then release the left mouse button to complete the move.

   Drag and drop is a method of moving objects in which you point to the selection and then drag it to a new location.

2. Select the range **A4:F4**. In the **Clipboard group**, click the **Copy** button.

   A moving border surrounds the selected range, and a message on the status bar indicates *Select destination and press ENTER or choose Paste*, confirming that your selected range has been copied to the Clipboard.

3. Display the **May** sheet, and then click cell **A4**. In the **Clipboard group**, click the **Paste arrow** to display the **Paste Options** gallery. Point at the second option in the second row—**Keep Source Column Widths**, and then compare your screen with **Figure 2**.

■ Continue to the next page to complete the skill

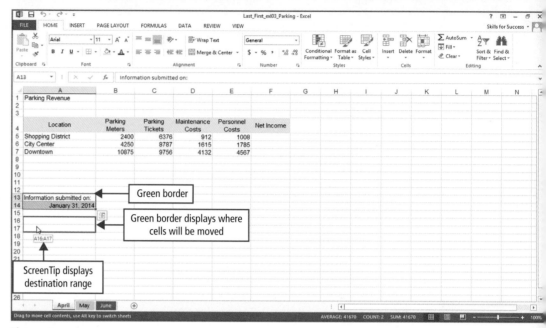

Figure 1

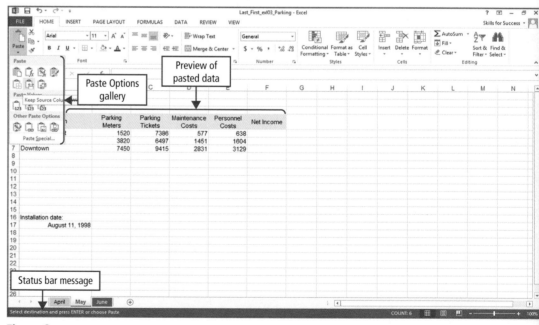

Figure 2

Paste Options

Option	Icon	Content and format pasted
Paste		Both the contents and cell formatting
Formulas		Only the formula
Formulas & Number Formatting		Both the formula and the number formatting
Keep Source Formatting		All content and cell formatting from original cells
No Borders		All content and cell formatting except borders
Keep Source Column Widths		All content and formatting including the column width format
Transpose		Orientation of pasted entries change—data in rows are pasted as columns
Formatting		Only the formatting

Figure 3

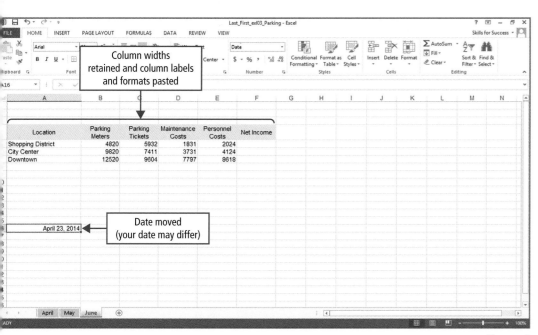

Column widths retained and column labels and formats pasted

Date moved (your date may differ)

Figure 4

4. In the **Paste Options** gallery, click the option **Keep Source Column Widths** to paste the column labels and to retain the column widths from the source worksheet. The table in **Figure 3** summarizes the Paste Options.

   When pasting a range of cells, you need to select only the cell in the upper left corner of the *paste area*—the target destination for data that has been cut or copied. When an item is pasted, it is not removed from the Clipboard, as indicated by the status bar message.

5. Display the **June** sheet, and then click cell **A4**. Using the technique just practiced, paste the column labels using the Paste Option **Keep Source Column Widths**.

6. Click cell **A17**, and then point to the upper green border surrounding the cell to display the pointer. Drag up to move the cell contents to cell **A16**. In the message box *There's already data here. Do you want to replace it?* click **OK** to replace the contents. Compare your screen with **Figure 4**.

7. Click the **April** worksheet tab. **Save** workbook.

- **You have completed Skill 4 of 10**

▶ You can group any number of worksheets in a workbook. After the worksheets are grouped, you can edit data or format cells in all of the grouped worksheets at the same time.

▶ Grouping worksheets is useful when you are creating or modifying a set of worksheets that are similar in purpose and structure.

1. Right-click the **April** worksheet tab, and then from the shortcut menu, click **Select All Sheets**.

2. At the top of the screen, on the title bar, verify that *[Group]* displays as shown in **Figure 1**.

   Here, all three worksheet tabs are shaded with a gradient color and *[Group]* displays on the title bar to indicate that the three worksheets are active as a group.

3. Select the range **A5:A7**, and then apply the **40% - Accent1** cell style.

4. Display the **May** worksheet to ungroup the sheets and to verify that the cell style you selected in the previous step displays as shown in **Figure 2**.

   In the worksheet tab area, both the *April* worksheet tab and the *June* worksheet tab display a solid color, indicating that they are no longer active in the group. At the top of your screen, *[Group]* no longer displays on the title bar.

   Selecting a single worksheet cancels a grouping. Because the worksheets were grouped, formatting was applied to all of the selected worksheets. In this manner, you can make the same changes to all selected worksheets at the same time.

■ **Continue to the next page to complete the skill**

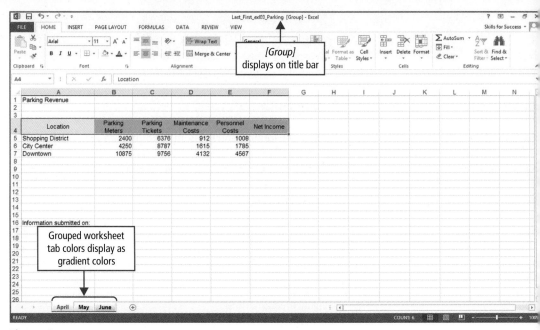

Figure 1

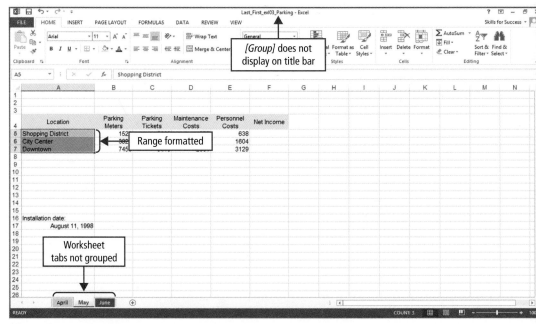

Figure 2

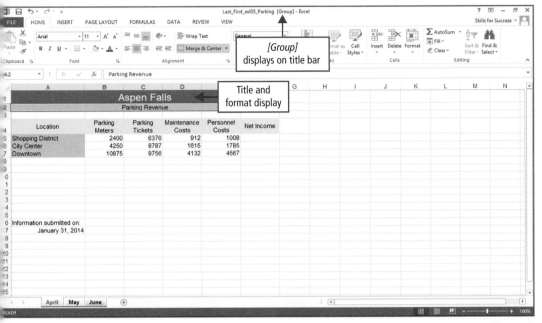

Figure 3

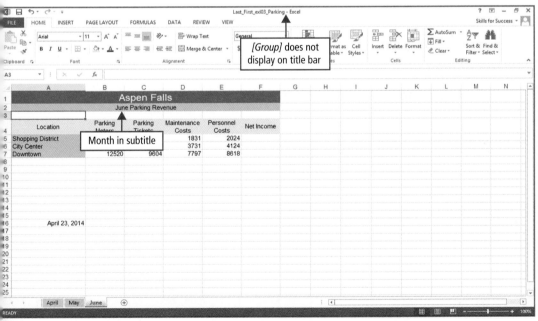

Figure 4

5. Right-click the **April** worksheet tab, and then from the shortcut menu, click **Select All Sheets**.

6. In cell **A1**, press Delete , type Aspen Falls and then press Enter . Select the range **A1:F1**, and then in the **Alignment group**, click the **Merge & Center** button. Apply the **Accent1** cell style. Click the **Font Size** button 11 ▾ , and then click **18**.

7. In cell **A2**, type Parking Revenue and then press Enter . Select the range **A2:F2**, and then click the **Merge & Center** button. Apply the **40% - Accent1** cell style, and then compare your screen with **Figure 3**.

8. Right-click the **April** worksheet tab, and then from the shortcut menu, click **Ungroup Sheets**. Verify that *[Group]* no longer displays on the title bar.

9. Double-click cell **A2** to edit the cell contents. Use the arrow keys to move to the left of the word *Parking*. Type April and add a space, and then press Enter . Display the **May** worksheet. Using the same technique, edit cell **A2** to May Parking Revenue Display the **June** worksheet, and then edit cell **A2** to June Parking Revenue Compare your screen with **Figure 4**.

10. Save 🖫 the workbook.

■ **You have completed Skill 5 of 10**

▶ When you combine several math operators in a single formula, ***operator precedence***—a set of mathematical rules for performing calculations within a formula—are followed. Expressions within parentheses are calculated first. Then, multiplication and division are performed before addition and subtraction.

▶ When a formula contains operators with the same precedence level, Excel evaluates the operators from left to right. Multiplication and division are considered to be on the same level of precedence. Addition and subtraction are considered to be on the same level of precedence.

1. Right-click the **June** worksheet tab, and then click **Select All Sheets**. Verify that *[Group]* displays on the title bar.

2. Click cell **F5**, enter the formula =(B5+C5)–(D5+E5) and then compare your screen with **Figure 1**.

> The formula *Net Income = Total Revenue – Total Cost* is represented by *(Parking Meters + Parking Tickets) – (Maintenance Cost + Personnel Cost)*. By placing parentheses in the formula, the revenue is first added together, the costs are added together, and then the total costs are subtracted from the total revenues. Without the parentheses, the formula would give an incorrect result.

3. On the **formula bar**, click the **Enter** button ☑. AutoFill the formula down through cell **F7**. Compare your screen with **Figure 2**.

■ **Continue to the next page to complete the skill**

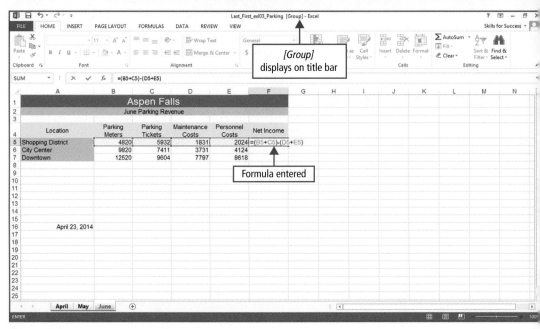

Figure 1

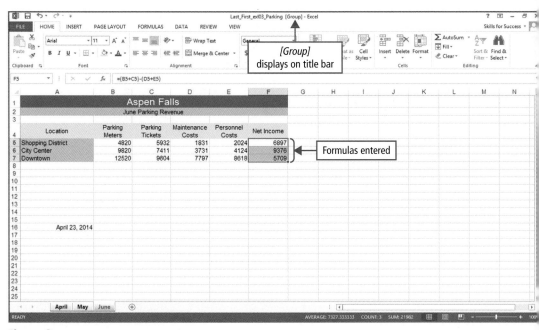

Figure 2

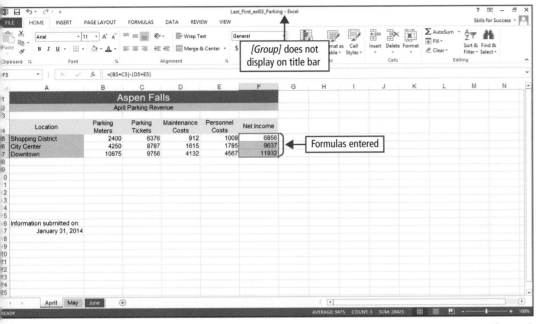

Figure 3

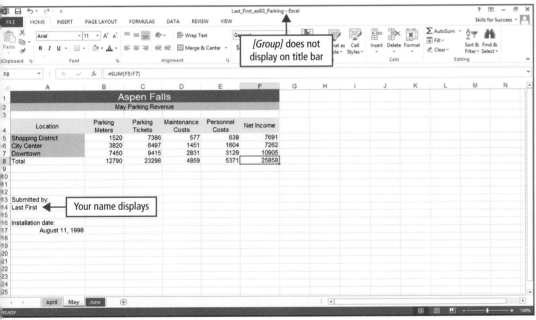

Figure 4

4. Display the **April** worksheet to ungroup the sheets and to verify that the formula results display in the worksheet. Compare your screen with **Figure 3**.

   Because the worksheets were grouped, the formulas have been entered on all selected worksheets.

5. Right-click the **April** worksheet tab, and then click **Select All Sheets**. Verify that *[Group]* displays on the title bar.

6. In cell **A8**, type Total and then press Enter. Select the range **B8:F8**, and then on the **Home tab**, in the **Editing group**, click the **AutoSum** button to insert the column totals.

7. Click cell **A13**, type Submitted by: and then press Enter. In cell **A14**, using your name, type Last First and then press Enter.

8. Click the **May** worksheet tab. Click cell **F8**, and then compare your screen with **Figure 4**.

   On the *May* worksheet, the formula in cell F8 displays as the value *25858*.

9. **Save** 🖫 the workbook.

■ **You have completed Skill 6 of 10**

▶ When worksheets are grouped, any changes made to a single worksheet are made to each worksheet in the group. For example, if you change the width of a column or add a row, all the worksheets in the group are changed in the same manner.

1. Right-click the **May** worksheet tab, and then click **Select All Sheets**.

2. In the row heading area, point to row 7 to display the ➡ pointer. Right-click, and then compare your screen with **Figure 1**.

3. From the shortcut menu, click **Insert** to insert a new blank row above the *Downtown* row in all of the grouped worksheets. In cell **A7**, type Midtown and press ⎯Tab⎯.

4. Click the **April** worksheet tab to make it the active worksheet and to ungroup the worksheets. Beginning in cell **B7**, enter the following *Midtown* data for April:

   2785   5012   3270   1860

5. Click the **May** worksheet tab, and then beginning in cell **B7**, enter the following *Midtown* data for May:

   2420   8190   1916   2586

6. Click the **June** worksheet tab, and then beginning in cell **B7**, enter the following *Midtown* data for June:

   2170   6546   4425   1925

7. Click each of the worksheet tabs, and then verify that you entered the values correctly. Click the **June** worksheet tab, and then compare your screen with **Figure 2**.

■ **Continue to the next page to complete the skill**

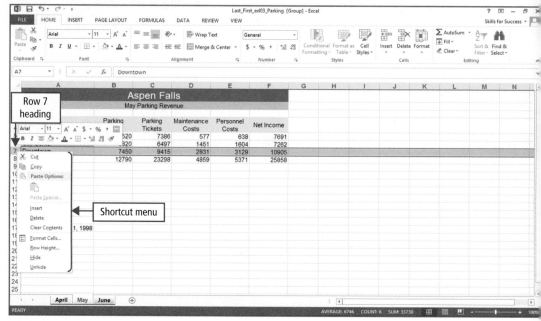

Figure 1

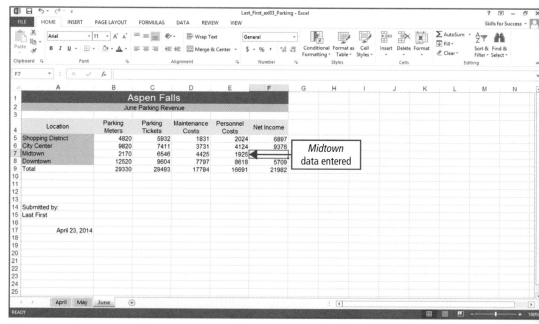

Figure 2

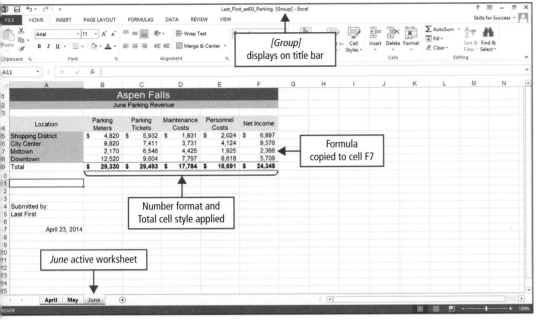

Figure 3

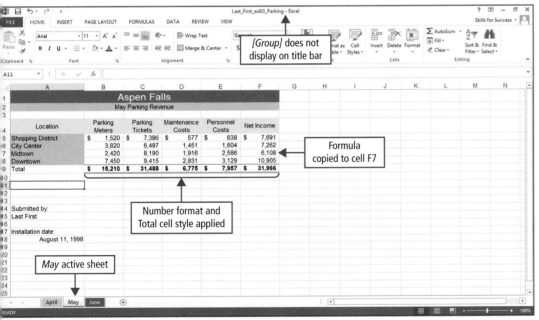

Figure 4

8. Right-click the **June** worksheet tab, and then click **Select All Sheets**. Click cell **F6**, and then AutoFill the formula down to cell **F7**.

> On the *June* worksheet, the formula in cell *F9* displays as the value *24348*.

9. Select the range **B5:F5**, hold down Ctrl, and then select the range **B9:F9**. With the nonadjacent ranges selected, in the **Styles group**, click the **Cell Styles** button, and then click **Currency [0]**.

10. Select the range **B6:F8**, and then apply the **Comma [0]** cell style.

11. Select the range **B9:F9**, and then apply the **Total** cell style. Click cell **A11**, and then compare your screen with **Figure 3**.

12. Display the **April** sheet, and then verify that the same formatting was applied.

13. Click the **May** worksheet tab to make it the active worksheet, and verify that the formulas and formatting changes were made. Compare your screen with **Figure 4**.

> On the *May* sheet, the formula in cell *F9* displays as the value *$31,966*.

14. Save 💾 the workbook.

■ **You have completed Skill 7 of 10**

EXL 3-8
VIDEO

▶ To organize a workbook, you can position worksheet tabs in any order you desire.

▶ You can add new worksheets to accommodate new information.

1. Right-click the **April** worksheet tab, and then from the shortcut menu, click **Unhide**. Compare your screen with Figure 1.

2. In the **Unhide** dialog box, verify *1st Qtr* is selected and then click **OK**. Use the same technique to **Unhide** the **2010** and the **2011** worksheets.

3. Right-click the **2010** worksheet tab, and then click **Delete**. Read the message that displays, and then click **Delete**. Use the same technique to **Delete** the **2011** worksheet.

> Because you can't undo a worksheet deletion, it is a good idea to verify that you selected the correct worksheet before you click Delete.

4. To the right of the **June** worksheet tab, click the **New Sheet** button ⊕ to create a new worksheet. Rename the new worksheet tab as Summary

5. In cell **A2**, type Second Quarter Parking Revenue and press Enter . In cell **A4**, type Month and then press Tab . Type the following labels in row **4**, pressing Tab after each label: Total Meter Revenue, Total Ticket Revenue, Total Maintenance Cost, Total Personnel Cost, Net Income

6. In cell **A5**, type April and then AutoFill the months down through cell **A7**.

7. Change the **Column Width** of columns **A:F** to 12 Click cell **A9**, and then compare your screen with Figure 2.

■ **Continue to the next page to complete the skill**

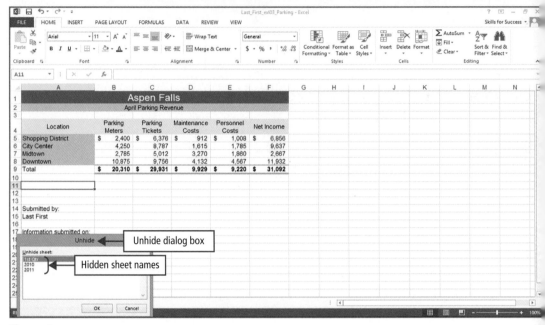

Figure 1

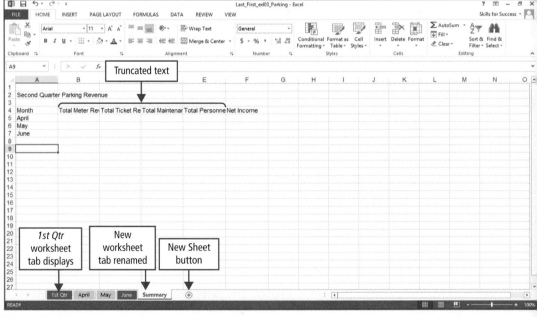

Figure 2

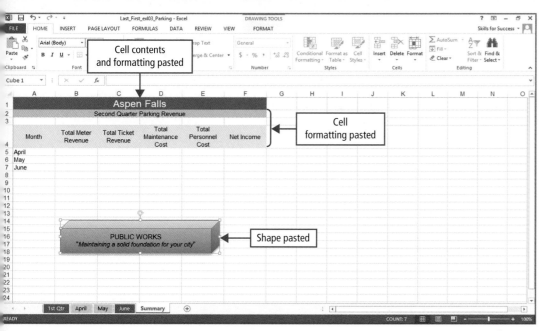

Figure 3

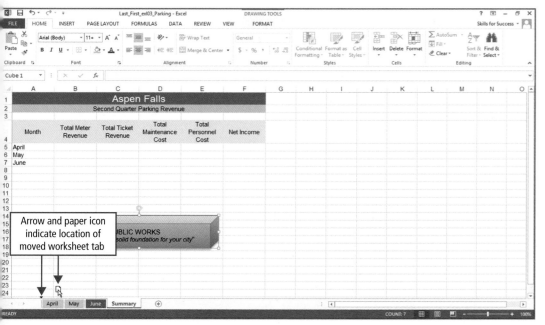

Figure 4

8. Display the **June** sheet. Click cell **A1**, and then in the **Clipboard group**, click the **Copy** button. Display the **Summary** sheet. Click cell **A1**, and then click the **Paste** button to paste the cell content and format.

9. Display the **June** sheet, and then press Esc to remove the moving border. Select the range **A2:F4**, and then click the **Copy** button. Display the **Summary** sheet, and then click cell **A2**. In the **Clipboard group**, click the **Paste arrow**. In the **Paste Options** gallery, under **Other Paste Options**, click the first option—**Formatting** to paste only the format.

10. Display the **1st Qtr** sheet. Click the shape, and then click the **Copy** button. Display the **Summary** sheet. In the **Clipboard group**, click the **Paste** button. Move the shape to approximately the range **B14:E18**. Compare your screen with **Figure 3**.

11. Right-click the **1st Qtr** worksheet tab, and then click **Hide**.

12. Click the **Summary** worksheet tab. Hold down the left mouse button and drag to the left to display an arrow and the pointer. Drag to the left until the arrow is to the left of the **April** worksheet tab, as shown in **Figure 4**.

13. Release the left mouse button to complete the worksheet move. **Save** the workbook.

■ **You have completed Skill 8 of 10**

EXL 3-9
VIDEO

► A ***summary sheet*** is a worksheet that displays and summarizes totals from other worksheets. A ***detail sheet*** is a worksheet with cells referred to by summary sheet formulas.

► Changes made to the detail sheets that affect totals will automatically recalculate and display on the summary sheet.

1. On the **Summary** sheet, click cell **B5**. Type = and then click the **April** worksheet tab. On the **April** sheet, click cell **B9**, and then press ⎡Enter⎤ to display the April sheet *B9* value in the Summary sheet *B5* cell.

2. In the **Summary** sheet, click cell **B5**. In the formula bar, notice that the cell reference in the underlying formula includes both a worksheet reference and a cell reference as shown in **Figure 1**.

   > By using a formula that refers to another worksheet, changes made to the Total in cell *B9* of the *April* sheet will be automatically updated in this *Summary* sheet.

3. Click cell **B6**, type = and then click the **May** worksheet tab. On the **May** sheet, click cell **B9**, and then press ⎡Enter⎤.

4. On the **Summary** sheet, repeat the technique just practiced to display the **June** sheet **B9** value in the **Summary** sheet **B7** cell.

5. On the **Summary** sheet, select the range **B5:B7**, and then AutoFill to the right through column **F**. Click cell **F7**, and then compare your screen with **Figure 2**.

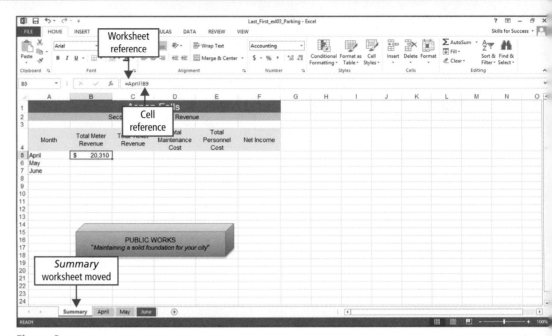

Figure 1

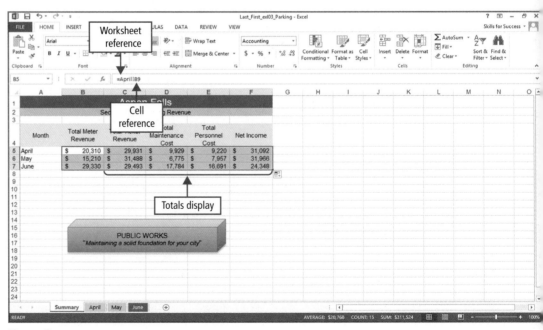

Figure 2

■ **Continue to the next page to complete the skill**

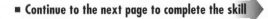

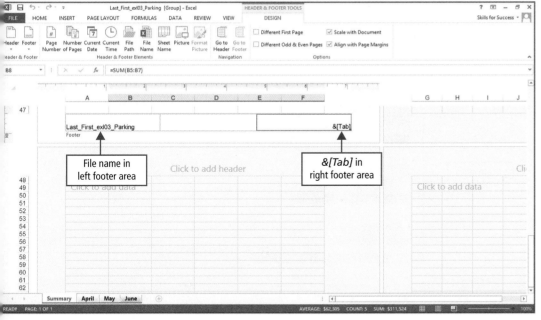

Figure 3

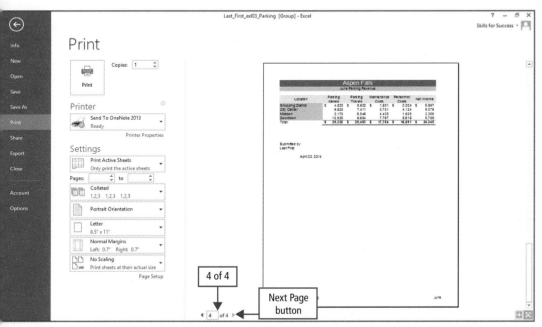

Figure 4

6. On the **Summary** sheet, click cell **A8**, type Total and then select the range **B8:F8**. In the **Editing group**, click the **AutoSum** button, and then apply the **Total** cell style.

7. Right-click the **Summary** worksheet tab, and then click **Select All Sheets**.

8. Insert the file name in the worksheet's left footer. Click the right section of the footer, and then in the **Header & Footer Elements group**, click the **Sheet Name** button, and then compare your screen with **Figure 3**.

    By grouping worksheets, you can insert headers and footers into each worksheet quickly and consistently.

9. Click in a cell just above the footer to exit the **Footer area**. On the lower right side of the status bar, click the **Normal** button ▦. Hold down Ctrl, and press Home to make cell **A1** the active cell on all selected worksheets.

10. With the sheets still grouped, click the **File tab**, and then click **Print**. At the bottom of the screen, click the **Next Page** button ▶ three times to view each of the four worksheets, and then compare your screen with **Figure 4**.

    Because the worksheets are grouped, all four worksheets are included in the preview.

11. **Save** ▦ the workbook.

- **You have completed Skill 9 of 10**

EXL 3-10
VIDEO

▶ A ***clustered bar chart*** is useful when you want to compare values across categories; bar charts organize categories along the vertical axis and values along the horizontal axis.

1. Click the **Back** button. Right-click the **Summary** worksheet tab, and then click **Ungroup Sheets**. On the **Summary** sheet, select the range **A4:E7**. On the **Insert tab**, in the **Charts group**, click the **Recommended Charts** button. In the **Insert Chart** dialog box, verify the first choice is selected—**Clustered Bar**, and then click **OK**.

2. On the **Design tab**, in the **Location group**, click the **Move Chart** button. In the **Move Chart** dialog box, select the **New sheet** option button, type 2nd Qtr Chart and then click **OK**.

3. On the **Design tab**, in the **Data group**, click the **Switch Row/Column** button to display the months on the vertical axis. Compare your screen with **Figure 1**.

   Because you want to look at revenue and costs by month, displaying the months on the vertical axis is useful.

4. In the **Chart Layouts group**, click the **Quick Layout** button, and then click **Layout 3**.

5. To the right of the chart, click the **Chart Styles** button, and then click **Style 3**.

6. Edit the **Chart Title** to 2nd Quarter Parking Revenue and Cost and then compare your screen with **Figure 2**.

■ **Continue to the next page to complete the skill** ▶

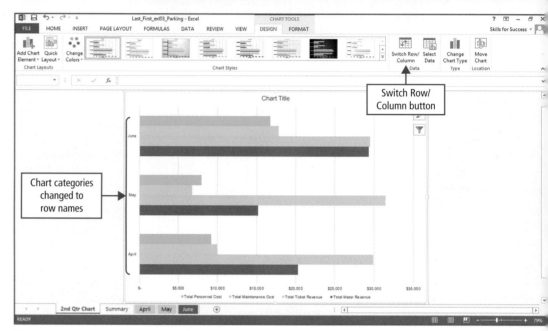

Figure 1

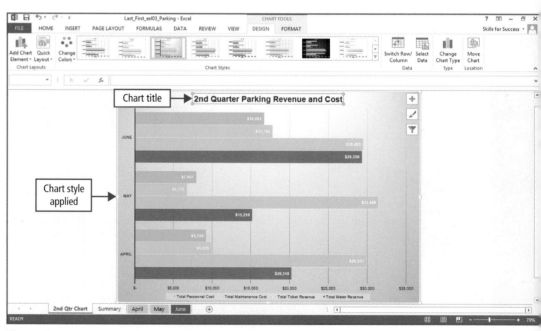

Figure 2

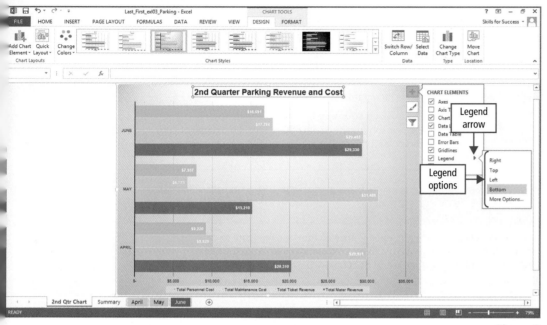

Figure 3

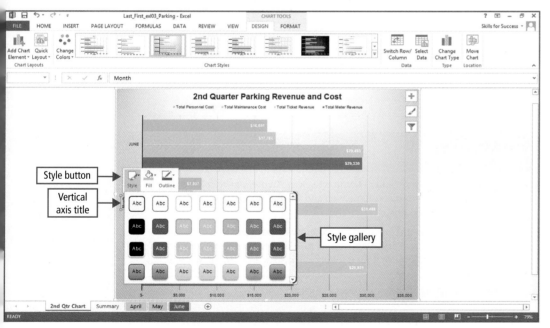

Figure 4

7. At the top right corner of the chart, click the **Chart Elements** button ⊞. Point to **Legend**, and then click the **Legend arrow**. Compare your screen with **Figure 3**.

8. In the list, click **Top** to move the legend to the top of the chart sheet.

9. In the **Chart Elements** gallery, point to **Axis Titles**, and then click the **Axis Titles arrow**. Select the **Primary Vertical** check box to add the vertical axis title. Click the **Chart Elements** button ⊞ to close the gallery.

10. On the left side of the chart, change the vertical **Axis Title** text to Month Right-click the *Month* title, and then on the Mini toolbar, click the **Style** button and compare your screen with **Figure 4**.

11. In the **Style** gallery, click the second thumbnail in the fourth row—**Subtle Effect - Blue, Accent 1**.

12. On the **Insert tab**, in the **Text group**, click the **Header & Footer** button. In the **Page Setup** dialog box, click the **Custom Footer** button. In the **Footer** dialog box, verify the insertion point is in the **Left section** and then click the **Insert File Name** button 📄. Click the **Right section** of the footer, and then click the **Insert Sheet Name** button 🖥. Click **OK** two times.

13. **Save** 💾 the workbook, and then **Close** ✖ Excel. Submit the project as directed by your instructor.

✔ **DONE! You have completed Skill 10 of 10, and your document is complete!**

The following More Skills are located at **www.pearsonhighered.com/skills**

More Skills 11 Create Organization Charts

You can add SmartArt graphics to a worksheet to create timelines, illustrate processes, or show relationships. When you click the SmartArt button on the Ribbon, you can select from among a broad array of graphics, including an organization chart. An organization chart graphically represents the relationships between individuals and groups in an organization.

In More Skills 11, you will insert and modify a SmartArt graphic to create an organization chart.

To begin, open your web browser, navigate to www.pearsonhighered.com/skills, locate the name of your textbook, and then follow the instructions on the website.

More Skills 12 Create Line Charts

Use a line chart when you want to compare more than one set of values over time. Time is displayed along the bottom axis and the data point values are connected with a line. The curves and directions of the lines make trends obvious to the reader.

In More Skills 12, you will create a line chart comparing three sets of values.

To begin, open your web browser, navigate to www.pearsonhighered.com/skills, locate the name of your textbook, and then follow the instructions on the website.

More Skills 13 Set and Clear Print Areas

If you are likely to print the same portion of a particular worksheet over and over again, you can save time by setting a print area.

In More Skills 13, you will set and then clear print areas in a worksheet.

To begin, open your web browser, navigate to www.pearsonhighered.com/skills, locate the name of your textbook, and then follow the instructions on the website.

More Skills 14 Create, Edit, and Delete Hyperlinks

You can insert a hyperlink in a worksheet that can link to a file, a location in a file, a web page on the World Wide Web, or a web page on an organization's intranet. Creating a hyperlink in a workbook is a convenient way to provide quick access to related information. You can edit or delete hyperlinks.

In More Skills 14, you will create hyperlinks to related information on the web and to other worksheets in the workbook.

To begin, open your web browser, navigate to www.pearsonhighered.com/skills, locate the name of your textbook, and then follow the instructions on the website.

Please note that there are no additional projects to accompany the More Skills Projects, and they are not covered in the End-of-Chapter projects.

The following table summarizes the **SKILLS AND PROCEDURES** covered in this chapter.

Skills Number	Task	Step	Keyboard Shortcut
1	Rename worksheet tabs	Right-click worksheet tab → Rename → Type new name → Enter	
1	Rename worksheet tabs	Double-click worksheet tab → Type new name → Enter	
1	Format worksheet tabs	Home tab → Cells group → Format → Tab Color	
1	Format worksheet tabs	Right-click worksheet tab → Tab Color	
2	Format dates	Home tab → Number group → Number Format arrow → More Number Formats	
2	Enter the current date		Ctrl + ;
3	Clear cell contents	Home tab → Editing group → Clear → Clear Contents	Delete
3	Clear cell formatting	Home tab → Editing group → Clear → Clear Formats	
3	Clear cell contents and formatting	Home tab → Editing group → Clear → Clear All	
4	Paste with options	Home tab → Clipboard group → Paste Arrow → Select desired option	
5	Group worksheets	Right-click worksheet tab → Select All Sheets	
5	Ungroup worksheets	Right-click worksheet tab → Ungroup Sheets or click a single worksheet tab	
8	Insert worksheets	Home tab → Cells group → Insert arrow → Insert Sheet	
8	Delete worksheet	Home tab → Cells group → Delete arrow → Delete Sheet	
8	Hide worksheet	Right-click worksheet tab → Hide	
8	Unhide worksheet	Right-click worksheet tab → Unhide → Worksheet name	
8	Move worksheet tab	Drag worksheet tab to new location	

Key Terms

Online Help Skills

1. Start **Excel 2013**, and then in the upper right corner of the start page, click the **Help** button ⓘ.

2. In the **Excel Help** window **Search help** box, type numbers to dates and then press [Enter].

3. In the search result list, click **Stop automatically changing numbers to dates**, and then compare your screen with **Figure 1**.

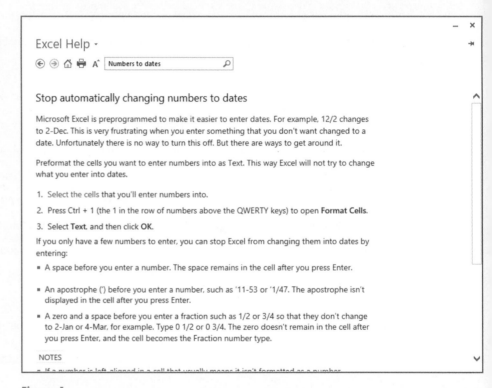

Figure 1

4. Read the article to answer the following question: What cell format can be applied to stop changing numbers into dates?

Matching

Match each term in the second column with its correct definition in the first column by writing the letter of the term on the blank line in front of the correct definition.

___ **1.** The labels along the lower edge of the workbook window that identify each worksheet.

___ **2.** Controls to the left of the worksheet tabs used to display worksheet tabs that are not in view.

___ **3.** A sequential number assigned to a date.

___ **4.** A temporary storage area for text and graphics.

___ **5.** A method of moving or copying the content of selected cells in which you point to the selection and then drag it to a new location.

___ **6.** The target destination for data that has been cut or copied using the Clipboard.

___ **7.** The mathematical rules that specify the order in which calculations are performed.

___ **8.** A worksheet that displays and recaps totals from other worksheets.

___ **9.** A worksheet that contains the detailed information in a workbook.

___ **10.** A chart type that is useful when you want to compare values across categories.

A Clipboard

B Clustered bar chart

C Detail sheet

D Drag and drop

E Operator precedence

F Paste area

G Serial number

H Summary sheet

I Tab scrolling buttons

J Worksheet tabs

BizSkills Video

1. Why should you arrive early for an interview?

2. What should you do at the end of an interview?

Multiple Choice (MyITLab®)

Choose the correct answer.

1. An active worksheet tab will display in this way.
   A. With a solid tab color
   B. With a gradient tab color
   C. Always as the first worksheet

2. Worksheets can be grouped in this way.
   A. Right-clicking a worksheet tab and then clicking Select All Sheets
   B. Double-clicking a worksheet tab
   C. Clicking the New Sheet button

3. Clearing the contents of a cell deletes this.
   A. Only the contents
   B. Only the formatting
   C. Both contents and formatting

4. When pasting a range of cells, this cell needs to be selected in the paste area.
   A. Bottom right cell
   B. Center cell
   C. Top left cell

5. Worksheets can be hidden in this way.
   A. Move the worksheet as the last sheet
   B. Right-click a worksheet tab and then click Hide
   C. Double-click a worksheet tab

6. If a workbook contains grouped worksheets, this word will display on the title bar.
   A. [Collection]
   B. [Set]
   C. [Group]

7. When a formula contains operators with the same precedence level, the operators are evaluated in this order.
   A. Left to right
   B. Right to left
   C. From the center out

8. Addition and this mathematical operator are considered to be on the same precedence level.
   A. Multiplication
   B. Division
   C. Subtraction

9. Changes made in a detail worksheet will automatically recalculate and display on this sheet.
   A. Summary
   B. Final
   C. Outline

10. The paste option Keep Source Column Widths will paste this.
    A. The cell formatting
    B. Only the column width formatting
    C. All content and cell formatting including the column width format

Topics for Discussion

1. Some people in an organization will only view the summary worksheet without examining the detail worksheets. When might this practice be acceptable and when might it cause mistakes?

2. Illustrate some examples of how a formula's results will be incorrect if parentheses are not used to group calculations in the order they should be performed. Think of a class where you have three exam grades and a final exam grade. If the three tests together count as 50 percent of your course grade, and the final exam counts as 50 percent of your course grade, how would you write the formula to get a correct result?

Skills Review  Grader

To complete this project, you will need the following file:

- exl03_SRPayroll

You will save your file as:

- Last_First_exl03_SRPayroll

1. Start **Excel 2013**. From your student data files, open **exl03_SRPayroll**. Save the workbook in your chapter folder as Last_First_exl03_SRPayroll

2. Right-click the worksheet tab, and then click **Select All Sheets**. Click cell **A19**. On the **Home tab**, in the **Editing group**, click the **Clear** button, and then click **Clear All**. Select the range **A4:F4**, and then apply the **40% - Accent3** cell style. In the **Alignment group**, click the **Wrap Text** and the **Center** buttons.

3. In cell **F5**, type =B5-(C5+D5+E5) and then press Enter to construct the formula to compute the Net Pay as *Total Gross Pay – (Income Tax + Social Security (FICA) Tax + Health Insurance)*. AutoFill the formula in cell **F5** down through cell **F12**. Compare your screen with **Figure 1**.

4. Verify that the worksheets are still grouped. Select the range **B6:F12**, and then apply the **Comma [0]** cell style. Select the range **B13:F13**, and then apply the **Total** cell style. Click the **Courthouse** worksheet tab.

5. To the right of the **Courthouse** worksheet tab, click the **New Sheet** button. Rename the new worksheet tab Summary and then change the **Tab Color** to **Orange**, **Accent 6**. Click the **Summary** worksheet tab, and drag it to the left of the *Community Center* worksheet tab. Compare your screen with **Figure 2**.

6. Right-click the worksheet tab, and then click **Select All Sheets**. Add the file name in the worksheet's left footer. Click the right footer section, and then in the **Header & Footer Elements group**, click the **Sheet Name** button. Return to Normal view, and then press Ctrl + Home.

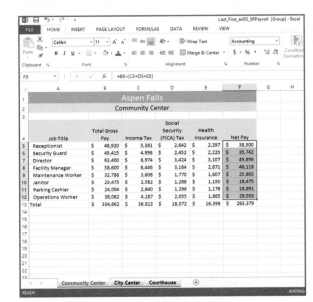

Figure 1

Figure 2

- Continue to the next page to complete this Skills Review

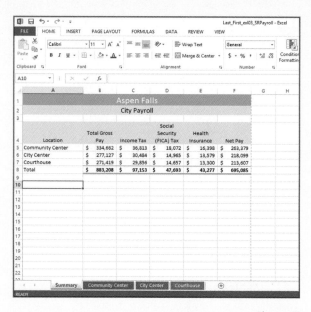

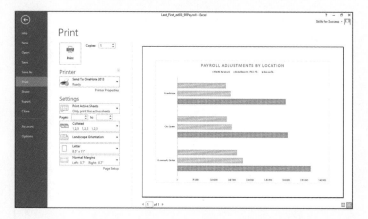

Figure 3

Figure 4

7. Display the **Community Center** sheet, select the range **A1:F4**, and then click **Copy**. Display the **Summary** sheet and then click cell **A1**. Click the **Paste arrow** and then click **Keep Source Column Widths**. In cell **A2**, replace the text with City Payroll in cell **A4**, replace the text with Location and then press Enter. Type the following labels in column **A**, pressing Enter after each label: Community Center, City Center, Courthouse, and Total

8. On the **Summary** sheet, click **B5**, type = and then click the **Community Center** worksheet tab. On the **Community Center** sheet, click cell **B13**, and then press Enter. Use the same technique in cells **B6** and **B7** to place the *Total Gross Pay* amounts from the *City Center* and the *Courthouse* sheets on the *Summary* sheet.

9. On the **Summary** sheet, select the range **B5:B7**. Click the **Quick Analysis Lens** button, click **Totals**, and then click the first option **Sum**. Select the range **B5:B8**, and then AutoFill the formulas to the right through column **F**. Select the range **B8:F8**, and then apply the **Total** cell style. Click cell **A10**, and then compare your screen with Figure 3.

10. On the **Summary** sheet, select the nonadjacent ranges **A4:A7** and **C4:E7**. On the **Insert tab**, in the **Charts group**, click the **Recommended Charts** button. In the **Insert Chart** dialog box, click **Clustered Bar**, and then click **OK**. On the **Design tab**, in the **Location group**, click the **Move Chart** button. In the **Move Chart** dialog box, select the **New sheet** option button, type Payroll Adjustments and then click **OK**.

11. On the **Design tab**, in the **Data group**, click the **Switch Row/Column** button. Click the **Chart Styles** button, and then click **Style 2**. Change the **Chart Title** to Payroll Adjustments by Location

12. On the **Summary** sheet, click cell **A12**, type Date Created and then click Enter. In cell **A13**, press Ctrl + ; (the semicolon), and then press Enter.

13. Right-click the **Summary** worksheet tab, and then click **Unhide**. In the **Unhide** dialog box, click **OK**. Right-click the **Art Center** worksheet tab, and then click **Delete**. In the message box, click **Delete**.

14. Group the worksheets, and then check the spelling.

15. Click the **File tab**, and then click **Print**. Compare your workbook with Figure 4.

16. Save the workbook, and then submit the workbook as directed by your instructor.

✓ **DONE! You have completed this Skills Review**

Skills Assessment 1

MyITLab®
Grader

To complete this workbook, you will need the following file:

- exl03_SA1Center

You will save your workbook as:

- Last_First_exl03_SA1Center

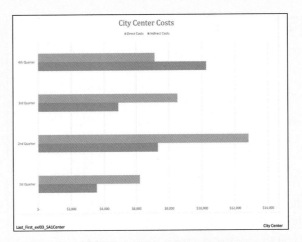

1. Start **Excel 2013**, and open the file **exl03_SA1Center**. **Save** the workbook in your chapter folder as Last_First_exl03_SA1Center

2. Group the worksheets. In cell **E5**, construct a formula to compute *Net Income = Income – (Indirect Costs + Direct Costs)*. AutoFill the formula down through cell **E7**.

3. In the nonadjacent ranges **B5:E5** and **B8:E8**, apply the **Currency [0]** cell style.

4. Insert a new worksheet. Rename the new worksheet tab Summary and apply the worksheet tab color **Brown, Accent 5**. Move the new worksheet tab to make it the first worksheet in the workbook.

5. Copy the range **A1:E4** from any of the detail worksheets, and then on the **Summary** sheet, click cell **A1**. Paste the range using the **Keep Source Column Widths** paste option. Change the subtitle of cell **A2** to City Center Annual Revenue and then change the label in cell **A4** to Quarter

6. In cell **A5**, type 1st Quarter and then AutoFill the labels in the range **A6:A8**. In cell **A9**, type Total

7. In the *Summary* worksheet, enter a formula in cell **B5** setting the cell to equal cell **B8** in the *1st Quarter* worksheet. Enter the *Income* total from the *2nd Quarter*, the *3rd Quarter*, and the *4th Quarter* worksheets in the range **B6:B8**.

8. Select the range **B5:B8**, and then use the **Quick Analysis Lens** button to insert the column total.

9. AutoFill the range **B5:B9** to the right through **column E**. In **row 9**, apply the **Total** cell style.

10. Insert a **Clustered Bar** chart using the nonadjacent ranges **A4:A8** and **C4:D8** as the source data. Move the chart to a chart sheet with the sheet name City Center

Aspen Falls
City Center Annual Revenue

Quarter	Income	Indirect Costs	Direct Costs	Net Income
1st Quarter	$ 17,700	$ 3,540	$ 6,195	$ 7,965
2nd Quarter	$ 36,590	$ 7,318	$ 12,806	$ 16,466
3rd Quarter	$ 24,320	$ 4,864	$ 8,511	$ 10,945
4th Quarter	$ 25,604	$ 10,270	$ 7,126	$ 8,208
Total	$ 104,214	$ 25,992	$ 34,638	$ 43,584

Aspen Falls
City Center Rental Revenue: 1st Quarter

Rental Item	Income	Indirect Costs	Direct Costs	Net Income
City Center Rental	$ 9,200	$ 1,840	$ 3,220	$ 4,140
AV Equipment	4,800	960	1,680	2,160
Display Equipment	3,700	740	1,295	1,665
Total	$ 17,700	$ 3,540	$ 6,195	$ 7,965

Figure 1

11. Apply the **Style 10** chart style. Change the **Chart Title** to City Center Costs

12. Group the worksheets. Add the file name in the left footer and the sheet name in the right footer. Return to Normal view, and then press [Ctrl] + [Home].

13. Check the spelling of the workbook, and then ungroup the sheets.

14. **Save** the workbook. Compare your completed workbook with **Figure 1**. Submit the workbook as directed by your instructor.

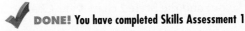

DONE! You have completed Skills Assessment 1

Skills Assessment 2

To complete this workbook, you will need the following file:

- exl03_SA2Taxes

You will save your workbook as:

- Last_First_exl03_SA2Taxes

---

1. Start **Excel 2013**, and open the file **exl03_SA2Taxes**. **Save** the workbook in your chapter folder as Last_First_exl03_SA2Taxes

2. Group the sheets. In cell **F5**, construct a formula to compute *Net Revenue = (Taxes Paid + Late Fees) – (Office Costs + Personnel Costs)*. AutoFill the formula down through **row 10**.

3. Select the nonadjacent ranges **B5:F5** and **B11:F11**, and then apply the **Currency [0]** cell style.

4. Ungroup the worksheets, and then hide the **April** worksheet. Compare the *January* worksheet with **Figure 1**.

5. Insert a new sheet, rename the worksheet tab 1st Qtr Summary and then change the worksheet tab color to **Brown, Text 2**. Move the worksheet to the first position in the workbook. Copy the range **A1:F4** from another sheet, and then paste the range at the top of the *1st Qtr Summary* sheet using the **Keep Source Column Widths** paste option.

6. On the **1st Qtr Summary** sheet, change the subtitle in cell **A2** to 1st Quarter Tax Revenue and then change the label in cell **A4** to Month In the range **A5:A7**, enter the months January, February, and March and in cell **A8**, type Total

7. In cell **B5**, enter a formula setting the cell to equal the total *Taxes Paid* in the *January* worksheet. In cells **B6** and **B7** of the **1st Qtr Summary** sheet, enter the total *Taxes Paid* from the *February* and the *March* worksheets.

8. Total column **B** and then AutoFill the range **B5:B8** to the right through column **F**. In the range **B8:F8**, apply the **Total** cell style.

9. Select the range **A4:C7**, and then insert a **Stacked Bar** chart. Move the chart to approximately the range **A10:F26**.

10. Apply the **Layout 9** chart layout and the **Style 2** chart style. Change the chart title to 1st Quarter

11. Group the worksheets and then check the spelling of the workbook. Add the file name in the left footer and the sheet name in the right footer. Return to Normal view, and then press Ctrl + Home.

12. **Save** the workbook. Compare your *1st Qtr Summary* sheet with **Figure 1**. Submit the workbook as directed by your instructor.

 DONE! You have completed Skills Assessment 2

Aspen Falls
1st Quarter Tax Revenue

Month	Taxes Paid	Late Fees	Office Costs	Personnel Costs	Net Revenue
January	$ 630,090	$ 274,527	$ 23,357	$ 284,629	$ 596,631
February	$ 654,466	$ 338,305	$ 22,029	$ 263,466	$ 707,276
March	$ 771,693	$ 407,095	$ 22,915	$ 320,350	$ 835,523
Total	$ 2,056,249	$ 1,019,927	$ 68,301	$ 868,445	$ 2,139,430

1ST QUARTER

■ January ■ February ■ March

LATE FEES
- $407,095
- $338,305
- $274,527

TAXES PAID
- $771,693
- $654,466
- $630,090

Aspen Falls
January Tax Revenue

Tax	Taxes Paid	Late Fees	Office Costs	Personnel Costs	Net Revenue
Motor Vehicle	$ 82,831	$ 58,255	$ 2,879	$ 49,255	$ 88,952
Sales	154,520	47,280	3,796	51,529	146,475
Franchise	72,956	46,998	4,915	60,061	54,978
Utilities	98,750	35,107	5,688	38,378	89,791
Property	120,000	40,762	3,200	24,320	133,242
Other	101,033	46,125	2,879	61,086	83,193
Totals	$ 630,090	$ 274,527	$ 23,357	$ 284,629	$ 596,631

Figure 1

Visual Skills Check

To complete this workbook, you will need the following file:

- exl03_VSWater

You will save your workbook as:

- Last_First_exl03_VSWater

Start **Excel 2013**, and open the file **exl03_VSWater**. Save the workbook in your chapter folder as Last_First_exl03_VSWater Complete the **Summary** sheet as shown in **Figure 1**. Create a summary sheet for the 4th Quarter with the totals from each month and the titles as shown in the figure. Name the worksheet tab 4th Qtr Summary and apply the worksheet tab color **Orange, Accent 1**. Move the **Summary** sheet to be the first worksheet. Insert a **Clustered Bar** chart based on the range **A4:D7**, and then move the chart below the data. Apply the **Style 12** chart style. On all sheets, add a footer with the file name in the left section and the sheet name in the right section. **Save** the workbook, and then submit the workbook as directed by your instructor.

 **DONE! You have completed Visual Skills Check**

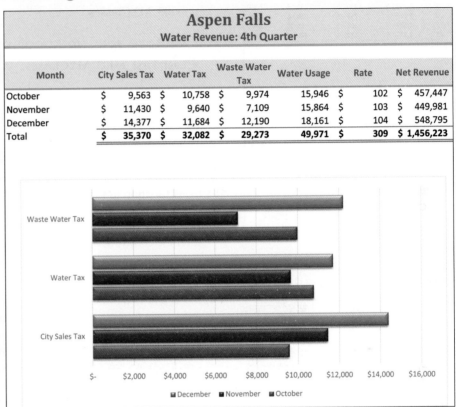

Aspen Falls
Water Revenue: 4th Quarter

Month	City Sales Tax	Water Tax	Waste Water Tax	Water Usage	Rate	Net Revenue
October	$ 9,563	$ 10,758	$ 9,974	15,946	$ 102	$ 457,447
November	$ 11,430	$ 9,640	$ 7,109	15,864	$ 103	$ 449,981
December	$ 14,377	$ 11,684	$ 12,190	18,161	$ 104	$ 548,795
Total	$ 35,370	$ 32,082	$ 29,273	49,971	$ 309	$ 1,456,223

Aspen Falls
Water Revenue: October

Building Type	City Sales Tax	Water Tax	Waste Water Tax	Water Usage	Rate	Net Revenue
Residential	$ 1,575	$ 1,890	$ 1,507	3,181	$ 19	$ 65,411
Commercial	4,233	5,762	5,671	5,440	27	162,546
Industrial	3,170	2,404	2,191	6,118	31	197,423
Apartments	585	702	605	1,207	25	32,067
Total	$ 9,563	$ 10,758	$ 9,974	15,946	$ 102	$ 457,447

Figure 1

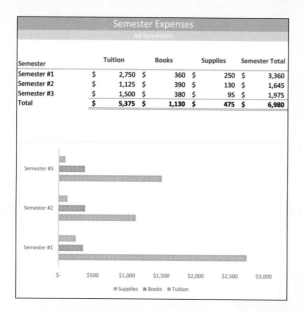

Figure 1

My Skills

To complete this workbook, you will need the following file:

- exl03_MYClasses

You will save your workbook as:

- Last_First_exl03_MYClasses

1. Start **Excel 2013**, and open the file **exl03_MyClasses**. **Save** the workbook in your chapter folder as Last_First_exl03_MYClasses

2. Group the worksheets. In cell **E5**, use the SUM function to total the row and then AutoFill the formula down through cell **E9**. In **row 10**, use the SUM function to total the columns.

3. Select cell **A2**, and then apply the **60% - Accent3** cell style.

4. Insert a new worksheet. Rename the new worksheet tab Semester Costs and apply the worksheet tab color **Blue, Accent 5**. Move the new worksheet tab to make it the first worksheet in the workbook.

5. Copy the range **A1:E4** from any of the detail worksheets, and then on the **Semester Costs** worksheet, click cell **A1**. Paste the range using the **Keep Source Column Widths** paste option. Change the subtitle of cell **A2** to All Semesters then change the label in cell **A4** to Semester and then change the label in cell **E4** to Semester Total

6. In cell **A5**, type Semester #1 and then AutoFill the label down through **A7**. In cell **A8**, type Total

7. In cell **B5** insert a formula to equal the value in cell **B10** in the *Semester #[?]1* worksheet. In the cells **B6** and **B7**, insert

formulas that equal the *Tuition* total from the *Semester #2* and *Semester #3* worksheets.

8. Use the **Quick Analysis Lens** button to insert the **column B** total, and then AutoFill the formulas in **column B** to the right through **column E**. Select the range **B8:E8**, and then apply the **Total** cell style.

9. Insert a **Clustered Bar** chart using the range **A4:D7** as the source data. Move and resize the chart to display below the data in approximately the range **A12:E28**.

10. Apply the **Style 2** chart style, and then delete the **Chart Title**. Move the legend to the bottom of the chart.

11. On the **Semester Costs** sheet, in cell **A36**, enter the current date, and then apply the **March 14, 2012**, date format.

12. Group the worksheets. Add the file name in the left footer and the sheet name in the right footer. Return to Normal view, and then press Ctrl + Home.

13. Check the spelling of the workbook, and then ungroup the sheets.

14. **Save** the workbook. Compare your completed workbook with **Figure 1**. Submit the workbook as directed by your instructor.

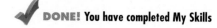 **DONE! You have completed My Skills**

Skills Challenge 1

To complete this workbook, you will need the following file:

- exl03_SC1Visitors

You will save your workbook as:

- Last_First_exl03_SC1Visitors

During each quarter, Carter Horikoshi, the Art Center Supervisor, tracked the revenue and costs at the Art Center. Open the file **exl03_SC1Visitors**, and then save the workbook in your chapter folder as Last_First_exl03_SC1Visitors Hide the Convention Center worksheet, and then move the remaining worksheets into the correct order. Assign a tab color to each worksheet tab. Group the worksheets, and then adjust the column widths to display all values. Format the labels in rows 1 through 4 consistently across all the worksheets. In cell F5, insert parentheses so that the sum of *Marketing Costs* and *Operating Costs* is subtracted from the sum of *Entrance Fees* and *Food Revenue*. Copy the corrected formula down. Format

the numbers appropriately. Unhide the Annual Summary worksheet, and move it as the first worksheet. Move and resize the bar chart to display below the data. On the Annual Summary sheet, format the values and the chart appropriately. Verify the formulas on the Summary sheet are correct. On all sheets, insert the file name in the left footer and the sheet name in the right footer. Check the spelling of the workbook and then verify that each sheet will print on one page. Save the workbook, and then submit the workbook as directed by your instructor.

 DONE! You have completed Skills Challenge 1

Skills Challenge 2

To complete this workbook, you will need the following file:

- exl03_SC2Durango

You will save your workbook as:

- Last_First_exl03_SC2Durango

During each month of the summer season, Duncan Chueng, the Park Operations Manager, tracked the revenue and cost at the various locations in the Durango County Recreation Area. Open the file **exl03_SC2Durango**, and then save the workbook in your chapter folder as Last_First_exl03_SC2Durango Using the skills you learned in the chapter, create a new summary worksheet with an appropriate sheet name. On the summary sheet, insert a clustered bar chart that displays the revenue for

each month. Format the chart appropriately. Move the summary sheet to the first position in the workbook. On all sheets, insert the file name in the left footer and the sheet name in the right footer. Adjust the page settings to print each worksheet on one page. Save the workbook, and then submit the workbook as directed by your instructor.

 DONE! You have completed Skills Challenge 2

CHAPTER 4

More Functions and Excel Tables

- The Excel Function Library contains hundreds of special functions that perform complex calculations quickly.
- Function Library categories include statistical, financial, logical, date and time, and math and trigonometry.
- Conditional formatting helps you see important trends and exceptions in your data by applying various formats such as colored gradients, data bars, or icons.

- You can convert data that is organized in rows and columns into an Excel table that adds formatting, filtering, and AutoComplete features.
- An Excel table helps you manage information by providing ways to sort and filter the data and to analyze the data using summary rows and calculated columns.

© alisonhancock

Aspen Falls City Hall

In this chapter, you will revise a spreadsheet for Jack Ruiz, the Aspen Falls Community Services Director. He has received permission from the City Council to create community gardens in open space areas in Aspen Falls. In order to promote the gardens, the city will provide materials to community members. He has a workbook with a list of materials and wants to know if any items need to be reordered and if new suppliers should be contacted for quotes when replacing the items. He is also tracking the donations received from local retail stores.

Using workbooks to track information is a primary function of a spreadsheet application. Because spreadsheets can be set up to globally update when underlying data is changed, managers often use Excel to help them make decisions in real time. An effective workbook uses functions, conditional formatting, summary statistics, and charts in ways that describe past trends and help decision makers accurately forecast future needs.

In this project, you will use the functions TODAY, NOW, COUNT, and IF to generate useful information for the director. You will apply conditional formatting to highlight outlying data and create sparklines to display trends. To update the underlying data, you will use the Find and Replace tool. Finally, you will create and format Excel tables, and then search the tables for data.

Time to complete all 10 skills – 60 to 90 minutes

Student data file needed for this chapter:

exl04_Garden

You will save your workbook as:

Last_First_exl04_Garden

Outcome

Using the skills in this chapter, you will be able to work with Excel worksheets like this:

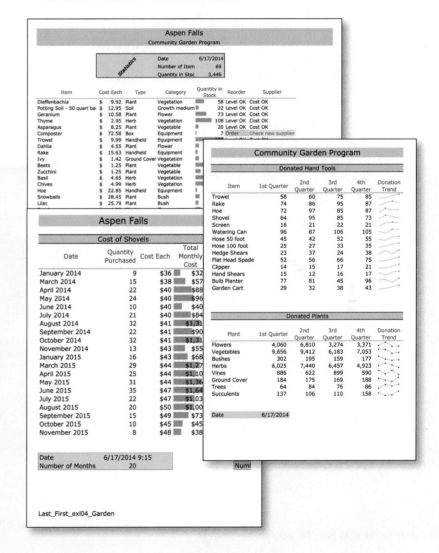

SKILLS

Skills 1-10 Training

At the end of this chapter you will be able to:

Skill 1 Insert the TODAY, NOW, and COUNT Functions

Skill 2 Insert the IF Function

Skill 3 Move Functions, Add Borders, and Rotate Text

Skill 4 Apply Conditional Formatting

Skill 5 Insert Sparklines

Skill 6 Use Find and Replace

Skill 7 Freeze and Unfreeze Panes

Skill 8 Create, Sort, and Filter Excel Tables

Skill 9 Filter Data

Skill 10 Convert Tables to Ranges, Hide Rows and Columns, and Format Large Worksheets

MORE SKILLS

Skill 11 Apply Conditional Color Scales with Top and Bottom Rules and Clear Rules

Skill 12 Insert the Payment (PMT) Function

Skill 13 Create PivotTable Reports

Skill 14 Use Goal Seek

EXL 4-1
VIDEO

► The **TODAY function** returns the serial number of the current date.

► The **NOW function** returns the serial number of the current date and time.

► The **COUNT function** counts the number of cells that contain numbers.

1. Start **Excel 2013**, and then open the student data file **exl04_Garden**. Click the **File tab**, and then click **Save As**. Click the **Browse** button, and then navigate to the location where you are saving your files. Click **New folder**, type Excel Chapter 4 and then press Enter two times. In the **File name** box, using your own name, name the workbook Last_First_exl04_ Garden and then press Enter.

2. On the **Inventory** sheet, click cell **E4**. On the **Formulas tab**, in the **Function Library group**, click the **Date & Time** button, and then click **TODAY**. Read the message that displays, compare your screen with **Figure 1**, and then click **OK** to enter the function.

   The TODAY function takes no arguments, and the result is **volatile**—the date will not remain as entered but rather will be updated each time this workbook is opened.

3. Click the **Donations** worksheet tab, scroll down, and then click cell **B36**. Use the technique just practiced to enter the **TODAY** function. Compare your screen with **Figure 2**.

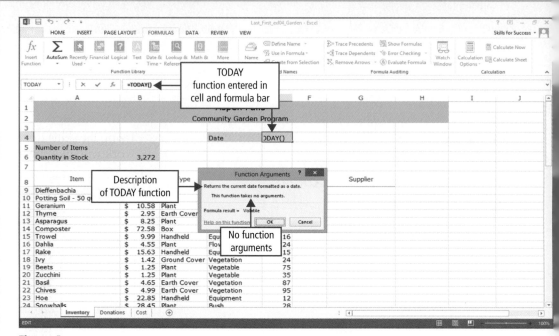

Figure 1

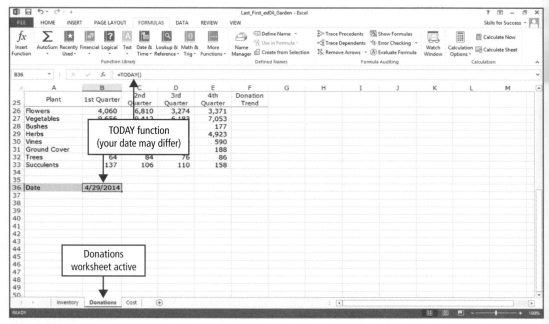

Figure 2

■ **Continue to the next page to complete the skill**

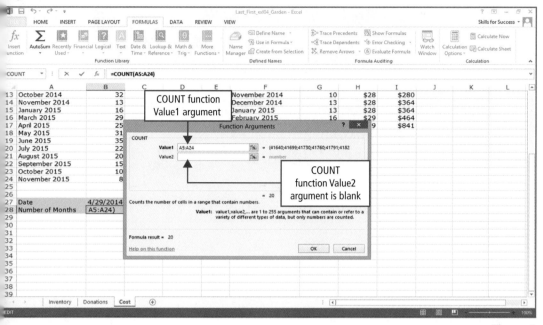

Figure 3

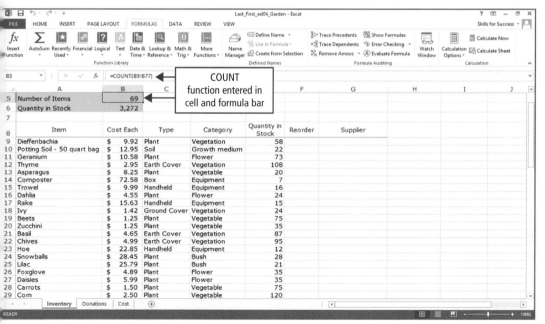

Figure 4

4. Click the **Cost** worksheet tab, scroll down and then click the merged cell **B27**. In the **Function Library group**, click the **Date & Time** button, and then click **NOW**. Read the message that displays, and then click **OK** to insert the function.

5. Click cell **B28**. In the **Function Library group**, click the **More Functions** button. Point to **Statistical**, and then click **COUNT**.

6. In the **Function Arguments** dialog box, in the **Value1** box, type A5:A24 and then compare your screen with **Figure 3**.

7. In the **Function Arguments** dialog box, click **OK**.

   The number of cells in the range A5:A24 that contain values is *20*.

8. Click cell **G28**. Use the technique just practiced to enter a **COUNT** function with the range F5:F17 as the **Value1** argument. The result should be *13*.

9. Click the **Inventory** worksheet tab, and then click cell **B5**. In the **Function Library group**, click the **More Functions** button, point to **Statistical**, and then click **COUNT**. If necessary, move the Function Arguments dialog box to the right to view column **B**. In the **Function Arguments** dialog box, with the insertion point in the **Value1** box, click cell **B9**. Press Ctrl + Shift + ↓ to select the range **B9:B77**. Click **OK** to display the result *69*. Compare your screen with **Figure 4**.

10. **Save** 🖫 the workbook.

■ **You have completed Skill 1 of 10**

▶ A **logical function** applies a logical test to determine whether a specific condition is met.

▶ A **logical test** is any value or expression that can be evaluated as TRUE or FALSE and **Criteria** are the conditions specified in the logical test.

▶ The **IF function** is a logical function that checks whether criteria are met and then returns one value when the condition is TRUE and another value when the condition is FALSE.

1. On the **Inventory** worksheet, click cell **F9**. In the **Function Library group**, click the **Logical** button, and then on the list, point to **IF**. Read the ScreenTip, and then click **IF**.

2. In the **Function Arguments** dialog box, with the insertion point in the **Logical_test** box, type E9<10

   A **comparison operator** compares two values and returns either TRUE or FALSE. Here, the logical test *E9<10* uses the less than comparison operator, and will return TRUE only when the value in E9 is less than 10. The table in **Figure 1** lists commonly used comparison operators.

3. Press ⎯Tab⎯ to move the insertion point to the **Value_if_true** box, and then type Order

4. Press ⎯Tab⎯ to move the insertion point to the **Value_if_false** box, type Level OK and then compare your screen with **Figure 2**.

   In function arguments, text values are surrounded by quotation marks. Here, quotation marks display around *Order* and will automatically be inserted around *Level OK* after you click OK.

■ **Continue to the next page to complete the skill** ➡

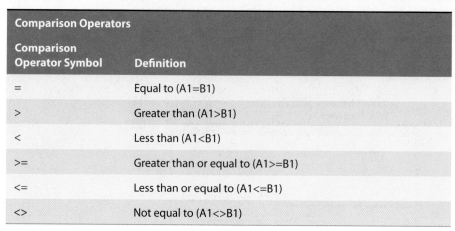

Comparison Operators	
Comparison Operator Symbol	**Definition**
=	Equal to (A1=B1)
>	Greater than (A1>B1)
<	Less than (A1<B1)
>=	Greater than or equal to (A1>=B1)
<=	Less than or equal to (A1<=B1)
<>	Not equal to (A1<>B1)

Figure 1

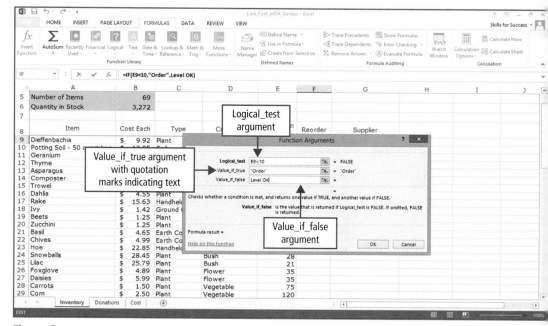

Figure 2

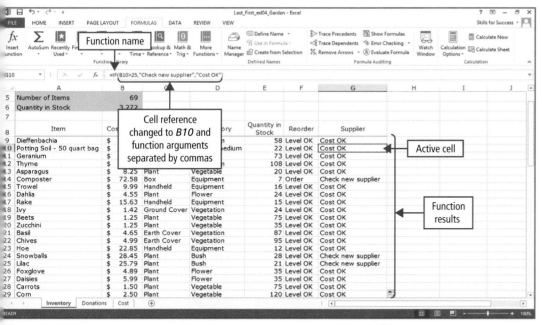

Figure 3

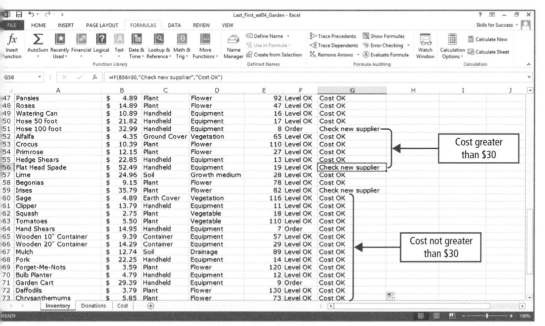

Figure 4

5. Click **OK** to display the result *Level OK*.

   The IF function tests whether E9 is less than 10. When this condition is TRUE, *Order* will display. Because E9 contains the value *58*, the condition is FALSE, and *Level OK* displays.

6. Click cell **G9**. In the **Function Library group**, click the **Logical** button, and then click **IF**. In the **Logical_test** box, type B9>25 and then in the **Value_if_true** box, type Check new supplier In the **Value_if_false** box, type Cost OK and then click the **OK** button to display *Cost OK*.

7. Select the range **F9:G9**. Point to the fill handle to display the ➕ pointer, and then double-click to AutoFill the functions down through row **77**. Click **G10**, and then compare your screen with **Figure 3**.

   In each row of column G, the function evaluates the value in column B. When the value in column B is greater than $25, the text *Check new supplier* displays. Otherwise, the text *Cost OK* displays.

   When a function has multiple arguments, each argument is separated by a comma.

   When the function was copied down to G10, the cell reference changed from B9 to B10.

8. Scroll down and verify that nine items meet the condition and display the text *Check new supplier*. Click cell **G9**. In the formula bar, change the number 25 to 30 and then, click the **Enter** button ✔. AutoFill the function down through cell **G77**. Scroll down to verify that five items meet the changed condition. Click cell **G56**, and then compare your screen with **Figure 4**.

9. Save 🖫 the workbook.

■ **You have completed Skill 2 of 10**

▶ When you move cells containing formulas or functions by dragging them, the cell references in the formulas or functions do not change.

▶ Borders and shading emphasize a cell or a range of cells, and rotated or angled text draws attention to text on a worksheet.

1. On the **Inventory** worksheet, press [Ctrl] + [Home]. Select the range **A5:B6**. Point to the top edge of the selected range to display the [↖] pointer. Drag the selected range to the right until the ScreenTip displays the range **D5:E6**, as shown in **Figure 1**, and then release the mouse button to complete the move.

2. Click cell **E5**. Notice that the cell references in the function did not change.

3. Click the **Donations** worksheet tab. Select the merged cell **A3**. On the **Home tab**, in the **Font group**, click the **Border arrow** [▦ ▾], and then click **Top and Bottom Border**.

4. Click the merged cell **A23**. In the **Font group**, click the **Border** button [▦ ▾] to apply a top and bottom border. Click cell **A5**, and then compare your screen with **Figure 2**.

5. Click the **Cost** worksheet tab. Click the merged cell **A3**. Hold down [Ctrl] and then click the merged cell **F3**. Use the technique just practiced to apply a top and bottom border.

■ Continue to the next page to complete the skill ▶

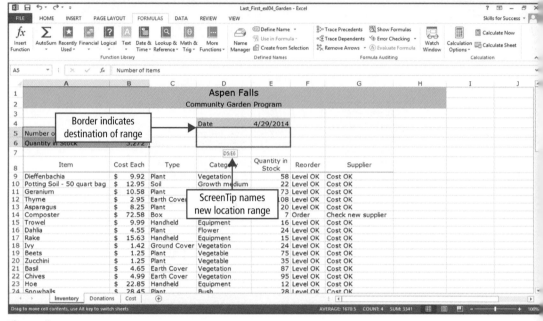

Figure 1

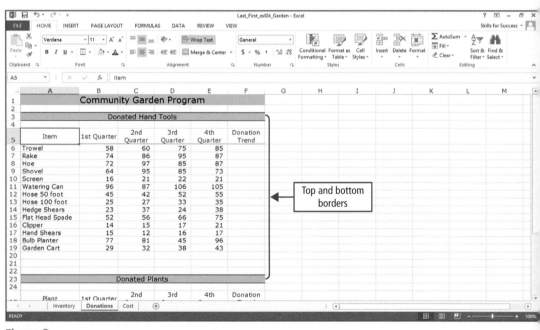

Figure 2

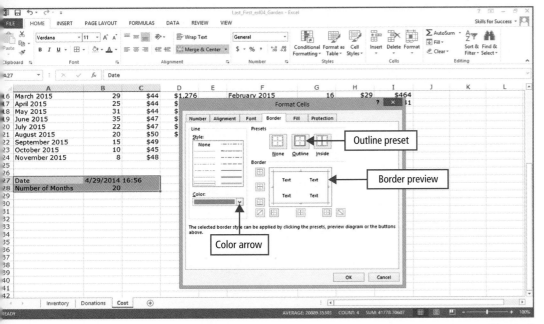

Figure 3

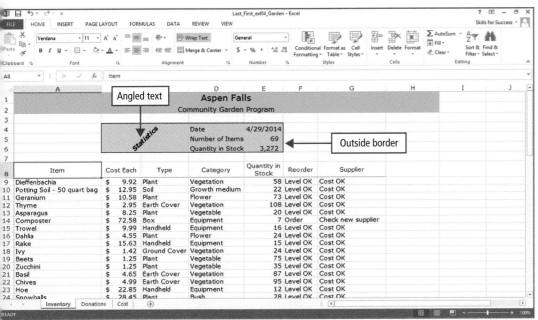

Figure 4

6. Scroll down, and then select the range **A27:C28**. In the **Font group**, click the **Border arrow** . At the bottom of the **Border** gallery, click **More Borders**.

7. In the **Format Cells** dialog box, click the **Color arrow**, and then click the fifth color in the first row—**Orange, Accent 1**. Under **Presets**, click **Outline**. Compare your screen with **Figure 3**, and then click **OK**.

8. Select the range **F28:G28**. Press F4 to repeat the last command, and then click cell **F30**.

   Pressing F4 will repeat the last command. In this instance it will apply an orange border to the selected range.

9. Click the **Inventory** worksheet tab. Click cell **B4**, type Statistics and then press Enter .

10. Select the range **B4:C6**. On the **Home tab**, in the **Alignment group**, click the **Merge & Center** button. Apply the **40% - Accent 4** cell style, and then click **Middle Align** , **Bold B**, and **Italic I**.

11. With the merged cell still selected, in the **Alignment group**, click the **Orientation** button , and then click **Angle Counterclockwise**.

12. Select the range **B4:E6**. In the **Font group**, click the **Border arrow** , and then click **Outside Borders**. Click cell **A8**, and then compare your screen with **Figure 4**.

13. **Save** the workbook.

■ **You have completed Skill 3 of 10**

▶ **Conditional formatting** is a format, such as cell shading or font color, that is applied to cells when a specified condition is true.

▶ Conditional formatting makes analyzing data easier by emphasizing differences in cell values.

1. On the **Inventory** worksheet, click cell **F9**. Press `Ctrl` + `Shift` + `↓` to select the range **F9:F77**.

2. Click the **Quick Analysis Lens** button, and then click **Text Contains**. In the **Text That Contains** dialog box, delete the text in the first box, and then type Order Compare your screen with **Figure 1**, and then click **OK**.

   Within the range F9:F77, cells that contain the text *Order* display with light red fill and dark red text formatting.

3. Using the technique just practiced, select the range **G9:G77**, and then open the **Text That Contains** dialog box. In the first box, type Check new supplier To the right of the format box, click the **arrow**, and then compare your screen with **Figure 2**.

   You can use the Text That Contains dialog box to specify the formatting that should be applied when a condition is true. If the formatting choice you need is not listed, you can open the Format Cells dialog box by clicking the Custom Format command.

■ **Continue to the next page to complete the skill**

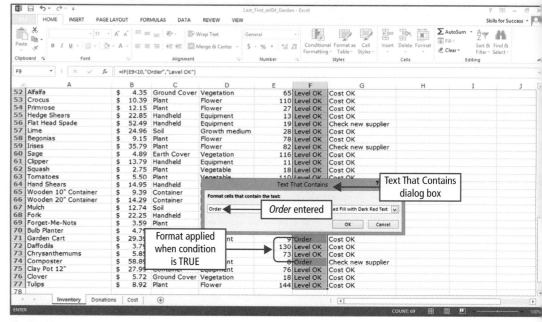

Figure 1

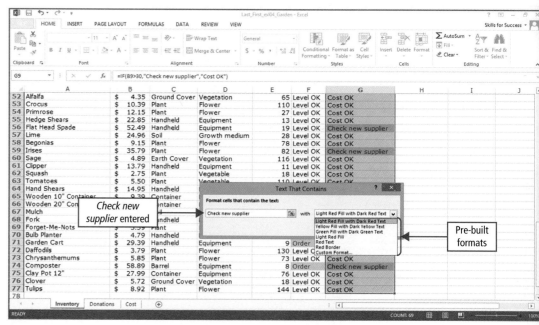

Figure 2

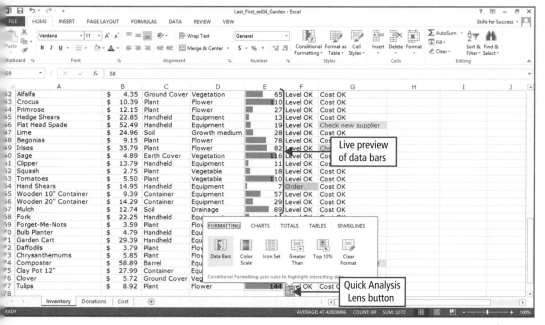

Figure 3

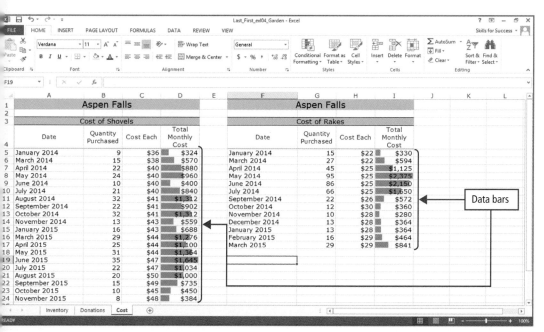

Figure 4

4. In the list of conditional formats, click **Green Fill with Dark Green Text**, and then click **OK**.

5. Select the range **E9:E77**. Click the **Quick Analysis Lens** button, and then point to **Data Bars**. Compare your screen with **Figure 3**.

> A **data bar** is a format that provides a visual cue about the value of a cell relative to other cells in a range. Data bars are useful to quickly identify higher and lower numbers within a large group of data, such as very high or very low levels of inventory.

6. In the **Quick Analysis** gallery, click **Data Bars** to apply the conditional formatting.

7. Scroll up, and then click cell **E15**. Type 190 and then press Enter to adjust all data bars to the new value.

> Data bars are sized relative to the maximum value within a range. Here, when a new maximum value of 190 was entered, all the data bars adjusted.

8. Click the **Cost** worksheet tab. Select the range **D5:D24**, and then use the technique just practiced to apply the default data bar conditional format.

9. Select the range **I5:I17**, and then apply the default data bar conditional format. Click cell **F19**, and then compare your screen with **Figure 4**.

10. Save the workbook.

■ **You have completed Skill 4 of 10**

▶ A **sparkline** is a chart contained in a single cell that is used to show data trends.

1. Click the **Donations** worksheet tab to make it the active sheet, and then select the range **B6:E19**.

2. Click the **Quick Analysis Lens** button, and then click **Sparklines**. In the **Sparklines** gallery, point to **Line** to display sparklines in **column F**. Compare your screen with **Figure 1**, and then click **Line**.

3. With the range **F6:F19** selected, on the **Design tab**, in the **Show group**, select the **High Point** check box to mark the highest point of data on each sparkline.

4. In the **Style group**, click the **Sparkline Color** button, and then click the fifth color in the first row—**Orange, Accent 1**. Click cell **E20**, and then compare your screen with **Figure 2**.

The sparklines in column F show that the donation levels of hand tools are generally increasing over time.

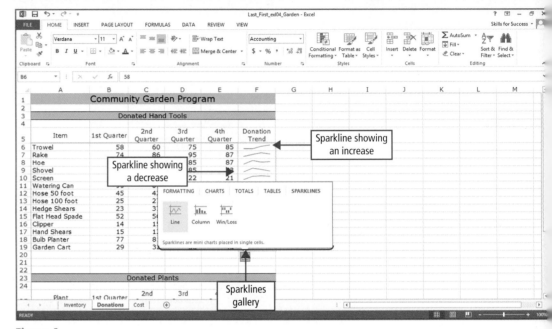

Figure 1

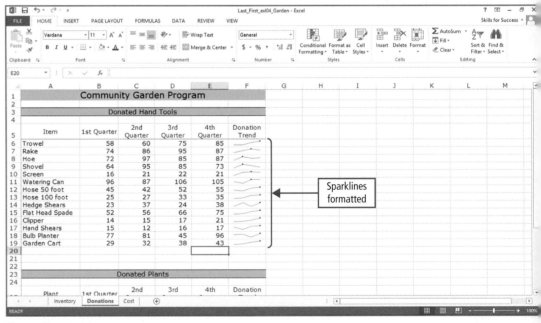

Figure 2

■ Continue to the next page to complete the skill

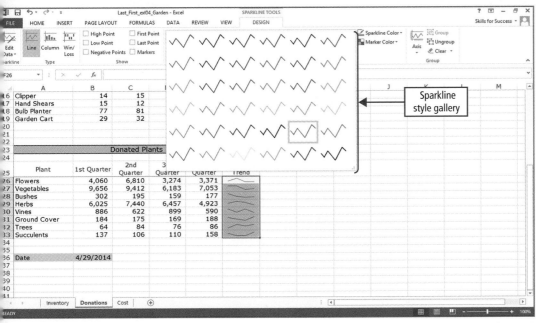

Figure 3

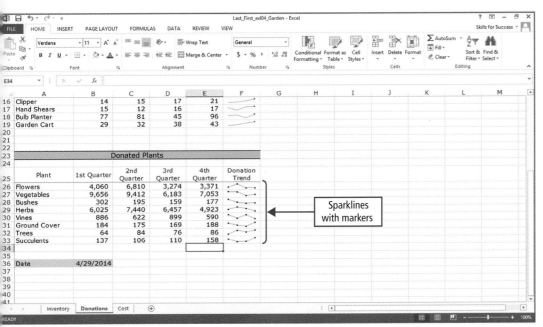

Figure 4

5. Scroll down and then select the range **B26:E33**. Use the techniques just practiced to insert the default **Line** sparklines.

6. With the range **F26:F33** selected, on the **Design tab**, in the **Style group**, click the **More** button ▾, and then compare your screen with **Figure 3**.

7. In the **Style** gallery, click the first color in the third row—**Sparkline Style Accent 1, (no dark or light)**.

8. In the **Style group**, click the **Marker Color** button. In the displayed list, point to **Markers**, and then click the second color in the first row—**Black, Text 1** to mark each data point on the sparklines. Click cell **E34**, and then compare your screen with **Figure 4**.

9. Right-click the **Donations** worksheet tab, and then click **Select All Sheets**. Add the file name to the worksheet's left footer and the sheet name to the right footer. Return to **Normal** view and then press Ctrl + Home to make cell **A1** the active cell on each of the grouped worksheets.

10. Right-click the **Donations** worksheet tab, and then click **Ungroup Sheets**. **Save** 🖫 the workbook.

■ **You have completed Skill 5 of 10**

▶ The **Replace** feature finds and then replaces a character or string of characters in a worksheet or in a selected range.

1. Click the **Inventory** worksheet tab, and then verify that cell **A1** is the active cell. On the **Home tab**, in the **Editing group**, click the **Find & Select** button, and then click **Replace**.

2. In the **Find and Replace** dialog box, in the **Find what** box, type Earth Cover and then press ⊞Tab. In the **Replace with** box, type Herb and then compare your screen with **Figure 1**.

3. Click the **Find Next** button, and then verify that cell **C12** is the active cell. In the **Find and Replace** dialog box, click the **Replace** button to replace the value in cell *C12* with *Herb* and to select the next occurrence of *Earth Cover* in cell *C21*.

4. In the **Find and Replace** dialog box, click the **Replace All** button. Read the message that displays. Compare your screen with **Figure 2**, and then click **OK**.

> The Replace All option replaces all matches of an occurrence of a character or string of characters with the replacement value. Here, six values were replaced. Only use the Replace All option when the search string is unique.

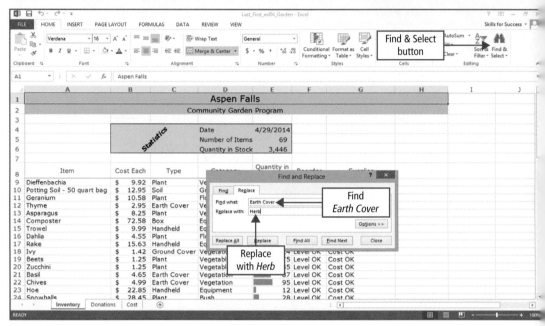

Figure 1

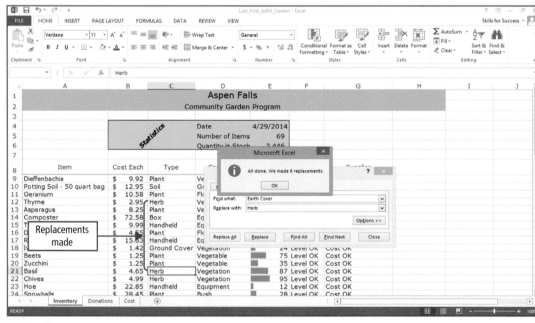

Figure 2

■ **Continue to the next page to complete the skill** ➤

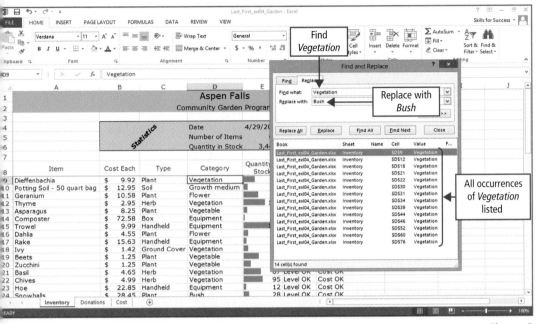

Figure 3

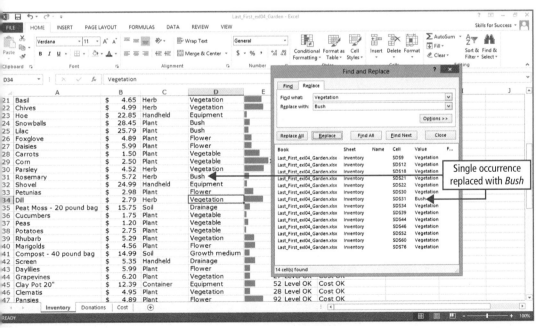

Figure 4

5. In the **Find and Replace** dialog box, in the **Find what** box, replace the text *Earth Cover* with Vegetation and then press [Tab]. In the **Replace with** box, replace the text *Herb* with Bush and then click the **Find All** button.

6. In the **Find and Replace** dialog box, point to the bottom border, and then with the ⬍ pointer, drag down to resize the dialog box until each listed occurrence displays as shown in **Figure 3**. If necessary, move the dialog box to display all occurrences.

   The Find All option finds all occurrences of the search criteria.

7. In the lower portion of the **Find and Replace** dialog box, in the **Cell** column, click **$D$31** to make cell **D31** the active cell, and then click the **Replace** button. Compare your screen with **Figure 4**.

   In this manner you can find all occurrences of cell text and use the list to replace only the occurrences you desire.

8. Use the technique just practiced to replace the two occurrences of the word Clay with the word Terracotta and then close all message and dialog boxes.

9. **Save** 🖫 the workbook.

■ **You have completed Skill 6 of 10**

▶ The **Freeze Panes** command keeps rows or columns visible when you are scrolling in a worksheet. The frozen rows and columns become separate panes so that you can always identify rows and columns when working with large worksheets.

1. On the **Inventory** sheet, scroll until **row 50** displays at the bottom of your window and the column labels are out of view. Compare your screen with **Figure 1**.

   When you scroll in large worksheets, the column and row labels may not be visible, which can make identifying the purpose of each row or column difficult.

2. Press Ctrl + Home, and then click cell **C15**. On the **View tab**, in the **Window group**, click the **Freeze Panes** button, and then click **Freeze Panes** to freeze the rows above and the columns to the left of C15—the active cell.

   A line displays along the upper border of row 15 and on the left border of column C to show where the panes are frozen.

3. Click the **Scroll Down** ⌄ and **Scroll Right** ⟩ arrows to display cell **M80**, and then notice that the top and left panes remain frozen. Compare your screen with **Figure 2**.

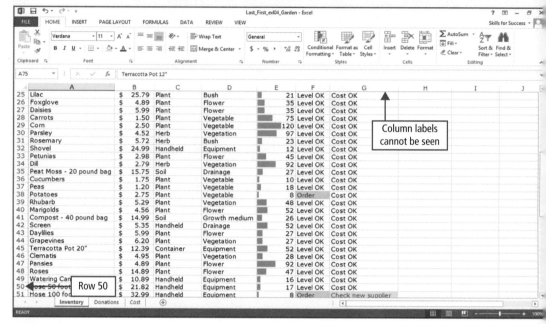

Figure 1

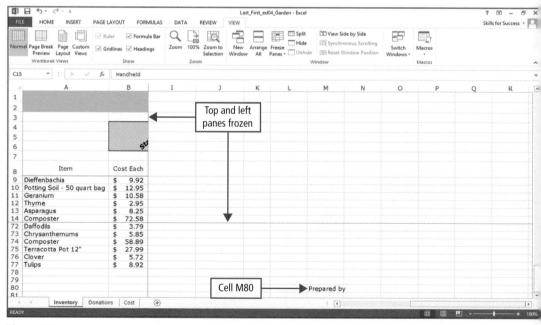

Figure 2

■ Continue to the next page to complete the skill ➤

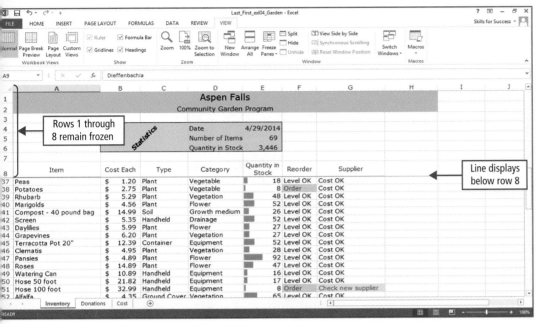

Figure 3

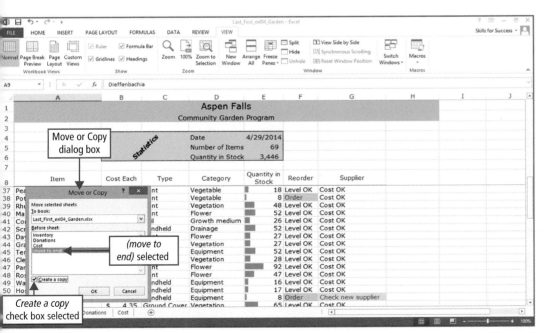

Figure 4

4. Click cell **M80** and then press ⬜Delete.

5. In the **Window group**, click the **Freeze Panes** button, and then click **Unfreeze Panes**.

   The rows and columns are no longer frozen, and the border no longer displays on row 15 and on column C.

6. Click cell **A9**. In the **Window group**, click the **Freeze Panes** button, and then click **Freeze Panes** to freeze the rows above **row 9**.

7. Watch the row numbers below **row 8** as you scroll down to **row 50**. Compare your screen with **Figure 3**.

   The labels in row 1 through row 8 stay frozen while the remaining rows of data continue to scroll.

8. Right-click the **Inventory** worksheet tab, and then from the list, click **Move or Copy**. In the **Move or Copy** dialog box, click **(move to end)**, and then select the **Create a copy** check box. Compare your screen with **Figure 4**.

9. In the **Move or Copy** dialog box, click **OK** to create a copy of the worksheet named *Inventory (2)*.

   A *(2)* displays in the name since two sheets in a workbook cannot have the same name.

10. Right-click the **Inventory (2)** worksheet tab, click **Rename**, type Sort by Cost and then press ⬜Enter.

11. In the **Window group**, click the **Freeze Panes** button, and then click **Unfreeze Panes** to unfreeze the panes.

12. Click the **Inventory** worksheet tab, and verify that on this worksheet, the panes are still frozen.

13. Save 🖫 the workbook.

■ **You have completed Skill 7 of 10**

EXL 4-8
VIDEO

▶ To analyze a group of related data, you can convert a range into an *Excel table*—a series of rows and columns that contain related data that has been formatted as a table. Data in an Excel table are managed independently from the data in other rows and columns in the worksheet.

▶ Data in Excel tables can be sorted in a variety of ways—for example, in ascending order or by color.

1. Click the **Sort by Cost** worksheet tab, and then click cell **A11**. On the **Home tab**, in the **Styles group**, click the **Format as Table** button. In the gallery, under **Light**, click the fifth choice—**Table Style Light 5**.

2. In the **Format as Table** dialog box, under **Where is the data for your table?** verify that the range =$A$8:$G$77 displays. Verify that the **My table has headers** check box is selected. Compare your screen with Figure 1, and then click **OK** to convert the range to an Excel table.

   When creating an Excel table, you only need to click in the data. The layout of column and row headings determines the default range provided in the Format As Table dialog box.

3. Click cell **H8**, type Total Cost and then press Enter to automatically add the formatted column to the Excel table.

4. In cell **H9**, type =B9*E9 and then press Enter to create a *calculated column*—a column in an Excel table that uses a single formula which adjusts for each row. Compare your screen with Figure 2.

■ Continue to the next page to complete the skill

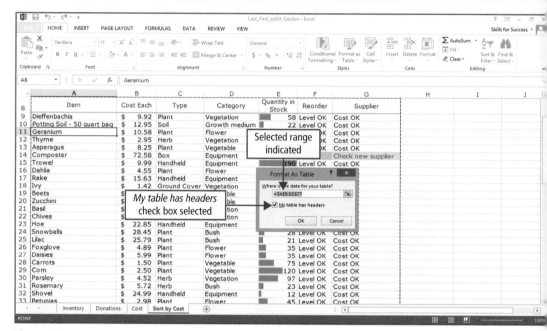

Figure 1

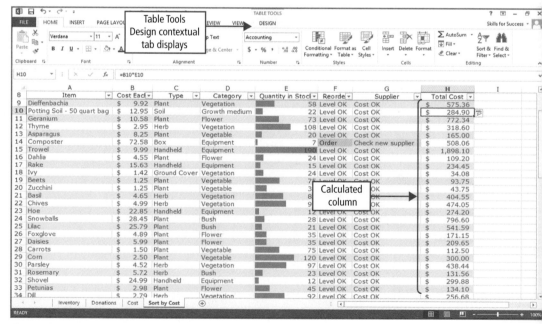

Figure 2

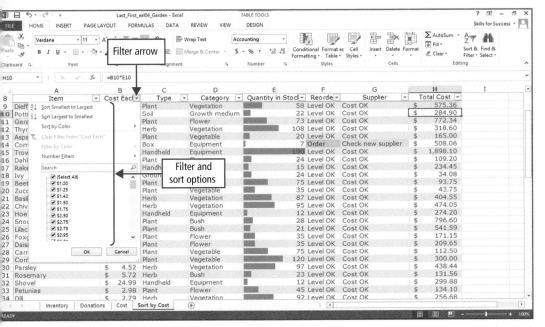

Figure 3

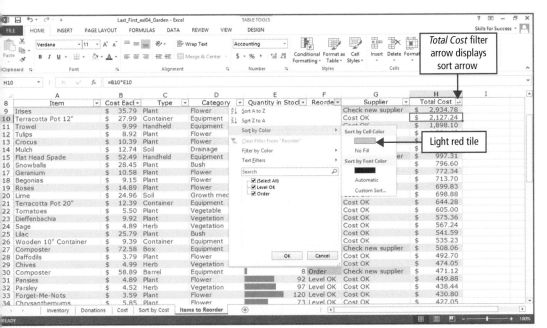

Figure 4

5. In the header row of the Excel table, click the **Cost Each filter arrow**, and then compare your screen with **Figure 3**.

6. In the **Filter** gallery, click **Sort Smallest to Largest**.

   The rows in the table are sorted by the *Cost Each* values, from the lowest to the highest, as indicated by the up arrow on the column's filter button.

7. In the header row, click the **Total Cost filter arrow**, and then click **Sort Largest to Smallest**.

   The rows in the table are now sorted from the highest to lowest *Total Cost* value, and the small arrow in the Total Cost filter arrow points down, indicating a descending sort. The previous sort on the *Cost Each* column no longer displays.

8. Right-click the **Sort by Cost** worksheet tab, and then click **Move or Copy**. In the **Move or Copy** dialog box, click **(move to end)**, select the **Create a copy** check box, and then click **OK**.

9. Rename the **Sort by Cost (2)** worksheet tab, as Items to Reorder

10. In the **Items to Reorder** worksheet, click the **Reorder filter arrow**, and then point to **Sort by Color**. Notice that the color formats in **column F** display in the list. Compare your screen with **Figure 4**.

    If you have applied manual or conditional formatting to a range of cells, you can sort by these colors.

11. In the list, under **Sort by Cell Color**, click the **light red tile** to place the six items that need to be ordered at the top of the Excel table.

12. Save 💾 the workbook.

■ **You have completed Skill 8 of 10**

▶ You can *filter* data to display only the rows of a table that meet specified criteria. Filtering temporarily hides rows that do not meet the criteria.

1. On the **Items to Reorder** worksheet, click the **Category filter arrow**. From the menu, clear the **(Select All)** check box to clear all the check boxes. Select the **Equipment** check box, as shown in **Figure 1**, and then click **OK** to display only the rows containing *Equipment*.

    The rows not meeting this criteria are hidden from view.

2. On the **Design tab**, in the **Table Style Options group**, select the **Total Row** check box to display the column total in cell **H78**.

    The **Total row** provides summary functions in drop-down lists for each column. Here, *Total* displays in cell A78. In cell H78, the number *$10,400.26* indicates the SUM of the Total Cost column for the filtered *Equipment* rows.

3. In the **Total** row, click cell **D78**, and then click the **arrow** that displays to the right of the selected cell. Compare your screen with **Figure 2**.

4. In the list of summary functions, click **Count** to count only the visible rows in **column D—*20***.

5. In the header row, click the **Type filter arrow**. From the menu, clear the **Handheld** check box, and then click **OK**.

    Filters can be applied to more than one column. Here, both the Type and Category columns are filtered.

■ **Continue to the next page to complete the skill** ▶

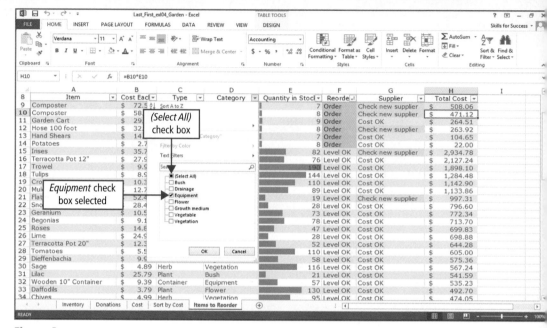

Figure 1

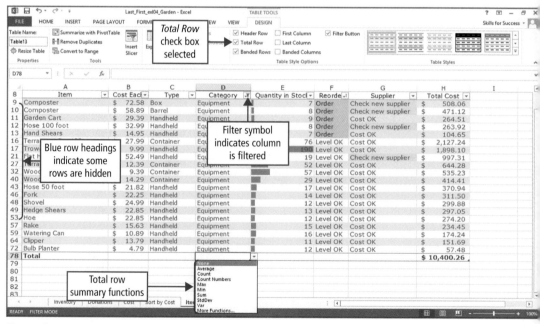

Figure 2

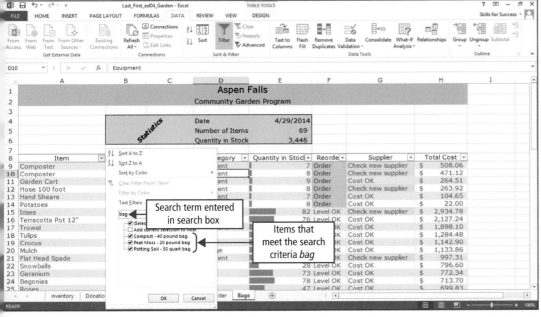

Figure 3

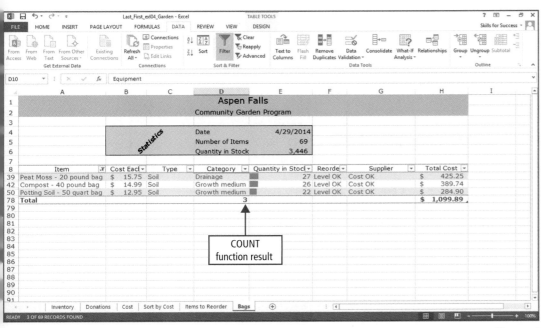

Figure 4

6. Right-click the **Items to Reorder** worksheet tab, and then using the techniques you just practiced, create a copy of the worksheet and move the sheet to the end. Rename the **Items to Reorder (2)** worksheet tab as Bags

7. With the **Bags** worksheet active, click any cell in the Excel table to make the Excel table active. On the **Data tab**, in the **Sort & Filter group**, click the **Clear** button to clear all the filters and to display all the rows in the Excel table.

8. In the header row, click the **Item filter arrow**. In the **Filter** list, click in the **Search** box, type bag and then compare your screen with **Figure 3**.

9. Click **OK** to display the three rows containing the text bag in the **Item** column. Compare your screen with **Figure 4**.

   In the Total row, the Category count in cell D78 and the Total Cost in cell H78 display the results of the filtered rows.

10. Save 💾 the workbook.

■ **You have completed Skill 9 of 10**

▶ An Excel table can be converted into a range retaining the table format.

▶ When a large worksheet is too wide or too long to print on a single page, row and column headings can be printed on each page.

1. Right-click the **Bags** worksheet tab, create a copy of the sheet, and move it to the end of the workbook. Rename the **Bags (2)** worksheet tab as All Items

2. In the **All Items** sheet, click cell **A8**. On the **Design tab**, in the **Tools group**, click the **Convert to Range** button. Read the message box, as shown in **Figure 1**, and then click **Yes**.

> When converting an Excel table into a range, all filters are removed and the heading row no longer displays filter buttons. Any existing sorts and formatting remain.

3. Click the **File tab**, and then click **Print**. Click the **Next Page** button ▶ three times to view the four pages.

4. Click the **Back** button ⬅. On the **Page Layout tab**, in the **Scale to Fit group**, click the **Width arrow**, and then click **1 page**. Click the **Height arrow**, and then click **1 page**.

5. Click the **Inventory** worksheet tab. In the **Scale to Fit group**, click the **Width** arrow, and then click **1 page**.

6. In the **Page Setup group**, click the **Print Titles** button, and then in the **Page Setup** dialog box, under **Print titles**, click in the **Rows to repeat at top** box. In the worksheet, click **row 8**, and then compare your screen with **Figure 2**.

▪ **Continue to the next page to complete the skill** ➤

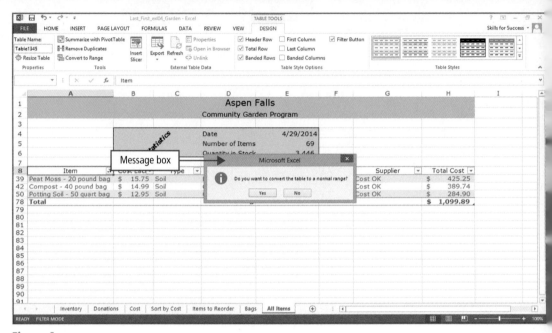

Figure 1

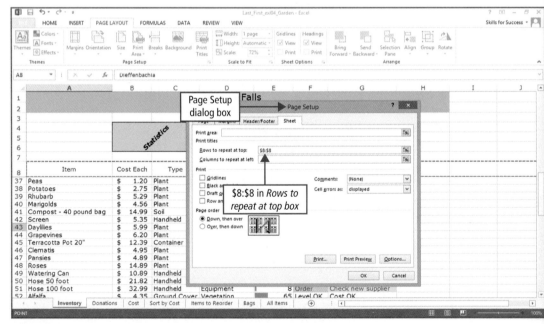

Figure 2

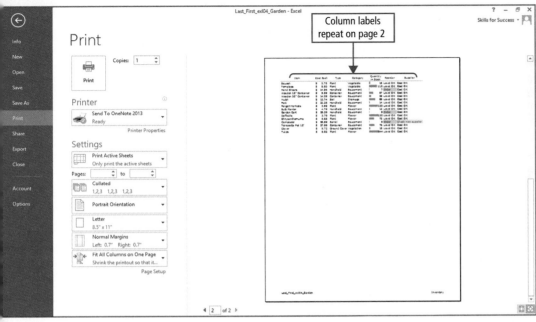

Figure 3

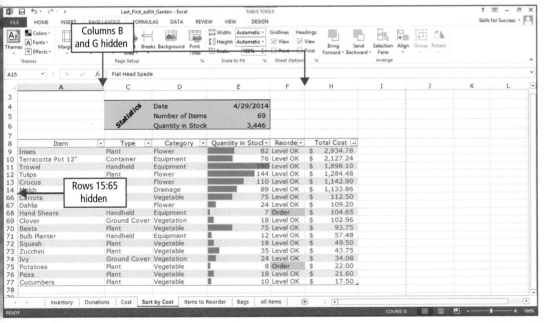

Figure 4

7. In the **Page Setup** dialog box, click the **Print Preview** button. Click the **Next Page** button ▸ to verify that the column labels from **row 8** display at the top of page 2. Compare your screen with **Figure 3**.

8. Click the **Back** button ⬅.

9. Click the **Cost** worksheet tab. Hold down Ctrl, and then click the **Items to Reorder** and the **Bags** worksheet tabs to group the three worksheets. In the **Page Setup group**, click the **Orientation** button, and then click **Landscape**. In the **Scale to Fit group**, click the **Width** arrow, and then click **1 page**.

   With the worksheets grouped, the orientation and scaling are applied to all three worksheets.

10. Click the **Sort by Cost** worksheet tab to select the worksheet and ungroup the three worksheets. Click cell **B13**. On the **Home tab**, in the **Cells group**, click the **Format** button, point to **Hide & Unhide**, and then click **Hide Columns**. Use the same technique to hide **column G**.

11. Select **rows 15:65**. In the **Cells group**, click the **Format** button, point to **Hide & Unhide**, and then click **Hide Rows**.

12. On the **Page Layout tab**, in the **Page Setup group**, click the **Orientation** button, and then click **Landscape**. Compare your screen with **Figure 4**.

13. **Save** 🖫 the workbook, and then **Close** ✕ Excel. Submit the workbook as directed by your instructor.

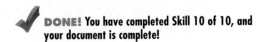

DONE! You have completed Skill 10 of 10, and your document is complete!

The following More Skills are located at **www.pearsonhighered.com/skills**

More Skills Apply Conditional Color Scales with Top and Bottom Rules and Clear Rules

You can apply color scales, which apply different colors to the cells, and top/bottom rules, which format the highest or lowest values. Conditional formatting rules can be cleared when no longer needed.

In More Skills 11, you will apply these additional types of conditional formats.

To begin, open your web browser, navigate to www.pearsonhighered.com/skills, locate the name of your textbook, and then follow the instructions on the website.

More Skills Insert the Payment (PMT) Function

The PMT function calculates the periodic payment for loans based on the loan amount, interest rate, and length of the loan. When you borrow money from a bank, the amount charged for your use of the borrowed money is called interest, and the interest amount is included in the PMT function.

In More Skills 12, you will use the PMT function to calculate various loan payments.

To begin, open your web browser, navigate to www.pearsonhighered.com/skills, locate the name of your textbook, and then follow the instructions on the website.

More Skills Create PivotTable Reports

A PivotTable report is an interactive way to summarize large amounts of data quickly, to analyze numerical data in depth, and to answer unanticipated questions about your data.

In More Skills 13, you will create a PivotTable report, pivot the data, and then filter the data.

To begin, open your web browser, navigate to www.pearsonhighered.com/skills, locate the name of your textbook, and then follow the instructions on the website.

More Skills Use Goal Seek

Goal Seek is a method to find a specific value for a cell by adjusting the value of another cell. With Goal Seek, you work backward from the desired outcome to find the necessary input to achieve your goal.

In More Skills 14, you will use Goal Seek to determine how much money can be borrowed to achieve a specific monthly payment.

To begin, open your web browser, navigate to www.pearsonhighered.com/skills, locate the name of your textbook, and then follow the instructions on the website.

Please note that there are no additional projects to accompany the More Skills Projects, and they are not covered in the End-of-Chapter projects.

The following table summarizes the **SKILLS AND PROCEDURES** covered in this chapter.

Skills Number	Task	Step	Icon	Keyboard Shortcut
1	Insert TODAY functions	Formula tab → Function Library group → Date & Time → TODAY		
1	Insert NOW functions	Formula tab → Function Library group → Date & Time → NOW		
1	Insert COUNT functions	Formula tab → Function Library group → More Functions → Statistical → COUNT		
2	Insert IF functions	Formula tab → Function Library group → Logical → IF		
3	Add borders	Home tab → Font group → Border arrow → Border	⊡ ▾	
3	Angle text	Home tab → Alignment group → Orientation	✎ ▾	
4	Apply conditional formatting to text	Quick Analysis Lens button → Text Contains		
4	Apply conditional formatting to data bars	Quick Analysis Lens button → Data Bars		
5	Insert sparklines	Quick Analysis Lens button → Sparklines		
5	Add sparkline high points	Design tab → Show group → High Point		
6	Use Find and Replace	Home tab → Editing group → Find & Select → Replace		Ctrl + H
7	Freeze panes	View tab → Window group → Freeze Panes		
7	Unfreeze panes	View tab → Window group → Unfreeze Panes		
8	Create Excel tables	Home tab → Styles group → Format as Table		
8	Filter Excel tables	Click the column filter arrow		
8	Sort Excel tables	Column filter arrow		
9	Search Excel tables	Column filter arrow → Search criteria		
9	Insert Total rows	Design tab → Table Style Options group → Total Row		
10	Convert Excel tables to ranges	Design tab → Tools group → Convert to Range		
10	Repeat rows at the top of each printed page	Page Layout tab → Page Setup group → Print Titles		
10	Hide columns	Home tab → Cells group → Format → Hide & Unhide → Hide Columns		
10	Hide rows	Home tab → Cells group → Format → Hide & Unhide → Hide Rows		

Key Terms

Online Help Skills

1. Start **Excel 2013**, and then in the upper right corner of the start page, click the **Help** button ? .

2. In the **Excel Help** window **Search help** box, type use formulas in Excel tables and then press Enter .

3. In the search result list, click **Using formulas in Excel tables**, and then compare your screen with **Figure 1**.

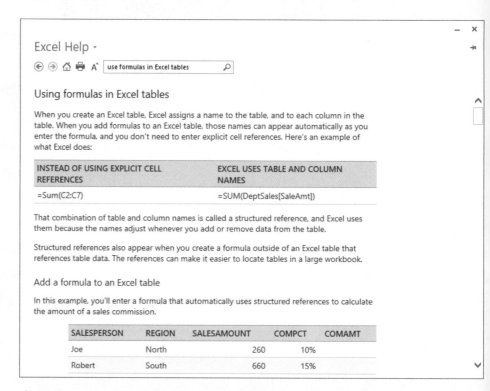

Figure 1

4. Read the article to answer the following questions: What are structured references and why would you use them?

Matching

Match each term in the second column with its correct definition in the first column by writing the letter of the term on the blank line in front of the correct definition.

___ **1.** An Excel function that returns the serial number of the current date.

___ **2.** The result of a function that will be updated each time the workbook is opened.

___ **3.** The type of function that tests for specific conditions and typically uses conditional tests to determine whether specified conditions are TRUE or FALSE.

___ **4.** Conditions that determine how conditional formatting is applied or what values are returned in logical functions.

___ **5.** A cell shading or font color that is applied to cells when a specified circumstance is met.

___ **6.** A chart inside a single cell used to show data trends.

___ **7.** A series of rows and columns that are formatted together.

___ **8.** A column in an Excel table that uses a single formula that adjusts for each row.

___ **9.** A command to display only the rows of a table that meet specified criteria.

___ **10.** A row in an Excel table that provides summary functions.

A Calculated column

B Conditional formatting

C Criteria

D Excel table

E Filter

F Logical function

G Sparkline

H TODAY function

I Total row

J Volatile

BizSkills Video

1. What are some of the positive behaviors of the second applicant?

2. If you were the interviewer, which applicant would you hire and why would you hire that person?

Multiple Choice (MyITLab®)

Choose the correct answer.

1. This function checks whether criteria are met and returns one value if TRUE and another value if FALSE.
   - A. IF
   - B. UNKNOWN
   - C. NEW

2. These symbols are inserted into logical functions to determine whether a condition is true or false—(<) and (=), for example.
   - A. Comparison operators
   - B. Mathematical operators
   - C. Logical symbols

3. Applying this format to text draws attention to the text on a worksheet.
   - A. Angle
   - B. Slope
   - C. Slant

4. This word describes a format, such as cell shading, that is applied to cells when a specified condition is true.
   - A. Filtered
   - B. Conditional
   - C. Calculated

5. This format provides a visual cue about the value of a cell relative to other cells.
   - A. Cell style
   - B. Quick style
   - C. Data bar

6. This command ensures that header rows and columns remain visible when a worksheet is scrolled.
   - A. Total Panes
   - B. Excel Panes
   - C. Freeze Panes

7. Data in an Excel table can be sorted in this way.
   - A. Large to largest
   - B. Smallest to largest
   - C. Small to smallest

8. This command displays only the rows of a table that meet specified criteria.
   - A. Filter
   - B. Standard
   - C. Chart

9. This row displays as the last row in an Excel table and provides summary statistics.
   - A. Total
   - B. Sorted
   - C. Changeable

10. This word describes the result of a function that is updated each time a workbook is opened.
    - A. Volatile
    - B. Changeable
    - C. Unstable

Topics for Discussion

1. Think about current news stories, including sports stories, and identify statistical data that is presented by the media. What are the advantages of using conditional formatting with this type of data?

2. Sorting and filtering are two of the most valuable ways to analyze data. If you were presented with an Excel table containing names and addresses, what are some of the ways you might sort or filter the data? If you were presented with an Excel table of a day's cash transactions at your college's cafeteria, what are some ways you could sort, filter, and total?

Skills Review

To complete this project, you will need the following file:

- exl04_SRAuction

You will save your file as:

- Last_First_exl04_SRAuction

1. Start **Excel 2013**, and then open the file **exl04_SRAuction**. Save the workbook in your chapter folder as Last_First_exl04_SRAuction

2. On the **Materials List** sheet, click cell **B4**. On the **Formulas tab**, in the **Function Library group**, click the **Date & Time** button, and then click **TODAY**. In the message box, click **OK**. Click cell **B5**. In the **Function Library group**, click the **More Functions** button. Point to **Statistical**, and then click **COUNT**. In the **Value1** box, enter the range B9:B48, and then press Enter . Compare your screen with **Figure 1**.

3. Select the range **A4:B6**. Point to the right border of the selected range, and then move the data to the range **D4:E6**.

4. In cell **B4**, type Surplus and then merge and center the title in the range **B4:C6**. On the **Home tab**, in the **Alignment group**, click the **Middle Align** button. Click the **Orientation** button, and then click **Angle Counterclockwise**. Select the range **B4:E6**. In the **Font group**, click the **Border arrow**, and then click **Outside Borders**.

5. Click cell **A1**. In the **Editing group**, click the **Find & Select** button, and then click **Replace**. In the **Find what** box, type Sedan In the **Replace with** box, type Car and then click **Replace All**. Click **OK**, and then **Close** the dialog box.

6. Click cell **G9**. On the **Formulas tab**, in the **Function Library group**, click **Logical**, and then click **IF**. In the **Logical_test** box, type E9="Yes" In the **Value_if_true** box, type B9*F9 In the **Value_if_false** box, type 0 and then click **OK**. AutoFill the function down through **G48**, and then compare your screen with **Figure 2**.

7. Click cell **A9**. On the **View tab**, in the **Window group**, click the **Freeze Panes** button, and then click **Freeze Panes**.

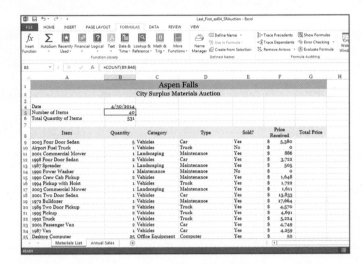

Figure 1

Figure 2

■ Continue to the next page to complete this Skills Review

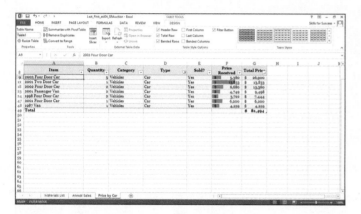

Figure 3

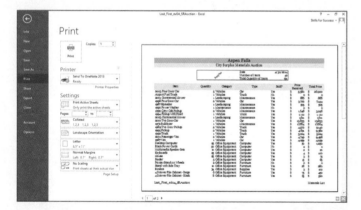

Figure 4

8. Right-click the **Materials List** worksheet tab, and then click **Move or Copy**. In the **Move or Copy** dialog box, click **(move to end)**, select the **Create a copy** check box, and then click **OK**. Rename the new worksheet tab as Price by Car

9. On the **Price by Car** sheet, in the **Window group**, click the **Freeze Panes** button, and then click **Unfreeze Panes**. On the **Home tab**, in the **Styles group**, click the **Format as Table** button, and then click **Table Style Light 17**. In the **Format As Table** dialog box, verify that the **My table has headers** check box is selected, and then click **OK**.

10. Click the **Type filter arrow**, and then clear the **(Select All)** check box. Select the **Car** check box, and then click **OK**. Click the **Total Price filter arrow**, and then click **Sort Largest to Smallest**. On the **Design tab**, in the **Table Style Options group**, select the **Total Row** check box.

11. Select the range **F9:F48**. Click the **Quick Analysis Lens** button, and then click **Data Bars**. Click cell **A9**, and then compare your screen with Figure 3.

12. Create a copy of the **Price by Car** sheet, move to the end, and then rename the new worksheet tab Pickups On the **Data tab**, in the **Sort & Filter group**, click the **Clear** button. Click the **Item filter arrow**. In the **Search** box, type Pickup and then click **OK**.

13. On the **Annual Sales** worksheet, select the range **B4:F9**. Click the **Quick Analysis Lens** button, click **Sparklines**, and then click the **Column** button.

14. Right-click the worksheet tab, and then click **Select All Sheets**. On the **Page Layout tab**, in the **Page Setup group**, click the **Orientation** button, and then click **Landscape**. In the **Scale to Fit group**, change the **Width** to **1 page**. Click the **Insert tab**, and add the file name in the left footer and the sheet name in the right footer. Return to **Normal** view, and then ungroup the worksheets.

15. Click the **Materials List** worksheet tab. On the **Page Layout tab**, in the **Page Setup group**, click the **Print Titles** button. In the **Page Setup** dialog box, click in the **Rows to repeat at top** box, click row **8**, and then click **OK**.

16. **Save** the workbook. Click the **File tab**, and then click the **Print tab**. Compare your workbook with Figure 4. Submit the workbook as directed by your instructor.

 DONE! You have completed this Skills Review

Skills Assessment 1
MyITLab®
Grader

To complete this project, you will need the following file:

- exl04_SA1Recycling

You will save your workbook as:

- Last_First_exl04_SA1Recycling

---

1. Start **Excel 2013**, and open the file **exl04_SA1Recycling**. Save the file in your chapter folder as Last_First_exl04_SA1Recycling

2. In **E3**, insert the **NOW** function. Select **A5:G5**, and apply a **Bottom Border**.

3. In **F6:F27**, insert **Line Sparklines** using the data in **columns B:E**. Show the **Low Point**.

4. In **G6**, insert the **IF** function. For the logical test, check whether the **FY 2014** result is greater than the **FY 2013** value in the same row. If the logical test is TRUE, Yes should display, and if it is FALSE, Needs Work should display. **Center** the results, and then AutoFill **G6** down through **G27**.

5. Select **G6:G27**. Apply a **Text Contains** conditional format that will display any cells that contain *Needs Work* formatted with **Light Red Fill**.

6. Create a copy of the sheet, and move the copy to the end of the workbook. Rename the new worksheet tab Improvements

7. On the **Improvements** sheet, format **A5:G27** as an Excel table, using the **Table Style Light 16**. Filter **column G** to display only the rows that improved from the previous year.

8. Display the **Total** row, and then display the four FY sums. In **G28**, select **None**.

9. Sort the **FY 2014** column from the smallest to the largest value.

10. Hide **column B**.

11. Group the worksheets. Change the page orientation to **Landscape**. Add the file name in the left footer and the sheet name in the right footer. Return to **Normal** view, and ungroup the sheets.

12. On the **Recycling** sheet, change the Page Setup to repeat the titles in **row 5**. On the **Improvements** sheet, change the **Height** scale to fit on one page.

13. **Save** the file. Click the **File tab**, click **Print**, and then compare your workbook with **Figure 1**. Submit the file as directed by your instructor.

DONE! You have completed Skills Assessment 1

Recycling Volumes Aspen Falls (in tons)						
					11/25/2012 16:32	
Type	FY 2011	FY 2012	FY 2013	FY 2014	Trend	Improved from previous year?
Glass	$ 10,820	$ 8,857	$ 10,928	$ 11,036		Yes
Tin Cans	$ 825	$ 650	$ 833	$ 842		Yes
White goods	$ 11,010	$ 12,250	$ 11,120	$ 11,230		Yes
Other ferrous	$ 61,150	$ 63,000	$ 61,762	$ 62,373		Yes
Aluminum cans	$ 1,150	$ 1,320	$ 1,262	$ 1,173		Needs Work
Non-ferrous	$ 13,160	$ 13,270	$ 13,292	$ 13,423		Yes
High Grade Paper	$ 1,830	$ 2,490	$ 1,848	$ 1,867		Yes
Newsprint	$ 14,790	$ 13,370	$ 14,938	$ 15,086		Yes
Cardboard	$ 19,640	$ 16,350	$ 21,836	$ 20,033		Needs Work
Other paper	$ 4,340	$ 5,900	$ 4,383	$ 4,427		Yes
PETE	$ 703	$ 960	$ 710	$ 717		Yes
HDPE	$ 417	$ 710	$ 421	$ 425		Yes
Other plastics	$ 588	$ 920	$ 594	$ 600		Yes
Yard waste	$ 57,200	$ 55,829	$ 59,772	$ 58,344		Needs Work
Wood waste	$ 10,630	$ 11,825	$ 11,736	$ 10,843		Needs Work
Batteries	$ 2,900	$ 3,030	$ 2,929	$ 2,958		Yes
Oil	$ 8,840	$ 6,360	$ 8,928	$ 9,017		Yes

Recycling Volumes Aspen Falls (in tons)					
				11/25/2012 16:32	
Type	FY 2012	FY 2013	FY 2014	Trend	Improved from previous year?
Gypsum	$ 180	$ 227	$ 230		Yes
HDPE	$ 710	$ 421	$ 425		Yes
Other plastics	$ 920	$ 594	$ 600		Yes
PETE	$ 960	$ 710	$ 717		Yes
Tin Cans	$ 650	$ 833	$ 842		Yes
Tires	$ 806	$ 1,020	$ 1,030		Yes
High Grade Paper	$ 2,490	$ 1,848	$ 1,867		Yes
Electronics	$ 1,050	$ 1,869	$ 1,887		Yes
Other	$ 2,500	$ 2,010	$ 2,030		Yes
Batteries	$ 3,030	$ 2,929	$ 2,958		Yes
Other paper	$ 5,900	$ 4,383	$ 4,427		Yes
Textiles	$ 6,208	$ 6,474	$ 6,538		Yes
Oil	$ 6,360	$ 8,928	$ 9,017		Yes
Glass	$ 8,857	$ 10,928	$ 11,036		Yes
White goods	$ 12,250	$ 11,120	$ 11,230		Yes
Non-ferrous	$ 13,270	$ 13,292	$ 13,423		Yes
Newsprint	$ 13,370	$ 14,938	$ 15,086		Yes
Other ferrous	$ 63,000	$ 61,762	$ 62,373		Yes
Total	142,511	144,287	145,715		

Figure 1

Skills Assessment 2

To complete this project, you will need the following file:

- exl04_SA2Equipment

You will save your workbook as:

- Last_First_exl04_SA2Equipment

---

1. Start **Excel 2013**, and open the file **exl04_SA2Equipment**. Save the workbook in your chapter folder as Last_First_exl04_SA2Equipment Insert the file name in the worksheet's left footer and the sheet name in the right footer. Return to **Normal** view.

2. In cell **A2**, insert the **TODAY** function.

3. Select the range **A4:G4**, and then apply **Outside Borders**.

4. In cell **F5**, insert the **IF** function. For the logical test, check whether the **Quantity in Stock** is less than **10**. If the logical test is TRUE, Order should display. If the logical test is FALSE, Level OK should display.

5. AutoFill the function in cell **F5** down through cell **F63**.

6. Select the range **F5:F63**, apply a **Text Contains** conditional format that will display any cells that indicate *Order* formatted with **Red Text**.

7. Find all occurrences of Removal and replace with Extrication

8. Format the range **A4:G63** as an Excel table, using the **Table Style Medium 10** table style.

9. Change the page orientation to **Landscape**, and then set the titles in **row 4** to repeat on each printed page.

10. Create a copy of the worksheet, and move the copied sheet to the end of the workbook. Rename the new worksheet tab Safety On the **Safety** worksheet, **Sort** the table in alphabetical order by **Category**. **Filter** the Excel table to display the **Safety** type.

11. Display the **Total** row, and then in cell **B64**, display the count for column B.

12. Hide **column D**.

13. **Save** your workbook, and then compare your workbook with **Figure 1**. Submit the workbook as directed by your instructor.

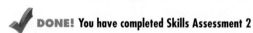

DONE! You have completed Skills Assessment 2

Quantity in Stock	Item	Cost Each	Type	Category	Stock Level	Total Cost
11	Radio Chest Harness	$35	Safety	Safety Equipment	Level OK	$ 385
87	Rope Gloves	$32	Gloves	Outerwear	Level OK	$ 2,784
28	Safety Harness	$199	Safety	Safety Equipment	Level OK	$ 5,572
29	Chest Harness	$99	Safety	Safety Equipment	Level OK	$ 2,871
35	EMS Jacket	$399	Coat	Outerwear	Level OK	$ 13,965
47	EMS Pants	$289	Pants	Outerwear	Level OK	$ 13,583
89	Breakaway Vest	$29	Vest	Outerwear	Level OK	$ 2,581
15	Mesh Vest	$17	Vest	Outerwear	Level OK	$ 255
25	Mesh Traffic Vest	$29	Vest	Outerwear	Level OK	$ 725
89	Reflective Nylon Vest	$11	Vest	Outerwear	Level OK	$ 979
16	Handheld Remote Siren	$289	Siren	Traffic	Level OK	$ 4,624
19	Siren	$189	Siren	Traffic	Level OK	$ 3,591
27	Traffic Baton	$19	Baton	Traffic	Level OK	$ 513
37	Flare Beacon Kit	$305	Light	Traffic	Level OK	$ 11,285
90	Flares with Stands	$99	Light	Traffic	Level OK	$ 8,910
26	Traffic Flashlight	$18	Light	Traffic	Level OK	$ 468
56	Night Barrier Tape	$15	Tape	Traffic	Level OK	$ 840
17	Water Rescue Kit	$119	Safety	Water Rescue	Level OK	$ 2,023
38	Water Rescue Vest	$99	Safety	Water Rescue	Level OK	$ 3,762
4	Water Tether System	$59	Safety	Water Rescue	Order	$ 236
18	Wildfire Helmet	$59	Helmet	Outerwear	Level OK	$ 1,062
17	Full-Brim Helmet	$59	Helmet	Outerwear	Level OK	$ 1,003
58	Firefighting Goggles	$49	Helmet	Safety Equipment	Level OK	$ 2,842
31	Water Throw Bag	$59	Safety	Water Rescue	Level OK	$ 1,829
32	Dry Bag	$18	Safety	Water Rescue	Level OK	$ 576

Aspen Falls					
11/24/2012					

Quantity in Stock	Item	Type	Category	Stock Level	Total Cost
9	Gas Mask	Safety	Safety Equipment	Order	$ 2,331
9	Gas Mask Pouch	Safety	Safety Equipment	Order	$ 315
13	Respirator	Safety	Safety Equipment	Level OK	$ 4,797
45	Disaster Safe Bag	Safety	Safety Equipment	Level OK	$ 585
57	Disaster Kit	Safety	Safety Equipment	Level OK	$ 5,643
11	Radio Chest Harness	Safety	Safety Equipment	Level OK	$ 385
28	Safety Harness	Safety	Safety Equipment	Level OK	$ 5,572
29	Chest Harness	Safety	Safety Equipment	Level OK	$ 2,871
17	Water Rescue Kit	Safety	Water Rescue	Level OK	$ 2,023
38	Water Rescue Vest	Safety	Water Rescue	Level OK	$ 3,762
4	Water Tether System	Safety	Water Rescue	Order	$ 236
31	Water Throw Bag	Safety	Water Rescue	Level OK	$ 1,829
32	Dry Bag	Safety	Water Rescue	Level OK	$ 576
Total		13			$ 30,925

Figure 1

Visual Skills Check

To complete this project, you will need the following file:

- exl04_VSArt

You will save your workbook as:

- Last_First_exl04_VSArt

Start **Excel 2013**, and then open the file **exl04_VSArt**. Save the workbook in your chapter folder as Last_First_exl04_VSArt Add the file name in the worksheet's left footer. Insert the current date using a date function. Your date may be different than shown. In **column F**, use a logical function indicating *Insure* for art with a value greater than $50,000. The conditional formatting in the **Insurance** column is **Light Red Fill with Dark Red Text**. Display Data Bars in **column C**. The Excel table is formatted using the **Table Style Light 14** table style. Filter and sort the Excel table, and display the functions on the **Total** row as shown in **Figure 1**. **Save** the workbook, and then submit the workbook as directed by your instructor.

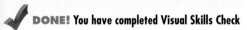 **DONE! You have completed Visual Skills Check**

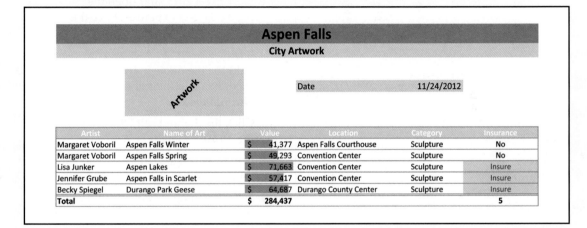

Artist	Name of Art	Value	Location	Category	Insurance
Margaret Voboril	Aspen Falls Winter	$ 41,377	Aspen Falls Courthouse	Sculpture	No
Margaret Voboril	Aspen Falls Spring	$ 49,293	Convention Center	Sculpture	No
Lisa Junker	Aspen Lakes	$ 71,663	Convention Center	Sculpture	Insure
Jennifer Grube	Aspen Falls in Scarlet	$ 57,417	Convention Center	Sculpture	Insure
Becky Spiegel	Durango Park Geese	$ 64,687	Durango County Center	Sculpture	Insure
Total		$ 284,437			5

Aspen Falls — City Artwork — Date 11/24/2012

Figure 1

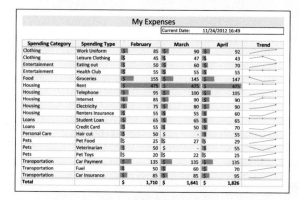

My Expenses

Spending Category	Spending Type	February	March	April	Trend
		Current Date:	11/24/2012 16:49		
Clothing	Work Uniform	85	90	92	
Clothing	Leisure Clothing	45	47	43	
Entertainment	Eating out	50	60	70	
Entertainment	Health Club	55	55	55	
Food	Groceries	155	145	147	
Housing	Rent	475	475	475	
Housing	Telephone	95	100	105	
Housing	Internet	85	90	90	
Housing	Electricity	75	80	90	
Housing	Renters Insurance	55	55	60	
Loans	Student Loan	65	65	65	
Loans	Credit Card	55	50	70	
Personal Care	Hair cut	50	-	55	
Pets	Pet Food	25	27	29	
Pets	Veterinarian	50	-	55	
Pets	Pet Toys	20	22	25	
Transportation	Car Payment	135	135	135	
Transportation	Fuel	50	60	70	
Transportation	Car Insurance	85	85	95	
Total		$ 1,710	$ 1,641	$ 1,826	

My Expenses

Spending Category	Spending Type	February	March	April	Trend
		Current Date:	11/24/2012 16:49		
Housing	Rent	475	475	475	
Food	Groceries	155	145	147	
Transportation	Car Payment	135	135	135	
Housing	Telephone	95	100	105	
Transportation	Car Insurance	85	85	95	
Clothing	Work Uniform	85	90	92	
Housing	Internet	85	90	90	
Housing	Electricity	75	80	90	
Entertainment	Eating out	50	60	70	
Loans	Credit Card	55	50	70	
Transportation	Fuel	50	60	70	
Loans	Student Loan	65	65	65	
Housing	Renters Insurance	55	55	60	
Entertainment	Health Club	55	55	55	
Total		$ 1,520	$ 1,545	$ 1,619	

Figure 1

My Skills

To complete this project, you will need the following file:

- exl04_MYExpenses

You will save your workbook as:

- Last_First_exl04_MYExpenses

1. Start **Excel 2013**, and open the file **exl04_MYExpenses**. Save the workbook in your chapter folder as Last_First_exl04_MYExpenses

2. Add the file name in the left footer and the sheet name in the right footer. Return to **Normal** view.

3. Click the merged cell **E2**, and then insert the **NOW** function.

4. Select the range **D2:F2**, and then apply the **Outside Borders**.

5. Select the range **C5:E23**, and then insert **Data Bars**.

6. In the range **F5:F23**, insert **Line Sparklines** using the data in the **columns C:E**. On the sparklines, show the **High Point**.

7. Format the range **A4:F23** as an Excel table, using **Table Style Light 19**. Sort the

Spending Category column to display in alphabetical order.

8. Display the **Total** row, display the sums for **C24:E24**, and in the **Trend** column, select **None**.

9. Change the **Width** scale to fit on one page.

10. Create a copy of the worksheet, and move the copied sheet to the end of the workbook. Rename the new worksheet tab High Expenses

11. On the **High Expenses** worksheet, sort the **April** column from largest to smallest. Hide **rows 19:23**.

12. **Save** your workbook. Click the **File tab**, click **Print**, and then compare your workbook with **Figure 1**. Submit the workbook as directed by your instructor.

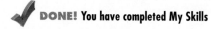 **DONE! You have completed My Skills**

Skills Challenge 1

Start **Excel 2013**, and then open the file **exl04_SC1Classes**. Save the workbook in your chapter folder as Last_First_exl04_SC1Classes Carter Horikoshi, the Art Center Supervisor, has started a workbook to track the art classes offered at different locations. He is concerned about large class sizes and wonders if he should hire an assistant for the instructors. Using the skills you practiced in this chapter, on the Classes worksheet, correct the date function. The panes no longer need to be frozen. In the Excel table, display all rows. In column D, the Data Bars should be applied to all cells. In column E, the logical function should calculate whether a class needs a Class Assistant—a class needs a Class Assistant if the class size is

greater than 30. The Excel table should be filtered to show the Computer Basics, Drawing, Painting, and Woodworking classes, and sorted from the largest to smallest class size. The titles in row 6 should repeat on each page. On the Enrollment sheet, the sparklines should be formatted to emphasize the high and low values in each row. The Enrollment sheet should print on one page. On both worksheets, add the file name in the left footer and the sheet name in the right footer. Save your workbook, and then submit the workbook as directed by your instructor.

 DONE! You have completed Skills Challenge 1

Skills Challenge 2

Start **Excel 2013**, and then open the file **exl04_SC2Water**, and save the workbook in your chapter folder as Last_First_exl04_SC2Water Diane Payne, the Public Works Director, is responsible for testing the city water supply. She has started a workbook to track the water test results. Using the skills you practiced in this chapter, insert functions in the Water worksheet that provide the current date and count the number of samples. Insert a logical function to determine if the High Test amount is greater than the Farm Water Limit for each quarter. Display Yes if TRUE and No if FALSE. Format the

data as an Excel table using the table style of your choice, and then filter the Excel table to display violations. On the Test Results worksheet, insert sparklines to display trends. On both worksheets, add the file name in the left footer and the sheet name in the right footer. Each worksheet should print on one page. Save your workbook, and then submit the workbook as directed by your instructor.

 DONE! You have completed Skills Challenge 2

CAPSTONE PROJECT

To complete this workbook, you will need the following file:
exl_CAPBudget

You will save your workbook as:
Last_First_exl_CAPBudget

1. Start **Excel 2013**, and open the student data file **exl_CAPBudget**. **Save** the workbook in your chapter folder as Last_First_exl_CAPBudget

2. Group the worksheets. Widen **columns B:E** to *13.00*. Change the height of **row 4** to *15.00*. In cell **E5**, insert a function to total the row, and then AutoFill **E5** down through **E14**. In the range **E6:E14**, apply the **Comma [0]** cell style. In the range **B15:E15**, insert a function to total the columns, and then apply the **Total** cell style.

3. With the worksheets still grouped, in cell **B16**, insert a function to calculate the average *North* budget item. In cell **B17**, insert a function to calculate the highest *North* budget item.

4. In cell **B18**, insert a function to calculate the lowest *North* budget item.

5. AutoFill the range **B16:B18** to the right through **column D**, and then compare your screen with **Figure 1**.

6. Ungroup the worksheets. Insert a new worksheet. Rename the new worksheet tab Summary and apply the worksheet tab color **Orange, Accent 2**. Move the new worksheet tab to make it the first worksheet in the workbook.

7. Copy the range **A1:E4** from any of the quarter worksheets, and then on the **Summary** worksheet, paste the range into **A1:E4** using the **Keep Source Column Widths** paste option.

8. On the **Summary** worksheet, change the subtitle of cell **A2** to Annual Budget and then change the label in cell **A4** to Quarter

9. On the **Summary** worksheet, in cell **A5** type 1st Quarter and then AutoFill **A5** down through cell **A8**. In cell **A9**, type Annual Total

10. On the **Summary** worksheet, enter a formula in cell **B5** setting the cell equal to cell **B15** in the **First Quarter** worksheet. **Save** the workbook, and then compare your screen with **Figure 2**.

■ Continue to the next page to complete the skill

Figure 1

Figure 2

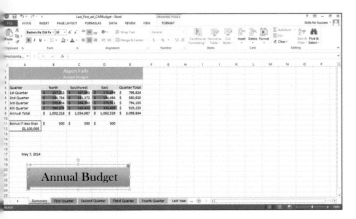

Figure 3

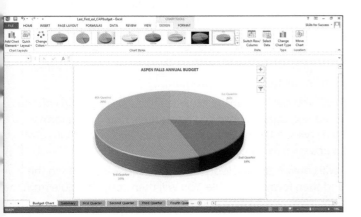

Figure 4

11. On the **Summary** worksheet, enter a formula for the *North* total from the **Second Quarter**, the **Third Quarter**, and the **Fourth Quarter** worksheets in the range **B6:B8**. AutoFill the range **B5:B8** to the right through **column E**.

12. On the **Summary** worksheet, in the range **B9:E9**, insert a function to calculate the column totals.

13. In cell **A11**, type Bonus if less than and then in cell **A12** type $1,100,000 Select the range **A11:A12**, and then apply the **Outside Borders**.

14. In cell **B11**, insert the **IF** function. For the logical test, check whether the *North* total is less than the value in cell **A12**. If the logical test is true, 500 should display, and if the logical test is false, 50 should display. In the function, use an absolute cell reference when referring to cell **A12**.

15. In cell **B11**, apply the **Currency [0]** cell style, and then AutoFill cell **B11** to the right through cell **D11**.

16. Select the range **B5:D8**, insert the default **Data Bars** conditional format.

17. In cell **A17**, insert the **TODAY** function. Format the date with the **March 14, 2012**, date format.

18. Unhide the **Last Year** worksheet. **Copy** the *Annual Budget* shape and then paste the shape in the **Summary** worksheet. Move the shape to approximately the range **A19:E24**, and then compare your screen with **Figure 3**.

19. **Hide** the **Last Year** worksheet.

20. Group the worksheets, and then press Ctrl + Home. Find and replace the four occurrences of Qtr with Quarter

21. With the worksheets still grouped, check and correct any spelling errors. Add the file name to the left footer and the sheet name to the right footer. Return to **Normal view**, and then make cell **A1** the active cell. Ungroup the worksheets.

22. Make the **Summary** worksheet the active worksheet. Insert a **3-D Pie** chart based on the nonadjacent ranges **A4:A8** and **E4:E8**. Move the pie chart to a chart sheet with the sheet name Budget Chart

23. For the pie chart, apply **Layout 1**, and then apply the **Chart Style 8**. Change the chart title to Aspen Falls Annual Budget and then for the data labels, change the font size to **12**. Add the file name in the chart sheet's left footer and the sheet name in the right footer. Compare your screen with **Figure 4**.

24. **Save**, and then **Close** the workbook. Submit the project as directed by your instructor.

 DONE! You have completed the Excel Capstone Project

Copy Word Tables into Excel Worksheets

▶ Each Microsoft Office application has different strengths. For example, you can use Word to convert text into tables, and Excel to insert functions and formulas into table cells.

▶ Exporting data from one application to another enables you to use the strengths of each application without having to retype the data.

▶ To move data from Word to Excel, you must organize the information into rows and columns. One way to format data is to create a table in Word.

© Vitaly Krivosheev

Aspen Falls City Hall

In this Integrated Project, you will create documents for the Aspen Falls Community Services Office, which has been working on various sustainability programs for the citizens of Aspen Falls, California. As part of their sustainability program, Aspen Falls is working with the local community college to increase the number of students riding city buses instead of driving their cars to campus. Students will be given a sticker to affix to their student ID, and then by showing this ID to a bus driver, the students can ride a city bus for free. You will assist Jack Ruiz, Community Services Director, to complete a letter to the college president stating more students will be permitted to participate in the free bus ride program.

In Word, you can use tabs to organize text into rows and columns. The tabbed text can be converted into a table that can be formatted with table styles. A Word table can be copied and pasted into other applications such as Excel.

You will convert tabbed Word text into a table, add data to the table, and then format the table. You will then copy the table from the Word document and paste it into an Excel worksheet.

Time to complete this project – 30 to 60 minutes

Student data files needed for this project:

exl_IP03Riders (Word)
exl_IP03Pass (Excel)

You will save your files as:

Last_First_exl_IP03Riders
(Word)

Last_First_exl_IP03Pass
(Excel)

Outcome

Using the skills in this project, you will be able to work with Office documents like this:

SKILLS

At the end of this project you will be able to:

▶ Convert text to a table
▶ Copy a Word table into an Excel workbook
▶ Match destination formatting when pasting

ASPEN FALLS COMMUNITY SERVICES
275 Elm Street, Room 122C
Aspen Falls, CA 93463

June 17, 2014

Dr. Dan Cheek
President
Aspen Falls Community College
817 Wisteria Lane
Aspen Falls, CA 93468

Dear Dr. Cheek:

We have been pleased with the involvement of the Aspen Falls Commun... sustainability programs. As you know, the city has been promoting "Ride... provides each student a sticker to affix to a student ID. By showing the st... student can ride a city bus for free. Student participation in this program...

We still have funds available for this program and are pleased to inform... who signed up after the deadline may now pick up a free city bus ride sti...

First Name	Last Name
Carmelina	Goforth
Florine	Dupont
Valentina	Blunt
Erik	Zook
Scotty	Whittle
Kareen	Whitehurst
First	Last

Thank you again for encouraging your students to take part in this sustai...

Sincerely,

Jake Ruiz
Community Services Director

Last_First_exl_IP03Riders

Aspen Falls Student Bus Passes		
First Name	Last Name	Bus Pass Issued
Dane	Borders	Yes
Junko	Bachman	Yes
Donovan	Tisdale	Yes
Hugh	Tavares	Yes
Brandi	Schmid	Yes
Viviana	Pickard	Yes
Willy	Jasper	Yes
Denita	Gulley	Yes
Riley	Fonseca	Yes
Genevie	Condon	Yes
Sulema	Clancy	Yes
Errol	Batista	Yes
Dodie	Wicks	Yes
Delmer	New	Yes
Zoe	Martell	Yes
Misha	Lo	Yes
Yuki	Littleton	Yes
Cedrick	Ison	Yes
Lady	Haag	Yes
Joy	Folsom	Yes
China	Brumfield	Yes
Terence	Broyles	Yes
Gregg	Brito	Yes
Lane	Mireles	Yes
Glen	McDonnell	Yes
Valeria	LeClair	Yes
Lupe	Hamblin	Yes
Jonelle	Gough	Yes
Abel	Fanning	Yes
Freddie	Binder	Yes
Rueben	Winfield	Yes
Kathrine	Whitworth	Yes
Carmelina	Goforth	No
Florine	Dupont	No
Valentina	Blunt	No
Erik	Zook	No
Scotty	Whittle	No
Kareen	Whitehurst	No
First	Last	No

1. Start **Excel 2013**, and then open the student data file **exl_IP03Pass**. Save the workbook in your chapter folder as Last_First_exl_IP03Pass

2. Add the file name in the worksheet's left footer, and then return to **Normal view**. **Minimize** the Excel window.

3. Start **Word 2013**, and then open the student data file **exl_IP03Riders**. **Save** the file in your chapter folder as Last_First_exl_IP03Riders Add the file name to the footer, and then close the footer.

4. At the bottom of the Word document, beginning with the text *First Name*, select the seven lines of tabbed text. Do not select the blank line above or below the tabbed text.

5. On the **Insert tab**, in the **Tables group**, click the **Table** button, and then click **Convert Text to Table**. Compare your screen with **Figure 1**.

6. In the **Convert Text to Table** dialog box, click **OK**.

7. On the **Design tab**, in the **Table Styles group**, click the **More** button. In the **Table Style gallery**, scroll down and then under **List Tables**, point at the fourth style—**List Table 1 Light - Accent 3**. Compare your screen with **Figure 2**, and then click the fourth style.

8. In the **Table Style Options group**, clear the **First Column** check box.

9. On the **Layout tab**, in the **Cell Size group**, click the **AutoFit** button, and then click **AutoFit Contents**.

■ **Continue to the next page to complete the skill**

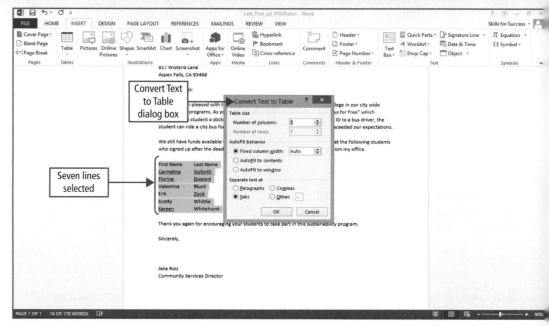

Figure 1

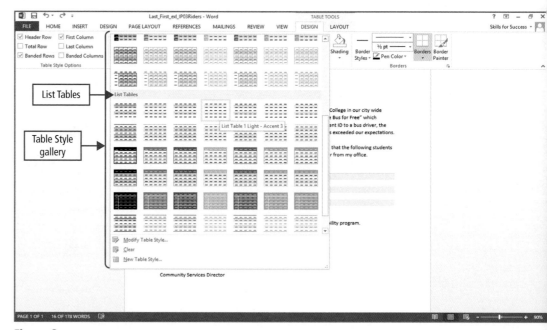

Figure 2

Figure 3

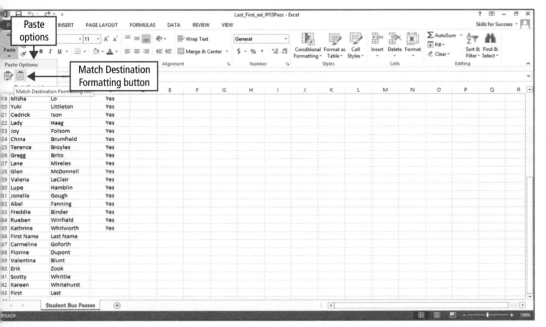
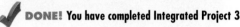

Figure 4

10. In the last table row, click in the cell with the text *Whitehurst*, and then press `Tab` to insert a new row. Type your first name, press `Tab`, and then type your last name. **Save** 🖫 the Word document.

11. On the **Layout tab**, in the **Table group**, click the **Select** button, and then compare your screen with **Figure 3**.

12. In the list, click **Select Table**. On the **Home tab**, in the **Clipboard group**, click the **Copy** button 🖹.

13. On the taskbar, click the **Excel** button 🔣 to make the Excel window active.

14. Scroll down, and then click cell **A36**. On the **Home tab**, in the **Clipboard group**, click the **Paste arrow**. Under **Paste Options**, point to the second button 📋—**Match Destination Formatting**. Compare your screen with **Figure 4**.

15. Click the **Match Destination Formatting** button 📋.

16. Click cell **A36**. In the **Cells group**, click the **Delete arrow**, and then click **Delete Sheet Rows** to delete the header row from the copied table.

17. Click cell **C36**, type No and then on the formula bar, click **Enter** ✓. AutoFill cell **C36** down through **C42**.

18. **Save** 🖫 the Excel workbook, and then **Close** ✖ the workbook. **Save** 🖫 the Word document, and then **Close** ✖ the document. Submit the project as directed by your instructor.

✔ **DONE! You have completed Integrated Project 3**

Link Data from Excel

- You can copy a chart from an Excel workbook and paste it into a Word document.
- When you copy data from Excel, you can paste it into a Word document as a table, or you can create a link between Excel and Word so that any changes made in an Excel document will also be reflected in a linked Word table.
- When you update data in an Excel file that has been linked to a Word document, the information will be updated in the Word document.
- Excel charts or data that have been pasted into a Word document can be formatted in the Word document.

© Africa Studio

Aspen Falls City Hall

In this Integrated Project, you will complete a memo for the Library Director, Douglas Hopkins. Mr. Hopkins has been working with the Friends of the Aspen Falls Public Library. The group operates a bookstore and donates the revenue to the public library. The group tracks their bookstore revenue in an Excel workbook and Mr. Hopkins plans to present the revenue information to the Board of Trustees. You will complete a memo to the Board of Trustees and include a chart and linked data from the Excel workbook in your memo.

Each Microsoft Office application has different strengths; for example, you can use Excel to create charts based on values in an Excel workbook. An Excel chart can be copied and then pasted into a Word document such as a memo or a report. You can link data from one file to another file, and when you update the data in the original file, the linked data will also be updated.

You will open an Excel workbook and a Word document, and you will paste a chart from the Excel worksheet into the Word document. You will also link data from the Excel worksheet to the Word document, and then update the link.

Time to complete this project – 30 to 45 minutes

Student data files needed for this project:

exl_IP04Report (Word)

exl_IP04BookSales (Excel)

You will save your files as:

Last_First_exl_IP04Report (Word)

Last_First_exl_IP04BookSales (Excel)

Outcome

Using the skills in this project, you will be able to create documents that look like this:

At the end of this project you will be able to:

▶ Copy Excel charts and paste them into Word documents

▶ Link Excel data to Word documents

▶ Link and keep the source formatting

▶ Update linked data

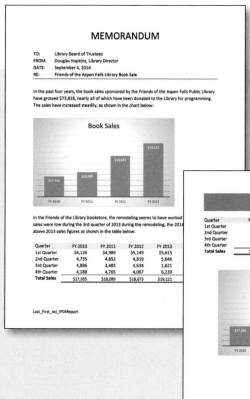

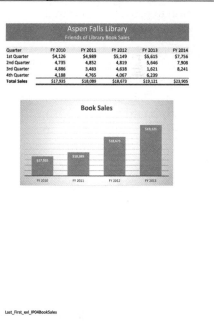

1. Start **Word 2013**, and then open the student data file **exl_IP04Report**. **Save** 🖫 the file in your chapter folder as Last_First_exl_IP04Report Add the file name to the footer, and then close the footer.

2. Start **Excel 2013**, and then open the student data file **exl_IP04BookSales**. **Save** 🖫 the workbook in your chapter folder as Last_First_exl_IP04BookSales Add the file name in the worksheet's left footer, and then return to **Normal view**.

3. In Excel, click the chart border to select the chart. Compare your screen with **Figure 1**.

4. On the **Home tab**, in the **Clipboard group**, click the **Copy** button 🖹.

5. On the taskbar, click the **Word** button 🔲 to make the Word window active. Position the insertion point in the first blank line below the paragraph that begins *In the past four years*.

6. In the **Clipboard group**, click the **Paste** button to paste the chart in the Word document. Compare your screen with **Figure 2**.

7. On the taskbar, click the **Excel** button 🔲 to make the Excel window active. Select the range **A4:F9**. On the **Home tab**, in the **Clipboard group**, click the **Copy** button 🖹.

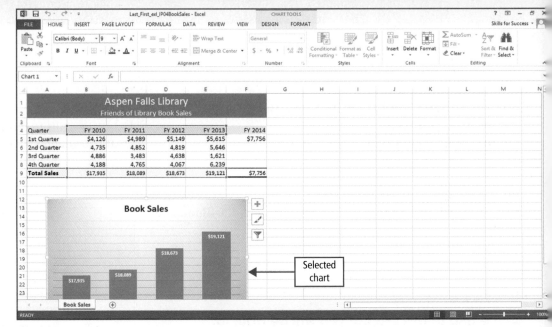

Figure 1

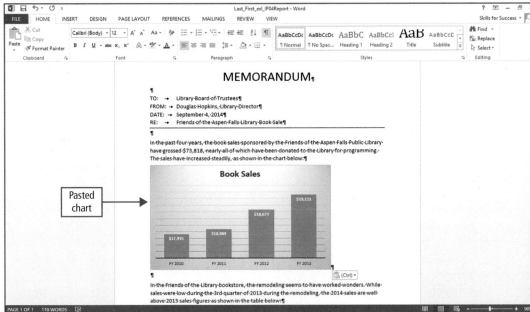

Figure 2

■ **Continue to the next page to complete the skill**

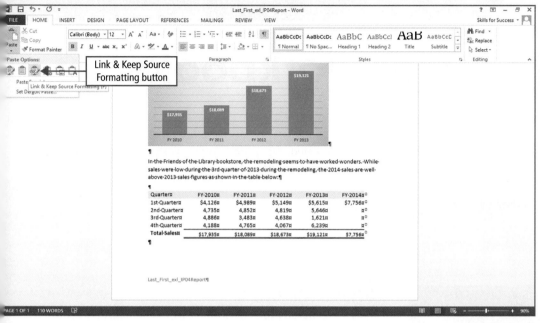

Link & Keep Source Formatting button

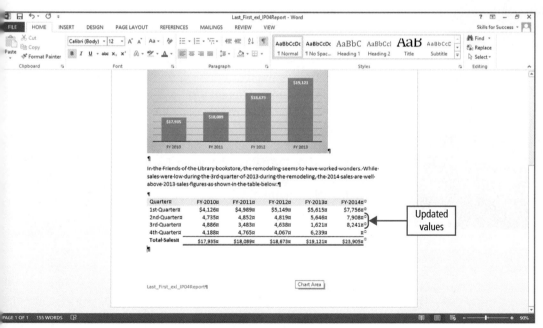

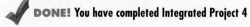

Updated values

Figure 3

Figure 4

8. On the taskbar, click the **Word** button.

9. Position the insertion point in the blank line at the end of the document. On the **Home tab**, in the **Clipboard group**, click the **Paste arrow**, and then under **Paste Options**, point to the third button —**Link & Keep Source Formatting**. Compare your screen with **Figure 3**.

   A preview of the data displays at the insertion point.

10. Click the **Link & Keep Source Formatting** button.

11. On the taskbar, click the **Excel** button. Press Esc to remove the moving border.

12. In cell **F6** type 7908 and then press Enter. In cell **F7** type 8241 and then press Enter.

13. **Save** the Excel file.

14. On the taskbar, click the **Word** button.

15. In the Word document, right-click the Excel table that you pasted previously, and then click **Update Link** to check for any changes in the linked Excel data. Compare your screen with **Figure 4**.

   In the Word document, the updated 2nd Quarter and 3rd Quarter values display, and the 2014 total is updated.

16. **Save** the Word document, and then **Close** x the document. **Close** X the Excel workbook. Submit the project as directed by your instructor.

DONE! You have completed Integrated Project 4

Refer to Cells in Other Workbooks

▶ An ***external reference***—a reference to a cell in another workbook—is useful when keeping worksheets together in the same workbook is not practical.

▶ An external reference must include the name of the workbook and the name of the worksheet.

▶ After a link is created, the source workbook should not be renamed or moved to a different location.

© Gunnar3000

Aspen Falls City Hall

In this Integrated Project, you will assist Kim Leah, Parks and Recreation Director, to complete a list of contacts for the city parks and golf courses. The Course Managers at the Aspen Lakes Golf Course and at the Hamilton Golf Course each maintain an Excel workbook that contains information about the employees working at their golf courses. You will link the contact information from these two workbooks into a third workbook that contains the parks contact information.

If employees are in different locations, sometimes it isn't practical to keep data in the same workbook. Data can be linked from one workbook to another workbook using external references.

You will link data from two Excel workbooks to a third workbook. You will update the data in the original workbooks and verify that the data is updated in the linked workbook, and then you will apply conditional formatting.

Time to complete this project – 30 to 60 minutes

Student data files needed for this project:

exl_IP05Golf1   exl_IP05Contacts
exl_IP05Golf2

Outcome

Using the skills in this project, you will be able to work with an Excel workbook like this:

You will save your files as:

Last_First_exl_IP05Golf1   Last_First_exl_IP05Contacts
Last_First_exl_IP05Golf2

SKILLS   MyITLab®

At the end of this project you will be able to:

▶ Link data from one Excel workbook to another

▶ Update linked data

▶ Insert conditional formatting

Aspen Falls Parks and Recreation
Employee Contact Information

First Name	Last Name	Position	Phone	Location
First	Last	Parks and Recreation Manager	(805) 555-1479	City Hall, Room 416
Amado	Pettinelli	Outdoor Recreation Supervisor	(805) 555-1417	City Hall, Room 440
Leah	Kim	Parks and Recreation Director	(805) 555-1410	City Hall, Room 412
Lorrine	Deely	Community Center Supervisor	(805) 555-1153	City Hall, Room 434
Booker	Berhe	Aquatics Supervisor	(805) 555-1350	City Hall, Room 432
Irving	Siravo	Capital Improvement Supervisor	(805) 555-1310	City Hall, Room 426
Keith	Hansen	Park Operations Manager	(805) 555-1112	City Hall, Room 414
Jacquetta	Ronald	Planning and Design Supervisor	(805) 555-1031	City Hall, Room 430
Neely	Ramsburg	Design and Development Manager	(805) 555-1403	City Hall, Room 420
Vic	Fowler	Aspen Lakes Course Manager	(805) 555-1010	Aspen Lakes Golf Course
Lee	Garrett	Golf Instructor	(805) 555-1787	Aspen Lakes Golf Course
Kyle	Burress	Golf Instructor	(805) 555-5851	Aspen Lakes Golf Course
Diego	Alvarez	Mechanic	(805) 555-7985	Aspen Lakes Golf Course
Ariana	Korpela	Landscaper	(805) 555-2775	Aspen Lakes Golf Course
Brooke	Whitlow	Bookkeeper	(805) 555-5595	Aspen Lakes Golf Course
Timothy	Dominik	Clubhouse Associate	(805) 555-2523	Aspen Lakes Golf Course
Jesse	Periera	Clubhouse Associate	(805) 555-6944	Aspen Lakes Golf Course
Chloe	Tauer	Maintenance Associate	(805) 555-3989	Aspen Lakes Golf Course
Rosaria	Cabiness	Food and Beverage	(805) 555-6814	Aspen Lakes Golf Course
Tracy	Lecroy	Hamilton Course Manager	(805) 555-1010	Hamilton Golf Course
Mandee	Covey	Golf Instructor	(805) 555-8675	Hamilton Golf Course
Ollie	Wizen	Golf Instructor	(805) 555-3593	Hamilton Golf Course
Dylan	Lee	Mechanic	(805) 555-9124	Hamilton Golf Course
Marissa	Madeiros	Landscaper	(805) 555-7781	Hamilton Golf Course
Sabrina	Mak	Bookkeeper	(805) 555-5221	Hamilton Golf Course
Chester	Schillinger	Clubhouse Associate	(805) 555-7279	Hamilton Golf Course
Byron	Hoese	Maintenance Manager	(805) 555-9737	Hamilton Golf Course

Last_First_exl_IP05Contacts

1. Start **Excel 2013**, and then open the student data file **exl_IP05Contacts**. **Save** 🔲 the workbook in your chapter folder as Last_First_exl_IP05Contacts

2. Click cell **A5**, type your first name, and then press [Tab]. In cell **B5** type your last name, and then press [Enter]. **Save** 🔲 the workbook, and then compare your screen with **Figure 1**.

3. **Open** the student data file **exl_IP05Golf1**. **Save** 🔲 the workbook in your chapter folder as Last_First_exl_IP05Golf1

4. Right-click the **Golf Lessons** worksheet tab, and then click **Select All Sheets**. Add the file name in the worksheet's left footer, and then return to **Normal view**. Right-click the worksheet tab, and then click **Ungroup Sheets**.

5. Click the **Aspen Lakes Contacts** worksheet tab, and then select the range **A4:E13**. On the **Home tab**, in the **Clipboard group**, click the **Copy** button 📋.

6. Make **Last_First_exl_IP05Contacts** the active workbook, and then click cell **A14**. On the **Home tab**, in the **Clipboard group**, click the **Paste arrow**. Under **Other Paste Options**, click the second button 📋—**Paste Link**. Click cell **A14**, and then compare your screen with **Figure 2**.

   The reference to the source workbook, worksheet, and cell displays in the formula bar.

7. Make **Last_First_exl_IP05Golf1** the active workbook. **Save** 🔲 the workbook and then **Close** ✕ the workbook.

■ **Continue to the next page to complete the skill**

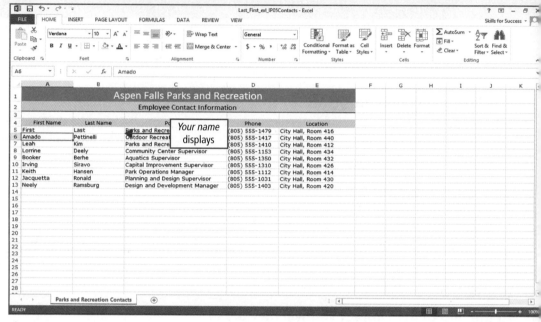

Figure 1

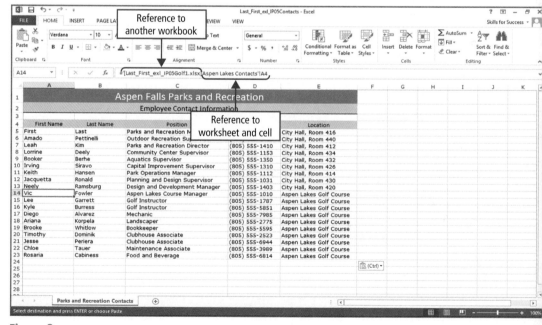

Figure 2

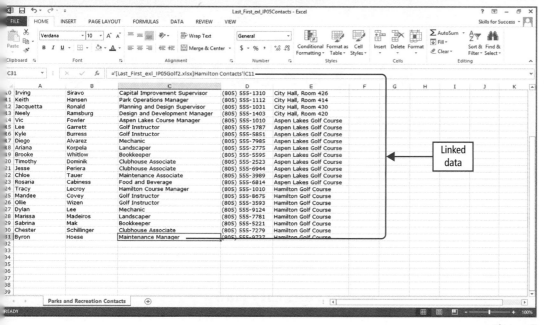

Figure 3

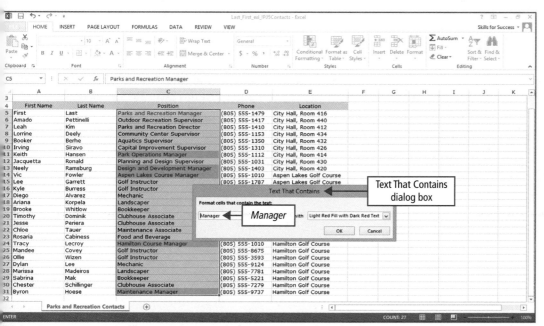

Figure 4

8. **Open** the student data file **exl_IP05Golf2**. **Save** the workbook in your chapter folder as Last_First_exl_IP05Golf2

9. Using the techniques just practiced **Select All Sheets**, add the file name in the worksheet's left footer, return to **Normal view**, and then **Ungroup Sheets**.

10. Click the **Hamilton Contacts** worksheet tab, and then select the range **A4:E11**. On the **Home tab**, in the **Clipboard group**, click the **Copy** button.

11. Make **Last_First_exl_IP05Contacts** the active workbook, and then click cell **A24**. In the **Clipboard group**, click the **Paste arrow**. Under **Other Paste Options**, click the **Paste Link** button.

12. Make **Last_First_exl_IP05Golf2** the active workbook, and then click cell **C11**. Type Maintenance Manager and then press Enter. **Save** the workbook.

13. Make **Last_First_exl_IP05Contacts** the active workbook. Click cell **C31**, and then compare your screen with **Figure 3**.

14. Select the range **C5:C31**. Click the **Quick Analysis Lens** button, and then click the **Text Contains** button. In the **Text That Contains** dialog box, in the first box replace the text with Manager Compare your screen with **Figure 4**, and then click **OK**.

16. **Save** the Excel workbooks, and then **Close** the workbooks. Submit the project as directed by your instructor.

DONE! You have completed Integrated Project 5

Create Workbooks Using Excel Online

▶ **Excel Online**, formerly Excel Web App, is a cloud-based application used to complete basic spreadsheet formulas using a web browser.

▶ Excel Online can be used to create or edit workbooks using a web browser instead of the Excel program—Excel 2013 does not need to be installed on your computer.

▶ When you create a document using Excel Online, it is saved on your OneDrive so that you can work with it from any computer connected to the Internet.

▶ You can use Excel Online to insert a chart and perform basic chart formatting tasks.

▶ If you need a feature not available in Excel Online, you can edit the workbook in Microsoft Excel and save it on your OneDrive.

© Maxim_Kazmin

Aspen Falls City Hall

In this project, you will assist Taylor and Robert Price, energy consultants for the city of Aspen Falls. They have asked you to use Excel Online to create a spreadsheet that shows the energy consumption of a city building.

Excel Online is used to create or open Excel workbooks from any computer or device connected to the Internet. When needed, you can edit text, enter formulas, or insert charts. You can save these workbooks on your OneDrive, and continue working with them later when you are at a computer that has Excel 2013 available.

In this project, you will use Excel Online to create a new workbook. You will enter data and then apply formats and number styles. You will insert formulas, functions, and a chart. Finally, you will open the workbook in Excel 2013 to format the chart and check the spelling in the worksheet.

Time to complete this project – 30 to 60 minutes

Student data file needed for this project:

New blank Excel Online workbook

Outcome

Using the skills in this project, you will be able to create and edit an Excel Online workbook like this:

You will save your file as:

Last_First_exl_WAEnergy

At the end of this project you will be able to:

► Create new Excel workbooks from OneDrive
► Enter data in Editing View
► Apply number styles
► Enter summary functions
► Enter formulas using absolute cell references
► Insert and format bar charts
► Edit workbooks created in Excel Online in Excel 2013

Aspen Falls
City Administrative Building

Total Square Footage	20,000
Energy Cost per Square Foot	$2.25
Annual Energy Cost	$45,000

Energy Consumption	Percent of Total Cost	Annual Cost
Building Heating	32%	$14,400
Water Heating	8%	$3,600
Lighting	15%	$6,750
Computers	18%	$8,100
Air Conditioning	27%	$12,150
		$45,000

Percent of Total Cost

- Building Heating
- Water Heating
- Lighting
- Computers
- Air Conditioning

27% 32% 18% 8% 15%

1. Start **Internet Explorer**, navigate to live.com and log on to your Microsoft account. If you do not have an account, follow the links and directions on the page to create one.

2. After logging in, navigate as needed to display the **OneDrive** page.

   OneDrive and Web App technologies are accessed through web pages that may change and the formatting and layout of some pages may often be different from the figures in this book. When this happens, you may need to adapt the steps to complete the actions they describe.

3. On the Ribbon, click Create, and then compare your screen with **Figure 1**.

4. On the menu, click Excel Workbook.

5. Above the Ribbon, point to the text *Book1* click one time, type Last_First_exl_WAEnergy and then click cell A1.

   Excel Online displays five tabs in Editing View: File, Home, Insert, Date, and View.

6. In cell **A1** type Aspen Falls and then press [Enter].

7. In cell **A2** type City Administrative Building and then press [Enter].

8. Select the range **A1:F1**, and then on the **Home tab**, in the **Alignment group**, click the **Merge & Center** button [Merge & Center]. Select the range **A2:F2**, and then click the **Merge & Center** button. Compare your screen with **Figure 2**.

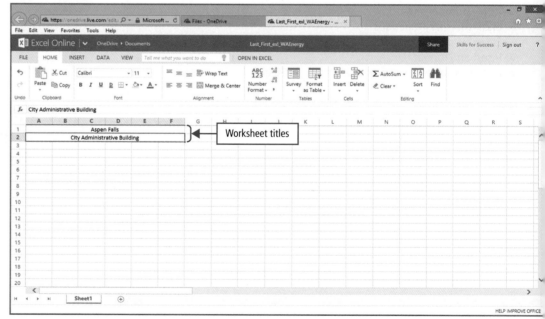

Figure 1

Figure 2

■ Continue to the next page to complete the skill

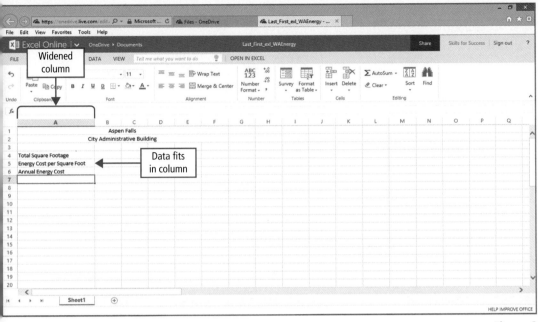

Figure 3

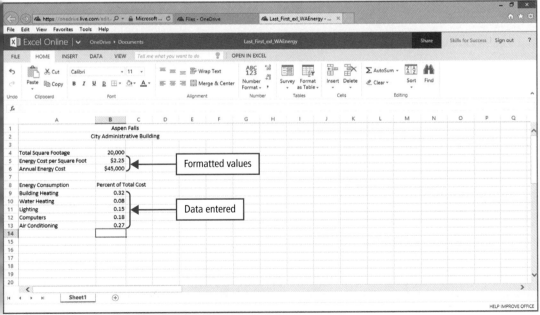

Figure 4

9. In cell **A4** type Total Square Footage and then press Enter.

10. In cell **A5** type Energy Cost per Square Foot and then press Enter.

11. In cell **A6** type Annual Energy Cost and then press Enter.

12. In the column heading area, point to the right boundary of **column A** to display the ✛ pointer. Double-click between **columns A** and **B** to display all of the contents of cell **A5** in the column. Compare your screen with **Figure 3**.

13. Make cell **B4** the active cell. Type 20,000 and then press Enter.

14. In cell **B5** type 2.25 and then press Enter.

15. In cell **B6** type =B4*B5 and then press Enter.

16. Click cell **B5**. On the **Home tab**, in the **Number group**, click the **Number Format** button, and then click **Currency**.

17. Click cell **B6**, and then apply the **Currency** number format. Click the **Decrease Decimal** button two times.

18. Click cell **A8**, type Energy Consumption and then press Enter.

19. In the range **A9:A13**, pressing Enter after each entry, type Building Heating, Water Heating, Lighting, Computers and then Air Conditioning

20. Click cell **B8**, type Percent of Total Cost and then press Enter.

21. In **B9:B13**, making sure you type the decimal in front of each number, type the following values: .32, .08, .15, .18 and then .27 Compare your screen with **Figure 4**.

■ **Continue to the next page to complete the skill**

22. Select the range **B9:B13**. In the **Number group**, click the **Number Format** button, and then click **Percentage**. Click the **Decrease Decimal** button ⌷⌷ two times.

23. Click **C8**, type Annual Cost and then press Enter.

24. Select the range **B8:C8**. In the **Alignment group**, click the **Wrap Text** button, click the **Middle Align** button ≡, and then click the **Center** button ≡.

25. Click **C9**, type =B9*$B$6 and then press Enter.

26. Click **C9**, point at the fill handle, and then compare your screen with **Figure 5**.

27. While still pointing at the fill handle, drag the fill handle to copy the formula down through cell **C13**.

> The absolute cell reference to $B6 is copied to each of the other formulas.

28. Click **C14**. In the **Editing group**, click the **AutoSum** button, and then press Enter.

29. Select the range **A8:B13**. On the **Insert tab**, in the **Charts group**, click the **Pie** button, and then point at the first chart—**2-D Pie**. Compare your screen with **Figure 6**, and then click the first chart.

> A contextual tab—the Chart Tools tab—displays on the Ribbon.

30. Move the chart to approximately the range **A16:F30**.

31. To the right of the tabs, click the **OPEN IN EXCEL** button. If prompted, enter your ID and password.

32. If prompted, at the top of the screen, on the **Protected View** bar, click **Enable Editing**.

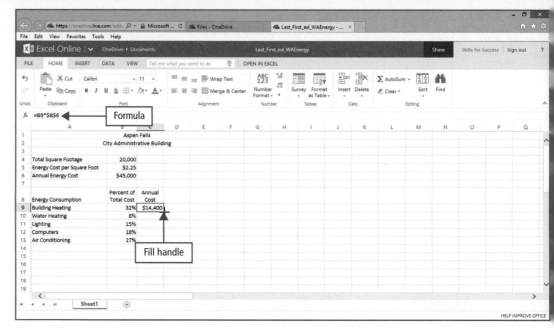

Figure 5

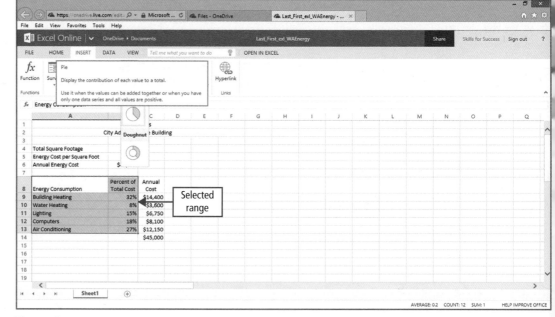

Figure 6

■ **Continue to the next page to complete the skill**

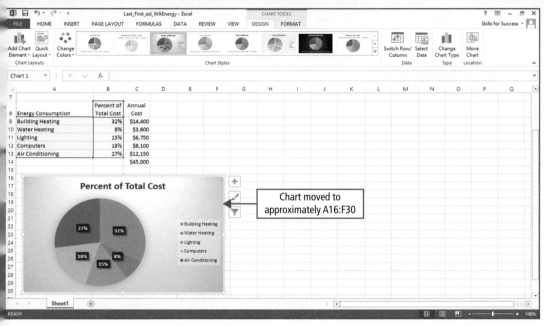

Figure 7

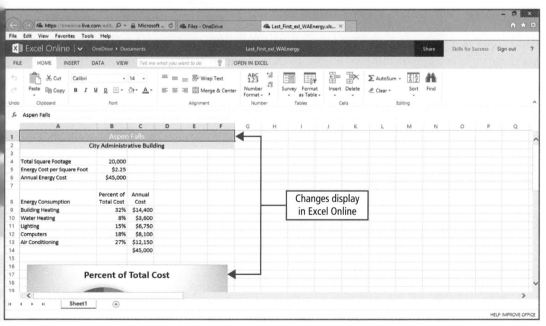

Figure 8

33. Click cell **A1**. On the **Home tab**, in the **Styles group**, click the **Cell Styles** button, and then click **Accent 4**. In the **Font group**, click the **Font Size** button [11 ▾], and then click **14**. In the **Cells group**, click the **Format** button, and then click **Row Height**. In the **Row Height** dialog box, type 20 and then click **OK**.

34. Click cell **A2**. In the **Styles group**, click the **Cell Styles** button, and then click **40% - Accent 4**. In the **Font group**, click the **Font Size** button [11 ▾], and then click **12**.

35. Click the chart to select the chart, and then on the **Design tab**, in the **Chart Styles group**, click the third style—**Style 3**. Compare your screen with **Figure 7**.

36. On the **Review tab**, in the **Proofing group**, click the **Spelling** button to check and correct any spelling errors. **Save** 🖫 your workbook and then **Close** [X] Excel 2013.

37. On the **OneDrive** page, open the workbook in Excel Online. Compare your screen with **Figure 8**.

   The cell styles and the chart style 3 have been applied. Features not supported by Excel Online, such as styles, cannot be changed in the Web App but they can be viewed.

38. Click the **View tab**, and then click **Reading View**. **Print** or **Share** the document as directed by your instructor.

39. In the top-right corner of the Internet Explorer window, click the **Sign out** link, and then **Close** [X] the browser window.

   ✔ **DONE! You have completed the Excel Online Project!**

Introduction to Access

Microsoft Access is a ***database system***—a program used to both store and manage large amounts data. In a database system, the ***database*** is a collection of structured tables designed to store large amounts of data. The data is managed using queries, forms, and reports.

Access tables organize data into rows and columns. Each row (record) stores data about each item in a collection. For example, in a table storing customer data, each row would represent an individual customer. The columns (fields) organize the types of data being collected such as first name, last name, street, and so on.

You can build a database from scratch or use one of the pre-built templates provided by Microsoft. You can also add pre-built tables, fields, and forms to an existing database.

After designing the tables, you are ready to enter data. Forms are built so that others can type the data quickly and accurately. You can also import data from files created by programs.

Queries are used to answer questions about the data. They filter and sort the data to display the information that answers the questions. Reports can be based on either tables or queries, and are created to display information effectively.

Access has several wizards and views that you can use to build your tables, forms, queries, and reports quickly. You can format these objects using techniques similar to those in other Office programs.

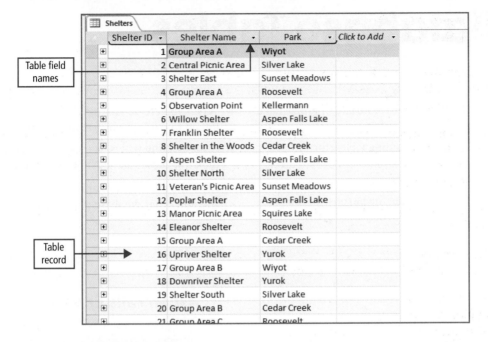

Table field names

Table record

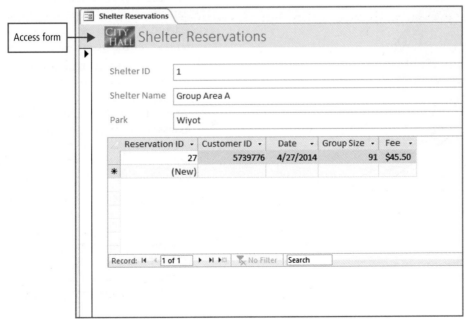

Access form

CHAPTER 1

Create Database Tables

- ▶ Microsoft Office Access is an application used to store and organize data, and access and display that data as meaningful information.

- ▶ A single Access file contains many objects including tables, forms, queries, and reports. Tables are used to store the data. The other objects are used to access the data stored in those tables.

- ▶ When you create a database, you first determine the purpose of the database. You can then plan how to organize the data into tables.

- ▶ When you create tables, you assign properties that match the data you intend to enter into the database tables.

- ▶ After creating tables, you establish the relationships between them and then test those relationships by adding sample data.

- ▶ After the table relationships are tested, you are ready to enter all the data and add other database objects such as forms, queries, and reports.

© Franck Boston

Aspen Falls City Hall

In this project, you will help Sadye Cassiano, Director of the Building Services Department of Aspen Falls City Hall, add two tables to the database that the department uses to track building permits. You will use Access to design and test prototypes of two related database tables that will be added to the city database.

The data stored in database tables is used in many ways. In Aspen Falls, building permits are considered public records, and the database will be used to publish permits on the city website. Internally, the city will use the data to adjust yearly property assessments, track city construction, track payments of fees, and contact the person filing a building permit. All of these tasks can be accomplished by accessing two tables in the database in different ways. Thus, the tables are the foundation of a database.

In this project, you will create a new database and then create one table in Datasheet view, and a second table in Design view. In both tables you will add fields and assign properties to those fields and create a relationship between the two tables. You will add data to one table by typing the data, and add data to the second table by importing it from an Excel spreadsheet. Finally, you will use Datasheet view to filter, sort, format, and print the tables.

Time to complete all 10 skills – 60 to 90 minutes

Student data file needed for this chapter:

acc01_PermitsData (Excel)

You will save your databases as:

Last_First_acc01_Permits (Access)
Last_First_acc01_PermitsData (Excel)

Outcome

Using the skills in this chapter, you will be able to work with Access tables like this:

Permit Number	Start Date	Project Title	Location	Fee
B8756215ELEC	7/24/2014	REMODEL MALASKY RESIDENCE	4863 S Biltmore Av	$54.23
B5666375ELEC	7/24/2014	ADDITION JAPP RESIDENCE	8493 N Bannock St	$44.20
B3680115ELEC	7/24/2014	REMODEL AHRENDES RESIDENCE	3858 S Glenn Brook P	$51.79
B1684124ELEC	7/24/2014	REMODEL HARTNETT RESIDENCE	8147 S 5Th St	$49.32
B3849977ELEC	7/29/2014	ADDITION BRANDL RESIDENCE	6031 S Hinsdale Ct	$53.79
B1090716ELEC	7/29/2014	REMODEL CUBIT RESIDENCE	3674 W Teabrook Av	$74.50
B9568069ELEC	8/1/2014	ADDITION TRIEU RESIDENCE	8668 E Hopkirk Av	$55.06
B4824848ELEC	8/1/2014	REMODEL MIYAGAWA RESIDENC	515 E Birch	$64.67
*				$0.00

SKILLS

MyITLab®
Skills 1-10 Training

At the end of this chapter you will be able to:

Skill 1 Create Databases
Skill 2 Create Tables in Datasheet View
Skill 3 Enter Data into Datasheets
Skill 4 Create Tables in Design View
Skill 5 Relate Tables
Skill 6 Enter Data in Related Tables
Skill 7 Import Data into Tables
Skill 8 Filter and Sort Datasheets
Skill 9 Format Datasheets
Skill 10 Preview and Print Datasheets

MORE SKILLS

Skill 11 Compact and Repair Databases
Skill 12 Work with the Long Text Data Type
Skill 13 Work with the Attachment Data Type
Skill 14 Work with the Hyperlink and Yes/No Data Types

▸ When you start Access, the Start screen displays so that you can either open an existing database or create a new blank database.

▸ Before you create a new database, you assign a name and location for the database file.

1. Start **Access 2013**, and then compare your screen with **Figure 1**.

   On the Access Start screen, you can create a database from a template, open a recent database, or create a blank database.

2. On the Access start page, click **Blank desktop database**. In the **Blank desktop database** dialog box, replace the suggested **File Name** value with Last_First_acc01_Permits

3. To the right of the **File Name** box, click the **Browse** button 📁 to open the File New Database dialog box.

4. In the **File New Database** dialog box, navigate to the location where you will be saving your work for this chapter.

5. In the **File New Database** dialog box, click **New folder**, and then type Access Chapter 1 Press Enter two times to create and open the new folder. Compare your screen with **Figure 2**.

   The Microsoft Access 2007 - 2013 file format is the default file format for Access 2013.

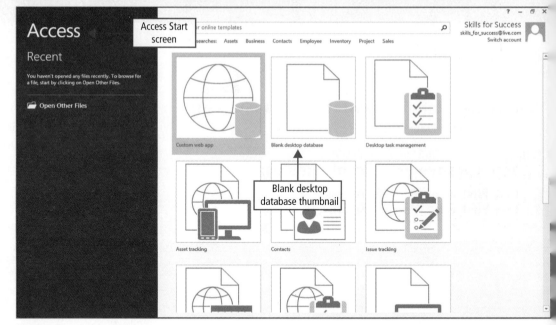

Figure 1

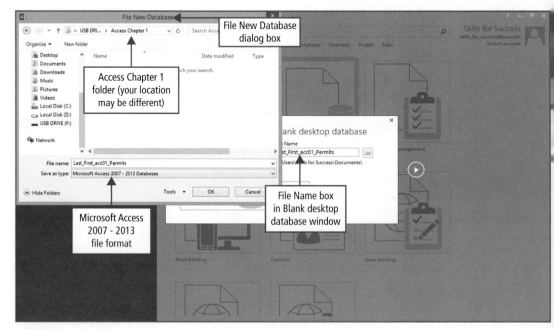

Figure 2

■ **Continue to the next page to complete the skill**

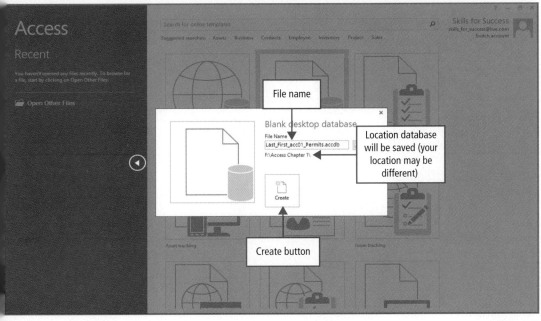

Figure 3

6. Click **OK** to accept the changes and close the File New Database dialog box.

7. Compare your screen with **Figure 3**, and then click the **Create** button.

8. Take a few moments to familiarize yourself with the Access window as described below and in **Figure 4**.

When you create a blank database, a new table is automatically started for you. The name *Table1* is temporarily assigned to the table, and the first column—*ID*—is the name of a *field*—a common characteristic of the data that the table will describe.

Database *tables* store the data in rows and columns and are presented in *datasheets*. In a datasheet, each row is a *record*—a collection of related data such as the contact information for a person. Each column is a field that each record will store such as city, state, or postal code.

Table1 currently displays in **Datasheet view**—a view that features the data but also has contextual tabs on the Ribbon so that you can change the table's design. In Datasheet view, the last row of the table is the *append row*—the row in which a new record is entered. *Table1* currently has no data.

9. Leave the table open for the next skill.

■ **You have completed Skill 1 of 10**

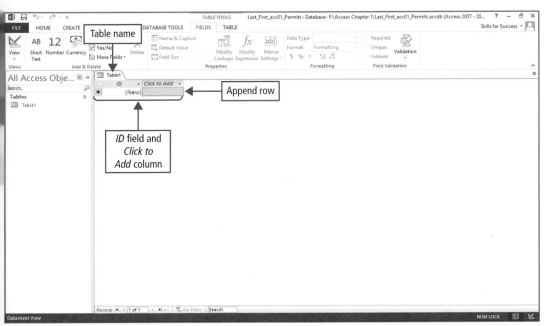

Figure 4

▶ When you design a table, you add field names and their properties.

▶ **Data Type** is a field property that specifies the type of information that a field will hold: for example, text, number, date, or currency.

1. In **Table1**, click the **ID** column header. On the **Fields tab**, in the **Properties group**, click **Name & Caption**. Replace the **Name** box value with ContractorID and in the **Caption** box, type Contractor ID (include a space between the two words).

2. Compare your screen with **Figure 1**, and then click **OK**.

> *Contractor ID*—the field's caption—displays at the top of the column and is slightly truncated. You will widen the column in a later step. **Captions** determine what displays in all datasheet, form, and report labels.

3. In the second column, click the text **Click to Add,** and then from the list of data types, click **Short Text**. Type CompanyName and then press Enter to move to the next column.

> The **Short Text data type** stores up to 255 characters of text.

4. On the **Fields tab**, in the **Add & Delete group**, click the **More Fields** button. Scroll to the bottom of the list of data types, click **Name**, and then compare your screen with **Figure 2**.

> **Quick Start fields** are a set of fields that can be added with a single click. For example, the Name Quick Start data type inserts the LastName and FirstName fields, assigns the Text data type, and adds a caption with a space between the two words.

■ **Continue to the next page to complete the skill**

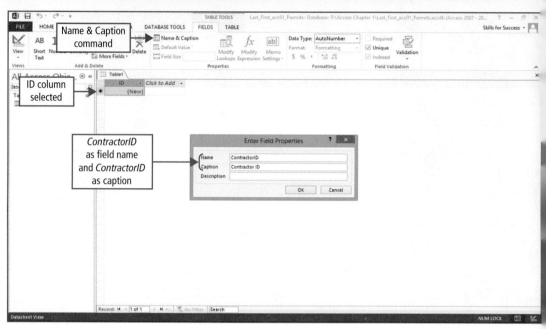

Figure 1

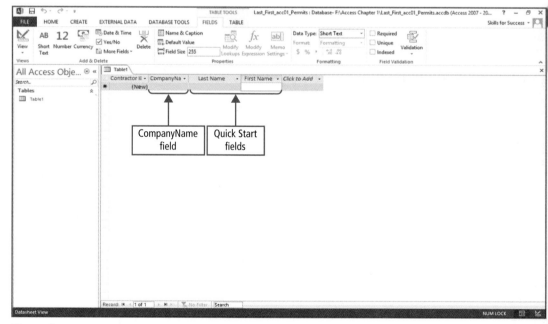

Figure 2

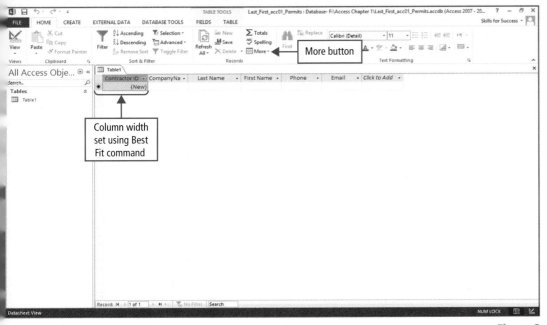

Figure 3

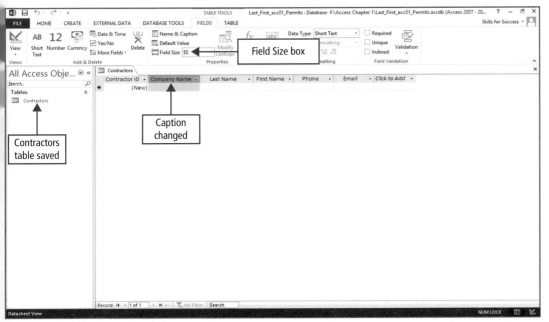

Figure 4

5. Click in the last column—**Click to Add,** and then click **Short Text**. Type Phone and then press Enter.

6. Repeat the technique just practiced to add a field name Email with the **Short Text** data type.

7. In the header row, click in the **Contractor ID** column. Click the **Home tab**. In the **Records group**, click **More**, and then click **Field Width**. In the **Column Width** dialog box, click **Best Fit**. Compare your screen with **Figure 3**.

   Column widths can be changed to match the width of their contents. As you add data, the widths may need to be adjusted.

8. Repeat the technique just practiced to adjust the **CompanyName** column width.

9. Click **Save**. In the **Save As** dialog box, type Contractors and then click **OK**.

   When you save a table that you have added or changed, its name displays in the Navigation Pane, and it becomes part of the database file.

10. Click **CompanyName** to select the column, and then click the **Fields tab**. In the **Properties group**, change the **Field Size** value to 50

    Field size limits the number of characters that can be typed into a text or number field.

11. With the Company Name field selected, in the **Properties group**, click **Name & Caption**. Change the **Caption** to Company Name and then click **OK**. Compare your screen with **Figure 4**.

12. Repeat the technique just practiced to change the **Field Size** property of the **Last Name**, **First Name**, **Phone**, and **Email** fields to 50 and then click **Save**.

■ **You have completed Skill 2 of 10**

▶ ACC 1-3
VIDEO

▶ When you are designing and building database tables, it is a good idea to enter some of the data that they will store. In this way, the design can be tested and adjusted if needed.

1. In the **Contractors** table datasheet, in the append row, click the first empty **Company Name** cell, and then type Front Poarch Construction Compare your screen with **Figure 1**.

> As soon as you enter data in the append row, it becomes a record, and the append row displays below the new record.

2. Press [Enter] to accept the data entry and move to the next column. Type Poarch Press [Enter], and then in the **First Name** column, type Ken

3. Continue in this manner to enter the **Phone** number, (805) 555-7721 and the **Email** address, poarch.ken@ poarchcontractors.com

4. Press [Enter] to finish the record and move the insertion point to the append row. Compare your screen with **Figure 2**.

> When you move to a different record or append row, the new or changed data is automatically saved to the database file on your drive.

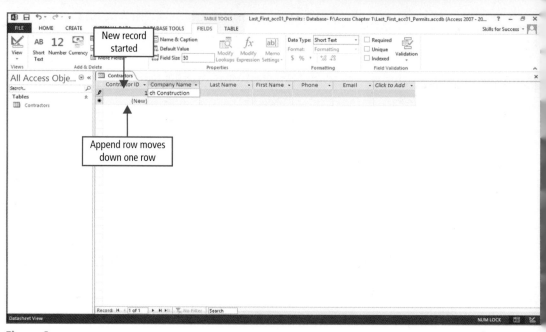

Figure 1

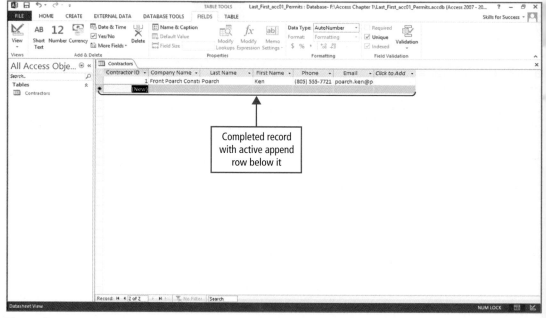

Figure 2

■ Continue to the next page to complete the skill

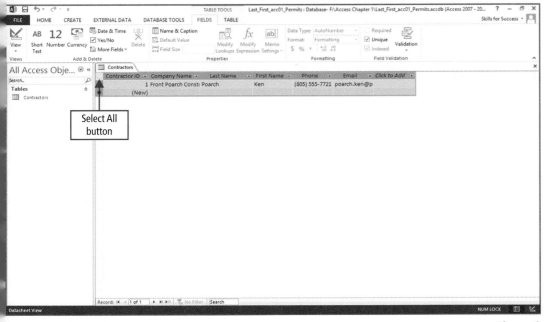

Figure 3

CompanyName	Last Name	First Name	Phone	Email
Front Poarch Construction	*Poarch*	*Ken*	*(805) 555-7721*	*poarch.ken@ poarchconstruction.com*
Mikrot Construction	Mikrot	Kim	(805) 555-6795	kmikrot@mikrot .com
Sobata Contractors	Sobata	Jeri	(805) 555-4789	jeri@sobatacon .com
(leave blank)	Jestis	Mee	(805) 555-8506	mee.jestis@ jestisandsons.com
Degasparre Remodelers	Degasparre	Artur	(805) 555-0770	artur@degasparre .com

Figure 4

5. To the left of the **Contractor ID** column heading, click the **Select All** button ▨. Compare your screen with **Figure 3**.

   ContractorID is the table's *primary key*—a field that uniquely identifies each record in a table. Primary key field names often include *ID* to help you identify them.

6. With all the cells still selected, repeat the technique practiced previously to apply **Best Fit** to the column widths.

   By selecting the entire datasheet, you can adjust column widths quickly. If your window is sized smaller than the datasheet, columns that are not in view will not be adjusted. You can adjust them by first maximizing the Access window or by scrolling to display them.

7. Starting with *Mikrot Construction*, add the records shown in the table in **Figure 4**. For the **Contractor ID**, accept the AutoNumber values.

   The ContractorID data type is *AutoNumber*—a field that automatically enters a unique, numeric value when a record is created. Once an AutoNumber value has been assigned, it cannot be changed. If your AutoNumber values differ from the ones shown in this chapter's figures, you do not need to change them.

8. Click **Save** 🖫, and then **Close** ☒ the table.

   When you close a database table, the database does not close. If you accidentally close the database, reopen it to continue.

■ **You have completed Skill 3 of 10**

▶ An alternate method for creating a table is to create it in **Table Design view**—a view that features table fields and their properties.

1. Click the **Create tab**, and then in the **Tables group**, click the **Table Design** button.

2. With the insertion point in the **Field Name** column's first row, type PermitID and then press Enter to automatically assign the Short Text data type.

3. On the **Design tab**, in the **Tools group**, click **Primary Key**.

4. In the **Field Properties** pane, change the **Field Size** value to 50 and the **Caption** to Permit Number Compare your screen with **Figure 1**.

   When working with a table in Design view, the Field Name, Data Type, and Description data are entered in rows. Other field properties are entered in the Field Properties pane.

5. Click in the next blank **Field Name** box, and then type StartDate

6. Press Enter, click the **Data Type arrow**, and then click **Date/Time**. In the **Field Properties** pane, click the **Format** box, click the **Format arrow** that displays, and then click **Short Date**. Add the **Caption** property Start Date and then compare your screen with **Figure 2**.

   The **Date/Time data type** stores serial numbers that are converted and formatted as dates or times.

7. Add a third field named ProjectTitle with the **Short Text** data type and the **Caption** property Project Title

8. Add a fourth field named Location with the **Short Text** data type.

■ Continue to the next page to complete the skill ▶

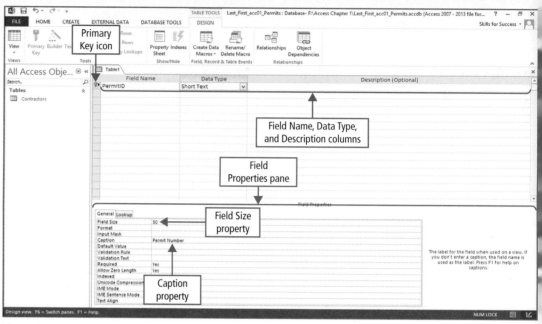

Figure 1

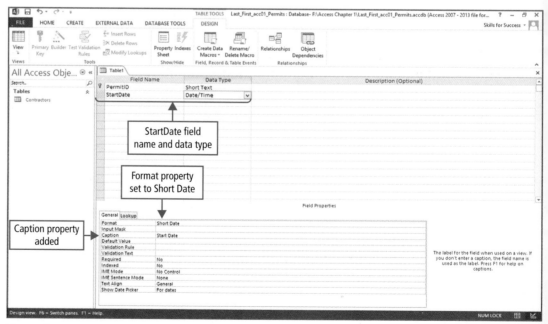

Figure 2

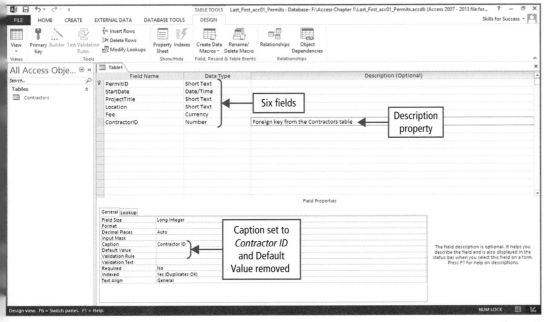

Figure 3

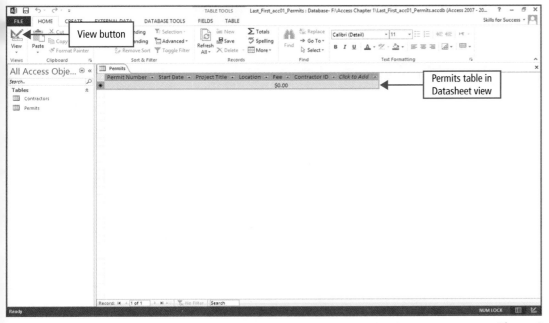

Figure 4

9. Add a fifth field named Fee with the **Currency** data type. Do not change any other field properties.

   The ***Currency data type*** stores numbers formatted as monetary values.

10. Add a sixth field named ContractorID with the **Number** data type and the caption Contractor ID In the **Default Value** box, delete the *0*.

    The ***Number data type*** stores numeric values.

11. In the **ContractorID Description** box, type Foreign key from the Contractors table Compare your screen with **Figure 3**.

    A ***foreign key*** is a field that is used to relate records in a second related table. The foreign key field is often the second table's primary key. Here, ContractorID is the primary key of the Contractors table. The ContractorID field will be used to join this table to the Contractors table.

    When you join tables, the common fields must share the same data type. Because the Contractors table automatically assigns a number in the ContractorID field, the foreign key field should be assigned the Number data type.

12. Click **Save** 🖫. In the **Save As** dialog box, type Permits and then click **OK**.

13. On the **Design tab**, in the **Views group**, click the **View** button to switch to Datasheet view. Click the **Select All** button [ ], and then adjust the column widths to **Best Fit**. Compare your screen with **Figure 4**.

14. **Save** 🖫 and then **Close** ✕ the table.

■ **You have completed Skill 4 of 10**

▶ Records in two tables can be related by placing the same field in both tables and then creating a relationship between the common fields.

1. Click the **Database Tools tab**, and then in the **Relationships group**, click the **Relationships** button to display the Relationships tab and Show Table dialog box.

> If the Show Table dialog box does not display, you can open it by clicking the Show Table button in the Relationships group.

2. In the **Show Table** dialog box, double-click **Permits** to add it to the Relationships tab. In the **Show Table** dialog box, double-click **Contractors**. Alternately, you can add tables to the Relationships tab by dragging them from the Navigation Pane.

3. Compare your screen with **Figure 1**, and then close the Show Table dialog box.

4. From the **Permits** table, drag the **ContractorID** field to the **ContractorID** field in the **Contractors** table. When the pointer displays, as shown in **Figure 2**, release the mouse button.

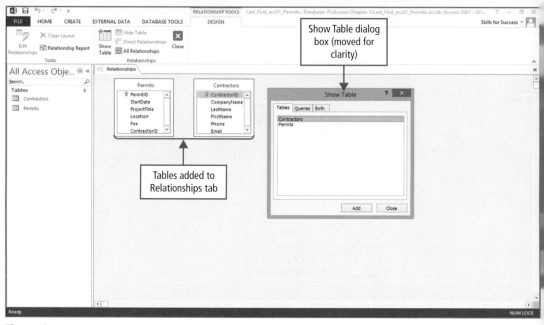

Figure 1

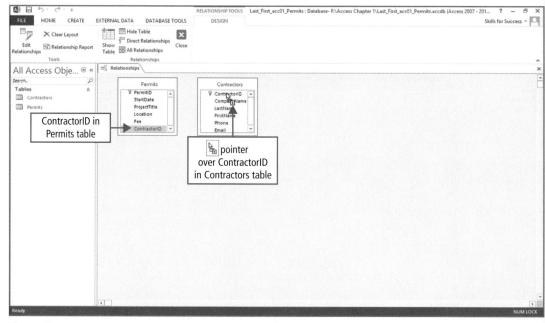

Figure 2

■ Continue to the next page to complete the skill

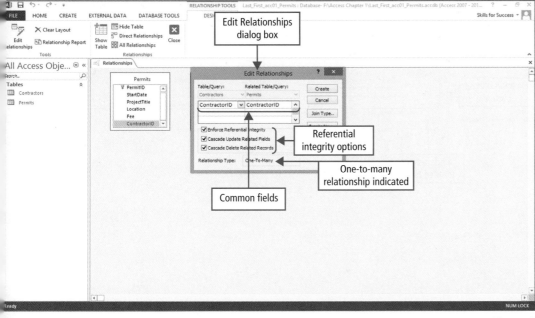

Figure 3

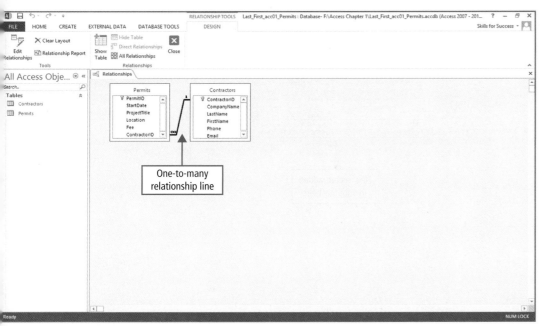

Figure 4

5. In the **Edit Relationships** dialog box, select the **Enforce Referential Integrity** check box. Select the **Cascade Update Related Fields** and **Cascade Delete Related Records** check boxes, and then compare your screen with **Figure 3**.

Tables are typically joined in a ***one-to-many relationship***—a relationship in which a record in the first table can have many associated records in the second table.

Referential integrity is a rule that keeps related values synchronized. For example, the foreign key value must be present in the related table. This option must be selected to create a one-to-many relationship.

With a ***cascading update***, if you edit the primary key values in a table, all the related records in the other table will update accordingly.

With a ***cascading delete***, you can delete a record on the *one* side of the relationship, and all the related records on the *many* side will also be deleted.

6. Click **Create**, and then compare your screen with **Figure 4**.

7. Click **Save** 🖫. On the **Design tab**, in the **Tools group**, click the **Relationship Report** button to create a report showing the database relationships.

When you create a relationship report, the report name is automatically assigned.

8. If your instructor asks you to print your work for this chapter, print the report.

9. Click **Save** 🖫, and then click **OK**. **Close** ☒ the report, and then **Close** ☒ the Relationships tab.

■ **You have completed Skill 5 of 10**

▶ When you enter data in related tables, referential integrity rules are applied. For example, a foreign key value must have a matching value in the related table.

▶ A ***subdatasheet*** displays related records from another table by matching the values in the field that relates the two tables. For example, all the permits issued to each contractor can be listed by matching the ContractorID value assigned to that permit.

1. In the **Navigation Pane**, double-click **Contractors** to open its datasheet.

2. Locate the record for Mee Jestis (Jestis, Mee), click the **Expand** button ⊞, and then compare your screen with **Figure 1**.

   When a table is on the *one* side of a relationship, a subdatasheet is available. Here, no permits have been issued to this contractor yet.

3. In the subdatasheet append row, under **Permit Number**, type B1018504RFSW

4. In the same record, under **Start Date**, click the cell, and then click the **Date Picker** button 🗓 that displays. In the **Date Picker**, click the **Today** button.

   Fields that have been assigned the Date/Time data type display a Date Picker when they are selected.

5. In the same record, enter a **Project Title** of REMODEL CHITTESTER RESIDENCE a **Location** of 6088 W Devon Way and a **Fee** of $217.71 Compare your screen with **Figure 2**.

■ **Continue to the next page to complete the skill**

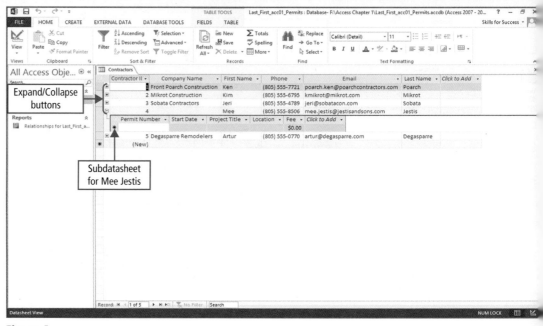

Figure 1

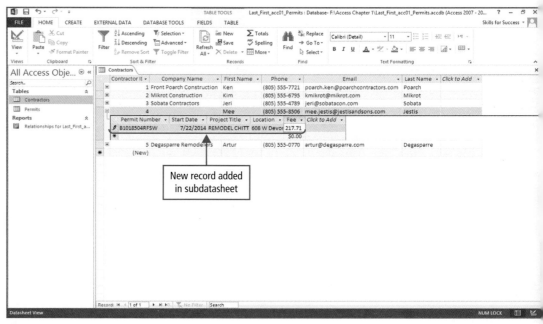

Figure 2

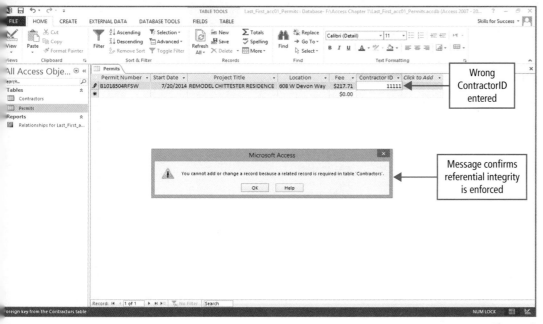

Figure 3

6. **Close** ☒ the table. In the **Navigation Pane**, under **Tables**, double-click **Permits** to open its datasheet.

7. Adjust the column widths to **Best Fit** to display all the data you entered in the subdatasheet previously.

> In this manner, records in a one-to-many relationship can be entered using a subdatasheet. Here, a new building permit record has been created, and the Contractor has been assigned. Because it is an AutoNumber, your ContractorID value may be different.

8. In the first record, change the **Contractor ID** to 11111 Click in the append row, and then compare your screen with **Figure 3**.

> It is a good idea to test referential integrity. Here, referential integrity is working correctly. You are not allowed to enter a Contractor ID that does not exist in the related Contractors table.

9. Read the message, click **OK**, and then press [Esc] to cancel the change and return to the correct Contractor ID.

10. In the table, repeat the techniques just practiced to add the three records shown in **Figure 4**. For all records, use the same Contractor ID used in the first record.

11. If necessary, adjust the column widths to fit the contents. **Save** ☐, and then **Close** ☒ the table.

■ **You have completed Skill 6 of 10**

Permit Number	Start Date	Project Title	Location	Fee
B1018504RFSW	Your date	REMODEL CHITTESTER RESIDENCE	6088 W Devon Way	217.71
B1052521RFSW	7/21/2014	ROOF ABADIE RESIDENCE	5943 S Balivi Ln	208.65
B1090716ELEC	7/29/2014	REMODEL CUBIT RESIDENCE	3674 W Teabrook Av	74.50
B1071316PLMB	8/19/2014	REMODEL LAA RESIDENCE	5901 S Farnyville Ln	58.00

Figure 4

▶ When Excel tables are arranged as a datasheet, the data can be imported into Access tables.

1. Start **Excel 2013**, and then on the Excel start page, click **Open Other Workbooks**. On the **Open** page, click **Computer**, and then click **Browse**. In the **Open** dialog box, navigate to the student files for this chapter, and then open the Excel file **acc01_PermitsData**.

2. On the **File tab**, click **Save As**, and then click **Browse**. In the **Save As** dialog box, navigate to your chapter folder. Name the file Last_First_acc01_PermitsData and then click **Save**.

3. Click cell **A1**, type PermitID and then press [Tab]. Continue in this manner to enter the column labels in this order: StartDate | ProjectTitle | Location | Fee Compare your screen with **Figure 1**.

   When you import data from Excel, it is best practice to insert the table's field names in the spreadsheet's header row. In this project, you will not import any ContractorID data.

4. Click **Save** 🖫, and then **Close** ✖ Excel.

5. In **Access**, click the **External Data tab**, and then in the **Import & Link group**, click **Excel**.

6. In the **Get External Data - Excel Spreadsheet** dialog box, click the **Browse** button. In the **File Open** dialog box, navigate to your **Access Chapter 1** folder, select **Last_First_acc01_PermitsData**, and then click **Open**.

7. Click the **Append a copy of the records to the table** option button, click the **arrow**, and then select the **Permits** table as shown in **Figure 2**.

▪ Continue to the next page to complete the skill ▶

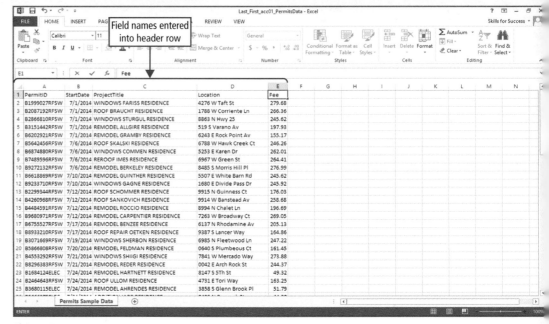

Figure 1

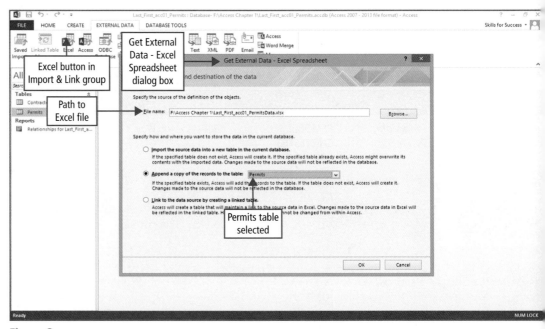

Figure 2

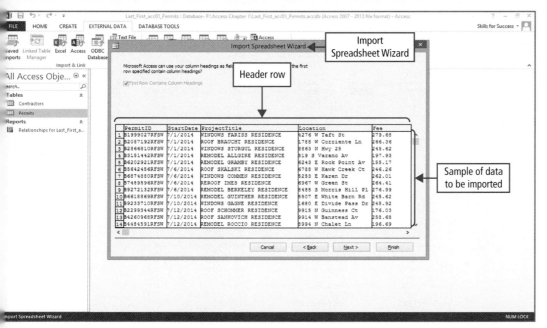

Figure 3

8. In the dialog box, click **OK** to open the **Import Spreadsheet Wizard** dialog box.

Because a workbook can contain multiple worksheets, you are asked to select the worksheet that contains the data you wish to import.

9. In the first screen of the **Import Spreadsheet Wizard**, verify that the **Permits Sample Data** worksheet is selected, and then click **Next**. Compare your screen with **Figure 3**.

In the wizard, it is recommended that you view the sample data and verify that it matches the field names in the header row. Here, the header that you inserted previously matches the field names in the Access table.

10. Click **Next** to display the last screen in the **Import Spreadsheet Wizard**. Verify that the **Import to Table** box displays the text *Permits,* and that the **I would like a wizard…** check box is cleared. Click **Finish** to complete the import.

11. In the **Save Import Steps** screen, verify that the **Save import steps** check box is cleared, and then click **Close**.

12. Open the **Permits** table in Datasheet view. Adjust the column widths to **Best Fit**, and then compare your screen with **Figure 4**.

The records are added to the table and then sorted by the primary key—*Permit Number*. The Contractor ID is blank because these permits were issued to homeowners who are completing the work themselves.

13. Click **Save** 🖫, and then leave the table open for the next skill.

■ **You have completed Skill 7 of 10**

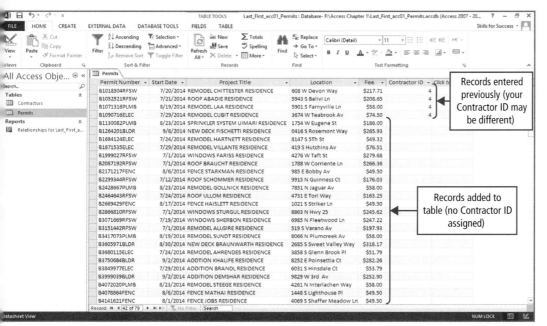

Figure 4

▶ Datasheets can be sorted and filtered to make the information more meaningful and useful.

1. With the **Permits** table open in Datasheet view click anywhere in the **Start Date** column. On the **Home tab**, in the **Sort & Filter group**, click the **Ascending** button. Compare your screen with **Figure 1**.

    By default, tables are sorted by their primary key field. Here, the Start Date column arrow changes to a sort arrow to indicate that the records have been sorted in ascending order by date.

2. In the **Fee** column, click the **Fee arrow**. In the **Filter** menu that displays, clear the **(Select All)** check box, and then select the **$58.00** check box.

3. Compare your screen with **Figure 2**, and then click **OK** to view the eight records that result.

    In this manner, the Filter menu can be used to select records with the values you choose.

4. Click the **Fee arrow**, and then click **Clear filter from Fee**.

5. Click the **Fee arrow**, point to **Number Filters**, and then click **Less Than**. In the **Custom Filter** dialog box, type 75 and then click **OK** to display 31 records.

■ Continue to the next page to complete the skill

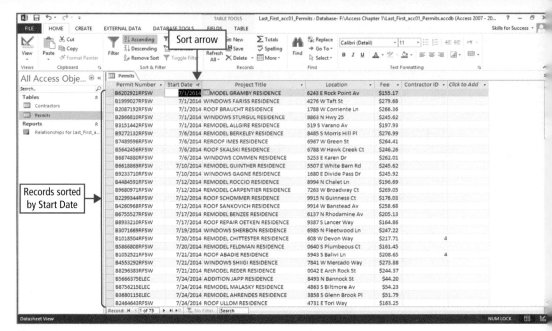

Figure 1

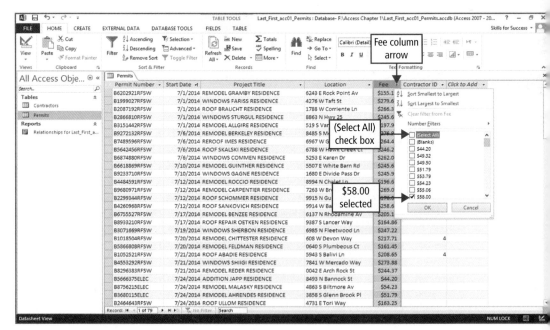

Figure 2

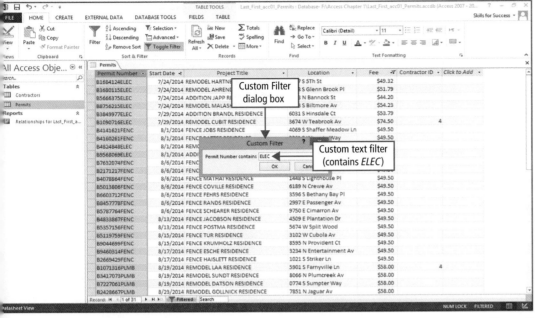

Figure 3

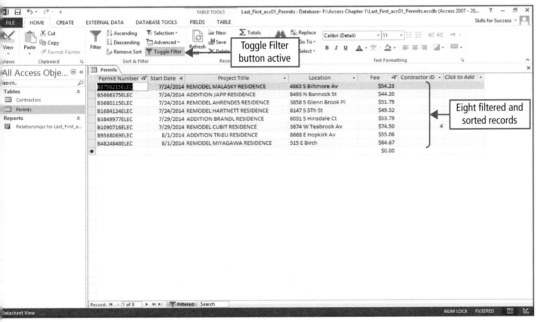

Figure 4

6. Click the **Permit Number arrow**. From the **Filter** menu, point to **Text Filters**, and then click **Contains**. In the **Custom Filter** dialog box, type ELEC

7. Compare your screen with **Figure 3**, and then click **OK** to display eight records.

   In this manner you can display records whose values contain the text or numbers you specify. Here, only the permits with permit numbers ending with ELEC and with fees less than $75 display.

8. Click **Save** 🖫, and then **Close** ✕ the table.

9. In the **Navigation Pane**, double-click **Permits** and notice that the 79 records are sorted by **Start Date**, but the filters are not applied.

10. On the **Home tab**, in the **Sort & Filter group**, click **Toggle Filter** to reapply the filter. Compare your screen with **Figure 4**.

    The sort order and filter that you create in a datasheet are saved as part of the table's design. When you open a table, it sorts in the order you specified, but the filter is not applied.

11. Leave the table open for the next skill.

■ **You have completed Skill 8 of 10**

▶ Datasheets can be formatted to make the data easier to read.

1. If necessary, open the **Permits** table, and then toggle the filter on.

2. On the **Home tab**, in the **Text Formatting group**, click the **Font Size arrow** 11 ▾, and then click **10**.

3. In the **Text Formatting group**, click the **Font arrow**. Scroll through the list of fonts as needed, and then click **Verdana**. Compare your screen with **Figure 1**.

> When you change the font size or font, the changes are applied to the entire datasheet.

4. Click the **Select All** button, and then apply the **Best Fit** column width.

5. With all the cells still selected, on the **Home tab**, in the **Records group**, click **More**, and then click **Row Height**.

6. In the **Row Height** dialog box, replace the existing **Row Height** value with 15 and then click **OK**.

7. Click anywhere in the **Contractor ID** column. On the **Home tab**, in the **Records group**, click **More**, and then click **Hide Fields**. Compare your screen with **Figure 2**.

Figure 1

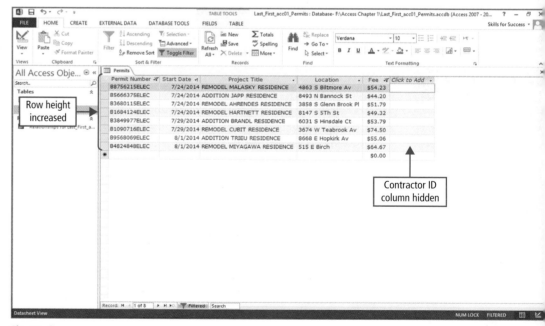

Figure 2

■ Continue to the next page to complete the skill ▶

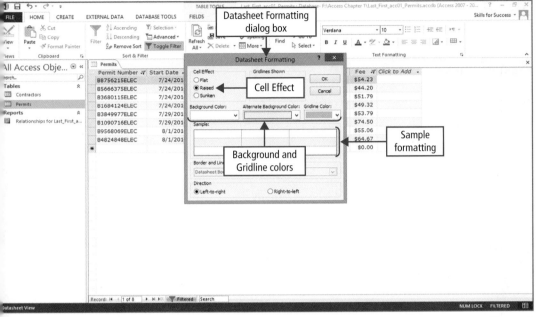

Figure 3

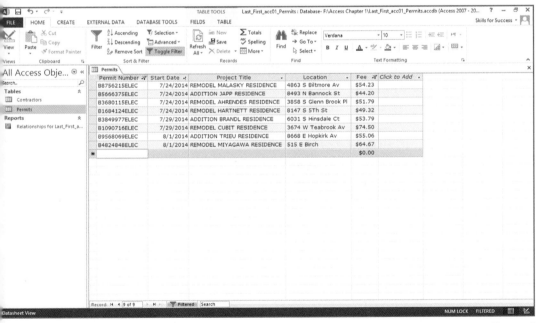

Figure 4

8. In the **Text Formatting group**, click the **Datasheet Formatting Dialog Box Launcher**.

9. In the **Datasheet Formatting** dialog box, under **Cell Effect**, select the **Raised** option button.

10. Click the **Background Color arrow**. In the gallery, click **Automatic**.

11. Click the **Alternate Background Color arrow**. In the gallery, under **Theme Colors**, click the sixth color in the second row—**Orange**, **Accent 2**, **Lighter 80%**.

12. Click the **Gridline Color arrow**. In the gallery, under **Theme Colors**, click the eighth color in the first row—**Gold**, **Accent 4**. Compare your screen with **Figure 3**.

   In the Datasheet Formatting dialog box, a sample of the selected formatting displays.

13. Click **OK** to apply the changes and to close the dialog box. Click in the append row, and then compare your screen with **Figure 4**.

14. Save the table design changes, and leave the table open for the next skill.

■ **You have completed Skill 9 of 10**

▶ Before printing, it is a good idea to preview the printed page(s) and make adjustments if necessary.

1. With the **Permits** table open in **Datasheet view**, click the **File tab**, and click **Print**. Compare your screen with **Figure 1**.

   The ***Quick Print*** command prints the object directly. You cannot make any adjustments to the object, choose a different printer, or change the printer settings.

   The ***Print*** command opens the Print dialog box so that you can select a different printer or different print options.

   The ***Print Preview*** command opens a preview of the table with Ribbon commands that enable you to make adjustments to the object you are printing.

2. On the **Print** page, click **Print Preview**. In the **Zoom group**, click the **Zoom arrow**, and then click **Zoom 100%**. Compare your screen with **Figure 2**. If necessary, scroll to the top of the page.

   The last column—Fee—will not print on page one. At the bottom of the preview, tools in the navigation bar are used to view the other printed pages.

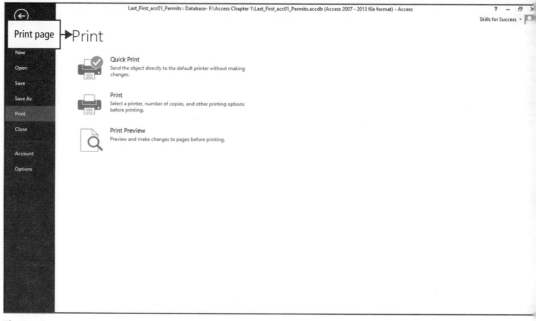

Figure 1

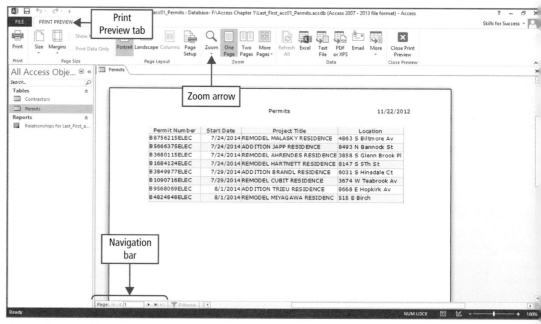

Figure 2

■ **Continue to the next page to complete the skill** ▶

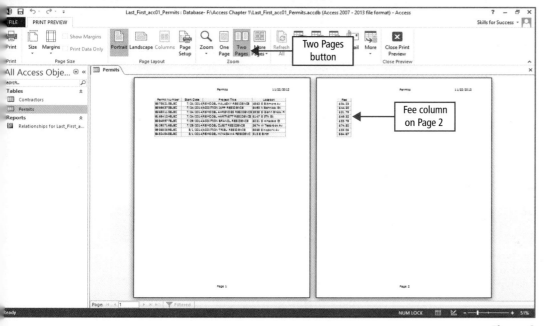

Figure 3

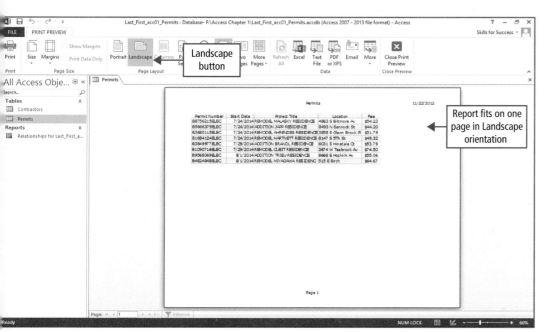

Figure 4

3. In the **Zoom group**, click **Two Pages**, and then compare your screen with **Figure 3**.

4. In the **Page Layout group**, click **Landscape**.

By default, tables print in *Portrait*—taller than wide. You can change the layout to *Landscape*—wider than tall—to accommodate a wider table with few records.

5. In the **Zoom group**, click **One Page**, and then compare your screen with **Figure 4**.

The buttons on the navigation bar are dimmed because the table now fits on one page.

6. If you are printing your work for this project, click the Print button, note the printer listed in the Print dialog box, and then click OK.

7. **Close** ✕ the table.

A table's page layout settings cannot be saved. The next time the table is open, the default Portrait view will be applied. Typically, when you want to print data from a table, an Access report is created. Report layout settings can be saved.

8. If you are printing your work for this project, use the technique just practiced to print the **Contractors** table with the portrait orientation.

9. With all tables closed, **Close** ✕ the Access window. Submit your work as directed by your instructor.

Because all the data and database objects are saved as you work with them, you do not need to click Save before quitting Access.

 DONE! You have completed Skill 10 of 10, and your databases are complete!

More Skills

The following More Skills are located at **www.pearsonhighered.com/skills**

More Skills Compact and Repair Databases

As tables, forms, queries, and reports are created and deleted, the size of the database file can grow quite large. Access provides a tool that rebuilds database files so that data and these objects are stored more efficiently. Applying the Compact and Repair tool decreases the size of a database file and improves database performance.

In More Skills 11, you will view the file size of a database before and after deleting several forms and reports. You will then compact and repair the database and observe the resulting change in file size.

To begin, open your web browser, navigate to www.pearsonhighered.com/skills, locate the name of your textbook, and follow the instructions on the website.

More Skills Work with the Long Text Data Type

To maintain efficient databases, the Short Text data type limits entries to 255 characters per record. When you need to store more characters, you can assign the Long Text data type which can store up to 65,535 characters.

In More Skills 12, you will attempt to enter more than 255 characters in a Short Text field. You will then convert the field to the Long Text type, and complete the record entry.

To begin, open your web browser, navigate to www.pearsonhighered.com/skills, locate the name of your textbook, and follow the instructions on the website.

More Skills Work with the Attachment Data Type

In Access, tables can store files such as Microsoft Word files, Excel files, or files created with a digital camera. Access provides a method to attach specific files to specific records. The attached files can then be opened and viewed in the application that created them.

In More Skills 13, you will create an Attachment field, attach several files to two records, and then open one of the attached files in another program.

To begin, open your web browser, navigate to www.pearsonhighered.com/skills, locate the name of your textbook, and follow the instructions on the website.

More Skills Work with the Hyperlink and Yes/No Data Types

A field can be used to store a hyperlink to a web page or file. These fields use the Hyperlink data type. Another data type, called Yes/No, can be assigned to a field that will have only two possible values, such as Yes or No.

In More Skills 14, you will create a new field, assign it the Hyperlink data type, and enter a web address into a record.

You will then create a Yes/No field and enter a Yes value into a record.

To begin, open your web browser, navigate to www.pearsonhighered.com/skills, locate the name of your textbook, and follow the instructions on the website.

Please note that there are no additional projects to accompany the More Skills Projects, and they are not covered in the End-of-Chapter projects.

The following table summarizes the **SKILLS AND PROCEDURES** covered in this chapter.

Skills Number	Task	Step	Icon
1	Create desktop databases	From the Access start screen, click Blank desktop database	
1	Create fields	Click the Click to Add column, and select the desired data type (Datasheet view)	
2	Insert Quick Start fields	Fields tab → Add & Delete group → More Fields	
2, 4	Set field properties	Click the field and use Fields tab commands Click the field and use Field Properties pane (Design view)	
3	Set Best Fit column widths	Home tab → Records group → More → Field Width	
3	Create new records in Datasheet view	Click append row, and type record data	
4	Define primary keys (Design view)	Design tab → Tools group → Primary Key	
4	Set data types (Design view)	Click Data Type arrow	
5	Add tables to Relationships tab	Database Tools → Relationships → Show Table	
5	Create a one-to-many relationship	Drag the field from the table to the related field in the other table and select the Enforce Referential Integrity check box	
6	Display subdatasheets	Click the Expand button	⊞
7	Import Excel data	External Data → Import & Link → Excel	
8	Sort datasheets	Home tab → Sort & Filter group → Ascending (or Descending)	
8	Filter datasheets	Click column Filter arrow	
8	Disable or enable filters	Home tab → Sort & Filter group → Toggle Filter	
9	Change datasheet fonts and font sizes	Home tab → Text Formatting group	
9	Set datasheet row height	Home tab → Records group → More → Row Height	
9	Hide datasheet fields	Home tab → Records group → More → Hide Fields	
9	Apply alternate row shading	Home tab → Datasheet Formatting Dialog Box Launcher	⌐
10	Preview a printed table	File tab → Print → Print Preview	
10	Change orientation	Print Preview tab → Page Layout group	

Key Terms

Online Help Skills

1. Start **Access 2013**, and then in the upper right corner of the Access start page, click the **Help** button [?].

2. In the **Access Help** window **Search help** box, type table relationships and then press [Enter].

3. In the search result list, click **Guide to table relationships**. Compare your screen with **Figure 1**.

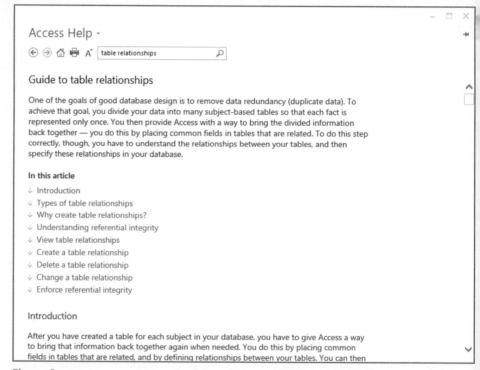

Figure 1

4. Read the article to the answer to the following question: Why create table relationships?

Matching

Match each term in the second column with its correct definition in the first column by writing the letter of the term on the blank line in front of the correct definition.

___ **1.** The object that stores the data by organizing it into rows and columns. Each column is a field and each row is a record.

___ **2.** The collection of related information that displays in a single row of a database table.

___ **3.** This specifies the kind of information that a field will hold; for example, text or numbers.

___ **4.** A field property that determines what displays in datasheets, forms, and report labels.

___ **5.** A data type that automatically assigns a unique numeric value to a field.

___ **6.** A field that uniquely identifies each record in a table.

___ **7.** A data type that stores numbers formatted as monetary values.

___ **8.** A set of fields that can be added with a single click. For example, the Address data type inserts five fields for storing postal addresses.

___ **9.** An Access view that features table fields and their properties.

___ **10.** A field on the *many* side of a relationship used to relate to the table on the *one* side of the relationship.

A AutoNumber

B Caption

C Currency

D Data type

E Foreign key

F Primary key

G Quick Start

H Record

I Table

J Table Design

BizSkills Video

1. Is there anything you would change about Theo's behavior at his performance evaluation? Why or why not?

2. How important do you think it is to set career development goals for yourself? Why?

Multiple Choice (MyITLab®)

Choose the correct answer.

1. An Access view that displays records in rows and fields in columns.
   A. Database
   B. Data grid
   C. Datasheet

2. Each individual characteristic in a record that displays as a single column in a datasheet.
   A. Field
   B. Record
   C. Subset

3. A data type that stores up to 255 characters of text.
   A. Currency
   B. Number
   C. Short Text

4. The blank row at the end of a datasheet used to add records to a table.
   A. Append
   B. Data entry
   C. New record

5. An Access field property that limits the number of characters that can be typed into a text or number field.
   A. Character Limit
   B. Character Size
   C. Field Size

6. A relationship in which a record in the first table can have many associated records in the second table.
   A. Cascading
   B. One-to-One
   C. One-to-Many

7. A referential integrity option in which you can edit the primary key values in a table, and all the related records in the other table will update accordingly.
   A. Cascading delete
   B. Cascading update
   C. One-to-many relationship

8. A rule that keeps related values synchronized.
   A. Data duplication
   B. Data redundancy
   C. Referential integrity

9. A command that opens the Print dialog box so that you can select a different printer or different print options.
   A. Quick Print
   B. Print
   C. Print Preview

10. An orientation of the printed page that makes it wider than it is tall.
    A. Print Preview
    B. Landscape
    C. Portrait

Topics for Discussion

1. What kind of information do you think a small business or organization would organize into a database?

2. Each database object has a special purpose. For example, a query is used to filter and sort records. Why do you think that the filter and sort tools are also available when you work with tables, forms, and reports?

Skills Review

MylTLab®
Grader

To complete this project, you will need the following file:

- acc01_SREmployees

You will save your database as:

- Last_First_acc01_SRDepartments

Figure 1

1. Start **Access 2013**, and then click **Blank desktop database**. Replace the **File Name** with Last_First_acc01_SRDepartments Click **Browse**, navigate to your chapter folder, and then click **OK**. Finish the process by clicking the **Create** button.

2. In **Table1**, select the **ID** column. On the **Fields tab**, in the **Properties group**, click **Name & Caption**. Change the **Name** to EmployeeID and the **Caption** to Employee ID and then click **OK**.

3. Click the **Click to Add** column. In the **Add & Delete group**, click **More Fields**, scroll down, and then click **Name**.

4. Click the **Click to Add** column, click **Date & Time**, and then type DateHired Repeat to add a **Short Text** field named DeptID

5. With the **DeptID** field selected, in the **Properties group**, click in the **Field Size** box, and then type 50

6. Click **Save**, type Employees and then click **OK**. Compare your screen with **Figure 1**, and then **Close** the table.

7. On the **External Data tab**, in the **Import & Link group**, click **Excel**. In the **Get External Data - Excel Spreadsheet** dialog box, click the **Browse** button. In the **File Open** dialog box, navigate to and select the student data file **acc01_SREmployees**, and then click **Open**. Click the **Append a copy of the records to the table** option button, and then click **OK**. In the first screen of the **Import Spreadsheet Wizard**, click **Finish**, and then click **Close** to complete the import process.

8. Double-click **Employees** to open the table in Datasheet view. Set the column widths to **Best Fit**.

9. Click the **DateHired** column, and then on the **Home tab**, in the **Sort & Filter group**, click **Ascending**.

10. Click the **DeptID arrow**, and then in the Filter list, clear the **(Select All)** check box. Select the **HR** check box, click **OK**, and then compare your screen with **Figure 2**.

Figure 2

■ Continue to the next page to complete this Skills Review

11. On the **Home tab**, in the **Text Formatting group**, change the font size to **10** and the font to **Verdana**.

12. In the **Text Formatting group**, click the **Datasheet Formatting Dialog Box Launcher**, and then in the dialog box, select the **Raised** cell effect. Click the **Background Color arrow**, and then click **Automatic**. Click the **Gridline Color arrow**, and then click the fifth color—**Blue, Accent 1**. Click **OK** to close the dialog box.

13. On the **File tab**, click **Print**, and then click **Print Preview**. In the **Page Layout group**, click **Landscape**. If you are printing this project, click **Print**. Otherwise, click the **Close Print Preview** button. **Save**, and then close the table.

14. On the **Create tab**, in the **Tables group**, click the **Table Design** button. Name the first field DeptID and then press Enter to assign the **Short Text** data type. On the **Design tab**, in the **Tools group**, click **Primary Key**.

15. With the **DeptID** field still selected, in the **Field Properties** pane, change the **Field Size** value to 50 and the **Caption** to Department ID

16. Add a second field named Department with the **Short Text** data type.

17. Click **Save**, type Departments and then click **OK**.

18. Click the **View** button to switch to **Datasheet view**, and then add the following departments:

Department ID	Department
BG	Buildings and Grounds
CD	Community Development
CI	Capital Improvement
F2	Fire
HR	Human Resources
PR	Parks and Recreation

19. Set the column width to **Best Fit**, and then compare your screen with Figure 3.

20. **Save**, and then close the table. On the **Database Tools tab**, click the **Relationships** button. In the **Show Table** dialog box, add **Employees**, add **Departments**, and then click **Close**.

21. Drag the **DeptID** field from the **Employees** table, point to **DeptID** in the **Departments** table, and then release the left mouse button.

22. In the **Edit Relationships** dialog box, select the **Enforce Referential Integrity** check box, and then click **Create**. If you receive a message, open the Departments table and carefully check your typing.

Figure 3

Figure 4

23. In the **Tools group**, click **Relationship Report**. Compare your screen with Figure 4. If you are printing this project, print the report.

24. Click **Save**, click **OK** to accept default name, and then close the report.

25. **Save** and **Close** all open objects, and then **Close** the Access window. Submit your printouts or database files as directed by your instructor.

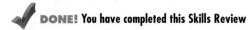 **DONE! You have completed this Skills Review**

Skills Assessment 1

To complete this database, you will need the following file:

- acc01_SA1UtilityData

You will save your database as:

- Last_First_acc01_SA1Utilities

1. Create a blank desktop database. Name the file Last_First_acc01_SA1Utilities and save it in your chapter folder.

2. In **Table1**, rename the **ID** field BillingID In the second column, add a **Short Text** field named AccountNumber

3. In the third column, add a **Date & Time** field with the name BillingDate In the fourth column, add a **Currency** field with the name Charge and then save the table as Billings **Close** the table.

4. Import the records in the **Electricity** worksheet from the student data file **acc01_SA1UtilityData**. Append the records to the **Billings** table.

5. Sort the **Billings** datasheet by the **Charge** column in descending order, and then filter the datasheet to display only the records from **Account Number** 2610-408376.

6. Change the font to **Verdana**, the font size **10**, and then set column widths to **Best Fit**.

7. Change the cell effect to **Raised**, the background color to **Automatic**, and the gridline color to **Blue-Gray**, **Text 2**. Compare your screen with **Figure 1**.

8. If you are printing this project, print the datasheet in landscape orientation. **Save** and then close the table.

9. Create a new table in Design view. Name the first field AccountNumber Set the field as the table's primary key, assign the **Short Text** data type, and set its caption to Account Number

10. Save the table as Residents and then switch to **Datasheet view**. In the second and third columns, add the **Name** Quick Start fields. In the fourth column, add a **Short Text** field named Street

11. Add the following records to the table:

Account Number	Last Name	First Name	Street
1673-467266	Alloway	Dorris	56553 S Paddington Way
2610-408376	Klasen	Franklin	99721 E Powder River Dr

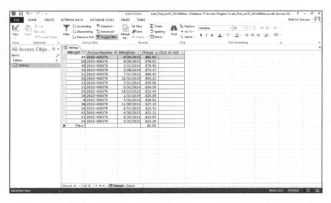

Figure 1

Figure 2

Account Number	Last Name	First Name	Street
2790-748496	Cavagnaro	Crystle	72343 N Riverford Pl
3794-907351	Carie	Ryann	45340 N Gurdon Dr

12. Set the column widths to **Best Fit**, and then compare your screen with **Figure 2**. **Save** and close the table.

13. Add the **Billings** and then the **Residents** table to the **Relationships** tab. Create a one-to-many relationship using the **AccountNumber** field as the common field. Do not select the cascading update or delete options.

14. Create a relationship report. **Save** the report using the name suggested in the **Save As** dialog box. **Close** the report. **Save** and **Close** the **Relationships** tab.

15. **Close** the Access window. Submit your work as directed by your instructor.

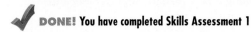 **DONE! You have completed Skills Assessment 1**

Skills Assessment 2

To complete this database, you will need the following file:

- acc01_SA2ClassData

You will save your database as:

- Last_First_acc01_SA2Interns

Figure 1

1. Create a blank desktop database. Name the file Last_First_acc01_SA2Interns and save it in your chapter folder.

2. In **Table1**, rename the **ID** field as InternID and then change its data type to **Number**. In the second and third columns, add the **Name** Quick Start fields. In the fourth column, add a **Short Text** field with the name Phone

3. Add the following records to the table:

Intern ID	Last Name	First Name	Phone
1	Yerigan	Kenton	(805) 555-7928
2	Mostowy	Clarice	(805) 555-3107
3	Hemstreet	Caroline	(805) 555-5548
4	Marcantel	Almeda	(805) 555-7000
5	Shriver	Cheyenne	(805) 555-6991

4. Set the column widths to **Best Fit**, and then **Save** the table as Interns Compare your screen with **Figure 1**, and then **Save** and close the table.

5. Create a new table in **Design view**. Name the first field ClassID Set the field as the table's primary key, assign the **AutoNumber** data type, and set its caption to Class ID

6. Add a **Short Text** field named Class as the second field. As the third field, add a **Date/Time** field name StartDate and set its caption to Start Date

7. In the fourth row, add a **Number** data type named InternID and set its caption to Intern ID Save the table as Sections and then close the table.

8. Add both tables to the **Relationships** tab. Create a one-to-many relationship using the **InternID** field as the common field. Do not select the cascading update or delete options.

9. Create a relationship report. **Save** the report using the name suggested in the **Save As** dialog box. **Close** the report. **Save** and then **Close** the Relationships tab.

Figure 2

10. Import the records in the **Sections** worksheet from the Excel student data file **acc01_SA2ClassData**. Append the records to the **Sections** table.

11. Sort the **Sections** datasheet by the **InternID** column in ascending order, and then filter the datasheet to display only the records for the **Introduction to Windows** class.

12. Change the font to **Cambria**, the font size to **12**, and then set column widths to **Best Fit**.

13. Change the cell effect to **Raised**, the background color to **Automatic**, and the gridline color to **Blue-Gray**, **Text 2**. Compare your screen with **Figure 2**.

14. If you are printing this project, print the datasheet in landscape orientation. **Save** and then close the table. **Close** Access.

 DONE! You have completed Skills Assessment 2

Visual Skills Check

To complete this database, you will need the following file:

- acc01_VSAssessments

You will save your database as:

- Last_First_acc01_VSAssessments

Open the student data file **acc01_VSAssessments**. On the **File tab**, click **Save As**, and then under **Save Database As**, click **Save As**. Use the **Save As** dialog box to save the file in your chapter folder with the name Last_First_acc01_VSAssessments Sort, filter, and format the **Assessments** table datasheet as shown in **Figure 1**. The table is sorted by the **Parcel** column and filtered by the **AssessorID** column. The font is **Verdana** size **10**, the columns are set to **Best Fit**, and the row height is **15**. The cell effect is **Raised**, the background color is **Automatic**, and the gridline color is **Blue, Accent 1, Darker 50%**.

Print the table in landscape orientation or submit the database file as directed by your instructor.

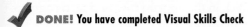 **DONE! You have completed Visual Skills Check**

AssessmentID	Year	Parcel	Valuation	AssessorID	Millage	Tax	Click to Add
1068	2010	1074.73862	$661,396.00	2	0.01264	$8,360.05	
1001	2009	1074.73862	$635,958.00	2	0.01206	$7,669.65	
1263	2014	1107.92107	$196,639.00	2	0.00982	$1,930.99	
1071	2010	1185.79277	$147,830.00	2	0.01264	$1,868.57	
1015	2009	1425.83907	$108,930.00	2	0.01206	$1,313.70	
1123	2011	1425.83907	$106,751.00	2	0.01256	$1,340.79	
1237	2014	1436.87414	$224,278.00	2	0.00982	$2,202.41	
1260	2014	1456.34750	$188,338.00	2	0.00982	$1,849.48	
1113	2011	1535.95379	$1,382,544.00	2	0.01256	$17,364.75	
1072	2010	1566.97107	$105,409.00	2	0.01264	$1,332.37	
1086	2010	1596.79257	$160,074.00	2	0.01264	$2,023.34	
1170	2012	1596.79257	$166,525.00	2	0.01188	$1,978.32	
1141	2012	1624.82671	$103,785.00	2	0.01188	$1,232.97	
1256	2014	1647.42795	$686,674.00	2	0.00982	$6,743.14	
1026	2009	1733.74385	$109,472.00	2	0.01206	$1,320.23	
1054	2010	1779.97568	$393,439.00	2	0.01264	$4,973.07	
1077	2010	1830.45633	$140,778.00	2	0.01264	$1,779.43	
1094	2011	1830.45633	$150,633.00	2	0.01256	$1,891.95	
1091	2011	1878.99577	$154,065.00	2	0.01256	$1,935.06	

Figure 1

My Skills

To complete this database, you will need the following file:

- acc01_MYAddresses

You will save your database as:

- Last_First_acc01_MYContacts

Figure 1

Figure 2

1. Create a blank desktop database. Name the file Last_First_acc01_MYContacts and save it in your chapter folder.

2. In **Table1**, rename the **ID** field as ContactID and add a caption of Contact ID

3. In columns two and three, add the Quick Start **Name** fields.

4. In columns four through eight, add the Quick Start **Address** fields.

5. In columns nine through twelve, add the Quick Start **Phone** fields.

6. With the **Fax Number** column selected, on the **Fields tab**, in the **Add & Delete group**, click the **Delete** button. Repeat this technique to delete the **Business Phone** field.

7. Save the table as Contacts and then set the column widths to **Best Fit**. Compare your screen with Figure 1.

8. Complete the first record by inserting your own contact information, and then save and close the table.

9. Import the contacts from the Excel student data file **acc01_MYAddresses**. Use the Addresses worksheet and append the data to the **Contacts** table.

10. Change the font to **Verdana**, and the font size **10**.

11. In the **Navigation Pane**, click the **Shutter Bar Open/Close Button** to close the pane. Set the column widths to **Best Fit**.

12. Change the cell effect to **Raised**, the background color to **Automatic**, and the gridline color to **Blue-Gray**, **Text 2**.

13. Select the **Contact ID** column, and then on the **Home tab**, in the **Records group**, click **More**, and then click **Hide Fields**. **Save** the table changes.

14. Click the **Shutter Bar Open/Close Button** one time to display the Navigation Pane. Click in the append row, and then compare your screen with Figure 2.

15. If you are printing this project, print the datasheet in landscape orientation. **Save** and then close the table.

16. Close the Access window. Submit your work as directed by your instructor.

 DONE! You have completed My Skills

Skills Challenge 1

To complete this database, you will need the following file:

- acc01_SC1ZonesData

You will save your files as:

- Last_First_acc01_SC1ZonesData (Excel)
- Last_First_acc01_SC1Zones (Access)

Open the student data file **acc01_SC1ZonesData** in Excel, and then save it in your chapter folder as Last_First_acc01_SC1ZonesData View the data stored in the spreadsheet, which describes the zones used in Aspen Falls. Label each column with a label that describes the column and can be used as database field names, and then close the spreadsheet.

Create a new database named Last_First_acc01_SC1Zones and save it in your chapter folder. Create a table to store the data in the Excel spreadsheet. Assign field names, data types, and

captions using the practices in this chapter's projects. Assign a primary key to the field that will uniquely identify each record. Name the table Zones and then import the Excel data into the table you just created. Set the field widths to Best Fit, and then close the table.

Print the table datasheet in landscape orientation or submit the database and spreadsheet files as directed by your instructor.

 DONE! You have completed Skills Challenge 1

Skills Challenge 2

To complete this database, you will need the following file:

- acc01_SC2Plants

You will save your database as:

- Last_First_acc01_SC2Plants

Open the student data file **acc01_SC2Plants**. On the **File tab**, click **Save As**, and then under **Save Database As**, click **Save As**. Use the **Save As** dialog box to save the file in your chapter folder with the name Last_First_acc01_SC2Plants View the **Relationships** tab, and notice that each plant is assigned a scientific name but the plant may have many common names—a one-to-many relationship. Open the **Plants** table and then expand the subdatasheet for *Asarum caudatum* to display three of its common names. Use the subdatasheets for

the other nine plants to enter the common names for each. To locate the common names, search the Internet using the plant's scientific name as the key term. For each plant, enter between one and three common names based on the information you find.

Submit your work as directed by your instructor.

 DONE! You have completed Skills Challenge 2

CHAPTER 2

Create Select Queries

- Databases typically store thousands of records in multiple, related tables. Queries answer questions about the data stored in tables by selecting and presenting the records and fields with the information you need.

- In a query, you select the fields with the data you want, and then add criteria that filter the records.

- Criteria test to see if conditions are true or false, and then select only those records in which the result of those tests are true.

- When you run a select query, a datasheet is created with just the records and fields you selected. The data in the underlying tables is not changed or deleted.

- You can create new fields by calculating values derived from existing fields. These types of fields can be added to both tables and queries.

- Query results can also be grouped by one or more fields so that statistics such as totals and averages for each group can be calculated.

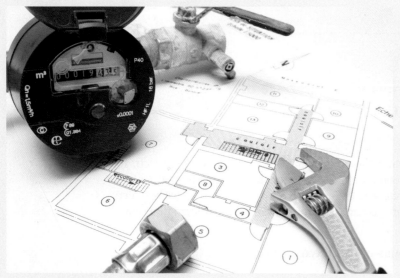

© John Leee / Fotolia

Aspen Falls City Hall

In this chapter, you will create database queries for Aspen Falls City Hall, which provides essential services for the citizens and visitors of Aspen Falls, California. In this project, you will assist Diane Payne, Public Works Director, to answer several questions about the Water Utility monthly billing cycles.

For each monthly billing cycle, the Public Works Department needs to calculate charges—an amount that is derived from each resident's water usage and that month's rate for water. As payments are recorded in the database, the amount due should be automatically adjusted. You will complete both of these tasks by adding calculated fields to a table.

The Public Works Department needs to find records for specific residents by searching for their account number, name, or meter number. You will create select queries that can perform these searches. The department also needs to know which residents are late in their payments and add a late fee when appropriate. To do this, you will add a calculated field to a query.

Finally, the city needs to analyze water usage statistics. To do this, you will add grouping to a query, and then provide summary statistics such as count, average, and total. Throughout the project, you will test your queries using a small sample of the city database used to track resident utility bills.

Time to complete all 10 skills – 60 to 90 minutes

Student data file needed for this chapter:

acc02_Water

You will save your files as:

Last_First_acc02_Water

Outcome

Using the skills in this chapter, you will be able to work with Access queries like this:

Billing Date	Billing Count	Average Usage	Total Billing	Total Due
31-Jan-13	50	67.7	$778.09	($18.27)
28-Feb-13	55	68.4	$865.72	$0.00
31-Mar-13	60	78.8	$1,069.96	($1.00)
30-Apr-13	65	76.9	$1,149.54	$51.18
31-May-13	69	89.4	$1,541.50	$0.00
30-Jun-13	71	113.0	$2,006.00	$24.75
31-Jul-13	74	126.7	$2,312.25	$0.45
31-Aug-13	79	126.7	$2,702.43	$87.21
30-Sep-13	80	128.1	$2,743.20	$55.58
31-Oct-13	82	112.7	$2,279.00	$73.00
30-Nov-13	84	83.9	$1,761.00	$8.00
31-Dec-13	83	61.3	$1,170.24	$17.02
31-Jan-14	84	46.8	$903.67	$0.00
28-Feb-14	83	37.8	$753.60	$2.94
31-Mar-14	83	50.1	$1,039.75	$18.75
30-Apr-14	83	53.3	$1,312.22	($17.08)
31-May-14	82	73.7	$1,993.20	($32.01)
30-Jun-14	80	94.4	$2,643.90	$6.30
31-Jul-14	80	138.1	$4,199.38	$4,199.38

Statistics

SKILLS

MyITLab®
Skills 1-10 Training

At the end of this chapter you will be able to

Skill 1 Create Queries with the Simple Query Wizard
Skill 2 Add Text Criteria
Skill 3 Add Calculated Fields to Tables
Skill 4 Create Queries in Design View
Skill 5 Add Comparison Operators
Skill 6 Add Date and Time Criteria
Skill 7 Group and Total Queries
Skill 8 Add Calculated Fields to Queries
Skill 9 Work with Logical Operators
Skill 10 Add Wildcards to Query Criteria

MORE SKILLS

Skill 11 Export Queries to Excel
Skill 12 Export Queries as Web Pages
Skill 13 Link to External Data Sources
Skill 14 Create Crosstab Queries

ACC 2-1
VIDEO

▶ *Queries* are used to ask questions about—query—the data stored in database tables. *Select queries* select and display the records that answer the question without having to change the data in the underlying table or tables.

1. Start **Access 2013**. On the **Recent** page, click **Open Other Files**. On the **Open** page, click **Computer**, and then click **Browse**. In the **Open** dialog box, navigate to the student data files for this chapter, select **acc02_Water**, and then click the **Open** button.

2. On the **File tab**, click **Save As**. With **Save Database As** selected, click the **Save As** button. In the **Save As** dialog box, navigate to the location you are saving your files for this project. Click **New folder**, type Access Chapter 2 and then press ⏎Enter two times. Name the file Last_First_acc02_Water Compare your screen with **Figure 1**, and then click **Save**.

3. If the security warning message displays, click Enable Content.

4. In the **Navigation Pane**, under **Tables**, select **Residents**.

5. Click the **Create tab**, and then in the **Queries group**, click the **Query Wizard** button. In the **New Query** dialog box, with **Simple Query Wizard** selected, click **OK** to start the Simple Query Wizard. Compare your screen with **Figure 2**.

The Simple Query Wizard's first screen is used to select the fields you want to display as columns in the query result. You can choose fields from any table or query, but they should be from tables that are related. Including unrelated tables will result in too many records in the query results.

■ **Continue to the next page to complete the skill** ➔

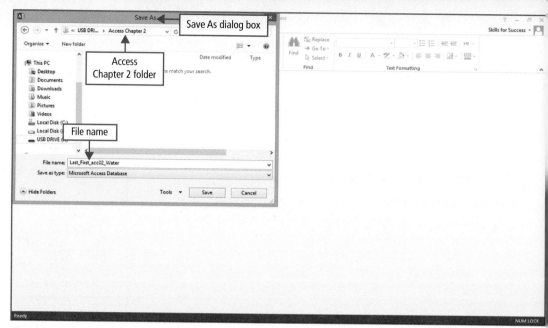

Figure 1

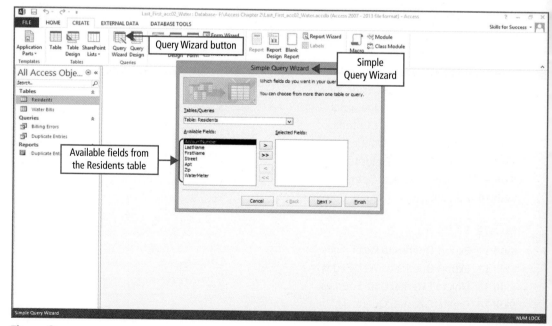

Figure 2

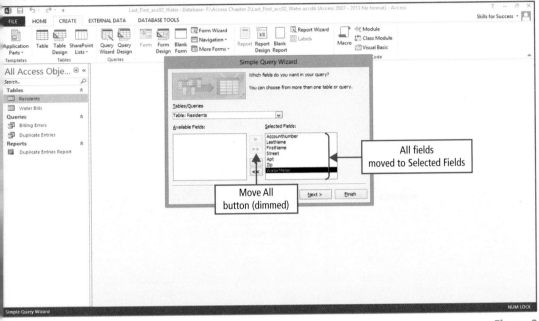

Figure 3

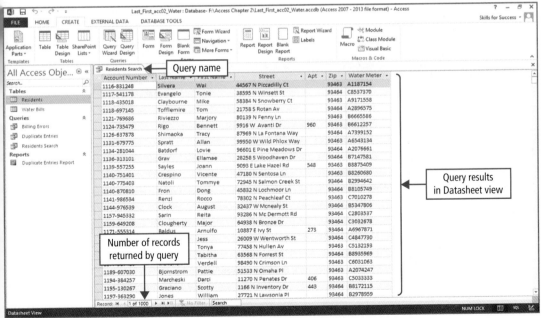

Figure 4

6. Click the **Move** button [>] one time, to move the **AccountNumber** field into Selected Fields.

7. Click the **Move All** button [>>] to move all the table's fields into Selected Fields. Compare your screen with **Figure 3**, and then click **Next**.

8. In the **What title do you want for your query** box, replace the existing text—*Residents Query*—with Residents Search

    In the last screen of the Simple Query Wizard, you type the name that will be given to the query and choose to either run the query or open it in Design view.

9. Click **Finish**, and then compare your screen with **Figure 4**.

    In this manner, the Simple Query Wizard quickly adds fields to a new query. When the query is run, the results display in Datasheet view. Here, all the records and fields from the Residents table have been selected and display.

10. Leave the query open for the next skill.

■ **You have completed Skill 1 of 10**

▶ **Criteria** are conditions in a query used to select the records that answer the query's question.

1. With the **Residents Search** query open in **Datasheet view**, click the **Home tab**. In the **Views group**, click the **View** button to switch to **Design view**. Alternately, in the lower right corner of the window, click the Design View button ▨. Compare your screen with **Figure 1**.

   Query Design view has two panes. The **query design workspace** displays the tables that the query will search. The **query design grid** displays the fields the query will display and the query settings that will be applied to each field.

2. If the table name—*Residents*—does not display under each field name in the design grid, on the Design tab, in the Show/Hide group, click Table Names so that it is selected.

3. In the intersection of the **LastName** column and **Criteria** row—the **LastName** column **Criteria** cell—type the letter h and then compare your screen with **Figure 2**.

   As you type in a criteria cell, **IntelliSense**—Quick Info, ToolTips, and AutoComplete boxes—displays guidelines for the feature you are typing. **AutoComplete** is a menu of commands that match the characters you type. The **Quick Info** message explains the purpose of the selected AutoComplete command.

■ **Continue to the next page to complete the skill** ➡

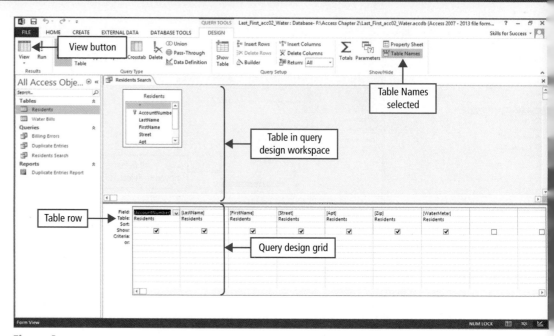

Figure 1

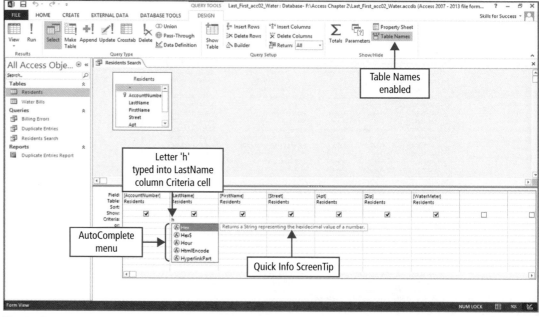

Figure 2

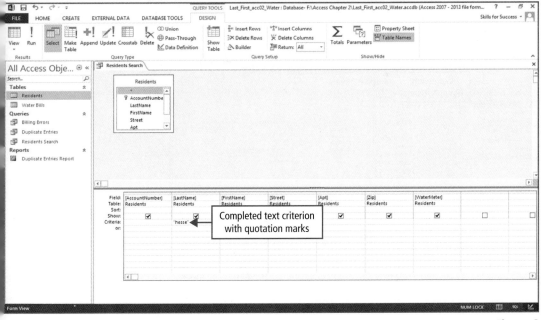

Figure 3

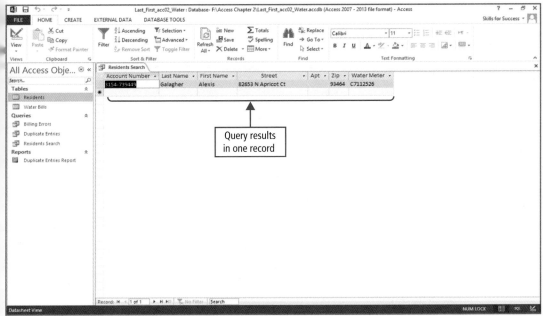

Figure 4

4. In the **LastName** column **Criteria** cell, complete the entry hesse Press `Tab`, and then compare your screen with **Figure 3**.

> Criteria that contain text must be surrounded by quotation marks. If you do not type the quotation marks, they will be automatically inserted before the query is run.

5. On the **Design tab**, in the **Results group**, click the **Run** button to display the three records that result.

> In this manner, criteria filters the data. Here, the query answers the question, *Which residents have a last name of Hesse?* By default, criteria are not case sensitive. Here, the criterion *hesse* matched the value *Hesse*.

6. On the **Home tab**, in the **Views group**, click the **View** button, to return to Design view.

7. In the **LastName** column **Criteria** cell, delete the quotation marks and text *"hesse"*.

8. In the **WaterMeter** column **Criteria** cell, type the quotation marks and text *"C7112526"*

> When you include the quotation marks around criteria, the AutoComplete and Quick Info messages do not display.

9. On the **Design tab**, in the **Results group**, click the **Run** button, and then compare your screen with **Figure 4**.

> The query answers the following question, *Who owns meter C7112526 and what is the address?*

10. If you are printing your work for this project, print the datasheet in landscape orientation.

11. Click **Save** 💾, and then **Close** ✖ the query.

■ **You have completed Skill 2 of 10**

▶ A ***calculated field*** is a field in a table or query that derives its values from other fields in the table or query.

1. In the **Navigation Pane**, under **Tables**, double-click **Water Bills** to open the datasheet.

2. Click anywhere in the **Usage** column to make it the active column.

3. Click the **Fields tab**, and then in the **Add & Delete group**, click **More Fields**. Near the bottom of the field list, point to **Calculated Field**, and then in the submenu that displays, click **Currency**.

4. In the **Expression Builder** dialog box, under **Expression Categories**, double-click **Rate** to insert it into the expression.

   An ***expression*** is a combination of fields, mathematical operators, and pre-built functions that calculates values in tables, forms, queries, and reports. In expressions, field names are enclosed between left and right square brackets.

5. Under **Expression Elements** click **Operators**, and then under **Expression Categories**, click **Arithmetic**.

6. Under **Expression Values**, double-click the multiplication operator—the asterisk (*)—to insert it into the expression.

7. Under **Expression Elements**, click **Water Bills**, and then under **Expression Categories**, double-click **Usage**.

8. Compare your screen with **Figure 1**, and then click **OK**.

9. In the datasheet, with the text *Field1* still selected, type Billing Press ⎯Tab⎯, and then compare your screen with **Figure 2**.

   The Billings column displays the result of multiplying each record's Rate by its Usage.

■ **Continue to the next page to complete the skill**

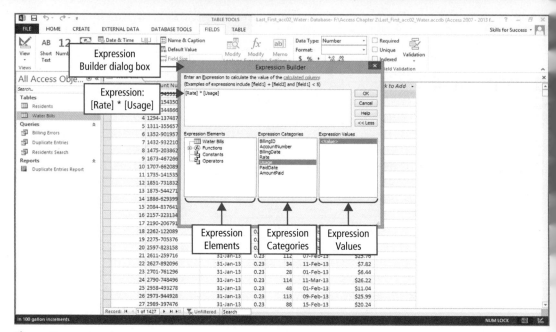

Figure 1

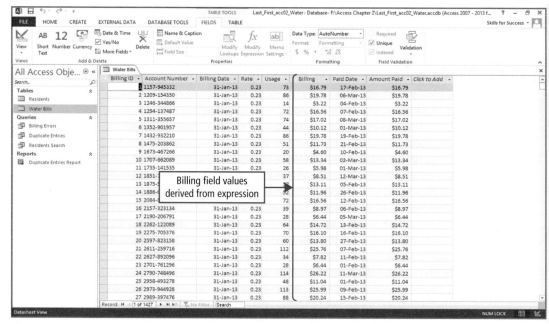

Figure 2

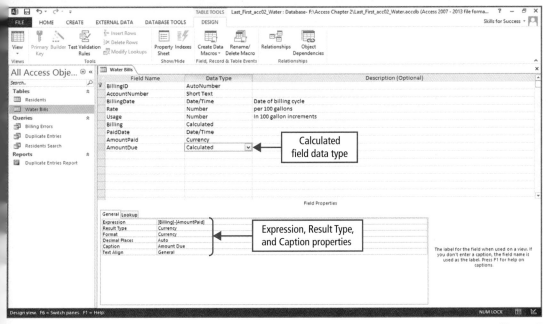

Calculated field data type

Expression, Result Type, and Caption properties

Figure 3

10. Click **Save** 🖫. On the **Home tab**, in the **Views group**, click **View** to switch to **Design view**.

11. In the **Field Name** column, click in the first empty cell, and then type AmountDue In the same row, display and click the **Data Type arrow**, and then click **Calculated** to open the Expression Builder.

12. In the **Expression Builder**, repeat the technique just practiced or type the following expression: [Billing] - [AmountPaid] and then click **OK**.

13. With the **AmountDue** field still active, in the **Field Properties** pane, click **Result Type**, click the **Result Type arrow**, and then click **Currency**.

A calculated field can be assigned any of the data types other fields are assigned. Here, the Currency data type is the most appropriate data type.

14. In the **Field Properties** pane, click in the **Caption** cell, and then type Amount Due Compare your screen with **Figure 3**.

15. Click **Save** 🖫, and then switch to Datasheet view. Set the **Amount Due** column width to **Best Fit**, and then compare your screen with **Figure 4**.

It is best practice to exclude spaces from field names. Labels, however, can display spaces. Here, the *Amount Due* caption displays at the top of the last column instead of the field name—*AmountDue*.

16. Click **Save** 🖫, and then **Close** ✕ the table.

■ **You have completed Skill 3 of 10**

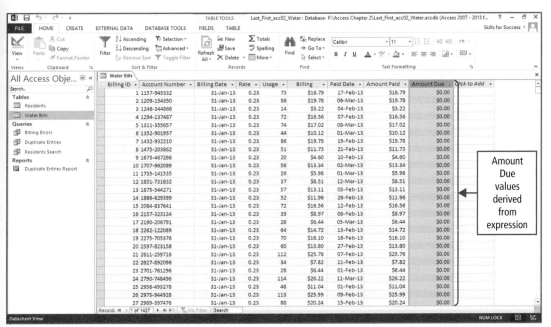

Amount Due values derived from expression

Figure 4

▶ To create a query in Design view, you first add the tables you will need to the query design workspace. You then add the fields you want to use to the design grid.

1. Click the **Create tab**, and then in the **Queries group**, click the **Query Design** button.

2. In the **Show Table** dialog box, double-click **Residents** to add the table to the query design workspace. Alternately, select the table in the dialog box, and then click the Add button.

3. Repeat the technique just practiced to add the **Water Bills** table. Compare your screen with **Figure 1**.

   Tables can be added to the query design workspace using the Show Table dialog box or by dragging them from the Navigation Pane.

4. **Close** the **Show Table** dialog box, and then compare your screen with **Figure 2**.

   This query needs to answer these questions: *What are the names of the customers that have an overdue balance, what are those balances, and from what time periods?* To answer these questions, fields from two tables are needed.

   When a query selects fields from multiple tables, the tables need to be related. By default, queries follow the relationship rules defined in the Relationships tab. Here, the two tables are joined in a one-to-many relationship using AccountNumber as the common field. A resident can have many water billing cycles.

■ Continue to the next page to complete the skill ▶

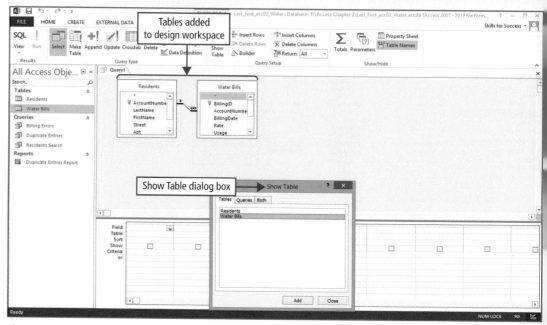

Figure 1

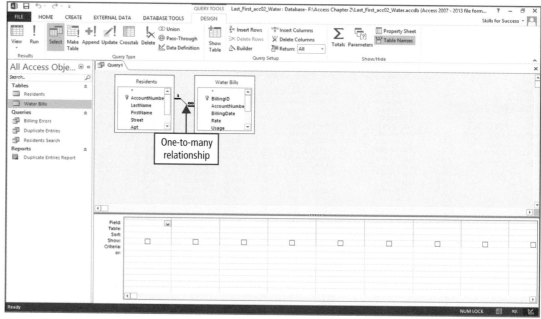

Figure 2

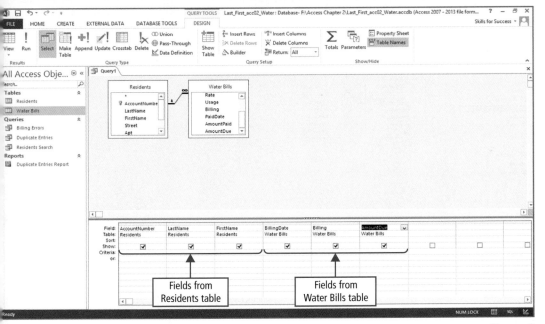

Fields from
Residents table

Fields from
Water Bills table

Figure 3

5. In the query design workspace, in the **Residents** table, double-click the **AccountNumber** field to add it to the first column of the design grid. Alternately, drag the field into the first column Field cell.

6. Repeat the technique just practiced to add the **LastName** and **FirstName** fields to the second and third column of the design grid.

7. Scroll down the **Water Bills** table list as needed and add the following fields in this order: **BillingDate**, **Billing**, and **AmountDue**. Compare your screen with **Figure 3**.

8. Click **Save** 🖫. In the **Save As** dialog box, type Late Billings and then press Enter.

9. On the **Design tab**, in the **Results group**, click **Run**. Compare your screen with **Figure 4**.

   Before adding criteria, it is a good idea to run the query to verify that it displays the fields you need. Here, you can see each billing cycle sorted by customer.

10. On the status bar, click the **Design View** button 🖾, and then leave the query open for the next skill.

■ **You have completed Skill 4 of 10**

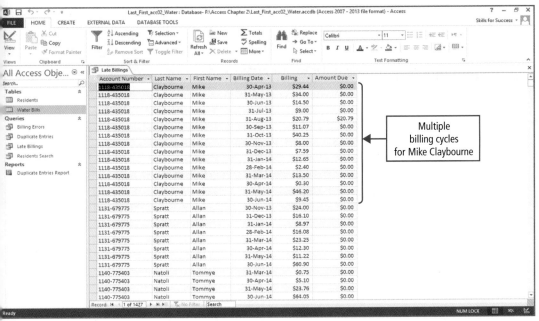

Multiple
billing cycles
for Mike Claybourne

Figure 4

▶ In query criteria, numbers are typically combined with ***comparison operators***—operators that compare two values including operators such as > (greater than) and < (less than).

1. If necessary, open the Late Billings query in Design view.

2. In the **Billing** column **Criteria** cell, type >80 Compare your screen with **Figure 1**.

3. On the **Design tab**, in the **Results group**, click the **Run** button to display the 15 records that answer the question, *Which billings are larger than 80?*

4. On the **Home tab**, click the **View** button to return to Design view.

5. In the **Billing** column **Criteria** cell, delete the criterion.

6. In the **Amount Due** column **Criteria** cell, type <0 and then **Run** the query to display the 12 records that answer the question: *Which customers have a negative balance?*

7. Switch to Design view. In the **Amount Due** column **Criteria** cell, replace the criteria with 0 **Run** the query to display the 1314 records that answer the question, *Which billings have a balance of zero?*

> When a value is to match exactly, simply type the value. The equals (=) operator is not needed. The commonly used comparison operators are summarized in the table in **Figure 2**.

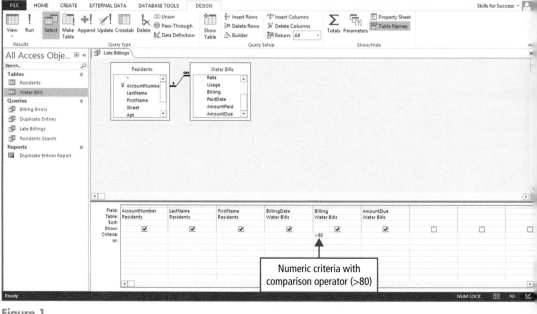

Numeric criteria with comparison operator (>80)

Figure 1

Common Comparison Operators

Operator	Purpose
=	Is true when the field's value is equal to the specified value
<>	Is true when the field's value does not equal the specified value
<	Is true when the field's value is less than the specified value
<=	Is true when the field's value is less than or equal to the specified value
>	Is true when the field's value is greater than the specified value
>=	Is true when the field's value is greater than or equal to the specified value

Figure 2

■ **Continue to the next page to complete the skill**

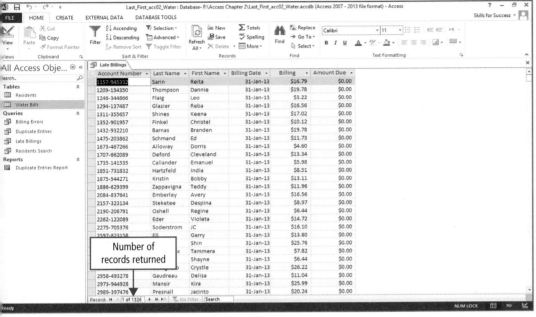

Number of records returned

Figure 3

8. Switch to Design view. In the **Amount Due** column **Criteria** cell, replace the criteria with <=0 **Run** the query, and then compare your screen with **Figure 3**.

 The query returns records for which the amount due is zero and the records for which the amount due is negative. In this manner, the <= operator returns records that are equal to or less than the number following the criterion.

9. Switch to Design view. In the **Amount Due** column **Criteria** cell, replace the criteria with >0 **Run** the query, and then scroll down the datasheet to view the last records in the results similar to **Figure 4**.

 The query answers the question, *Which billings have a balance due?* An additional criterion is needed to return only those records for which the amount due is late.

10. Click **Save** 🔲 and leave the query open for the next skill.

■ **You have completed Skill 5 of 10**

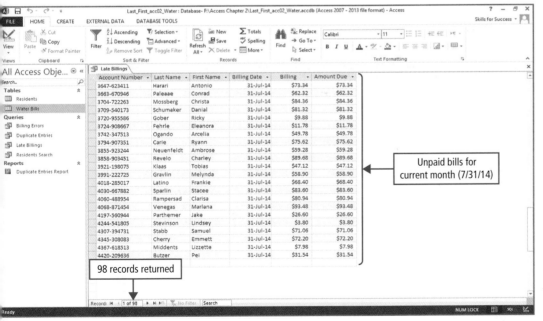

Unpaid bills for current month (7/31/14)

98 records returned

Figure 4

▶ In Access, dates and times are stored as numbers. The underlying numbers display as dates in database objects. For example, the number 37979 displays as *12/24/2003* if the Short Date format is assigned to the Date/Time field.

▶ When you add criteria to more than one query column, both criteria must be true if the record is to be included in the results.

1. With the **Late Billings** query open in Design view, click in the **BillingDate** column **Criteria** cell, and then type <7/1/2014 Press ⟦Tab⟧, and then compare your screen with **Figure 1**.

   Because all dates are stored as serial numbers, you can include arithmetic and comparison operators in your criteria.

   When dates are used as query criteria, they are enclosed in number signs (#). If you do not include them, they will be inserted when the query is run.

2. On the **Design tab**, in the **Results group**, click the **Run** button, and then compare your screen with **Figure 2**.

   This query answers the question, *Which billings before July 1, 2014 still have a balance due?* In this manner, both the billing date and amount due comparisons must be true for the record to be included in the query results.

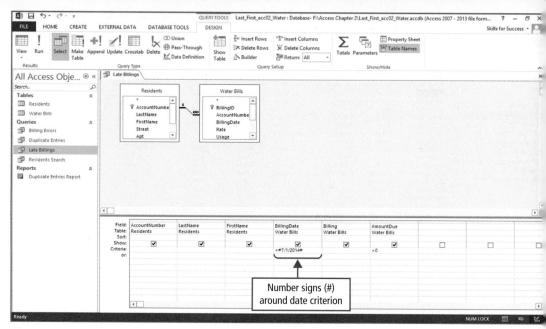

Figure 1

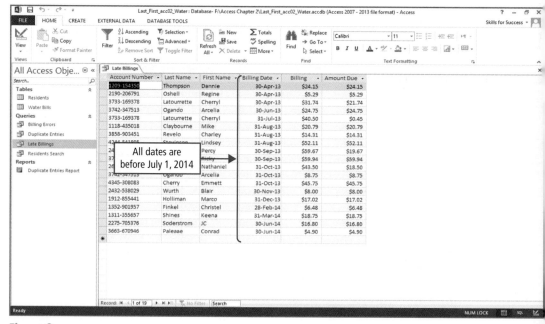

Figure 2

■ **Continue to the next page to complete the skill**

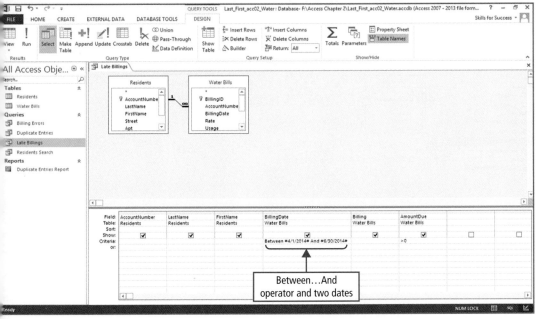

Between...And operator and two dates

Figure 3

Overdue bills between 4/1/2014 and 6/30/2014

Figure 4

3. Switch to Design view. In the **BillingDate** column **Criteria** cell, replace the criteria with >=4/1/2014 **Run** the query to display the 81 billing cycles with balances due that occurred on or after April 1, 2014.

4. Switch to Design view. In the **BillingDate** column **Criteria** cell, replace the existing criterion with Between 4/1/2014 And 6/30/2014

5. Click an empty cell, and then with the ⊞ pointer, increase the width of the **BillingDate** column to display all its criteria, and then compare your screen with **Figure 3**.

> The **Between...And operator** is a comparison operator that finds all numbers or dates between and including two values. Here, the billing cycle must be between April 1 and June 30, 2014, to display in the query.

> When you widen a query column in the design grid, the column will return to its original width when the query is closed.

6. **Run** the query, and then compare your screen with **Figure 4**.

> The query answers the question, *Which billings from the second quarter of 2014 have a balance due?*

7. Click **Save** 🔲. If you are printing this project, print the datasheet in Landscape view. **Close** ☒ the query.

■ **You have completed Skill 6 of 10**

▶ The Total row is added to queries when you need **summary statistics**—calculations for groups of data such as totals, averages, or counts.

1. On the **Create tab**, in the **Queries group**, click the **Query Design** button. In the **Show Table** dialog box, add the **Water Bills** table, and then **Close** the dialog box.

2. On the **Design tab**, in the **Show/Hide group**, click **Totals**. Add **BillingDate** to the first column, and then compare your screen with **Figure 1**.

> The Total row is used to determine how queries should be grouped and summarized. By default, each column is set to Group By. The **Group By** operator designates which query column contains the group of values to summarize as a single record, one for each set. Here, totals will be calculated for each month.

3. In the **Water Bills** list of fields, double-click **BillingDate** to add the field to the second column. Click the **BillingDate** column **Total** cell to display its arrow. Click the cell's **Total arrow**, and then from the menu, click **Count**.

> The **Count** operator calculates the number of records in each group. Here, the number of billings for each month will be calculated.

4. Repeat the technique just practiced to add the **Usage** field to the third column, and then change its **Total** cell value to **Avg**. Compare your screen with **Figure 2**.

> The **Avg** operator calculates the average of the values in each group.

■ **Continue to the next page to complete the skill**

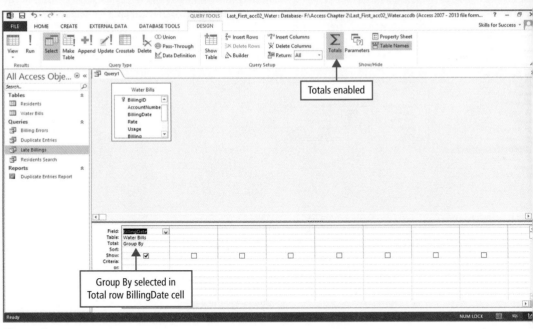

Figure 1

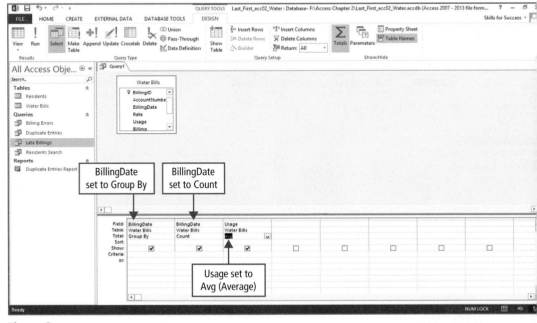

Figure 2

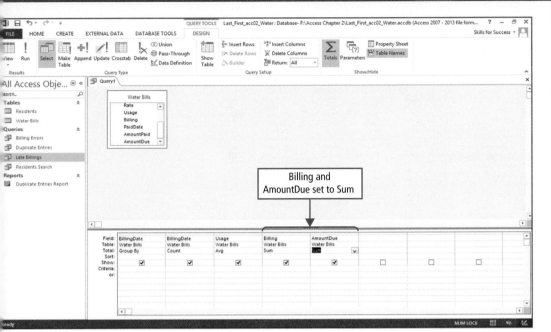

Billing and
AmountDue set to Sum

Figure 3

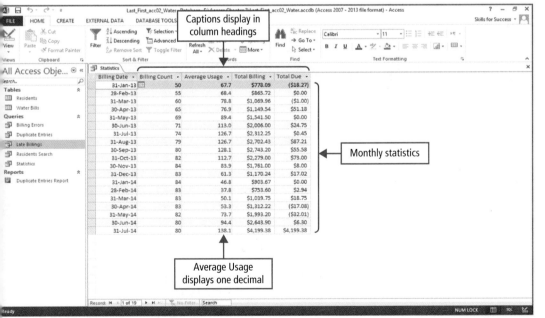

Captions display in
column headings

Monthly statistics

Average Usage
displays one decimal

Figure 4

5. Add the **Billing** and **AmountDue** fields, and set their **Total** cells to **Sum**. Compare your screen with **Figure 3**.

> The **Sum** operator calculates the total of the values in each group.

6. Save the query with the name Statistics and then **Run** the query to display the statistics for each month.

> Pound signs in a numeric field indicate that the values are too wide for the column. Here, some of the averages have too many decimals for the number to display in the given column width.

7. Switch to **Design view**. Click in the **Usage** column to make it active, and then on the **Design tab**, in the **Show/Hide group**, click **Property Sheet**.

8. In the property sheet, click **Format**, click the **Format arrow** that displays, and then click **Fixed**. Display and click the **Decimal Places arrow**, and then click **1**. Click in the **Caption** cell, and then type Average Usage

9. Repeat the technique just practiced to change the caption of the second **BillingDate** to Billing Count Change the **Billing** caption to Total Billing and the **AmountDue** caption to Total Due

10. **Close** ☒ the property sheet. **Run** the query, set the column widths to **Best Fit**, and then compare your screen with **Figure 4**.

> The captions that were set previously in the property sheet display in the datasheet header row.

11. **Save** 🖫 the query. If you are printing this project, print the datasheet in Landscape orientation.

12. **Close** ☒ the query.

■ **You have completed Skill 7 of 10**

▶ You can insert calculated fields into queries. In queries, calculated fields need an *alias*—a descriptive label used to identify a field in expressions, datasheets, forms, and reports.

1. Click the **Create tab**, and then in the **Queries group**, click the **Query Design** button. In the **Show Table** dialog box, add the **Residents** table, add the **Water Bills** table, and then **Close** the dialog box.

2. From the **Residents** table, add the **AccountNumber**, **LastName**, and **FirstName** fields to the design grid.

3. From the **Water Bills** table, add **BillingDate**, and then in the **BillingDate** column **Criteria** cell, type <4/1/14

4. From the **Water Bills** table, add **AmountDue**, and then in the **AmountDue** column **Criteria** cell, type >0 **Run** the query, and then compare your screen with **Figure 1**.

5. Click **Save** 🖫, and then in the **Save As** dialog box, type Late Fees and then click **OK**.

6. Switch to Design view. In the **AmountDue** column, clear the **Show** cell check box so that the column will not display in the datasheet.

7. With the I pointer, click in the first blank column **Field** row. On the **Design tab**, in the **Query Setup group**, click the **Builder** button.

8. In the **Expression Builder** dialog box, type the following expression: Penalty:[AmountDue]* 0.25 taking care to include the colon. Compare your screen with **Figure 2**.

The alias in a calculated field ends with a colon. Here, *Penalty* will be the alias.

■ **Continue to the next page to complete the skill**

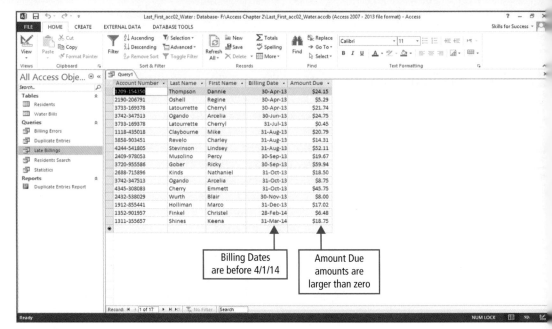

Figure 1

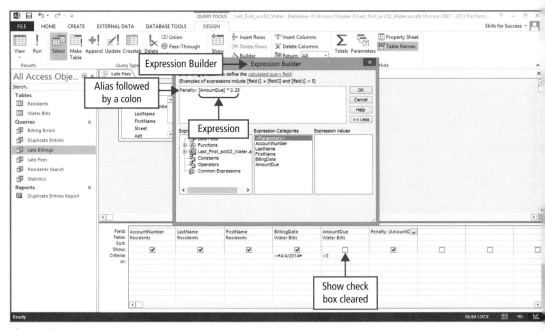

Figure 2

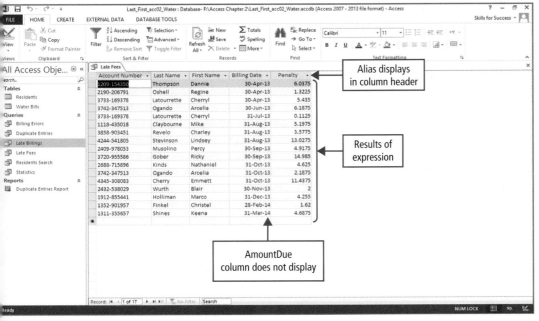

Figure 3

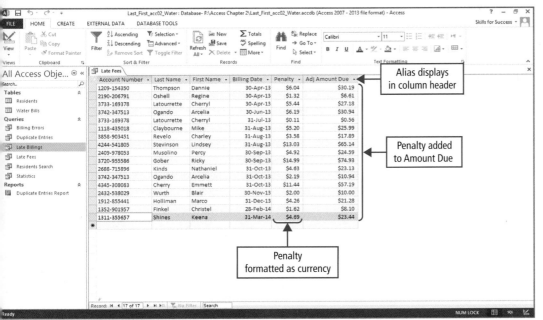

Figure 4

9. Click **OK** to close the Expression Builder and insert the expression.

10. **Run** the query, and then compare your screen with **Figure 3**. If the Enter Parameter dialog box displays, click Cancel, and then repeat steps 6 through 8 carefully checking your typing.

   In the last column, the alias *Penalty* displays in the header row. The result of the expression displays in each record. Here, a 25% penalty is derived by multiplying 0.25 by the amount due.

11. Click **Save** 🖫, and then switch to Design view. If necessary, click in the Penalty column to make it active.

12. Click the **Property Sheet** button to open it. In the property sheet, display and click the **Format arrow**, and then click **Currency**. **Close** ☒ the property sheet.

13. Click the first blank column **Field** cell, and then in the **Query Setup group**, click **Builder**.

14. In the **Expression Builder** dialog box, type the following alias and expression:
   Adj Amount Due: [AmountDue] + [Penalty]

   Because an alias represents a field name, when an alias is used in an expression, it is enclosed in square brackets. Here, the Penalty alias is used to add the penalty to the original amount due.

15. Click **OK**, and then **Run** the query. Set the column widths to **Best Fit**, and then compare your screen with **Figure 4**.

16. Click **Save** 🖫. If you are printing this project, print the datasheet in Landscape orientation.

17. **Close** ☒ the query.

■ **You have completed Skill 8 of 10**

▶ When criteria are in more than one column, the placement of the criteria in the design grid rows determines whether one or both of the criteria must be true for the record to display.

1. In the **Navigation Pane**, under **Queries**, right-click **Billing Errors**, and then from the shortcut menu, click **Design View**.

2. In the **Usage** column, click the **Sort** cell, click the **arrow** that displays, and then click **Ascending**.

3. **Run** the query, notice that the **Usage** values that are empty or negative are listed first.

4. Switch to Design view. In the **Usage** column **Criteria** cell, type Is Null Below the value just typed, in the **Usage** column or cell, type <0 Compare your screen with **Figure 1**.

   The **Is Null** and **Is Not Null** operators test if a field is empty or not empty.

5. **Run** the query to display only the records for which the **Usage** value is empty or less than 0.

6. **Save** 🖫, and then **Close** ✖ the query. In the **Navigation Pane**, right-click **Billing Errors**, and then click **Design View**. Compare your screen with **Figure 2**.

   When two criteria are placed in *different* rows in the design grid, the **Or logical operator**—a logical comparison of two criteria that is true if either of the criteria outcomes is true—applies. Because the two criteria in this query can be combined into a single row, they were automatically combined with the Or operator separating them.

■ Continue to the next page to complete the skill ▷

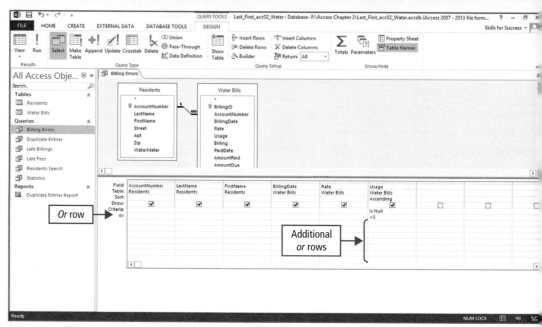

Figure 1

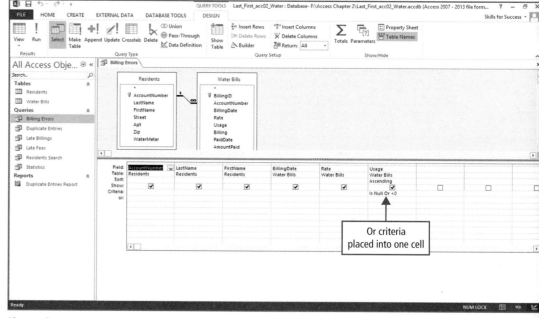

Figure 2

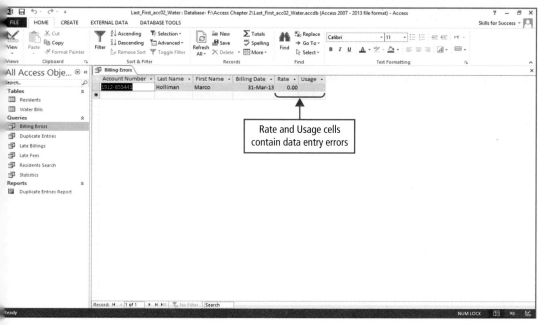

Figure 3

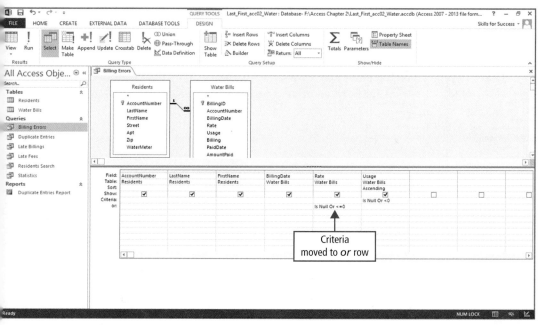

Figure 4

7. In the **Rate** column **Criteria** cell, type Is Null Or <=0

8. **Run** the query, and notice that both the **Usage** and **Rate** columns contain errant values—Rate should not be 0 and Usage should not be empty—as shown in **Figure 3**.

   When two criteria are placed in the same row, the **And logical operator**—a logical comparison of two criteria that is true only when both criteria outcomes are true—applies. Here, records are selected only where the Usage and Rate columns both have errors.

9. Switch to Design view. In the **Rate** column **Criteria** row, delete the criteria. In the **Rate** column **or** row (the row below the Criteria row), type Is Null Or <=0 and then compare your screen with **Figure 4**.

   Here, records are selected if either the Usage or Rate column have errors.

10. **Run** the query to display six records that match the criteria. If you are printing your work for this project, print the datasheet.

11. **Save** 🖫 and then **Close** ✖ the query.

- **You have completed Skill 9 of 10**

▶ A **wildcard** is a special character, such as an asterisk, used in query criteria to allow matches for any combination of letters or characters.

▶ Using wildcards, you can expand your search criteria to find a more accurate subset of the data.

1. In the **Navigation Pane**, under **Queries**, right-click **Duplicate Entries**, and then, from the shortcut menu, click **Design View**.

2. In the **LastName** column **Criteria** cell, type Jones In the **FirstName** column **Criteria** cell, type William and then **Run** the query to display the record for William Jones.

> William Jones reports that he receives three bills each month. However, with the current criteria, his record is listed one time.

3. Switch to Design view. In the **FirstName** column **Criteria** cell, replace the existing criterion with Will* **Run** the query, and then compare your screen with **Figure 1**.

> The **asterisk (*) wildcard** character matches any combination of characters. Here, the two first names begin with *Will* but end differently.

4. Switch to Design view, and then compare your screen with **Figure 2**.

> When you include wildcards, the criterion needs to start with the Like operator. If you don't type the Like operator, it will be inserted automatically when the query is run.

■ **Continue to the next page to complete the skill**

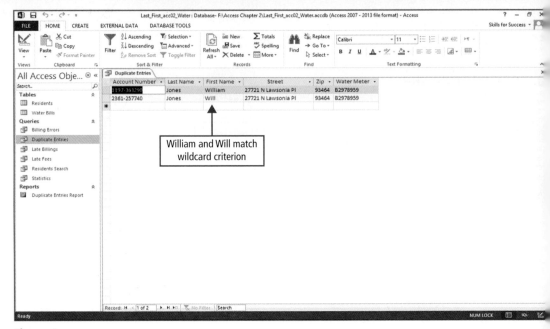

William and Will match wildcard criterion

Figure 1

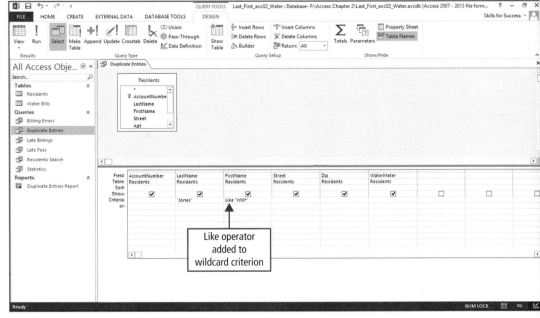

Like operator added to wildcard criterion

Figure 2

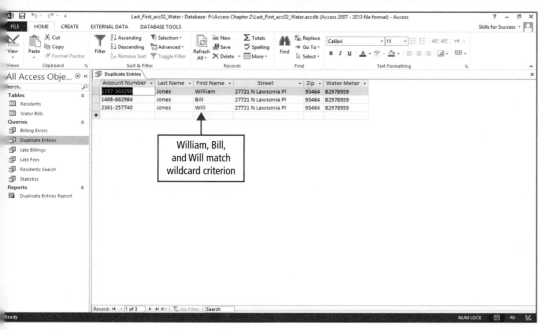

William, Bill, and Will match wildcard criterion

Figure 3

5. In the **FirstName** column **Criteria** cell, replace the existing criterion with Like "?ill*" **Run** the query to display the three duplicate records for William Jones. Compare your screen with **Figure 3**.

The **question mark (?) wildcard** character matches any single character. Common wildcard characters supported by Access are summarized in the table in **Figure 4**.

6. Save 💾, and then **Close** ❌ the query.

7. In the **Navigation Pane**, under **Reports**, double-click **Duplicate Entries Report**. If you are printing this project, print the report.

Recall that reports are often used to display the results of queries. Here, the report displays the results of the Duplicate Entries query.

8. **Close** ❌ the report.

Because you did not make any design changes to the report, you do not need to save it.

9. **Close** ❌ Access. Submit your printouts or database file as directed by your instructor.

DONE! You have completed Skill 10 of 10, and your database is complete!

Common Access Wildcard Characters		
Character	**Description**	**Example**
*	Matches any number of characters.	Don* matches Don and Donna, but not Adonna.
?	Matches any single alphabetic character.	D?n matches Don and Dan, but not Dean.
[ ]	Matches any single character in the brackets.	D[ao]n matches Don and Dan, but not Den.
#	Matches any single numeric character.	C-#PO matches C-3PO, but not C-DPO.

Figure 4

More Skills

The following More Skills are located at **www.pearsonhighered.com/skills**

More Skills Export Queries to Excel

There are times when you need to work with data in a table or query using another application. Access can export database tables and queries into several file formats that are used by other applications. For example, you can export a table to a Word document or an Excel spreadsheet.

In More Skills 11, you will export a query to an Excel spreadsheet and then open the query in Excel.

To begin, open your web browser, navigate to www.pearsonhighered.com/skills, locate the name of your textbook, and then follow the instructions on the website.

More Skills Export Queries as Web Pages

You can export queries as web pages so that they can be shared on the Internet. When published as a web page, anyone connected to the Internet can view the query results using a web browser.

In More Skills 12, you will export a query as a web page, and then open the web page in Internet Explorer.

To begin, open your web browser, navigate to www.pearsonhighered.com/skills, locate the name of your textbook, and then follow the instructions on the website.

More Skills Link to External Data Sources

You can link to data stored in other files. These files can be created in other applications such as Excel or Access. When you link to external data, you can include them in queries and reports. You cannot change any data, however, unless you open the external file.

In More Skills 13, you will link to an external Excel worksheet and an external Access table. You will open and view both tables

and join them in a relationship that does not enforce referential integrity.

To begin, open your web browser, navigate to www.pearsonhighered.com/skills, locate the name of your textbook, and then follow the instructions on the website.

More Skills 14 Create Crosstab Queries

The Crosstab Query Wizard creates a special query that calculates the results of two groupings. One group displays down the left column, and the other group displays across the top. Each remaining cell in the query displays a total, an average, or other summary statistic for each pair of groupings.

In More Skills 14, you will create a crosstab query.

To begin, open your web browser, navigate to www.pearsonhighered.com/skills, locate the name of your textbook, and then follow the instructions on the website.

Please note that there are no additional projects to accompany the More Skills Projects, and they are not covered in the End-of-Chapter projects.

The following table summarizes the **SKILLS AND PROCEDURES** covered in this chapter.

Skills Number	Task	Step
1	Create queries (Simple Query Wizard)	Create tab → Queries group → Query Wizard
2	Add query criteria	In the Criteria row, type the criteria in the column(s) with the values you wish to filter
3	Add calculated fields to tables (Datasheet view)	Fields tab → Add & Delete group → More Fields → Calculated Field → click the desired data type
3	Add calculated fields to tables (Design view)	Data Type arrow → Calculated
4	Create queries (Design view)	Create tab → Queries group → Query Design
4	Add tables to queries in Design view	Design tab → Query Setup group → Show Table
7	Group and total queries	Design tab → Show/Hide group → Totals Group first column(s), set Totals row to statistic for other column(s)
	Criteria:	
2	Equals the word five	"five"
5	Equals the number 5	5
5	Greater than 5	>5
5	Less than or equal to 5	<=5
5	Does not equal 5	Not 5 or <>5
6	Is after July 5, 2014	>#7/5/2014#
6	Is between July 5 and 10, 2014	Between #7/5/2014# And #7/10/2014#
8	Equals the Rate field plus 5 and is labeled Extra	Extra: [Rate]+5
9	Cell is empty	Is Null
9	One or both criteria are true	"Will" Or "Bill"
9	Both criteria must be true	"Will" And "Bill"
10	Contains the word five	Like "*five*"
10	Can be Bill or Will but not Cerill	Like "?ill"

Key Terms

Online Help Skills

1. **Start** Access 2013, and then in the upper right corner of the start page, click the **Help** button ⟨?⟩.

2. In the **Access Help** window **Search help** box, type query criteria and then press ⟨Enter⟩.

3. In the search result list, click **Examples of query criteria**, and then compare your screen with **Figure 1**.

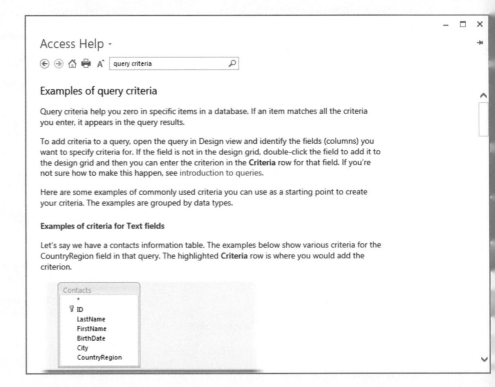

Figure 1

4. Read the article to answer the following question: How might you use *Not*, *In*, and *Len* in your criteria?

Matching

Match each term in the second column with its correct definition in the first column by writing the letter of the term on the blank line in front of the correct definition.

___ **1.** A database object used to ask questions about the data stored in database tables.

___ **2.** Conditions in a query used to select the records that answer the query's question.

___ **3.** A field in a table or query that derives its values from other fields in the table or query.

___ **4.** Less than (<) and greater than (>) are examples of this type of operator.

___ **5.** In the query design grid, two criteria placed in the same row use this logical operator.

___ **6.** To add summary statistics to a query, this row must be added to the query.

___ **7.** When two criteria are placed in different rows in the query design grid, this logical operator will be applied.

___ **8.** An operator that tests if a field is empty.

___ **9.** This wildcard character can represent any combination of characters.

___ **10.** This wildcard character can represent any single character.

A And

B Asterisk (*)

C Calculated

D Comparison

E Criteria

F Or

G Query

H Question mark (?)

I Null

J Total

BizSkills Video

1. If you could apply just one of the tips provided in this video to help manage your current priorities, which one would you choose? Why?

2. What techniques do you currently use to set a plan for your day? What other techniques could help you do this better?

Multiple Choice (MyITLab®)

Choose the correct answer.

1. A query that displays records without changing the data in a table.
   - A. Select
   - B. Simple
   - C. View

2. In a query, criteria are added in this view.
   - A. Datasheet
   - B. Design
   - C. Workspace

3. An IntelliSense box that explains the purpose of the selected AutoComplete.
   - A. Balloon
   - B. Quick Info
   - C. ScreenTip

4. In a query, results are displayed in this view.
   - A. Datasheet
   - B. Design
   - C. Design grid

5. A combination of fields, mathematical operators, and pre-built functions that calculates values.
   - A. Comparison operator
   - B. Expression
   - C. Quick Info

6. In query criteria, dates are surrounded by this character.
   - A. >
   - B. !
   - C. #

7. A calculation for a group of data such as a total, an average, or a count.
   - A. Calculated column
   - B. Group formula
   - C. Summary statistic

8. An operator that finds all numbers or dates between and including two values.
   - A. And…Between
   - B. Between…And
   - C. In…Between

9. A descriptive label used to identify a field in expressions, datasheets, forms, and reports.
   - A. Alias
   - B. Label
   - C. Name

10. The operator that is placed at the beginning of criteria that contain wildcards.
    - A. Like
    - B. Similar
    - C. Wildcard

Topics for Discussion

1. You have created queries using the Simple Query Wizard and using Design view. Which method do you prefer, and why? What situations may be better suited to using the Simple Query Wizard? What situations may be better suited to using Design view?

2. Data that can be calculated from existing fields can be entered manually into its own field, or it can be included as a calculated field in a table or query. Which method would produce the most accurate results, and why?

Skills Review  MyITLab®
Grader

To complete this project, you will need the following file:

- acc02_SRElectricity

You will save your database as:

- Last_First_acc02_SRElectricity

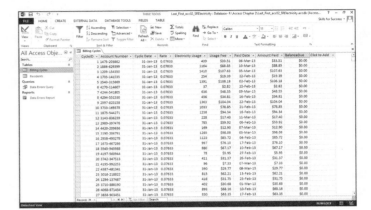

Figure 1

1. Start **Access 2013**, and then open the student data file **acc02_SRElectricity**. Save the database in your **Access Chapter 2** folder with the name Last_First_acc02_SRElectricity If necessary, enable the content.

2. Open the **Billing Cycles** table in Datasheet view. In the last column, click the **Click to Add arrow**, point to **Calculated Field**, and then from the submenu, click **Currency**.

3. In the **Expression Builder**, add the following expression:
   [UsageFee] - [AmountPaid]

4. Click **OK**, and then replace the selected text *Field1* with BalanceDue

5. Compare your screen with **Figure 1**, and then **Save** and **Close** the table.

6. On the **Create tab**, in the **Queries group**, click **Query Design**. **Add** both tables to the query workspace, and then **Close** the Show Table dialog box.

7. From the **Residents** table, add the **AccountNumber**, **LastName**, and **FirstName** fields to the design grid.

8. From the **Billing Cycles** table, add the **CycleDate**, **UsageFee**, and **BalanceDue** fields to the design grid.

9. In the **CycleDate** column **Criteria** cell, type Between 6/1/2014 And 6/30/2014

10. In the **BalanceDue** column **Criteria** cell, type >1 Or Is Null

11. Click **Save**, type Penalties Query and then click **OK**.

12. Click the first blank **Field** cell, and then in the **Query Setup group**, click **Builder**. In the **Expression Builder**, add the following expression: Penalty: [BalanceDue] * 0.2 Click **OK**. In the **Show/Hide group**, click **Property Sheet**, and then change the calculated field's **Format** to **Currency**. **Close** the property sheet.

13. **Run** the query, compare your screen with **Figure 2**, and then **Save** and **Close** the query.

Figure 2

■ Continue to the next page to complete this Skills Review

Figure 3

Figure 4

14. On the **Create tab**, in the **Queries group**, click **Query Wizard**, and then in the **New Query** dialog box, click **OK**.

15. In the **Simple Query Wizard**, click the **Tables/Queries arrow**, and then click **Table: Residents**.

16. Click **AccountNumber** and then click the **Move** button. Repeat the procedure to move **LastName** and **FirstName**.

17. Click the **Tables/Queries arrow**, and then click **Table: Billing Cycles**. Move **CycleDate** and **UsageFee** into **Selected Fields**, and then click **Next** two times. In the last Wizard screen, change the query name to Resident Statistics and then click **Finish**.

18. Switch to **Design view**, and then in the **LastName** column **Sort** cell, set the value to **Ascending**.

19. On the **Design tab**, in the **Show/Hide group**, click **Totals**. Change the **LastName**, **FirstName**, and **CycleDate** columns **Total** cells to **First**. Change the **UsageFee** column **Total** cell to **Avg**.

20. Click in the **LastName** column, open the property sheet. In the property sheet **Caption** box, type Last Name Click the **FirstName** column, and then change the **Caption** property to First Name

21. Click the **UsageFee** column. In the property sheet, change the **Format** to **Currency**, the **Caption** to Average Bill and then **Close** the property sheet.

22. In the **CycleDate** column **Criteria** cell, type <1/1/2014 Clear the **CycleDate** column **Show** cell check box, and then **Run** the query.

23. Compare your screen with **Figure 3**, and then **Save** and **Close** the query.

24. Open **Data Errors Query**, and then switch to Design view. In the **LastName** column **Criteria** cell, type Like Thomps?n

25. In the **FirstName** column **Criteria** cell, type Ralph

26. In the **ElectricityUsage** column **or** cell, type Is Null

27. **Run** the query and then compare your screen with **Figure 4**. **Save**, and then **Close** the query.

28. Open **Data Errors Report**. If you are printing your work, print the report.

29. **Close** the report, and then **Close** Access. Submit your work as directed by your instructor.

 DONE! You have completed this Skills Review

Skills Assessment 1

MyITLab®
Grader

To complete this project, you will need the following file:

- acc02_SA1Properties

You will save your file as:

- Last_First_acc02_SA1Properties

Figure 1

1. Start **Access 2013**, and then open **acc02_SA1Properties**. Save the database in your chapter folder as Last_First_acc02_SA1Properties

2. In the last column of **Parcels** table datasheet, add a **Currency** calculated field that is derived by multiplying the **Value** field by 0.01206 Name the field Taxes and then **Save** and **Close** the table.

3. Use the Simple Query Wizard to start a query with the **Owner** field from the **Parcels** table, and the **ZoneName** field from the **Zones** table. Name the query Tax Payments and then **Finish** the wizard.

4. In the **Tax Payments** query, add text criteria with a wildcard so that only records with *Residential* in their zone name result.

5. In the **Tax Payments** query, set the **ZoneName** column so that it does not show when the query is run.

6. Add a calculated field with the alias Payments that divides the **Taxes** field by two (Taxes/2). Set the field's **Format** property to **Currency**. **Run** the query and compare your results with **Figure 1**. **Save** and **Close** the query.

7. Create a new query in Design view, and then add the **Zones** and **Parcels** tables.

8. From the **Zones** table, add the **ZoneName** field, and then from the **Parcels** table, add the **Value** field three times.

9. Add the **Totals** row and group the query by **ZoneName**.

10. Set the first **Value** column summary statistic to **Count** each group, and then change its **Caption** property to Number of Parcels

11. Set the second **Value** column summary statistic to **Sum** each group, and then change its **Caption** property to Total Value

12. Set the third **Value** column summary statistic to average (**Avg**) each group, and then change its **Caption** property to Average Value

13. Set the third **Value** column **Sort** order to **Descending**.

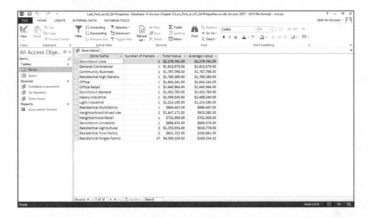

Figure 2

14. **Save** the query with the name Zone Values and then **Run** the query. Set the datasheet column widths to **Best Fit**, and then compare your results with **Figure 2**. **Save**, and then **Close** the query.

15. Open the **Outdated Assessments** query in Design view. In the **LastAssessed** column, add criteria so that values that are either before 1/1/2013 *or* are empty (Null) will display in the query datasheet. Run the query and verify that 24 records result. **Save** and **Close** the query.

16. Open the **Assessments Needed** report to view the 24 records from the Outdated Assessments query. If you are printing your work, print the report.

17. **Close** the report and then **Close** Access. Submit your work as directed by your instructor.

 DONE! You have completed Skills Assessment 1

Skills Assessment 2

To complete this project, you will need the following file:

- acc02_SA2Fleet

You will save your database as:

- Last_First_acc02_SA2Fleet

Figure 1

1. Start **Access 2013**, and then open the student data file **acc02_SAFleet**. Save the database in your chapter folder as Last_First_acc02_SA2Fleet

2. In the last column of the **Fleet Services** table, add a calculated field that is derived from the product of the **Miles** and **MileageRate** fields (Miles * MileageRate). Name the field MileageFee Assign it the **Currency** result type and add the caption Mileage Fee **Save** and **Close** the table.

3. Use the Simple Query Wizard to start a query with the **Department** field from the **Departments** table and the **StartDate** field from the **Fleet Services** table. Name the query Police and Fire Travel and accept all other wizard defaults.

4. In the **Police and Fire Travel** query, add text criteria so that the **Department** can be from the Fire or Police department. Run the query, verify that 29 records result, and then **Save**.

5. In Design view, set the query to sort in ascending order by **StartDate**. Add criteria so that only records with a **StartDate** between 1/1/2014 and 7/31/2014 result.

6. Add a calculated field with the alias Charge that adds the BaseFee and MileageFee columns (BaseFee + MileageFee). **Run** the query and compare your results with **Figure 1**. **Save** and **Close** the query.

7. Create a new query in Design view, and then add the **Departments**, **Employees**, and then the **Fleet Services** tables.

8. From the **Departments** table, add the **Department** field, and then from the **Fleet Services** table, add the **ServiceID** field, and then add the **Miles** field two times.

9. Group the query by **Department**, and then **Count** the **ServiceID** in each group. Set the first **Miles** column to total each group, and the second **Miles** column to average each group.

Figure 2

10. Set the **ServiceID** column **Caption** property to Trips and the first **Miles** column **Caption** property to Total Miles

11. Set the second **Miles** column properties so that the datasheet displays no decimals and the column's caption will be Average Trip Length **Close** the property sheet.

12. **Save** the query with the name Department Travel and then **Run** the query. Set the datasheet column widths to **Best Fit**, and then compare your results with **Figure 2**. **Save**, and then **Close** the query.

13. **Close** Access, and then submit your work as directed by your instructor.

 DONE! You have completed Skills Assessment 2

Visual Skills Check

To complete this project, you will need the following file:

- acc02_VSPermits

You will save your database as:

- Last_First_acc02_VSPermits

Open the database **acc02_VSPermits**, and then using your own name, save the database as Last_First_acc02_ VSPermits

Create a query with the results shown in **Figure 1**. Name the query Fence Permits Due and add the columns as shown. Add a calculated field with the alias Balance and then add criteria that answer the question, *Which fencing projects have balances due?* Six records should result.

Submit your work as directed by your instructor.

Figure 1

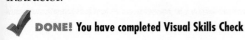 **DONE! You have completed Visual Skills Check**

My Skills

To complete this project, you will need the following file:

- acc01_MYBaseball

You will save your database as:

- Last_First_acc02_MYBaseball

1. Start **Access 2013**, and then open **acc02_MYBaseball**. Save the database in your chapter folder as Last_First_acc02_MYBaseball

2. In the **League Statistics** table datasheet, click the **At Bats (AB)** column, and then add a **Number** calculated field. For the expression, divide the **Hits** field by the **AtBats** field. Name the field BattingAverage You will format the numbers in a later step.

3. **Save** the table, and then switch to Design view. In the **BattingAverage Description (Optional)** cell, type Hits divided by AtBats

4. In the **BattingAverage** field properties, change the **Result Type** to **Single**, the **Format** to **Fixed**, and the **Decimal Places** to **3**. Add Batting Average (BA) as the field's caption.

5. In the first available row, add a new calculated field named ERA For the expression, multiply the **EarnedRuns** field by 9, and then divide by the **InningsPitched** field (EarnedRuns * 9 / InningsPitched).

6. In the **ERA Description (Optional)** cell, type Earned run average (EarnedRuns * 9 / InningsPitched)

7. In the **ERA** field properties, change the **Result Type** to **Single**, the **Format** to **Fixed**, and the **Decimal Places** to **1**.

8. **Save** the table, and switch to Datasheet view. Set the column widths to **Best Fit**, and then compare your screen with **Figure 1**. **Save** and **Close** the table.

9. Create a new query in Design view that includes every field in the **League Statistics** table *except for* PlayerID, LastName, and FirstName. **Save** the query with the name Team Stats

10. Change the query to calculate the averages for each team.

11. Change the **Hits** column properties so that one decimal displays and the column heading displays as Avg Team Hits

12. Change the **AtBats** column properties so that one decimal displays and the column heading displays as Avg Team AB

13. Change the **BattingAverage** column properties so that three decimals display and the column heading displays as Team BA

14. Change the **EarnedRuns** column properties so that one decimal displays and the column heading displays as Avg Team ER

15. Change the **InningsPitched** column properties so that one decimal displays and the column heading displays as Avg Team IP

16. Change the **ERA** column properties so that one decimal displays and the column heading displays as Avg Team ERA

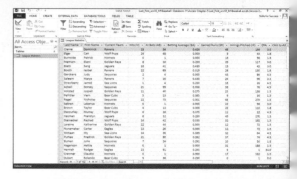

Figure 1

Figure 2

17. Run the query, set the column widths to **Best Fit**, and then compare your screen with **Figure 2**.

18. **Save** the query, and then **Close** Access. Submit your work as directed by your instructor.

 DONE! You have completed My Skills

Skills Challenge 1

To complete this project, you will need the following file:

- acc02_SC1Classes

You will save your database as:

- Last_First_acc02_SC1Classes

Open **acc02_SC1Classes** and save the database in your chapter folder as Last_First_acc02_SC1Classes Open the Instructor Class Counts query, and then add a column so that each instructor's first name is included and the two interns with the last name of *Shriver* have an accurate count. Cheyenne Shriver should have a total of one, and Kenton Shriver should have a total of five.

Open the Intern Contacts List query, and then fix the query so that each intern is listed only once. To do this, you do not need to add any criteria, change any properties, use the Total row, or apply any filters to the datasheet.

Open the Word Classes query, and then fix the criteria and add columns so that it answers the question, *Where are all the Word classes offered and what are their start dates and times?*

Submit your work as directed by your instructor.

 DONE! You have completed Skills Challenge 1

Skills Challenge 2

To complete this project, you will need the following file:

- acc02_SC2Rentals

You will save your database as:

- Last_First_acc02_SC2Rentals

Open **acc02_SC2Rentals** and save the database in your chapter folder as Last_First_acc02_SC2Rentals Create a query named Refunds that answers the following question: *Which July renters of community center rooms get a refund?* Identify the renters by including the RenterID field. Display the date and hours each room was rented and the refund amount.

To calculate the balance due, subtract the deposit from the rental fee. The rental fee can be determined by multiplying the number of hours rented by the room's hourly rate. Define

the calculated field's alias as Balance and format the column to display as currency. (The currency format encloses negative numbers—refunds—in parenthesis instead of using a negative sign.) Be sure to limit the query results to July 2014 and only to those receiving a refund.

Submit your work as directed by your instructor.

 DONE! You have completed Skills Challenge 2

CHAPTER 3

Create Forms

- Forms are used to edit, delete, and add records stored in database tables and are designed to make data entry quick and accurate.

- Forms are often designed for entering data for the specific needs of the database. For example, a college database may provide one form for entering new students, another form for registering students for classes, and another form for assigning instructors to teach those classes.

- Forms are designed to be viewed on a computer screen and are rarely printed. Instead, reports are typically used when data needs to be printed.

- Forms show one record at a time so that you can work with just that data.

- Forms can take advantage of one-to-many relationships. The main form shows one record at a time from the first table, and below that, all the related records in the other table display in a subform.

- There are several methods for creating forms, including the Form Wizard and the Form Tool.

- Forms can be arranged in Word-like tables so that you can quickly position labels and text in cells to create a custom layout for your form.

- Forms can be based on queries so that you can work with a subset of the data.

- Some forms have buttons that open other database objects—tables, queries, other forms, and reports. These forms can be built quickly using the Navigation Form command.

© Goodluz

Aspen Falls City Hall

In this chapter, you will create forms for Aspen Falls Utilities. You will work under the supervision of Diane Payne, Public Works Director, to design forms for entering records about city residents and their water bills. You will also build a form that data entry personnel will use to open and close the database forms.

There are several methods for creating forms in Access. The method you choose depends on the type of form you need and personal preference. No matter which method you choose, all forms need to provide a way to locate and update records quickly and accurately. Most forms also provide a way to add new records. The form's header displays information about the form's purpose, and the detail area displays labels and text boxes with values from the underlying table.

Some forms are used to open and close other forms and reports. These forms provide a way to navigate the database and can be set up in a way that hides the Navigation Pane. Using this method, you can provide a custom database interface based on the needs of the individuals who will use it.

To complete this project, you will create a form using a wizard and then format that form. You will use the form to edit records. You will create another form using the Form tool that displays records from two related tables on the same screen and then enter new records using this form. You will also build a form based on a select query. Finally, you will create a Navigation Form that opens the other three forms, and then set up the form to hide the Navigation Pane when the form is in use.

Time to complete all 10
skills – 60 to 90 minutes

Student data files needed for this chapter:

acc03_Water

acc03_WaterLogo

You will save your files as:

Last_First_acc03_Water

Last_First_acc03_WaterSnip (1 – 4)

Outcome

Using the skills in this chapter, you will be able to
work with Access forms like this:

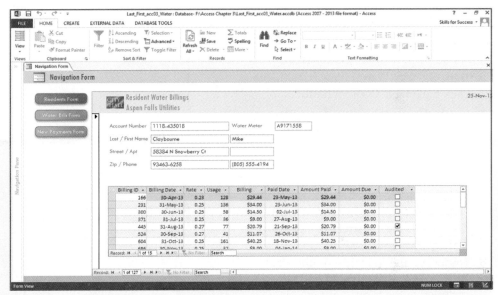

SKILLS

Skills 1-10 Training

At the end of this chapter you will be able to:

Skill 1   Use the Form Wizard

Skill 2   Use Forms to Modify Data

Skill 3   Format Forms in Layout View

Skill 4   Add Controls and Conditional Formatting

Skill 5   Use the Form Tool

Skill 6   Work with Tabular Layouts

Skill 7   Add Input Masks

Skill 8   Change Data in One-to-Many Forms

Skill 9   Create Forms from Queries

Skill 10 Create Navigation Forms

MORE SKILLS

Skill 11 Validate Fields

Skill 12 Create Databases from Templates

Skill 13 Create Macros

Skill 14 Create Access Apps

▶ Access has several tools for creating forms. The Form Wizard is an efficient method when you do not need to include all the fields from a table.

1. Start **Access 2013**, and then open the student data file **acc03_Water**. On the **File tab**, click **Save As**. With **Save Database As** selected, click the **Save As** button. In the **Save As** dialog box, navigate to the location where you are saving your files for this project. Click **New folder**, type Access Chapter 3 and then press Enter two times. Name the file Last_First_acc03_Water and then click **Save**.

2. If the Security Warning message displays, click the Enable Content button.

3. On the **Create tab**, in the **Forms group**, click the **Form Wizard** button. Click the **Tables/Queries arrow**, and then click **Table: Water Bills**. Compare your screen with **Figure 1**.

   By default, the table or query that is selected in the Navigation Pane will be selected in the first screen of the Form Wizard.

4. Under **Available Fields**, double-click **BillingID** so that the field will be included in the form.

5. With **AccountNumber** selected, click the **Move** button > to place it into **Selected Fields**.

6. Use either technique just practiced to move the following fields into **Selected Fields** in this order: **BillingDate**, **Rate**, **Usage**, **Billing**, **PaidDate**, **AmountPaid**, and **AmountDue**. Do *not* move the Audited field. Compare your screen with **Figure 2**.

■ Continue to the next page to complete the skill ▶

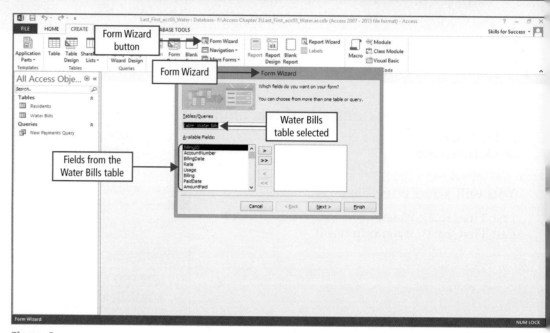

Figure 1

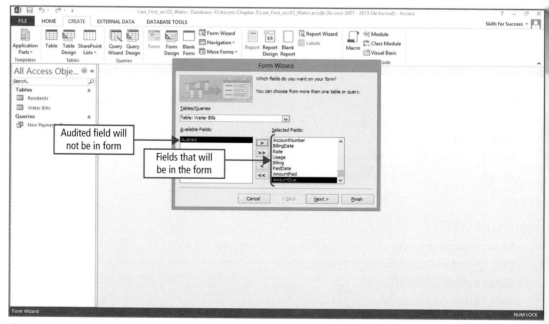

Figure 2

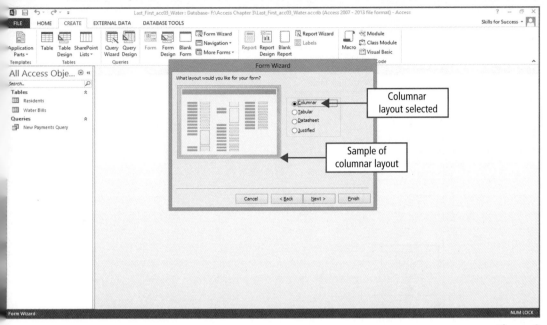

Figure 3

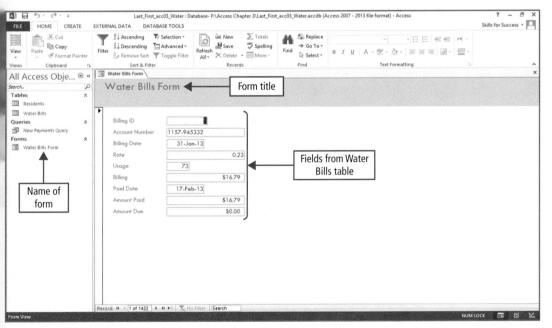

Figure 4

7. In the **Form Wizard**, click **Next**, and then compare your screen with **Figure 3**.

   You can use the Form Wizard to pick different layouts for your form. A *layout* determines how data and labels are arranged in a form or report. For example, the *columnar layout* places labels in the first column and data in the second column.

8. With **Columnar layout** selected, click **Next**. Under **What title do you want for your form**, change *Water Bills* to Water Bills Form

9. In the **Form Wizard**, click **Finish** to create the form and open it in **Form view**. Compare your screen with **Figure 4**.

   The title that you type in the last screen of the Form Wizard becomes the name of the form in the Navigation Pane, and the theme last used in the database is applied to the form. Here, the Integral theme has been applied.

10. Leave the form open for the next skill.

■ **You have completed Skill 1 of 10**

▶ Forms are designed to input data into tables. When you edit data or add records, the changes are stored automatically in the underlying table.

1. Take a few moments to familiarize yourself with the **Water Bills Form** as shown in **Figure 1**.

    Most forms display in *Single Form view*—a view that displays one record at a time with field names in the first column and the field values in the second column. If a field has a caption property assigned, that value will display in the label. For example, the *BillingID* field displays as *Billing ID*.

    At the bottom of the form, the Navigation bar shows how many records are in the underlying table and has buttons for moving from one record to another.

2. On the Navigation bar, click the **Next record** button ▶ to display record 2 of 1422—*Billing ID 2*.

3. Click the **Paid Date** box, type the date 06-Feb-13 Press [Enter] to move to the next field, **Amount Paid**, and then type 19.78 Watch the **Amount Due** value automatically update as you press [Enter], and then compare your screen with **Figure 2**.

    The AmountDue field is a calculated field that automatically updates when the Rate, Usage, or AmountPaid fields are changed. The change you made to the AmountPaid field was changed in the table, and the AmountDue box updated to display the new value. In this manner, forms can be used to edit table data while viewing one record at a time.

■ **Continue to the next page to complete the skill** ▶

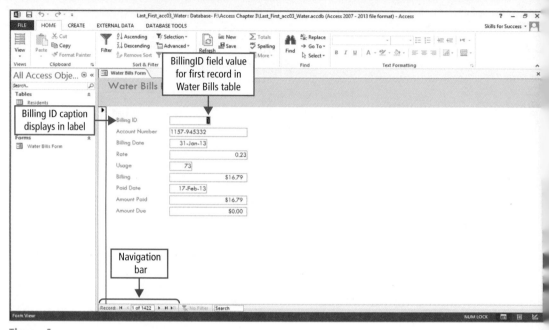

Figure 1

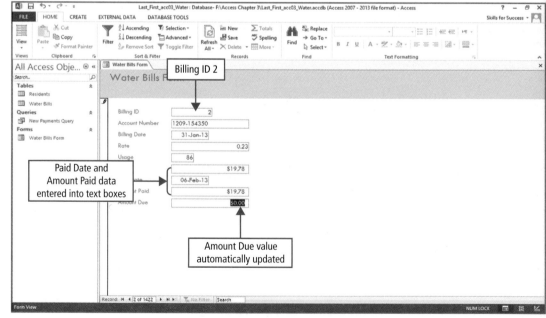

Figure 2

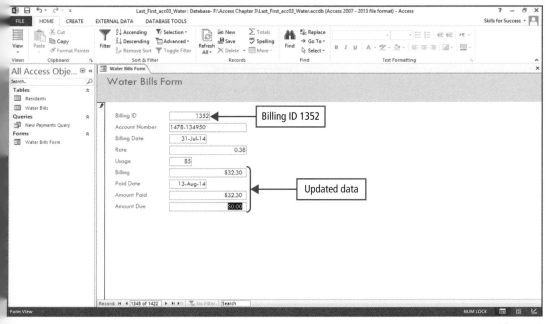

Figure 3

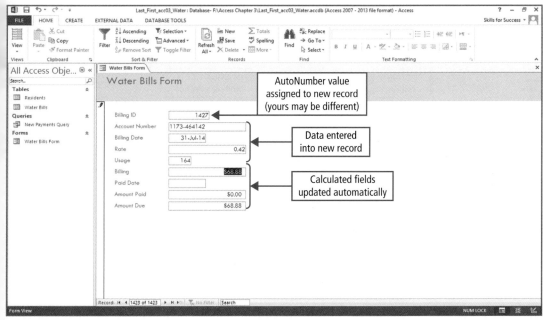

Figure 4

4. Press **Enter** to move to the next record—*Billing ID 3*. With **Billing ID** active, on the **Home tab**, in the **Find group**, click the **Find** button.

5. In the **Find and Replace** dialog box **Find What** box, type 1352 Press **Enter**, and then **Close** ☒ the dialog box.

6. In the record for *Billing ID 1352*, enter a **Paid Date** of 13-Aug-14 and an **Amount Paid** of 32.30 Press **Enter** to update the record. Compare your screen with **Figure 3**.

7. On the Navigation bar, click the **New (blank) record** button ▸*. Press **Enter** to move the insertion point to the **Account Number** box. Type 1173-464142 and then press **Enter**.

> You can move to the next field in a form by pressing **Enter** or **Tab**. In this way, you can continue typing values without having to use the mouse. Keeping your hands over the keyboard speeds data entry and increases accuracy.

8. In the **Billing Date** box, type 31-Jul-14 and then press **Enter**. In the **Rate** box, type 0.42 and then press **Enter**.

9. In the **Usage** box, type 164 Watch the **Billing** and **Amount Due** values update automatically as you press **Enter**, and then compare your screen with **Figure 4**.

> In the Water Bills table, the Billing field is a calculated field that multiplies the Rate value by the Usage value. Here, the July billing for this account is $68.88.

10. Leave the table open for the next skill.

> You do not need to save any changes because data was automatically saved as you entered it.

■ **You have completed Skill 2 of 10**

▶ *Layout view* is used to format a form or report while you are viewing a sample of the data.

1. With the **Water Bills Form** open, on the **Home tab**, in the **Views group**, click the **View** button to switch to Layout view. If the Field List pane displays, Close ✕ the pane.

2. On the **Design tab**, in the **Tools group**, click the **Property Sheet** button as needed to open the property sheet.

3. On the Navigation bar, click the **First record** button ◄. Click the **AccountNumber** text box, and then compare your screen with **Figure 1**.

In Layout view, you can select individual *controls*—objects in a form or report such as labels and text boxes—and format them. A *label* is a control in a form or report that describes other objects in the report or form. A *text box* is a control in a form or report that displays the data from a field in a table or query. Here, the label displays the caption *Account Number,* and the AccountNumber text box displays the value *1157-945332.*

4. With the **AccountNumber** text box control still selected, click the Ribbon **Format tab**. In the **Font group**, click the **Align Right** button.

5. Click the **Billing ID** text box to select it. Press and hold Shift while clicking the eight other text boxes with the ⟨ pointer. Release the Shift key, and then compare your screen with **Figure 2**.

■ Continue to the next page to complete the skill ▶

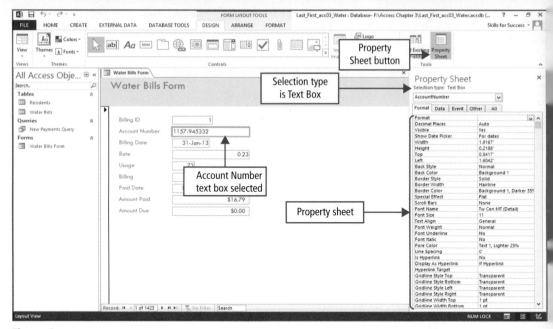

Figure 1

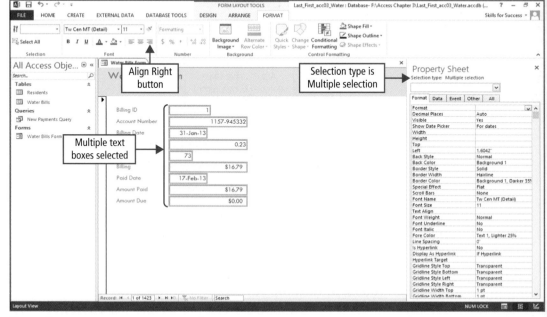

Figure 2

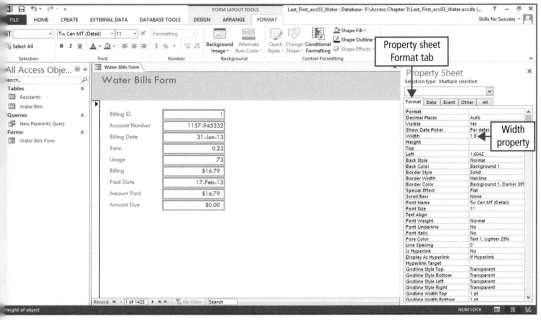

Figure 3

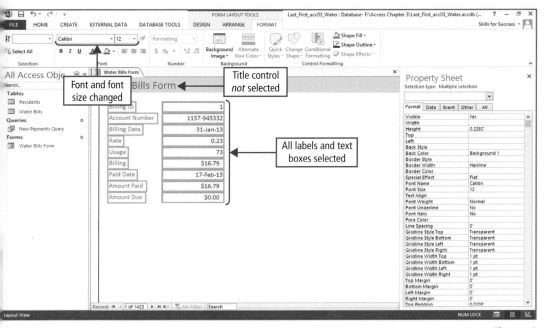

Figure 4

6. On the property sheet **Format tab**, click in the **Width** box, type 1.5" and then press Enter to simultaneously set the width of all nine text boxes. Compare your screen with **Figure 3**.

In this manner, you can select multiple controls and then format them at the same time.

7. On the **Format tab**, in the **Selection group**, click **Select All** to select all the form controls. In the **Font group**, click the **Font arrow**. Scroll down the list of fonts, and then click **Calibri**.

8. With all the controls still selected, press and hold Ctrl while clicking the **Title** control with the text *Water Bills Form* to remove it from the current selection, and then release the Ctrl key.

9. On the **Format tab**, in the **Font group**, click the **Font size arrow** 11 ▾ , and then click **12** to increase the font size by one point. Compare your screen with **Figure 4**.

10. Click **Save** 🖫 to save the design changes, and then leave the form open for the next skill.

When you make changes to the form's design, you need to save those changes. Here, the form's design was changed; however, none of the data was changed.

■ **You have completed Skill 3 of 10**

▶ Controls such as logos and titles can be added to forms to identify a company and the purpose of the form.

▶ You can format values so that when a condition is true, the value will be formatted differently than when the condition is false.

1. If it is not already open, open Water Bills Form in Layout view.

2. In the form header, click the **Title** control with the text *Water Bills Form*. Be careful to select the control and not the text in the control—an orange border should surround the control as shown in **Figure 1**.

3. Press Delete to remove the Title control.

4. On the **Design tab**, in the **Header / Footer group**, click the **Logo** button. In the **Insert Picture** dialog box, navigate to the student data files for this project. Select **acc03_WaterLogo**, and then click **OK** to insert the control.

5. On the **Design tab**, in the **Header / Footer group**, click the **Title** button, and then type Monthly Billings

6. Click the **Amount Due** text box. Click the **Format tab**, and then in the **Control Formatting group**, click the **Conditional Formatting** button.

7. In the **Conditional Formatting Rules Manager**, click the **New Rule** button. In the **New Formatting Rule** dialog box, under **Format only cells where the**, click the second **arrow**. Compare your screen with **Figure 2**.

> The second box contains a drop-down list of ***comparison operators***—operators such as greater than and less than that compare two values.

■ **Continue to the next page to complete the skill** ▶

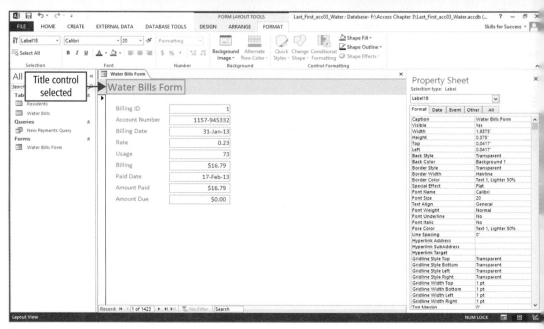

Figure 1

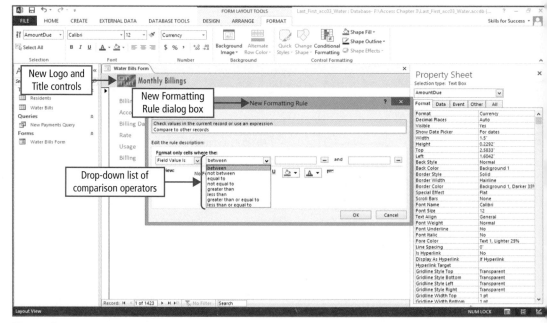

Figure 2

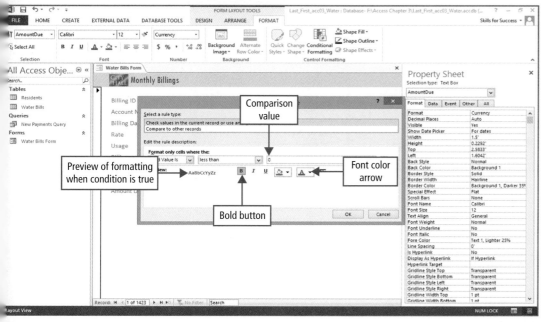

Figure 3

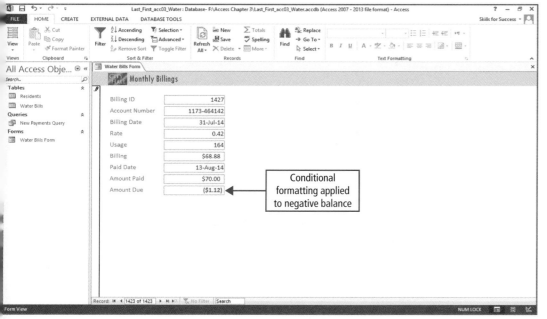

Conditional formatting applied to negative balance

Figure 4

8. In the conditions list, click **less than**. Click in the third box, and then type 0

9. In the **New Formatting Rule** dialog box, click the **Font color arrow** [A ▾], and then click the second color in the last row—**Red**.

10. In the dialog box, click the **Bold** button [B], and then preview the conditional formatting, as shown in **Figure 3**.

11. Click **OK** two times to accept the changes and close the two dialog boxes. Click **Save** [💾], and then on the **Home tab**, click the **View** button to switch to Form view. Alternately, on the status bar, click the Form View button [▦].

12. On the Navigation bar, click the **Last record** button [▶|]. In the **Paid Date** field, type 13-Aug-14 Press [Enter], and then in the **Amount Paid** box, type 70 Press [Enter], click in the **Amount Due** box to deselect the text, and then compare your screen with **Figure 4**.

13. Press [⊞], type snip and then press [Enter] to start the **Snipping Tool**. In the **Snipping Tool** window, click the **New arrow**, and then click **Full-screen Snip**.

14. Click the **Save Snip** button [💾]. In the **Save As** dialog box, navigate to your **Access Chapter 3** folder, save the snip as Last_First_acc03_WaterSnip1 and then **Close** [×] the **Snipping Tool** window.

15. **Save** [💾] the design changes, and then **Close** [×] the form.

■ **You have completed Skill 4 of 10**

▶ You can use the Form Tool to quickly create a form for any table or query that is selected in the Navigation Pane.

1. Click the **Database Tools tab**, and then click the **Relationships** button. Drag the **AccountNumber** field from the **Residents** table, point to the **AccountNumber** field in the **Water Bills** table, and then when the 🔲 displays, release the left mouse button.

2. In the **Edit Relationships** dialog box, select the **Enforce Referential Integrity** check box. Compare your screen with **Figure 1**, and then click **Create**.

   The Residents and Water Bills tables need to have a one-to-many relationship so that each resident's account information can be linked to their monthly water bills.

3. **Close** ✖ the Relationships tab.

4. In the **Navigation Pane**, select the **Residents** table. Click the **Create tab**, and then in the **Forms group**, click the **Form** button to create a one-to-many form. Compare your screen with **Figure 2**. If necessary, Close ✖ the property sheet.

   When a one-to-many relationship exists, a main form and subform will be created when you use the Form Tool. In a ***one-to-many form***, the main form displays in Single Form view, and the related records display in a subform in Datasheet view. Here, a single resident displays in the main form, and that resident's monthly billings display in the subform.

■ **Continue to the next page to complete the skill** ➤

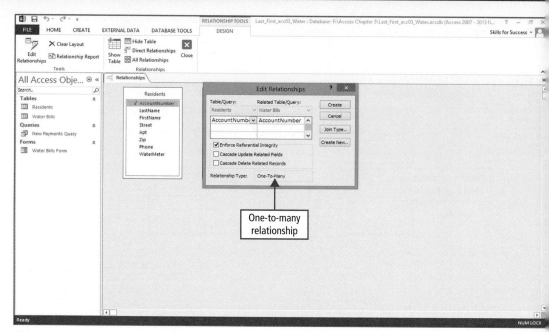

Figure 1

One-to-many relationship

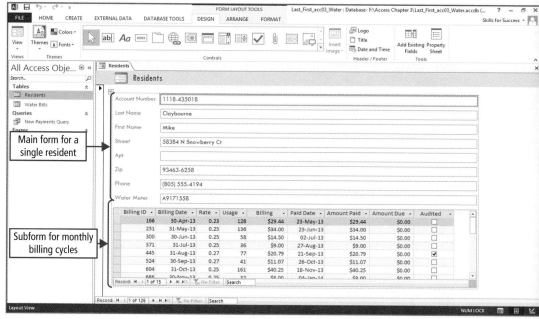

Main form for a single resident

Subform for monthly billing cycles

Figure 2

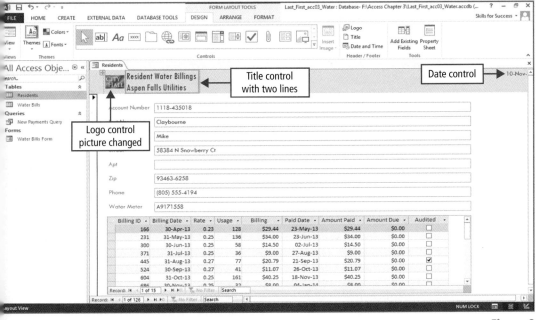

Figure 3

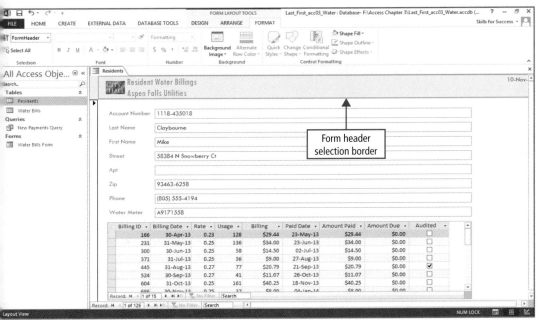

Figure 4

5. On the **Design tab**, in the **Header / Footer group**, click the **Logo** button, and then use the **Insert Picture** dialog box to insert **acc03_WaterLogo** as the form's logo.

6. In the **Header / Footer group**, click the **Date and Time** button. In the **Date and Time** dialog box, select the middle date—**dd-mmm-yy**—option button, clear the **Include Time** check box, and then click **OK**.

7. In the **Header / Footer group**, click the **Title** button to select the text in the form's **Title** control. Type Resident Water Billings and then press Ctrl + Enter to insert a new line in the control. Type Aspen Falls Utilities press Enter to finish editing the text, and then compare your screen with **Figure 3**.

   To change text in a control, you need to be in **Edit mode**. As you type in Edit mode, the Title control adjusts its size to fit the new text.

8. With the **Title** control still selected, click the **Format tab**. In the **Font group**, click the **Font Color arrow** [A ▾], and then click the last color in the first row—**Teal, Accent 6**.

9. In the header, click a blank area to the right of the form title to select the entire header. On the **Format tab**, in the **Font group**, click the **Background Color arrow** [▾], and then click the last color in the second row—**Teal, Accent 6, Lighter 80%**. Compare your screen with **Figure 4**.

10. Click **Save** [💾]. In the **Save As** dialog box, type Residents Form and then press Enter. Leave the form open for the next skill.

■ **You have completed Skill 5 of 10**

▶ Forms created with the Form tool use a *tabular layout*—a layout in which the controls are positioned as table cells in rows and columns. You can insert, delete, and merge columns and then position controls within these tables as needed.

1. With **Residents Form** open in **Layout view**, click the **Account Number** text box to select the control.

2. Point to the selected control's right border to display the ⟷ pointer. Drag the right border to the left. When the column is aligned with the **Usage** column in the subform as shown in **Figure 1**, release the left mouse button to resize the entire column. (You will resize the subform later in this skill.)

3. With the **Account Number** text box still selected, click the **Arrange tab**. In the **Rows & Columns group**, click the **Insert Right** button two times to insert two new columns.

4. Point to the label with the text *Water Meter*, and then with the 🔛 pointer, drag and drop the label into the first cell in the first blank column.

5. Repeat the previous technique to move the **WaterMeter** text box—*A9171558*—into the blank cell to the right of the **Water Meter** label. Compare your screen with **Figure 2**.

6. Move the **First Name** text box—*Mike*—into the blank cell to the right of the **Last Name** text box.

7. Double-click the **Last Name** label, change the label text to Last / First Name and then press Enter.

■ **Continue to the next page to complete the skill**

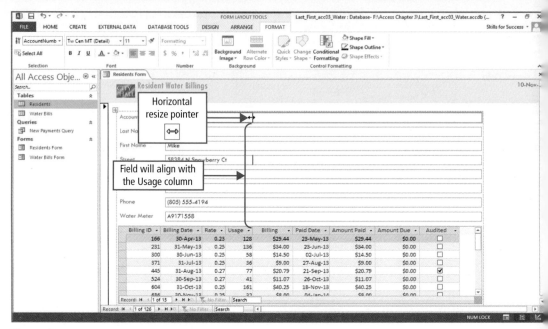

Figure 1

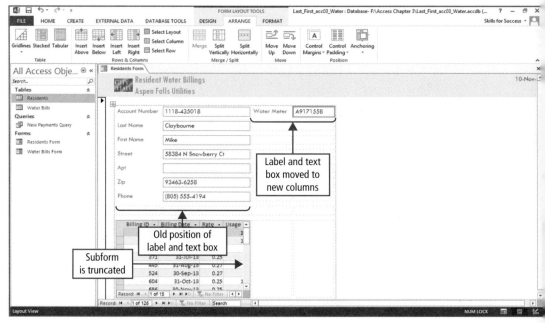

Figure 2

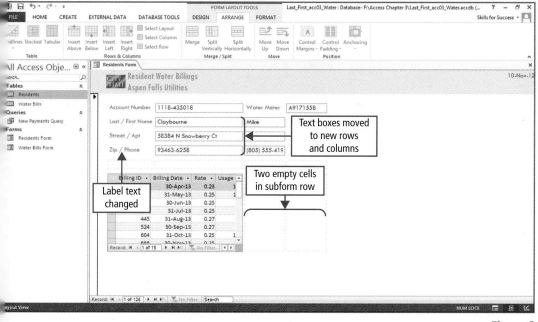

Figure 3

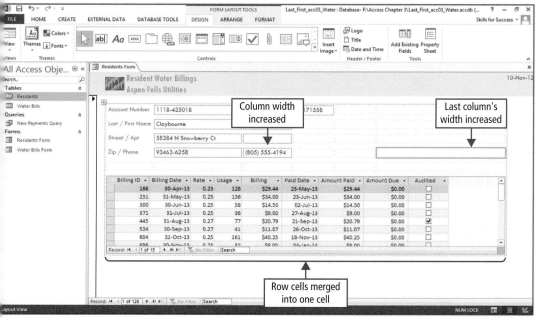

Figure 4

8. In the fifth row, click to select the **Apt** text box—it has a blank value. Drag to move the control into the empty cell to the right of the **Street** text box. In the first column of the same row, change the **Street** label text to Street / Apt

9. Move the **Phone** text box to the right of the **Zip** text box, and then change the **Zip** label text to Zip / Phone

10. In the third row, click the **First Name** label. On the **Arrange tab**, in the **Rows & Columns group**, click **Select Row**. With the row selected, press [Delete] to remove the unused row from the table.

11. Repeat the technique just practiced to delete the unused **Apt** and **Phone** rows. Compare your screen with **Figure 3**.

12. In the row with the subform, click in the empty cell on the right, and then in the **Rows & Columns group**, click the **Insert Right** button two times to add two new columns. Click the **Select Row** button, and then with the five cells selected, in the **Merge / Split group**, click the **Merge** button.

13. In the main form, click the **PhoneNumber** text box to select it. On the **Design tab**, in the **Tools group**, click the **Property Sheet** button, and then change the **Width** value to 1.2″

14. Click in a blank cell in the last column, and then in the property sheet, change the **Width** value to 3.2″ **Close** [X] the property sheet, and then compare your screen with **Figure 4**.

15. Click **Save** [🖫], and leave the form open for the next skill.

■ **You have completed Skill 6 of 10**

▶ An ***input mask*** is a set of special characters that control what can and cannot be entered in a field.

1. With **Residents Form** open in Layout view, click the **Phone** text box. On the **Design tab**, in the **Tools group**, click the **Property Sheet** button.

2. In the property sheet, click the **Data tab**. On the property sheet **Data tab**, click **Input Mask**, and then click the **Build** button ⌷···⌷ that displays in the box. Compare your screen with **Figure 1**.

3. With **Phone Number** selected in the **Input Mask Wizard**, click **Next**. Click the **Placeholder character arrow**, and then click the number sign (#). Click in the **Try It** box, and then compare your screen with **Figure 2**.

   The Try It box displays a sample of the input mask in which you can try entering sample data. ***Placeholder characters*** are the symbols in an input mask that are replaced as you type data into the field. Here, the parentheses, space, and hyphen are in place, and number signs display where each number can be typed.

4. In the **Try It** box, click the first number sign, and then watch the box as you type 10 digits—any digit can be typed in this preview.

■ Continue to the next page to complete the skill ➡

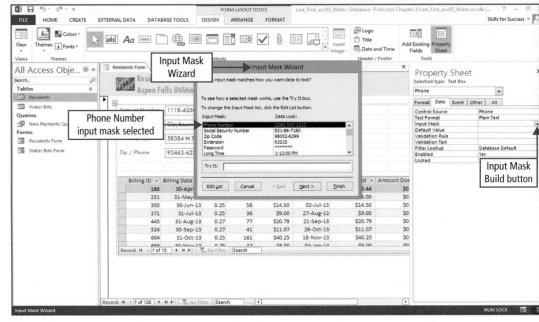

Figure 1

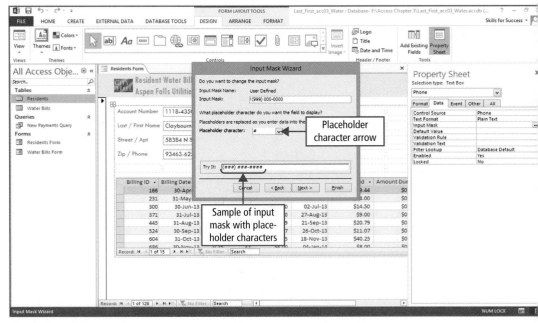

Figure 2

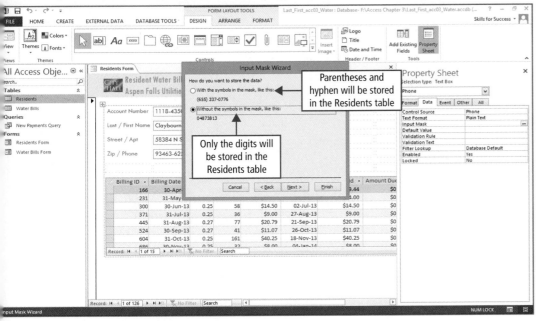

Figure 3

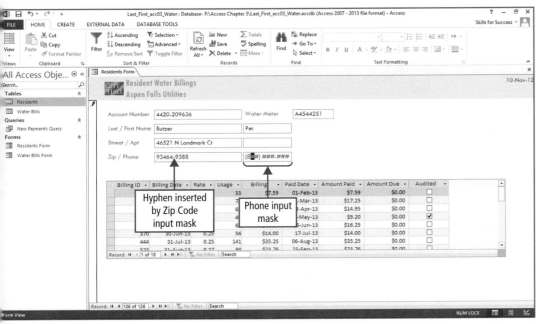

Figure 4

5. Click **Next**, and then compare your screen with **Figure 3**.

The Phone Number input mask has one option that stores the number, parentheses, space, and hyphen in the table; the other option stores only the digits in the phone number.

6. Select the **With the symbols in the mask** option button, click **Next**, and then click **Finish**.

In the property sheet Input Mask box, special characters have been inserted. These characters are needed for the input mask to perform correctly.

7. Select the **Zip** text box, and then use the property sheet to start the Input Mask Wizard. In the **Input Mask Wizard**, click **Zip Code**, and then accept the wizard defaults by clicking **Finish**.

8. **Close** ☒ the property sheet, and then **Save** 🖫 the form.

9. Click the **View** button to switch to Form view. In the main form's Navigation bar—the lower Navigation bar—click the **Last record** ▶ button. Click in the left side of the **Zip** box, and then watch as you type 934649388

10. Press Enter to move to the **Phone** box, type 8 and then compare your screen with **Figure 4**.

11. Watch the **Phone** field as you type the rest of the phone number: 045556894

The input mask converts the digits to *(804) 555-6894* and stores that value in the table.

12. Leave the form open for the next skill.

■ **You have completed Skill 7 of 10**

▶ In a one-to-many form, you can work with the data from two tables on a single screen.

1. If necessary, open **Residents Form** in Form view.

2. Using the technique practiced in a previous skill, use the **Find and Replace** dialog box to navigate to the record for **Account Number** 4367-618513 and then close the dialog box.

3. In the subform datasheet for Lizzette Middents, click in the third record's **Paid Date** cell, and then type 13-Aug-14

4. Press Enter, and then in the **Amount Paid** cell, type 7.98 Press Enter, and then compare your screen with **Figure 1**.

    A payment from Lizzette Middents has just been recorded in the Water Bills table.

5. In the main form's Navigation bar, click the **Next record** button ▶. In the subform Navigation bar for Pei Butzer, click the **New (blank) record** button ▶* to scroll to the bottom of the datasheet and create a new record.

6. Press Enter, and then in the **Billing Date** cell, type 31-Jul-14 Press Enter, and type 0.38 as the **Rate**. Press Enter, and then type 83 as the **Usage**. Press Enter to update the **Billing** and **Amount Due** columns, and leave the rest of the row blank. Compare your screen with **Figure 2**.

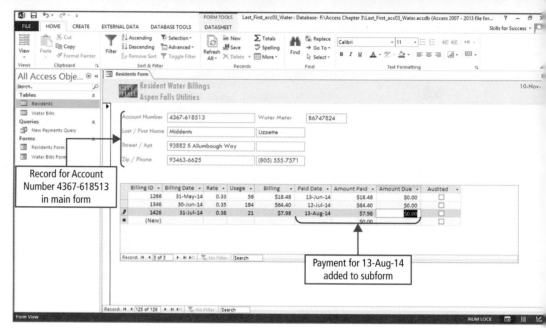

Figure 1

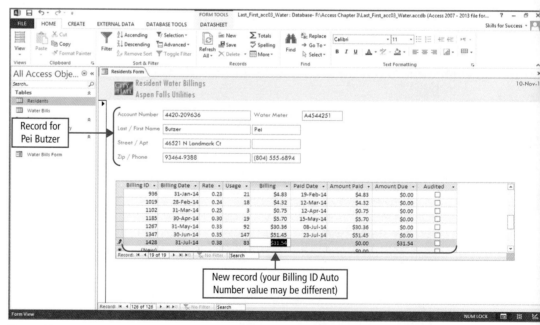

Figure 2

■ **Continue to the next page to complete the skill**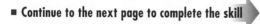

Account Number	4421-879567	Water Meter	C4847198
Last Name	Bransom	First Name	Alfred
Street	12133 S Azure Ln	Apt	A110
Zip	93464-5635	Phone	(805) 555-2685

Figure 3

7. In the main form's Navigation bar, click the **New (blank) record** button ▶✱ to create a new Resident record.

8. In the main form, enter the data shown in **Figure 3**, pressing [Enter] to move to each text box.

9. In the subform for **Alfred Bransom**, click in the first row **Billing Date** cell. Type 31-Jul-14 and press [Enter]. In the **Rate** cell, enter 0.38 and then in the **Usage** cell enter 27 Press [Enter] and then compare your screen with **Figure 4**.

In this manner, a one-to-many form can add records to two tables. Here, a new resident was added to the Residents table, and then the first billing for that resident was added to the Water Bills table.

10. Repeat the skills practiced in a previous skill to start the **Snipping Tool** and create a **Full-screen Snip**. Save the snip in your chapter folder with the name Last_First_acc03_WaterSnip2 and then **Close** ✕ the **Snipping Tool** window.

11. Close ✕ the form.

■ **You have completed Skill 8 of 10**

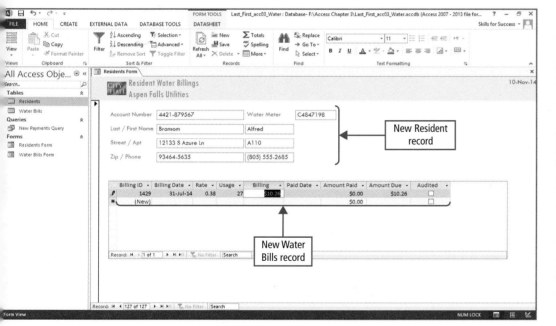

Figure 4

▶ When you need to edit data for a specific subset of data, you can base the form on a query.

▶ A form based on a query displays only the records returned by the query's criteria.

1. In the **Navigation Pane**, under **Queries**, right-click **New Payments Query**, and then from the shortcut menu, click **Design View**. If the property sheet displays, **Close** ☒ it.

2. In the **AmountDue** column **Criteria** cell, type >0 and then compare your screen with **Figure 1**.

> In the New Payments Query, fields from two related tables are selected. The criteria will filter only those records for which an amount is due.

3. Click **Save** 🖫. On the **Design tab**, in the **Results group**, click **Run** to display 50 records. **Close** ☒ the query.

4. Under **Queries**, verify that **New Payments Query** is selected. Click the **Create tab**, and then in the **Forms group**, click the **Form** button. Compare your screen with **Figure 2**.

> The form displays all the fields from the select query. In this manner, you can build forms with fields from related tables in Single Form view or filter data by adding criteria to the query.

■ **Continue to the next page to complete the skill** ▶

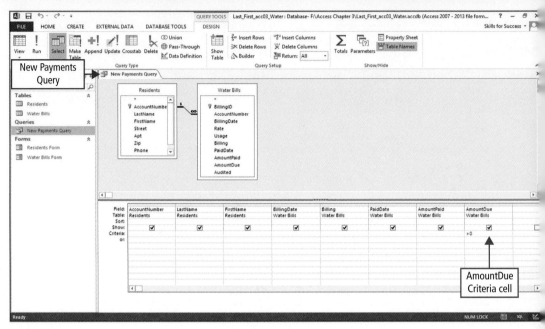

Figure 1

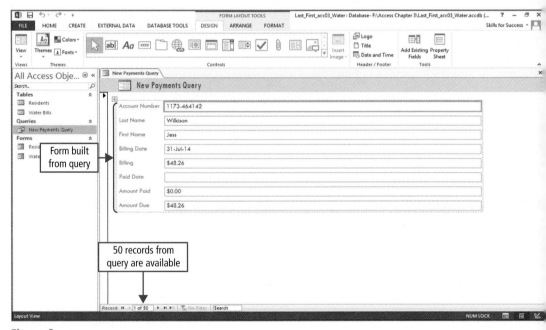

Figure 2

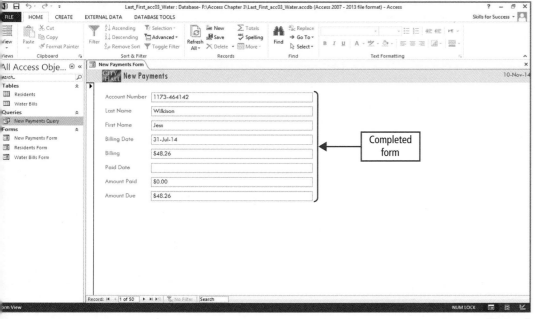

Figure 3

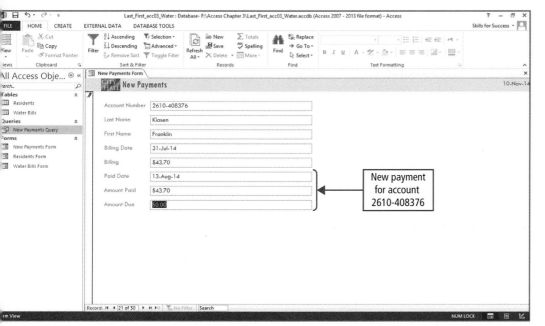

Figure 4

5. On the **Design tab**, in the **Tools group**, click the **Property Sheet** button to open the sheet. Verify that the first text box is selected, and then on the property sheet **Format tab**, change the **Width** value to 4" **Close** ⊠ the property sheet.

6. Repeat the technique practiced previously to insert the **acc03_WaterLogo** file as the form's logo, and then change the **Title** control's text to New Payments

7. Insert a **Date and Time** control with the middle date—**dd-mmm-yy**—option button selected and the **Include Time** check box cleared.

8. Click **Save** 🖫. In the **Save As** box, type New Payments Form and then press Enter.

9. Click the **View** button to switch to Form view, and then compare your screen with **Figure 3**.

10. **Find** the record for **Account Number** 2610-408376 In the **Paid Date** text box, enter 13-Aug-14 and then press Enter. In the **Amount Paid** field, enter 43.70 Press Enter, and then compare your screen with **Figure 4**.

11. Create a **Full-screen Snip**, save the snip in your chapter folder as Last_First_acc03_WaterSnip3 and then **Close** ⊠ the Snipping Tool window.

12. **Close** ⊠ the form.

■ **You have completed Skill 9 of 10**

▶ **Navigation forms** are forms that contain a Navigation Control with tabs that you can use to quickly open forms and reports.

1. On the **Create tab**, in the **Forms group**, click the **Navigation** button, and then compare your screen with **Figure 1**.

   The gallery provides a visual summary of the several layouts available in a Navigation form.

2. In the **Navigation Form** gallery, click **Vertical Tabs Left** to create the form.

3. Near the top-left corner of the new form, click to select the **[Add New]** button, and then click the **Format tab**. In the **Control Formatting group**, click the **Quick Styles** button, and then click the last style in the last row—**Intense Effect – Teal, Accent 6**.

4. With the button still selected, in the **Control Formatting group**, click the **Change Shape** button, and then click the third shape—**Rounded Rectangle**.

5. Drag **Residents Form** from the **Navigation Pane** to the **[Add New]** button in the Navigation form, and then release the left mouse button. Repeat this technique to add **Water Bills Form** and then **New Payments Form** to the Navigation form. Compare your screen with **Figure 2**. If the Field List list displays, **Close ✕** it.

6. Click the **Design tab**, and then click the **Property Sheet** button. In the property sheet, below **Selection type**, click the **arrow**, and then click **Form** to display the form's properties.

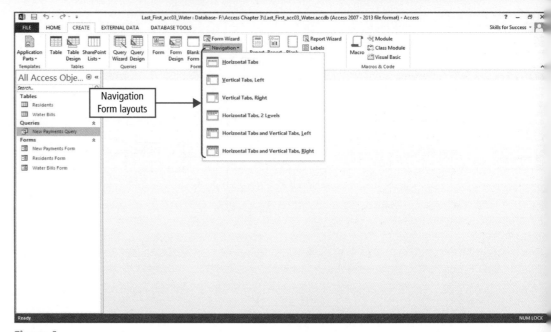

Figure 1

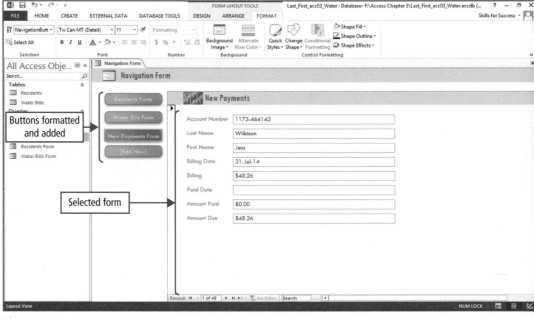

Figure 2

■ **Continue to the next page to complete the skill** ➤

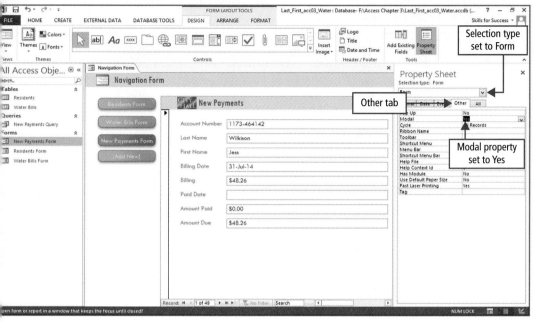

Figure 3

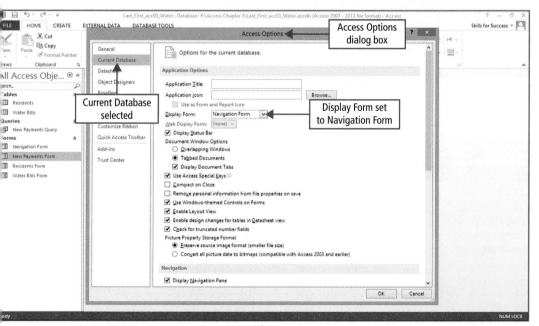

Figure 4

7. On the property sheet, click the **Other tab**, and then click **Modal**. Click the **Modal arrow**, and then click **Yes**. Compare your screen with **Figure 3**.

When a ***modal form*** opens, the Navigation Pane is collapsed.

8. Click **Save** 🔲, and then click **OK** to accept the default name for the form. **Close** ✕ the property sheet, and then **Close** ✕ the form.

9. Click the **File tab**, and then click **Options**. On the left side of the **Access Options** dialog box, click **Current Database**. Click the **Display Form arrow** to display a list of all the database forms, and then click **Navigation Form**. Compare your screen with **Figure 4**.

In the Application Options dialog box, you can pick one form that opens automatically when the database is opened.

10. Click **OK**, read the message that displays, and then click **OK**.

11. **Close** ✕ and then reopen the database to verify that Navigation Form opens as a modal form.

12. Create a **Full-screen Snip**, save the snip in your chapter folder as Last_First_ acc03_WaterSnip4 and then **Close** ✕ the Snipping Tool window.

13. **Close** ✕ the form to display the Navigation Pane, and then **Close** ✕ Access.

14. If you are printing this project, open the snips in Paint, and then print them. Otherwise, submit the database file as directed by your instructor.

 DONE! You have completed Skill 10 of 10, and your database is complete!

The following More Skills are located at **www.pearsonhighered.com/skills**

More Skills Validate Fields

Designing databases involves setting field properties so that those who use the databases enter data correctly. For example, the data type, field size, and input mask properties all limit the types of data that can be entered into a field. Validation rules are also written so that the desired values are entered into fields.

In More Skills 11, you will set the Field Size and Format field properties to validate data. You will then add a validation rule that limits what can be typed into the field.

To begin, open your web browser, navigate to www.pearsonhighered.com/skills, locate the name of your textbook, and then follow the instructions on the website.

More Skills Create Databases from Templates

Online templates can provide a way to build a full-featured database quickly. When you start Access, several templates are available for common business practices such as managing contacts and tasks.

In More Skills 12, you will create a database from the Task Management template provided by Microsoft. You will then

use the database to enter a new task, enter a new contact, and then assign the task to the contact. You will then view one of the template's reports.

To begin, open your web browser, navigate to www.pearsonhighered.com/skills, locate the name of your textbook, and then follow the instructions on the website.

More Skills Create Macros

Macros are used to perform a sequence of steps with a single click of the mouse. Using macros in forms and reports saves time and automates common tasks.

In More Skills 13, you will create two macros using two different methods and then use the macros to update a report that is based on a query.

To begin, open your web browser, navigate to www.pearsonhighered.com/skills, locate the name of your textbook, and then follow the instructions on the website.

More Skills Create Access Apps

Access databases can be stored on the Cloud and then shared on the web by creating an Access app. Also known as Access Web apps, Access apps are stored on an SQL Azure or SQL Server. If you have an Office 365 account, you may have access to one of these servers. After they are created, Web apps can be accessed from a web browser.

In More Skills 14, you will read how to create and use an Access app and answer five questions about the process. If you have SQL Azure or an SQL Server account, you can perform the steps in this skill to create the Access app yourself.

To begin, open your web browser, navigate to www.pearsonhighered.com/skills, locate the name of your textbook, and then follow the instructions on the website.

Please note that there are no additional projects to accompany the More Skills Projects, and they are not covered in the End-of-Chapter projects.

The following table summarizes the **SKILLS AND PROCEDURES** covered in this chapter.

Skills Number	Task	Step	Icon	Keyboard Shortcut
1	Create forms with the Form Wizard	Create tab → Forms group → Form Wizard		
2	Locate a record in a form	Click in the field to be searched. Then, Home → Find group → Find		Ctrl + F
2	Create new records	In the Navigation bar, click New (blank) record	▶	
3	Format form controls	Select the control(s) in Layout view, and then use the groups on the Format tab		
3	Set control widths and heights	On the property sheet Format tab, change the Width or Height property		F4
4	Apply conditional formatting	Format tab → Control Formatting group → Conditional Formatting → New Rule		
4	Add logos	Design tab → Header / Footer group → Logo		
5	Create forms with the Form Tool	Select table or query in Navigation Pane. Then, Create tab → Forms group → Form		
5	Create one-to-many forms	In the Navigation Pane, select the table that will be the main form. Then, Create tab → Forms group → Form		
5	Add date and time controls	Design tab → Header / Footer group → Date and Time		
6	Insert columns and rows	Arrange tab → Rows & Columns group		
6	Delete columns and rows	Arrange tab → Rows & Columns group → Select Column or Select Row. Then, press Delete		
6	Merge columns and rows	Select cells. Then, Arrange tab → Merge / Split group → Merge		
6	Edit label control text	Double-click the label control		
7	Add input masks to form text box controls	Property sheet Data tab → Input Mask → Build button		
8	Edit data in one-to-many forms	Use the main form Navigation bar to locate the desired record. Change data in either the main form or the subform datasheet		
10	Create Navigation Forms	Create tab → Forms group → Navigation Form		
10	Automatically close the Navigation Pane when the form is open	Property sheet Other tab → Modal → Yes		
10	Automatically set a form to open when the database is first opened	File → Options → Current Database → Display Form		
10	Format button controls	Format tab → Control Formatting group → Quick Styles (and other commands in the group)		

Key Terms

Online Help Skills

1. Start **Access 2013**, and then in the upper right corner of the start page, click the **Help** button ?.

2. In the **Access Help** window **Search help** box, type split form and then press Enter.

3. In the search result list, click **Create a split form**, and then compare your screen with **Figure 1**.

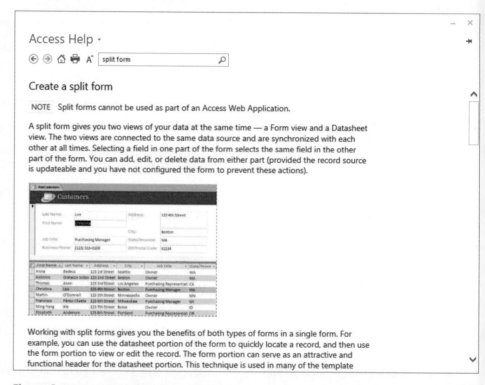

Figure 1

4. Read the article to answer the following questions: How is a split form like a one-to-many form? How is a split form different from a one-to-many form? What are the advantages of a split form?

Matching

Match each term in the second column with its correct definition in the first column by writing the letter of the term on the blank line in front of the correct definition.

___ **1.** A tool used to create a form that provides a way to select tables and fields before the form is created.

___ **2.** The arrangement of data and labels in a form or report—columnar or tabular, for example.

___ **3.** A form control that displays the name of a form by default; the actual text can be edited later.

___ **4.** A set of special characters that control what can and cannot be entered in a field.

___ **5.** A layout with cells arranged in rows and columns into which controls are placed.

___ **6.** By default, subforms display in this view.

___ **7.** By default, main forms display in this layout.

___ **8.** A type of form that has a subform that displays related records from another table.

___ **9.** A form that can be used to quickly switch between forms and reports in the database.

___ **10.** To set a form to open automatically when the database is opened, open the Access Options dialog box, and then display the options for this category.

A Current Database

B Datasheet view

C Form Wizard

D Input mask

E Layout

F Navigation form

G One-to-many form

H Single Form view

I Tabular layout

J Title

BizSkills Video

1. What do you think are the biggest sources of conflict in the meeting portrayed in the video?

2. What suggestions do you have to reduce the conflict in the group portrayed in the video?

Multiple Choice (MyITLab®)

Choose the correct answer.

1. An Access view used to format a form or report while you are viewing a sample of the data.
   A. Design view
   B. Form view
   C. Layout view

2. A layout that places labels in the first column and data in the second column.
   A. Columnar
   B. Datasheet
   C. Tabular

3. Controls on a form or report that describe each field—often the field name—in the underlying table.
   A. IntelliSense Quick Info boxes
   B. Labels
   C. Text boxes

4. Controls on a form or report that display the data from each field in the underlying table or query.
   A. Labels
   B. Text boxes
   C. Titles

5. The property sheet tab that contains the Input Mask property.
   A. Data
   B. Format
   C. Other

6. The symbol in an input mask that is replaced as you type data into the field.
   A. Data character
   B. Input character
   C. Placeholder character

7. Formatting that evaluates the values in a field and formats that data according to the rules you specify; for example, only values over 1000 will have bold applied.
   A. Conditional formatting
   B. Logical formatting
   C. Rules-based formatting

8. A form contained within another form that contains records related to the record displayed in the main form.
   A. Parent form
   B. Relationship form
   C. Subform

9. When you want to build a form for a subset of table data, you can base the form on this.
   A. Blank Form tool
   B. Filtered table
   C. Query

10. To automatically close the Navigation Pane whenever the form is open, this form property needs to be set to *Yes*.
    A. Full Width
    B. Modal
    C. Open Exclusive

Topics for Discussion

1. You have created forms using two different methods: the Form tool and the Form Wizard. Which method do you prefer and why? What are the primary advantages of each method?

2. Recall that forms are used to enter data into a database. Consider the types of data businesses might store in a database. For example, a school needs a class registration form to enter students into classes. What type of forms might other businesses need to enter data?

Skills Review

To complete this project, you will need the following files:

- acc03_SRElectricity
- acc03_SRLogo

You will save your file as:

- Last_First_acc03_SRElectricity

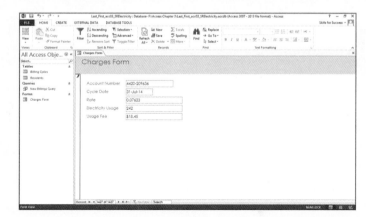

Figure 1

1. Start **Access 2013**, and then open the student data file **acc03_SRElectricity**. Save the database in your **Access Chapter 3** folder with the name Last_First_acc03_ SRElectricity If necessary, enable the content.

2. On the **Create tab**, in the **Forms group**, click the **Form Wizard** button. In the **Form Wizard**, select the **Billing Cycles** table, and then move **AccountNumber**, **CycleDate**, **Rate**, **ElectricityUsage**, and **UsageFee** into **Selected Fields**. Click **Next** two times, name the form Charges Form and then **Finish** the wizard.

3. On the **Home tab**, in the **Views group**, click **View** to switch to Layout view.

4. With the **Account Number** text box control selected, press and hold [Ctrl], while clicking the other four text boxes. Click the **Format tab**, and then in the **Font group**, click the **Align Left** button.

5. Click the **Home tab**, and then click the **View** button to switch to Form view. In the Navigation bar, click **New (blank) record**, and then enter the following billing: **Account Number** is 4420-209636 **Cycle Date** is 31-Jul-14 **Rate** is 0.07623 and **Electricity Usage** is 242 Click in the **Usage Fee** field, and then compare your screen with **Figure 1**.

6. **Save** and then **Close** the form. In the **Navigation Pane**, click **New Billings Query** one time to select it. Click the **Create tab**, and then in the **Forms group**, click the **Form** button.

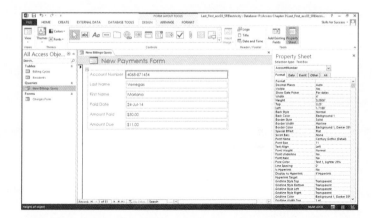

Figure 2

7. Double-click the **Title** control, and then change the text to New Payments Form

8. Click the **Account Number** text box, and then click as needed to open the property sheet. On the property sheet **Format tab**, change the **Width** property to 4" and then compare your screen with **Figure 2**.

9. Click **Save**, type New Payments Form and then click **OK**. **Close** the form.

■ Continue to the next page to complete this Skills Review

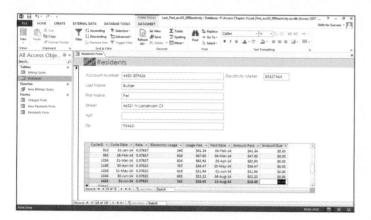

Figure 3

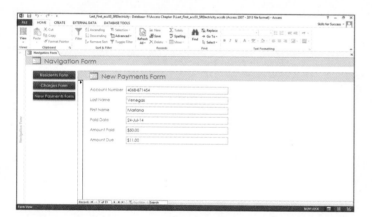

Figure 4

10. In the **Navigation Pane**, click **Residents** one time to select it. Click the **Create tab**, and then in the **Forms group**, click the **Form** button. Click **Save**, type Residents Form and then click **OK**.

11. On the **Design tab**, in the **Header / Footer group**, click **Logo**, and then use the **Insert Picture** dialog box to insert the file **acc03_SRLogo**.

12. Click the **Zip** text box, and then click the property sheet **Data tab**. Click the **Input Mask** box, and click the displayed **Build** button. In the **Input Mask Wizard**, select **Zip Code**, and then click **Finish**.

13. Using the property sheet, set the width of the column of the **Account Number** text box to 4" With the column still active, click the **Arrange tab**, and then in the **Rows & Columns group**, click the **Insert Right** button three times.

14. Drag the **Electricity Meter** label to the first empty cell to the right of the **Account Number** text box. Drag the **Electricity Meter** box control to the first empty cell to the right of the **Electricity Meter** label. Use the property sheet to set the width of the column with the **Electricity Meter** label to 1.5" and then **Close** the property sheet.

15. Click in the row with the subform. On the **Arrange tab**, in the **Rows & Columns group**, click **Select Row**. In the **Merge / Split group**, click **Merge**.

16. Click **Save**, and then switch to Form view. **Find** the record for **Account Number** 4420-209636 and then **Close** the Find and Replace dialog box.

17. In the subform, click the **Last record** button, and then in the last record, type a **Paid Date** of 13-Aug-14 and an **Amount Paid** of 18.45 Compare your screen with **Figure 3**, and then **Close** the form.

18. On the **Create tab**, in the **Forms group**, click **Navigation**, and then click **Vertical Tabs, Left**.

19. Select the **[Add New]** button, and then click the **Format tab**. In the **Control Formatting group**, click the **Quick Styles** button, and then click the second style in the last row—**Intense Effect – Dark Red, Accent 1**.

20. Drag **Residents Form** to the **[Add New]** button. Repeat to add **Charges Form** and then **New Payments Form**.

21. Display the property sheet, and then, under **Selection type**, select **Form**. On the property sheet **Other tab**, change the **Modal** property to **Yes**.

22. Click **Save**, click **OK**, and then switch to Form view. Compare your screen with **Figure 4**.

23. **Close** Access and submit the project as directed by your instructor.

 DONE! You have completed this Skills Review

Skills Assessment 1

MyITLab®
Grader

To complete this database, you will need the following files:

- acc03_SA1Classes
- acc03_SA1Logo

You will save your database as:

- Last_First_acc03_SA1Classes

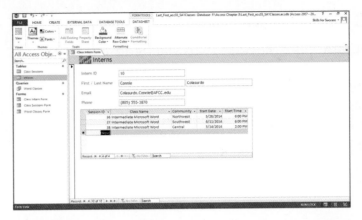

Figure 1

1. Start **Access 2013**, and then open the student data file **acc03_SA1Classes**. Save the database in your chapter folder with the name Last_First_acc03_SA1Classes If necessary, enable the content.

2. Use the **Form Wizard** to create a form with all the fields from the **Class Sessions** table *except* SessionID. Name the form Class Sessions Form and accept all other wizard defaults.

3. Set the width of all the form's text boxes to 3" and their text alignment to left.

4. Use the form to add the following record: **Class Name** is Intermediate Microsoft Word **Community Center** is Central and **Intern ID** is 10 Leave the other fields blank. **Save** and then **Close** the form.

5. Use the **Form Tool** to create a form based on the **Word Classes** query. Change the **Title** control text to Word Classes Form **Save** the form as Word Classes Form and then **Close** the form.

6. Use the **Form Tool** to create a form with a main form based on the **Interns** table and a subform based on the **Class Sessions** table. Change the form's logo using the file **acc03_SA1Logo**.

7. Add a **Phone Number** input mask to the **Phone** text box control that uses the number sign (#) as the placeholder character. Accept all other wizard defaults.

8. Add a column to the right of the table, and then move the **Last Name** text box control into the first cell to the right of the **First Name** text box.

9. Delete the unused row with the **Last Name** label, and then change the *First Name* label text to First / Last Name

10. Set the width of the table's first column to 1.5" and the width of the second and third columns to 2.6" In the subform row, merge all of the cells.

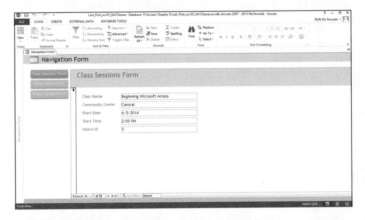

Figure 2

11. **Save** the form with the name Class Intern Form and then switch to **Form view**. Navigate to the last **Intern** record, and then in the subform for Connie Colasurado, complete the last record by adding a **Start Date** of 5/14/2014 and **Start Time** of 2:00 PM Compare your screen with **Figure 1**, and then **Close** the form.

12. Create a **Navigation Form** with the **Vertical Tabs**, **Left** layout. Apply the **Intense Effect – Green**, **Accent 1** Quick Style to the **[Add New]** button, and then add buttons in the following order: **Class Sessions Form**, **Class Intern Form**, and then **Word Classes Form**.

13. Set the form's **Modal** property to **Yes**. Click **Save**, and then click **OK**. Reopen the form, and then compare your screen with **Figure 2**.

14. **Close** the form, **Close** Access, and submit the project as directed by your instructor.

 DONE! You have completed Skills Assessment 1

Skills Assessment 2

To complete this database, you will need the following files:

- acc03_SA2Rentals
- acc03_SA2Logo

You will save your database as:

- Last_First_acc03_SA2Rentals

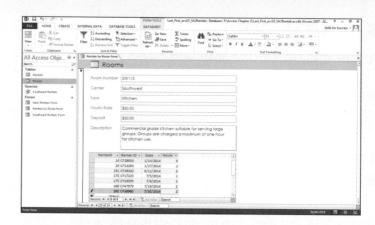

Figure 1

1. Start **Access 2013**, and then open the student data file **acc03_SA2Rentals**. Save the database in your chapter folder with the name Last_First_acc03_SA2Rentals If necessary, enable the content.

2. Use the **Form Wizard** to create a form with fields from the **Rentals** table in this order: **RenterID**, **Date**, and **RoomNumber**. Name the form New Rentals Form and accept all other wizard defaults.

3. Set the width of all the form's text boxes to 2" and their text alignment to left.

4. Use the form to add the following record: **Renter ID** is CF38960 **Date** is 7/30/2014 and **Room Number** is SW115 **Save** and then **Close** the form.

5. Use the **Form Tool** to create a form based on the **Southeast Rentals** query. Change the form's logo using the file **acc03_SA2Logo**. **Save** the form as Southeast Rentals Form and then **Close** the form.

6. Use the **Form Tool** to create a form with a main form based on the **Rooms** table with a subform based on the **Rentals** table.

7. For the **Deposit** text box control, create a new conditional formatting rule: If the field value is greater than 75 the font should be **Green** (column 6, last row) and **Bold**.

8. Use the property sheet to set the **Description** text box control's **Width** to 4.5" and the **Height** to 1"

9. **Save** the form with the name Rentals by Room Form and then switch to **Form view**. In the main form, navigate to **Room Number SW115**. In the subform for that room, complete the last record by entering 2 in the **Hours** field. Compare your screen with **Figure 1**, and then **Close** the form.

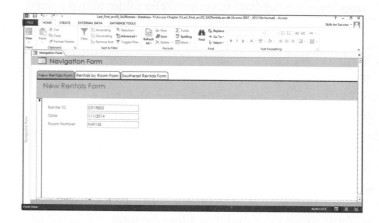

Figure 2

10. Create a **Navigation Form** with the **Horizontal Tabs** layout. Apply the **Colored Outline - Purple, Accent 6** Quick Style (column 7, row 1) to the **[Add New]** button, and then change its shape to **Round Same Side Corner Rectangle** (shape 5).

11. Add buttons in the following order: **New Rentals Form**, **Rentals by Room Form**, and then **Southeast Rentals Form**.

12. Set the form's **Modal** property to **Yes**. Click **Save**, and then click **OK**. Reopen the form, and then compare your screen with **Figure 2**.

13. **Close** the form, **Close** Access, and submit the project as directed by your instructor.

 DONE! You have completed Skills Assessment 2

Visual Skills Check

To complete this database, you will need the following files:

- acc03_VSArtCenter
- acc03_VSLogo

You will save your database as:

- Last_First_acc03_VSArtCenter

Open the database **acc03_VSArtCenter**, and then using your own name, save the database in your **Access Chapter 3** folder as Last_First_acc03_VSArtCenter

Open **Students Form** in **Layout view**, and then arrange and format the label and text box controls as shown in **Figure 1**. The **First Name** and **Last Name** labels are bold, the **City** label text has been changed to City / State / Zip and unused rows have been deleted.

Create the Navigation form shown in **Figure 1**. The form is named Navigation Form the title text has been changed to Art Classes Navigation Form and the logo was inserted from the file **acc03_VSLogo**. The buttons have been formatted with the **Subtle Effect - Dark Blue**, **Accent 1** Quick Style, the **Rounded Rectangle** shape, and the button text is bold. The form properties have been changed so that the Navigation Pane automatically closes whenever the form is open.

Submit the project as directed by your instructor.

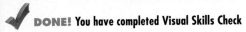

DONE! You have completed Visual Skills Check

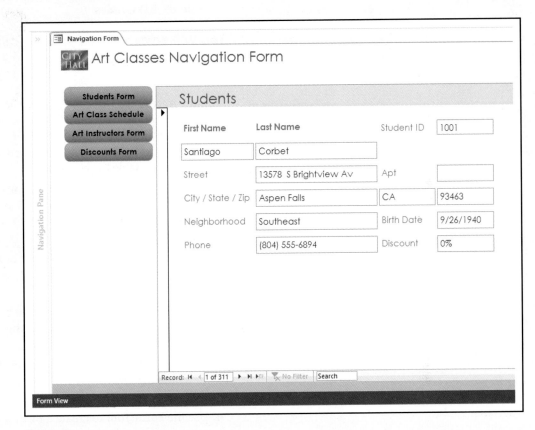

Figure 1

Figure 1

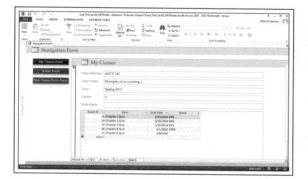

Figure 2

My Skills

To complete this database, you will need the following file:

- acc03_MYGrades

You will save your database as:

- Last_First_acc03_MYGrades

1. Start **Access 2013**, and then open the student data file **acc03_MYGrades**. Save the database in your chapter folder with the name Last_First_acc03_MYGrades If necessary, enable the content.

2. Use the **Form Wizard** to create a form with all of the fields from the **Scores** table *except* ScoreID. Name the form Scores Form and accept all other wizard defaults.

3. Set the width of all the form's text boxes to 2.5" and their text alignment to left. **Save**, and then **Close** the form.

4. Use the **Form Tool** to create a form based on the **Missing Scores** query. Change the **Title** control text to New Scores

5. Set the width of the text box controls to 3.5" **Save** the form as New Scores Entry Form and then **Close** the form.

6. Use the **Form Tool** to create a form with a main form based on the **Classes** table with a subform based on the **Scores** table.

7. In the main form, change the **Title** control to My Classes and then use the property sheet to set the **Height** of the row with the subform to 3.2"

8. **Save** the form with the name My Classes Form and then switch to **Form view**. Compare your screen with Figure 1.

9. In the main form, create a new record using the data from the class that is assigning this project to you. In the subform, fill in the data for all of the assignments, quizzes, tests, or other grading opportunities that have been posted for your class. If you received scores on any of these, enter those scores. When you are done, **Close** the form.

10. Create a **Navigation Form** with the **Vertical Tabs**, **Left** layout. Apply the **Moderate Effect - Brown**, **Accent 4** Quick Style (column 5, row 5) to the [**Add New**] button.

11. Add buttons in the following order: **My Classes Form**, **Scores Form**, and then **New Scores Entry Form**.

12. Set the form's **Modal** property to **Yes**. Click **Save**, and then click **OK**. Reopen the form, and then compare your screen with Figure 2.

13. **Close** the form, **Close** Access, and submit the project as directed by your instructor.

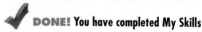 **DONE! You have completed My Skills**

Skills Challenge 1

To complete this database, you will need the following file:

- acc03_SC1Farms

You will save your database as:

- Last_First_acc03_SC1Farms

Open **acc03_SC1Farms** and save the database in your **Access Chapter 3** folder as Last_First_acc03_SC1Farms Use the Form Tool to create a form that displays all the records and fields from the Farms table. Using the techniques practiced in this chapter, arrange the labels and text boxes so that anyone who uses the form can fill in the data in a logical order. Add columns and rows and merge cells as needed, and resize them to better fit the data they contain. Delete any unused rows or columns. Update the label text so that the labels clearly

describe the data. For example, add spaces between words and where appropriate, describe all the controls in a single row. Format the controls with the farm's name so they stand out from the rest of the controls.

Create and print a snip of the form or submit the database file as directed by your instructor.

 DONE! You have completed Skills Challenge 1

Skill Challenge 2

To complete this database, you will need the following file:

- acc03_SC2Wildlife

You will save your database as:

- Last_First_acc03_SC2Wildlife

Open **acc03_SC2Wildlife**, and then save the database as Last_First_acc03_SC2Wildlife Create a one-to-many form based on the Wildlife table in the main form, and the Alternate Names table in the subform. Format the form to fit the data it will hold making sure to leave room for about five lines of text in the Description text box. Research each of the animals in the Wildlife table in order to complete the form. You can find the information you need at a website such as Wikipedia. Using

the information you find, fill in the form. The first record—Tule Elk—has been completed as an example. Place alternate names in the subform. If an alternate name cannot be found, leave the subform blank for that animal. Submit the project as directed by your instructor.

 DONE! You have completed Skills Challenge 2

CHAPTER 4

Create Reports

- Access reports are designed to present information derived from tables and queries.

- You can use several methods to add fields to reports. You can then format and arrange the fields to make the information more meaningful.

- The records in reports can be grouped, sorted, and filtered to make the information more useful.

- You can build a report with fields from an entire table or those fields that are selected when you run a query using the Report tool.

- When you want to select certain fields from one or more tables, you can create a report using the Blank Report tool.

- When you need to print addresses on self-adhesive labels, you can create a labels report.

- As you work with reports, each view has a special purpose that can be modified in Layout view. Report view shows the report's screen version and Print Preview shows the report's printed version.

© Auremar

Aspen Falls City Hall

In this chapter, you will create reports for Aspen Falls Utilities. You will work under the supervision of Diane Payne, Public Works Director, to build a report about water bills for city residents and create mailing labels using resident addresses. You will also build a report that provides statistics about monthly water usage.

Good reports filter and sort the data found in the database tables in a way that provides useful information. Many reports are started by first creating a query so that the query can provide the fields and criteria needed by the report. After a report is created, you can add additional grouping, sorting, and filters so that just the records and fields you need display.

Reports can be designed in Layout view, and then viewed in Report view or printed. Reports that will be printed typically need to be narrower than reports that are designed to be viewed on a computer screen. For this reason, it is a good practice to view reports in Print Layout View, and then make adjustments as needed to present the report effectively on the printed page.

You will create reports using the Report Wizard, Blank Report tool, Report tool, and Labels tool. You will also format, group, sort, and filter reports to display the information more effectively. Finally, you will summarize report data by adding totals.

Time to complete all 10 skills – 60 to 90 minutes

Student data files needed for this chapter:

acc04_Water (Access)

acc04_WaterLogo (JPG)

You will save your file as:

Last_First_acc04_Water

Outcome

Using the skills in this chapter, you will be able to create Access reports like this:

Month Ending	Sample Count	Ave. Usage*	Ave. Billing	Total Due
31-Jan-14	84	46.8	$10.76	$0.00
28-Feb-14	83	37.8	$9.08	$2.94
31-Mar-14	83	50.1	$12.53	$18.75
30-Apr-14	83	53.3	$15.81	($17.08)
31-May-14	82	73.7	$24.31	($32.01)
30-Jun-14	80	94.4	$33.05	$6.30
31-Jul-14	80	138.1	$52.49	$4,199.38

2014 Water Statistics — 22-Sep-14 8:11 AM

Total Sample 575

Averages 70.6 $22.57

*100's of gallons

Net Total Due $4,178.28

Page 1 of 1

SKILLS

MyITLab®
Skills 1-10 Training

At the end of this chapter you will be able to:

Skill 1   Build Queries for Reports

Skill 2   Create Reports Using the Report Tool

Skill 3   Format Reports

Skill 4   Add Totals to Reports

Skill 5   Preview and Print Reports

Skill 6   Create Reports with the Blank Report Tool

Skill 7   Group and Sort Reports

Skill 8   Modify Report Layouts

Skill 9   Filter Reports

Skill 10   Create Label Reports

MORE SKILLS

Skill 11   Import Objects from Other Databases

Skill 12   Export Reports to Word

Skill 13   Save Reports as PDF Documents

Skill 14   Save Reports as Web Pages and Save Export Steps

▶ ACC 4-1
VIDEO

▶ Reports are often based on queries. You add the fields that you need in the report into the query, add criteria, and then build the report using the query as the data source.

1. Start **Access 2013**, and then open the student data file **acc04_Water**. On the **File tab**, click **Save As**. With **Save Database As** selected, click the **Save As** button. In the **Save As** dialog box, navigate to the location you are saving your files for this project. Click **New folder**, type Access Chapter 4 and then press [Enter] two times. Name the file Last_First_acc04_Water and then click **Save**.

2. If the Security Warning message displays, click the Enable Content button.

3. Click the **Create tab**, and then in the **Queries group**, click the **Query Wizard** button. In the **New Query** dialog box, verify that **Simple Query Wizard** is selected, and then click **OK**.

4. In the **Simple Query Wizard**, click the **Table/Queries arrow**, and then click **Table: Water Bills**.

5. Double-click the following fields to move them into **Selected Fields** in this order: **BillingDate**, **BillingID**, **Usage**, **Billing**, and **AmountDue**. Compare your screen with **Figure 1**, and then click **Finish**.

6. Click the **Home tab**, and then click the **View** button to switch to **Design view**. On the **Design tab**, in the **Show / Hide group**, click **Totals** to display the **Total** row. Compare your screen with **Figure 2**.

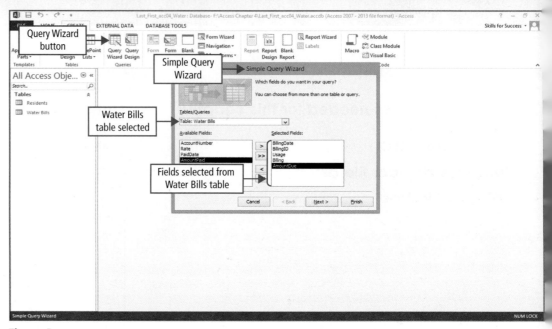

Figure 1

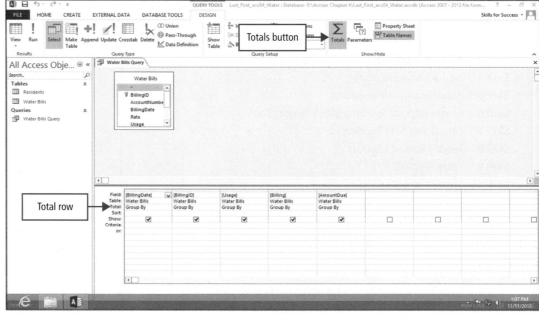

Figure 2

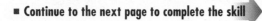

■ **Continue to the next page to complete the skill**

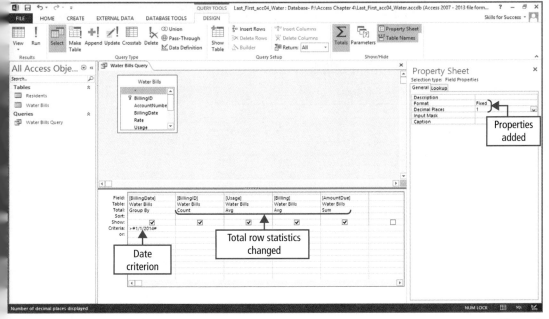

Figure 3

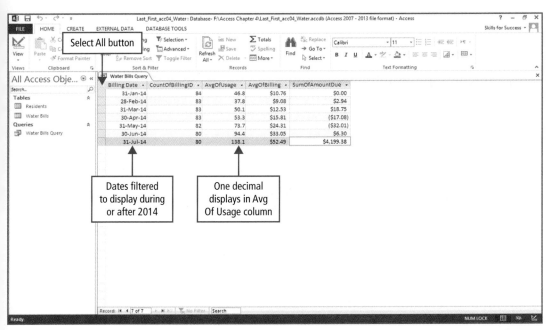

Figure 4

7. Click the **Total** cell for the **BillingID** column, click the arrow that displays, and then click **Count**.

8. Repeat the same technique to change the **Usage** column **Total** cell to **Avg**, the **Billing** column **Total** cell to **Avg**, and the **AmountDue** column **Total** cell to **Sum**.

9. In the **BillingDate** column **Criteria** cell, type >1/1/2014

10. Click in the **Usage** column **Criteria** cell, and then in the **Show/Hide group**, click **Property Sheet** to open it. In the property sheet, change the **Format** to **Fixed** and the **Decimal Places** to 1. Compare your screen with **Figure 3**.

11. **Close** ☒ the property sheet, and then **Run** the query.

12. In the upper left corner of the query datasheet, click the **Select All** button ▨ to select all the columns. On the **Home tab**, in the **Records group**, click the **More** button, and then click **Field Width**. In the **Column Width** dialog box, click **Best Fit**. Click a cell to deselect the columns, and then compare your screen with **Figure 4**.

This query displays statistics about Aspen Falls water usage and bills for each month in 2014. This shows how a query can select the data that needs to be presented in a report.

13. Click **Save** 🖫, and then **Close** ☒ the query.

■ **You have completed Skill 1 of 10**

▶ Reports can be created quickly by selecting a table or query in the Navigation Pane, and then clicking the Report button.

1. In the **Navigation Pane**, under **Queries**, click **Water Bills Query** one time to select it.

2. Click the **Create tab**, and then in the **Reports group**, click the **Report** button to create the report and open it in *Layout view*—a view that can be used to format a report while viewing the report's data.

3. Click the **Save** button 🖫. In the **Save As** dialog box, replace the suggested report name with 2014 Statistics and then click **OK**. Compare your screen with **Figure 1**.

   Access reports have three main sections: the header(s), details, and footer(s). In each section, text boxes display the Data and Label controls label the text boxes. In this report, the labels are above each column in a tabular layout.

4. On the **Design tab**, in the **Themes group**, click the **Themes** button, and then click the last thumbnail—**Wisp**.

5. In the **Themes group**, click the **Colors** button, and then in the **Colors** gallery, click **Marquee**.

6. In the **Themes group**, click the **Fonts** button, and then near the bottom of the **Fonts** gallery, click **Gill Sans MT**. Compare your screen with **Figure 2**.

   This is how you can refine a theme by changing its colors to a different color theme and its fonts to a different fonts theme.

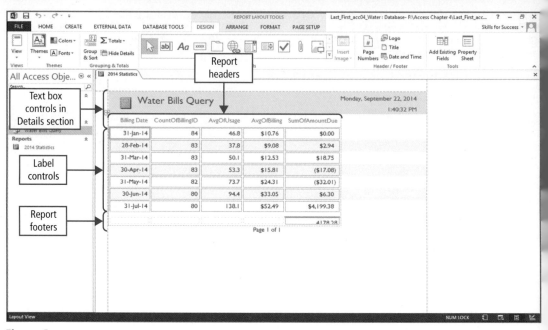

Figure 1

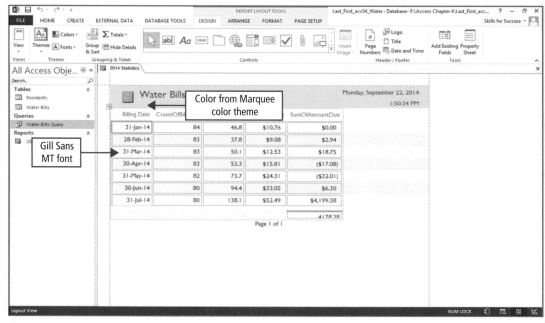

Figure 2

■ **Continue to the next page to complete the skill** ▶

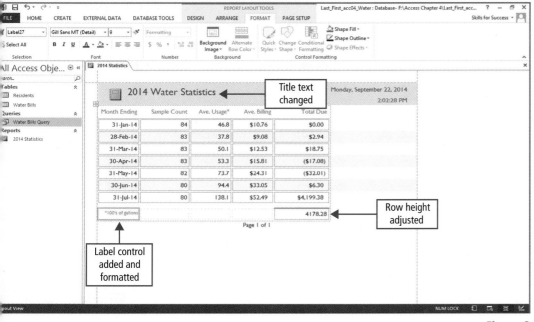

Figure 3

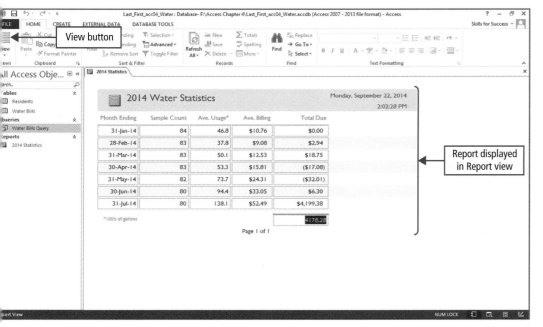

Figure 4

7. In the report header, double-click the title *Water Bills Query* to enter Edit mode, and then change its text to 2014 Water Statistics

8. Double-click the **Billing Date** label control, and then change the label's text to Month Ending Repeat this technique to change **CountOfBillingID** to Sample Count, **AvgOfUsage** to Ave. Usage*, **AvgOfBilling** to Ave. Billing and **SumOfAmountDue** to Total Due

9. Click the last cell—the cell with the value *4178.28*. Point to the cell's lower orange border to display the ↕ pointer, and then double-click to AutoSize the cell's height.

10. Click in the empty cell below the **Month Ending** column, and then type *100's of gallons Press Enter to complete the entry.

11. With the cell *100's of gallons* selected, click the **Format tab**. In the **Font group**, click the **Font Size arrow**, and then click 9. Compare your screen with **Figure 3**.

12. Click the **Home tab**, and then in the **Views group**, click the **View** button to switch to **Report view**. Alternately, in the status bar, click the Report View button . Compare your screen with **Figure 4**.

> ***Report view*** is a view optimized for onscreen viewing of reports.

13. Click **Save** , and then leave the report open for the next skill.

- **You have completed Skill 2 of 10**

▶ Report controls can be formatted using the Property Sheet and the commands on the Format tab.

1. With the **2014 Water Statistics** report open, on the **Home tab**, click the **View** button to switch to **Layout view**. Alternately, on the status bar, click the Layout View button ▦.

2. On the **Design tab**, in the **Header / Footer group**, click the **Logo** button. In the **Insert Picture** dialog box, navigate to the student files, select **acc04_WaterLogo**, and then click **OK**.

3. Select the **Title** control, and then on the **Design tab**, in the **Tools group**, click **Property Sheet**.

4. In the property sheet **Format tab**, change the **Title** control's **Width** to 2.6" In the report, select the **Date** control, and then in the property sheet, change its **Width** to 2.4" Compare your screen with **Figure 1**.

   Because the Time control is in the same layout column as the Date control, the width of both controls can be adjusted at the same time.

5. With the **Date** control still selected, click the Ribbon's **Format tab**. Change the **Font size** to 9, and then apply **Italic** ☐*I*.

6. In the **Font group**, click the **Format Painter** button ☐, and then with the ☐ pointer, click the **Time** control to apply the formatting from the previous step. Compare your screen with **Figure 2**.

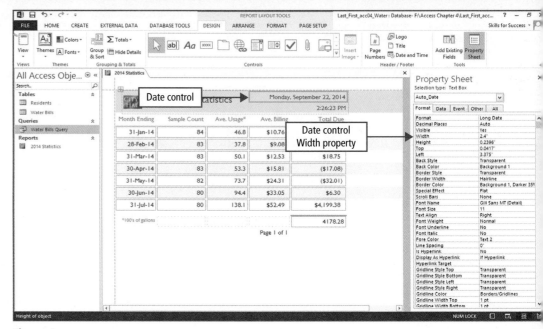

Figure 1

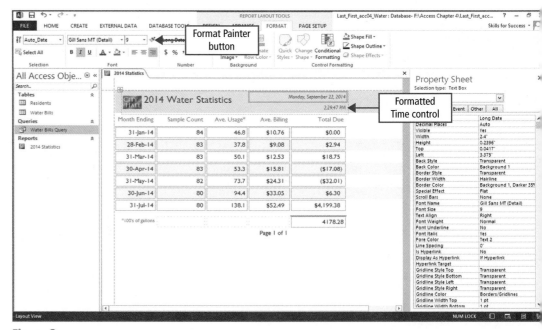

Figure 2

■ **Continue to the next page to complete the skill** ➤

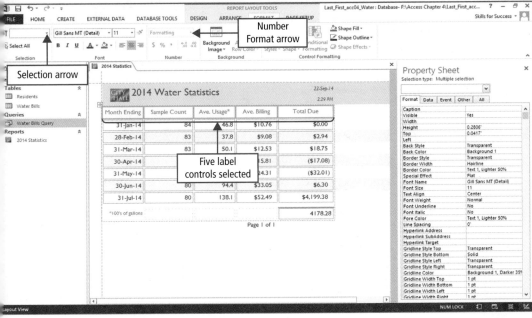

Figure 3

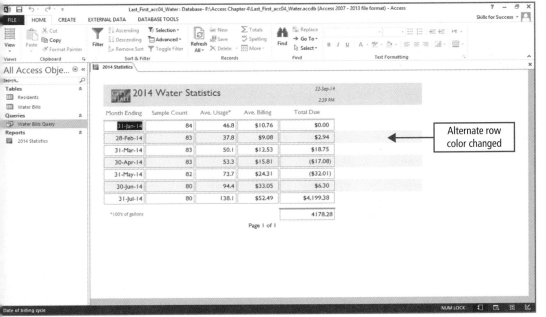

Figure 4

7. With the **Date** control still selected, on the Ribbon's **Format tab**, in the **Number group**, click the **Number Format arrow**, and then click **Medium Date**. Select the **Time** control, and then change the **Number Format** to **Medium Time**.

8. Above the first column, click the **Label** control with the text *Month Ending*. Press and hold [Shift] while clicking the four other labels. Be careful not to move the mouse while clicking the left button.

9. With the five labels selected, on the **Format tab**, in the **Font group**, click the **Center** button. Compare your screen with **Figure 3**.

10. On the **Format tab**, in the **Selection group**, click the **Selection arrow**, and then click **Detail**. On the **Format tab**, in the **Background group**, click the **Alternate Row Color arrow**, and then in the color gallery's second row, click the sixth color—**Green, Accent 2, Lighter 80%**.

    To change the color of banded rows, you need to select the ***Detail control***—the area of a report that repeats for each record in the table or query.

11. On the status bar, click the **Report View** button, and then compare your screen with **Figure 4**.

12. Click **Save**, and leave the report open for the next skill.

■ **You have completed Skill 3 of 10**

▶ You can add *summary statistics*—calculations for groups of data such as totals, averages, and counts—to report columns.

1. With the **2014 Water Statistics** report still open, switch to **Layout view** 📊.

2. In the report's last row, click in a blank cell, and then click the **Arrange tab**. In the **Rows & Columns group**, click the **Insert Above** button two times to insert two blank rows.

3. Click in the first cell of the upper blank row just inserted, and then type Total Sample

4. Click a number in the **Sample Count** column to make it active, and then click the **Design tab**. In the **Grouping & Totals group**, click the **Totals** button, and then click **Sum** to add a total for the active column.

5. Click the **Sum** control just inserted, point to its lower border, and then double-click with the ⬍ pointer to AutoSize the row's height. Compare your screen with **Figure 1**.

6. Click a number in the **Ave. Usage** column to make it active. On the **Design tab**, in the **Grouping & Totals group**, click the **Totals** button, and then click **Average**. Repeat this technique to add an average for the **Ave. Billing** column. Compare your screen with **Figure 2**.

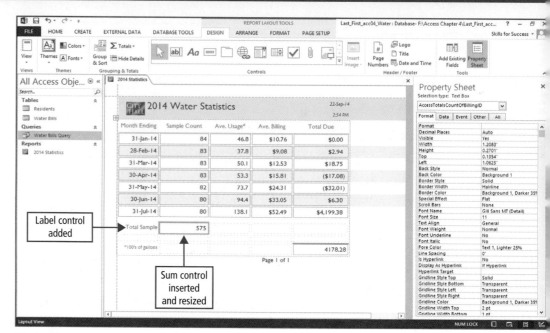

Figure 1

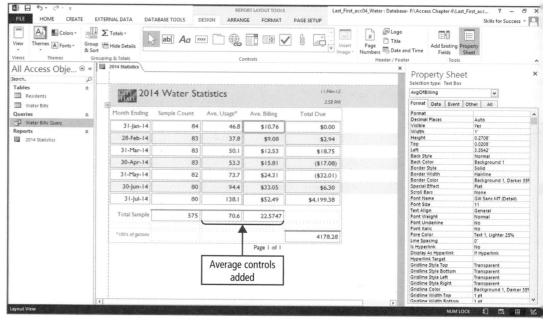

Figure 2

■ Continue to the next page to complete the skill

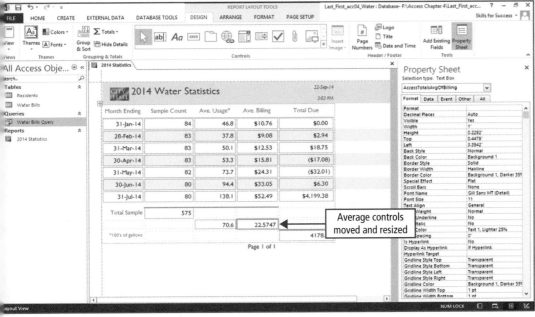

Average controls moved and resized

Figure 3

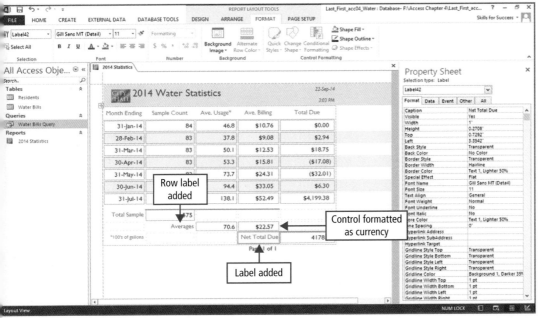

Row label added

Control formatted as currency

Label added

Figure 4

7. Point to the middle of the cell with the **Ave. Usage** column **Average** control—*70.6*. With the pointer, drag the control down one cell. Repeat to move the **Average** control of the **Ave. Billing** column down one cell.

8. Point to the lower border of the selected **Average** control, and then double-click with the pointer to AutoSize the row's height. Compare your screen with **Figure 3**.

9. With the **Ave. Billing** column **Average** control still selected, click the Ribbon's **Format tab**, and then in the **Number group**, click the **Currency** button $.

10. Click in the blank cell below the **Sample Count** column **Sum** control, and then type Averages

11. Click in the blank cell below the **Ave. Billing** column **Average** control, and then type Net Total Due Press Enter, and then compare your screen with **Figure 4**.

12. Click **Save**, and leave the report open for the next skill.

■ **You have completed Skill 4 of 10**

▶ It is a good practice to preview reports before printing them to see if they need any formatting adjustments.

1. With the **2014 Water Statistics** report open, click the **Home tab**. In the **Views group**, click the **View arrow**, and then click **Print Preview**. Compare your screen with **Figure 1**. If the entire page does not display, in the **Zoom group**, click the **One Page** button.

   In Print Preview view, the Print Preview tab is the only Ribbon tab, and the report displays as it will print on paper. Here, the page number footer—*Page 1 of 1*—displays at the bottom of the printed page.

2. In the **Close Preview group**, click the **Close Print Preview** button to return to **Layout view**. If your report displays in a different view, on the status bar, click the **Layout View** button.

3. Click the **Format tab**. In the **Selection group**, click the **Selection arrow**, and then click **Report** to select the report and display its properties in the property sheet. If necessary, open the **Property Sheet**.

4. Near the middle of the **Property Sheet Format tab**, double-click the **Fit to Page** box to change the value to **No**. Change the **Width** property to 5.8" Press Enter, and then compare your screen with **Figure 2**.

   By default, a report is set to the width of a printed sheet of paper. By removing this setting, you can decrease the width of the report to fit the contents.

■ **Continue to the next page to complete the skill**

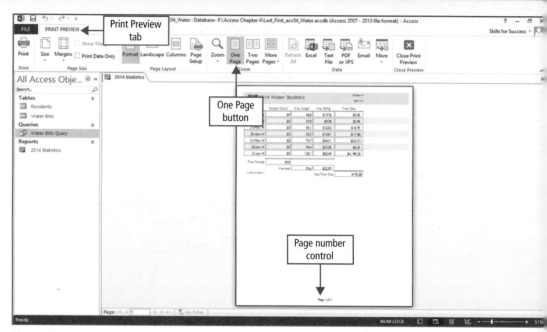

Figure 1

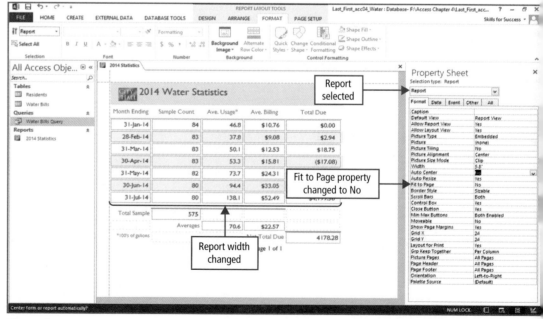

Figure 2

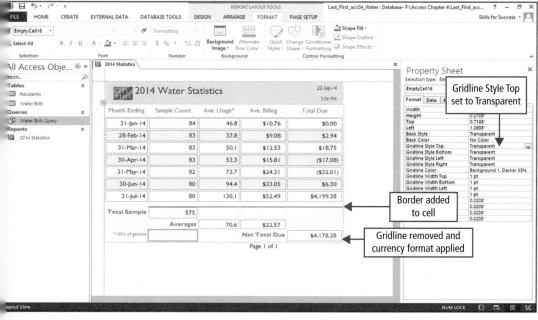

Figure 3

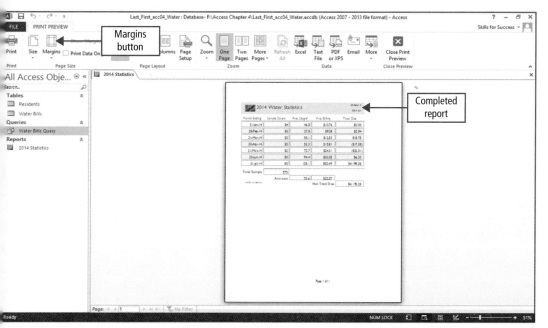

Figure 4

5. Below the **Month Ending** column, select the label with the text *Total Sample*. On the **Format tab**, in the **Font group**, click **Bold** B, and then click **Align Right** ☰. Double-click **Format Painter** 🖌, and then click the **Averages** and **Net Total Due** labels to apply the same formatting. Click the **Format Painter** button 🖌 so that it is no longer active.

6. Click the **Net Total Due Label** control, point to its right border, and then with the ↔ icon, double-click to AutoSize the column width.

7. Click in the first empty cell below *$4,199.38*. On the property sheet **Format tab**, double-click **Gridline Style Top** to change its value to **Solid**. Double-click **Gridline Width Top** to change its value to **2 pt**.

8. Click in the last cell—*$4,178.28*. On the property sheet **Format tab**, click **Gridline Style Top** one time, click the displayed **arrow**, and then click **Transparent**. On the **Format tab**, in the **Number group**, click **Currency** $. Click in a blank cell in the report, and then compare your screen with **Figure 3**.

9. **Close** X the property sheet. On the status bar, click the **Print Preview** button 🔍.

10. In the **Page Size group**, click the **Margins** button, and then click **Wide**. Compare your screen with **Figure 4**.

11. If you are printing this project, click **Print**, and then use the **Print** dialog box to print the report.

12. Click **Save** 💾, and then **Close** X the report.

■ **You have completed Skill 5 of 10**

▶ The Blank Report tool is used when you want to build a report by adding fields one at a time.

1. On the **Create tab**, in the **Reports group**, click the **Blank Report** button.

2. In the **Field List** pane, click **Show all tables**. In the **Field List**, to the left of **Residents**, click the **Expand** button ⊞.

3. In the **Field List**, double-click **AccountNumber** to add the field to the report. Compare your screen with **Figure 1**.

   As you add fields with the Blank Report tool, the other tables move to the lower sections of the Field List pane. Here, the Water Bills table is a related table—it contains the AccountNumber as a foreign key.

4. In the **Field List**, double-click **LastName** and **FirstName** to add them to the report.

5. In the **Field List**, under **Fields available in related tables**, **Expand** ⊞ the **Water Bills** table.

6. Double-click **BillingDate**, and then compare your screen with **Figure 2**.

   When you add a field from another table, that table moves to the upper pane of the Field List.

■ **Continue to the next page to complete the skill** ➡

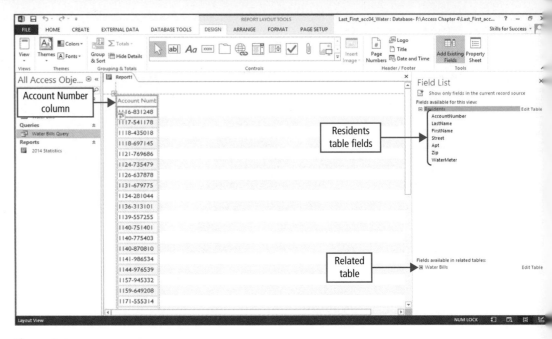

Figure 1

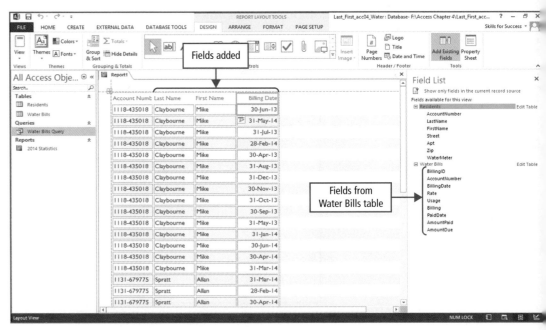

Figure 2

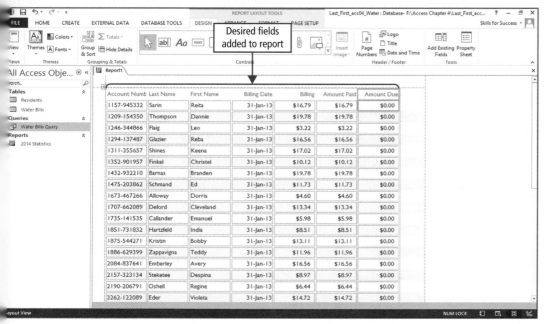

Figure 3

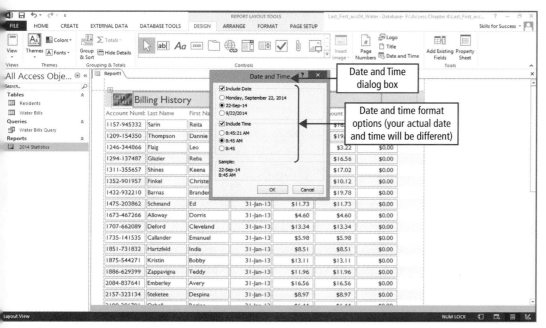

Figure 4

7. In the **Field List**, under **Water Bills**, double-click **Billing, AmountPaid**, and then **AmountDue**, to add the three fields to the report.

8. **Close** ⌧ the **Field List** pane, and then compare your screen with **Figure 3**.

9. In the **Header / Footer group**, click the **Logo** button. In the **Insert Picture** dialog box, navigate to the student files, select **acc04_WaterLogo**, and then click **OK** to create a report header and insert the logo in it.

10. On the **Design tab**, in the **Header / Footer group**, click the **Title** button, type Billing History and then press Enter .

11. In the **Header / Footer group**, click the **Date and Time** button. In the **Date and Time** dialog box, under **Include Date**, select the middle option button—**dd-mmm-yy**. Under **Include Time**, click the middle option button—**hh:mm PM**. Compare your screen with **Figure 4**, and then click **OK**.

12. Click **Save** 🖫. In the **Save As** dialog box, type Billing History Report and then press Enter . Leave the report open for the next skill.

■ **You have completed Skill 6 of 10**

► Report data can be grouped and sorted to make the report information more useful.

► Reports created with the Blank Report tool lay out controls in a table. You can position controls by dragging them into other cells, and you can format text controls by selecting the cell they are in.

1. If necessary, open the **Billing History** report in **Layout view**. On the **Design tab**, in the **Grouping & Totals group**, click the **Group & Sort** button as needed to display the **Group, Sort, and Total** pane.

2. In the **Group, Sort, and Total** pane, click the **Add a group** button. In the list of fields, click **AccountNumber** to group the billings within each account.

3. In the report, click **Account Number** to select the label. Point to the right border, and then with the ↔ pointer, double-click to AutoSize the label width. Compare your screen with **Figure 1**.

4. Click the first text box control with the text *Claybourne*, and then, with the ⟰ pointer, drag the control into the empty cell below the **Last Name** label.

5. Repeat this technique to move the control with the text *Mike* into the empty cell below the **First Name** label. Compare your screen with **Figure 2**.

> Because the resident names do not change within each group of account numbers, they can be in the same row as the Account Number. In this way, the names are not repeated in each billing row.

■ **Continue to the next page to complete the skill** ▶

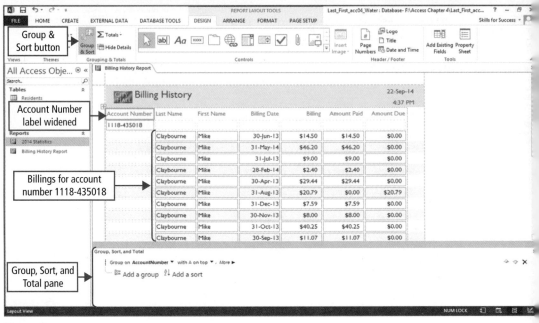

Figure 1

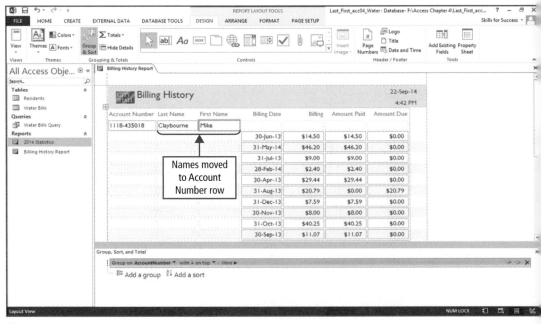

Figure 2

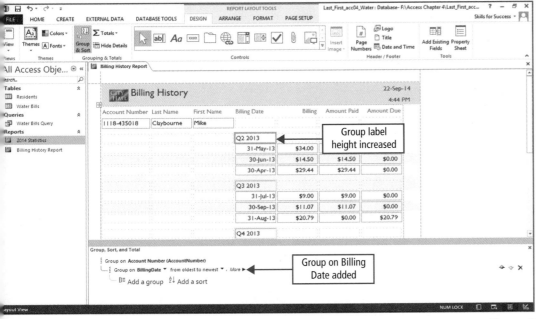

Figure 3

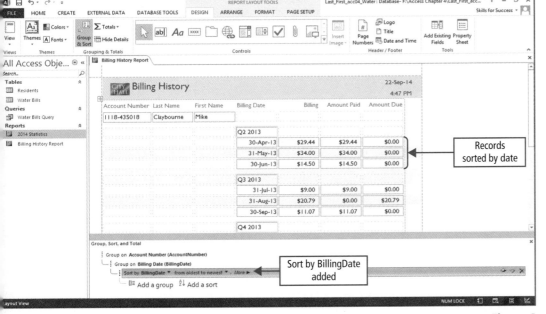

Figure 4

6. In the **Group**, **Sort**, **and Total** pane, click the **Add a group** button, and then in the list of fields, click **BillingDate** to group the Billing Cycles by quarter.

7. Click the first quarter label with the text *Q2 2013*. Point to the lower border, and then with the ⬍ pointer, double-click to AutoSize the row height. Compare your screen with **Figure 3**.

   Fields that contain dates can be grouped by several time intervals including days, months, quarters, and years. By default, they are grouped into yearly quarters with the oldest quarters displayed first.

8. In the **Group**, **Sort**, **and Total** pane, click the **Add a sort** button, and then in the list of fields, click **BillingDate** to sort by month within each yearly quarter. Compare your screen with **Figure 4**.

9. On the **Design tab**, in the **Grouping & Totals group**, click the **Group & Sort** button to close the pane.

10. **Save** 🖫 the report and leave it open for the next skill.

■ **You have completed Skill 7 of 10**

► In a tabular layout, you can insert and delete rows and columns and then move controls so that they better communicate the report's information.

1. If necessary, open the **Billing History** report in **Layout view**. Point to the cell with the text *Q2 2013*. With the ⟨pointer⟩ pointer, drag the control into the first empty cell below the cell with the text *Claybourne*.

2. Click in the first **Billing Date** cell with the text *30-Apr-13*. Press and hold [Shift] while clicking the **Amount Due** cell in the same row. Compare your screen with **Figure 1**.

3. With the four cells selected, point to the cell with the text *30-Apr-13*, and then drag the cell into the empty cell below the **Q2 2013** control. Compare your screen with **Figure 2**.

4. Below the report header, click the **Billing Date** label, and then press [Delete] to remove the label from the report.

5. Repeat the techniques practiced in this skill to move the **Billing** label to the empty cell to the right of the **Q2 2013** control.

6. Move the **Amount Paid** label to the empty cell to the right of the **Billing** label.

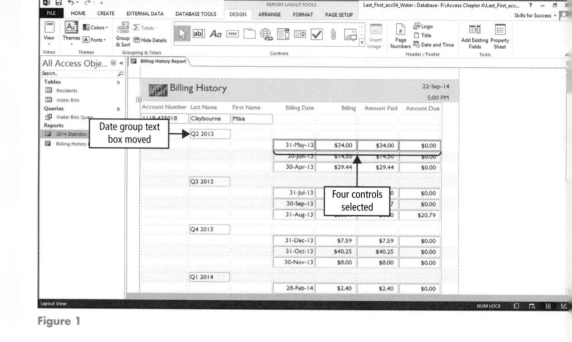

Figure 1

■ Continue to the next page to complete the skill

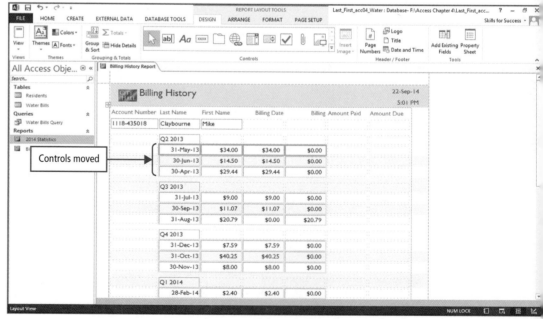

Figure 2

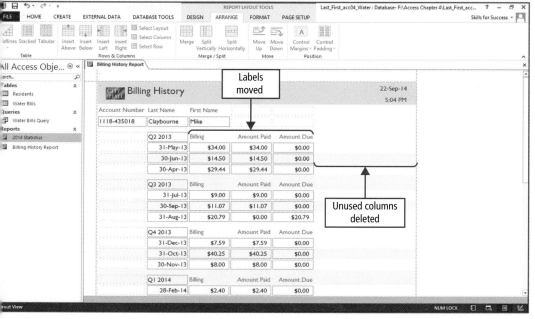

Figure 3

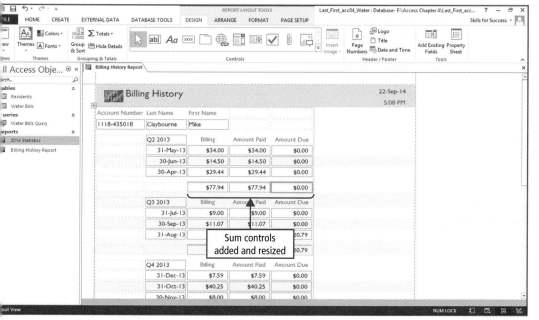

Figure 4

7. Move the **Amount Due** label to the empty cell to the right of the **Amount Paid** label.

8. Click in one of the blank columns on the right side of the report. Click the **Arrange tab**, and then in the **Rows & Columns group**, click **Select Column**. Press [Delete] to remove the column from the report. Repeat this technique to delete the other blank column, and then compare your screen with **Figure 3**.

9. Use the Shift-click technique to select these labels: **Billing**, **Amount Paid**, and **Amount Due**. Click the **Format tab**, and then in the **Font group**, click the **Center** button ☰.

10. Click in any cell below the **Billing** label to make the column active. Click the **Design tab**. In the **Grouping & Totals group**, click the **Totals** button, and then click **Sum** to add a summary statistic for each quarter.

11. Repeat the technique just practiced to insert the **Sum** total to the **Amount Paid** and **Amount Due** columns.

12. Click one of the cells with a **Sum** control that was inserted in the previous step. Point to the lower border, and then with the ↕ pointer, double-click to AutoSize the row's height. Compare your screen with **Figure 4**.

13. Click **Save** 🖫 and leave the report open for the next skill.

■ **You have completed Skill 8 of 10**

▶ Reports can be filtered in a variety of ways so that you can view just the information you need.

1. With the **Billing Report** open in **Layout view**, switch to **Report view**.

2. Click in the text box with the last name *Claybourne*. Click the **Home tab**. In the **Sort & Filter group**, click the **Filter** button. In the **Filter** list, point to **Text Filters**, and then click **Equals**.

3. In the **Custom Filter** dialog box, type *swickard* and then click **OK**. Compare your screen with **Figure 1**.

   When you apply a filter, only the subset of records that match the filter criteria display, and the Toggle Filter button is active. Here, the billing history for only Evie Swickard displays.

4. In the report, click in a control that displays a **Billing Date** value. On the **Home tab**, in the **Sort & Filter group**, click the **Filter** button. In the **Filter** list, point to **Date Filters**, and then click **Between**.

5. In the **Between Dates** dialog box, in the **Oldest** box, type 7/1/13 In the **Newest** box, type 9/30/13 Click **OK**, and then compare your screen with **Figure 2**.

   When you add filters, the previous filters remain in effect. Here, only the records for Evie Swickard in the third quarter of 2013 display. At the end of this report, three rows of totals display: one for the quarter, the account number, and the entire report.

■ **Continue to the next page to complete the skill**

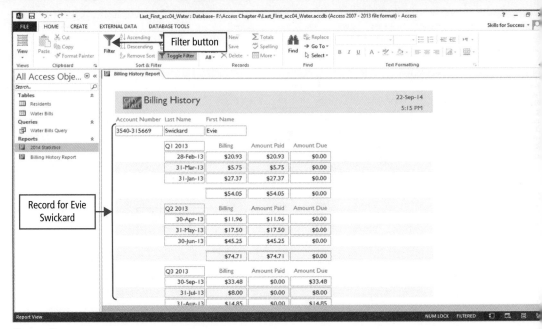

Figure 1

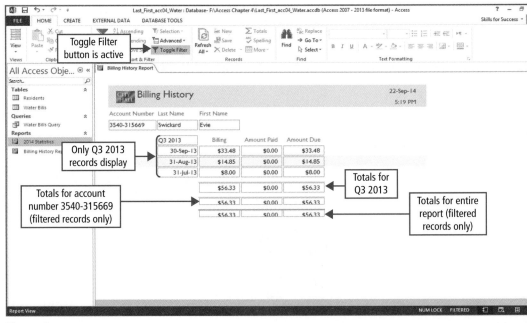

Figure 2

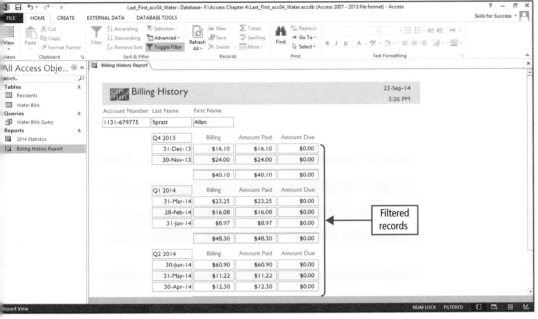

Filtered records

Figure 3

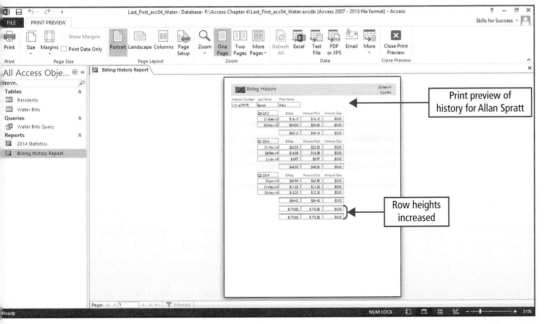

Print preview of history for Allan Spratt

Row heights increased

Figure 4

6. **Save** 🔲, and then **Close** ✖ the report. In the **Navigation Pane**, double-click **Billing History Report** to open it in **Report view**. In the **Sort & Filter group**, click the **Toggle Filter** button to reapply the filter created previously.

> By default, any filters saved in a report are not active when you open the report.

7. In the **Sort & Filter group**, click **Advanced**, and then click **Clear All Filters**.

> The Clear All Filters command removes all filters from the report. Once the filter is cleared, it can no longer be enabled by clicking the Toggle Filter button.

8. Scroll down to the second account, to display the history for *Allan Spratt*. Click in the text box with the text *Spratt*. On the **Home tab**, in the **Sort & Filter group**, click the **Selection** button, and then click **Equals "Spratt"**. Compare your screen with **Figure 3**.

9. On the status bar, click the **Layout View** button 🔳. Using the technique practiced previously, AutoSize the height of the last two rows—the rows with the **Sum** controls.

10. On the status bar, click the **Print Preview** button 🔳. In the **Zoom group**, click **One Page** as needed to display the entire page, and then compare your screen with **Figure 4**.

11. If you are printing your work, print the report.

12. Click **Save** 🔲, and then **Close** ✖ the report.

■ **You have completed Skill 9 of 10**

▶ A *label report* is a report formatted so that the data can be printed on a sheet of labels.

1. In the **Navigation Pane**, under **Tables**, click **Residents** one time to select the table.

2. On the **Create tab**, in the **Reports group**, click the **Labels** button.

3. In the **Label Wizard**, be sure that the **Filter by manufacturer** box displays the text *Avery*. Under **What label size would you like**, select the label size where **Product number** is **C2160**, as shown in **Figure 1**.

   Each manufacturer identifies its label sheets using a product number. Access formats the report to match the dimensions of the selected sheet size.

4. Click **Next**. If necessary, change the **Font name** to **Arial** and the **Font weight** to **Light**. Change the **Font size** to **10**.

5. Click **Next**. Under **Available fields**, click **FirstName**, and then click the **Move >** button to add the field to the **Prototype label**.

6. With the insertion point in the **Prototype label** and to the right of *{FirstName}*, add a space, and then **Move >** the **LastName** field into the first line of the **Prototype label**.

7. Press [Enter], and then **Move >** the **Street** field into the second line of the **Prototype label**. Compare your screen with **Figure 2**.

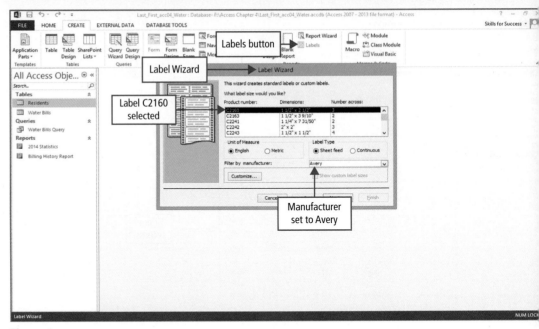

Figure 1

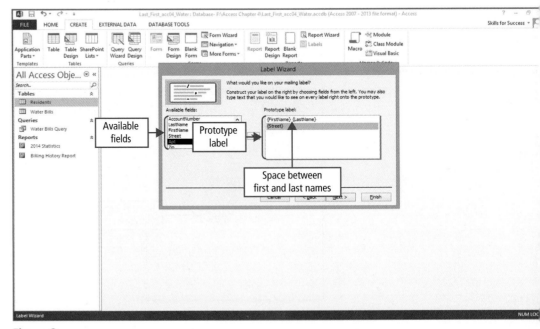

Figure 2

■ Continue to the next page to complete the skill ➤

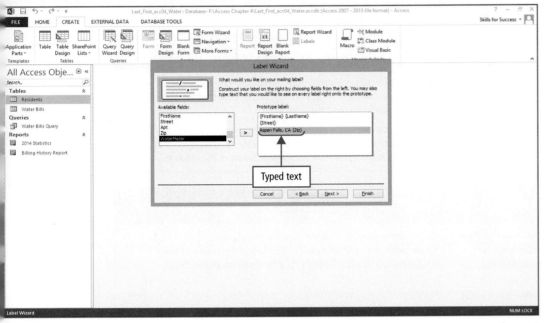

Figure 3

Figure 4

8. Press `Enter`, and then type Aspen Falls, CA Add a space, and then **Move** `>` the **Zip** field. Compare your screen with **Figure 3**.

   You can create labels using a combination of typed characters and fields from a table or query.

9. Click **Next** two times. Under **What name would you like for your report**, replace the existing name with Residents Mailing Labels

10. Click **Finish** to open the report in Print Preview. Compare your screen with **Figure 4**.

11. If you are printing your work for this project, print the first page of labels by setting the **From** and **To** values in the **Print** dialog box to 1.

    When printing a label report, your printer may require additional steps. Most printers will not print until a sheet of labels or sheet of paper is placed in the manual feed tray. If you are working in a computer lab, check with your lab technician or instructor for what is required in your situation.

12. **Close** `X` the report, and then **Close** `X` Access. Submit your work as directed by your instructor.

 DONE! You have completed Skill 10 of 10, and your database is complete!

More Skills

The following More Skills are located at **www.pearsonhighered.com/skills**

More Skills (11) Import Objects from Other Databases

You can import tables, forms, queries, reports, and other Access objects from other Access databases.

In More Skills 11, you will build a database by importing objects from other database files. You will import four tables, two queries, one form, and three reports.

To begin, open your web browser, navigate to www.pearsonhighered.com/skills, locate the name of your textbook, and then follow the instructions on the website.

More Skills (12) Export Reports to Word

You can export reports to other file formats so that you can view the data in other applications. For example, you can export a report so that it can be opened in Word or sent as an e-mail attachment.

In More Skills 12, you will export a report to another file format and then open that file in Word.

To begin, open your web browser, navigate to www.pearsonhighered.com/skills, locate the name of your textbook, and then follow the instructions on the website.

More Skills (13) Save Reports as PDF Documents

You can export reports to other file formats so that you can view the data in other applications. PDF documents can be read from any computer with a PDF reader application such as Word, Windows 8 Reader, or Acrobat Reader.

In More Skills 13, you will export an Access report as a PDF file. You will view the exported document in Windows 8 Reader.

To begin, open your web browser, navigate to www.pearsonhighered.com/skills, locate the name of your textbook, and then follow the instructions on the website.

More Skills (14) Save Reports as Web Pages and Save Export Steps

You can export reports so that they can be opened in a web browser. In this manner, reports can be published and shared on the Web. When you expect to export a report or other database object frequently, you can save the export steps. The export task can then be completed by clicking a single command.

In More Skills 14, you will export a report as a Hypertext Markup Language (HTML) document and view the report in your web browser. You will then save the export steps.

To begin, open your web browser, navigate to www.pearsonhighered.com/skills, locate the name of your textbook, and then follow the instructions on the website.

Please note that there are no additional projects to accompany the More Skills Projects, and they are not covered in the End-of-Chapter projects.

The following table summarizes the **SKILLS AND PROCEDURES** covered in this chapter.

Skills Number	Task	Step
1	Open the property sheet	Design tab → Tools group → Property Sheet
2	Build reports from queries	With the query selected in the Navigation pane, Create tab → Reports group → Report
2	Modify themes	Design tab → Themes group → Colors or Fonts
2	Edit label text	Double-click the label control to enter Edit mode
2	Add labels (Tabular layout)	Click in a blank table cell. Type the label text.
3	Format labels and text boxes	With the control selected, Format tab → Font group
3	Insert logos	Design tab → Header / Footer group → Logo
3	Select a specific control	Format tab → Selection group → Selection arrow
3	Change alternate row colors	Select Detail control, and then Format tab → Background group → Alternate Row Color
4	Change number formats	Format tab → Number group → Number Format arrow
4	Add totals to reports	Click in column, and then Design tab → Grouping & Totals group → Totals
4	AutoSize labels and text boxes	With the control selected, double-click a border
5	Modify cell borders	In the property sheet, change Gridline Style properties
5	Change margins	Print Preview tab → Page Size group → Margins
6	Create reports with the Blank Report Tool	Create tab → Reports group → Blank Report. In the Field list, double-click or drag to add fields to the report.
6	Insert title controls	Design tab → Header / Footer group → Title
6	Add date and time controls	Design tab → Header / Footer group → Date and Time
7	Group and sort reports	Group, Sort, and Total pane → Add a group or Add a sort
8	Delete rows and columns	Arrange tab → Rows & Columns group → Select Column or Select Row → press Delete
9	Apply custom text and date filters	With a field selected, Home tab → Sort & Filter group → Filter button → Text Filters or Date Filters
9	Remove filters	Home tab → Sort & Filter group → Advanced → Clear All Filters
9	Toggle filters on	Home tab → Sort & Filter group → Toggle Filter
9	Filter by selection	Click in field with desired value. Home tab → Sort & Filter group → Selection
10	Create label reports	Create tab → Reports group → Labels

Key Terms

Online Help Skills

1. Start Access 2013, and then in the upper right corner of the start page, click the **Help** button ?.

2. In the **Access Help** window **Search help** box, type conditional formatting and then press Enter.

3. In the **Search result** list, click **Highlight data with conditional formatting**, and then compare your screen with **Figure 1**.

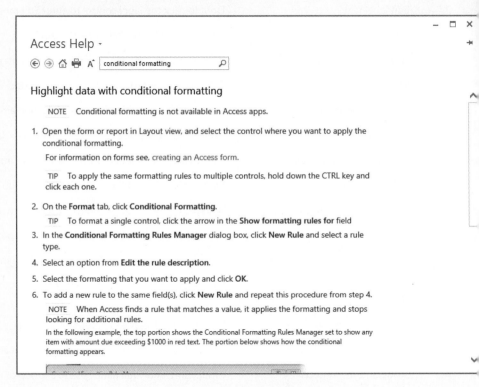

Figure 1

4. Read the article to answer the following question: How does adding conditional formatting add meaning to report data?

Matching  MyITLab®

Match each term in the second column with its correct definition in the first column by writing the letter of the term on the blank line in front of the correct definition.

___ **1.** To change a theme, Colors theme, or Fonts theme, use this tab.

___ **2.** The Font group is located on this tab.

___ **3.** This is used when you want to build a report by adding fields one at a time or arrange them in a different layout.

___ **4.** A small picture that can be added to a report header, typically to the left of the title.

___ **5.** To set the width of a report control to a precise dimension in Layout view, this pane can be used.

___ **6.** An area at the beginning of a report that contains labels, text boxes, and other controls.

___ **7.** The Format Painter button can be found in this group.

___ **8.** To change the alternate row color, this report control should be selected.

___ **9.** To display a subset of records on a report that matches a given criterion.

___ **10.** This button creates and applies a filter automatically using the value in the active field.

A Blank Report tool

B Design

C Detail

D Filter

E Fonts

F Format

G Logo

H Property sheet

I Report header

J Selection

BizSkills Video

1. What are some examples of good e-mail etiquette?

2. What are some things to avoid when e-mailing co-workers?

Multiple Choice (MyITLab®)

Choose the correct answer.

1. A tool that can create a report with a single click.
   - **A.** Blank Report tool
   - **B.** Report tool
   - **C.** Report Wizard

2. The method used to edit text in a label control in Layout view.
   - **A.** Click the control two times
   - **B.** Right-click the control, then click Edit
   - **C.** Click the control, and then on the Design tab, click Edit

3. A method used to add a label control in Layout view.
   - **A.** On the Design tab, in the Controls group, click Text Box
   - **B.** Click in an empty cell and type the label text
   - **C.** On the Insert tab, in the Labels group, click Add

4. This pane is used to add fields to a report in Layout view.
   - **A.** Add Fields
   - **B.** Blank Report
   - **C.** Field List

5. Buttons to insert logo, title, and date and time controls are found in this group on the Design tab.
   - **A.** Controls
   - **B.** Header / Footer
   - **C.** Tools

6. This pane is used to group and sort reports.
   - **A.** Group pane
   - **B.** Group and Sort pane
   - **C.** Group, Sort, and Total pane

7. To delete a report column in Layout view, this method can be used.
   - **A.** Click in the column, and then press [Delete]
   - **B.** Click in the column, and then on the Arrange tab, click Delete Column
   - **C.** Click in the column. On the Arrange tab, click Select Column, and then press [Delete]

8. To apply a custom filter, this method can be used.
   - **A.** Click in the field, and then on the Home tab, click the Filter button
   - **B.** Click in the field, and then on the Home tab, click the Custom button
   - **C.** Click in the field, and then on the Home tab, click the Selection button

9. When you close a report that has a filter applied, the following describes what happens when the report is opened the next time.
   - **A.** The filter created previously was deleted
   - **B.** The filter was saved, but it is not enabled
   - **C.** The filter was saved, and it is enabled

10. A report formatted so that the data can be printed on a sheet of labels.
   - **A.** Label report
   - **B.** Mail report
   - **C.** Merge report

Topics for Discussion

1. You have created reports using two different methods: the Report tool and the Blank Report tool. Which method do you prefer and why? What are the primary advantages of each method?

2. You have filtered reports using two different methods: One method added criteria to a query and then built the report from the query. The other method added filters after the report was finished. Which method do you prefer and why? What are the primary advantages of each method?

Skills Review

MyITLab®
Grader

To complete this project, you will need the following files:

- acc04_SRElectricity (Access)
- acc04_SRLogo (JPG)

You will save your file as:

- Last_First_acc04_SRElectricity

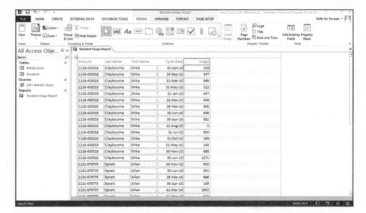

Figure 1

1. Start **Access 2013**, and then open the student data file **acc04_SRElectricity**. Save the database in your **Access Chapter 4** folder with the name Last_First_acc04_SRElectricity If necessary, enable the content.

2. Click the **Create tab**, and then in the **Reports group**, click **Blank Report**. In the **Field List**, click **Show all tables**, and then expand the **Residents** table. Double-click to add these fields in the following order: **Account**, **LastName**, and then **FirstName**.

3. In the **Field List**, expand the **Billing Cycles** table, double-click **CycleDate** and then **Usage** to add them to the report.

4. Click **Save**, type Resident Usage Report and then click **OK**. **Close** the Field List, and then compare your screen with **Figure 1**.

5. On the **Design tab**, in the **Header / Footer group**, click **Title**, type Electricity Usage by Resident and then press Enter.

6. On the **Design tab**, in the **Grouping & Totals group**, click **Group & Sort**. In the **Group, Sort, and Total** pane, click **Add a group**, and then click **Account**. **Close** the **Group, Sort, and Total** pane.

7. Drag the field with the value *Claybourne* into the blank cell below the **Last Name** label. Drag the field with the value *Mike* into the blank cell below the **First Name** label.

8. Click the field displaying **Account** *1118-435018*, and then click the **Home tab**. In the **Sort & Filter group**, click **Selection**, and then click **Equals "1118-435018"**.

9. On the **Design tab**, in the **Views group**, click the **View arrow**, and then click **Print Preview**. Compare you screen with **Figure 2**. If you are printing this project, print the report. Click **Save**, and then **Close** the report.

10. In the **Navigation Pane**, select **Residents**. Click the **Create tab**, and then in the **Reports group**, click the **Labels** button.

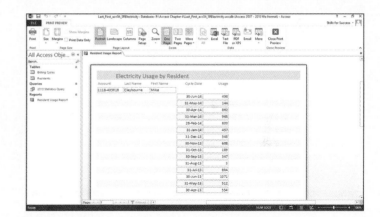

Figure 2

■ Continue to the next page to complete this Skills Review

Figure 3

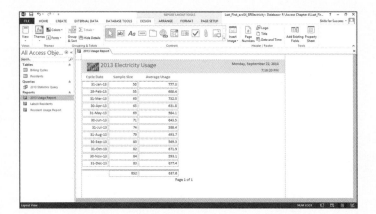

Figure 4

11. In the **Label Wizard**, select **Avery C2160**, and then click **Next** two times. Double-click **FirstName** to add it to the **Prototype label**. Add a space, and then add **LastName**. Press [Enter], and then add **Street**. Press [Enter], type Aspen Falls, CA Add a space, and then add the **Zip** field. Compare your screen with **Figure 3**, and then click **Finish**. If you are printing your work, print the first page of the report. **Close** the report.

12. Open **2013 Statistics Query** in **Design view**. In the **CycleDate** column **Criteria** cell, type <1/1/2014 Click **Save**, and then **Close** the query.

13. In the **Navigation Pane**, select **2013 Statistics Query**. Click the **Create tab**, and then in the **Reports group**, click the **Report** button. Click **Save**, type 2013 Usage Report and then click **OK**.

14. In the **Header / Footer group**, click the **Logo** button. In the **Insert Picture** dialog box, navigate to the student files for this chapter, click **acc04_SRLogo**, and then click **OK**.

15. In the **Header / Footer group**, click the **Title** button, type 2013 Electricity Usage and then press [Enter].

16. Double-click the **CountOfCycleID** label control, and then double-click the text to select it. Type Sample Size and then press [Enter]. Repeat this technique to change the **AvgOfUsage** label text to Average Usage

17. Click to select the **Cycle Date** label. Press and hold [Shift] while clicking the **Sample Size** and **Average Usage** labels. Click the **Format tab**, and then in the **Font group**, click **Bold** and **Center**.

18. On the **Format tab**, in the **Selection group**, click the **Selection arrow**, and then click **Detail**. In the **Background group**, click the **Alternate Row Color arrow**, and then click **No Color**.

19. Click a field in the **Sample Size** column, and then click the **Design tab**. In the **Grouping & Totals group**, click **Totals**, and then click **Sum**. Repeat this technique to add an **Average** total to the **Average Usage** column.

20. Below the **Sample Size** values, click the cell with the value *852*. Point to the top border, and then double-click to AutoSize the row. Click the total cell with the value *12*, and then press [Delete] to remove the control.

21. Compare you screen with **Figure 4**. If you are printing this project, print the report.

22. Click **Save**, **Close** the report, and then **Close** Access. Submit the project as directed by your instructor.

 DONE! You have completed this Skills Review

Skills Assessment 1
MyITLab®
Grader

To complete this database, you will need the following files:

- acc04_SA1Parcels (Access)
- acc04_SA1Logo (JPG)

You will save your database as:

- Last_First_acc04_SA1Parcels

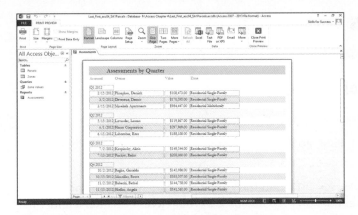

Figure 1

1. Start **Access 2013**, and then open the student data file **acc04_SA1Parcels**. Save the database in your **Access Chapter 4** folder with the name Last_First_acc04_SA1Parcels If necessary, enable the content.

2. Use the **Blank Report** tool to create a report with these fields in the following order: **Owner**, **Value**, **Assessed**, and **Zone**. Save the report as Assessments

3. Apply the **Organic** theme, and then add a **Title** control with the text Assessments by Quarter

4. Group the report by the **Assessed** field, and then sort the **Assessed** field within each group in oldest to newest order. For the yearly quarter label controls, AutoSize the control height.

5. Use the **Property Sheet** to set the width of the **Owner** column to 2" and the width of the **Zone** column to 2" Change the alignment of the **Value** label to **Align Left**.

6. For the **Detail** control, change the **Alternate Row Color** to **Orange, Accent 5, Lighter 80%** (column 9, row 2).

7. Create a custom **Text Filter** to display only the records in which the **Zone** contains the word Residential

8. Switch to **Print Preview**, and then compare you screen with **Figure 1**. If you are printing this project, print the report. **Save**, and then **Close** the report.

9. Create a **Labels** report based on the **Parcels** table. In the **Label Wizard**, select **Avery C2160**, and accept the default label format settings. In the first line of the **Prototype label**, add the **Owner** field. In the second line, add the **Street** field. In the third line, type Aspen Falls, CA add a space, and then add the **Zip** field. Accept all other wizard defaults, and then **Close** the report.

10. Modify the **Zone Values** query so that the second **Value** column computes an average for the group. **Save**, and then **Close** the query.

Figure 2

11. Use the **Report** tool to create a report based on the **Zone Values** query. **Save** the report as Average Zone Values

12. Add a logo using the file **acc04_SA1Logo**. Select the three column labels, and then apply **Bold** and **Center**.

13. Change the **AvgOfValue** label control text to Average Value and then add a control that calculates the column's average. Format the calculated control as **Currency**, and then AutoSize its height.

14. Switch to **Report view**, and then compare your screen with **Figure 2**. If you are printing this project, print the report.

15. Click **Save**, **Close** the report, and then **Close** Access. Submit the project as directed by your instructor.

 **DONE! You have completed Skills Assessment 1**

Skills Assessment 2

To complete this database, you will need the following file:

- acc04_SA2Rentals

You will save your database as:

- Last_First_acc04_SA2Rentals

---

1. Start **Access 2013**, and then open the student data file **acc04_SA2Rentals**. Save the database in your **Access Chapter 4** folder with the name Last_First_acc04_SA2Rentals If necessary, enable the content.

2. Use the **Blank Report** tool to create a report with these fields in the following order: **Center** and **Room Number** from the **Rooms** table; and **Date** and **Hours** from the **Rentals** table. Save the report as Rentals Report

3. Apply the **Facet** theme, and then add a **Title** control with the text Community Center Rentals

4. Group the report by **Center**, and then group it again by **RoomNumber**. Sort by **Date** from oldest to newest within each group.

5. Below the **Hours** column, add a control that calculates the column's total.

6. For the **Detail** control, change the **Alternate Row Color** to **Orange, Accent 4, Lighter 80%** (column 8, row 2).

7. Use filter by **Selection** to display only the rentals for Room CE110. AutoSize the height of the three summary controls in the **Hours** column.

8. Switch to **Print Preview**, and then compare your screen with **Figure 1**. If you are printing this project, print the report. **Save**, and then **Close** the report.

9. Create a **Labels** report based on the **Renters** table. In the **Label Wizard**, select **Avery C2160**, and accept the default label format settings. In the **Prototype label**, add fields and spaces to create labels in the following format:

First Last
Street
City, State Zip

Accept all other wizard defaults. If you are printing this project, print the first page of the report. **Close** the report.

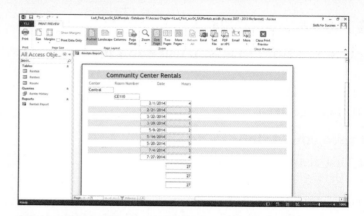

Figure 1

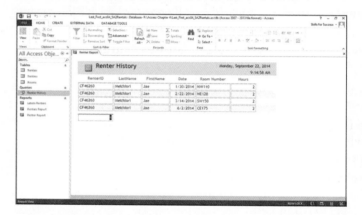

Figure 2

10. Modify the **Renter History** query to display only the records with **RenterID** CF46260 **Save**, and then **Close** the query.

11. Use the **Report** tool to create a report based on the **Renter History** query. **Save** the report as Renter Report

12. Resize the column widths so that the report is one page wide, and then delete the **Page Number** control.

13. Select the six column labels, and then apply **Bold** and **Center**. AutoSize the height of the **Count** control in the **RenterID** column.

14. Switch to **Report view**, and then compare your screen with **Figure 2**. If you are printing this project, print the report.

15. Click **Save**, **Close** the report, and then **Close** Access. Submit the project as directed by your instructor.

 DONE! You have completed Skills Assessment 2

Visual Skills Check

To complete this database, you will need the following files:

- acc04_VSPhones
- acc04_VSLogo

You will save your database as:

- Last_First_acc04_VSPhones

Open the student data file **acc04_VSPhones**, and then save the database in your **Access Chapter 4** folder as Last_First_acc04_VSPhones

Use the Blank Report tool to create the report shown in **Figure 1**. In the report header, add the title, date, and time controls as shown. The logo is from the file **acc04_VSLogo**. Group the report by *Department* and sort it by *LastName*. Position, size, and delete controls as shown in **Figure 1**. Set the *Department* label control to size **14**, **Bold**, and merge cells so that the label spans the first two columns. Set the alternate row color of the group header row to **No Color**.

Save the report as Phone List Print the report or submit the database file as directed by your instructor.

 DONE! You have completed Visual Skills Check

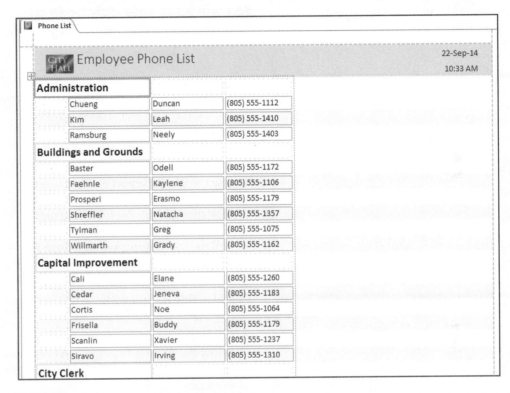

Figure 1

Figure 1

Figure 2

My Skills

To complete this database, you will need the following file:

- acc04_MYBaseball

You will save your database as:

- Last_First_acc04_MYBaseball

1. Start **Access 2013**, and then open the student data file **acc04_MYBaseball**. Save the database in your **Access Chapter 4** folder with the name Last_First_acc04_MYBaseball If necessary, enable the content.

2. Use the **Blank Report** tool to create a report with these fields from the **League Statistics** table in the following order: **Team**, **FirstName**, **LastName**, **Hits**, **AtBats**, and **BattingAverage**. Save the report as Batting Averages

3. Apply the **Integral** theme, and then add a **Title** control with the text Batting Averages

4. Group the report by **Team**, and then below the **Batting Average (BA)** column, add a control that calculates the column's averages.

5. For the **Detail** control, change the **Alternate Row Color** to **Teal, Accent 6, Lighter 80%** (last column, row 2).

6. Use filter by **Selection** to display only statistics for the *Golden Rays* team. AutoSize the height of the two summary controls in the **Batting Average (BA)** column.

7. Switch to **Print Preview**, and then compare your screen with **Figure 1**. If you are printing this project, print the report. **Save**, and then **Close** the report.

8. Create a **Labels** report based on the **Coaches** table. In the **Label Wizard**, select **Avery C2160**, and accept the default label format settings. In the **Prototype label**, add fields and spaces to create labels in the following format:

   First Last
   Street
   City, State Zip
   Accept all other wizard defaults. If you are printing this project, print the first page of the report. **Close** the report.

9. Modify the **Pitching Stats** query so that the **ERA** column calculates the average for each team. **Save**, and then **Close** the query.

10. Use the **Report** tool to create a report based on the **Pitching Stats** query. **Save** the report as Team Pitching

11. Change the **Title** control text to Team Pitching Statistics For the four column labels, apply **Bold** and **Center**.

12. Add a sort so that the **Team ERA** column is ordered from smallest to largest. Delete the **Count** control in the **Team** column.

13. Switch to **Report view**, and then compare your screen with **Figure 2**. If you are printing this project, print the report.

14. Click **Save**, **Close** the report, and then **Close** Access. Submit the project as directed by your instructor.

 DONE! You have completed My Skills

Skills Challenge 1

To complete this database, you will need the following file:

- acc04_SC1Reviews

You will save your database as:

- Last_First_acc04_SC1Reviews

Open the student data file **acc04_SC1Reviews** and save the database in your **Access Chapter 4** folder as Last_First_acc04_SC1Reviews Open Employee Evaluations in Layout view, and then add grouping so that each employee's evaluations display under his or her name. Position and sort the fields and labels to make the report easier to understand. Add Totals to the Attendance and Customer Relations columns that calculate the average values for each column, and format the numbers to display two decimals. Format the report to make it easier

to read, and adjust the column widths and heights to fit the content each needs to display. Add a Title control that describes the purpose of the report, and then filter the report to display the evaluations for Jack Hooley.

Print the report or submit the database file as directed by your instructor.

 DONE! You have completed Skills Challenge 1

Skills Challenge 2

To complete this database, you will need the following file:

- acc04_SC2Students

You will save your database as:

- Last_First_acc04_SC2Students

Open the student data file **acc04_SC2Students** and save the database in your **Access Chapter 4** folder as Last_First_acc04_SCStudents Create a query that can be used to create a mailing labels report. In the query, include the necessary name and address fields from the **Students** table, and then filter the query so that only participants from the Central neighborhood display. Save the query as Central Students Query. Use the **Label Wizard** to create a label report. Arrange

the fields in the standard mailing address format. Include spacing and punctuation where appropriate. Do not include the Neighborhood field in the label. Accept all other default wizard settings.

Print the report or submit the database file as directed by your instructor.

 DONE! You have completed Skills Challenge 2

CAPSTONE PROJECT

Student data files needed for this project:

acc_CSShelters (Access)
acc_CSShelterData (Excel)
acc_CSLogo (JPG)

You will save your file as:

Last_First_acc_CSShelters (Access)

1. Start **Access 2013**, and then open the student data file that came with this project, **acc_CSShelters**. Use the **Save As** dialog box to save the database to your drive with the name Last_First_acc_CSShelters If necessary, enable the content.

2. Create a new table in **Design view**. Add a field named ShelterID with the **AutoNumber** data type. Set the field as the table's primary key, and then change the field's **Caption** property to Shelter ID

3. Add a field named ShelterName with the **Short Text** data type. Change the field's **Field Size** property to 50 and its **Caption** property to Shelter Name

4. Add a field named Park with the **Short Text** data type, and change the field's **Field Size** property to 50

5. **Save** the table with the name Shelters and **Close** the table.

6. Import the data in the Excel file **acc_CSShelterData** by appending the data to the **Shelters** table.

7. Open the **Shelters** table, set the column widths to **Best Fit**, and then compare your screen with **Figure 1**. **Save**, and then **Close** the table.

8. Relate the database's two tables in a one-to-many relationship by enforcing referential integrity between the **ShelterID** fields. For the relationship, select both cascading options. **Save**, and then **Close** the Relationships tab.

9. Create a query in **Design view**, add both database tables, and then add the following fields: **ShelterName**, **ReservationDate**, **GroupSize**, and **Fee**. Add criteria so that only reservations for the month of July 2014 display. **Save** the query with the name July Reservations

10. **Run** the query. Compare your screen with **Figure 2**, and then **Close** the query.

■ **Continue to the next page to complete the skill**

Figure 1

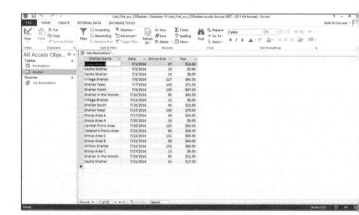

Figure 2

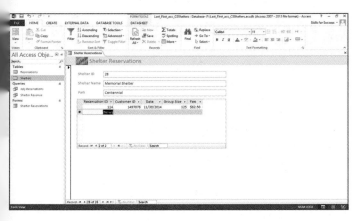

Figure 3

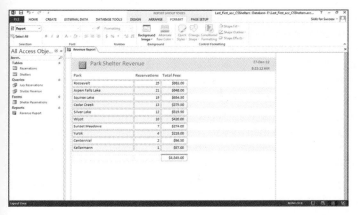

Figure 4

11. Create a query in **Design view**, add both database tables, and then add the following fields: **Park**, **ReservationDate**, and **Fee**. **Save** the query with the name Shelter Revenue

12. Group the **Shelter Revenue** query by **Park**. In the **ReservationDate** column, add a **Count** total, and then in the **Fee** column, add a **Sum** total.

13. **Save**, and then **Run** the query. Verify that 10 records display, and then **Close** the query.

14. Use the **Form** tool to create a form and subform with the main form based on the **Shelters** table. **Save** the form with the name Shelter Reservations

15. Apply the **Retrospect** theme, insert the logo from the file **acc_CSLogo**, and then change the form's title text to Shelter Reservations

16. Use the **Property Sheet** to change the width of the **Shelter ID** text box control to 4.8" and then **Close** the **Property Sheet**.

17. In the main form, add a new record with Memorial Shelter as the shelter name and Centennial as the park name. In the subform, add a reservation with a **Customer ID** of 1497076 The date is 11/30/2014 and the **Group Size** is 125

18. Compare your screen with **Figure 3**. **Save**, and then **Close** the form.

19. Use the **Report** tool to create a report based on the **Shelter Revenues** query. **Save** the report as Revenue Report

20. Change the report title to Park Shelter Revenue and then change the **Date** control's **Number Format** to **Medium Date**.

21. Add a sort that orders the **CountOfReservationDate** column from largest to smallest.

22. Change the second column label to Reservations and the third column label to Total Fees

23. For all three column labels, change the font size to **12**, apply **Bold**, and apply **Align Left**. AutoSize the second column's width.

24. Below the **Total Fees** column, AutoSize the height of the **Total** control, and then change the control's **Number Format** to **Currency**.

25. **Close** the **Group**, **Sort**, **and Total** pane, and then delete the control with the page number. Compare your screen with **Figure 4**.

26. **Save**, and then **Close** the report. **Close** Access, and then submit the project as directed by your instructor.

 DONE! You have completed Access Capstone Project

Create Envelopes from Access Queries

▶ Recall that in Word, you can merge data into different types of documents such as letters, envelopes, mailing labels, or email messages.

▶ You can use Access to store data such as addresses, filter that data in an Access query, and then use the results of the query to create mail merge documents in Word.

© Tsiumpa / Fotolia

Aspen Falls City Hall

In this Integrated Project, you will create documents for the Aspen Falls City Hall, which provides essential services for the citizens and visitors of Aspen Falls, California. You will help Carter Horikoshi, Art Center Supervisor, create envelopes addressed to art students who live in the Central neighborhood.

You can use tables and queries in Access databases as data sources for mail merge documents. Queries are used to filter the records before using them as a mail merge data source. When you set a Word document as an envelope, the document changes to the size of a standard envelope with placeholders for the return and recipient addresses. Typically, the return address is typed, and the recipients' addresses are retrieved from the database table or query.

You will add criteria to an Access query and then use that query as the data source for a mail merge. In Word, you will create a document that can print an envelope for each student who lives in the Central neighborhood.

Time to complete this project – 30 to 60 minutes

Student data file needed for this project:

acc_IP06Addresses (Access)

You will save your files as:

Last_First_IP06Addresses (Access)
Last_First_IP06Merged (Word)

Outcome

Using the skills in this project, you will be able to work with an Office document like this:

Your Name
500 S Aspen St
Aspen Falls, CA 93463

Eliseo Brennan
14824 W Dogwood Ln
Aspen Falls, CA 93463

SKILLS MyITLab®

At the end of this project you will be able to:

► Add criteria to an Access query
► Create an envelope as a mail merge document
► Use an Access query as a data source
► Type a return address and insert an address block merge field
► Preview and print an envelope for a selected record

1. Start **Access 2013**, and then from the student files, open the student data file **acc_IP06Addresses**.

2. Use the **Save As** dialog box to save the database to your drive with the name Last_First_acc_IP06Addresses If necessary, enable the content.

3. In the **Navigation Pane**, right-click **Central Addresses**, and then click **Design View**. In the **Neighborhood** column **Criteria** cell, type Central and then compare your screen with **Figure 1**.

4. Click **Save** 🖫, and then **Run** the query to display 10 records. **Close** ✕ the query, and then **Close** ✕ Access.

5. Start **Word 2013**, and then click **Blank document**. Click the **Mailings tab**. In the **Start Mail Merge group**, click the **Start Mail Merge** button, and then click **Envelopes**.

   When you start a mail merge, you need to choose a document type. Here, the document will be an envelope.

6. In the **Envelope Options** dialog box, verify that the **Envelope Size** is set to **Size 10**, and then click **OK**.

7. In the upper left corner of the envelope, type your first and last names, and then press Enter . Type 500 S Aspen St and then press Enter . Type Aspen Falls, CA 93463 Compare your screen with **Figure 2**.

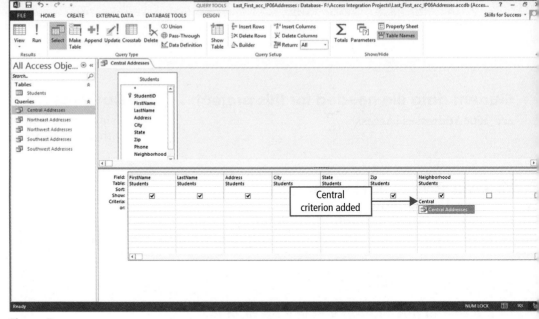

Figure 1

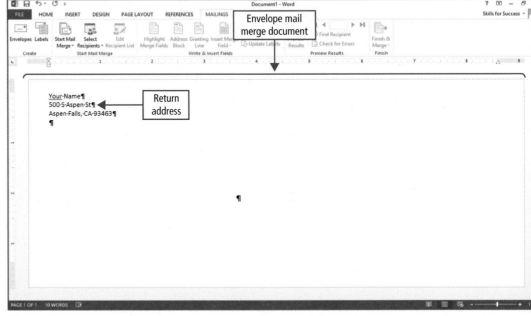

Figure 2

■ **Continue to the next page to complete the skill**

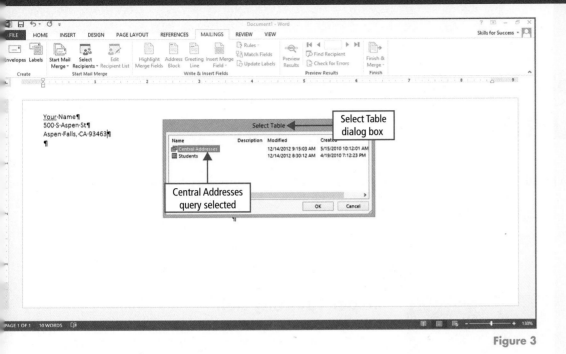

Select Table dialog box

Central Addresses query selected

Figure 3

8. On the **Mailings tab**, in the **Start Mail Merge group**, click the **Select Recipients** button, and then click **Use an Existing List**.

9. In the **Select Data Source** dialog box, navigate to and click **Last_First_acc_ IP06Addresses**, and then click **Open**. In the **Select Table** dialog box, verify that **Central Addresses** is selected. Compare your screen with **Figure 3**, and then click **OK**.

10. In the center of the envelope, click to left of the paragraph mark (¶) to display the address placeholder. In the **Write & Insert Fields group**, click the **Address Block** button, and then click **OK**.

11. In the **Preview Results group**, click **Preview Results**. In the **Preview Results group**, click the **Next Record** button ▶ two times.

12. In the **Finish group**, click the **Finish & Merge** button, and then click **Edit Individual Documents**. In the **Merge to New Document** dialog box, select the **Current record** option button, and then click **OK**. Compare your screen with **Figure 4**.

13. Click **Save** 🔲, and then in the **Save As** dialog box navigate to the location you are saving your work. Name the file Last_First_acc01_IP06Merged and then click **Save**. **Close** ✖ the document.

14. **Close** ✖ the original envelope document without saving changes, and then submit the project as directed by your instructor.

✔ **DONE! You have completed Integrated Project 6**

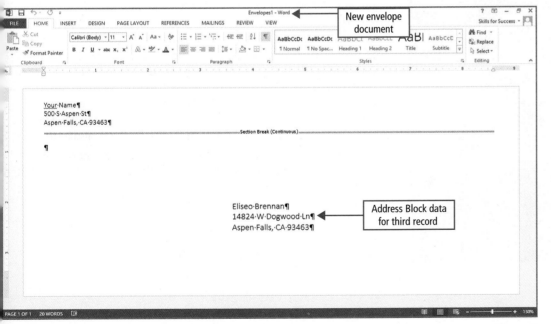

New envelope document

Address Block data for third record

Figure 4

Export Access Data to Word Documents

▶ Data stored in Access tables can be exported into files that can be opened by other programs.

▶ When Access tables or queries are exported as Rich Text Format (RTF) files, they can be imported into Word documents.

▶ Access data is imported into Word as a table that can be formatted using Word's table tools.

© Milan Surkala / Fotolia

Aspen Falls City Hall

In this Integrated Project, you will create documents for the Aspen Falls City Hall, which provides essential services for the citizens and visitors of Aspen Falls, California. You will write a memo to City Manager Maria Martinez listing the members of one of the city's councils.

Any Access table or query can be exported into a file that can be opened in Word. Queries are used when you need to first filter the data using criteria. The file that is created during the export is a *Rich Text Format (RTF)* file—a document in a file format designed to work with many different types of programs. If you are already working with a Word document, you can insert the text from the RTF file. This allows you to include Access data in reports, memos, and letters.

You will create an Access query to display the members of the Public Works Council. You will export the results of the query and then import the data as a table in a Word memo. You will then format the table.

Time to complete this
project – 30 to 60 minutes

Student data files needed for this project:

acc_IP07Councils (Access)
acc_IP07Memo (Word)

You will save your files as:

Last_First_acc_IP07Councils (Access)
Last_First_acc_IP07PublicWorks (RTF file)
Last_First_acc_IP07Memo (Word)

SKILLS MyITLab®

At the end of this project you will be able to

▶ Create an Access query in design view, add criteria, and hide a
   column
▶ Export an Access query as an RTF file
▶ Modify a memo
▶ Import data in an RTF file into Word
▶ Adjust table column widths using Autofit

Outcome

Using the skills in this project, you will be able to work
with an Office document like this:

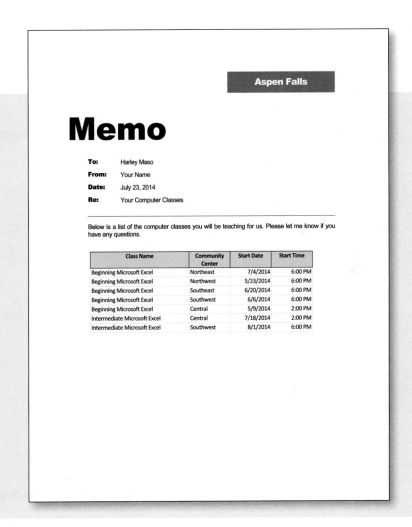

1. Start **Access 2013**, and then from the student files, open the student data file **acc_IP07Councils**.

2. Use the **Save As** dialog box to save the database to your drive with the name Last_First_acc_IP07Councils If necessary, enable the content.

3. Click the **Create tab**, and then in the **Queries group**, click **Query Design**. **Add** the **Councils** and **Members** tables to the query, and then **Close** the dialog box.

4. Add the **FirstName**, **LastName**, and then the **CouncilName** fields to the query design grid.

5. In the **CouncilName** column **Criteria** cell, type Public Works In the **CouncilName** column **Show** cell, clear the check box.

6. Click **Save**, type Public Works and then click **OK**. Compare your screen with **Figure 1**.

7. **Run** the query, verify that seven records display, and then **Close** ☒ the query.

8. In the **Navigation Pane**, verify that **Public Works** is still selected. Click the **External Data tab**. In the **Export group**, click **More**, and then click **Word**.

9. In the **Export - RTF File** dialog box, click the **Browse** button. In the **File Save** dialog box, navigate to the location you are saving your work. Name the file Last_First_acc_IP07PublicWorks and then click **Save**. Compare your screen with **Figure 2**.

10. Click **OK** to complete the export. **Close** the **Export - RTF File** dialog box, and then **Close** ☒ Access.

11. Start **Word 2013**, and then from the student data files, open **acc_IP07Memo**.

■ **Continue to the next page to complete the skill**

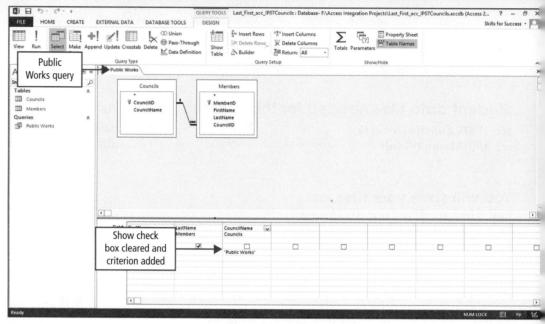

Figure 1

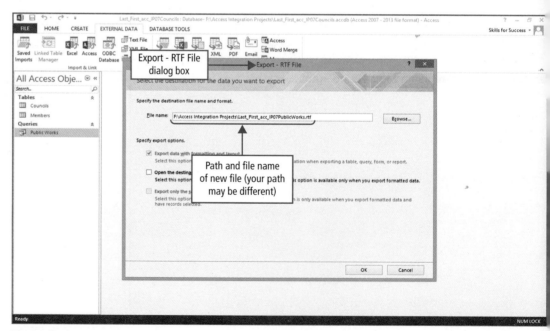

Figure 2

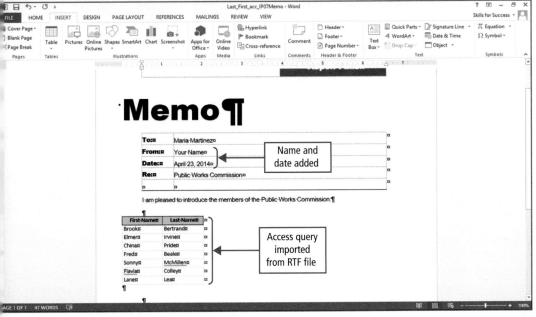

Figure 3

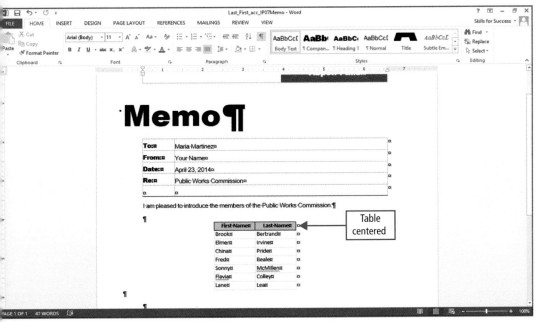

Figure 4

12. Click the **File tab**, and then click **Save As**. Use the **Save As** page to open the **Save as** dialog box and navigate to the location you are saving your work. Name the file Last_First_acc_IP07Memo and then click **Save**.

13. Click in the cell to the right of *From,* and then type your name. In the cell to the right of *Date,* type the current date.

14. Click in the blank paragraph below the table, and then type the following: I am pleased to introduce the members of the Public Works Commission:

15. Press Enter two times, and then click the **Insert tab**. In the **Text group**, click the **Object arrow**, and then click **Text from File**.

16. In the **Insert File** dialog box, select **Last_First_acc_IP07PublicWorks** that you created previously, and then click **Insert**. Compare your screen with **Figure 3**.

17. Point to the table, and then click the table's **Selector** button ⊞ to select the table.

18. Click the **Layout tab**, and in the **Table group**, click the **Properties** button. In the **Table Properties** dialog box, under **Alignment**, click **Center**, and then click **OK**. Click to deselect the table, and then compare your screen with **Figure 4**.

19. **Save** 🖫 the document, and then **Close** ✕ Word. Submit the files as directed by your instructor.

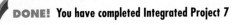 **DONE! You have completed Integrated Project 7**

Create OneNote Notebooks

▸ ***OneNote*** is a program used to collect notes, drawings, and media from multiple participants.

▸ A OneNote document is a loose structure of digital pages called a ***notebook***.

▸ Notebooks can be shared by saving them to OneDrive and using OneNote Online, formerly OneNote Web App, to edit them.

▸ OneNote notebooks are divided into sections, and each section can have multiple pages.

▸ In a OneNote notebook, participants enter text, graphics, or audio anywhere on a page. You can use these notebooks to collect and foster ideas that will be published in a more formal format later.

© 3ddock / Fotolia

Aspen Falls City Hall

In this Office Online Project, you will create documents for the Aspen Falls City Hall, which provides essential services for the citizens and visitors of Aspen Falls, California. Using OneNote Online, you will help City Manager Maria Martinez create a OneNote notebook for the city council.

To create a shared notebook, you save it to OneDrive. You can then invite others to work on the notebook. Those who you invite add text, pictures, tables, or other objects to the notebook in the web browser. You are able to track the changes each author makes and return the page to a previous version if you do not want to accept the changes they made. An online notebook helps teams collaborate from any computer connected to the Internet. When all the OneNote features are needed, the notebook can be opened in the Desktop OneNote.

In this project, you will use OneDrive and OneNote Online to create a notebook. You will add sections and pages and add text, graphics, and other objects to the pages in the notebook.

Time to complete this project – 30 to 60 minutes

Student data file needed for this project:

acc_WAPhoto

Outcome

Using the skills in this project, you will be able to work with a OneNote Online notebook like this:

You will save your files as:

City Council Notebook (OneDrive)
Last_First_acc_WASnip1
Last_First_acc_WASnip2

SKILLS

At the end of this project you will be able to

► Create a OneNote notebook on OneDrive
► Name notebook sections and pages
► Add notebook sections and pages
► Add text, tables, and pictures to pages
► Display pages in Reading view
► Show authors and share notebooks

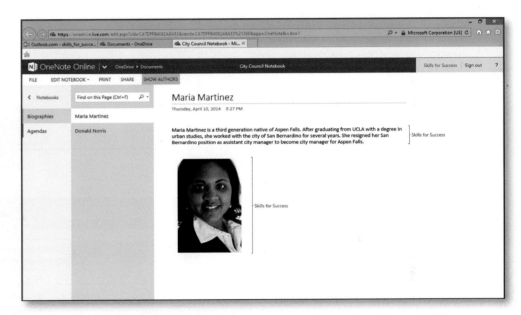

1. Start desktop **Internet Explorer** or another web browser, navigate to live. com and log on to your Windows account. If you do not have an account, follow the links and directions on the page to create one.

2. After logging in, navigate as needed to display your **OneDrive** page. Compare your screen with **Figure 1**.

   OneDrive and Office Online technologies are accessed through web pages that can change often, and the formatting and layout of some pages may often be different than the figures in this book. You may need to adapt the steps to complete the actions they describe.

3. On the toolbar, click **Create**, and then click **OneNote notebook**. In the **New Microsoft OneNote notebook** dialog box, name the file City Council Notebook and then click the **Create** button to save the document to your OneDrive and start OneNote Online.

4. With the insertion point in the blank page title, type Maria Martinez Compare your screen with **Figure 2**.

   In OneNote, notes are organized in notebooks. Each notebook is divided into sections, and each section can have multiple pages. Here, the notebook is named City Council Notebook, the section is untitled, and the first page is titled Maria Martinez.

   The changes you make in OneNote Online are automatically saved. For this reason, there is no save button.

■ Continue to the next page to complete the skill

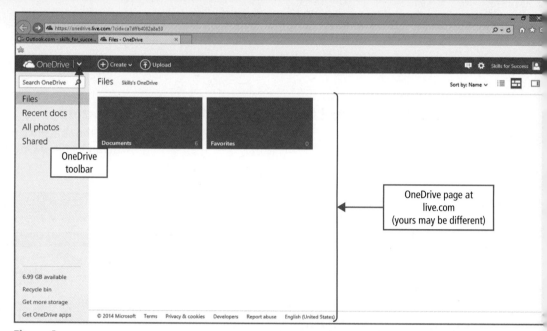

Figure 1

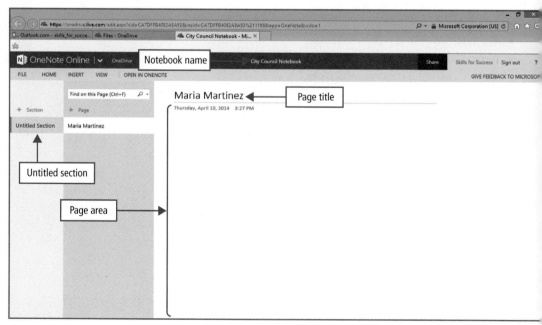

Figure 2

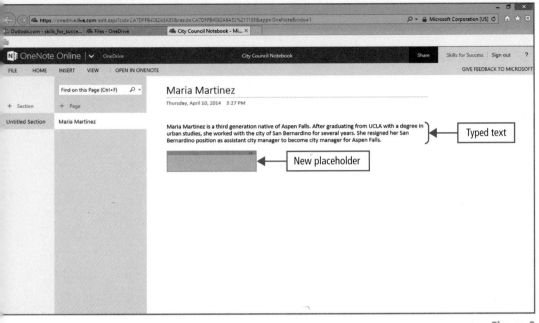

Figure 3

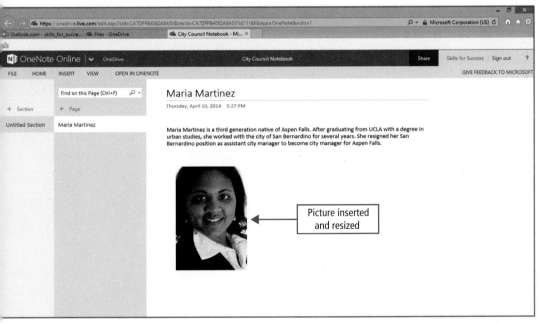

Figure 4

5. Press `Tab` to move the insertion point into the page, and then type the following: Maria Martinez is a third generation native of Aspen Falls. After graduating from UCLA with a degree in urban studies, she worked with the city of San Bernardino for several years. She resigned her San Bernardino position as assistant city manager to become city manager for Aspen Falls.

6. Click in a blank area in the middle of the page to create a new placeholder. Point to the title bar of the new placeholder, and then with the pointer, drag to position the placeholder below the text typed previously so that it is in a position similar to the one shown in **Figure 3**.

An object can be inserted anywhere on the page. It can then be moved by dragging its placeholder.

7. Click in the new placeholder that you positioned in the previous step. Click the **Insert tab**, and then in the **Pictures group**, click **Picture**.

8. In the **Choose File to Upload** dialog box, navigate to the student data files that you downloaded for this project. Click **acc_WAPhoto**, and then click **Open**.

9. Wait a few moments for the picture to upload and display. Click the picture to select it and display the **Picture Tools Format tab**.

10. Click the **Format tab**, and then in the **Image Size group**, select the value in the **Scale** box. Type 50% click in a blank area to deselect the photo, and then compare your screen with **Figure 4**.

■ **Continue to the next page to complete the skill**

11. In the left pane, right-click **Untitled section**, and then from the shortcut menu, click **Rename**. In the **Section Name** dialog box, name the section Biographies and click **OK**.

12. To the right of **Section**, click the **Page** button, and then type Donald Norris

13. Press Tab to move the insertion point to the page, and then type Donald, you need to post your bio. Thanks. Compare your screen with **Figure 5**.

14. Click the **Insert tab**, and then in the **Notebook group**, click **New Section**. In the **Section Name** dialog box, type Agendas and then click **OK**.

15. With the insertion point in the title of the new untitled page, type April Meeting to title the page.

16. Press Tab to move the insertion point into the first line of the page. Click the **Insert tab**, and then in the **Tables group**, click the **Table** button. In the **Table** gallery, click to the second cell in the third row to insert a **2x3 Table**.

17. In the six table cells, type the following:

Item	Presenter
Aspen Falls Lake Flood Mitigation	Donald Norris
Community College Internships	Evelyn Stone and George Gato

18. Compare your screen with **Figure 6**.

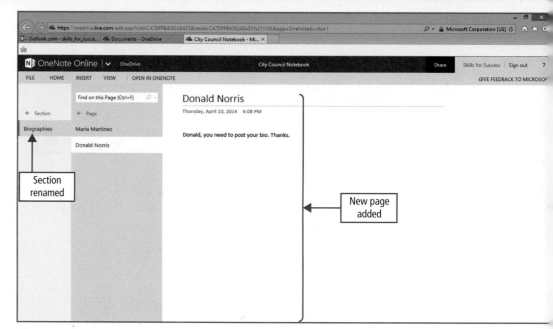

Figure 5

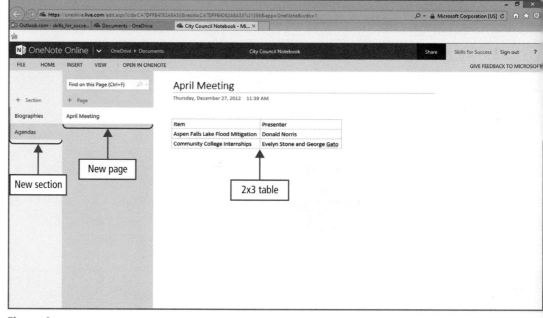

Figure 6

■ **Continue to the next page to complete the skill**

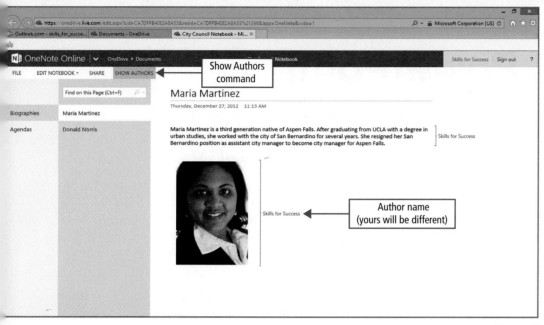

Figure 7

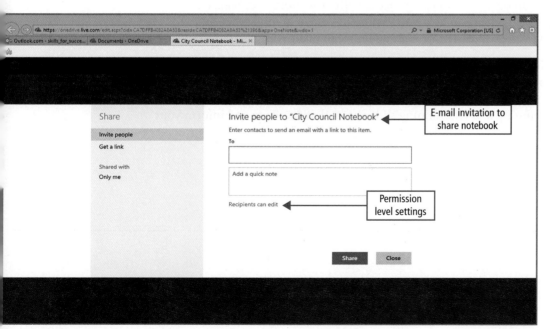

Figure 8

19. Click the **View tab**, and then in the **Notebook Views group**, click **Reading View**. In the left pane, click **Maria Martinez** to display the page. Click the **Show Authors** command, and then compare your screen with **Figure 7**.

> When you display the authors, each author's contributions are marked so that you can track each author's contributions to the notebook.

20. Press [⊞], type snip and then press [Enter] to start the **Snipping Tool**. Create a **Full-screen Snip**. Save 💾 the snip as Last_First_acc_WASnip1 and then **Close** ❌ the **Snipping Tool mark-up** window.

21. In the left pane, click Agendas, and then click **April Meeting** to display the page. Create a **Full-screen Snip** named Last_First_acc_WASnip2 and **Close** ❌ the **Snipping Tool mark-up** window.

22. Click the **Share** command, then compare your screen with **Figure 8**.

> In Reading view, you can click Share to invite others to view the notebook. You can allow them to make changes as authors or limit them only to Reading view.

23. If your instructor has asked you to share the notebook, enter the e-mail address of the person you are to share it with, and then click **Share**. Otherwise, in the **Send a link to "City Council Notebook" in email** dialog box, click **Done**.

24. Click the **Sign out** link, and then **Close** ❌ the browser window. Submit the snips as directed by your instructor.

✔ **DONE! You have completed the OneNote Online Project!**

Introduction to PowerPoint

Microsoft PowerPoint 2013 is a ***presentation software program***—an application used to create slides to communicate a message to an audience.

You can use PowerPoint to insert, format, and add effects to text on slides. You can add text in the form of a bulleted or numbered list, captions, or titles.

When using PowerPoint, you will use three main views. In Normal view, you'll see a thumbnail image of each slide next to a larger view of the slide you are working on. In Slide Sorter view, you will see a bird's-eye view of your presentation. When presenting, you will use Slide Show view, where the current slide fills the screen. In Slide Show view, you can access Presenter view, which provides you with additional presentation information.

You can change layouts and add images to your slides. Images, either from your own files or from online sources, including office.com, can help to explain your message further, hold your audience's attention, and evoke an emotion or feeling. Slide layouts can be easily changed.

You can add other graphics into your slides using shapes with or without text, SmartArt graphics, or WordArt. Charts and tables can help you to present data in an organized and easy-to-understand format and make it easier for your audience to make comparisons.

PowerPoint can be used for collaboration. For example, you can save presentations to the Internet and invite others to view them or make changes to them. You can also track the changes each collaborator makes to the file, and then accept or reject those changes. You can use PowerPoint to create interesting and entertaining slide shows that captivate and inform your audience.

Image

Text effects

Slide layout

Aspen Falls City Government

We are glad to have you on our team!

CHAPTER 1

Getting Started with PowerPoint 2013

▶ Microsoft PowerPoint is a presentation software program that can be used to effectively relay information, images, and video to an audience through a slide show.

▶ There are multiple views in PowerPoint: Normal, Slide Sorter, Reading, Slide Show, and Presenter. Each view is designed for particular tasks.

▶ Normal view is commonly used to create, edit, and format a presentation.

▶ Slide Show view is used to give a presentation; the slides are displayed as full screen.

▶ In Presenter View, a presenter can view upcoming slides while displaying the current slide to the audience on the screen.

© Auremar

Aspen Falls City Hall

In this chapter, you will edit a presentation for Maria Martinez, the City Manager of Aspen Falls, California. Maria will use this presentation when representing the city to businesses, investors, and other agencies.

In your career, you may need to create professional presentations to help convey your message to an audience. Keep in mind that your audience will remember more information if you present it to them in a variety of ways—verbally, in writing, and visually. Using PowerPoint slides as a presentation aid will help you do this.

A slide, generally shown behind the presenter, can contain text to emphasize the most important information. Images can be used to emphasize a point, increase interest, or render an emotion. Animation or motion on the screen can attract—and help to hold—the audience's attention. You can create handouts from your slides and distribute them to your audience so that they can retain the handout for reference.

A general rule of thumb for PowerPoint is to follow the 7 by 7 rule—a maximum of seven lines per slide and no more than seven words per line. Another PowerPoint standard is to use no font smaller than 18 to 24 points. Slides should always look uncluttered and use simple designs.

In this project, you will open and save an existing presentation and then edit the presentation, adding, editing, and adjusting text and images. You will change slide layouts, insert new slides, and rearrange slides. You will apply transitions, view the slide show, and create presentation handouts and notes.

Time to complete all 10 skills – 60 to 75 minutes

Student data files needed for this chapter:

ppt01_Lifestyle   ppt01_CityHall
ppt01_Vision

You will save your files as:

Last_First_ppt01_Lifestyle
Last_First_ppt01_LifestyleSnip

Outcome

Using the skills in this chapter, you will be able to create slides like this:

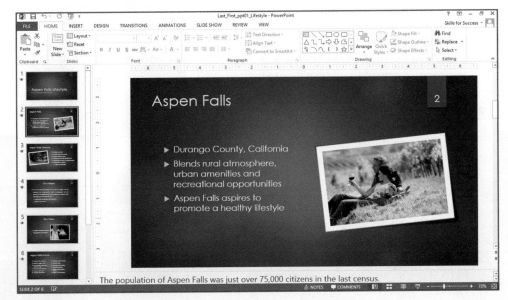

SKILLS

Skills 1-10 Training

At the end of this chapter, you will be able to:

Skill 1   Open, View, and Save Presentations
Skill 2   Edit and Replace Text
Skill 3   Format Slide Text
Skill 4   Check Spelling and Use the Thesaurus
Skill 5   Insert Slides and Modify Slide Layouts
Skill 6   Insert and Format Pictures
Skill 7   Organize Slides in Slide Sorter View
Skill 8   Apply Slide Transitions and View Slide Shows
Skill 9   Insert Headers and Footers and Print Handouts
Skill 10   Add Notes Pages and Use Presenter View

MORE SKILLS

Skill 11   Add Online Pictures
Skill 12   Print Presentations, Notes Pages, and Custom Ranges
Skill 13   Move and Delete Slides in Normal View
Skill 14   Change Slide Size and Orientation

▶ When you start PowerPoint 2013, the **Start screen** displays. From the Start screen, you can view a list of recently opened presentations, create a new presentation, or open an existing presentation.

▶ A **slide** is an individual page in a presentation and can contain text, pictures, tables, charts, and other multimedia or graphic objects.

▶ Save your changes frequently so that you do not lose any of your editing or formatting changes.

1. Start **PowerPoint 2013**, and then take a moment to familiarize yourself with the components of the PowerPoint Start screen as shown in **Figure 1**.

2. On the Start screen, click **Open Other Presentations**. On the **Open** page, click **Computer**, and then click **Browse**. In the **Open** dialog box, navigate to the student data files for this chapter. Select **ppt01_Lifestyle**, and then click the **Open** button—or double-click the file name— to open the presentation and display **Slide 1**.

3. Take a moment to identify the main parts of the PowerPoint window as shown in **Figure 2**.

The PowerPoint window is divided into two main parts—the Slide pane and the left pane, which contains thumbnail images of the slides. In addition, the status bar indicates the displayed slide number and the number of slides in the presentation, and it contains buttons for the Notes and Comments panes, various views, and Fit slide to current window.

■ **Continue to the next page to complete the skill**

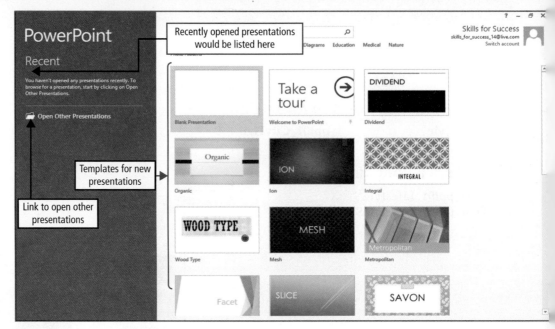

Figure 1

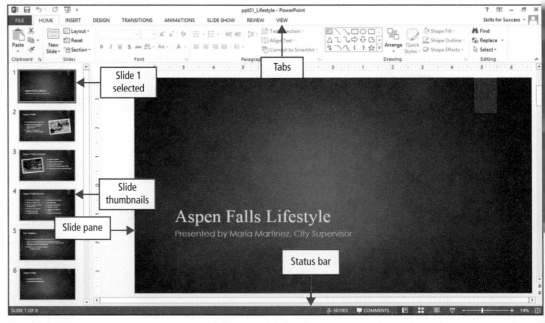

Figure 2

Microsoft PowerPoint Screen Elements

Screen Element	Description
Tabs	In PowerPoint, the default tabs on the Ribbon include File, Home, Insert, Design, Transitions, Animations, Slide Show, Review, and View.
Slide thumbnails	Small preview images of each slide.
Slide pane	An area of the Normal View window that displays the current slide.
Status bar	A horizontal bar at the bottom of the window that displays the current slide number, number of slides in the presentation, and the Notes, Comments, various views, and Fit slide to current window buttons.

Figure 3

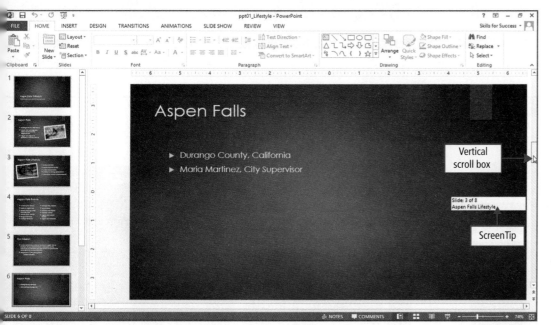

Figure 4

4. Locate the items described in **Figure 3**.

   At the left side of the PowerPoint window, the slide **thumbnails**—miniature images of presentation slides—and slide numbers display. You can click a slide thumbnail to display it in the Slide pane. At the right side of the window, a scroll bar displays a scroll box and the Next Slide and Previous Slide buttons used to navigate in your presentation.

5. At the left of the PowerPoint window, click the **Slide 2** thumbnail to display the slide in the Slide pane. Click the slide thumbnails for **Slides 3** through **6** to view each slide.

   As you view each slide, the vertical scroll box at the right side of the PowerPoint window moves, indicating the relative location in the presentation of the slide that you are viewing.

6. With **Slide 6** displayed, at the right side of the PowerPoint window, point to the vertical scroll box, and then hold down the mouse button. Drag up to display **Slide 3**, and release the mouse button. A ScreenTip displays the slide number and slide title, as shown in **Figure 4**.

7. On the **File tab**, click **Save As**. Click the **Browse** button and navigate to the location where you are saving your files, create a folder named PowerPoint Chapter 1 and then using your own name, save the presentation as Last_First_ppt01_Lifestyle

■ **You have completed Skill 1 of 10**

▶ In **Normal view**, the PowerPoint window is divided into two areas—the Slide pane and the left pane, which contains thumbnails of each slide.

▶ Individual lines of bulleted text on a slide are referred to as **bullet points**.

▶ Bullet points are organized in list levels similar to an outline. A **list level** is a hierarchy of bullets and sub-bullets. Each level of bullet has its own formatting.

▶ You can use the Replace command to change multiple occurrences of the same text in a presentation.

1. Move to **Slide 2**, which contains two **placeholders**—boxes with dotted borders that are part of most slide layouts and that hold text or objects such as pictures, charts, and tables. The dotted border is not visible until click, or place your insertion point in, the placeholder.

2. In the second bullet point, click to the left of the letter *o* in the word *opportunities* so that the insertion point displays before the word, as shown in **Figure 1**.

3. Type recreational and then press SpaceBar to insert the text to the left of the word *opportunities*.

4. Move to **Slide 3**. In the right content placeholder, click at the end of the last bullet point—*Pedestrian friendly neighborhoods*—and then press Enter.

   Pressing Enter at the end of a bullet point adds a new bullet point at the same list level.

5. Type Sustainable lifestyle and press Enter.

6. Press Tab to create a second-level, indented bullet point. Type Focus on tomorrow and then compare your slide with **Figure 2**.

■ **Continue to the next page to complete the skill**

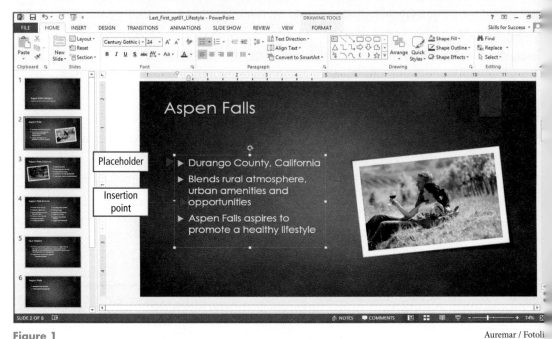

Figure 1

Auremar / Fotolia

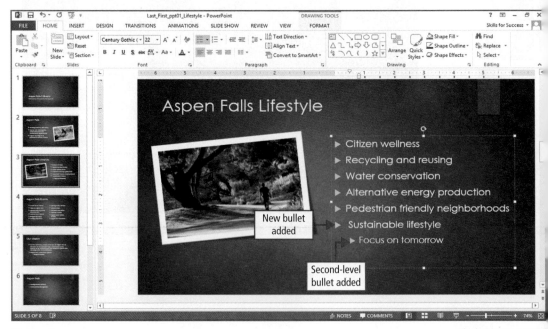

Figure 2

Charles Shapiro / Fotolia

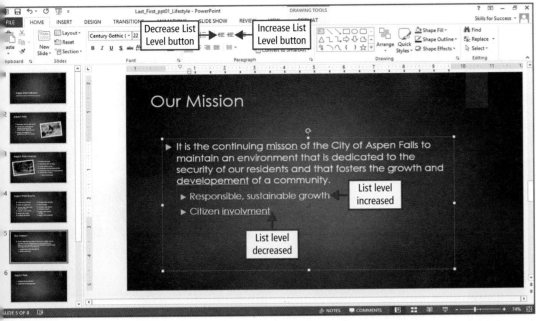

Figure 3

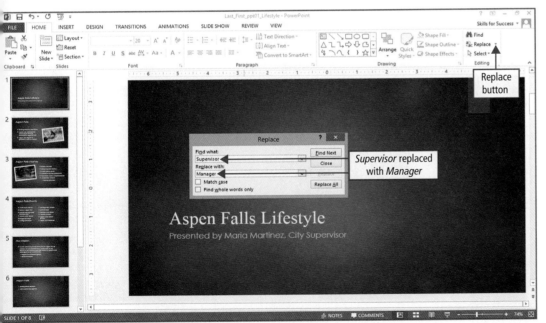

Figure 4

7. Move to **Slide 5**. Click anywhere in the second bullet point—*Responsible, sustainable growth*. On the **Home tab**, in the **Paragraph group**, click the **Increase List Level** button.

> The selection is formatted as a second-level bullet point, indicated by the indent and smaller font size.

8. Click anywhere in the third bullet point beginning with the word *Citizen*. On the **Home tab**, in the **Paragraph group**, click the **Decrease List Level** button. Compare your screen with **Figure 3**.

> A second-level bullet point is applied, as indicated by the decreased indent and the increased font size.

9. Move to **Slide 1** and notice the word *Supervisor* in the subtitle placeholder.

> This is the incorrect title for Maria. There is more than one instance in the presentation in which the word *Supervisor* is used instead of the word *Manager*.

10. On the **Home tab**, in the **Editing group**, click the **Replace** button. In the **Find what** box, type Supervisor and then click in the **Replace with** box. Type Manager and then compare your screen with **Figure 4**.

11. In the **Replace** dialog box, click the **Replace All** button to display a message box indicating that two replacements were made. Click **OK** to close the message box, and then in the **Replace** dialog box, click the **Close** button. **Save** the presentation.

■ **You have completed Skill 2 of 10**

▶ A *font*, which is measured in *points*, is a set of characters with the same design and shape.

▶ Font styles and effects emphasize text and include bold, italic, underline, shadow, small caps, and outline.

▶ The placement of text within a placeholder is referred to as *text alignment*. Text can be aligned left, centered, aligned right, or justified.

─────────────────────

1. On **Slide 1**, select the title text—*Aspen Falls Lifestyle*

2. On the **Mini toolbar**, click the **Font Size arrow**, and then click **72**.

3. With the title text still selected, on the **Home tab**, in the **Font group**, click the **Font arrow**. Scroll up and through the **Font list**, and then point to **Century Gothic** to display the Live Preview of the font, as shown in **Figure 1**.

4. In the **Font list**, click **Century Gothic**.

5. Place your insertion point anywhere in the subtitle. Click a border of the subtitle placeholder as shown in **Figure 2**.

   A solid border around a placeholder indicates that the entire placeholder and all of the contents within it are selected. With the placeholder selected, any formatting changes will be made to the entire contents of the placeholder.

6. In the **Font group**, click the **Launcher** to display the Font dialog box. Under **Effects**, select **Small Caps**, and then click **OK**.

   With small caps, lowercase characters are capitalized but are smaller than characters that are typed as capital letters.

■ **Continue to the next page to complete the skill**

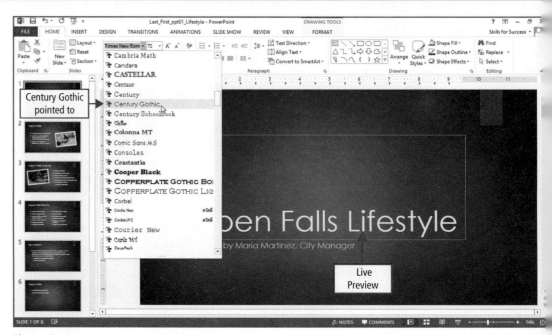

Figure 1

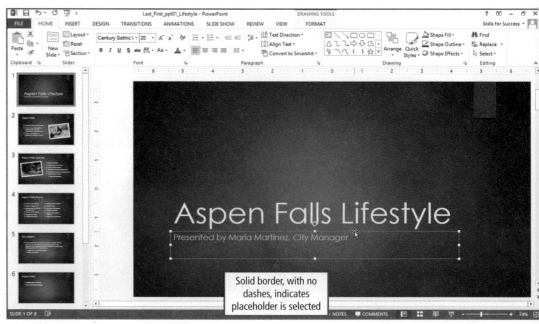

Figure 2

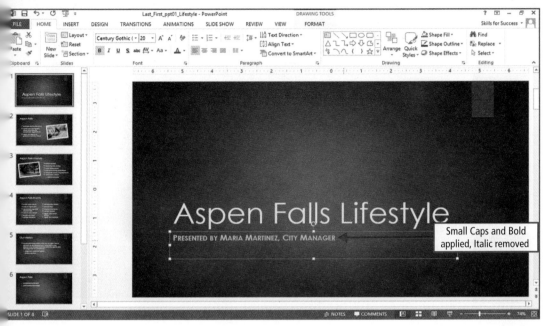

Figure 3

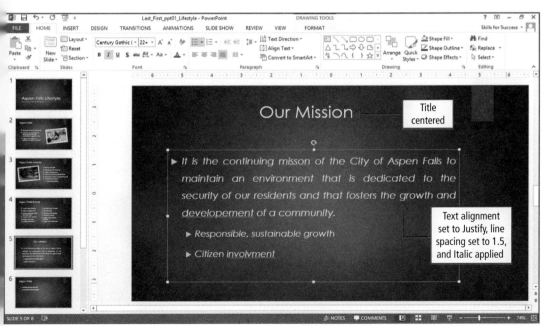

Figure 4

7. With the subtitle placeholder still selected, in the **Font group**, click the **Bold** button B, and then click the **Italic** button I.

8. Review the changes you have made, and then on the **Home tab**, in the **Font group**, click the **Italic** button I to turn off the italic formatting. Compare your slide with **Figure 3**.

   The italic formatting may have made the text more difficult to read, so it was removed. You can use the Mini toolbar, the Ribbon, or the Font dialog box to apply font styles and effects.

9. Move to **Slide 5** and click the title, and then click the border of the title placeholder to select it.

10. On the **Home tab**, in the **Paragraph group**, click the **Center** button ≡ to center align the title text.

11. Place your insertion point anywhere in the content placeholder. Click the border of the placeholder to select it; the placeholder will now have a solid border. With the content placeholder selected, on the **Home tab**, in the **Paragraph group**, click the **Justify** button ≡ to distribute the bulleted text evenly between the placeholder margins.

12. With the content placeholder still selected, in the **Paragraph group**, click the **Line Spacing** button. In the displayed list, click **1.5** to increase the space between lines in the paragraph.

13. On the **Home tab**, in the **Font group**, click the **Italic** button I. Compare your slide with **Figure 4**.

14. **Save** ⊟ the presentation.

■ **You have completed Skill 3 of 10**

▶ You can check for spelling errors in a presentation by looking for words marked with a red wavy underline. These words are flagged because they are not in the Office 2013 main dictionary.

▶ You can also correct spelling errors using a shortcut menu or the spell check feature.

▶ The ***thesaurus*** is a research tool that provides a list of ***synonyms***—words with the same meaning—for text that you select.

1. With **Slide 5** displayed in Normal view, notice that the word *involment* is flagged with a red wavy underline, indicating that it is misspelled.

2. Point to *involment* and click the right mouse button to display the shortcut menu with suggested solutions for correcting the misspelled word, as shown in **Figure 1**.

3. From the shortcut menu, click **involvement** to correct the spelling of the word.

4. Move to **Slide 4**. In the right content placeholder, notice misspelled word or words.

     In the content placeholder, if the word Cinquo is flagged as misspelled, right click and then click Ignore All. Proper names and non-English-language words are sometimes flagged as misspelled although they are spelled correctly. When you use the Ignore All command, the red wavy underline is removed for the current document only. If you are working on your personal computer, you can add words to the dictionary using the Add to Dictionary command. However, many colleges and workplaces do not allow this option.

5. Right-click the word *Triathalon*. From the shortcut menu, click **Triathlon**. Compare your slide with **Figure 2**.

■ **Continue to the next page to complete the skill** ▶

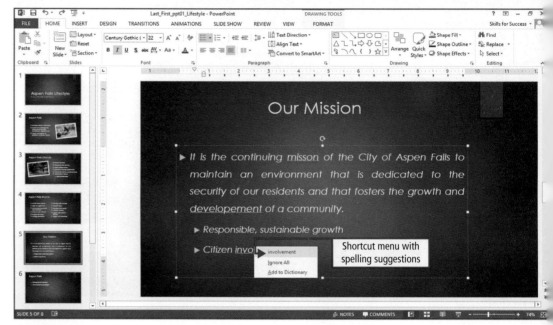

Figure 1

Figure 2

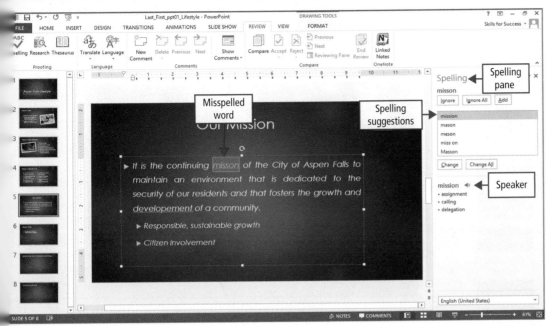

Figure 3

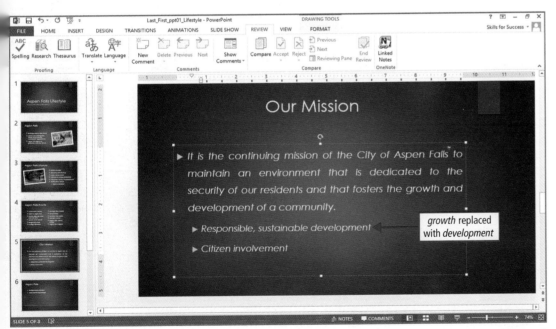

Figure 4

6. On the **Review tab**, in the **Proofing group**, click the **Spelling** button to display the **Spelling** pane as shown in **Figure 3**.

   You can use the Spelling pane to check the spelling of an entire presentation. Here, the incorrect spelling of the word *mission* on Slide 5 is highlighted on the slide and is also displayed in the Spelling pane. The Spelling pane provides options for correcting spelling, ignoring spelling, adding words to the custom dictionary, and a speaker icon, which, when clicked, plays a recording of the spoken word.

7. Check that your computer's speakers are on and not muted, or plug in headphones. In the lower half of the **Spelling** pane, click the **Speaker** icon and listen to the correct pronunciation of the word. Then, in the box containing spelling suggestions, be sure that **mission** is selected, and then click the **Change** button.

8. Use the **Spelling** pane to correct the spelling of one more word. When a message box indicates that the spell check is complete, click **OK**.

9. On **Slide 5**, in the bullet point beginning with *Responsible,* point to the word *growth,* and then click the right mouse button to display the shortcut menu.

10. Near the bottom of the shortcut menu, point to **Synonyms** to display the thesaurus list of suggested words to replace *growth.* Click **development** to replace *growth* with *development.* Compare your screen with **Figure 4**.

11. **Save** the presentation.

- **You have completed Skill 4 of 10**

- ▶ The arrangement of the text and graphic elements or placeholders on a slide is referred to as its *layout*.
- ▶ Users can choose different layouts for the arrangement of slide elements.

1. Display **Slide 5** in Normal view. On the **Home tab**, in the **Slides group**, click the top half of the **New Slide** button to add a new slide with the same layout as the current slide. Alternately, you can press Ctrl + M to insert a new slide.

2. Click in the title placeholder, and then type Our Vision

3. On the **Home tab**, in the **Paragraph group**, click the **Center** button.

4. Place your insertion point in the content placeholder. Type Our goal is to become one of the best places to live in the world. In the text you just typed, place your insertion point before the *O* in *Our*, and then press Enter three times to move the text in the placeholder downward. Compare your slide with **Figure 1**.

5. With **Slide 6** still selected, on the **Home tab**, in the **Slides group**, click the **Layout** button to display the *Layout gallery*—a visual representation of several content layouts that you can apply to a slide. The Layout gallery varies with the slide design. Some slide designs have 17 or more layouts, while others have as few as 6 to choose from.

6. Click **Two Content**, and then compare your screen with **Figure 2**.

   The slide layout is changed to one that includes a title and two content placeholders. The existing text is arranged in the placeholder on the left side of the slide. For now, the placeholder on the right will remain empty.

■ **Continue to the next page to complete the skill** ▶

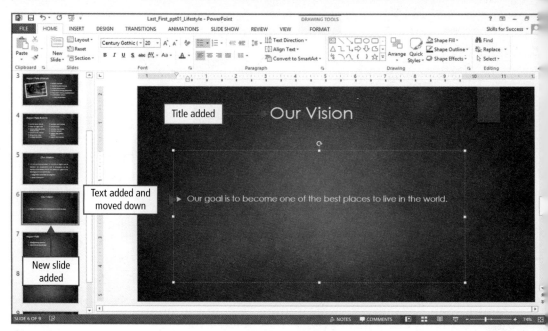

Figure 1

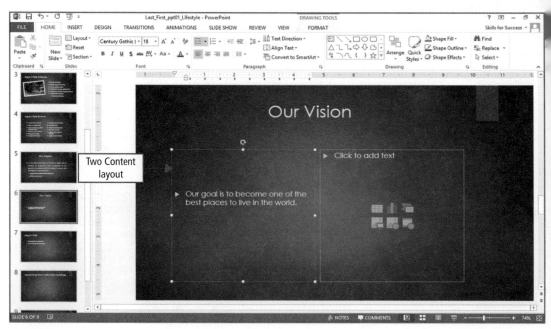

Figure 2

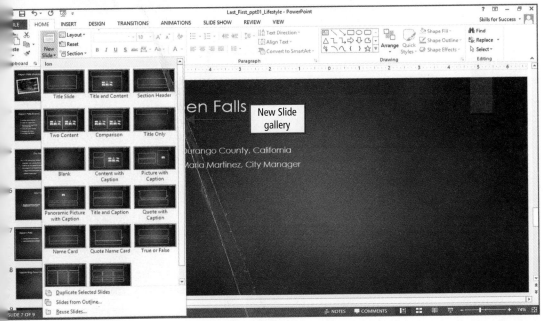

New Slide gallery

Figure 3

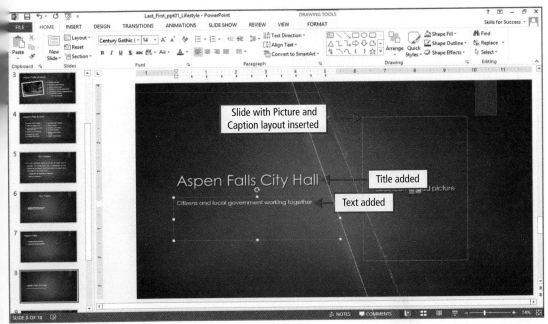

Slide with Picture and Caption layout inserted

Title added

Text added

Aspen Falls City Hall

Citizens and local government working together

Figure 4

7. If necessary, scroll down, and then click **Slide 7**. On the **Home tab**, in the **Slides group**, click the lower half of the **New Slide** button—the **New Slide arrow**—and compare your screen with **Figure 3**.

   When you click the upper half of the New Slide button, a new slide is inserted with the same layout as the previous slide. When you click the New Slide arrow, a gallery displays in which you can select a layout for the slide that you want to insert.

8. In the **Layout** gallery, click **Picture with Caption**.

9. Click in the title placeholder, and then type Aspen Falls City Hall

10. Select the title placeholder, and then on the **Home tab**, in the **Font group**, click the **Text Shadow** button $\boxed{\text{S}}$.

11. In the text placeholder, type Citizens and local government working together and compare your screen with **Figure 4**.

12. Move to **Slide 7**. On the **Home tab**, in the **Slides group**, click the **Layout** button. From the layout gallery, select **Name Card** to change the existing layout.

    You set the layout when you insert a slide using the New Slide button, or you can adjust the layout of an existing slide using the Layout button.

13. **Save** $\boxed{\text{🖫}}$ the presentation.

■ **You have completed Skill 5 of 10**

PPT 1-6
VIDEO

▶ **Pictures** are images created with a scanner or digital camera and saved with a graphic file extension such as .jpg, .png, .tif, or .bmp.

1. On **Slide 6**, in the right content placeholder, click the **Pictures** button.

2. In the **Insert Picture** dialog box, navigate to your student files for this chapter, click **ppt01_Vision**, and then click **Insert**. Compare your screen with **Figure 1**.

   The picture is selected as indicated by the **sizing handles**—squares or circles surrounding a selected object that can be used to adjust its size. When you point to a sizing handle on a corner of the image, a resize pointer or displays, indicating that you can resize the image proportionally, both vertically and horizontally. When you point to a sizing handle in the middle of any side on the image, a vertical resize pointer or horizontal resize pointer displays, indicating the direction in which you can size the image.

3. With the image on Slide 6 still selected, point to the **Format tab**.

   The Picture Tools tab displays only when you have an image selected. This **contextual tab** contains commands related to the selected object.

4. On the **Format tab**, in the **Picture Styles group**, click the **More** button to display the **Picture Styles** gallery, and then compare your screen with **Figure 2**.

   A **picture style** is a pre-built set of formatting borders, effects, and layouts applied to a picture.

■ **Continue to the next page to complete the skill**

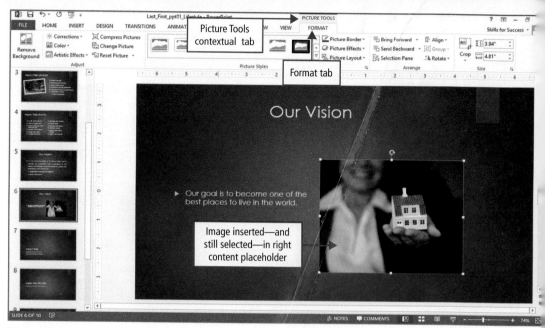

Figure 1

Thunder / Fotolia

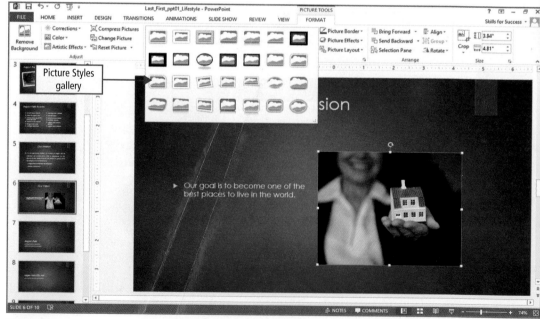

Figure 2

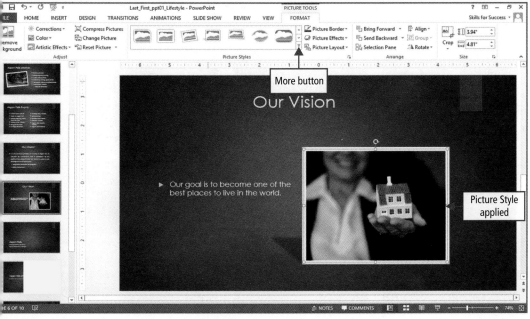

Figure 3

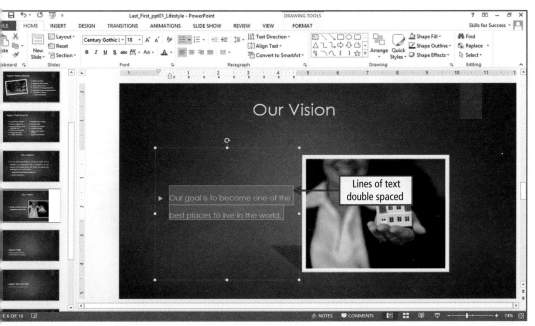

Figure 4

5. In the **Picture Styles** gallery, move your pointer over several of the thumbnails to preview the styles and display their names.

6. Using the ScreenTips to verify your selection, point to the fourth picture style in the third row—**Perspective Shadow, White**. Click to apply the picture style, and then compare your screen with **Figure 3**.

7. In the left placeholder, select both lines of bulleted text. On the **Home tab**, in the **Paragraph group**, click the **Line Spacing** button, and then click **2.0**. Compare your slide with **Figure 4**.

2.0 line spacing means that the lines of text are double spaced. The additional line spacing balances the text with the picture.

8. Move to **Slide 8**. In the picture placeholder on the right, click the **Pictures** button. In the **Insert Picture** dialog box, navigate to your student files for this chapter, click **ppt01_CityHall**, and then click **Insert**.

9. On the **Format tab**, in the **Picture Styles group**, click the same style you applied to the previous picture—**Perspective Shadow**, **White**.

10. Save the presentation.

■ **You have completed Skill 6 of 10**

▶ *Slide Sorter view* displays all of the slides in your presentation as thumbnails.

▶ Slide Sorter view can be used to rearrange and delete slides, to apply formatting to multiple slides, and to review and reorganize a presentation.

▶ In Slide Sorter view, you can select multiple slides by holding down ⎙Shift⎙ or ⎙Ctrl⎙.

1. Display **Slide 1** in Normal view. On the task bar at the bottom of the PowerPoint window, locate the **View** buttons, and then click the **Slide Sorter** button ⊞ to display the slide thumbnails. Compare your screen with **Figure 1**.

2. If necessary, scroll down in the presentation so that Slides 7 through 10 are visible. Click **Slide 7** and notice that a thick outline surrounds the slide, indicating that it is selected.

   On a touch screen device, you can tap—touch one time with your fingertip or stylus—to select a slide.

3. Press and hold ⎙Shift⎙ and click **Slide 10** so that Slides 7 through 10 are selected. Release ⎙Shift⎙.

   Using ⎙Shift⎙ enables you to select a group of sequential slides.

4. With the four slides selected, press and hold ⎙Ctrl⎙, and then click **Slides 7** and 8. Notice that only Slides 9 and 10 are selected. Release ⎙Ctrl⎙. Compare your screen with **Figure 2**.

   Using ⎙Ctrl⎙ enables you to select or deselect individual slides.

■ **Continue to the next page to complete the skill**

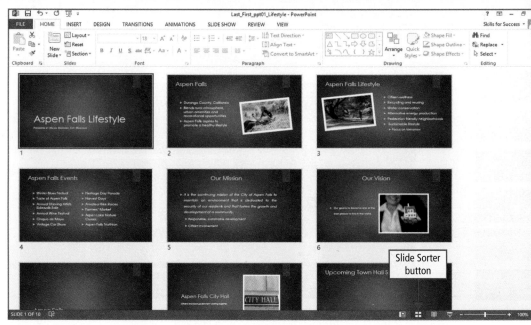

Figure 1

FotoLuminate / Foto

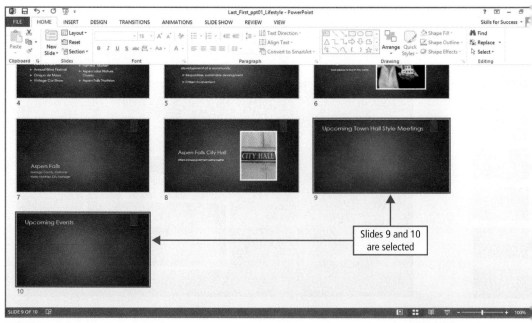

Figure 2

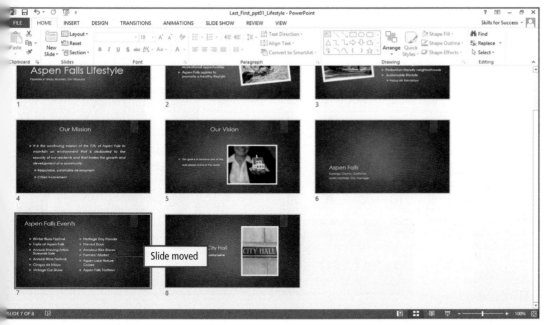

Figure 3

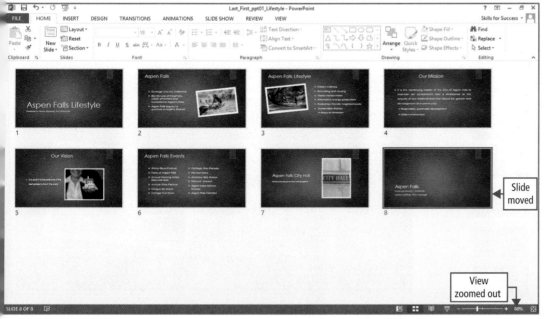

Figure 4

5. Press Delete to delete **Slides 9** and **10**. Notice that your presentation now contains eight slides because of the deletion.

6. If necessary, use the scroll bar so that **Slide 4** is visible, and then click **Slide 4** to select it.

7. Point to **Slide 4**, hold down the left mouse button, and then drag the slide straight down until it is positioned to the left of **Slide 8**. Release the mouse button and then compare your screen with **Figure 3**.

   On a touch screen device, you can tap to select a slide and then tap and drag to move slide thumbnails.

8. Click the **Slide 6** thumbnail and drag it downward so that it displays as the last slide in the presentation.

9. On the task bar, locate the **Zoom Slider**. Notice that the current zoom level is 100%. On the left side of the zoom slider, click the **Zoom Out** button two times so that all slides are visible and the zoom level is **80%**. Compare your screen with **Figure 4**.

   On a touch screen device, you can zoom out by using a pinch gesture—placing two fingers apart on the screen and pinching them together. You can zoom in using a spread gesture—placing two fingers together on the screen and spreading them apart.

10. Double-click **Slide 1** to return the presentation to Normal view with Slide 1 displayed.

11. **Save** the presentation.

- **You have completed Skill 7 of 10**

PPT 1-8
VIDEO

▶ When a presentation is viewed as a slide show, the entire slide fills the screen. When connected to a projection system, an audience can view your presentation on a large screen.

▶ **Slide transitions** are motion effects that occur in a slide show as you move from one slide to another.

▶ You can choose from a variety of transitions, and you can control the speed and method with which the slides advance during a presentation.

1. Display **Slide 2** in Normal view and then click the **Transitions tab**. In the **Transition to This Slide group**, click the **More** button ⬇ to display the **Transitions** gallery. Compare your screen with **Figure 1**.

   The slide transitions are organized in three groups—Subtle, Exciting, and Dynamic Content.

2. Click several of the transitions to view the transition effects, using the **More** button ⬇ as necessary to redisplay the gallery.

3. In the **Transition to This Slide group**, click the **More** button ⬇, and then under **Exciting**, click the last option in the first row—**Page Curl**.

4. In the **Transition to This Slide group**, click the **Effect Options** button, and then compare your screen with **Figure 2**. Click several of the effects to view them, clicking the Effect Options button to redisplay the gallery as needed.

   The Effect Options gallery lists the directions from which a slide transition displays and additional formats.

5. On the Effect Options list, click **Single Left** to change the effect.

■ **Continue to the next page to complete the skill**

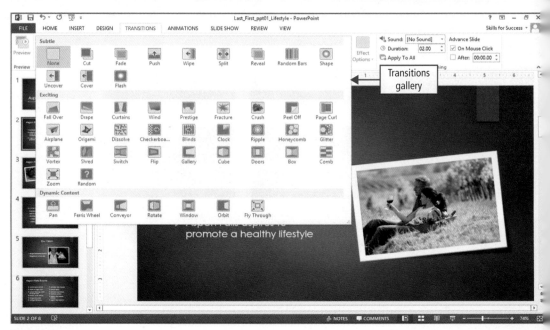

Figure 1

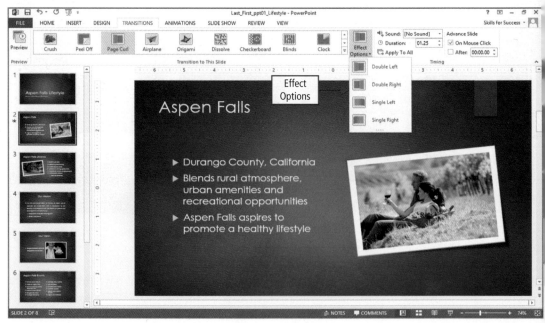

Figure 2

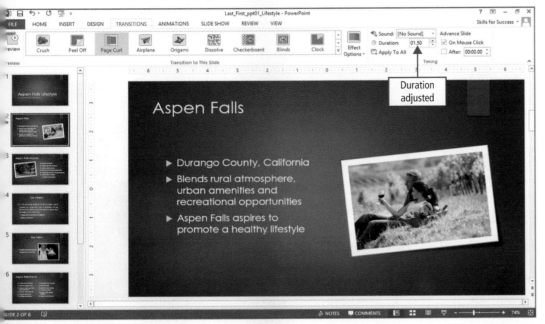

Figure 3

Figure 4

6. In the **Timing group**, click the **Duration box up spin arrow** one time to display *01.50*. Compare your screen with **Figure 3**.

7. Verify that under **Advance Slide**, the **On Mouse Click** check box is selected so that the slides advance when the mouse button is clicked.

8. In the **Timing group**, click the **Apply To All** button to apply the transition setting to all of the slides.

   The star that appears to the left of the slide thumbnails indicates that motion—in this case a transition—is present on the slide.

9. Click the **Slide Show tab**. In the **Start Slide Show group**, click **From Beginning**. Compare your screen with **Figure 4**.

10. Click the left mouse button to advance to the second slide, noticing the transition.

11. On **Slide 2**, in the lower left corner, locate the **Slide Controls**. Click the **Next Slide button** to advance to **Slide 3**.

    On a touch screen device, you can tap any of the Slide Controls to use them.

12. With **Slide 3** displayed, press the SpaceBar or Enter to move to **Slide 4**. Continue to advance through the presentation using your preferred method.

13. After the last slide displays, click to display a black slide with the text *End of slide show, click to exit*.

    A ***black slide*** displays at the end of the slide show to indicate that the presentation is over.

14. Click the left mouse button to return to **Slide 1** in Normal view, and then **Save** the presentation.

■ **You have completed Skill 8 of 10**

▶ A *header* is text that prints at the top of each page of slide handouts. A *footer* is text that displays at the bottom of every slide or that prints at the bottom of a sheet of slide handouts or notes pages.

▶ The *Snipping Tool* is an application that is used to create screenshots called *snips*.

▶ *Slide handouts* are printed images of slides on a sheet of paper.

1. Click the **Insert tab**, and then, in the **Text group**, click the **Header & Footer** button to display the Header and Footer dialog box.

   In the Header and Footer dialog box, the Slide tab is used to insert a footer on individual slides. The Notes and Handouts tab is used to add headers and footers to printouts.

2. In the **Header and Footer** dialog box, on the **Slides tab**, click the **Slide number** box to select it. Then, at the bottom of the dialog box, click **Don't show on title slide**. Compare your screen with Figure 1.

   A slide number will appear on each slide in the space indicated in the Preview section on the right except on the first slide. The placement of the slide number varies with the slide design.

3. Click the **Notes and Handouts tab**. Under **Include on page**, select—place a check mark in—the **Date and Time** box, and verify it is set to **Update automatically**.

4. Select the **Footer** check box, and then in the Footer box, using your own first and last name, type Last_First_ppt01_ Lifestyle Compare your screen with Figure 2, and then click the **Apply to All** button.

■ **Continue to the next page to complete the skill**

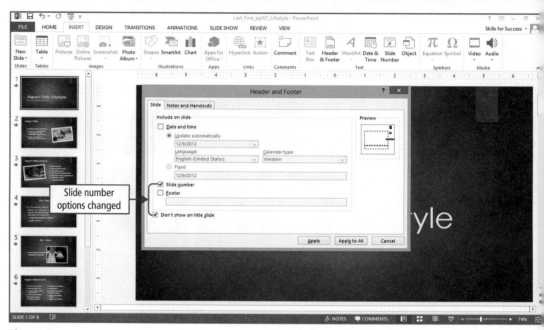

Figure 1

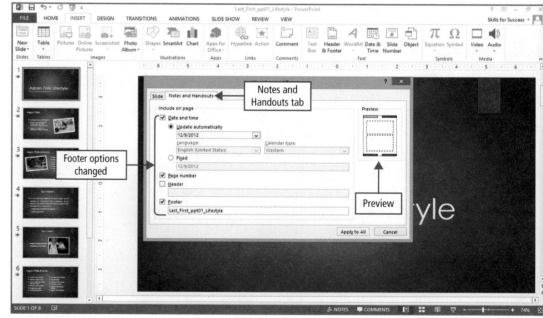

Figure 2

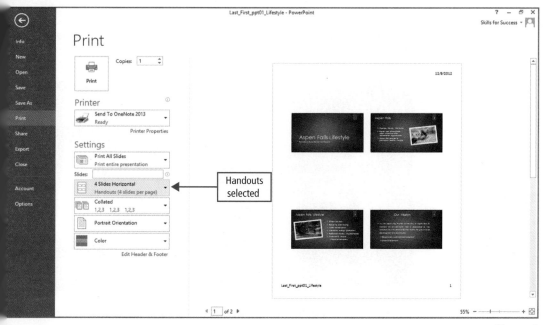

Figure 3

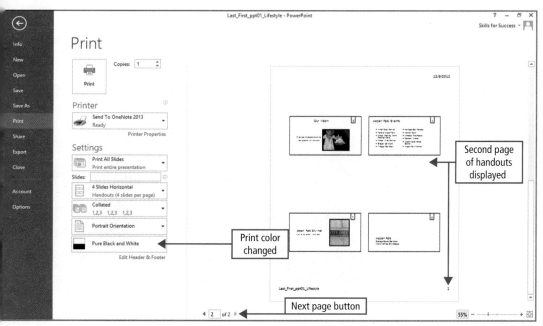

Figure 4

5. On the **File tab**, click **Print**.

The Print page has tools you can use to select your desired print settings and displays a preview of your presentation exactly as it will print.

6. On the **Print page**, under **Settings**, click **Full Page Slides**. In the gallery, under **Handouts**, click **4 Slides Horizontal**. Compare your screen with **Figure 3**.

Depending upon your printer, your slides may display in color, grayscale, or black and white. Your presentation includes eight slides, and the first handout displays the first four slides. The footer displays on the handouts, not on the slides.

7. On the left side of the window, under **Settings**, click the **Color** button, and then click **Pure Black and White**.

8. On the left side of the window, toward the bottom of the screen, click the **Next Page** button ▶ to display the second page of slide handouts, containing Slides 5 through 8. Compare your screen with **Figure 4**.

9. Press ⊞ to switch to the **Start screen**. With the Start Screen displayed, type Snip Open the **Snipping Tool** app. In the **Snipping Tool dialog box**, click the **New arrow**, and then click **Full-screen Snip**.

10. Click the **Save Snip button** 💾, and then in the **Save As** dialog box, navigate to your **PowerPoint Chapter 1** folder. **Save** the snip as Last_First_ppt01_LifestyleSnip and then **Close** ⊠ the Snipping Tool markup window. Press Esc to return to the presentation, and then click **Save** 💾.

■ **You have completed Skill 9 of 10**

▶ The ***Notes pane*** is an area of the Normal View window used to type notes that can be printed below an image of the slide. You can read your notes either on printed Notes pages or on screen using Presenter view.

▶ ***Notes pages*** are printouts that contain the slide image on the top half of the page and speaker notes on the lower half of the page.

▶ In ***Presenter view***, you can view your notes and slide on the computer screen. Only the slide is projected to the audience. Presenter view requires only one monitor.

▶ During a presentation, you may find it helpful to refer to your notes for specific statistical information or important points.

1. Display **Slide 2**. On the status bar, click the **Notes button** as needed to display the **Notes** pane. Click in the **Notes** pane and type The population of Aspen Falls was just over 75,000 citizens in the last census. Compare your screen with **Figure 1**.

2. On **Slide 6**. Click in the **Notes** pane and type Volunteers are needed, and welcomed, at all events. Please contact Deborah Davidson for more information at ddavidson@aspenfalls.org. Compare your screen with **Figure 2**.

3. Press F5 to start the presentation from the beginning, and then click to advance to the second slide.

   Notice that on Slide 2 the speaker notes you entered do not appear on screen. Your screen exactly matches the view being projected to the audience. If you are using dual monitors, your view may differ.

▪ **Continue to the next page to complete the skill**

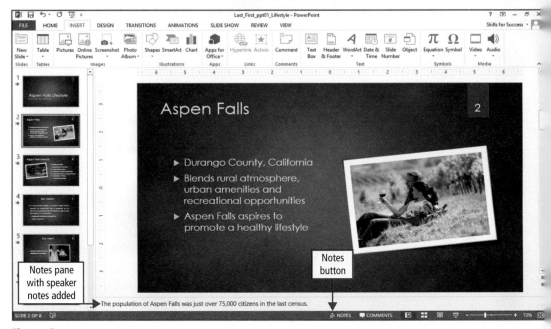

Figure 1

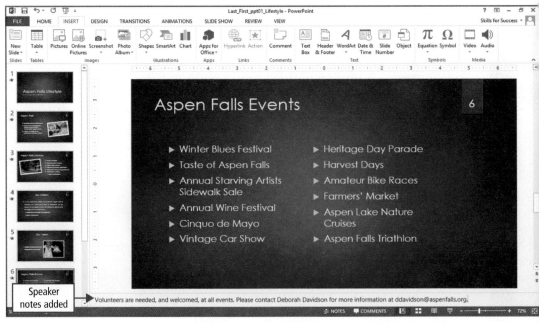

Figure 2

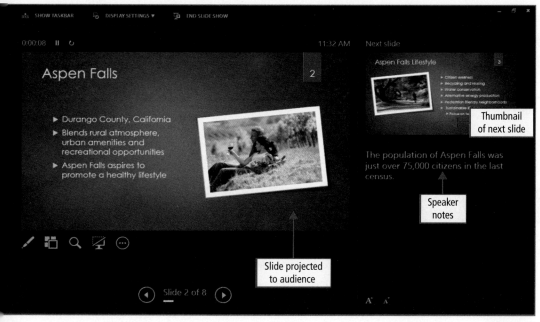

Figure 3

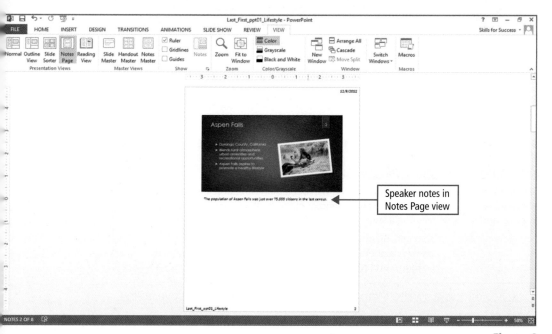
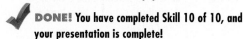

Figure 4

4. Still in Slide Show view, with Slide 2 displayed, right-click any area of the slide. From the shortcut menu, click **Show Presenter View**. Compare your screen with **Figure 3**.

   Presenter view displays three items—the current slide, speaker notes, and a thumbnail of the next slide. This view is shown only on the presenter's screen and is not projected on the screen the audience views. If you are using dual monitors, Presenter view may appear automatically, or the slide may appear on one monitor and the remaining information on the other. Keep these differences in mind as you use Presenter view.

5. Click the **Advance to the Next Slide** button 🔘 to advance to Slide 3, and then continue to click to advance through the presentation, noticing the speaker notes on Slide 6. Click to end the slide show and return to Normal view.

6. Move to **Slide 1**, and then click the **View tab**. In the **Presentation Views group**, click **Notes Page**. Scroll down to display **Slide 2** and compare your screen with **Figure 4**.

   The lower half of Notes pages for any slides that do not contain notes will remain blank.

7. On the **Status Bar**, click the **Normal button** 🔲 to return to Normal view.

8. On the Quick Access Toolbar, click **Save** 🔲 and then **Close** ☒ PowerPoint. Submit as directed by your instructor.

   ✔ **DONE!** You have completed Skill 10 of 10, and your presentation is complete!

The following More Skills are located at **www.pearsonhighered.com/skills**

More Skills Add Online Pictures

You can add images, including clip art and photos, from online sources to your presentation. These images are available from online sources including office.com and bing.com.

In More Skills 11, you will open a presentation and then search for and insert images from online sources. You will resize the inserted images.

To begin, open your web browser, navigate to www.pearsonhighered.com/skills, locate the name of your textbook, and follow the instructions on the website.

More Skills Print Presentations, Notes Pages, and Custom Ranges

In addition to showing a slide show on screen, you can create printouts to accompany a presentation. Printouts can be used as an aid for the presenter or as supplemental materials for the intended audience.

In More Skills 12, you will create screen captures—or Snips—of several presentation views—full page slides, pages with speaker notes, outlines, and audience handouts with spaces for notes.

To begin, open your web browser, navigate to www.pearsonhighered.com/skills, locate the name of your textbook, and follow the instructions on the website.

More Skills Move and Delete Slides in Normal View

Slides can be moved in Normal view. You can select multiple slides using Ctrl, and then delete or drag the selected slides to a new location in the presentation.

In More Skills 13, you will open a presentation, select and delete two slides, and select and move two slides.

To begin, open your web browser, navigate to www.pearsonhighered.com/skills, locate the name of your textbook, and follow the instructions on the website.

More Skills Change Slide Size and Orientation

Projectors and screens have two main formats—standard and wide screen. Slides can be sized to fit their intended use. Handouts can also be adjusted to either a landscape or portrait orientation.

In More Skills 14, you will open a presentation and then change the slide size and orientation. You will document your work by creating a snip.

To begin, open your web browser, navigate to www.pearsonhighered.com/skills, locate the name of your textbook, and follow the instructions on the website.

Please note that there are no additional projects to accompany the More Skills Projects, and they are not covered in the End-of-Chapter projects.

The following table summarizes the **SKILLS AND PROCEDURES** covered in this chapter.

Skills Number	Task	Step	Icon	Keyboard Shortcut
1	Save a presentation	File tab → Save As	💾	Ctrl + S
2	Increase list level in a bulleted list	Select bulleted point to be increased → Home tab → Paragraph group → Increase Indent button		Tab
2	Decrease list level in a bulleted list	Select bulleted point to be decreased → Home tab → Paragraph group → Decrease Indent button		Shift + Tab
2	Replace text	Home tab → Editing group → Replace		Ctrl + H
3	Apply a Font Effect	Select text → Home tab → Font group → Launcher button → Select Font effect		
3	Apply Bold	Select text → Home tab → Font group → Bold button	B	Ctrl + B
3	Apply Italic	Select text → Home tab → Font group → Italic button	I	Ctrl + I
3	Increase Line Spacing	Select text → Home tab → Paragraph group → Line Spacing button		
4	Check spelling	Review tab → Proofing group → Spelling button		F7 or Alt + R S
4	Find a synonym	Right-click word → Synonym		
5	Insert a new slide	Home tab → Slides group → New Slide button		Ctrl + M
5	Change slide layout	Home tab → Slides group → Layout button		
6	Insert a picture	Insert tab → Images group → Pictures button		
6	Apply a Picture Style	Picture Tools Format tab → Picture Style group		
7	Delete a slide	Select slide thumbnail → Right-click → Delete		Delete
7	Move a slide	Select slide → drag		
7	Select multiple slides	Select first slide → Press and hold Shift or Ctrl → Select next slide		Shift or Ctrl
7	Switch to Slide Sorter view	Status bar → Slide Sorter or View tab → Presentation Views group → Slide Sorter	▦	
8	Add a transition	Transitions tab → Transitions to this Slide group → Transitions gallery		
8	Start Slide Show	Status bar → Slide Show or Slide Show tab → Start Slide Show group		F5
9	Insert Headers and Footers	Insert tab → Text group → Header & Footer		
10	Use Presenter View	While in Slide Show, Right-click → Presenter view		
10	Add speaker notes	Status bar → Notes button		
10	Print presentations and handouts	File tab → Print		

Key Terms

Online Help Skills

1. With PowerPoint open, in the upper right corner of the screen, click the Microsoft PowerPoint Help ⊘ button, or press F1.

2. In the **PowerPoint Help** window, use the Search box to locate and open the article *Jump to a slide in Slide Show view*. Compare your screen with **Figure 1**.

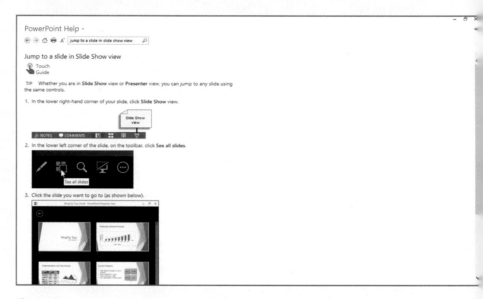

Figure 1

3. Read the article and answer the following questions: In what situation might you want to jump to a different slide during a presentation? How might this be beneficial?

Matching

Match each term in the second column with its correct definition in the first column. Write the letter of the term on the blank line in front of the correct definition.

___ **1.** The initial screen that displays when you open PowerPoint 2013; from here you can open a Recent file or create a new presentation from a template.

___ **2.** The setting that determines the indent, font size, and bullet type for slide bullets.

___ **3.** A line of text on a slide that starts with a special character and is assigned with a specific indent.

___ **4.** The boxes on slides used to hold objects such as titles, subtitles, pictures, and other content.

___ **5.** A feature that changes the horizontal placement of text within a placeholder.

___ **6.** A set of characters with the same design and shape.

___ **7.** A circle or square surrounding a selected object that is used to adjust its size.

___ **8.** A slide that displays at the end of the slide show to indicate that the presentation is over.

___ **9.** An area of the Normal View window used to type notes that can be printed below a picture of each slide.

___ **10.** A printout that contains the slide image in the top half of the page and speaker notes typed in the Notes pane in the lower half of the page.

A Black slide

B Bullet point

C Font

D List level

E Notes page

F Notes pane

G Placeholder

H Sizing handle

I Start screen

J Text alignment

BizSkills Video

1. After viewing the video, summarize some of the common elements of appropriate professional apparel for work.

2. How might a person's appearance impact his or her professional image? Is this fair?

Multiple Choice

Choose the correct answer.

1. The button that is used to move a bullet point, or line of text, to the right in preset increments.
   - **A.** Increase List Level
   - **B.** Decrease List Level
   - **C.** Line Spacing

2. Words with the same meaning.
   - **A.** Synonyms
   - **B.** Antonyms
   - **C.** Prepositions

3. The arrangement of the text and graphic elements or placeholders on a slide.
   - **A.** Layout
   - **B.** Gallery
   - **C.** Design

4. The view in which all of the slides in your presentation are displayed as thumbnails.
   - **A.** Normal View
   - **B.** Slide Sorter
   - **C.** Reading View

5. Tabs that display only when certain objects such as pictures are selected.
   - **A.** Contextual tabs
   - **B.** ScreenTips
   - **C.** Tool galleries

6. A prebuilt set of formatting borders, effects, and layouts applied to a picture.
   - **A.** Artistic effects
   - **B.** Picture styles
   - **C.** Picture designs

7. A motion effect that occurs in Slide Show view when you move from one slide to the next during a presentation.
   - **A.** Animation
   - **B.** Slide transition
   - **C.** Custom effect

8. Text that prints at the top of a sheet of slide handouts or notes pages.
   - **A.** Page numbers
   - **B.** Header
   - **C.** Footer

9. Text that displays at the bottom of every slide or that prints at the bottom of a sheet of slide handouts.
   - **A.** Page numbers
   - **B.** Header
   - **C.** Footer

10. View that displays the current slide, notes, and preview of upcoming slide to the presenter.
    - **A.** Presenter View
    - **B.** Slide Show View
    - **C.** Notes Page View

Topics for Discussion

1. Review the design templates available from the Start screen in PowerPoint. How are presentations and templates designed for different audiences? For example, how might the design used in a presentation created for children differ from the design used in a presentation created for a group of financial investors?

2. How might adding speaker notes to a presentation be helpful? What are some best practices for using speaker notes?

Skills Review  MyITLab® Grader

To complete this project, you will need the following files:

- ppt01_SRSustainability
- ppt01_SRPlant

You will save your files as:

- Last_First_ppt01_SRSustainability
- Last_First_ppt01_SRSnip

Figure 1

1. Start **PowerPoint 2013**, and then open the student data file **ppt01_SRSustainability**. On the **File tab**, click **Save As**, and then click **Browse**. In the **Save As** dialog box, navigate to your chapter folder, and save the file as Last_First_ppt01_SRSustainability

2. Display **Slide 2** and click so that your insertion point appears to the left of the *p* in *printed*. Type Decrease and then press [SpaceBar].

3. Display **Slide 1**. On the **Home tab**, in the **Editing group**, click the **Replace** button. In the **Find what** box, type Drive and then click in the **Replace with** box. Type Campaign and then click **Replace All**. **Close** the Replace dialog box.

4. On **Slide 1**, select the title placeholder. On the **Home tab**, in the **Font group**, click the **Launcher**. Select **Small Caps**, and then click **OK**.

5. On the **Review tab**, in the **Proofing group**, click the **Spelling** button. Use the **Spelling** task pane to correct the spelling of two words, and then click **OK**.

6. On **Slide 2**, in the third bullet point, right-click the word *policy,* point to **Synonyms** and then click the word **strategy**. Compare your screen with **Figure 1**.

7. Display **Slide 4**. On the **Home tab**, in the **Slides group**, click the **Layout** button, and then click **Two Content**.

8. In the right content placeholder, click the **Pictures** button. In the **Insert Picture** dialog box, navigate to your student files, and then click **ppt01_SRPlant**. Click **Insert**.

9. With the picture selected, on the **Format tab**, in the **Picture Styles group**, select **Rounded Diagonal Corner, White**.

10. On the **Status bar**, click the **Slide Sorter** button.

11. In Slide Sorter view, select **Slide 4**, and then drag it so that it appears directly after **Slide 1**. Compare your screen with **Figure 2**.

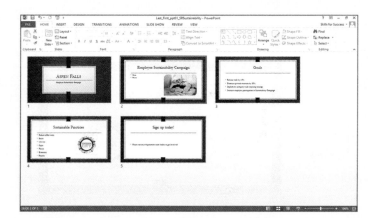

Figure 2

Rido / Fotolia

- Continue to the next page to complete this Skills Review

Figure 3

Marina Zlochin / Fotolia

Figure 4

12. In Slide Sorter view, select **Slide 5**, and then press ⌷Delete⌷.

13. Double-click **Slide 2** to return to **Normal view**. On the **Transitions tab**, in the **Transitions to This Slide group**, click the **More arrow**. At the bottom of the gallery, click **Fly Through**.

14. On the **Transitions tab**, in the **Transitions to This Slide group**, click the **Effect Options** button, and then select **In with Bounce**. In the **Timing group**, click **Apply To All**. Compare your screen with Figure 3.

15. Display **Slide 4**. Select the bullet points *Paper*, *Plastic*, and *Electricity*. With these three bullet points selected, press ⌷Tab⌷.

16. On the **Status bar**, click the **Notes** button. In the **Notes pane**, type Employees are encouraged to share new ideas for promoting sustainability. Compare your screen with Figure 4.

17. Display **Slide 3**. In the Notes pane, type Incentive program to be announced.

18. On the **Insert tab**, in the **Text group**, click **Header & Footer**. On the **Slide tab**, select the **Slide Number** check box. Select **Don't show on title slide**, and then click **Apply to All**.

19. On the **Insert tab**, in the **Text group**, click **Header & Footer**. On the **Notes and Handouts tab**, select **Date and Time** and verify that **Update Automatically** and **Page Number** are selected. Check **Footer**, and then in the footer box, type Last_First_ppt01_SRSustainability Click **Apply to All**.

20. On the **File tab**, click **Print**. Under **Settings**, click the **Full Page Slides** button and then select **4 Slides Horizontal**. Under **Settings**, click the **Color** button and then click **Pure Black and White**.

21. Press ⊞, type Snip and then press ⌷Enter⌷. In the Snipping Tool dialog box, click the **New arrow**, and then click **Full-screen Snip**.

22. Click **Save Snip**, navigate to your **PowerPoint Chapter 1** folder, and then save the snip as Last_First_ppt01_SRSnip **Close** the Snipping Tool markup window.

23. Press ⌷Esc⌷ to return to the presentation, click **Save**, and then **Close** PowerPoint.

24. Submit your printouts or files as directed by your instructor.

✔ **DONE! You have completed this Skills Review**

Skills Assessment 1

MyITLab®
Grader

To complete this project, you will need the following files:

- ppt01_SA1Bike
- ppt01_SA1BikeLane
- ppt01_SA1BikePark

You will save your files as:

- Last_First_ppt01_SA1Bike
- Last_First_ppt01_SA1Snip

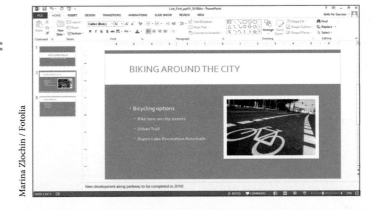

Marina Zlochin / Fotolia

Figure 1

1. From your student data files, locate and open **ppt01_SA1Bike**. Save it in your **Chapter 1** folder as Last_First_ppt01_SA1Bike

2. On **Slide 2**, in the second bullet point, before the word *on*, add the word lane and add a space.

3. Change the slide layout to **Two Content**. In the content placeholder on the right side of the slide, add the image **ppt01_SA1BikeLane**.

4. With the image still selected, apply the **Beveled Matte, White** picture style.

5. In the left content placeholder, select all of the text. Change the line spacing to **1.5** and the font size to **24**.

6. Select the last three bullet points, beginning with *Bike* and ending with *trails,* and then increase the list indent one level.

7. Add the sentence New development along parkway to be completed in 2016! as speaker notes on Slide 2. Compare your screen with **Figure 1**.

8. After **Slide 3**, insert a new **Slide 4** with the **Picture with Caption** layout. Add the title Bike Aspen Falls accepting the default title formatting.

9. In the picture placeholder, insert the image **ppt01_SA1BikePark**. Apply the **Beveled Matte, White** picture style. In the caption placeholder, type Off road trail at Aspen Lake Park and then increase the font size to **24**.

10. Move **Slide 3** so that it appears as the last slide in the presentation.

11. Use the Spelling pane to correct any spelling errors in the presentation.

12. On **Slide 4**, in the content placeholder, delete the word *fun* and replace it with the word family

13. On **Slide 4**, use the thesaurus to replace the word *Promotes* with the synonym Encourages

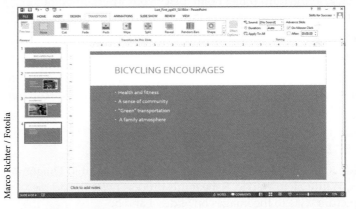

Marco Richter / Fotolia

Figure 2

14. Use Find and Replace to replace all occurrences of the word *Biking* with the word Bicycling

15. On **Slide 4**, increase the font size for all bulleted text to **24**. Click a blank area of the slide to deselect the placeholder. Compare your screen with **Figure 2**.

16. Apply the **Push** transition to all slides.

17. Add the **Slide number** to all slides except for the title slide.

18. Add the **file name** to the **Footer** for the Notes and Handouts pages, and add the **Date and Time**, setting it to update automatically.

19. Create a Full Screen **Snip** of **Handouts** with **Four Slides Vertical** per page, set to print in **Pure Black and White**. Save the Snip as Last_First_ppt01_SA1Snip

20. **Save** your presentation. **Close** PowerPoint, and then submit the files as directed by your instructor.

 DONE! You have completed Skills Assessment 1

Skills Assessment 2

To complete this project, you will need the following files:

- ppt01_SA2Health   - ppt01_SA2CheckUp

You will save your file as:

- Last_First_ppt01_SA2Health

1. From your student data files, locate and open **ppt01_SA2Health**. Save it in your chapter folder as Last_First_ppt01_SA2Health

2. On **Slide 2**, in the third bullet point, place your insertion point before the word *citizens*, and add the words Aspen Falls

3. On **Slide 2**, change the **Slide Layout** to **Title and Content**.

4. On **Slide 3**, replace the word *Guidance* with the synonym Leadership

5. Use the **Spelling** pane to correct the spelling of one word. Ignore the spelling of any business name.

6. On **Slide 3**, in the left placeholder, insert the image **ppt01_SA2CheckUp**.

7. On **Slide 3**, select the image, and then apply the **Rounded Diagonal Corner**, **White** picture style. Repeat this process twice to add the same picture style to the images on Slides 4 and 5.

8. On **Slide 4**, increase the **Line Spacing** of all bulleted text to **2.0**. Compare your screen with **Figure 1**.

9. On **Slide 5**, increase the **Font Size** for all bulleted text to **32**.

10. **Delete** the existing **Slide 6**.

11. After **Slide 5**, insert a new Slide 6 with the **Section Header** layout.

12. In the title placeholder, type Aspen Falls Healthy Living

13. In the text placeholder, type Contact Jack Ruiz, Community Services Director, for more information – jruiz@aspenfalls.org Compare your screen with **Figure 2**.

14. Add the **Blinds** transition, change the **Effect Options** to **Horizontal**, and then apply the transition to all slides.

15. Add the date, page number, and file name as a footer to all the Notes and Handouts pages.

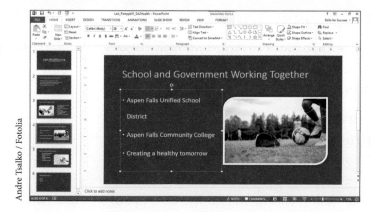

Figure 1

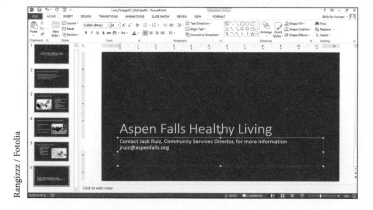

Figure 2

16. On **Slide 6**, using the Notes pane, add the speaker notes Jack can be reached at (805) 555–1010.

17. **Save** and then submit the presentation as directed by your instructor. **Close** PowerPoint.

 **DONE! You have completed Skills Assessment 2**

Visual Skills Assessment

To complete this project, you will need the following files:

- ppt01_VSPlanning
- ppt01_VSPlanningImage

You will save your file as:

- Last_First_ppt01_VSPlanning

In this project, you will edit a slide so it looks like the slide shown in **Figure 1**. To begin, open the presentation named **ppt01_VSPlanning**, and save it as Last_First_ppt01_VSPlanning in your **PowerPoint Chapter 1** folder.

The slide layout is **Two Content**. Increase the title **Font Size** to **66**, and apply **Bold** and **Small Caps**. Apply the list levels as shown in the figure. The font size of the first bullet is **32** points; the remaining bullets' font sizes are **30** points. The Line Spacing is **1.5** lines. The image is **ppt01_VCPlanningImage**. The style shown is applied to the picture. The **Transition** is named **Glitter**, and the **Effect Options** are set to **Hexagons from Bottom**. Spelling errors in the presentation are corrected. The date, page number, and file name appear in the footer of all of the Notes and Handouts pages. Submit the file as directed by your instructor.

 DONE! You have completed Visual Skills Assessment

Dulsita/Fotolia

Figure 1

My Skills

To complete this project, you will need the following files:

- ppt01_MSCareerDevelopment

You will save your file as:

- Last_First_ppt01_MSCareerDevelopment

1. From your student data files, locate and open **ppt01_MSCareerDevelopment**. Save it in your PowerPoint Chapter 1 folder as Last_First_ppt01_MSCareerDevelopment

2. On **Slide 1**, in the **subtitle placeholder**, type your first and last names. Select the text in the **subtitle placeholder**, and then apply the **Font Effect** named **Small Caps**.

3. Insert a new **Slide 2** with the **Title and Content** layout.

4. In the title placeholder, type Career Development Strategies

5. In the content placeholder, type five bulleted points: Join professional organizations and Participate in ongoing education and Continue to develop new skills and Present a professional image and Utilize a mentor

6. Increase the **Font Size** to **28**. Increase the **Line Spacing** of all bulleted text to **1.5** lines.

7. Add the Slide number to all slides.

8. Add the **Transition** named **Random Bars** to both slides in the presentation.

9. To all of the Notes and Handouts pages, add the date, page number, and file name as a footer.

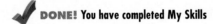 **DONE!** You have completed My Skills

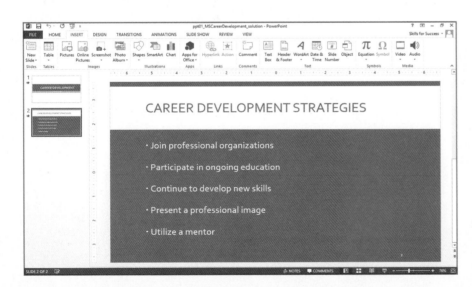

Figure 1

Skills Challenge 1

To complete this project, you will need the following files:

- ppt01_SC1Invest
- ppt01_SC1InvestImage

You will save your file as:

- Last_First_ppt01_SC1Invest

Locate and open the presentation **ppt01_SC1Invest**. Save the presentation in your chapter folder as Last_First_ppt01_SC11Invest Maria Martinez, City Manager, and Richard Mack, Assistant City Manager, will use this presentation when they meet with business investors who are considering investing in businesses in Aspen Falls. Using the skills you practiced in this chapter, adjust the font of the title on the title slide so that it appears on one line, and then adjust all other fonts in the presentation so they meet the standard rules of design listed in the chapter opening. Adjust the line spacing of all bulleted points so that the text fits well on the slides. Change the layout on Slide 3 so that on the right side of the slide you can add the image **ppt01_SC1InvestImage**. In the left content placeholder on Slide 3, increase the indent for all names, leaving the titles at their original level. Add a Picture Style to both images in the presentation. Correct all spelling errors in the presentation. To all of the Notes and Handouts pages, add the date, page number, and file name as a footer.

 DONE! You have completed Skills Challenge 1

Skills Challenge 2

To complete this project, you will need the following files:

- ppt01_SC2Events

You will save your file as:

- Last_First_ppt01_SC2Events

Locate and open the presentation **ppt01_SC2Events**, and save it in your chapter folder as Last_First_ppt01_SC2Events Add the current year in the appropriate place. Adjust the font sizes in the presentation, make at least one other enhancement to the fonts in the presentation—change fonts, apply Bold, or apply a Font Effect—and correct the spelling errors. Increase the indent level of approriate information on Slide 2, and then locate and add an appropriate image anywhere in the presentation. Apply a Picture Style to the image you inserted. Add a transition to both slides. To all of the Notes and Handouts pages, add the date, page number, and file name as a footer. Save the presentation and submit as directed.

 DONE! You have completed Skills Challenge 2

CHAPTER 2

Format a Presentation

- ▶ Formatting is the process of changing the appearance of the text, layout, or design of a slide.
- ▶ You can apply formatting to text and images to enhance your slides in a manner that assists you in conveying your message to your audience.
- ▶ You can apply themes to your presentation to create dynamic and professional slides.

- ▶ The design of a presentation can be customized by changing font colors, bullet symbols, and slide backgrounds.
- ▶ Before applying formatting, you can use the Live Preview feature to view the effect of different formatting on your slides.

© Yuri Arcurs

Aspen Falls City Hall

In this chapter, you will create a new presentation for Evelyn Stone, director of human resources for Aspen Falls. This presentation will be shown during orientation for new employees. It contains important information to guide the new employees and will serve to inform and set a positive, welcoming atmosphere.

In your career, you may create presentations to guide an audience through a process or to provide an itinerary. When presenting this type of information, it is often best to break the information into numbered or bulleted lists. You can also add images and WordArt to attract and hold your audience's attention, emphasize information on the slide, and elicit a certain emotion.

Slide design is important to the success of your presentation. Uncluttered, clean-looking slides make it easier for your audience to understand your main points. To increase your own efficiency, you can insert slides from other presentations, copy formatting using the Format Painter, and copy and paste information. Design your presentation with your message in mind. Choose a theme, layout, and images that will appeal to and interest your audience.

In this project, you will create a new presentation and add slides with different layouts. You will apply a theme and then select a different variant for the entire presentation; later you will adjust the variant on a single slide.

Time to complete all 10 skills – 60 to 75 minutes

Student data files needed for this chapter:

ppt02_Photo1   ppt02_Photo3
ppt02_Photo2   ppt02_Photo4

You will save your file as:

Last_First_ppt02_Orientation

Outcome

Using the skills in this chapter, you will be able to work with PowerPoint presentations like this:

SKILLS

MyITLab®
Skills 1-10 Training

At the end of this chapter you will be able to:

Skill 1   Create New Presentations
Skill 2   Change Themes and Variants
Skill 3   Change Font Colors and Effects
Skill 4   Format Slide Backgrounds with Fill
Skill 5   Add Pictures and Textures to Slide Backgrounds
Skill 6   Format Text with WordArt
Skill 7   Change Character Spacing
Skill 8   Modify Bulleted and Numbered Lists
Skill 9   Move and Copy Text and Objects
Skill 10 Use Format Painter and Clear All Formatting

MORE SKILLS

Skill 11 Edit Slide Masters
Skill 12 Save and Apply Presentation Templates
Skill 13 Create Slides from Microsoft Word Outlines
Skill 14 Design Presentations with Contrast

DOC RABE / Fotolia

▶ When you start PowerPoint, you can search available templates and themes to find a look that fits your needs.

▶ When you select a template, a new, blank presentation in that design appears.

1. Start **PowerPoint**. On the **Start screen,** view the templates available on the right side of the screen as shown in **Figure 1**.

    The Start screen displays some of the available templates, links to recently opened presentations or to other presentations that are already open, and a search box that you can use to search online templates and themes. A **template** is a file upon which a presentation can be based. This page displays only when you first start PowerPoint. If you already have a blank presentation started, you can click File and then New to view a gallery of available templates.

2. On the right side of the **Start screen,** click several template thumbnails to display a preview of each of the templates and the variants of the theme. After viewing the template, or templates, you selected, **Close** ✕ the preview window to return to the Start screen.

3. Click the **Ion** thumbnail. Along the bottom of the preview window, click the **More Images arrow** to view images of some of the slide layouts, and then click the **Create** button to create a presentation using the Ion template.

4. Click in the title placeholder, and then type Employee Orientation

5. Click in the subtitle placeholder. Type Aspen Falls City Government accepting the default All Caps formatting, and then compare your screen with **Figure 2**.

■ **Continue to the next page to complete the skill**

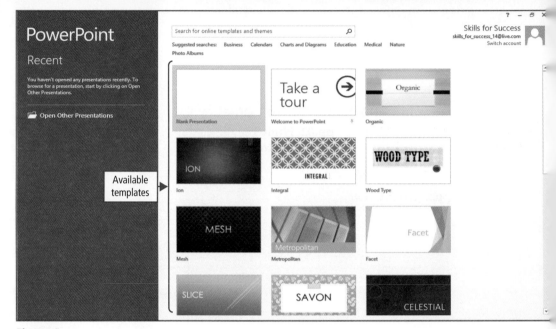

Figure 1

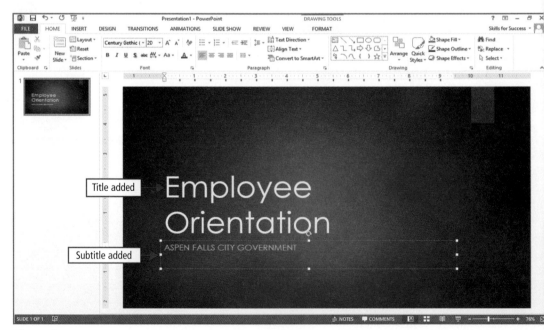

Figure 2

Figure 3

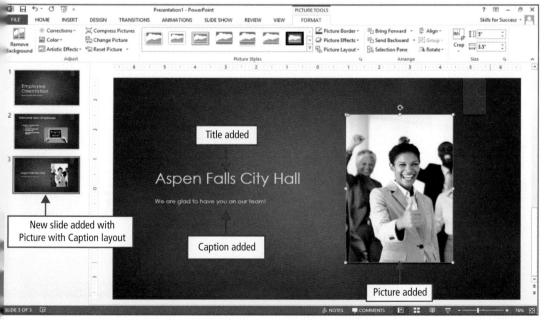

Figure 4

6. On the **Home tab,** in the **Slides group,** click the **New Slide arrow.** Click the **Two Content** thumbnail to insert a slide with the **Two Content** layout. In the title placeholder, type Welcome New Employees

7. In the left content placeholder, type Itinerary – First Day of Work and press Enter .

8. Press Tab , and type the following four bullet points, pressing Enter after each line:

   City Hall tour

   Department introduction

   Welcome lunch

   New employee orientation meeting

9. In the right content placeholder, click the **Pictures** button. In the **Insert Picture** dialog box, navigate to your student files for this chapter, click **ppt02_Photo1,** and then click **Insert.** Compare your screen with **Figure 3**.

10. On the **Home tab,** in the **Slides group,** click the **New Slide arrow.** In the gallery, click **Picture with Caption.** In the title placeholder, type Aspen Falls City Hall In the text placeholder, type We are glad to have you on our team!

11. In the picture placeholder, using the method described in Step 9, insert the student data file **ppt02_Photo2.** Compare your screen with **Figure 4**.

12. On the Quick Access Toolbar, click **Save**. On the Save As page, click the **Browse** button. Navigate to the location where you are saving your files, and create a folder named PowerPoint Chapter 2 Using your own name, save the presentation as Last_First_ppt02_Orientation

■ **You have completed Skill 1 of 10**

▶ The presentation **theme** is a set of unified design elements—colors, fonts, and effects—that provides a unique look for your presentation. The theme can be selected as the presentation is created, or it can be applied later. Each template has a theme, and the types and numbers of slide layouts vary among templates.

▶ **Theme variants** are variations of the current theme, with different accent colors. You can change the variant for all slides in the presentation or for a single slide.

1. On **Slide 1**, on the **Design tab**, in the **Themes group**, click the **More** button [▾] to display the Themes gallery.

2. Under **Office,** point to the first thumbnail—**Office Theme,** as shown in **Figure 1**.

   Theme names can be identified by their ScreenTips. The first theme in the Office group is the Office Theme, followed by other themes.

3. Point to several themes, and preview the changes to the first slide.

   Each theme includes background colors, font styles, colors, effects, and slide layouts specific to the theme.

4. In the **Themes gallery,** use ScreenTips to locate the **Retrospect** theme, and then click it to apply this theme to all of the slides in the presentation. Compare your screen with **Figure 2**.

■ Continue to the next page to complete the skill ▶

Figure 1

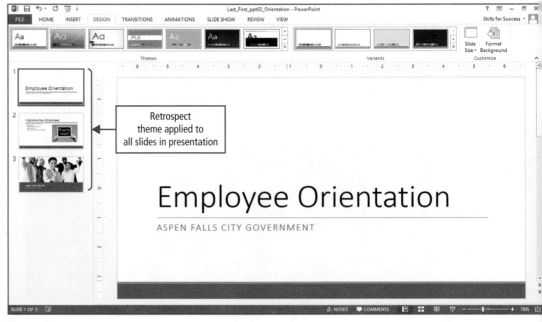

Figure 2

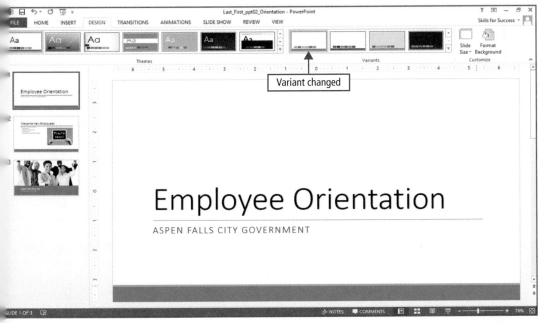

Variant changed

Figure 3

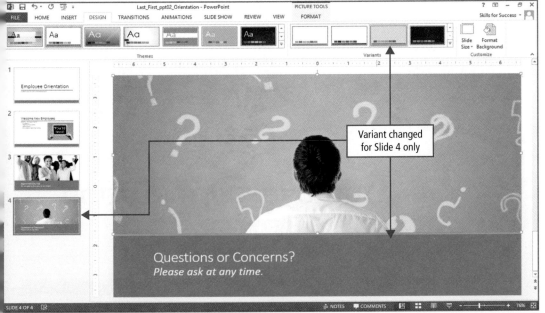

Variant changed for Slide 4 only

Questions or Concerns?
Please ask at any time.

Rangizzz / Fotolia

Figure 4

5. On the **Design tab**, in the **Variants group**, click the **More** button, click the first variant in the second row, and then compare your screen with **Figure 3**.

6. On **Slide 3**, select the caption *We are glad to have you on our team!* On the Mini toolbar, change the **Font Size** to **28**, and then click the **Italic** button.

   After applying a new theme to a presentation, you should review each slide and make formatting changes as necessary. The fonts, layouts, and spacing associated with one theme may require that existing text and objects be resized or moved to display in a manner that is consistent and attractive in the new theme.

7. On the **Home tab**, in the **Slides group**, insert a **New Slide** with the **Picture with Caption** layout. In the title placeholder, type Questions or Concerns? and then in the caption placeholder, type Please ask at any time. Select the text in the caption placeholder, and then increase the **Font Size** to **28** and add **Italic**.

8. In the picture placeholder, click the **Picture** button, and insert the student data file **ppt02_Photo3**.

9. Still on **Slide 4**, on the **Design tab**, in the **Variants group**, click **More**, point to the third variant in the second row, and then right-click. On the shortcut menu, click **Apply to Selected Slides**, and then compare your slide with **Figure 4**. **Save** the presentation.

   The theme variant is changed for only the selected slide.

■ **You have completed Skill 2 of 10**

► You can customize your presentation by changing the font colors and effects.

► When you are using several pictures in a presentation, choose font colors that complement the pictures you select.

1. Move to **Slide 1**. In the title placeholder, select *Employee Orientation*. On the **Home tab,** in the **Font group,** click the **Font arrow**. Scroll down and select **Trebuchet MS**.

2. With the text in the title placeholder still selected, on the **Home tab,** in the **Font group,** click the **Text Shadow** button ⓢ.

3. Click a blank area of the slide to deselect the text, and then compare your screen with **Figure 1**.

   Adding text shadow helps the text to stand out from the slide background and adds additional depth to the presentation.

4. Select the subtitle text *ASPEN FALLS CITY GOVERNMENT,* and then on the **Home tab,** in the **Font group,** click the **Text Shadow** button ⓢ. Compare your screen with **Figure 2**.

■ **Continue to the next page to complete the skill**

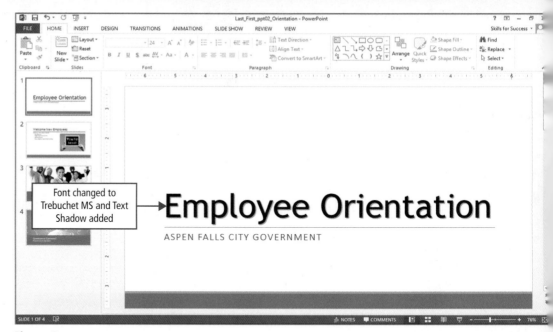

Figure 1

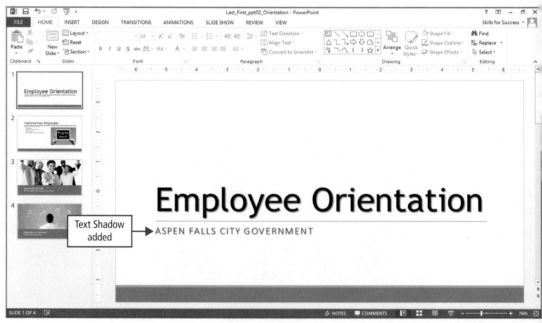

Figure 2

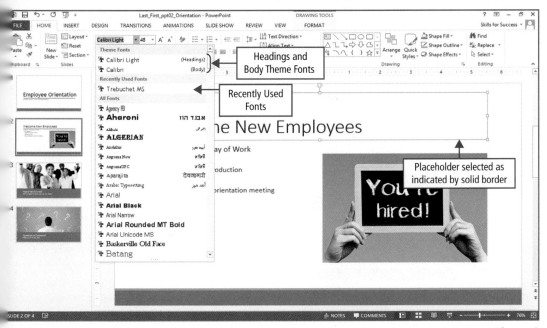

Figure 3

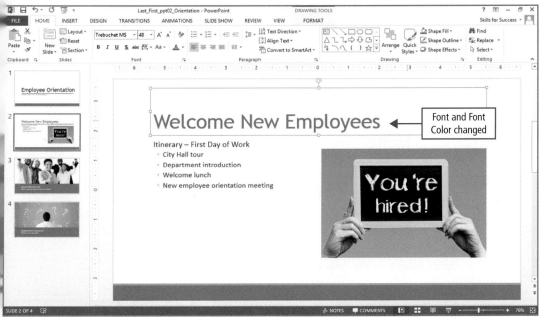

Figure 4

5. On **Slide 2,** click anywhere in the title placeholder, and then click the placeholder border to select it. Click the **Home tab,** and then in the **Font group,** click the **Font arrow.** Notice that at the top of the Font list, under Theme Fonts, *Calibri Light (Headings)* and *Calibri (Body)* display, as shown in **Figure 3.**

> The ***headings font*** is applied to slide titles, and the ***body font*** is applied to all other text. Sometimes the heading and body fonts are the same, but they are different sizes. In other font themes, the heading and body fonts are different. ***Recently Used Fonts*** is a listing of fonts you have selected and applied in the existing presentation. Using the Font list, you can apply theme fonts, recently used fonts, or a different font from the list of all fonts.

6. Under **Recently Used Fonts,** click **Trebuchet MS.**

7. With the title placeholder still selected, on the **Home tab,** in the **Font group,** click the **Font Color arrow** ![A]. Select the fifth color in the fifth row—**Turquoise, Accent 1, Darker 25%.** Compare your screen with **Figure 4.**

8. Save ![save icon] the presentation.

■ **You have completed Skill 3 of 10**

▶ You can customize the presentation design by changing the background of your slides.

▶ Modifications to slide backgrounds can be applied to a single slide or to all of the slides in the presentation.

▶ Previously modified backgrounds can be reset so that the original background associated with the presentation is applied to the slide.

1. Move to **Slide 1**. On the **Design tab**, in the **Customize group**, click **Format Background** to display the Format Background pane as shown in **Figure 1**.

   The Format Background pane is used to modify or reset the backgrounds for a single slide or for all slides in a presentation.

2. In the **Format Background** pane, under **Fill,** select **Gradient Fill** to display the gradient fill options.

3. Click the **Preset gradients** button, and then select the last color in the second row—**Top Spotlight - Accent 6**—and then compare your screen with **Figure 2**.

   The effects and color choices in the Format Background pane are based on the selected theme and variant. Here, the gradient choices all work well with the Retrospect theme and the selected color variant. Changes to the background may be made to a single slide, as you have done in this step, or to all slides in the presentation using the Apply to All button.

■ **Continue to the next page to complete the skill**

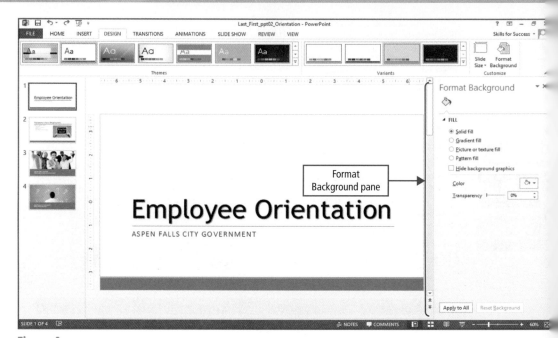

Figure 1

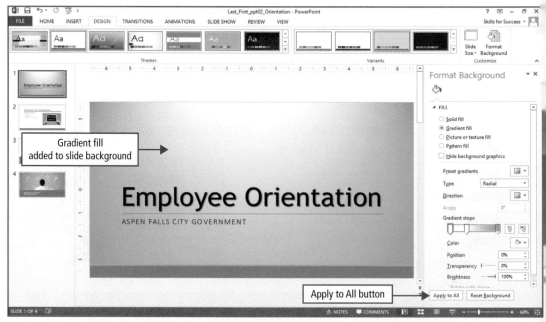

Figure 2

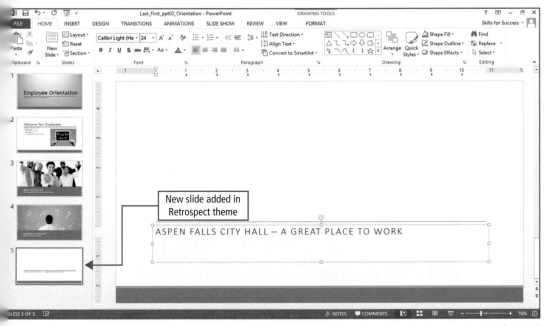

New slide added in Retrospect theme

ASPEN FALLS CITY HALL – A GREAT PLACE TO WORK

Figure 3

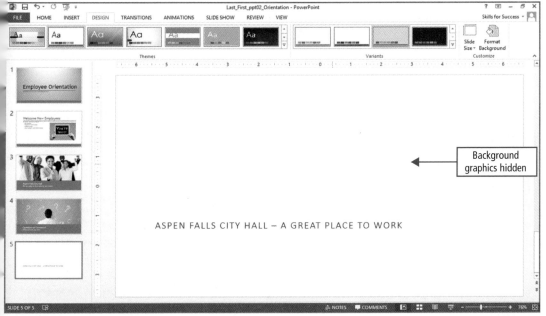

Background graphics hidden

ASPEN FALLS CITY HALL – A GREAT PLACE TO WORK

Figure 4

4. **Close** ☒ the **Format Background** pane.

   The background style is applied only to Slide 1.

5. Display **Slide 4,** and then on the **Home tab,** in the **Slides group,** click the **New Slide arrow.**

   The slide layouts available are now broken into two groups. The first group shows the layouts with the customized background with the gradient fill. The second group shows the original layouts.

6. In the **New Slide gallery,** under **Retrospect,** click **Section Header.** On the slide, click the title placeholder, and then click a border of the placeholder. Press Delete to remove the placeholder. In the subtitle placeholder, type Aspen Falls City Hall – A great place to work **Accept** the default All Caps setting in which the text appears. Compare your slide with **Figure 3.**

7. On the **Design tab,** in the **Customize group,** click **Format Background.** Alternately, you can right-click the slide background, and then from the shortcut menu, click Format Background.

8. In the **Format Background** pane, select the **Hide background graphics** check box. **Close** ☒ the **Format Background** pane, and then compare your screen with **Figure 4.**

9. **Save** 🖫 the presentation.

■ **You have completed Skill 4 of 10**

PPT 2-5
VIDEO

▶ You can add a picture or a texture to the slide background.

▶ When an image is inserted in the background, font colors, sizes, and effects may need to be adjusted so that the slide text is still easy to read.

1. With **Slide 5** displayed, on the **Design tab,** in the **Customize group,** click the **Format Background** button. In the **Format Background** pane, under **Fill,** select **Picture or texture fill**.

2. Under **Insert picture from,** click **File**. In the **Insert Picture** dialog box, navigate to the student files for this chapter, select **ppt02_Photo4,** and then click **Insert** to insert the picture as the slide background. Compare your screen with **Figure 1**.

3. In the **Format Background** pane, in the **Transparency** box, type 80 Alternately, drag the Transparency slider to the right or use the up or down arrows to adjust the transparency percentage. Compare your screen with **Figure 2**.

> You will format the slide text to stand out in a later skill. Here, the text is difficult to read due to lack of contrast between the font and the image in the background.

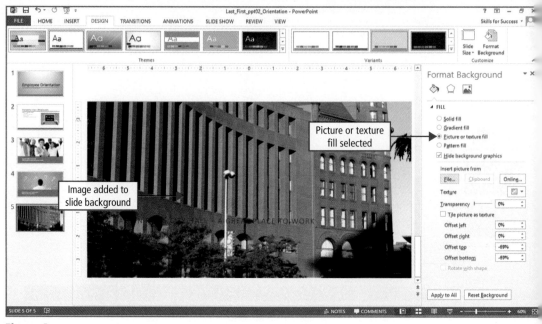

Figure 1

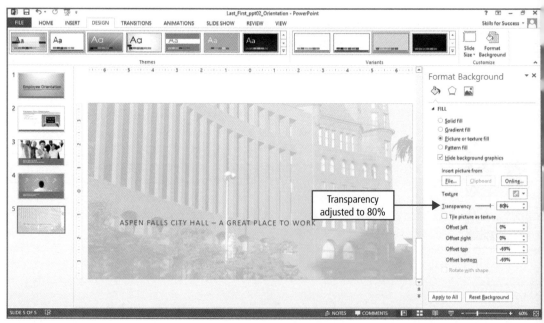

Figure 2

■ **Continue to the next page to complete the skill**

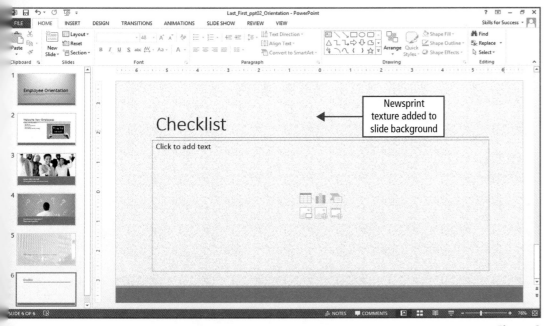

Figure 3

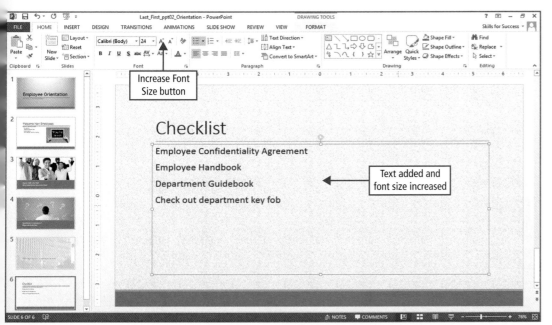

Figure 4

4. With **Slide 5** selected, on the **Home tab**, in the **Slides group**, click the **New Slide arrow**. In the lower half of the gallery, under **Retrospect**, click the **Title and Content** thumbnail. Take care not to select a thumbnail from the top half of the gallery. In the title placeholder, type Checklist and then press Esc so that no placeholders on the slide are selected.

5. In the **Format Background** pane, click **Picture or texture fill**. Click the **Texture** button, and then click the third texture in the third row—**Newsprint**. If necessary, use the **Transparency** slider to adjust the transparency of the texture to **80%**. **Close** ✕ the **Format Background** pane, and then compare your screen with **Figure 3**.

   When applying a texture to the slide background, be sure to choose a texture that coordinates with the background colors and complements the content of your slide.

6. In the content placeholder, type Employee Confidentiality Agreement Press Enter. Type Employee Handbook Press Enter. Type Department Guidebook Press Enter. Type Check out department key fob

7. Select the content placeholder, and then, on the **Home tab**, in the **Font group**, click the **Increase Font Size** button A˄ one time to change the **Font Size** to **24** points. Compare your screen with **Figure 4**.

8. **Save** 🖫 the presentation.

■ **You have completed Skill 5 of 10**

▶ ***WordArt*** is a pre-built set of fills, outlines, and effects used to create decorative text.

▶ You can convert existing text to WordArt or create new WordArt from scratch.

1. On **Slide 5**, select the text placeholder containing the text *Aspen Falls City Hall – A great place to work*. On the **Format tab**, in the **WordArt Styles group**, click the **More** button to display the WordArt gallery as shown in **Figure 1**.

2. Point to several WordArt styles to preview them with Live Preview.

3. In the **WordArt gallery**, click the second style in the second row—**Gradient Fill – Dark Green, Accent 1, Reflection**.

4. With the placeholder still selected, in the **WordArt Styles group**, click the **Text Fill** button, and then click the second color in the first row—**Black, Text 1**.

   In this manner, a WordArt style can be modified. Here the darker color provides more contrast between the text and slide background. Colors can be modified to match other font or theme colors in your presentation or to create a contrast with the slide background.

5. With the placeholder still selected, on the **Home tab**, in the **Font group**, click the **Font Size arrow**, click **44**, and then click the **Bold** B . Compare your screen with **Figure 2**.

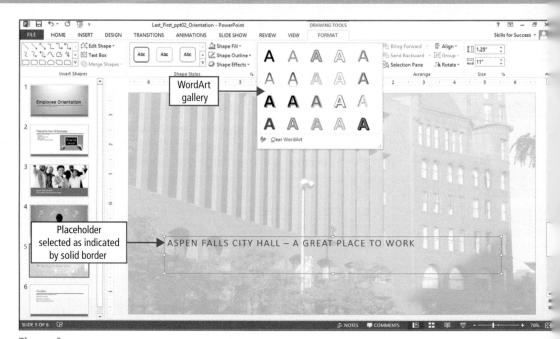

Figure 1

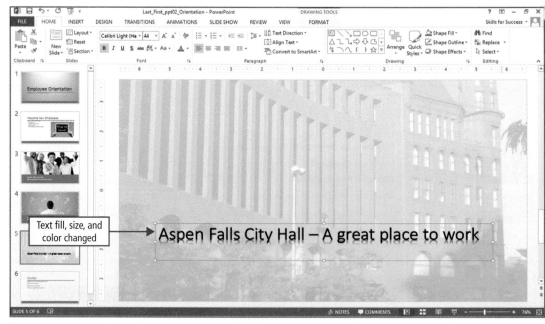

Figure 2

■ Continue to the next page to complete the skill

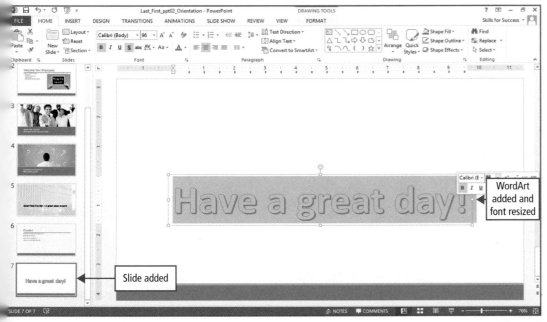

Figure 3

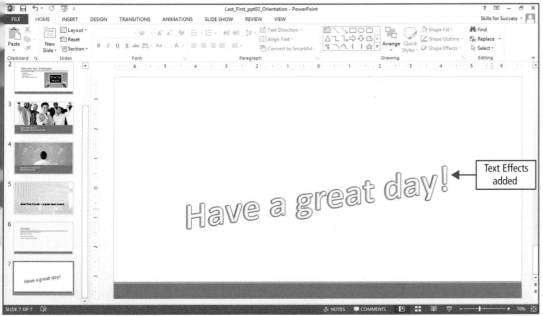

Figure 4

6. Move to **Slide 6**. On the **Home tab**, in the **Slides group**, click the **New Slide arrow**, and under **Retrospect**, click **Blank**.

> A blank slide layout contains no title or content placeholders.

7. On the **Insert tab**, in the **Text group**, click the **WordArt** button. In the **WordArt gallery** click the fourth option in the third row—**Fill – White, Outline – Accent 2, Hard Shadow – Accent 2**. Type Have a great day! Select the text you just typed, on the Mini toolbar, click the **Font Size arrow**, and then click **96** to increase the **Font Size**. Compare your screen with **Figure 3**.

8. With the WordArt still selected, on the **Format tab**, in the **WordArt Styles group**, click the **Text Effects button**. Point to several of the options to view the available galleries. Point to **Bevel**, then point to several of the options to preview their effect on the text, and then click the first option in the second row—**Angle**.

9. On the **Format tab**, in the **WordArt Styles group**, click the **Text Effects** button. Point to **3-D Rotation**, and then point to several of the options to preview their effect on the text. Under **Parallel**, click the second option in the second row—**Off Axis 1 Right**. Click a blank area of the slide to deselect the WordArt placeholder. Compare your screen with **Figure 4**.

10. **Save** 🖫 the presentation.

■ **You have completed Skill 6 of 10**

PPT 2-7
VIDEO

▶ Spacing between characters can be adjusted to change the look of the text or to adjust the text to better fit a placeholder.

1. Display **Slide 1**, and then select the text in the title placeholder, *Employee Orientation*.

2. On the **Home tab**, in the **Font group**, click the **Character Spacing** button [AV], and then in the list, select **Very Tight**. Compare your screen with **Figure 1**.

   The font size remains 80 points, but the spacing between characters has been decreased, allowing more text to fit into a smaller area.

3. Select the text in the subtitle placeholder, *Aspen Falls City Government*, and then, on the **Home tab**, in the **Font group**, click the **Character Spacing** button [AV]. At the bottom of the list, click **More Spacing**.

4. In the **Font** dialog box, on the **Character Spacing tab**, click the **Spacing arrow**, and then click **Expanded**. In the **By** box type 6 Click **OK** to apply the Character Spacing. On the **Home tab**, in the **Paragraph group**, click the **Center** button [≡]. Compare your screen with **Figure 2**.

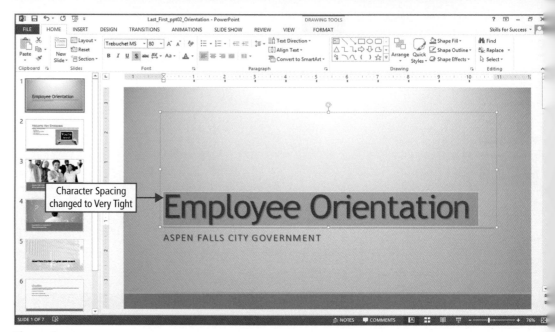

Figure 1

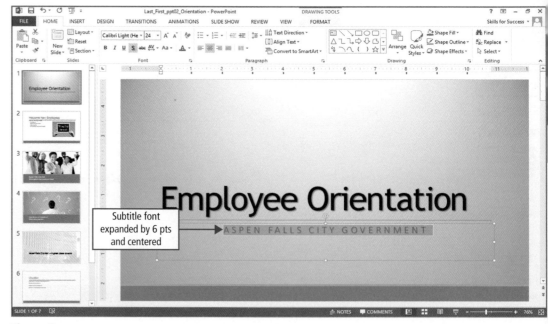

Figure 2

■ Continue to the next page to complete the skill ▶

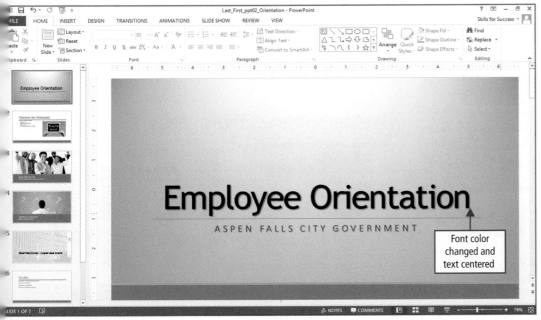

Font color changed and text centered

Figure 3

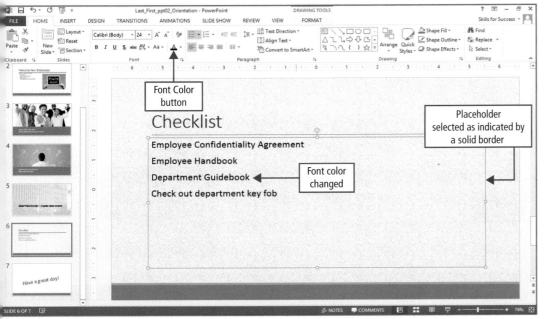

Font Color button

Placeholder selected as indicated by a solid border

Font color changed

Figure 4

5. With **Slide 1** still displayed, select the text in the title placeholder, *Employee Orientation*.

   The modified background of this slide has decreased the contrast between the background color and the font color, which may make it difficult to read in poor lighting conditions or for viewers with visual impairments.

6. On the **Home tab**, in the **Paragraph group**, click the **Center** button. In the **Font group**, click the **Font Color arrow** to display the Font Color gallery.

7. In the first row of the gallery, click the second color—**Black, Text 1**—to change the color of the selected text, as shown in **Figure 3**.

   In the Font group, the Font Color button displays the color that you just applied to the selection. If you want to apply the same color to another selection, you can click the Font Color button without displaying the color gallery.

8. Display **Slide 6**, and then select the content placeholder. On the **Home tab**, in the **Font group**, click the **Font Color** button to change the font color to the same shade of black used in the previous step. Compare your slide with **Figure 4**.

9. **Save** the presentation.

■ **You have completed Skill 7 of 10**

▶ A presentation theme includes default bullet styles for the bullet points in content placeholders. You can customize a bullet symbol by changing its style, color, or size.

▶ A numbered list can be applied to bullet points in place of bullet symbols.

1. Display **Slide 2**, and then in the content placeholder, select the four lines of bulleted text. On the **Home tab**, in the **Paragraph group**, click the **Numbering** button, and then compare your screen with **Figure 1**. If you clicked the Numbering arrow and a gallery displays, in the first row, click the second numbering option—1, 2, 3.

> The default color for the numbers just applied—Turquoise, Accent 1—is part of the current theme—Retrospect.

2. With the four numbered list items still selected, click the **Numbering arrow**, and then below the gallery, click **Bullets and Numbering**.

3. In the **Bullets and Numbering** dialog box, on the **Numbered tab**, click the **Color** button. Under **Theme Colors**, in the last row, click the fifth color—**Turquoise, Accent 1, Darker 50%**, and then click **OK**.

4. Select all of the text in the content placeholder—including the first line—click the **Font Size arrow** 20, and then click 24. Click a blank area of the slide to deselect the text, and then compare your screen with **Figure 2**.

■ Continue to the next page to complete the skill

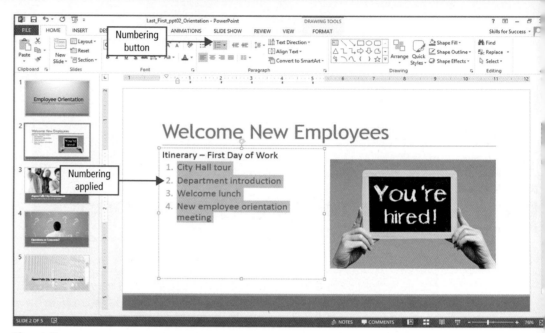

Figure 1

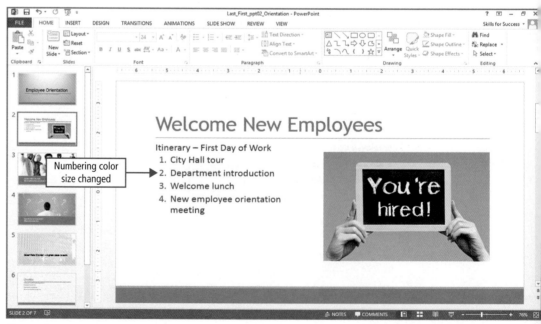

Figure 2

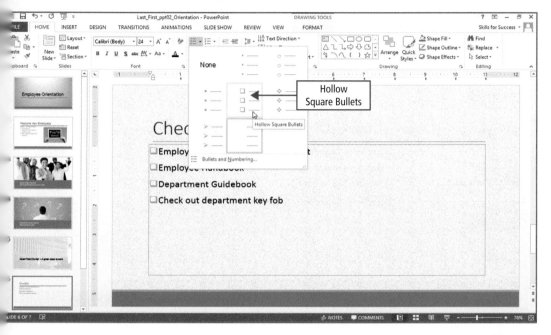

Figure 3

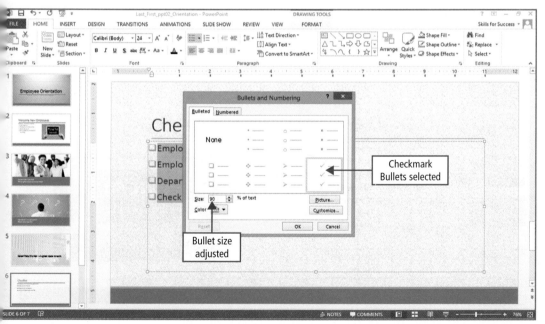

Figure 4

5. Move to **Slide 6**. In the content placeholder, select the four lines of text.

6. On the **Home tab**, in the **Paragraph group**, click the **Bullets arrow** ⊞· to display the Bullets gallery.

   The gallery displays several bullet characters that you can apply to the selection.

7. Point to the **Hollow Square Bullets** thumbnail as shown in **Figure 3**, and then click the thumbnail to apply the bullet style to the selection.

8. With the four bullet points still selected, click the **Bullets arrow** ⊞·, click **Bullets and Numbering**.

9. In the **Bullets and Numbering** dialog box, on the **Bulleted tab**, in the second row of the **Bullet gallery**, click **Checkmark Bullets**.

10. In the **Size** box, replace the number with 90 and compare your screen with **Figure 4**, and then click **OK** to apply the bullet style and size.

    The size of the checkmark bullets is adjusted to 90% of the size of the text after it. In this case, the size of the checkmarks will be 90% of the size of the 24 point font.

11. **Save** 🖫 the presentation.

■ **You have completed Skill 8 of 10**

▶ The Cut command removes selected text or graphics from your presentation and places the selection in the Office Clipboard.

▶ The *clipboard* is a temporary storage area maintained by your operating system.

▶ The Copy command duplicates a selection and places it on the Office Clipboard.

1. On **Slide 6**, in the content placeholder, position the pointer over the fourth checkmark—the checkmark before *Check out department key fob*—to display the pointer [⊕].

2. With the pointer [⊕] positioned over the fourth checkmark, click to select the entire line of text. Compare your screen with **Figure 1**.

> Clicking a list number or bullet symbol is an efficient way to select the entire bullet point or list line.

3. On the **Home tab**, in the **Clipboard group**, click the **Cut** button [✂] to remove the bullet from the slide and copy it to the clipboard.

4. Move to **Slide 2**. Place the insertion point before the third item in the numbered list, *Welcome lunch*. In the **Clipboard group**, click the Paste button to insert the selection and display the **Paste** Options button as shown in **Figure 2**.

> The Paste Options button provides options for formatting pasted text. When you paste into a numbered list, the list automatically renumbers to accommodate the newly pasted information.

■ Continue to the next page to complete the skill ▶

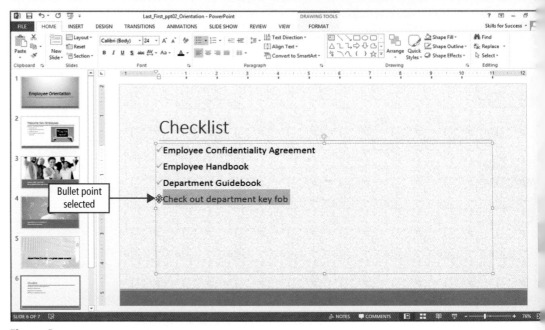

Figure 1

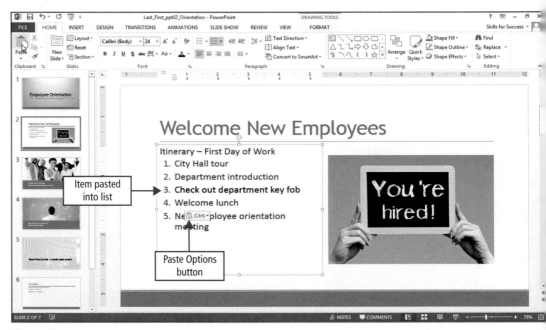

Figure 2

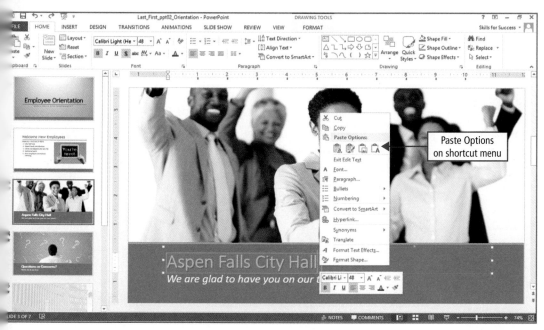

Figure 3

Figure 4

5. Click the **Paste Options** button 📋 to view the four options. Click **Keep Text Only**.

   Keep Source Formatting applies the original formatting of the pasted text. *Use Destination Theme* applies the formatting of the slide to which the text is pasted. *Picture* pastes the text as a picture. *Keep Text Only* removes all formatting from the selection. The Paste Options button remains on the screen until you perform another action.

6. Move to **Slide 1**, and then select the subtitle text *Aspen Falls City Government*. Point to the selection, and then right-click to display the shortcut menu. From the shortcut menu, click **Copy**.

   There are multiple methods you can use to cut, copy, and paste text, including the shortcut menu and the buttons in the Clipboard group. You can also use the keyboard shortcuts—Ctrl + X to cut, Ctrl + C to copy, and Ctrl + V to paste.

7. Move to **Slide 3**. Select the title text— *Aspen Falls City Hall*. Right-click the selected text to display the shortcut menu as shown in **Figure 3**, and then notice the four paste options.

8. On the shortcut menu, under **Paste Options**, point to each button to view how each paste option displays the text, and then click the last button—**Keep Text Only** 📋.

9. Select the title text. Apply **Bold** **B**, and then change the **Font Size** to **44**. Compare your slide with **Figure 4**.

10. **Save** 🖫 the presentation.

■ **You have completed Skill 9 of 10**

PPT 2-10
VIDEO

▶ *Format Painter* is used to copy formatting from one selection of text to another.

▶ When you need to copy formatting to multiple selections, double-click the Format Painter button. To copy formatting to a single selection, click the Format Painter one time.

▶ You can use the Clear All Formatting button to revert to the font formatting associated with the original slide layout.

1. Display **Slide 2**, and click anywhere in the title placeholder. On the **Home tab**, in the **Clipboard group**, double-click the **Format Painter** button.

2. Click the Slide 6 thumbnail to move to **Slide 6**. Point to the text in the title placeholder, and compare your screen with **Figure 1**.

> When Format Painter is active, the pointer displays.

3. With the pointer, drag through the title text—*Checklist*.

4. In the content placeholder, select all three bulleted points to apply the same formatting to the bulleted text. Notice that the pointer is still active.

5. On **Slide 4**, use the same method to select and apply the same formatting to the text *Please ask at any time*. On the **Home tab**, in the **Clipboard group**, click the **Format Painter** button to turn off Format Painter. Alternately, press [Esc].

6. With the text still selected, on the **Home tab**, in the **Font group**, click the **Clear All Formatting** button to revert to the default font formatting for this slide layout. Increase the **Font Size** to **24** and then compare your slide with **Figure 2**.

> Use the Clear All Formatting button to revert to the original formatting on a slide.

■ **Continue to the next page to complete the skill**

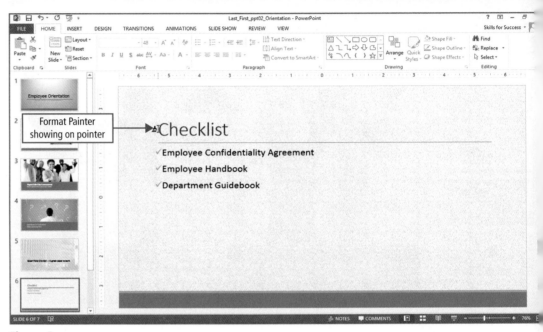

Figure 1

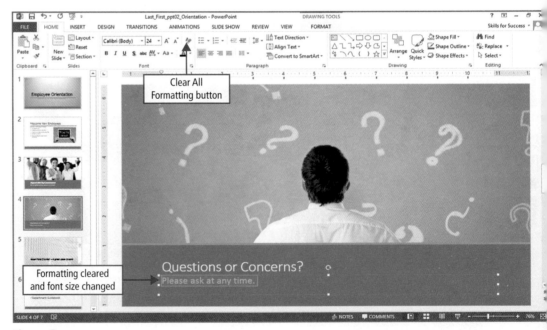

Figure 2

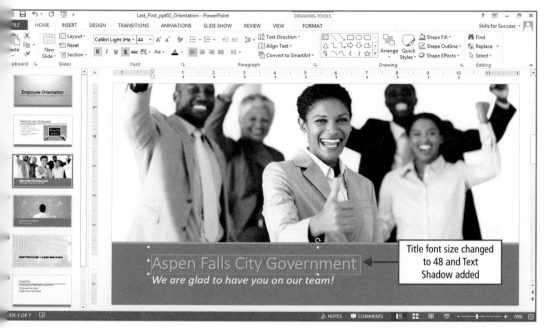

Figure 3

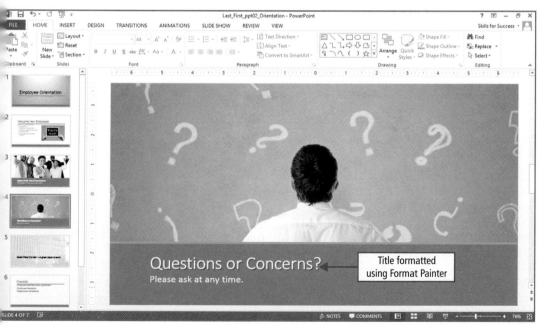

Figure 4

7. On **Slide 6**, select the bulleted list, and change the **Font Size** to **36**.

8. Move to **Slide 3**. Select the text in the title placeholder. On the **Home tab**, in the **Font group**, click the **Increase Font Size** $\boxed{\text{A}^{\cdot}}$ button one time to change the font size to **48**, and then click the **Text Shadow** button $\boxed{\text{S}}$. Compare your slide with **Figure 3**.

9. With the text still selected, on the **Home tab**, in the **Clipboard group**, click the **Format Painter** button 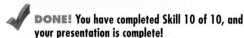 one time.

10. Display **Slide 4**, and then select the title text *Questions or Concerns?* to apply the same formatting as the title text on **Slide 3**.

> Because the Format Painter button was clicked one time, Format Painter is no longer active after the formatting was copied one time.

11. Click a blank area of the slide to deselect the text, and then compare your slide with **Figure 4**.

12. Insert a **Header & Footer** on the **Notes and Handouts** pages that includes the **Date and Time** updated automatically, a **Page Number**, and the **Footer** with the file name Last_First_ppt02_Orientation

13. **Save** $\boxed{\boxminus}$ the presentation. Submit your project as directed by your instructor. **Close** PowerPoint.

✔ **DONE! You have completed Skill 10 of 10, and your presentation is complete!**

The following More Skills are located at **www.pearsonhighered.com/skills**

 More Skills 11   **Edit Slide Masters**

When you are formatting a presentation and want to change the format for every slide in the presentation, modify the slide master. The slide master holds information about the colors, fonts, and other objects that display on your slides.

In More Skills 11, you will edit a slide master by changing the title font and background and bullet styles. You will also add a logo to the slide master so that it will appear on every slide in the presentation.

To begin, open your web browser, navigate to www.pearsonhighered.com/skills, locate the name of your textbook, and then follow the instructions on the website.

 More Skills 12   **Save and Apply Presentation Templates**

You can design your own custom presentation and save it as a template so that you can easily apply the template to another presentation.

In More Skills 12, you will save a presentation as a template and then apply the template to another presentation.

To begin, open your web browser, navigate to www.pearsonhighered.com/skills, locate the name of your textbook, and then follow the instructions on the website.

 More Skills 13   **Create Slides from Microsoft Word Outlines**

The bullet points in a PowerPoint presentation are based on an outline in which the list levels are assigned to varying outline levels. An outline based on paragraph styles in Microsoft Word can be imported into PowerPoint to create slides.

In More Skills 13, you will import a Microsoft Word outline to create slides in a PowerPoint presentation.

To begin, open your web browser, navigate to www.pearsonhighered.com/skills, locate the name of your textbook, and then follow the instructions on the website.

 More Skills 14   **Design Presentations with Contrast**

Contrast is an important element of slide design because it enables the audience to clearly view presentation text, images, and objects.

In More Skills 14, you will review design principles that will assist you in creating contrast on your slides. You will view two slides and compare the difference in contrast created by using color and images.

To begin, open your web browser, navigate to www.pearsonhighered.com/skills, locate the name of your textbook, and then follow the instructions on the website.

Please note that there are no additional projects to accompany the More Skills Projects, and they are not covered in the End-of-Chapter projects.

The following table summarizes the **SKILLS AND PROCEDURES** covered in this chapter.

Skills Number	Task	Step	Icon	Keyboard Shortcut
1	Create new presentation	Start page → Template		
1	Add a new slide	Home tab → New Slide		Ctrl + M
2	Change theme	Design tab → Themes group		
2	Change theme variant	Design tab → Variants group		
2	Change slide layout	Home tab → Slides group → Layout button		
3	Change font color	Home tab → Font group → Font Color button	A·	
3	Add text shadow	Home tab → Font group → Text Shadow button	S	
4	Change slide background	Design tab → Customize group → Format Background button		
6	Insert WordArt	Insert tab → Text group → WordArt button		
6	Convert text to WordArt	Select text → Format tab → WordArt Styles group → More button		
8	Add bullets	Home tab → Paragraph group → Bullets button	≔·	
8	Add numbering	Home tab → Paragraph group → Numbering button	≔·	
9	Cut text or object	Select text or object → Home tab → Clipboard group → Cut button	✂	Ctrl + X
9	Copy text or object	Select text or object → Home tab → Clipboard group → Copy button	📋	Ctrl + C
9	Paste text or object	Home tab → Clipboard group → Paste button		Ctrl + V
10	Copy formatting	Home tab → Clipboard group → Format Painter button	🖌	
10	Clear all formatting	Home tab → Font group → Clear All Formatting button	🧹	

Key Terms

Online Help Skills

1. With PowerPoint open, in the upper right corner of the screen, click the **Microsoft PowerPoint Help** ⸢?⸣ button, or press ⸢F1⸣.

2. In the **PowerPoint Help** window, use the **Search** box to locate and open the article *Keyboard shortcuts for use while creating a presentation in PowerPoint 2013.* Compare your screen with **Figure 1**.

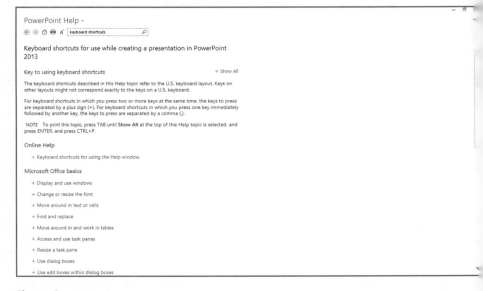

Figure 1

3. Read the article and answer the following question: What are two shortcuts that you might find most helpful, and why?

Matching

Match each term in the second column with its correct definition in the first column by writing the letter of the term on the blank line in front of the correct definition.

____ **1.** When you point to an item in a gallery, this appears on screen and displays the name of the item.

____ **2.** A set of unified design elements that provides a look for your presentation, using colors, fonts, and graphics.

____ **3.** Variations of the current theme, with different accent colors.

____ **4.** The Paste Option used to paste text as an image.

____ **5.** Listing of fonts you have selected and applied in the existing presentation.

____ **6.** Tool used to copy text formatting from one part of a presentation to another.

____ **7.** A text style used to create decorative effects in a presentation.

____ **8.** The font applied to all text in a presentation, except for the slide title.

____ **9.** A command that removes selected text or graphics from a presentation and then moves the selection to the Clipboard.

____ **10.** A temporary storage area maintained by the operating system.

A Body font

B Clipboard

C Cut

D Format Painter

E Picture

F ScreenTip

G Theme

H Theme variant

I Recently Used Fonts

J WordArt

BizSkills Video

1. Reflect on Joel and Sara's communication styles before, during, and after the meeting. List several ways in which each of them communicated in a non-professional or inappropriate manner.

2. Office communication includes not only speaking, but also written communication. What steps can you take to ensure that you come across professionally in written communication, including e-mail messages, reports, and presentations?

Multiple Choice

Choose the correct answer.

1. The process of changing the appearance of the text, layout, or design of a slide.
   A. Editing
   B. Designing
   C. Formatting

2. On the Start screen, click these to display a preview of each of the templates and the variants of the theme.
   A. Template thumbnails
   B. Theme list
   C. Slide pane

3. Variations of the current theme, with different accent colors.
   A. Variant
   B. Color scheme
   C. Template

4. The effects and color choices in the Format Background pane are based on this.
   A. The image styles
   B. The slide layout
   C. The theme and variant

5. A slide layout that contains no title or content placeholders.
   A. Empty
   B. Normal
   C. Blank

6. The amount of room between letters of slide text.
   A. Alignment
   B. Character spacing
   C. Layout

7. The command used to duplicate a selection.
   A. Format Painter
   B. Cut
   C. Copy

8. In Paste Options, this selection removes all formatting from a selection of pasted text.
   A. Use Destination Theme
   B. Keep Source Formatting
   C. Keep Text Only

9. A command used to revert to font formatting associated with the original slide layout.
   A. Clear All Formatting
   B. Reset Format
   C. Reset Slide Layout

10. The mouse action necessary when Format Painter is to be used on multiple selections.
    A. Single-click
    B. Double-click
    C. Triple-click

Topics for Discussion

1. PowerPoint 2013 includes different design themes and variants. What should you consider when choosing a design theme for the presentations that you create?

2. Format Painter is an important tool used to maintain consistent formatting in a presentation. Why is consistency important when you format the slides in your presentations?

Skills Review

To complete this project, you will need the following files:

- ppt02_SRIntern1
- ppt02_SRIntern2

You will save your file as:

- Last_First_ppt02_SRInternship

1. Start **PowerPoint**. On the **Start screen**, click the **Integral** theme thumbnail. Click the first variant in the second row. Click **Create**. Add the title Aspen Falls Internship Program and the subtitle 2014 On the **File tab**, click **Save As**, and then click **Browse**. In the **Save As** dialog box, navigate to your chapter folder. Save the file as Last_First_ppt02_SRInternship

2. Insert a **New Slide** with the **Title and Content** layout. Add the title Program Goals and apply **Bold** to the text in the title placeholder. In the text placeholder, type four bullet points, pressing Enter after each: Professional growth and Beneficial service and Innovation and Skill development

3. Select the content placeholder. In the **Paragraph group**, click the **Numbered List** button. Change the **Font Size** to **32** and apply **Bold** and **Text Shadow**.

4. On the **Design tab**, in the **Customize group**, click the **Format Background** button. In the **Format Background** pane, select **Picture or texture fill**. Under **Insert picture from**, click the **File** button. From your student files, insert **ppt02_SRIntern1**. Compare your screen with **Figure 1**.

5. Insert a **New Slide** with the **Two Content** layout. Add the title Process and apply **Bold**. In the left placeholder, type four points: Complete application and Send letter of reference and Provide photo id and Participate in interview pressing Enter after each entry.

6. On **Slide 2**, click the content placeholder. On the **Home tab**, in the **Clipboard group**, click the **Format Painter**.

7. On **Slide 3**, use the **Format Painter** to apply the formatting to all of the text in the content placeholder. On the **Home tab**, in the **Paragraph group**, click the **Bullets arrow**, and then click **Bullets and Numbering**. Click **Arrow Bullets**, and then adjust the **Size** to **80%** of text. Click **OK**.

8. In the right placeholder, click the **Pictures** button, and insert the image **ppt02_SCIntern2**. Compare your screen with **Figure 2**.

Figure 1

Minerva Studio / Fotolia

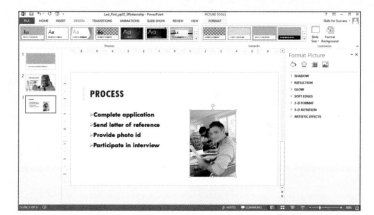

Figure 2

Goodluz / Fotolia

■ Continue to the next page to complete this Skills Review

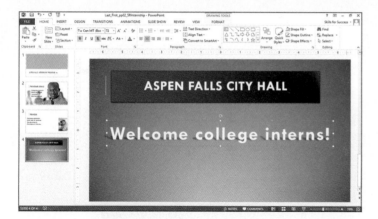

Figure 3

Figure 4

9. After Slide 3, insert a new **Slide 4** with the **Title Only** layout. In the title placeholder, type Aspen Falls City Hall and then **Center** and **Bold** the text.

10. On **Slide 4**, select the placeholder, and then on the **Format tab**, in the **Shape Styles group**, click the **More** button. Click the first thumbnail in the last row—**Intense Effect – Brown, Dark 1**.

11. Click a blank area of the slide to deselect the title placeholder. In the **Format Background** pane, select **Gradient Fill**. Click the **Preset gradients** button, and then click the fourth thumbnail in the fourth row—**Bottom Spotlight – Accent 4**. **Close** the Format Background pane.

12. On the **Insert tab**, in the **Text group**, click the **WordArt** button. Select the fourth option in the third row—**Fill – White, Outline – Accent 2, Hard Shadow – Accent 2**.

13. Accept the default location, and replace the WordArt text with Welcome college interns!

14. Select the WordArt placeholder. On the **Format tab**, in the **WordArt Styles group**, click the **Text Effects** button, and then click **Shadow**. Under **Perspective**, click the first option—**Perspective Diagonal Upper Left**. On the **Home tab**, in the **Font group**, increase the **Font Size** to 72.

15. With the WordArt placeholder still selected, on the **Home tab**, in the **Font group**, click the **Character Spacing** button, and then click **Loose**. Compare your screen with Figure 3.

16. With the WordArt placeholder still selected, on the **Home tab**, in the **Clipboard group**, click the **Format Painter** button.

17. Move to **Slide 1**, and with the **Format Painter**, select the text **2014** to apply the same formatting that was applied to the WordArt on Slide 4.

18. Select the subtitle text—*2014*—and then, on the **Home tab**, in the **Font group**, click the **Font arrow**, and click **Broadway**. Click a blank area of the slide so that no placeholders are selected.

19. Insert a **Header & Footer** on the **Notes and Handouts** with the **Date and Time**, the **Page Number**, and the **Footer** Last_First_ppt02_SRInternship

20. **Save** the presentation, and then compare your presentation with Figure 4. Submit the file as directed by your instructor. **Close** PowerPoint.

 DONE! You have completed this Skills Review

Skills Assessment 1

MyITLab®
Grader

To complete this presentation, you will need the following files:

- ppt02_SA1Thumbs
- ppt02_SA1Phone

You will save your presentation as:

- Last_First_ppt02_SA1SocialMedia

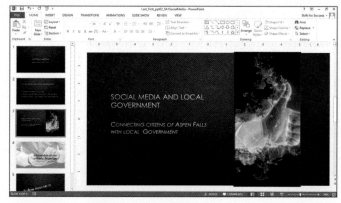

Detelina Petkova / Fotolia

Figure 1

1. Start **PowerPoint**, and then create a new presentation with the **Mesh theme**. Do not change the variant. Save the file in your **PowerPoint Chapter 2** folder as Last_First_ppt02_SA1SocialMedia

2. In the title placeholder, type Social Media and then in the subtitle placeholder, type Aspen Falls City Hall Change the subtitle **Font Size** to **32**, the **Character Spacing** to **Loose**, and the **Font Color** to **Light Blue**.

3. Insert a **New Slide** with the **Title and Content** layout. In the title placeholder, type Social Media and Local Government

4. In the content placeholder, type the following bullet points: Official Aspen Falls page and Open line of communication with citizens and Posts closely monitored and responded to

5. Use the **Format Painter** to apply the formatting from the subtitle on **Slide 1** to the bullet points on **Slide 2**.

6. Insert a **New Slide** with the **Picture with Caption** layout. **Copy** the title from **Slide 2**, and **Paste** the selection to the title placeholder on **Slide 3**. In the picture placeholder, insert the image **ppt02_SA1Thumbs**. In the text placeholder, type Connecting citizens of Aspen Falls with local government Select the text placeholder, change the **Font Size** to **24**, and apply **Italic**.

7. Insert a **New Slide** with the **Section Header** layout. In the title placeholder, type Information at our citizens' fingertips In the text placeholder, type Aspen Falls

8. Select the title placeholder. Use the **Format tab** to apply the **WordArt Style—Fill – Blue-Gray, Background 2, Inner Shadow**. Change the **Font Size** to **54**. Select the text placeholder, and apply the same WordArt style.

9. Insert the image **ppt02_SA1Phone** into the slide background, and then adjust the transparency to **50%**.

10. Insert a new **Slide 5** with a **Blank** layout. Insert **WordArt** in the **Fill – White, Text 1, Shadow**, with the text Follow Aspen Falls, CA! Include the exclamation point. Accept the default location for the WordArt. Increase the **Font Size** of the WordArt to **66**. To the WordArt, add the **Text Effect 3-D Rotation, Perspective Contrasting Right**.

11. Insert a **Header & Footer** on the **Notes and Handouts**. Include the date, page number, and the Footer Last_First_ppt02_SA1SocialMedia

12. Compare your presentation with **Figure 1**. **Save** your presentation, and then submit the file as directed by your instructor. **Close** PowerPoint.

 DONE! You have completed Skills Assessment 1

Skills Assessment 2

To complete this presentation, you will need the following files:

- ppt02_SA2Phone1
- ppt02_SA2Phone2

You will save your presentation as:

- Last_First_ppt02_SA2CallCenter

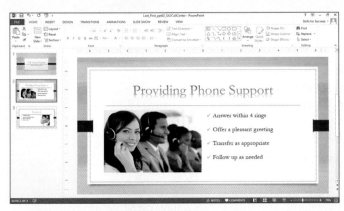

Wavebreakmediamicro / Fotolia; vgstudio / Fotolia

Figure 1

1. Start **PowerPoint**, and then create a new presentation with the **Organic** theme and the default variant for that theme. Save the file in your **PowerPoint Chapter 2** folder as Last_First_ppt02_SA2CallCenter

2. On **Slide 1**, in the title placeholder, type Call Center Training and then apply the second WordArt style in the second row—**Gradient Fill – Orange, Accent 1, Reflection**.

3. In the subtitle placeholder on **Slide 1**, type Aspen Falls City Hall Change the **Font** to **Verdana**, and then change the **Font Size** to **28**.

4. Insert a new **Slide 2** with the **Two Content** layout. Add the title Providing Phone Support In the left content placeholder, insert the image **ppt02_SA2Photo1**.

5. In the right content placeholder, type the following points: Answer within 4 rings and Offer a pleasant greeting and Transfer as appropriate and Follow up as needed

6. Select the four bullet points, and then change the **Font Color** to **Black, Text 1**, change the **Font Size** to **28**, and adjust the **Line Spacing** to **1.5**.

7. With the four bullet points still selected, change the bullets to **Checkmark Bullets**, and adjust them to **75%** of text.

8. Insert a new **Slide 3** with the **Two Content** layout. Change the **Background** to **Gradient Fill**.

9. In the title placeholder, type Teamwork In the right content placeholder, insert the image **ppt02_SA2Photo2**. In the left content placeholder, type the following points and then format them as a numbered list: Attempt to assist and Ask a team member for input and Refer to a supervisor and Follow up Change the **Font Size** to **28** for all text in the left content placeholder.

10. On **Slide 3**, select the text *Follow up* and change the **Font Color** to **Green, Accent 1**, apply **Bold**, and then change the **Character Spacing** to **Loose**.

11. Use the **Format Painter** to copy the formatting from the Slide 1 title—*Call Center Training*—to the titles on **Slides 2** and **3**.

12. Insert a **Header & Footer** on the **Notes and Handouts**. Include the date, page number, and the Footer Last_First_ppt02_SA2CallCenter

13. Compare your completed presentation with **Figure 1**. **Save** your presentation, and then submit the file as directed by your instructor. **Close** PowerPoint.

 DONE! You have completed Skills Assessment 2

Visual Skills Check

To complete this presentation, you will need the following file:

- ppt02_VSBadge

You will save your presentation as:

- Last_First_ppt02_VSNewHire

Start a new, blank presentation, and create the first two slides of a presentation as shown in **Figure 1**. These two slides use the **Basis** theme. The Slide 1 WordArt style is **Fill – White – Accent 1, Shadow**, and its character spacing is **Loose**. The gradient named **Bottom Spotlight – Accent 1** appears in the background. On **Slide 2**, the image is from your student files— **ppt02_VSBadge**. The Format Painter was used to apply the formatting on Slide 1 to the title on Slide 2. For the numbered list, the font color is **Green, Accent 1, Darker 50%**, and the numbers are sized at **90%** and are the same font color as the text. Save the presentation as Last_First_ ppt02_VSNewHire and then insert the date, file name, and page number in the **Notes and Handouts** footer. Submit the file as directed by your instructor.

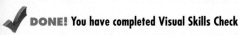 **DONE!** You have completed Visual Skills Check

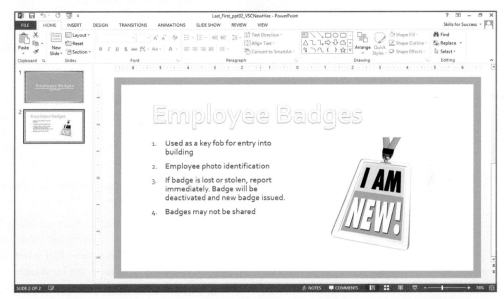

Figure 1

iQoncept / Fotolia

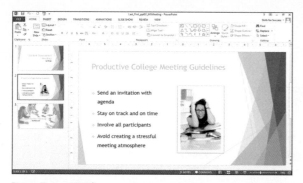

Picture-Factory / Fotolia

Figure 1

My Skills

To complete this presentation, you will need the following files:

- ppt02_MYMeeting1
- ppt02_MYMeeting2

You will save your presentation as:

- Last_First_ppt02_MYMeeting

1. Start **PowerPoint**, and then create a new presentation with the **Facet** theme, with the second variant in the first row. Save the file in your **PowerPoint Chapter 2** folder as Last_First_ppt02_MYMeeting

2. On **Slide 1**, in the title placeholder, type Student Government Meetings

3. In the subtitle placeholder on **Slide 1**, type the name of your college and then apply the first WordArt style—**Fill – Black, Text 1, Shadow**. Increase the **Font Size** to **24**.

4. Insert a new **Slide 2** with the **Two Content** layout. In the title placeholder, type Productive College Meeting Guidelines In the right content placeholder, insert the image **ppt02_MYMeeting1**, and apply the **Beveled Matte, White** picture style.

5. On **Slide 2**, in the left content placeholder, type the following points: Send an invitation with agenda and Stay on track and on time and Involve all participants and Avoid creating a stressful meeting atmosphere

6. Select the four bullet points, change the **Font Size** to **24**, and adjust the **Line Spacing** to **1.5**.

7. With the four bullet points still selected, change the bullets to **Star Bullets**, and change the size of the bullets to **70%** of text.

8. Insert a new **Slide 3** with the **Section Header** layout. Change the background for the newly inserted slide to **Picture Fill**, and insert the image **ppt02_MYMeeting2**. Set the image's transparency to **50%**.

9. In the title placeholder, type Productive Meetings Center the title text, and apply bold and text shadow. Change the **Font Size** to **48**.

10. In the text placeholder, type Beneficial to all! Use the **Format Painter** to apply the **Slide 1** subtitle formatting to the text *Beneficial to all!*, and then **Center** the text.

11. Insert a **Header & Footer** on the **Notes and Handouts**. Include the date, page number, and the Footer Last_First_ppt02_MYMeeting

12. Compare your completed presentation with **Figure 1**. **Save** your presentation, and then submit the file as directed by your instructor. **Close** PowerPoint.

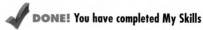 **DONE! You have completed My Skills**

Skills Challenge 1

To complete this presentation, you will need the following files:

- ppt02_SC1CellPhone
- ppt02_SC1CellPicture

You will save your presentation as:

- Last_First_ppt02_SC1CellPhone

Using the skills you have practiced in this chapter, correct the errors and issues with the presentation named **ppt02_SC1CellPhone**. Add the image named **ppt02_SC1CellPicture** to the Slide 1 slide background. Pick a theme and variant that have a background that complements the image used on Slide 1. Adjust the fonts or background so that the text is easy to read. On Slide 2, add numbering to the bullet points that begin the text *No surfing* and *No texting* and *Limit personal* and *Phones must be*. Adjust the numbers so that they are smaller than the text.

Resize the fonts on Slide 2 so they are easy to read and adjust the line spacing so that the text fills the placeholder.

Use WordArt to enhance the appearance of one of the titles in the presentation. Change the font color, and add one other enhancement to the text *Please use your break times for these activities*. Insert a new Slide 3 with the Section Header layout. Copy the title and subtitle from Slide 1. Paste them into the appropriate placeholders on Slide 3, and adjust font colors and sizes as needed. Save the presentation as Last_First_ppt02_SC1CellPhone Add a footer to the Notes and Handouts pages with the date, file name and page number, and then check spelling in the presentation. Submit as directed by your instructor.

 DONE! You have completed Skills Challenge 1

Skills Challenge 2

To complete this presentation, you will need the following file:

- New blank presentation

You will save your presentation as:

- Last_First_ppt02_SC2College

Using the skills you have practiced in this chapter, create a presentation with six slides describing a college at which you would like to continue your education after graduating from your current program. Apply an appropriate theme, and change the fonts and colors themes. On at least one slide, format the slide background with a picture that depicts the college that you choose. On the first slide, format the slide title by using a WordArt style. Include in your presentation a numbered list that indicates at least four reasons why you would like to attend this college. The remaining slides may include information about the programs, culture, and benefits of attending this college.

Format the last slide with the Section Header layout, and enter text that briefly summarizes your presentation. Check the spelling in the presentation. Add a footer to the Notes and Handouts pages with the date, page number, and footer text Last_First_ppt02_SC2College and page number. Save the presentation as Last_First_ppt02_SC2College and then submit as directed by your instructor.

 DONE! You have completed Skills Challenge 2

CHAPTER 3

Enhance Presentations with Graphics

- Appropriate presentation graphics visually communicate your message and help your audience understand the points you want to convey.

- It is a good practice to evaluate the graphics that you use, the text on your slides, and your spoken words to ensure that your presentation is coherent, precise, and accurate.

- It is helpful to review the procedures in your organization so that you are familiar with how presentations are shared using slide libraries and other file-sharing procedures.

- When effective and illustrative diagrams are needed, you can use SmartArt graphics to list information and show processes and relationships.

- Replacing bullet points with SmartArt graphics can add interest and variety to a presentation.

© auremar / Fotolia

Aspen Falls City Hall

In this chapter, you will create a presentation promoting Aspen Falls' new employee enrichment program. This program aims to improve career satisfaction and productivity for employees. It is being modeled after a similar program created at a local company—Samway Investments. It was so successful in increasing productivity that Maria Martinez, the City Manager, asked managers at Samway for permission to use their information. The managers agreed and have provided some of their materials, including a presentation.

In your career, you may reuse materials, including slides, created for a previous project. This will save you time and allow you to work efficiently and cooperatively. To keep your presentations engaging and appealing, you can search Microsoft's Online Pictures gallery and insert pictures. You may insert shapes to communicate your message, and modify those shapes to add interest. With SmartArt, you can take a plain bulleted list and change it to an easy-to-read diagram with clear separation between different elements. Videos add interest to your presentation, and you can use PowerPoint to add borders and styles and to correct the colors.

In this project, you will start with a new blank presentation, and reuse slides from another presentation. You will insert, size, move, and align images and shapes, add text and apply styles to shapes. You will also insert and format a SmartArt graphic and a video.

**Time to complete all 10
skills – 60 to 75 minutes**

Student data files needed for this chapter:

New blank PowerPoint presentation
ppt03_EnrichmentSamway
ppt03_EnrichmentProductivity
ppt03_EnrichmentVideo

You will save your file as:

Last_First_ppt03_Enrichment

Outcome

Using the skills in this chapter, you will be able to
work with PowerPoint presentations like this:

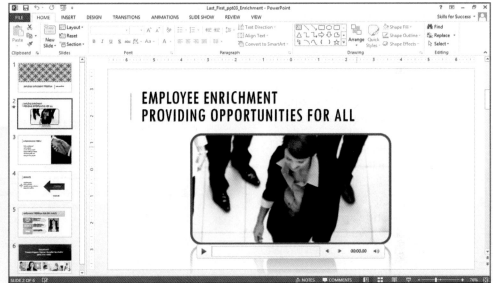

Minerva Studio / Fotolia

SKILLS

Skills 1-10 Training

At the end of this chapter you will be able to:

Skill 1 Insert Slides from Other Presentations

Skill 2 Insert, Size, and Move Online Pictures

Skill 3 Modify Picture Shapes, Borders, and Effects

Skill 4 Insert, Size, and Move Shapes

Skill 5 Add Text to Shapes and Insert Text Boxes

Skill 6 Apply Gradient Fills and Group and Align Graphics

Skill 7 Convert Text to SmartArt Graphics and Add Shapes

Skill 8 Modify SmartArt Layouts, Colors, and Styles

Skill 9 Insert Video Files

Skill 10 Apply Video Styles and Adjust Videos

MORE SKILLS

Skill 11 Compress Pictures

Skill 12 Save Groups as Picture Files

Skill 13 Change Object Order

Skill 14 Insert a Screen Shot in a Presentation

▶ Presentation slides can be shared so that frequently used content does not need to be recreated.

1. Start **PowerPoint 2013**, and then create a new presentation with the **Integral** template and default variant.

2. In the title placeholder, type Employee Enrichment Program and then in the subtitle placeholder, type Aspen Falls City Hall Compare your screen with **Figure 1**.

   When a placeholder has text formatted in all caps, it is a good idea to type the text with normal capitalization in case you change the formatting or theme later.

3. On the **Quick Access Toolbar**, click **Save** 🔲. Navigate to the location where you are saving your files, create a folder named PowerPoint Chapter 3 and then using your own name, save the document as Last_First_ppt03_Enrichment

4. On the **Home tab**, in the **Slides group**, click the **New Slide arrow**, and then in the gallery, click **Two Content**. In the title placeholder, type Enrichment Program Kick-Off Events

5. In the left placeholder, type Wellness Lunch and Learn and then press Enter. Press Tab to increase the list level. Type Health and wellness presenter and then press Enter. Type Lunch by Toole Inn and then press Enter.

6. Press Shift + Tab to decrease the list level. Type De-stress for Less Seminar and then press Enter. Press Tab. Type Products and demos from merchants at Sea View Mall and then press Enter. Type Aromatherapy classes Compare your screen with **Figure 2**.

■ **Continue to the next page to complete the skill** ➡

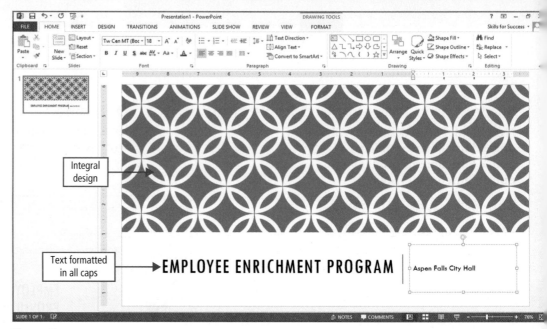

Figure 1

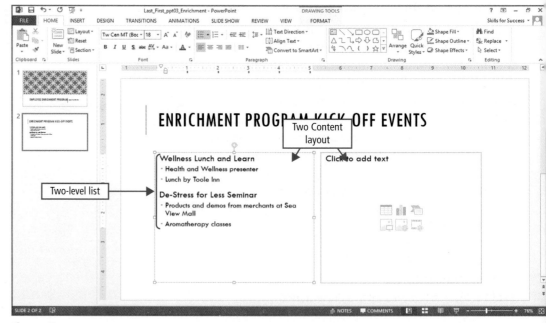

Figure 2

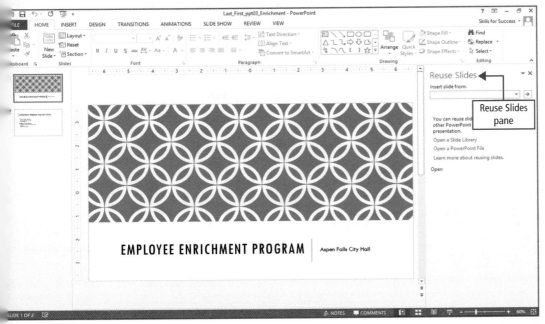

Figure 3

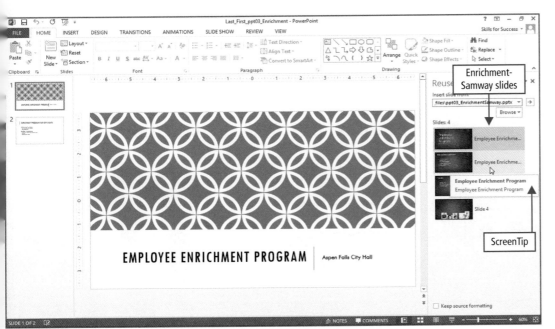

Figure 4

7. Move to **Slide 1**. On the **Home tab**, in the **Slides group**, click the **New Slide arrow**. Below the gallery, click **Reuse Slides** to display the **Reuse Slides** pane as shown in **Figure 3**.

8. In the **Reuse Slides** pane, click **Browse**, and then click **Browse File**. In the **Browse** dialog box, navigate to the student files for this chapter, click **ppt03_EnrichmentSamway**, and then click **Open**.

   You can use the Reuse Slides pane to insert all of the slides from another presentation, or insert only the slides you need.

9. At the bottom of the **Reuse Slides** pane, verify that the **Keep source formatting** check box is cleared. Point to the second slide thumbnail—*Employee Enrichment Program*—to view a ScreenTip with the slide title as shown in **Figure 4**.

10. Still pointing to the second slide in the **Reuse Slides** pane, click the **Employee Enrichment Program** slide to insert it in the current presentation.

    With the *Keep source formatting* option cleared, the formatting of the current presentation is applied to the inserted slide.

11. In the **Reuse Slides** pane, right-click the third slide—*Benefits*.

    On the shortcut menu, you have the option to insert only the selected slide or to insert all of the slides in the current presentation.

12. Click **Insert Slide**, and then in the upper right corner of the **Reuse Slides** pane, click the **Close** button ⊠ to close the pane.

13. Save ⊟ the presentation.

■ **You have completed Skill 1 of 10**

▶ Online Pictures are available from a wide variety of sources in many different formats, including .jpg, .tif, and .bmp files.

1. Display **Slide 4**. In the right content placeholder, click the **Online Pictures** button to display the **Insert Pictures** dialog box.

    Online pictures from the Office.com Clip Art gallery are images from a variety of online sources, made available by Microsoft and other companies. These images are royalty free and include photos and other types of illustrations.

2. In the **Insert Pictures** dialog box, in the **Office.com Clip Art** box, type teamwork success and then press Enter. Browse the search results and compare your screen with **Figure 1**.

3. In the **Search Results**, scroll as necessary to locate and then click the picture of two women high-fiving. Click the **Insert** button to insert the image into the right content placeholder in your presentation. If you are unable to locate the picture shown in the figure, insert a similar picture. Compare your screen with **Figure 2**.

    The image is inserted into the right content placeholder and sized to fit.

4. With the image selected, on the **Format tab**, in the **Size group**, in the **Height** box type 3.5 and then press Enter.

    When a shape's height is changed the width is automatically adjusted, unless the aspect ratio is unlocked.

■ Continue to the next page to complete the skill

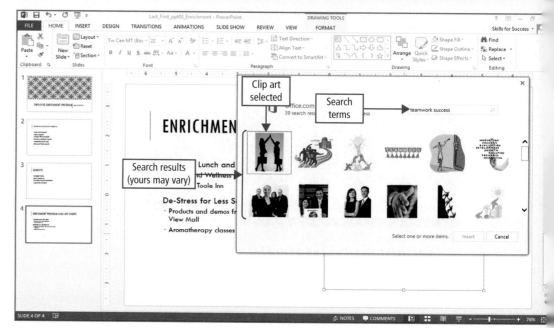

Figure 1

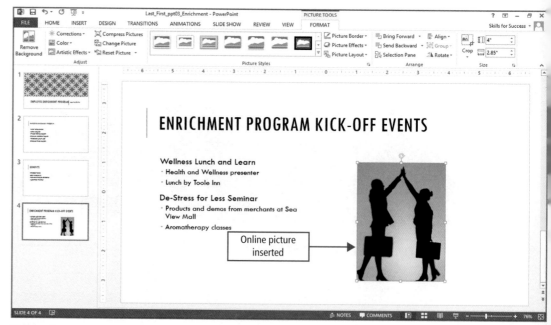

Figure 2

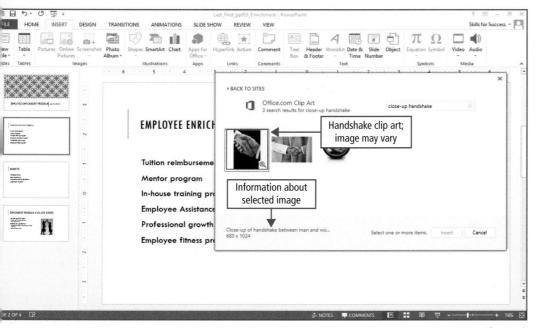

Figure 3

5. Display **Slide 2**. On the **Insert tab**, in the **Images group**, click the **Online Pictures** button. In the **Office.com Clip Art** box, type close-up handshake and then press Enter .

6. In the search results, point to any of the images shown to display information about the image—the name of the clip containing the search words you entered, the size of the clip and, if applicable, the author or company—in the lower left corner of the search box.

7. Click the image selected in Figure 3, and then click **Insert**. If you are unable to locate the same picture, choose a similar picture.

8. Point to the picture to display the pointer. With the pointer, drag the image to the right, so that it is aligned with the top, right, and bottom edges of the slide. Compare your screen with Figure 4.

9. Save the presentation.

■ **You have completed Skill 2 of 10**

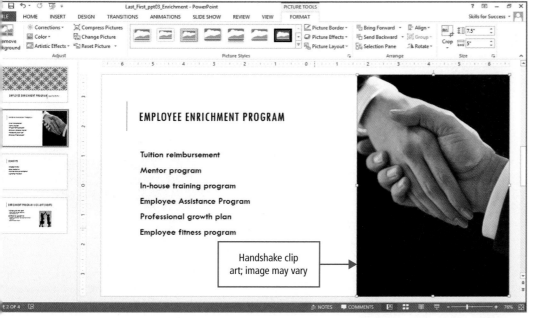

Figure 4

▶ Pictures are usually rectangular, but they can be changed to a number of different shapes available in PowerPoint.

▶ *Picture effects* are picture styles that include shadows, reflections, glows, soft edges, bevels, and 3-D rotations.

1. Display **Slide 3**. In the right content placeholder, click the **Pictures** button. From your student data files, insert the image named **ppt03_EnrichmentProductivity**.

2. On the **Format tab**, in the **Size group**, click the **Crop arrow**. Point to **Crop to Shape** to display the **Shape** gallery, and then compare your screen with **Figure 1**.

3. Under **Block Arrows**, click the second shape—**Left Arrow**—to change the shape of the picture.

4. In the **Picture Styles group**, click the **Picture Effects** button. Point to **Preset** and then point to each thumbnail to preview the effects on the cropped image using live preview.

5. Click the last option in the first row—**Preset 4**. If necessary, point to the picture to display the pointer, and drag to position the picture as shown in **Figure 2**.

6. Display **Slide 4**, and then select the picture. On the **Format tab**, in the **Picture Styles group**, click the **Picture Effects** button. Point to **Shadow**, and then point to, but do not click, several of the options to preview the shadow effects.

■ **Continue to the next page to complete the skill** ▶

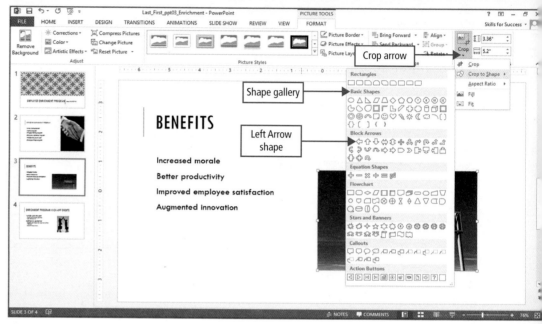

Figure 1

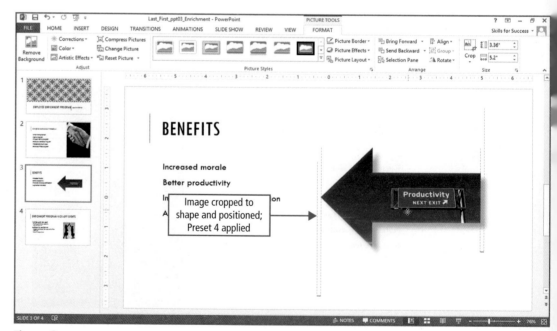

Figure 2

Eyeidea / Fotolia

Figure 3

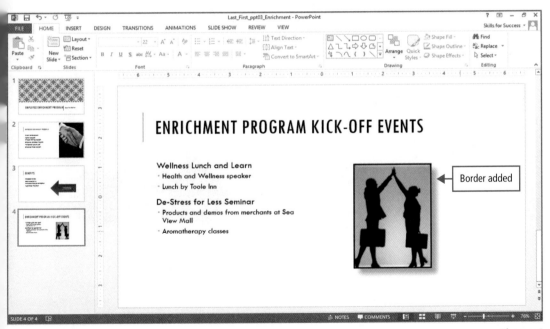

Figure 4

7. Point to **Reflection**, and then preview the various reflection effects. View the effects in several other galleries.

8. Point to **Presets** to display the gallery. Click the last option in the first row—**Preset 4**—to apply the same effect as applied on **Slide 3**. Compare your screen with **Figure 3**.

   Preset effects are a combination of other effects, like a bevel and a shadow.

9. With the picture still selected, on the **Format tab**, in the **Picture Styles group**, click the **Picture Border** button. Under **Theme Colors**, click the second color in the first row, **Black, Text 1**, to add a narrow border to the image.

   When you apply multiple effects to an image in this manner, choose effects that complement the picture, other effects, and the presentation theme.

10. Click the **Picture Border** button again, and then point to **Weight**. Click **3 pt** to apply a thicker border.

11. Click a blank area on the slide so that nothing is selected, and then compare your screen with **Figure 4**.

12. **Save** 🖫 the presentation.

■ **You have completed Skill 3 of 10**

▶ You can use shapes as design elements, particularly on slides with a simple background design.

1. Move to **Slide 3**. If the rulers are not displayed in the **Normal view slide** pane, on the **View tab**, in the **Show group**, select the **Ruler** check box.

2. On the **Insert tab**, in the **Illustrations group**, click the **Shapes** button, and then under **Equation Shapes**, click the first shape—**Plus**.

3. Click anywhere near the bottom center of the slide to insert the shape. Point to the center of the shape to display the ⬚ pointer, and then drag up and to the left, as shown in **Figure 1**.

   Smart Guides are dashed lines that appear on the slide when pictures, shapes, text, or placeholders are nearly even or evenly spaced. The ruler displays *guides*—lines that give you a visual indication of where the pointer is positioned.

4. With the shape selected, on the **Format tab**, in the **Shape Styles group**, click the **More** button ⬚ to display the gallery. Click the third option in the last row—**Intense Effect - Blue**, **Accent 2**.

5. On the **Format tab**, in the **Size group**, change the shape **Height** to 1.1" Adjust the **Width** to 1.1" Compare your screen with **Figure 2**.

   When a shape's height or width is changed, only that dimension and not the other is changed.

■ Continue to the next page to complete the skill

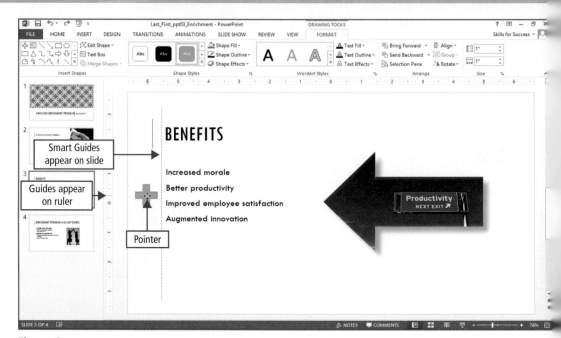

Figure 1

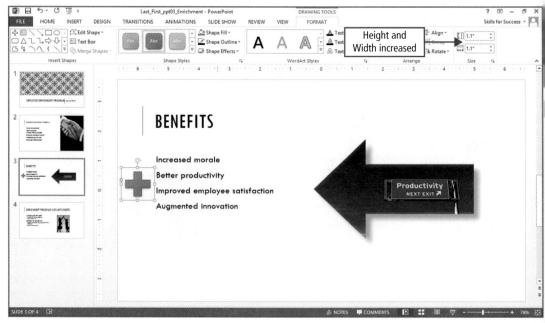

Figure 2

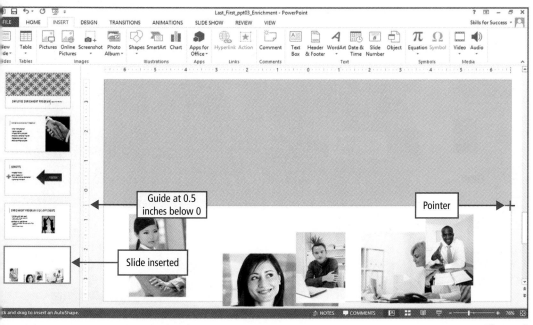

ptmatikphoto / Fotolia; Goodluz / Fotolia; Alliance / Fotolia

Figure 3

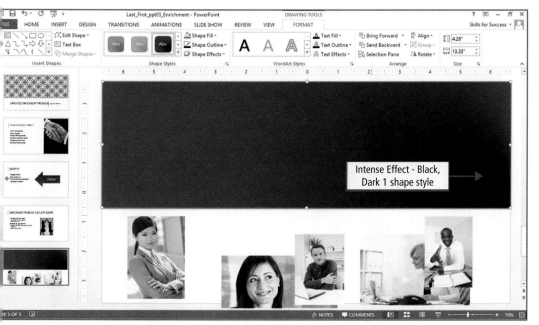

Figure 4

6. Move to **Slide 4**. On the **Home tab**, in the **Slides group**, click the **New Slide arrow**, and then click **Reuse Slides** to display the **ppt03_EnrichmentSamway** slides in the **Reuse Slides** pane. If the slides from **ppt03_EnrichmentSamway** do not display in the **Reuse Slides** pane, click the **Browse** button, click **Browse File**, navigate to your student files, and then open **ppt03_EnrichmentSamway**.

7. In the **Reuse Slides** pane, click **Slide 4** to insert it in the presentation, and then **Close** ☒ the pane.

8. On the **Insert tab**, in the **Illustrations group**, click the **Shapes** button. Under **Rectangles**, click the first shape— **Rectangle**. With the ➕ pointer, drag from the upper-left corner of the slide to the right edge of the slide and down to the half-inch mark—**0.5** inches below **0** on the vertical ruler. Compare your screen with **Figure 3**.

9. With the rectangle selected, on the **Format tab**, in the **Shape Styles group**, click the **More** button ⬇, and then click the first style in the last row— **Intense Effect - Black, Dark 1**.

10. Compare your screen with **Figure 4**, and if necessary, drag the rectangle so that it is positioned as shown in the figure.

11. **Save** 💾 the presentation.

■ **You have completed Skill 4 of 10**

▶ A ***text box*** is an object used to position text anywhere on a slide.

▶ In addition to being used as design elements, shapes can also be used as containers for text.

1. On **Slide 5**, if necessary, select the rectangle.

   To insert text in a shape, select the shape, and then begin to type.

2. Type Questions? Press Enter , and then type Contact Eugene Garner, Benefits Specialist Press Enter , type (805) 555-1020 and then compare your screen with **Figure 1**.

   When you type text in a shape, it is centered both horizontally and vertically within the shape.

3. Select the three lines of text, and then change the **Font Size** to **40**.

4. With the three lines of text still selected, on the **Format tab**, in the **WordArt Styles group**, click the **More** button ⯆ . Click the last style in the third row—**Fill - Ice Blue**, **Background 2**, **Inner Shadow**.

5. In the **WordArt Styles group**, click the **Text Fill arrow** to display the gallery. Click the first color in the first row— **White**, **Background 1**. Click a blank area of the slide so that nothing is selected, and then compare your slide screen with **Figure 2**.

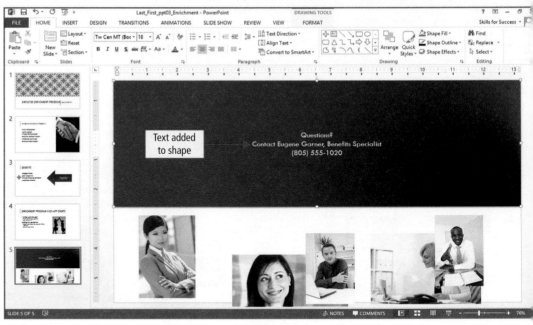

Figure 1

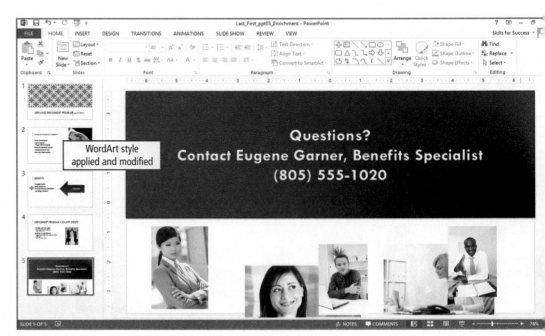

Figure 2

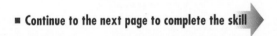

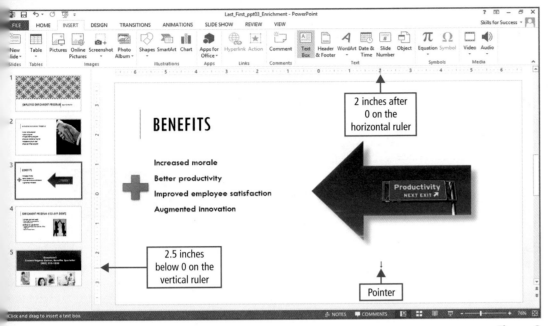

Figure 3

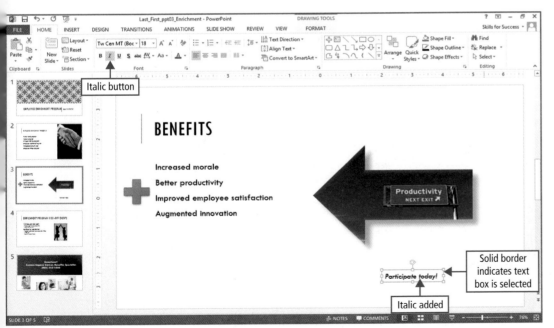

Figure 4

6. Display **Slide 3**. On the **Insert tab**, in the **Text group**, click the **Text Box** button 📇. Position the ↓ pointer on the slide aligned at **2** inches after **0** on the horizontal ruler and at **2.5** inches below **0** on the vertical ruler as shown in **Figure 3**.

7. Without moving the pointer, click one time to insert a text box. Type Participate today!

   Text boxes automatically resize to fit the text you type. If needed, text boxes can be resized using the sizing handles, or moved by clicking and dragging.

8. Click anywhere on the slide so that the text box is not selected.

   Unlike shapes, when a text box is inserted, it does not include borders or fill colors. Text inserted in a text box appears to be floating on the slide and is formatted in the same font as the body font used in content placeholders.

9. Click the text in the text box and then click a border of the text box to select it. Recall that a solid border indicates that the object is selected. On the **Home tab**, in the **Font group**, click the **Italic** button 𝐼. Compare your screen with **Figure 4**. If your text box is not positioned as shown in the figure, select the text box and then use the ↑, ↓, ←, or → keys on your keyboard to *nudge*—move an object in small increments using the directional arrow keys—the text box so that it is positioned as shown.

10. Save 🖫 the presentation.

■ **You have completed Skill 5 of 10**

▶ A *group* is a collection of multiple objects treated as one unit that can be copied, moved, or formatted.

1. On **Slide 3** select the plus sign shape. On the **Format tab**, in the **Shape Styles group**, click the **Shape Fill** button. Preview the styles, and then, under **Theme Colors**, click the fourth option in the second row—**Dark Teal**, **Text 2**, **Lighter 80%**.

2. In the **Shape Styles group**, click the **Shape Fill** button. Point to **Gradient**, and then under **Variations**, in the second row, point to the last thumbnail—**From Top Left Corner**—as shown in **Figure 1**, and click to apply a gradient fill to the shape.

   A *gradient fill* is a gradual progression of colors and shades, usually from one color to another, or from one shade to another shade of the same color. A gradient fill is used to add a fill to a shape or placeholder. Gradients come in light and dark variations.

3. Display **Slide 4**. Click the title placeholder and then click the placeholder border to select it. On the **Format tab**, in the **Shape Styles group**, click the **Shape Fill** button and then click **Gradient**. Under **Light Variations**, click the last option in the last row—**Linear Diagonal - Bottom Right to Top Left**. Compare your screen with **Figure 2**.

■ **Continue to the next page to complete the skill** ▶

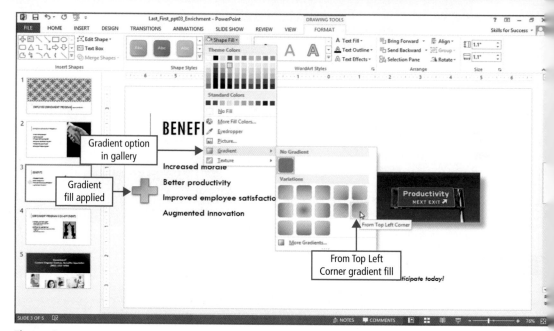

Figure 1

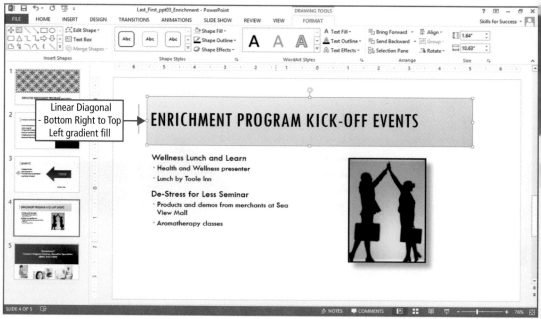

Figure 2

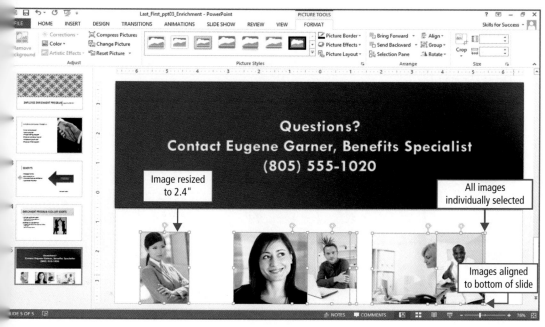

Figure 3

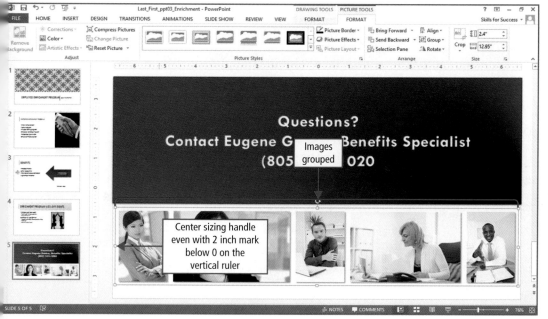

Figure 4

4. Display **Slide 5**. Select the furthest left image, and then on the **Format tab**, in the **Size group**, change the **Height** to 2.4"

5. Hold down Shift, and then click each picture at the bottom of the slide so that all five of the images are selected.

6. On the **Format tab**, in the **Arrange group**, click the **Align** button, and verify that **Align to Slide** is selected; if it is not, select it and then click the Align button again. Click **Align Bottom**. Compare your screen with **Figure 3**.

    The Align Bottom option aligns the selected objects to the bottom of the slide.

7. With the pictures selected, on the **Format tab**, in the **Picture Styles group**, click the **Picture Effects** button. Point to **Shadow**, and then under **Outer**, click the first option in the first row—**Offset Diagonal Bottom Right**.

8. With the pictures selected, on the **Format tab**, in the **Arrange group**, click the **Align** button, and then click **Distribute Horizontally**.

    When aligned to the slide the pictures are evenly distributed horizontally.

9. With the pictures selected, in the **Arrange group**, click the **Group** button, and then click **Group**. With the grouped pictures selected, use the [cursor] pointer to drag the images straight up, so that the horizontal center sizing handle is aligned with the 2 inch mark below **0** on the vertical ruler. Compare your screen with **Figure 4**.

10. **Save** 🔲 the presentation.

■ **You have completed Skill 6 of 10**

▶ A **SmartArt graphic** is a visual representation of information that can be used to communicate your message or ideas effectively.

▶ SmartArt graphics can be created from scratch by inserting the graphic and then adding text.

▶ You can convert text that you have already typed—such as a list—into a SmartArt graphic, add additional text and pictures, and then apply colors, effects, and styles that coordinate with the presentation theme.

1. Display **Slide 4**, and then click anywhere in the bulleted list. On the **Home tab**, in the **Paragraph group**, click the **Convert to SmartArt Graphic** button. At the bottom of the gallery, click **More SmartArt Graphics** to open the **Choose a SmartArt Graphic** dialog box. Compare your screen with **Figure 1**.

The Choose a SmartArt Graphic dialog box is divided into three sections. The left pane lists the SmartArt graphic types. The center section displays the layouts for the selected type. The right section displays a preview of the selected layout, along with a description of the layout.

2. In the left pane of the **Choose a SmartArt Graphic** dialog box, click each of the SmartArt graphic types to view the layouts in each category, and then in the center pane, click several layouts to view their descriptions.

The eight types of SmartArt layouts are summarized in **Figure 2**.

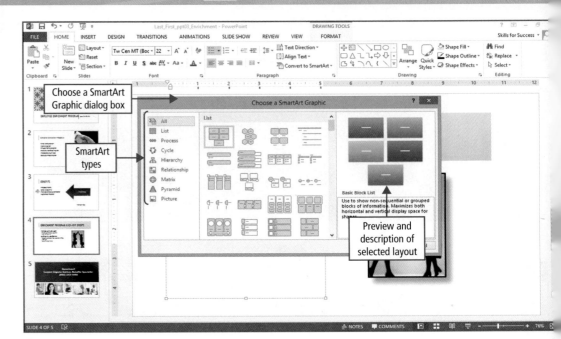

Figure 1

Microsoft PowerPoint SmartArt Layout Types	
Type	**Purpose**
List	Illustrates nonsequential information.
Process	Illustrates steps in a process or timeline.
Cycle	Illustrates a continual process.
Hierarchy	Illustrates a decision tree or creates an organization chart.
Relationship	Illustrates a connection.
Matrix	Illustrates how parts relate to a whole.
Pyramid	Illustrates proportional relationships, with the largest component on the bottom or top.
Picture	Communicates message and ideas using pictures in each shape.

Figure 2

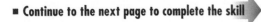

■ **Continue to the next page to complete the skill**

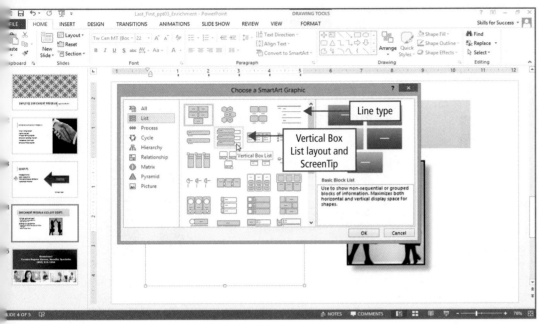

Figure 3

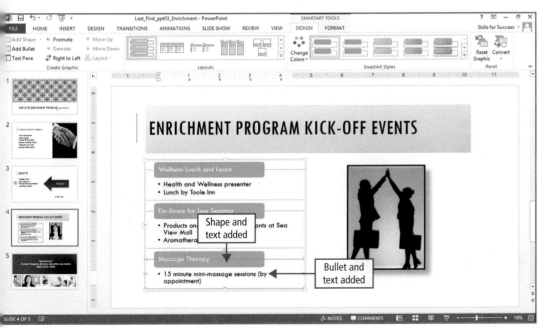

Figure 4

3. In the left pane of the **Choose a SmartArt Graphic** dialog box, click **List**, and then in the center pane, use the ScreenTips to locate **Vertical Box List**. Compare your screen with **Figure 3**.

4. Click **Vertical Box List**, and then click **OK** to convert the bulleted list to a SmartArt graphic.

   The Text Pane button may be selected on the Ribbon, and the Text Pane may display to the left of the SmartArt graphic.

5. If the **Text** Pane displays, **Close** ⊠ it.

6. Click anywhere in the text *De-stress for Less Seminar*. On the **SmartArt Tools Design tab**, in the **Create Graphic group**, click the **Add Shape** button. Type Massage Therapy

7. On the **SmartArt Tools Design tab**, in the **Create Graphic group**, click the **Add Bullet** button. Type 15 minute mini-massage sessions (by appointment) Compare your screen with **Figure 4**.

8. **Save** 🖫 the presentation.

■ **You have completed Skill 7 of 10**

PPT 3-8
VIDEO

▶ After you create a SmartArt graphic, you can change the layout to one that provides the best visual representation of your information.

▶ The colors that you apply to a SmartArt graphic are coordinated with the presentation color theme.

▶ SmartArt styles include gradient fills and 3-D effects.

1. On **Slide 4**, if necessary, select the SmartArt graphic. On the **SmartArt Tools Design tab**, in the **Layouts group**, click the **More** button ⤓, and then use ScreenTips to locate and click **Vertical Arrow List**.

2. Click anywhere in the text *Health and wellness presenter* in the first arrow shape. On the **Home tab**, in the **Font group**, notice that the font size is 17 points. Recall that in a professional presentation, all fonts should be at least 18 to 24 points.

3. Click a blank area of the SmartArt graphic to select the entire graphic—individual shapes should not be selected. Compare your screen with **Figure 1**.

4. With the ⟷ pointer, drag the SmartArt's right center sizing handle to the right, to align the side with the **0.5** inch mark after **0** on the horizontal ruler.

5. Click anywhere in the text *Health and wellness presenter* in the first arrow shape. On the **Home tab**, in the **Font group**, notice that the font size is **18** points. Compare your screen with **Figure 2**.

The font was automatically resized to fit the larger size of the SmartArt and now meets design standards.

■ **Continue to the next page to complete the skill**

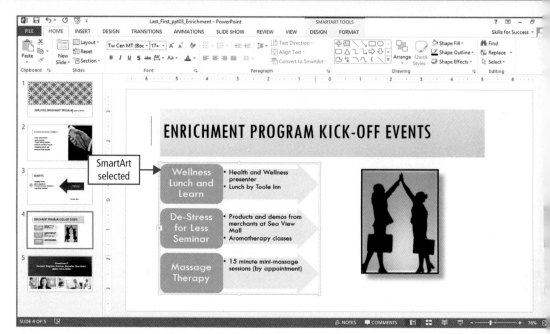

Figure 1

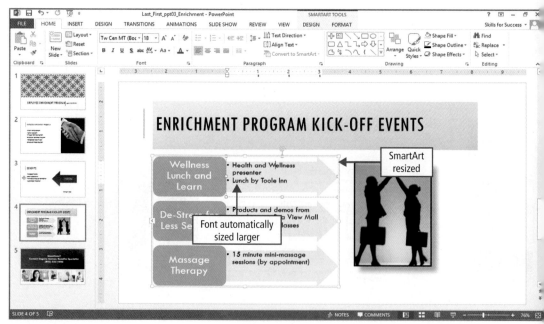

Figure 2

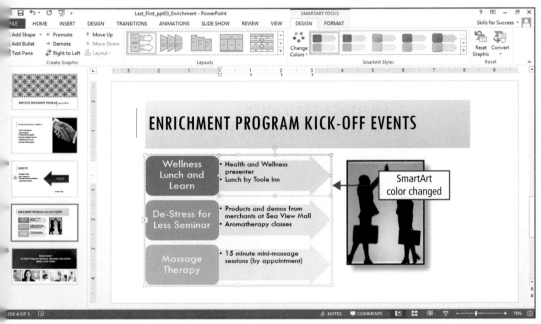

Figure 3

6. On **SmartArt Tools Design tab**, in the **SmartArt Styles group**, click the **Change Colors** button to display the **Color** gallery. Point to several options to preview the colors.

   The colors that display in the gallery coordinate with the slide design.

7. Under **Colorful**, click the second style—**Colorful Range - Accent Colors 2 to 3**. Compare your screen with **Figure 3**.

8. On the **SmartArt Tools Design tab**, in the **SmartArt Styles group**, click the **More** button ⟱ to display the **SmartArt Styles** gallery. Point to several of the styles to view their effects on the SmartArt. Then, under **3-D**, click the first style—**Polished**. Click in a blank area of the slide, and then compare your screen with **Figure 4**.

9. Save 🖫 the presentation.

■ **You have completed Skill 8 of 10**

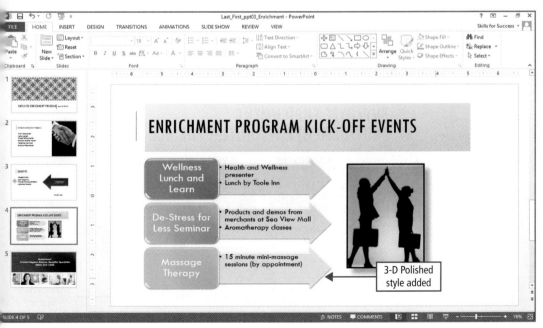

Figure 4

PPT 3-9
VIDEO

▶ You can insert, size, and move video files in a presentation, and you can control when the video will begin to play during a slide show.

1. Display **Slide 1**, and then insert a **New Slide** with the **Title and Content** layout. In the title placeholder, type Employee Enrichment Press [Enter] and type Providing Opportunities for All

2. In the content placeholder, click the **Insert Video** button 🎬, and then in the **Insert Video** dialog box, to the right of **From a file**, click the **Browse** button. Navigate to your student files and then click **ppt03_EnrichmentVideo**. Click **Insert**. Compare your screen with **Figure 1**.

> The video displays in the center of the slide, and playback and volume controls display in the control panel below the video. Video formatting and editing tools display on the Ribbon. On the Insert tab, in the Media group, clicking the Video button is an alternate method to insert videos.

3. On the control panel below the video, point to the **Play/Pause** button ▶ so that it is highlighted as shown in **Figure 2**.

4. Click the **Play/Pause** button ▶ to view the video. Alternately, press [Alt] + [P].

> As the video plays, the control panel displays the time that has elapsed since the start of the video.

■ **Continue to the next page to complete the skill** ▶

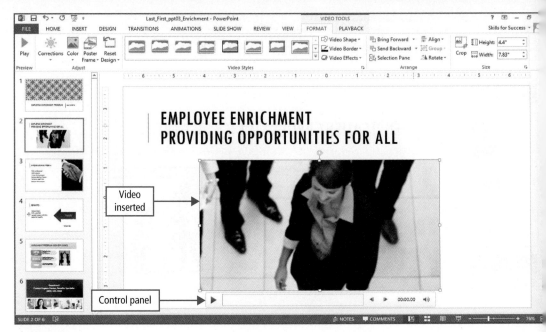

Figure 1

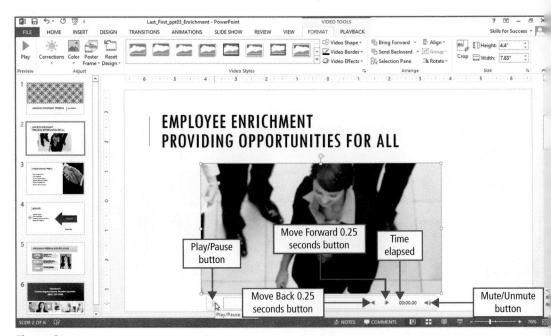

Figure 2

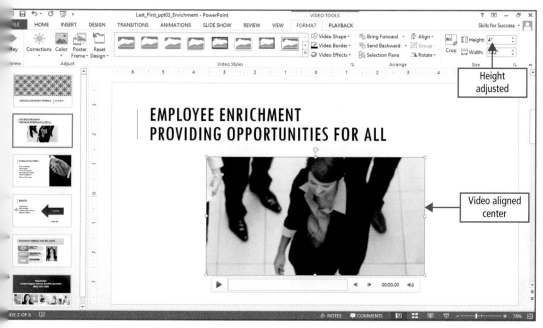

Figure 3

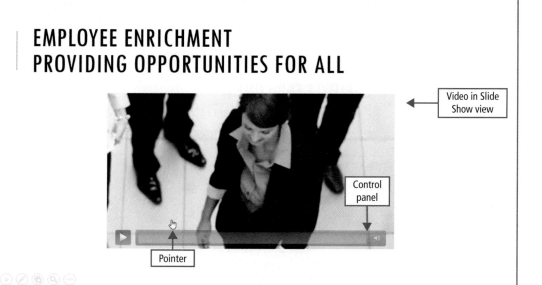

Figure 4

5. On the **Format tab**, in the **Size group**, click in the **Height** box. Type 4" and then press Enter. Notice that the video width adjusts proportionately.

6. On the **Format tab**, in the **Arrange group**, click the **Align** button, and then click **Align Center** to center the video horizontally on the slide. Compare your screen with **Figure 3**.

7. Toward the right side of the status bar, click the **Slide Show** button to display **Slide 2** in the slide show. Point to the video to display the pointer, and then compare your screen with **Figure 4**.

> When you point to the video during the slide show, the player controls display.

8. With the pointer displayed, click the mouse button to view the video. When the video is finished, press Esc to exit the slide show.

9. If necessary, select the video. On the **Playback tab**, in the **Video Options group**, click the **Start** arrow, and then click **Automatically**. On the **Slide Show** tab, in the **Start Slide Show** group, click the **From Current Slide** button to display **Slide 2** in the slide show. When the video is finished, press Esc to exit the slide show.

> When you set a video to start automatically, the video will play when the slide displays in the slide show. You can use this option if you want the video to begin playing without clicking the mouse button.

10. Save the presentation.

■ **You have completed Skill 9 of 10**

▶ You can apply styles and effects to a video and change the video shape and border.

▶ You can recolor a video so that it coordinates with the presentation theme.

1. On **Slide 2**, if necessary, select the video. On the **Format tab**, in the **Video Styles group**, click the **More** button ▽. In the **Video Styles** gallery, under **Intense**, click the third style—**Reflected Rounded Rectangle**. Click a blank area of the slide to view the style you just applied, and then compare your screen with **Figure 1**.

2. Select the video. On the **Format tab**, in the **Video Styles group**, click the **Video Border** button. Under **Theme Colors**, click the fourth option in the first row—**Dark Teal, Text 2**.

3. Click the **Video Border** button again, and then click **Weight** and **6 pt**.

4. With the video selected, on the **Format tab**, in the **Adjust group**, click the **Color** button.

    The Recolor gallery displays colors from the presentation theme that you can apply to the video.

5. Point to several of the thumbnails to view the color change, and then click the second thumbnail—**Grayscale**—to change the color of the video. Compare your slide with **Figure 2**.

6. On the **Format tab**, in the **Adjust group**, click the **Color** button, and then click the first thumbnail—**No Recolor**—to change the video color back to the original.

■ **Continue to the next page to complete the skill**

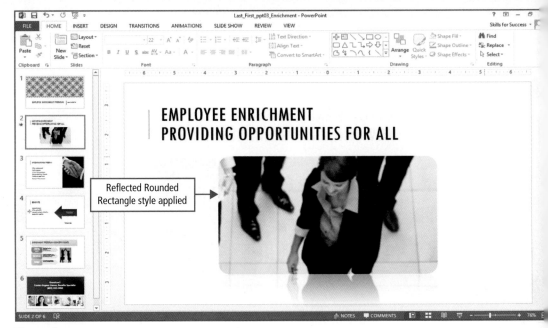

Figure 1

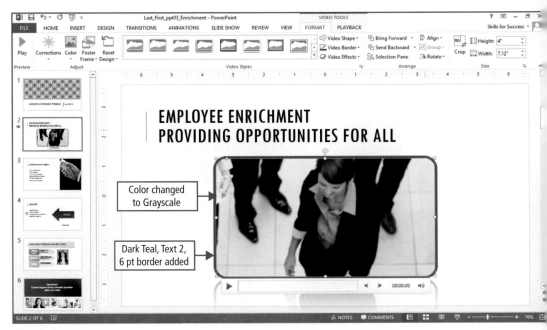

Figure 2

Figure 3

7. With the video selected, on the **Format tab**, in the **Adjust group**, click the **Corrections** button to display the **Brightness and Contrast** gallery.

> The Brightness and Contrast gallery displays combinations of brightness and contrast adjustments that you can apply to a video to improve color and visibility.

8. In the third column, point to the fourth thumbnail to display the ScreenTip **Brightness: +0% Contrast: +20%** as shown in **Figure 3**.

9. Click **Brightness: +0% Contrast: +20%** to apply the correction to the video, and then click anywhere on the slide so that the video is not selected. Compare your screen with **Figure 4**.

10. On the **Slide Show tab**, in the **Start Slide Show group**, click **From Beginning**, and then advance through the presentation. When the black slide displays, click one more time to return to **Normal view**.

11. Insert a **Header & Footer** on the **Notes and Handouts**. Include the **Date and time**, the **Page Number**, and a **Footer** with the text Last_First_ppt03_ Enrichment **Apply to All** pages.

12. **Save** 🗄 the presentation. **Close** ☒ PowerPoint. Submit as directed by your instructor.

✓ **DONE!** You have completed Skill 10 of 10, and your presentation is complete!

Figure 4

The following More Skills are located at **www.pearsonhighered.com/skills**

More Skills Compress Pictures

The large file sizes of pictures from digital cameras or scanners can slow the delivery of a presentation and make your presentation files large. You can compress the presentation pictures so that the file size is smaller.

In More Skills 11, you will open a presentation, view the file size, compress the pictures in the presentation, and then view the changes to the file size.

To begin, open your web browser, navigate to www.pearsonhighered.com/skills, locate the name of your textbook, and then follow the instructions on the website.

More Skills Save Groups as Picture Files

A group can be saved as a picture file so that you can insert it on another slide, insert it in another presentation, or use it in other programs. Saving a group as a picture facilitates easy sharing among presentations and applications.

In More Skills 12, you will open a presentation, create a group, and then save the group as a picture. You will then insert the picture into other slides in the presentation.

To begin, open your web browser, navigate to www.pearsonhighered.com/skills, locate the name of your textbook, and then follow the instructions on the website.

More Skills Change Object Order

When objects such as shapes and pictures are inserted on a slide, they often overlap. The first object inserted is positioned at the bottom of the stack, and the next object inserted is above the first object. You can change the order in which objects overlap by moving them backward and forward in the stack.

In More Skills 13, you will create a presentation and change the order of inserted objects.

To begin, open your web browser, navigate to www.pearsonhighered.com/skills, locate the name of your textbook, and then follow the instructions on the website.

More Skills Insert a Screen Shot in a Presentation

You can include a screen shot of any window on your desktop in your presentation.

In More Skills 14, you will open a memo and a presentation. You will add a screen shot of the memo to the second slide in the presentation.

To begin, open your web browser, navigate to www.pearsonhighered.com/skills, locate the name of your textbook, and then follow the instructions on the website.

Please note that there are no additional projects to accompany the More Skills Projects, and they are not covered in the End-of-Chapter projects.

he following table summarizes the **SKILLS AND PROCEDURES** covered in this chapter.

Skills Number	Task	Step
1	Insert slides from other presentations	Home tab → New Slide arrow → Reuse Slides
2	Insert online pictures	Insert tab → Online Pictures
3	Crop a picture to a shape	Format tab → Crop arrow → Crop to Shape
3	Add picture effects	Format tab → Picture Effects
3	Add a border to pictures	Format tab → Picture Border
4	Insert shapes	Insert tab → Shapes
5	Add text to shapes	Select shape → type text
5	Insert text boxes	Insert tab → Text Box
6	Group objects	Press Shift , select items → Format tab → Group
7	Convert text to SmartArt	Place insertion point in text → Home tab → Convert to SmartArt Graphic button
9	Insert videos	Insert tab → Video button
10	Apply video styles	Format tab → Video Styles

Key Terms

Online Help Skills

1. With **PowerPoint** open, in the upper right corner of the screen, click the **Help** button ⌐?¬, or press F1.

2. In the **PowerPoint Help** window, use the **Search** box to locate and open the article *Video and audio formats supported in PowerPoint*. Maximize the window and compare your screen with **Figure 1**.

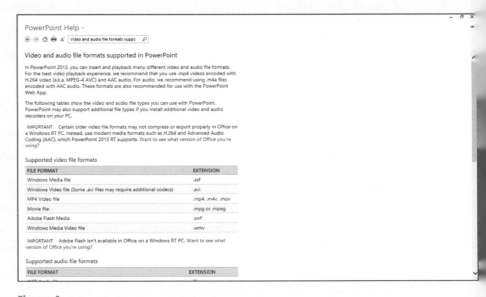

Figure 1

3. Read the article and answer the following questions: What video format does Microsoft recommend for use in PowerPoint presentations? List at least two other types of video files that could be inserted into a presentation.

Matching

Match each term in the second column with its correct definition in the first column by writing the letter of the term on the blank line in front of the correct definition.

___ **1.** The command used to insert slides from another presentation.

___ **2.** Formatting options applied to pictures that include shadows, reflections, glows, soft edges, bevels, and 3-D rotations.

___ **3.** Lines that display in the rulers to give you a visual indication of where the pointer is positioned.

___ **4.** Objects such as lines, rectangles, and circles that can be used as design elements on a slide.

___ **5.** An object used to position text anywhere on a slide.

___ **6.** The action of moving an object in small increments by using the directional arrow keys.

___ **7.** Multiple objects treated as one unit that can be copied, moved, or formatted.

___ **8.** A fill effect in which one color fades into another.

___ **9.** A visual representation of information that you can use to communicate your message or ideas effectively by choosing from many different layouts.

___ **10.** A command used to change a list into a SmartArt graphic.

A Convert to SmartArt Graphic

B Gradient fill

C Group

D Guides

E Nudge

F Picture effects

G Reuse Slides

H Shapes

I SmartArt graphic

J Text box

BizSkills Video

1. How is customer service important to customer retention? How does this impact the overall success, or failure, of a company?

2. If a company provides customer service training to all of its customer service staff, how might photos and videos help to communicate their message?

Multiple Choice MyITLab®

Choose the correct answer.

1. The task pane that is used to insert slides from another presentation.
   - A. Insert Slides
   - B. Browse Slides
   - C. Reuse Slides

2. This does not automatically include borders or shading when inserted on a slide.
   - A. Rectangle shape
   - B. Text box
   - C. SmartArt

3. The default alignment applied to text typed in a shape.
   - A. Left
   - B. Center
   - C. Right

4. A SmartArt layout type that illustrates nonsequential information.
   - A. Process
   - B. Cycle
   - C. List

5. A SmartArt layout type that illustrates a continual process.
   - A. Hierarchy
   - B. Cycle
   - C. Process

6. A SmartArt layout type that illustrates a decision tree or creates an organization chart.
   - A. Relationship
   - B. Hierarchy
   - C. Pyramid

7. A SmartArt layout type that illustrates connections.
   - A. Relationship
   - B. Hierarchy
   - C. Pyramid

8. The tab in which video Start options are found.
   - A. Format
   - B. Playback
   - C. Design

9. The button that displays video Brightness and Contrast options.
   - A. Color
   - B. Design
   - C. Corrections

10. The button that displays the video Recolor gallery.
    - A. Color
    - B. Design
    - C. Corrections

Topics for Discussion

1. Some PowerPoint presenters advocate using only slides that consist of a single statement and a graphic so that the presentation reads like a story. Other presenters advocate using slides that combine the "single statement and graphics" approach with slides that include detail in the form of bullet points, diagrams, and pictures. What is the advantage of each of these approaches? Which approach would you prefer to use?

2. Sharing presentation slides among employees in an organization is a common practice. What types of information and objects do you think should be included on slides that are shared within an organization?

Skill Review

To complete this project, you will need the following files:

- ppt03_SRPastTuition
- ppt03_SRImage
- ppt03_SRVideo

You will save your file as:

- Last_First_ppt03_SRTuition

1. **Start** PowerPoint 2013, and then create a new presentation using the **Facet** theme and the default variant. On **Slide 1**, in the title placeholder, type Tuition Reimbursement Plan Change the **Font Size** for the text in the title placeholder to **44**. In the subtitle placeholder, type An Aspen Falls Employee Benefit

2. On the **Home tab**, in the **Slides group**, click the **New Slide arrow**, and then click **Reuse Slides**.

3. In the **Reuse Slides** pane, click the **Browse** button, and then click **Browse File**. From your student files, click **ppt03_SRPastTuition**, and then click **Open**. In the **Reuse Slides** pane, click **Slides 2, 3**, and **4** to insert them, and then **Close** the pane. **Save** your presentation in your **PowerPoint Chapter 3** folder as Last_First_ppt03_SRTuition

4. On **Slide 2**, in the right content placeholder, click the **Online Pictures** button. In the **Insert Pictures** dialog box, in the **Office.com Clip Art** box, type textbook and press Enter. Click the picture of a woman carrying a stack of textbooks and an apple. Click the **Insert** button. Compare your screen with **Figure 1**.

5. With the picture selected, on the **Format tab**, in the **Size group**, change the **Height** to 4"

6. On the **Format tab**, in the **Size group**, click the **Crop arrow**, and then click **Crop to Shape**. Under **Rectangles**, click **Round Diagonal Corner Rectangle**. In the **Picture Styles group**, click the **Picture Effects** button, point to **Bevel**, and then under **Bevel**, click **Soft Round**.

7. On the **Insert tab**, in the **Text group**, click **Text Box**. Align the pointer at **0.5** inches before **0** on the horizontal ruler and at **3** inches below **0** on the vertical ruler, and then click one time to insert the text box. Type Earn your college degree Click a blank area of the slide, and then compare your slide with **Figure 2**.

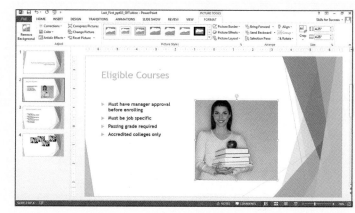

Figure 1

Xy / Fotolia

Figure 2

- **Continue to the next page to complete this Skills Review**

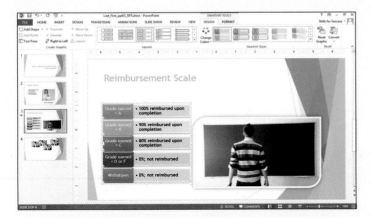

Figure 3

Figure 4

8. On **Slide 3**, in the right content placeholder, click the **Insert Video** button. From your student files, insert **ppt03_SRVideo**. On the **Format tab**, in the **Size group**, change the **Video Height** to 3.6"

9. On the **Playback tab**, in the **Video Options group**, click the **Start arrow**, and then click **Automatically**. On the **Format tab**, in the **Video Styles group**, click the **More** button, and then under **Moderate**, select **Rounded Diagonal Corner, White**.

10. On **Slide 3**, click the bulleted list. On the **Home tab**, in the **Paragraph group**, click the **Convert to SmartArt Graphic** button. In the gallery, click the second option in the first row—**Vertical Block List**.

11. Click the text *Grade earned = D or F*. On the **Design tab**, in the **Create Graphic group**, click the **Add Shape** button, type Withdrawn and then click the **Add Bullet** button. Type 0%; not reimbursed

12. With the SmartArt selected, change the SmartArt colors to **Colorful - Accent Colors**, and then apply the first **3-D** SmartArt style—**Polished**. Compare your slide with **Figure 3**.

13. Display **Slide 4**. Hold down Shift, and then click each picture. On the **Format tab**, in the **Arrange group**, click the **Align** button, and then, if necessary, select **Align to Slide**. Click the **Align** button again, and then click **Align Top**.

14. With the pictures selected, click the **Align** button. Click **Distribute Horizontally**.

15. In the **Picture Styles group**, click the **Picture Effects** button. Point to **3-D Rotation**, and then under **Parallel**, click **Off Axis 1 Right**. In the **Arrange group**, click the **Group** button, and then click **Group**. Drag the grouped images straight down, so that the vertical center sizing handle is aligned with the **2** inch mark before 0 on the vertical ruler. Click a blank area of the slide to deselect the grouped images.

16. On the **Insert tab**, in the **Illustrations group**, click **Shapes**. Under **Rectangles**, click **Rectangle**. Align the pointer with the **0** inch mark on the vertical ruler. Drag to draw a rectangle across the slide from the left edge to the right edge and down to the bottom of the slide. In the **Shape Styles group**, click the **Shape Fill** button and then under **Standard Colors**, click **Light Green**. Click **Shape Fill**, and then click **Gradient**. Under **Dark Variations**, click **From Center**.

17. In the shape, type Congratulations graduates! and then change the **Font Size** to 40 for all of the text in the shape.

18. View the slide show. Insert a **Header & Footer** on all **Notes and Handouts** pages with the date, page number, and the footer text Last_First_ppt03_ SRTuition Compare your presentation with **Figure 4**, and then **Save**. **Close** and then submit the file as directed by your instructor.

 DONE! You have completed this Skills Review

Skills Assessment 1

MyITLab®
Grader

To complete this presentation, you will need the following files:

- ppt03_SA1Online
- ppt03_SA1Courses
- ppt03_SA1Video

You will save your presentation as:

- Last_First_ppt03_SA1Online

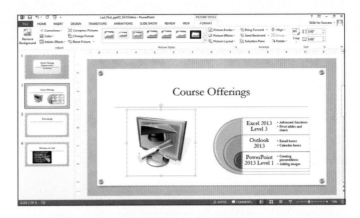
Figure 1

1. **Start** PowerPoint 2013, and then from your student files, open **ppt03_SA1Online**. With **Slide 1** showing in **Normal view**, display the **Reuse Slides** pane, and then insert **Slide 2** —**Course Offerings** —from the student data file **ppt03_SA1OnlineCourses**. **Save** your presentation in your **PowerPoint Chapter 3** folder as Last_First_ppt03_SA1Online

2. On **Slide 2**, convert the text in the right content placeholder to SmartArt in the **Target List** layout. Change the SmartArt **Color** to **Colorful Range - Accent Colors 5 to 6**, and then apply the **Inset** SmartArt style.

3. On **Slide 2**, in the left content placeholder, use **Online Pictures** to search for Online education images. Insert the image of a monitor, diploma, and cap. If this image is not available, locate and insert a similar image. Compare your screen with **Figure 1**.

4. On **Slide 3**, insert a **Left Arrow** shape. Draw the shape, adjusting the size to a **Height** of 2" and a **Width** of 3" Move the shape so that the tip of the arrow is at the **1** inch mark to the right of **0** on the horizontal ruler and bottom of the shape is even with the **2** inch mark below **0** on the vertical ruler.

5. In the shape, type Enroll today! Increase the **Font Size** to **24**. Apply the **Brown**, **18 pt glow**, **Accent color 1** glow shape effect.

6. On **Slide 3**, in the left content placeholder, insert the video named **ppt03_SA1Video** from your student files. Adjust the **Video Height** to 3.2" and add the **Simple Frame**, **White** video style.

7. With the video still selected, change the video **Color** to **Grayscale**. Compare your screen with **Figure 2**.

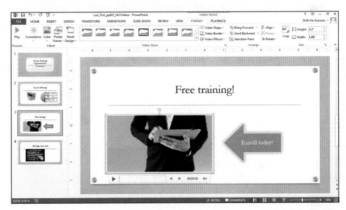
Figure 2

Doc Rabe Media / Fotolia

8. On **Slide 4**, select the image and then click **Align** and then **Align Center**. With the image still selected, crop it to the **Flowchart: Document** shape.

9. On the **Notes and Handouts** pages, include the date, a page number, and a footer with the text Last_First_ppt03_SA1Online **Save** and, **Close**, and submit as directed by your instructor.

 **DONE! You have completed Skills Assessment 1**

Skills Assessment 2

To complete this presentation, you will need the following files:

- ppt03_SA2Mentor
- ppt03_SA2Email

You will save your presentation as:

- Last_First_ppt03_SA2Mentor

Figure 1

1. **Start** PowerPoint 2013, and then from your student files, open **ppt03_SA2Mentor**. Move to **Slide 2**. Display the **Reuse Slides** pane, and from the student data file **ppt03_SA2Email**. Insert **Slide 1** —**Mentor Coordinators**. **Save** your presentation in your **PowerPoint Chapter 3** folder as Last_First_ppt03_SA2Mentor

2. On **Slide 2**, in the content placeholder, insert the online picture of one person climbing stairs to a desk being helped by a person sitting at the desk (use the search terms mentoring assistance). If this image is not available, locate and insert a similar image. Resize the image to a **Height** of 3.1"

3. On **Slide 2**, on the **Insert tab**, click **Shape** and then click **Flowchart: Punched Tape**. Position your pointer at the intersection of **0** on the horizontal ruler and **0** on the vertical ruler and click to insert the shape. Change the **Height** to 2" and the **Width** to 3.5"

4. In the shape, insert the text Climb to the top! Apply the **Intense Effect - Plumb**, **Accent 1** shape style, and then increase the **Font Size** to **28**. Apply the **Circle Bevel** shape effect. Select the image and the shape, use the **Align** button to **Align to slide**, and then **Distribute them horizontally**. Compare your screen with **Figure 1**.

5. On **Slide 3**, convert the content placeholder text to the **Segmented Process** SmartArt—found in the **List** or **Process** layouts. Change the SmartArt **Color** to **Primary Theme Colors Dark 2 Fill**, and then apply the **Powder** 3-D SmartArt style.

6. On **Slide 4**, select all of the images, and then crop all of them at once to the **Folded Corner** shape.

7. On **Slide 4**, with all of the images still selected, apply the **Align Middle** and **Distribute Horizontally** alignment options.

8. On **Slide 4**, apply the **Full Reflection**, **8 pt offset** Picture Effect to all of the pictures, and then compare your screen with **Figure 2**.

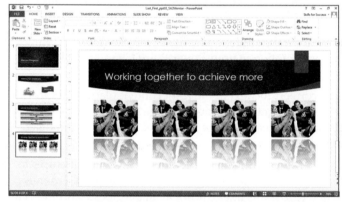

Yuri Arcurs / Fotolia

Figure 2

9. On the **Notes and Handouts** pages, include the date, a page number, and a footer with the text Last_First_ppt03_SA2Mentor **Save** and **Close**, and then submit as directed by your instructor.

 DONE! You have completed Skills Assessment 2

Visual Skills Check

To complete this presentation, you will need the following file:

- ppt03_VSPark

You will save your presentation as:

- Last_First_ppt03_VSPark

Start PowerPoint 2013, and then from your student files, open **ppt03_VSPark**. Format and edit the slide as shown in **Figure 1**. **Save** the file as Last_First_ptp03_VSPark in your **PowerPoint Chapter 3** folder.

The list in the left content placeholder has been converted to SmartArt. An additional shape and bullet have been added, with the text shown. The SmartArt's color has been changed to **Colorful Range – Accent Colors 4 to 5**, and the **Polished 3-D** SmartArt style has been applied. The image in the right content placeholder was found in Office.com Clip Art, searching with the term Walking Path A **Circle Bevel Picture Effect** has been applied to the image. The **From Center** gradient fill was added to the title placeholder, the font size was changed to **60** points, and the text was centered. On the **Notes and Handouts** pages, include the date, a page number, and a footer with the text Last_First_ppt03_VSPark **Save** and **Close**, then submit as directed by your instructor.

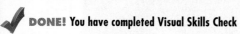 **DONE!** You have completed Visual Skills Check

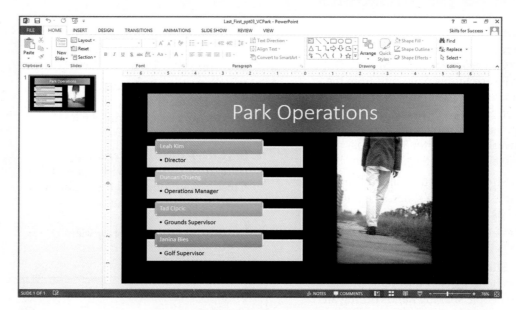

Figure 1

My Skills

To complete this presentation, you will need the following files:

- ppt03_MYCareerSearch
- ppt03_MYCareerAdvice

You will save your presentation as:

- Last_First_ppt03_MYCareerSearch

1. **Start** PowerPoint 2013, and then from your student files, open **ppt03_ MYCareerSearch**. Select **Slide 2**. Display the **Reuse Slides** pane, and from the student data file **ppt03_MSCareerAdvice**. Insert **Slide 1 —Making it to the top. Save** the presentation in your **PowerPoint Chapter 3** folder as Last_First_ppt03_MYCareerSearch

2. On **Slide 1**, insert the **Folded Corner** basic shape. Change the shape's height to 1.5" and its width to 1.5" Move the shape to the upper right corner of the slide and then insert the text Build a strong network!

3. On **Slide 2**, in the right content placeholder, insert the online picture of two people shaking hands during an interview (use the search term interview). If this image is not available, locate and insert a similar image. Resize the image to a height of **3.5"**.

4. On **Slide 2**, in the left content placeholder, convert the text to a **Horizontal Bullet List** SmartArt graphic, and then apply the **Polished** 3-D SmartArt style.

5. On **Slide 3**, select the left content placeholder, apply a **Gradient** with a **Dark Variation From Center** shape fill, and then apply the **Preset 4** shape effect. For the placeholder text, increase the font size to **24** and apply **Bold**.

6. On **Slide 3**, crop the image to the **Round Diagonal Corner Rectangle** shape, and then apply the **Preset 4** picture effect.

7. On the **Notes and Handouts** pages, include the date, a page number, and a footer with the text Last_First_ppt03_MYCareerSearch

8. **Save** the presentation, and then compare your screen with **Figure 1**. **Close** PowerPoint, and then submit as directed by your instructor.

DONE! You have completed My Skills

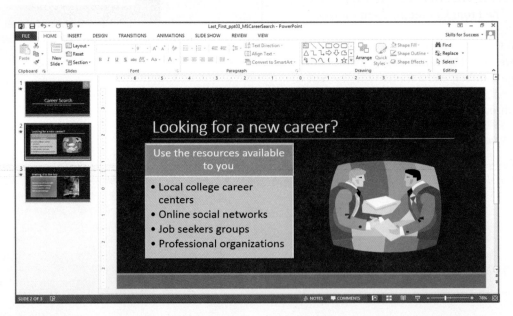

Figure 1

Skills Challenge 1

To complete this presentation, you will need the following file:

- ppt03_SC1Fire

You will save your presentation as:

- Last_First_ppt03_SC1Fire

Locate and open the presentation ppt03_SC1Fire. Save the presentation in your chapter folder as Last_First_ppt03_SC1Fire Rachel Brewer, the city's Fire Marshall, will use these slides as she presents at a volunteer recognition event. Using the skills you practiced in this chapter, add a gradient fill to the subtitle placeholder on Slide 1, and then adjust the font style, size, and color so that the subtitle will be easy for the audience to read. On Slide 2, convert the text in the left content placeholder into SmartArt. Choose a layout that effectively

conveys the slide's message, applying styles and colors as needed. Select the video and then correct the color by increasing the brightness and contrast. Apply a video style.

On the Notes and Handouts pages, include the date, a page number, and a footer with the text Last_First_ppt03_SC1Fire Save, Close, and then submit as directed by your instructor.

 DONE! You have completed Skills Challenge 1

Skills Challenge 2

To complete this presentation, you will need the following files:

- ppt03_SC2EAP
- ppt03_SC2EAPVideo

You will save your presentation as:

- Last_First_ppt03_SC2EAP

Locate and open the presentation ppt03_SC2EAP, and save it in your chapter folder as Last_First_ppt03_SC2EAP Add a shape to Slide 1 with the text EAP Size the shape appropriately, so that it draws attention and is easily readable. Add an effect and a gradient to the shape and position it in an appropriate place on the slide. Search online for an image that complements the slide design and the content of the presentation and insert it on Slide 2 in the right content placeholder. Add a border that matches the color of the image you added, adjust the weight of the border, and add an effect to the picture. Convert the text in the left content placeholder to SmartArt, using a style that emphasizes the information in the placeholder. Adjust the size of the SmartArt as needed. Insert a new Slide 3 with the Title and Content layout. In the

title placeholder, type Your EAP – Here to help In the content placeholder, insert the video from your student file named ppt03_SC2_EAPVideo. Add a complementary style to the video and size it to better fill the space on the slide.

Save the presentation. On the Notes and Handouts pages, include the date, a page number, and a footer with the text Last_First_ppt03_ESC2AP and then check spelling in the presentation. Save, Close, and then submit as directed by your instructor.

 DONE! You have completed Skills Challenge 2

CHAPTER 4

Present Data Using Tables, Charts, and Animation

- ▶ Tables and charts are used to present information in a graphic format that helps the audience to better understand the data being presented.
- ▶ Presenters can use charts to display numeric data, particularly when making comparisons between data.
- ▶ Styles can be used to format the chart or table and corresponding data in a manner that matches and complements the rest of the presentation.

- ▶ Animation effects are used to draw attention to important slide elements.
- ▶ Timing can be used to precisely control the pace of a slide show and the order in which each element of the presentation appears.

© Sergey Nivens

Aspen Falls City Hall

In this chapter, you will enrich a presentation regarding business growth in Aspen Falls, California. This presentation will be used to inform the audience about industries with high-growth potential and to encourage continued expansion of businesses. Statistical data about these issues will be easier to understand when presented in tables and charts.

In your career, you may need to present numerical or comparative information to an audience. You can use a table or chart to present this information. Tables and charts will help your audience to understand growth trends, make comparisons, or understand the composition of a whole.

Animations can help to draw your audience's attention to the screen. During a slide show you can use annotation to draw on a slide.

When adding tables, charts, animations, and annotations to your presentation, keep in mind the axiom that "less is more." Summarize data as much as possible, and present only the most important information. If needed, detailed studies can be presented to your audience in the form of handouts.

In this project, you will add a table and charts to a presentation. You will then add and modify animations. Finally, you will work with the presentation in Slide Show view, moving through the presentation and creating an annotation on a slide.

Time to complete all 10 skills – 60 to 75 minutes

Student data file needed for this chapter:

ppt04_Growth

You will save your file as:

Last_First_ppt04_Growth

Outcome

Using the skills in this chapter, you will be able to work with PowerPoint presentations like this:

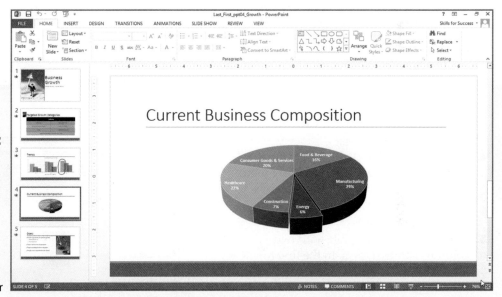

SKILLS

MyITLab®
Skills 1-10 Training

At the end of this chapter you will be able to:

Skill 1 Insert Tables
Skill 2 Modify Table Layouts
Skill 3 Apply Table Styles
Skill 4 Insert Column Charts
Skill 5 Edit and Format Charts
Skill 6 Insert Pie Charts
Skill 7 Apply Animation Effects and Change Duration
Skill 8 Modify Animation Timings and Use Animation Painter
Skill 9 Delay or Remove Animation
Skill 10 Navigate Slide Shows

MORE SKILLS

Skill 11 Save Presentations to CDs
Skill 12 Insert Hyperlinks in Presentations
Skill 13 Create Photo Albums
Skill 14 Add Images to Tables

▶ In a presentation, a **table** is used to organize and present information in columns and rows.

▶ In tables, text is typed into a **cell**—the intersection of a column and row.

1. Start **PowerPoint 2013**. On the **Start screen**, click **Open Other Presentations**. On the **Open** screen, click **Computer**, and then click **Browse**. In the **Open** dialog box, navigate to the student data files for this chapter. Select **ppt04_Growth**, and then click the **Open** button. On the **File tab**, click **Save As**. Navigate to the location where you are saving your files, create a folder named PowerPoint Chapter 4 and then using your own name, save the presentation as Last_First_ppt04_Growth

2. Move to **Slide 2**, and in the title placeholder, type Targeted Growth Categories

3. In the content placeholder, click the **Insert Table** button 🗊.

4. In the **Insert Table** dialog box, in the **Number of columns** box, type 2 and then press Tab. In the **Number of rows** box, if necessary, type 2 and then compare your screen with **Figure 1**.

5. Click **OK** to create a table with two columns and two rows. In the first row, in the first cell, type Technology and then press Tab.

   If your insertion point is in the first cell, pressing Tab moves the insertion point to the next cell in the same row. At the end of a row, pressing Tab moves your insertion point to the first cell in next row. Alternately, you can use the arrow keys on your keyboard, or use your mouse to move to another cell.

6. Type Home Health Care and then compare your screen with **Figure 2**.

■ **Continue to the next page to complete the skill**

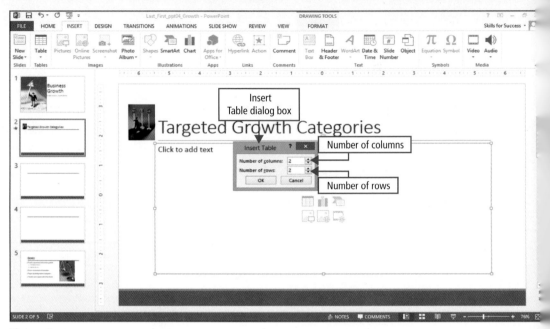

Figure 1

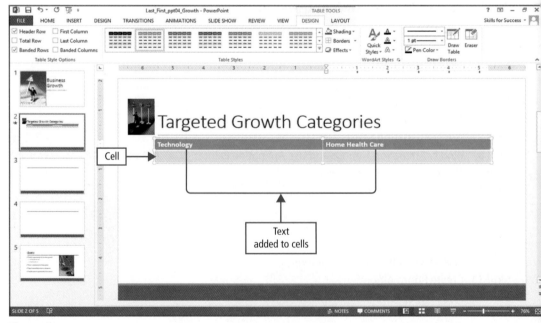

Figure 2

Figure 3

7. Press `Tab` to move the insertion point to the first cell in the second row. With the insertion point positioned in the first cell of the second row, type Fitness Products and Services

8. Press `Tab`. Type Green Construction and then press `Tab` to insert a new blank row. Compare your table with **Figure 3**.

  When the insertion point is positioned in the last cell of a table, pressing `Tab` inserts a new blank row at the bottom of the table. Alternately, on the Table Tools Layout tab, in the Rows & Columns group, you can click the Insert Below button to add a new row below the current row.

9. In the first cell of the third row, type Energy and then press `Tab`. Type Temporary Employment and then compare your screen with **Figure 4**.

10. **Save** 🖫 the presentation.

■ **You have completed Skill 1 of 10**

Figure 4

PPT 4-2 VIDEO

▶ You can modify the layout of a table by inserting or deleting rows and columns and by changing the height and width of rows and columns.

▶ The height and width of the entire table can also be modified.

1. In the first row of the table, click in any cell. On the **Layout tab**, in the **Rows & Columns group**, click the **Insert Above** button.

    A new first row is inserted.

2. Type Industry and then compare your screen with **Figure 1**.

3. Click so that your insertion point appears anywhere in the last row of the table, and then on the **Layout tab**, in the **Rows & Columns group**, click **Insert Below**.

4. In the last row of the table, in the first cell, type Aspen Falls Chamber of Commerce Study, 2013 Compare your screen with **Figure 2**.

5. At the center of the lower border surrounding the table, point to the center sizing handle to display the pointer ⬍.

6. With the pointer ⬍, drag down until the lower edge of the table extends to the **2.5 inch** mark below zero on the vertical ruler, and then release the mouse button to resize the table.

■ **Continue to the next page to complete the skill** ▶

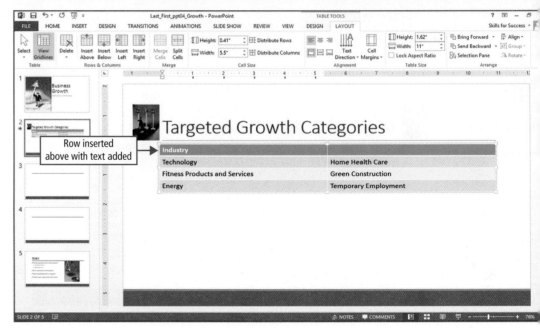

Figure 1

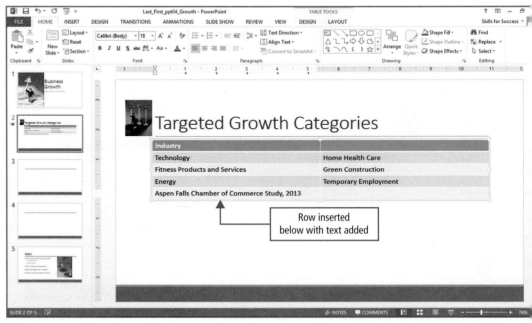

Figure 2

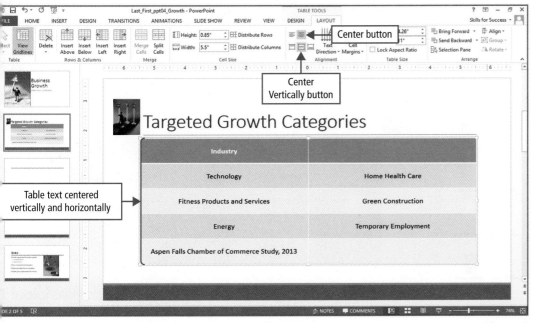

Figure 3

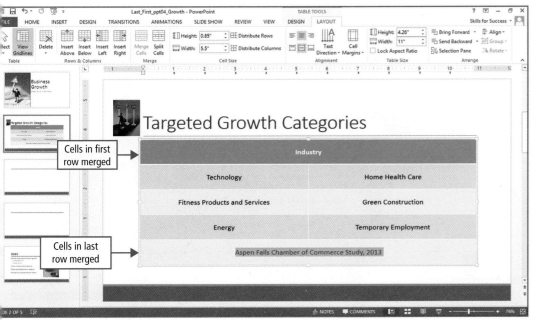

Figure 4

7. With the table still selected, on the **Layout tab**, in the **Alignment group**, click the **Center** button ▤.

8. In the **Alignment group**, click the **Center Vertically** button ▤. Compare your screen with **Figure 3**.

   All of the text in the table is centered horizontally and vertically within the cells.

9. Position the pointer to the left of the first row in the table to display the **Select Row** pointer ➡. Click to select the entire first row. On the **Layout tab**, in the **Merge group**, click **Merge Cells**. Repeat this process to merge the cells in the last row of the table, and then compare your screen with **Figure 4**.

   When **merged**, selected cells are combined into a single cell. Alternately, you can select a row of cells by clicking and dragging to select with your mouse. Only one row in a table may be merged at a time. When merging only the top, leftmost cell should contain data; otherwise the data in the remaining cells will be lost.

10. Save ▤ the presentation.

■ **You have completed Skill 2 of 10**

▶ A **table style** includes borders and fill colors that are applied to the entire table in a manner consistent with the presentation theme.

▶ The styles and color categories available vary depending on the theme.

1. On **Slide 2**, click in any cell in the table. On the **Table Tools Design tab**, in the **Table Styles group**, click the **More** button ⏷. In the **Table Styles gallery**, point to several styles and watch as Live Preview displays the table with the selected style. Scroll all the way to the bottom of the gallery to view all of the styles.

2. Under **Best Match for Document**, click the fifth style in the first row—**Themed Style 1 - Accent 4**—and compare your screen with **Figure 1**.

3. Click anywhere in the first row of the table. On the **Table Tools Design tab**, in the **Table Styles group**, click the **Shading arrow** 🖌. Click **Eyedropper**. In the upper portion of the slide, in the image, with the **Eyedropper**, click in the dark area beneath one of the signs and the figure of a man in the area shown in **Figure 2**.

With the color-matching *eyedropper*, you can select color from any object or image on your slide and apply the color to another area of your slide, creating a cohesive color scheme.

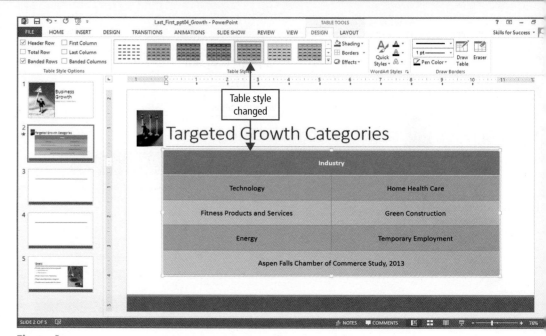

Figure 1

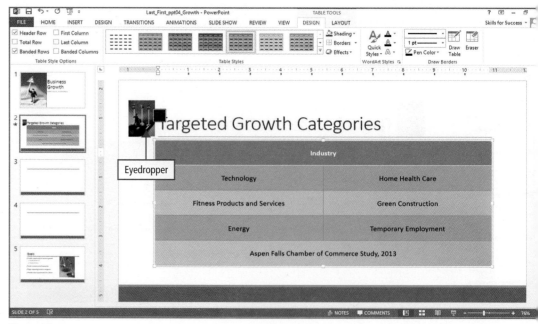

Figure 2

■ Continue to the next page to complete the skill ▷

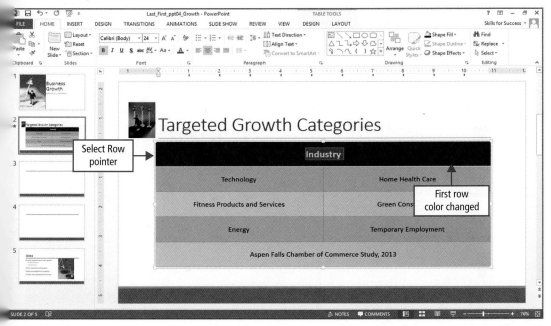

Figure 3

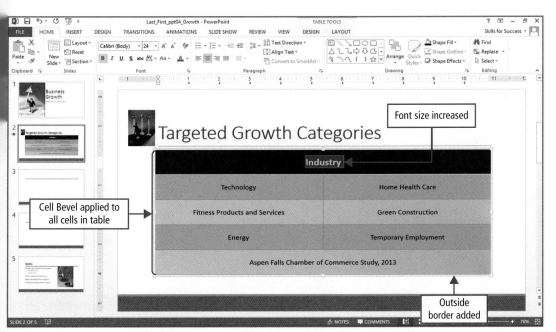

Figure 4

4. Move the pointer to the left of the first row in the table to display the **Select Row** pointer →.

5. With the **Select Row** pointer → pointing to the first row in the table, click to select the entire row and to display the **Mini toolbar**. On the **Mini toolbar**, change the **Font Size** 20 to **24**. Compare your screen with **Figure 3**.

6. Click a border of the table to select the entire table. On the **Table Tools Design tab**, in the **Table Styles group**, click the **Effects** button. Point to **Cell Bevel**, and then point to several bevels to view the effect on the table.

7. Under **Bevel**, click the second thumbnail in the first row—**Relaxed Inset**—to apply the effect to the entire table

8. With the table still selected, on the **Table Tools Design tab**, in the **Table Styles group**, click the **Borders arrow**, and then click **Outside Borders**. Compare your screen with **Figure 4**.

9. **Save** the presentation.

■ **You have completed Skill 3 of 10**

▶ A ***chart*** is a graphic representation of numeric data.

▶ A ***column chart*** is useful for illustrating comparisons among related categories.

▶ When creating a chart, you may need to delete unwanted data from the worksheet so that it does not display in the chart.

1. Display **Slide 3** in Normal view. In the title placeholder, type Trends

2. In the content placeholder, click the **Insert Chart** button. In the left pane of the **Insert Chart** dialog box, click several of the chart types to view the chart gallery and a preview of the selected chart. Then, click **Column**, as shown in **Figure 1**.

3. With the first chart—**Clustered Column**—selected, click **OK**. Compare your screen with **Figure 2**.

> The Chart in Microsoft PowerPoint window contains sample data. The column headings—*Series 1, Series 2,* and *Series 3*—display in the chart ***legend***, which identifies the patterns or colors that are assigned to the data in the chart. The row headings—*Category 1, Category 2, Category 3,* and *Category 4*—display along the bottom of the chart as ***category labels***—labels that identify the categories of data in a chart.

4. In the **Chart in Microsoft PowerPoint** window, click cell **B1**, which contains the text *Series 1.* Type Technology and press Tab to move to the next cell. In cell C1, type Healthcare. Press Tab, and then in cell D1, type Staffing Press Enter.

> On the slide, notice that the chart legend is updated to reflect the change.

■ **Continue to the next page to complete the skill**

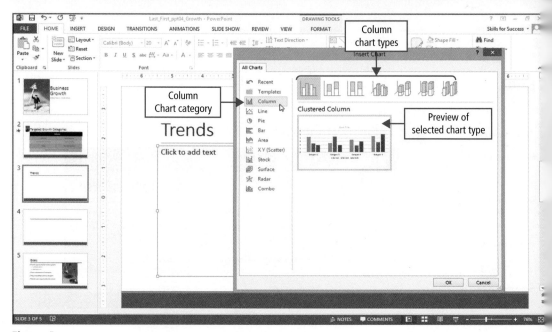

Figure 1

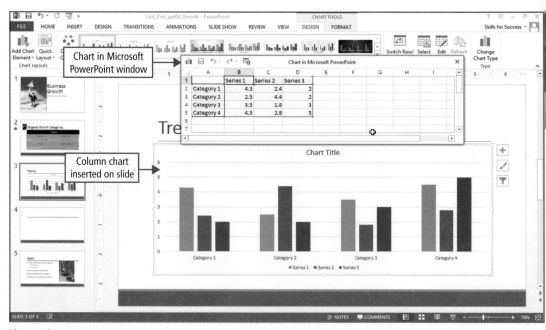

Figure 2

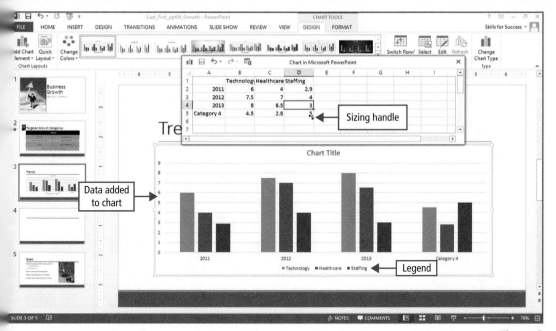

Figure 3

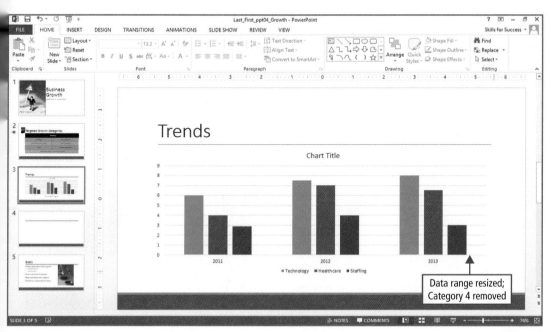

Figure 4

5. In cell **A2**, type 2011 Press ⌷Enter⌷, and type 2012 Press ⌷Enter⌷, and type 2013

6. Click cell **B2**, type 6 Press ⌷Enter⌷ to move to cell **B3**, and type 7.5 Press ⌷Enter⌷, and type 8 Click cell **C2**, and type 4 Press ⌷Enter⌷, and type 7 Press ⌷Enter⌷, and type 6.5 Click cell **D2**, and type 2.9 Press ⌷Enter⌷, and type 4 Press ⌷Enter⌷, and type 3

7. Still in the Chart in Microsoft PowerPoint window, point to the lower right corner of cell **D5** to display the pointer ↖ as shown in **Figure 3**.

8. With the pointer ↖, drag straight up so that only the range A1:D4 is selected. Release the mouse button. Select the data in cells A5:D5, and then press ⌷Delete⌷. Close the Chart in Microsoft PowerPoint window, and compare your screen with **Figure 4**.

   Alternately, in the Chart in Microsoft PowerPoint window, you can right-click the row 5 heading—the number 5 which appears on the left side of the worksheet—and then, on the shortcut menu, click Delete to remove the entire row and resize the data range.

9. Save 🖫 the presentation.

■ **You have completed Skill 4 of 10**

▶ After a chart is created, you can edit the data values using the Chart in Microsoft PowerPoint window. Changes made immediately display in the PowerPoint chart.

▶ Charts are formatted by applying predefined styles and by modifying chart elements.

1. On **Slide 3**, if necessary, click the chart so that it is selected. On the **Chart Tools Design tab**, in the **Data group**, click **Edit Data** to display the **Chart in Microsoft PowerPoint** window.

> Each of the cells containing the data that you entered are ***data points***—individual data plotted in a chart. Each data point is represented in the chart by a ***data marker***—a column, bar, or other symbol that represents a single data point. Related data points form a ***data series*** and are assigned a unique color or pattern represented in the chart legend. Here there is a data series for the past three years.

2. In the **Chart in Microsoft PowerPoint** window, click cell **D4**, which contains the value 3. Type 5 and then press Enter . Compare your screen with **Figure 1**.

> In the chart, the column is increased to reflect the change to the data.

3. In the **Chart in Microsoft PowerPoint** window, click cell **C1**, which contains the text *Healthcare*. Type Health and then watch the chart legend as you press Enter . Compare your screen with **Figure 2**.

4. In the **Chart in Microsoft PowerPoint** window, click the **Close** button ✕ .

■ **Continue to the next page to complete the skill**

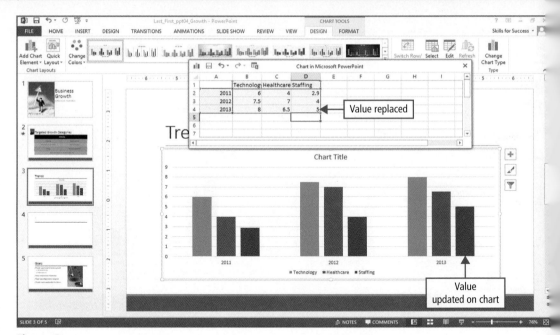

Figure 1

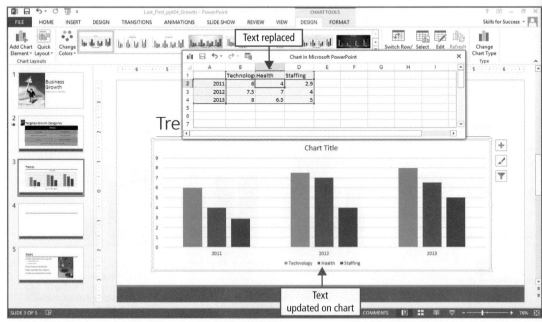

Figure 2

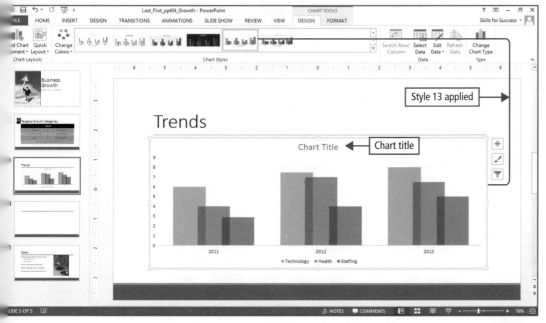

Figure 3

5. With the chart still selected, on the **Chart Tools Design tab**, in the **Chart Styles group**, click the **More** button ⊽ to display the **Chart Styles gallery**.

> A *chart style* is a pre-built set of effects, colors, and backgrounds designed to work with the presentation theme. For example, you can have flat or beveled columns, colors that are solid or transparent, and backgrounds that are dark or light.

6. The thumbnails in the **Chart Styles gallery** are numbered sequentially. Locate and click **Style 13**. Compare your slide with **Figure 3**.

7. Click the **Chart Title** placeholder, and then type Growth Rate in Percent Compare your screen with **Figure 4**.

8. **Save** 🖫 the presentation.

■ **You have completed Skill 5 of 10**

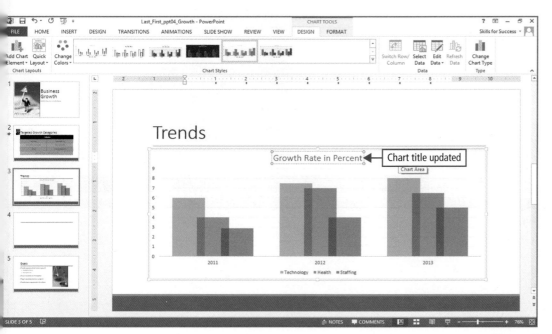

Figure 4

▶ A *pie chart* is used to illustrate percentages or proportions and includes only one data series.

1. Display **Slide 4**. In the title placeholder, type Current Business Composition

2. In the content placeholder, click the **Insert Chart** button. In the left pane of the **Insert Chart** dialog box, click **Pie**. Toward the top of the dialog box, click the second chart—**3-D Pie**—and then click **OK**.

3. In the displayed **Chart in Microsoft PowerPoint** window, in cell B1 type Percentage, and then in cells A2:B7 enter the remaining data as shown in **Figure 1**, pressing Enter after each entry.

    As you press Enter, the data range expands to include the new data.

4. **Close** the **Chart in Microsoft PowerPoint** window, and then compare your screen with **Figure 2**.

	Percentage
Food & Beverage	16
Manufacturing	29
Energy	6
Construction	7
Healthcare	22
Consumer Goods & Services	20

Figure 1

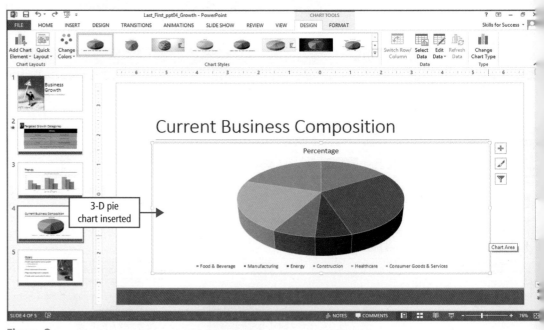

Figure 2

■ Continue to the next page to complete the skill ▶

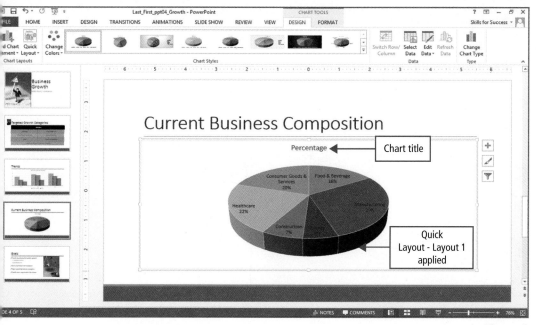

Figure 3

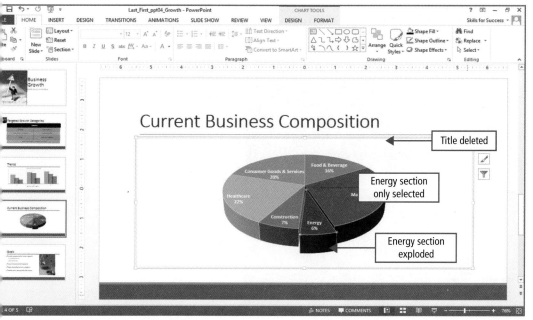

Figure 4

5. With the chart still selected, on the **Chart Tools Design tab**, in the **Chart Layouts group**, click the **Quick Layout** button and then click the first layout—**Layout 1**. Compare your screen with **Figure 3**.

> Recall that a pie chart includes one data series. Thus, the legend is usually omitted, and *data labels*—text that identifies data markers—are positioned on or outside of the pie slices. Layout 1 displays a title and the category names and the percentage that each slice represents of the total.

6. Click a border of the chart title, and then press Delete so that the title is removed.

> When the title is deleted, the chart is resized to fill the space.

7. With the chart still selected, on the **Home tab**, in the **Font group**, click the **Font Color arrow** A. In the first row, click the first color—**White, Background 1**—and then click **Bold** B.

> When the chart is selected, formatting changes can be made to the text using the Home tab and Font group.

8. To emphasize the growth in the *Energy* category, click any section of the pie, and then click the *Energy* section, so that just the *Energy* section is selected. Be sure that you are not selecting the label placeholder. Click, hold, and drag the Energy section straight down slightly to explode the section. Compare your screen with **Figure 4**.

> To *explode* a section of the pie, select and then drag it out to add emphasis.

9. **Save** ⊟ the presentation.

■ **You have completed Skill 6 of 10**

▶ *Animation* adds a special visual effect to an image, chart, or text on a slide.

▶ An *Entrance effect* is an animation that appears as an object or text is moved onto the screen. An *Emphasis effect* is an animation that emphasizes an object or text that is already displayed. An *Exit effect* is an animation that appears as an object or text is moved off the screen.

▶ You can change the duration of an animation effect by making it longer or shorter.

1. Display **Slide 1** in Normal view. On the **Transitions tab**, in the **Transition to This Slide group**, click the **More** button ⟱, and then click **Peel Off**. Click the **Effect Options** button, and then click Right.

2. In the **Timing group**, in the **Duration** box, type .75 and press Enter to speed up the animation effect. In the **Timing group**, click the **Apply To All** button.

   You can set the duration of a transition or animation by typing a value in the Duration box, or you can use the up and down spin arrows to increase and decrease the duration in increments.

3. On **Slide 1**, click to select the image on the left side of the slide. On the **Animations tab**, in the **Animation group**, click the **More** button ⟱ to display the **Animation gallery**. If necessary, scroll through the Animation gallery to view the types of animation effects. Compare your screen with **Figure 1**.

4. Under **Entrance**, click **Fly In** to apply the effect. Compare your screen with **Figure 2**.

   The number 1 displays to the left of the image, indicating that the image is the first object in the slide animation sequence and it will appear on the first mouse click during the slide show. The number will not display during the slide show.

■ **Continue to the next page to complete the skill**

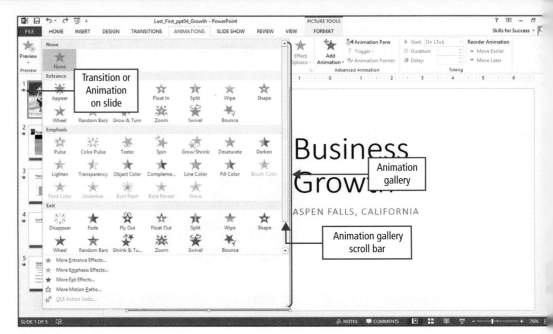

Figure 1

Figure 2

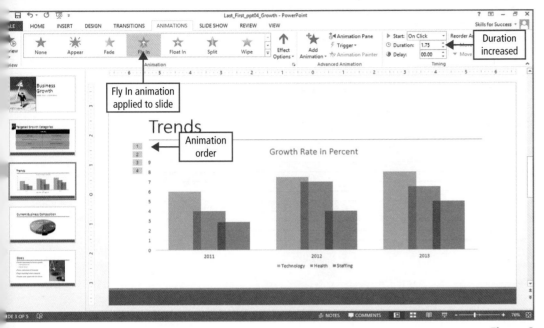

Figure 3

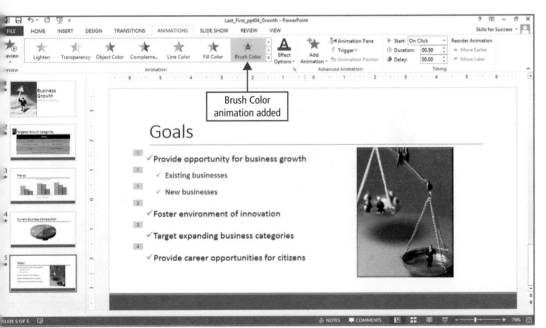

Figure 4

5. Move to **Slide 3**. Click the upper right corner of the chart placeholder so that the entire chart, and no individual element of the chart, is selected. On the **Animations tab**, in the **Animation group**, click **Fly In**.

6. On the **Animations tab**, in the **Animation group**, click the **Effect Options** button. Under **Sequence**, click **By Series**. Preview the effect as it appears automatically on the slide. In the **Duration** box, type 1.75 press Enter and then compare your screen with **Figure 3**.

   The numbers 1, 2, 3, and 4 display to the left of the content placeholder, indicating the order in which the animation will display. The number 1 indicates the animation of the chart area or background. Numbers 2, 3, and 4 indicate the animation of the data series. Providing this animation in a slower duration helps the viewer to see the overall increase in growth.

7. Move to **Slide 5**. Click in the left content placeholder, and then click a border of the placeholder to select it. On the **Animations tab**, in the **Animation group**, click the **More** button ▾. Under **Emphasis**, click **Brush Color**. Preview the effect as it appears automatically on the screen, and then compare your screen with **Figure 4**.

8. Still on **Slide 5**, select the image in the right content placeholder. In the **Animation group**, click the **More** button ▾. Under **Exit**, click **Wheel**.

9. Press F5 to view the show from the beginning, using your mouse button to click through the animations, noticing all of the animations—the ones you added and the one that was already in the presentation on Slide 2. When you reach the black slide, click one more time to return to Normal view.

10. **Save** 🖫 the presentation.

■ **You have completed Skill 7 of 10**

▶ Timing options control when animated items display in the animation sequence.

▶ *Animation Painter* is a tool used to copy animation settings from one object to another.

1. Display **Slide 1**, and then select the image. Recall that the number 1 displayed to the left of the image indicates that the image is first in the slide animation sequence.

2. On the **Animations tab**, in the **Timing group**, click the **Start** arrow to display three options—*On Click, With Previous,* and *After Previous.* Compare your screen with **Figure 1**.

> **On Click** begins the animation sequence when the mouse button is clicked or the [SpaceBar] is pressed. **With Previous** begins the animation sequence at the same time as any animation preceding it or, if it is the first animation, with the slide transition. **After Previous** begins the animation sequence immediately after the completion of the previous animation.

3. Click **After Previous**.

> The number 1 is changed to 0, indicating that the animation will begin immediately after the slide transition; the presenter need not click the mouse button or press [SpaceBar] to display the image.

4. With the image selected, on the **Animations tab**, in the **Advanced Animation group**, click the **Animation Painter** button. Move to **Slide 2**, and point to the table to display the **Animation Painter** pointer as shown in **Figure 2**.

■ **Continue to the next page to complete the skill**

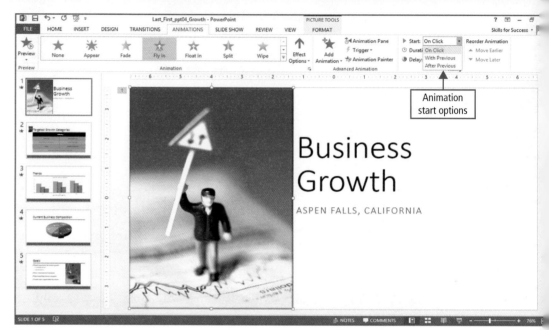

Figure 1

Figure 2

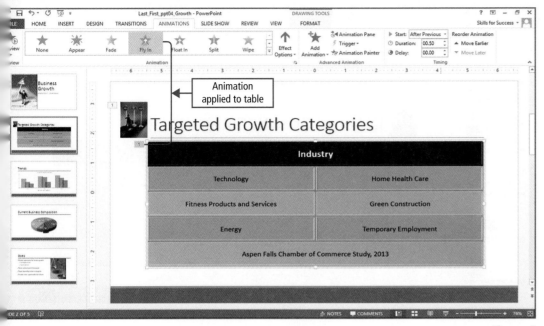

Figure 3

Figure 4

5. With the Animation Painter pointer, click the table to apply the same animation to it. Compare your screen with **Figure 3**.

> The table displays a number 1, indicating that the animation will begin with the animation applied to the image in the upper left corner of the slide. This animation was included in the original file.

6. Move to **Slide 5**. Click the image in the right content placeholder to select it. Notice that this image is currently the fifth animation—the Exit effect will be applied on the presenter's fifth mouse click.

7. With the image selected, on the **Animations tab**, in the **Timing group**, click the **Start arrow**. Click **With Previous**, and then compare your screen with **Figure 4**.

> The image animation number changes to 4, indicating that this animation will appear with the animation of the fourth bullet point. Alternately, in the timing group, you can use the Move Earlier and Move Later buttons to change the animation order of selected objects.

8. On your keyboard, press [F5] to view the slide show. Click through the presentation in Slide Show view to view the entire presentation.

9. Save 🖫 the presentation.

■ **You have completed Skill 8 of 10**

▶ When an animation effect interferes with the flow of the presentation, you can remove the effect.

▶ Animation can be *delayed* so that it starts after a predetermined amount of time.

1. Display **Slide 2** in Normal view. Select the image in the upper left corner of the slide. Notice that this image contains animation.

2. With the image selected, on the **Animations tab**, in the **Animation group**, click the **More** button ▼. At the top of the gallery, under **None**, click the first thumbnail—**None**—to remove the animation from the image. Compare your screen with **Figure 1**.

> It is not necessary to animate every object on every slide. In this slide, the slide transition and table animation draw sufficient attention to the table. The animation of the image detracted from the emphasis on the table.

3. Move to **Slide 3**, and click to select the chart. On the **Animations tab**, in the **Preview group**, click **Preview**.

> The preview shows the sequence automatically, without the need to click. When in Slide Show view, each of the animations would appear on a mouse click, including the chart area.

4. To the left of the chart, click the **1**, which indicates the first mouse click. With the **1** selected, on the **Animations tab**, in the **Animation group**, click the More button ▼, and then click **None**. On the **Animations tab**, in the **Preview group**, click **Preview** to view the modified animation. Compare your screen with **Figure 2**.

■ **Continue to the next page to complete the skill**

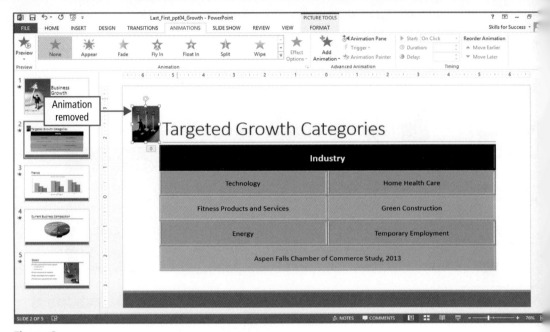

Figure 1

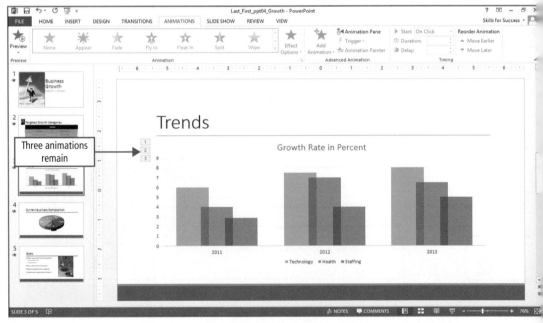

Figure 2

Figure 3

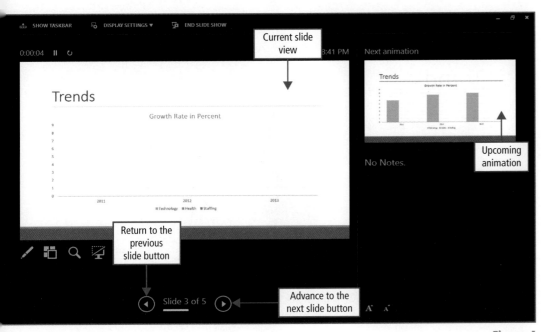

Figure 4

The animation was removed from the background of the chart, so that it appears automatically, rather than requiring a click.

5. Move to **Slide 5**. Select the image in the right content placeholder. On the **Animations tab**, in the **Timing group**, in the **Delay** box, type 3.5 Press Enter, and then compare your screen with **Figure 3**.

   The image will be animated on Exit effect 3.5 seconds after the last mouse click.

6. Press F5 to start the slide show from the beginning. While Slide 1 is displayed, right-click, and then click **Show Presenter View**. Click the **Advance to next slide arrow** to move through the presentation, until you reach **Slide 3**. Compare your screen with **Figure 4**.

   The upcoming animations—not just the next slide—are shown on the preview on the right side of the presenter view window.

7. Finish viewing the slide show, and return to Normal view.

8. Save 🖫 the presentation.

■ **You have completed Skill 9 of 10**

▶ During a slide show, when you point to the lower left corner of the slide, a ***navigation toolbar*** displays in the lower left corner of the slide. You can use the navigation toolbar to go to any slide while the slide show is running. You can use this toolbar, Presenter View, or simply click your mouse, spacebar, or Enter key to move through a presentation in Slide Show view.

1. On the **Slide Show tab**, in the **Start Slide Show group**, click the **From Beginning** button. Click the mouse button to display **Slide 2**.

2. Point to the lower left corner of the slide, and notice that left- and right-pointing arrows display, as shown in **Figure 1**.

    The left-pointing arrow—the Return to the previous slide button ⊙—is a navigation tool that, when clicked, displays the previous slide or animation. The right-pointing arrow—the Advance to the next slide button ⊙—displays the next slide or animation.

3. In the lower left corner of the slide, in the navigation toolbar, notice that a pen ⊘ displays.

    The pen can be used to ***annotate***—write on the slide—while the slide show is running.

4. Move the pointer to the right, and notice that a **See all slides** button ⊞ displays. Click this button, and then click the **Slide 3** preview to move to that slide. Click one time over the slide to display the first animation, the *Technology* category.

5. Click the **Pen** button ⊘, and then click **Pen**. With the pen pointer, circle the *2013 Technology* column as shown in **Figure 2**.

    Ink annotations can be kept or discarded at the end of a presentation.

■ **Continue to the next page to complete the skill** ▶

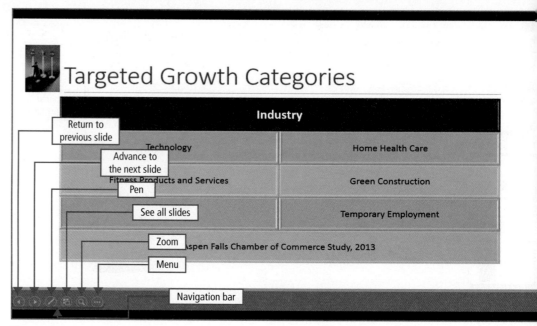

Figure 1

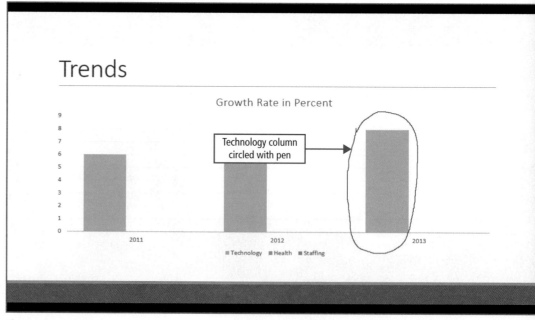

Figure 2

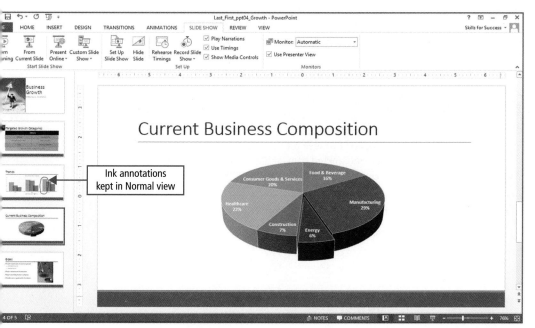

Figure 3

Figure 4

6. In the navigation toolbar, click the **Advance to the next slide** button three times to go through the animations on Slide 3 and display Slide 4 in Slide Show view.

7. With Slide 4 displayed, click the **Pen** button, and then click **Laser Pointer**. Point to the *Energy* section of the pie chart, and compare your screen to **Figure 3**.

8. Press Esc to turn the laser pointer off.

9. On your keyboard, press B.

   The B key is a toggle key that displays a black screen. During a slide show, you can pause a presentation so that a discussion can be held without the distraction of the presentation visuals. Rather than turning off the projection system or ending the slide show, you can display the slide as a black screen and then redisplay the same slide when you are ready to resume the presentation. Alternately, the W key will display a white screen.

10. On your keyboard, press B to redisplay **Slide 4**. Press Esc to end the slide show.

11. When prompted, click to **Keep** your ink annotations. Compare your screen with **Figure 4**.

12. Insert a **Header & Footer** on the **Notes and Handouts**. Include the **Page number** and a **Footer** with the text Last_First_ ppt04_Growth and **Apply to All** pages.

13. **Save** 🖫 the presentation. Submit the file as directed by your instructor. **Close** PowerPoint.

✔ **DONE! You have completed Skill 10 of 10, and your presentation is complete!**

The following More Skills are located at **www.pearsonhighered.com/skills**

More Skills ⑪ Save Presentations to CDs

You can package your presentation and save it to a CD so that it can be viewed on almost any computer. You can save your presentation directly to a CD, or, as you will do in this project, you can save it to a folder, which can be later saved to a CD or other device.

In More Skills 11, you will prepare a presentation to be saved on and viewed from a CD.

To begin, open your web browser, navigate to www.pearsonhighered.com/skills, locate the name of your textbook, and then follow the instructions on the website.

More Skills ⑫ Insert Hyperlinks in Presentations

Hyperlinks include text, buttons, and images that, when clicked during a slide show, activate another slide or a website.

In More Skills 12, you will open a presentation and insert a hyperlink to a website.

To begin, open your web browser, navigate to www.pearsonhighered.com/skills, locate the name of your textbook, and then follow the instructions on the website.

More Skills ⑬ Create Photo Albums

You can use PowerPoint 2013 to create a photo album presentation that is composed primarily of pictures.

In More Skills 13, you will create a photo album with several pictures.

To begin, open your web browser, navigate to www.pearsonhighered.com/skills, locate the name of your textbook, and then follow the instructions on the website.

More Skills ⑭ Add Images to Tables

You can add images to tables to add visual interest and provide more information for your audience.

In More Skills 14, you will add images to an existing table.

To begin, open your web browser, navigate to www.pearsonhighered.com/skills, locate the name of your textbook, and then follow the instructions on the website.

Please note that there are no additional projects to accompany the More Skills Projects, and they are not covered in the End-of-Chapter projects.

he following table summarizes the **SKILLS AND PROCEDURES** covered in this chapter.

Skills Number	Task	Step	Icon	Keyboard Shortcut
1	Insert table	Placeholder → Insert table button	⊞	
2	Add a Table Style	Table Tools Design tab → Table Styles group → More button → Table Styles gallery		
2	Center text in a table horizontally	Select table → Layout tab → Alignment tab → Center button	≡	Ctrl + E
2	Center text in a table vertically	Select table → Layout tab → Alignment tab → Center Vertically button	▤	
4	Insert chart	Placeholder → Insert chart button	▮▮	
4	Add a Chart Style	Chart Tools Design tab→ Chart Styles group→ More button → Chart Styles gallery		
5	Edit an existing chart	Chart Tools Design tab → Data group → Edit Data → Chart in Microsoft PowerPoint window → Edit data		
7	Add slide transition	Transitions tab → Transition to This Slide group→ Transition → Effect Options button→ Select Effect option → Timing group → Apply To All		
7	Add animation	Select object → Animations tab → Animation group → More button → Animation gallery		
8	Use Animation Painter	Select object with animation → Animations tab→ Advanced Animation group → Animation Painter button → Select object to be animated	▨I	
9	Remove animation	Select object → Animations tab → Animation group → More button → Animation gallery → None		
10	Next Slide - Slide Show	Left mouse click, Spacebar, Enter, or Next Slide arrow		
10	Previous Slide - Slide Show	Previous Slide arrow		
10	Pen - Slide Show	Navigation toolbar → Pen → Pen		
10	Laser Pointer - Slide Show	Navigation toolbar → Pen → Laser Pointer		Ctrl + Mouse Click and hold
10	Black Slide - Slide Show	End of slide show, or press B		B
10	White Slide - Slide Show	Press W while in Slide Show view		W

Key Terms

Online Help Skills

1. With PowerPoint open, in the upper right corner of the screen, click the Microsoft PowerPoint Help button 🔵, or press F1.

2. In the **PowerPoint Help** window, use the Search box to locate and open the article *Add a trend or average line to a chart*. Compare your screen with **Figure 1**.

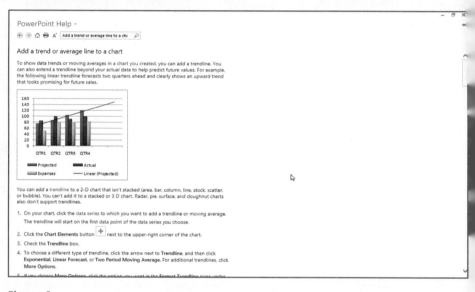

Figure 1

3. Read the article and answer the following questions: Why might it be beneficial to add a trend or average line to a chart? How might this help your audience to understand the data you are presenting?

Matching

Match each term in the second column with its correct definition in the first column by writing the letter of the term on the blank line in front of the correct definition.

___ **1.** In a table or worksheet, the intersection of a column and row.

___ **2.** A format used to organize and present information in columns and rows.

___ **3.** Predefined formatting that applies borders and fill colors to a table so that it is consistent with the presentation theme.

___ **4.** A graphic representation of numeric data.

___ **5.** A chart type useful for illustrating comparisons among related categories.

___ **6.** Text that identifies the categories of data in a chart.

___ **7.** Text that identifies a data marker in a chart.

___ **8.** A column, bar, area, dot, pie slice, or other symbol that represents a single data point.

___ **9.** Individual data plotted in a chart.

___ **10.** Visual or sound effects added to an object on a slide.

A Animation

B Cell

C Chart

D Column chart

E Category label

F Data label

G Data marker

H Data point

I Table

J Table style

BizSkills Video

1. In the video, professionals reflected on the lessons they learned from mistakes made in their career. Think of a mistake you made in your college career or a job you have had. What have you learned from that mistake and how will this knowledge help you in your future career?

2. What setbacks have you experienced in your college career? How did you, or will you, overcome it?

Multiple Choice

Choose the correct answer.

1. A pre-built set of effects, colors, and backgrounds applied to a chart that is designed to work with the presentation theme.
   A. Chart layout
   B. Chart style
   C. Chart effect

2. Tool used to copy color from one slide object to another.
   A. Eyedropper
   B. Animation Painter
   C. Copy button

3. A chart element that identifies the patterns or colors that are assigned to the data in the chart.
   A. Data series
   B. Data label
   C. Legend

4. A type of chart used to illustrate percentages or proportions using only one series of data.
   A. Column chart
   B. Line chart
   C. Pie chart

5. A type of animation that appears as a slide element comes onto the screen.
   A. Entrance effect
   B. Emphasis effect
   C. Exit effect

6. Animation that emphasizes an object or text that is already displayed.
   A. Entrance effect
   B. Emphasis effect
   C. Exit effect

7. Postpone animation, so that it appears at a predetermined amount of time after the last animation.
   A. Delay
   B. Duration
   C. Exit effect

8. A feature that copies animation settings from one object to another.
   A. Format Painter
   B. Animation Painter
   C. Copy and Paste

9. The action of writing on a slide while the slide show is running.
   A. Annotate
   B. Edit
   C. Navigation

10. A pointer used while slide show is in progress.
    A. Animation
    B. Highlighter
    C. Laser pointer

Topics for Discussion

1. You can apply multiple animations to each slide. Is it a good idea to limit the amount of animation you use? Why or why not?

2. Recall that a column chart is used to compare data and a pie chart is used to illustrate percentages or proportions. Give examples of the types of data that an organization might use in a column or a pie chart.

Skills Review

MyITLab®
Grader

To complete this project, you will need the following file:

- ppt04_SRGiving

You will save your file as:

- Last_First_ppt04_SRGiving

1. Start **PowerPoint 2013**, and then from your student files, open **ppt04_ SRGiving**. On the **File tab**, click **Save As**. Navigate to your PowerPoint Chapter 4 folder and then using your own name, save the presentation as Last_First_ppt04_SRGiving

2. Move to **Slide 2**. In the content placeholder, click the **Insert Table** button. In the **Insert Table** dialog box, in the **Number of columns** box, type 3 and then click **OK**.

3. In the first cell, type Literacy Council and press Tab. Type Food Pantry Press Tab, and type Aspen Falls Youth Club Press Tab. With the insertion point positioned in the first cell of the second row, type Green Aspen Falls and press Tab. Type Aspen Falls Cultural Committee and press Tab. Type Advocates Group

4. Click any cell in the first row. On the **Layout tab**, in the **Rows & Columns group**, click the **Insert Above** button. In the first cell in of the new row, type Employee-Selected Charities Compare your screen with **Figure 1**.

5. With your insertion point still in the first cell of the table, on the **Layout tab**, in the **Cell Size group**, click the **Distribute Rows** button. On the **Layout tab**, in the **Table group**, click the **Select** button, and then click **Select Table**. In the **Alignment group**, click the **Center** button, and then click the **Center Vertically** button.

6. Select all of the cells in the first row of the table. On the **Layout tab**, in the **Merge group**, click **Merge Cells**.

7. On the **Table Tools Design tab**, in the **Table Styles group**, click the **More** button. Under **Best Match for Document**, click the second style in the second row—**Themed Style 2 - Accent 1**. Compare your screen with **Figure 2**.

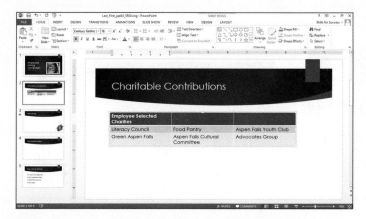

Figure 1

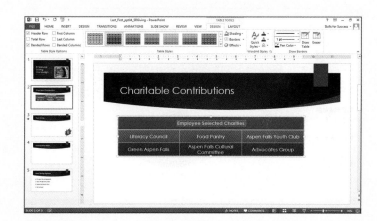

Figure 2

■ Continue to the next page to complete this Skills Review

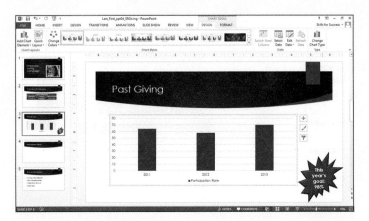

Figure 3

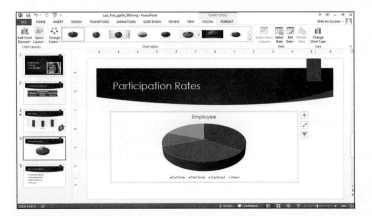

Figure 4

8. Move to **Slide 3**. In the content placeholder, click the **Insert Chart** button. On the left side of the **Insert Chart** dialog box, click **Column**. With the first chart—**Clustered Column**—selected, click **OK**.

9. In the **Chart in Microsoft PowerPoint** window, click cell **B1**. Type Participation Rate In cell **A2**, type 2011 Press [Enter], and type 2012 Press [Enter], and type 2013 In cell **B2**, type 64 Press [Enter], and type 58 Press [Enter], and type 70 Press [Enter]. Point to the sizing handle in the lower right corner of cell **D5**, and drag up and to the left so that only the range A1:B4 is selected. Release the mouse button. **Close** the Chart in Microsoft PowerPoint window.

10. Select the chart title placeholder, press [Delete], and compare your screen with **Figure 3**.

11. Move to **Slide 4**. In the content placeholder, click the **Insert Chart** button. On the left side of the Insert Chart dialog box, click **Pie**, click **3-D Pie**, and then click **OK**. In the worksheet, in cell **B1**, type Employee In cell **A2**, type Full time In cell **A3**, type Part time In cell **A4**, type Contract In cell **A5**, type Intern In cell **B2**, type 35 In cell **B3**, type 34 In cell **B4**, type 12 In cell **B5**, type 19 **Close** the Chart in Microsoft PowerPoint window, and compare your screen with **Figure 4**.

12. Move to **Slide 5**. Select the content placeholder, and then, on the **Animations tab**, in the **Animation group**, click the **More** button. Under **Entrance**, click **Zoom**.

13. With the content placeholder still selected, and the animation applied, on the **Animations tab**, in the **Advanced Animation group**, click the **Animation Painter** button. Move to **Slide 1**. Click the picture toward the right side of the slide to apply the animation from the bulleted list on Slide 5 to the picture on Slide 1.

14. With the image on Slide 1 selected, on the **Animations tab**, in the **Timing group**, in the **Duration box**, type 2 and then press [Enter].

15. With the image still selected, in the **Timing group**, click the **Start arrow**, and then click **With Previous**. In the **Delay** box, type 2 and then press [Enter].

16. Move to **Slide 3**. Select the starburst shape in the lower right corner of the slide. On the **Animations tab**, in the **Animation group**, click the **More button**, and then click **None** to remove the animation from this shape.

17. View the slide show. Insert a **Header & Footer** on all **Notes and Handouts** pages with the date, page number, and the footer text Last_First_ppt04_SRGiving and then **Save**. **Close** PowerPoint, and submit the file as directed.

 DONE! You have completed this Skills Review

Skills Assessment 1  MyITLab®
Grader

To complete this presentation, you will need the following file:

- ppt04_SA1Community

You will save your presentation as:

- Last_First_ppt04_SA1Community

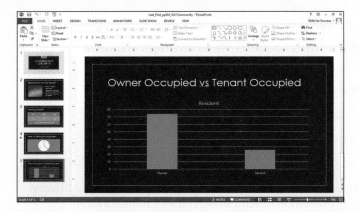

Figure 1

1. Start **PowerPoint 2013**. From your student files, open **ppt04_SA1Community**. Save the presentation in your **PowerPoint Chapter 4** folder as Last_First_ppt04_SA1Community

2. Display **Slide 3**. In the content placeholder, insert a table with 3 columns and 3 rows. In the three cells in the first row, type: 2011 and 2012 and 2013 In the second row, type the following from left to right: 2% and 1% and 3%. In the first cell in the third row, type County real estate records, 2013

3. Size the table so that its lower edge aligns at the **3 inch** mark below zero on the vertical ruler. Distribute the rows, and then apply the **Themed Style 2 - Accent 4** Table Style. Center the text horizontally and vertically within the cells. Increase the font size to **28** for the entire table. Add a **Soft Round** Cell Bevel to all cells in the table. Merge the cells in the bottom row.

4. Display **Slide 4**. Insert a **Pie** chart. In the **Chart in Microsoft PowerPoint** window, in cell **B1**, verify the word *Sales* appears. Beginning in cell **A2**, enter the following data:

New	37
Existing	63

5. In the **Chart in Microsoft PowerPoint** window, resize the data range so that only *A1:B3* appear. **Close** the **Chart in Microsoft PowerPoint** window. Change the chart style to **Style 10**, and then delete the chart title. Increase the size of all fonts in the chart to **18**.

6. Animate the pie chart by applying the **Swivel** entrance effect, and then change the **Effect Options** to **By Category**. Remove the animation from the chart background.

7. Display **Slide 5**. Add a **Clustered Column** chart with the following data, and change the data range so only this data displays:

	Resident
Owner	74
Tenant	26

8. Delete the legend below the clustered column chart.

9. Display **Slide 2**, and then remove the animation effect from the image in the left content placeholder.

10. Insert a **Header & Footer** on all **Notes and Handouts** pages with the date, page number, and the footer text Last_First_ppt04_SA1Community

11. Save, and then compare your presentation with **Figure 1**. Submit as directed by your instructor. **Close** PowerPoint.

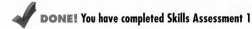 **DONE! You have completed Skills Assessment 1**

Skills Assessment 2

To complete this presentation, you will need the following file:

- ppt04_SA2Invest

You will save your presentation as:

- Last_First_ppt04_SA2Invest

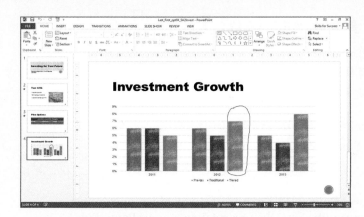

Figure 1

1. Start **PowerPoint**. From your student files, open **ppt04_SA2Invest**. **Save** the presentation in your **PowerPoint Chapter 4** folder as Last_First_ppt04_SA2Invest

2. On **Slide 2**, apply the **Wipe** entrance effect to the text in the left content placeholder. Use the Animation Painter to copy the same formatting to the image in the right content placeholder.

3. Move to **Slide 3**. In the content placeholder, insert a table with 3 columns and 2 rows. In the first row, type the following heading: Available Plans and then **Merge** the cells in the first row. In the second row, type Pretax and Traditional and Tiered

4. Size the table so that its lower edge aligns at the **1 inch** mark below zero on the vertical ruler. Apply the **Themed Style 2 - Accent 5** Table Style. Center the table text horizontally and vertically. Change the **Font Size** to **28** for the entire table. Apply the **Circle** Cell Bevel effect to the entire table. **Animate** the table by applying the **Wipe** animation.

5. Move to **Slide 4**, and then remove the animation from the title placeholder. In the content placeholder, insert a **Clustered Column** chart. In the **Chart in Microsoft PowerPoint** window, in cell **B1**, type Pretax In cell **C1**, type Traditional and in cell **D1**, type Tiered Beginning in cell **A2**, enter the following data:

2011	6%	6%	5%
2012	6%	5%	9%
2013	5%	4%	8%

6. Delete the value in cell A5, and then resize the data range so that only *A1:D4* appear on the chart. Apply the **Style 14** chart style.

7. Edit the chart data by changing the *2012 Tiered* data in cell **D3** to 7%

8. Delete the chart title.

9. Open the presentation in Slide Show view, and then on **Slide 4**, use the **Pen** to circle the *2012 Tiered* column. **End** the Slide Show. **Keep** your ink annotations.

10. Insert a **Header & Footer** on all **Notes and Handouts** pages with the date, page number, and the footer text Last_First_ppt04_SA2Invest

11. **Save**, and then compare your screen with **Figure 1**. Submit your presentation as directed. **Close** PowerPoint.

 DONE! You have completed Skills Assessment 2

Visual Skills Check

To complete this presentation, you will need the following file:

- New blank PowerPoint presentation

You will save your presentation as:

- Last_First_ppt04_VSHealthcare

Start PowerPoint. Add the slide title shown. Create the table as shown in **Figure 1**. **Save** the file as Last_First_ppt04_VSHealthcare in your **PowerPoint Chapter 4** folder. To complete this presentation, use the **Ion Boardroom** theme and the **Title and Content** layout. Type and align the text as shown in the figure, and apply the **Dark Style 1 - Accent 1** table style. In the first table row, change the **Font Size** to **24** and **Bold**. Change the font of the remaining data in the table to **18**. Apply the **Divot** cell Bevel effect to the entire table, and add an outside border to the table. Insert a **Header & Footer** on all **Notes and Handouts** pages with the date, page number, and the footer text Last_First_ppt04_VSHealthcare Submit your presentation as directed.

 **DONE! You have completed Visual Skills Check**

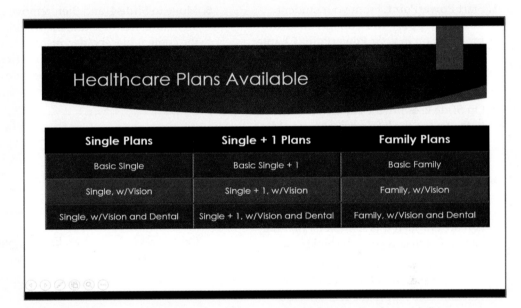

Figure 1

My Skills

To complete this presentation, you will need the following file:

- **ppt04_MYCollege**

You will save your presentation as:

- **Last_First_ppt04_MYCollege**

1. Start **PowerPoint**. From your student files, open **ppt04_MYCollege**. **Save** the presentation in your **PowerPoint Chapter 4** folder as Last_First_ppt04_MYCollege In the subtitle placeholder, replace the existing text with your first and last names.

2. On **Slide 2**, apply the **Fly In** animation to the text in the left content placeholder. Adjust the **Duration** of the animation to 01.25 seconds.

3. Move to **Slide 3**. In the content placeholder, insert a table with enough rows and columns to list all of the courses in which you are enrolled this semester. Enter the name of each course in the table.

4. Size the table so that its lower edge aligns at the **2 inch** mark below zero on the vertical ruler. Apply the **Dark Style 1 - Accent 2** Table Style. **Center** the table text horizontally and vertically. Change the **Font Size** to **28** for the entire table. Apply the **Cool Slant** Cell Bevel effect to the entire table. Use the **Animation Painter** to copy the animation from the bulleted list on Slide 2 to the table.

5. Move to **Slide 4**, and then remove the animation from the title placeholder. In the content placeholder, insert a **Clustered Column** chart. In the **Chart in Microsoft PowerPoint** window, add the following data (source: nces.ed.gov/fastfacts):

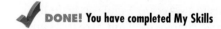

	Average Earnings
High school diploma	$21,000
Bachelor's degree	$45,000

6. Open the presentation in Slide Show view, and then on **Slide 4**, use the **Pen** to circle the text *Bachelor's degree*. **End** the Slide Show. **Keep** your ink annotations.

7. Insert a **Header & Footer** on all **Notes and Handouts** pages with the date, page number, and the footer text Last_First_ppt04_MyCollege

8. **Save**, and then compare your screen with **Figure 1**. Submit your presentation as directed. **Close** PowerPoint.

DONE! You have completed My Skills

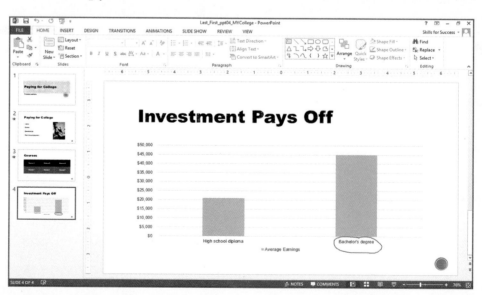

Figure 1

Skills Challenge 1

To complete this presentation, you will need the following file:

- ppt04_SC1Winery

You will save your presentation as:

- Last_First_ppt04_SC1Winery

Start **PowerPoint**. From your student files, open ppt04_SC1Winery. Save the presentation in your PowerPoint Chapter 4 folder as Last_First_ppt04_SC1Winery Using the skills you have practiced in this chapter, add a transition to both slides in the presentation. To the first image on the first slide add animation. Using the Animation Painter, copy the animation from the first image to the other two images on the slide. Adjust the animation of all three images so that they appear With Previous. Use the Animation Painter again to copy the same animation to the chart on Slide 2. On Slide 2, change

the Animation Effects so that the data appears By Category. If necessary, change the chart animation so that the background of the chart appears With Previous and each of the other animations appear On Click. With the chart selected, change the Chart Style. In Slide Show view, use the Highlighter to highlight the category label that represents the category with the highest percentage of visitors. Keep your ink annotations.

 DONE! You have completed Skills Challenge 1

Skills Challenge 2

To complete this presentation, you will need the following file:

- ppt04_SC2Forum

You will save your presentation as:

- Last_First_ppt04_SC2Forum

Start **PowerPoint**. From your student files, open ppt04_SC2Forum. Save the presentation in your PowerPoint Chapter 4 folder as Last_First_ppt04_SC2Forum View the presentation in Slide Show view, and notice the animation on Slide 2. In Normal view, edit the chart data to remove the Consultant category, and resize the data range so that only the Small, Medium, and Large categories appear. Change the Chart Style. Remove the animation from the chart on Slide 2, and replace it with something less obtrusive. Change the animation so

that all of the data appears at the same time. Use the Animation Painter to copy the new formatting you applied to the chart to the title on the first slide. Insert a Header & Footer on all Notes and Handouts pages with the date, page number, and the footer text Last_First_ppt04_SC2Forum Save, and then submit your presentation as directed. Close PowerPoint.

 DONE! You have completed Skills Challenge 2

Student data file needed for this project:
ppt_CPVote

You will save your file as:
Last_First_ppt_CPVote

1. **Start PowerPoint 2013**, and then create a new presentation with the **Dividend theme**. Select the second variant in the first row. **Save** the file to your drive with the name Last_First_ppt_CPVote

2. On **Slide 1**, add the title Vote Aspen Falls and adjust the **Character Spacing** to **Very Loose**. Add the subtitle Increase the Vote Campaign, By Maria Martinez Accept the default All Caps formatting of the title and subtitle text throughout the presentation.

3. On **Slide 1**, insert **WordArt** in **the Fill - White, Outline - Accent 1, Glow - Accent 1** style. Accept the default location for the WordArt. Add the text Get out and vote! to the WordArt.

4. Insert a new **Slide 2** with the **Two Content** layout. Add the title Voter Information

5. In the left content placeholder, add the photo **ppt_CPVote** from your student data files.

6. In the right content placeholder, add the following two-level bulleted list:
   Who is qualified to vote
   　　Resident for minimum of 28 days
   　　US citizen
   　　At least 18 years of age
   　　Registered or registering

7. Increase the **Line Spacing** for the bulleted list to **1.5**, and then compare your screen with **Figure 1**.

8. Insert a new **Slide 3** with the **Two Content** layout. Add the title Poll Location

9. In the left content placeholder, add **SmartArt** with the **Vertical Box List** layout. In the top shape, type Aspen Falls City Hall Add a **Bullet** with the text 500 S Aspen St, Aspen Falls, CA Delete all other shapes in the SmartArt placeholder.

10. In the right content placeholder, insert **Office.com Clip Art**. Search for *Voter*, and insert the image shown in **Figure 2**.

■ Continue to the next page to complete the skill

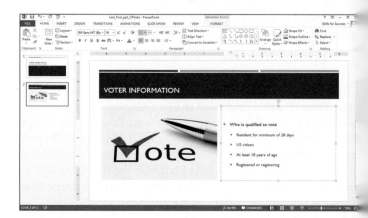

Figure 1

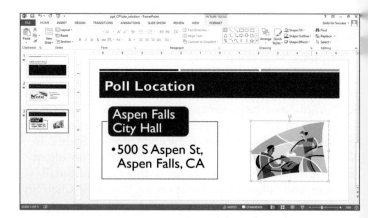

Figure 2

11. Increase the **Height** of the image to **3.2 inches**.

12. Insert a new **Slide 4** with the **Title and Content** layout. Add the title Elections

13. In the content placeholder, insert a **Table** with two columns and two rows, and add the following text:

Spring Primary	Spring Election
Partisan Primary	General Election

14. Change the **Table Style Options** so that **Header Row** is not selected, and then change the **Table Style** to **Themed Style 2 - Accent 1**. Add a **Circle Cell Bevel** to the table.

15. With the table selected, increase the table **Height** to **3.5 inches**, and then **Center** the text **Vertically** and **Horizontally**. Increase the **Font Size** to **24**. Click a blank area of the slide so that the table is no longer selected, and then compare your screen with **Figure 3**.

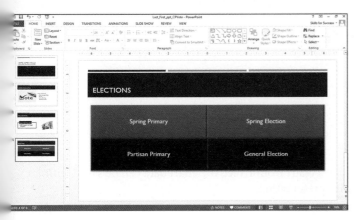

Figure 3

16. Insert a new **Slide 5** with the **Title and Content** layout. Add the title Voter Demographics

17. On **Slide 5**, in the content placeholder, insert a **Pie Chart** with the following data:

	Race
White	46
Asian	25
African American	12
Native American	0.6
Pacific Islander	0.2
Other	10
Two or More	5

18. Add **Chart Style 12** to the pie chart.

19. Use the **Format Painter** to copy the formatting from the WordArt on **Slide 1** to the titles on **Slides 2, 3, 4,** and **5**, and then compare your screen with **Figure 4**.

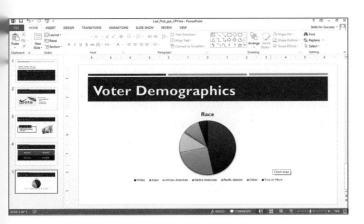

Figure 4

20. Add the **Fly-In Animation** to the pie chart on **Slide 5**.

21. Add the **Wind Transition**, and adjust the **Effect Options** to **Left.** Apply the transition to all slides.

22. Add a footer to the **Notes and Handouts** pages with date, page number, and the text Last_First_ppt_CPVote

23. **Save** 🖫 and then **Close** ✕ PowerPoint. Submit the project as directed by your instructor.

 DONE! You have completed the PowerPoint Capstone Project

Copy and Paste Between Office Programs

▶ You can paste text from a Word document into a PowerPoint presentation.

▶ Objects created in PowerPoint can be pasted into Word. For example, you can copy a SmartArt graphic from a PowerPoint presentation and paste it into a Word document.

▶ You can also copy a chart from Excel and paste it into a PowerPoint presentation.

▶ When you copy a chart from Excel, the chart data can be saved with the PowerPoint presentation.

© Magspace

Aspen Falls City Hall

In this Integrated Project, you will prepare a PowerPoint presentation and a Word handout for the Aspen Falls city council about trends in attendance at local events. City planners are working with the tourism department and the city council to update the venues, dates, and security needed based on attendance at each event. Tourism Director Todd Austin will make the presentation to the city council, city planners, and citizens of Aspen Falls.

In your career, you will often create files in different programs about the same topic. You may create a report in Word, a presentation in PowerPoint, and a spreadsheet in Excel about an upcoming project or event. It would be inefficient to recreate the same information in each file, so you will copy the information from one file to another.

In this project, you will paste a chart from an Excel spreadsheet and a bulleted list from a Word document into a PowerPoint presentation. You will also paste a SmartArt object from PowerPoint into Word.

Time to complete this project – 30 to 45 minutes

Student data files needed for this project:

ppt_IP08_Attendance (PowerPoint)
ppt_IP08_AttendanceReport (Word)
ppt_IP08_AttendanceTrends (Excel)

You will save your files as:

Last_First_ppt_IP08_Attendance (PowerPoint)
Last_First_ppt_IP08_AttendanceReport (Word)

Outcome

Using the skills in this project, you will be able to work with Word and PowerPoint files like this:

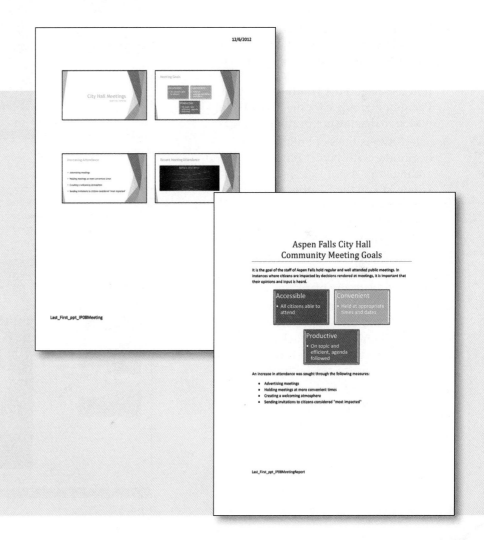

SKILLS MyITLab®

At the end of this project you will be able to:

▶ Copy a bulleted list from a Word document and paste it into a PowerPoint presentation

▶ Copy a SmartArt graphic from a PowerPoint presentation and paste it into a Word document

▶ Copy an Excel chart and paste it into a PowerPoint presentation

1. Start **Microsoft PowerPoint 2013**. On the start page, click **Open Other Presentations**. On the **Open** page, click **Computer**, and then click **Browse**. In the **Open** dialog box, navigate to the student data files for this chapter. Select **ppt_IP08Attendance**, and then click the **Open** button. On the **File tab**, click **Save As**. Navigate to the location where you are saving your files, create a folder named PowerPoint Special Projects and then save the presentation as Last_First_ppt_IP08Attendance

2. Start **Word**, open **ppt_IP08_AttendanceReport**, and then save it in your **PowerPoint Special Projects** folder as Last_First_ppt_IP08AttendanceReport If necessary, on the **Home tab**, in the **Paragraph group**, click the **Show/Hide** ¶ button to display nonprinting characters.

3. Select the six lines of bulleted text, beginning with *Winter Blues Festival* and ending with *Aspen Falls Triathlon*. On the **Home tab**, in the **Clipboard group**, click the **Copy** 📋 button.

4. Switch to the **PowerPoint** presentation, and display **Slide 3**. Click in the content placeholder, and then on the **Home tab**, in the **Clipboard group**, click the **Paste** button. Delete any blank lines.

5. Click a border of the placeholder to select it, and then on the **Home tab**, in the **Paragraph group**, click the **Line Spacing arrow** 📏. Click **1.5**, and then compare your screen with **Figure 1**.

6. Display **Slide 2**, and select the SmartArt object. Verify that none of the individual shapes in the SmartArt object are selected. If any of the shapes are selected, click a blank area of the SmartArt box to deselect the shape. Compare your screen with **Figure 2**.

■ **Continue to the next page to complete the skill**

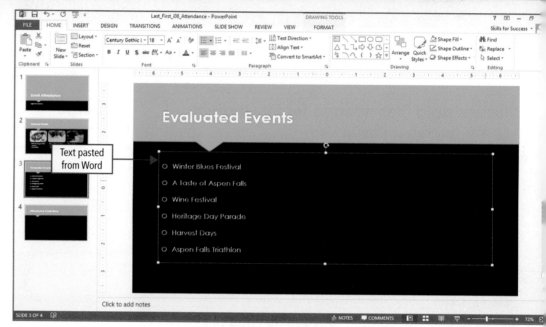

Figure 1

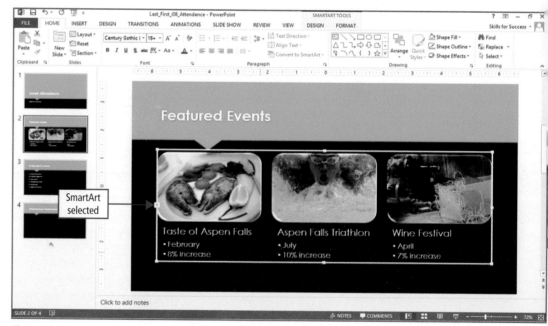

Figure 2

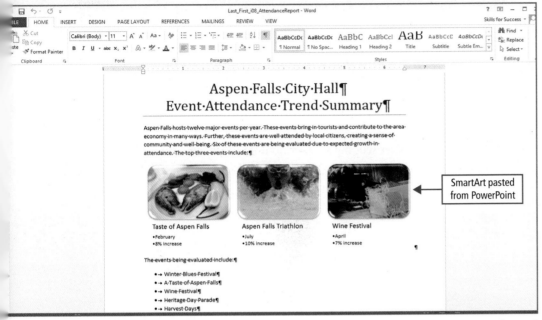

Figure 3

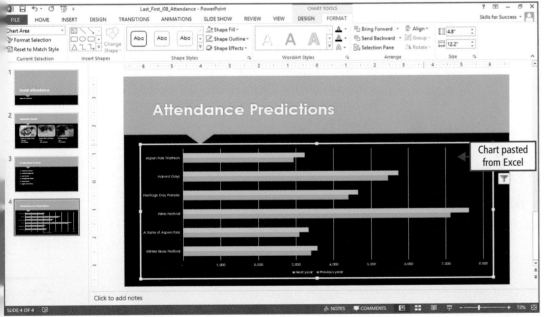

Figure 4

7. With the SmartArt object selected, press `Ctrl` + `C` to copy the SmartArt object.

8. On the taskbar, switch to **Word** 🔲. Click the blank line below the first paragraph, and then press `Ctrl` + `V` to paste the SmartArt object. Compare your screen with **Figure 3**.

9. Insert a footer in the Word document that displays the file name. **Save** 🔲 and then **Close** ⨯ the Word document.

10. Start **Excel**, and then from your student files, open **ppt_IP08_AttendanceTrends**.

11. Right-click in a blank area of the chart to display the shortcut menu, and then click **Copy**.

12. On the taskbar, click the **PowerPoint** button 🔲, and then display **Slide 4**. Right-click in the content placeholder, and then from the shortcut menu, under **Paste Options**, point to the first button— **Use Destination Theme & Embed Workbook**.

13. Click **Use Destination Theme & Embed Workbook** to paste the chart. With the chart selected, on the **Format tab**, in the **Height** box 🔲, type 4.8 and then press `Enter`. In the **Width** box 🔲, type 12.2 and then press `Enter`. In the **Arrange group**, click the **Align** button, and then click **Align Center**. On the chart, delete the title. Compare your screen with **Figure 4**.

14. Add a footer to the **Notes and Handouts** pages with date, page number, and the text Last_First_ppt_IP08_Attendance **Save** and **Close** the presentation, and then **Close** the Excel file without saving. Submit the Word and PowerPoint files as directed by your instructor.

✔ **DONE! You have completed Integrated Project 8**

Send PowerPoint Handouts to Word

- ▶ Presentation handouts can be sent to Word in several different formats.
- ▶ When you send handouts to Word, you can use Word's document formatting features to format the document appropriately.

- ▶ After sending speaker notes to Word, you can use Word to add or delete notes to create an effective handout.

© Kurhan

Aspen Falls City Hall

In this Integrated Project, you will prepare, edit, and format presentation handouts for the Aspen Falls City Engineer, Donald Norris. Donald will present this information to construction contractors at a city meeting and would like the contractors to have a handout with the same information.

In your career, you might create Word handouts from your PowerPoint presentation to distribute to your audience or even to attach to an email message.

You will use the Create Handouts feature in PowerPoint to send the handouts to Microsoft Word, where you will edit and format the handouts.

Time to complete this project – 30 to 45 minutes

Student data file needed for this project:

ppt_IP09Construction (PowerPoint)

You will save your file as:

Last_First_ppt_IP09ConstructionHandouts (Word)

Outcome

Using the skills in this project, you will be able to create a Word document that looks like this:

SKILLS MyITLab®

At the end of this project you will be able to:

▶ Create Handouts in Word from a PowerPoint presentation
▶ Edit presentation handouts in Word
▶ Format presentation handouts in Word

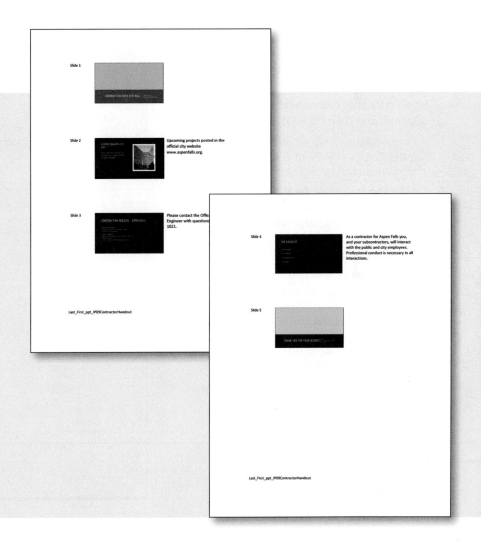

1. Start **PowerPoint**, and then open the student data file **ppt_IP09_Construction**.

2. On the **File tab**, click **Export**, and then click **Create Handouts**. Compare your screen with **Figure 1**.

   On the Export page, you can choose several different save and delivery options. The Create Handouts option is used to create a Word document with slides and presentation notes.

3. On the right side of the **Export page**, click the **Create Handouts** button.

   In the Send To Microsoft Word dialog box, you can choose how the presentation will be displayed in Microsoft Word.

4. In the **Send To Microsoft Word** dialog box, verify that **Notes next to slides** is selected, and then click **OK**.

   On the taskbar, a Word button displays, indicating that the Word document has been created.

5. On the taskbar, click the **Word** button. If necessary, on the **Home tab**, in the **Paragraph group**, click the **Show/Hide** button to display nonprinting characters. Compare your screen with **Figure 2**.

   The slides are inserted into the Word document in a three-column table format. The first column indicates the slide number. The second column displays the slide. The third column contains notes typed in the PowerPoint speaker notes pane. If notes are not created for a slide, then the cell in the third column will be blank.

6. Scroll down to view each slide. Notice that the document contains two pages with three slides per page, and that for Slides 3 and 4, notes display in the third column.

■ **Continue to the next page to complete the skill**

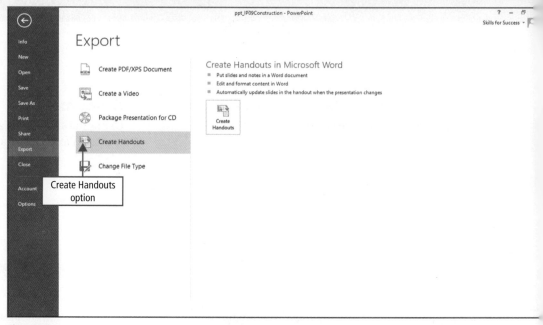

Figure 1

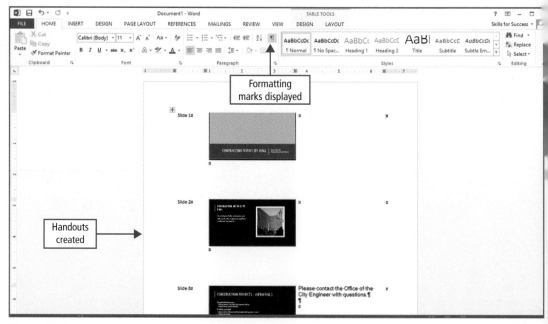

Figure 2

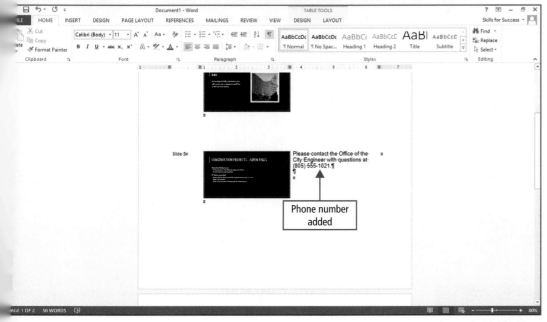

Figure 3

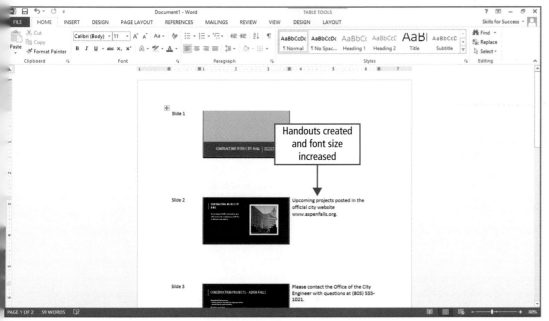

Figure 4

7. Scroll to display **Slide 3**. Click at the end of the text in the third column following the word *questions*, and then type at (805) 555-1021 Compare your screen with **Figure 3**.

8. Click anywhere in the first column. On the **Layout tab**, in the **Table group**, click the **Select** button, and then click **Select Column**. On the **Home tab**, in the **Styles group**, click the **More** button ⬇, and then click **Heading 2** to apply the style to all of the slide numbers.

9. Scroll to display **Slide 2**. Click in the third column, and then type Upcoming projects posted on the official city website, www.aspenfalls.org.

> Notice that the font, font size, and spacing of the text that you typed are different from the notes that were part of the PowerPoint presentation.

10. With the insertion point positioned in the third column, on the **Layout tab**, in the **Table group**, click the **Select** button, and then click **Select Column** to select all of the third column. Change the **Font** to **Calibri** and the **Font Size** to **12**. Click the **Show/Hide** button to turn off the nonprinting characters. Click a blank area of the document so that no text is selected. Compare your screen with **Figure 4**.

11. **Save** 🖫 the Word document in your **PowerPoint Special Projects** folder with the file name Last_First_ppt_IP09ContractorHandout

12. Insert a footer in the Word document that displays the file name, and then **Save** 🖫.

13. **Close** ✕ the Word document, and then **Close** the PowerPoint window without saving. Submit the Word document as directed by your instructor.

 DONE! You have completed Integrated Project 9

Create Presentations Using PowerPoint Online

▶ Office Online Apps can be used to create new files or to edit files that were created in Office programs.

▶ With PowerPoint Online, formerly PowerPoint Web App, you can create or edit a presentation in *Editing view,* and you view the presentation in *Slide Show view*.

▶ You can also use PowerPoint Online to insert images, apply styles, and add SmartArt.

© mangostock / Fotolia

Aspen Falls City Hall

In this project, you will use PowerPoint Online to create a presentation for the Aspen Falls IT Department. This presentation will be used by Cathy Story, the head of the IT department, in employee training to reinforce the department's mission.

In PowerPoint Online, you will create a new presentation and insert two slides. You will insert Clip Art and SmartArt, and add text. You will add Transitions and Animations and then view the presentation in Slide Show view.

Time to complete this project – 30 to 60 minutes

You will save your file as:

Last_First_ppt_WATechnology

Outcome

Using the skills in this project, you will be able to edit and format a PowerPoint Online presentation like this:

SKILLS

At the end of this project you will be able to use PowerPoint Online to:

- ▶ Create a presentation
- ▶ Add a Presentation Theme
- ▶ Add new slides
- ▶ Insert Clip Art
- ▶ Add Transitions
- ▶ Add Animations
- ▶ View a Presentation in Slide Show View

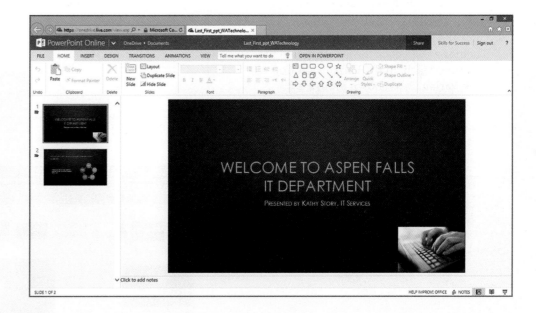

1. Start **Internet Explorer** or another web browser, navigate to live.com and log on to your Windows Live account. If you do not have a Windows Live account, follow the links and instructions on the page to create one.

2. Toward the top of the screen, click **Create** and then click **PowerPoint presentation**.

3. Above the Ribbon, point to the text *Presentation1*, click one time, type Last_First_ppt_WATechnology and then click a blank area in the presentation. Compare your screen with **Figure 1**.

4. Click the **Design** tab, and then in the Themes group, click the last option in the first row, **Mesh**. In the Variants group, click **Variant 3**, as shown in **Figure 2**.

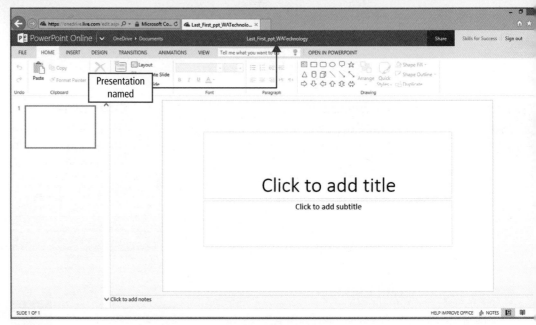

Figure 1

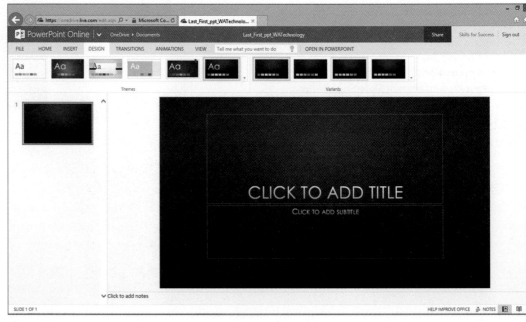

Figure 2

■ **Continue to the next page to complete the skill**

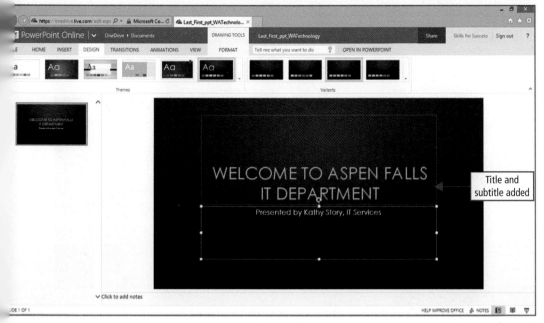

Figure 3

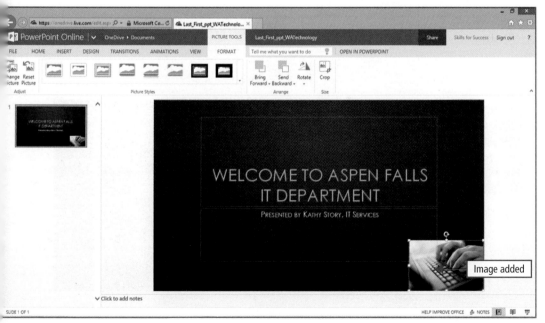

Figure 4

5. In the new presentation, on **Slide 1**, in the title placeholder, type Welcome to Aspen Falls Press Enter, and then type IT Department In the subtitle placeholder, type Presented by Cathy Story, IT Services and then compare your screen with **Figure 3**.

6. On the **Insert tab**, in the **Images group**, click **ClipArt**. In the ClipArt dialog box, in the **Search** box, type Technology, press Enter, and then click the image of hands on a keyboard. Click **Insert**. With the pointer, drag the image to the lower right corner of the slide and compare your screen with **Figure 4**.

7. On the **Home tab**, in the **Slides group**, click **New Slide**. In the **New Slide dialog box**, click **Two Content**, and then click **Add Slide**.

8. On **Slide 2**, in the title placeholder, type Information Technology Department Mission

9. In the left content placeholder, type Provide high-quality, collaborative technical support for the employees of Aspen Falls.

10. In the right content placeholder, click the **Insert SmartArt** button. On the **SmartArt Tools Design tab**, in the **Layouts group**, click the **More arrow**, and then, in the second row, click the second layout, **Basic Cycle**.

■ **Continue to the next page to complete the skill**

11. On the **SmartArt Tools Design tab**, in the **Create Graphic group**, click the **Edit text** button.

12. Type the following five bullet points, and then compare your screen with **Figure 5**.

Employee
Help Desk
IT Technician
IT Supervisor
Department Leader

13. Click a blank area of the slide to update the SmartArt graphic, and then click the SmartArt graphic in the right content placeholder to select it.

14. With the SmartArt selected, on the **SmartArt Tools Design tab**, in the **SmartArt Styles group**, click the **Change Colors** button. Under **Colorful**, click the first option **Colorful - Accent Colors**.

15. In the **SmartArt Styles group**, click the **More arrow** ▼, and in the second row, click the fourth style, **Powder**. Compare your screen with **Figure 6**.

16. On the **Transitions tab**, in the **Transitions to This Slide group**, click **Push**. In the **Transitions group**, click **Apply to All**.

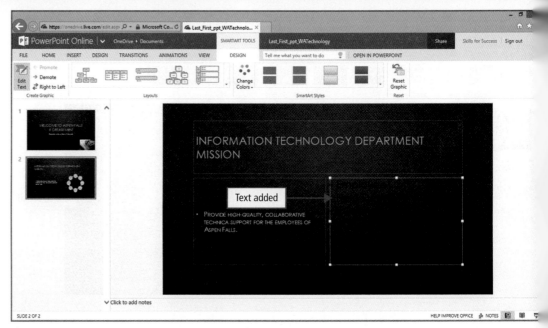

Figure 5

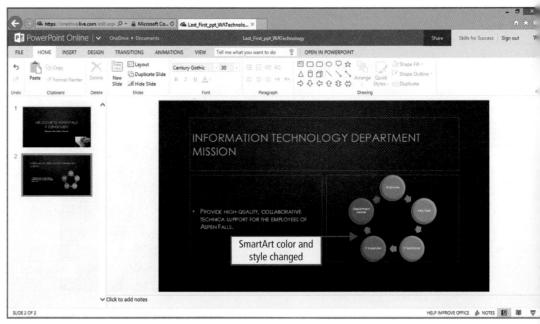

Figure 6

■ **Continue to the next page to complete the skill** ▶

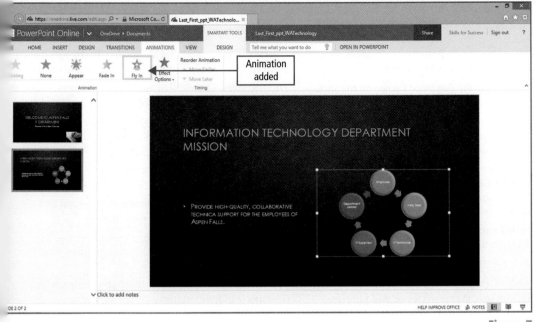

Figure 7

17. With the SmartArt still selected, on the **Animations tab**, in the **Animation group**, click **Fly-In**. Compare your screen with **Figure 7**.

18. On the **View tab**, in the **Presentation Views group**, click the **Slide Show** button. If necessary, allow the pop-up to appear. Click to move to the second slide, and then click to make each SmartArt animation appear.

19. When you have clicked through the animations, end the slide show by clicking, and return to PowerPoint Online.

20. **Print**, **Download**, or **Share** the document as directed by your instructor.

    In PowerPoint Online, there is no Save button because your presentation is saved automatically.

21. In the top left corner of the **Internet Explorer** window, click the **sign out** link, and then **Close** ⊠ the browser window.

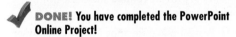

DONE! You have completed the PowerPoint Online Project!

Glossary

.docx extension The file extension typically assigned to Word documents.

.pdf extension The file extension assigned to PDF documents.

3-D Short for three-dimensional.

Absolute cell reference The exact address of a cell, regardless of the position of the cell that contains the formula, that remains the same when the formula is copied. An absolute cell reference takes the form $A$1.

Accelerator A feature that searches the web for information related to the text that you select.

Action argument An additional instruction that determines how the macro action should run.

Active cell The cell outlined in green in which data is entered when you begin typing.

Active content A program downloaded with a web page that provides additional functionality.

ActiveX script A small program that allows websites to provide content such as learning management systems.

Add-on A small program added to a web browser to add functionality.

After Previous Begins the animation sequence immediately after the completion of the previous animation.

Alias A descriptive label used to identify a field in expressions, datasheets, or forms and reports.

Alignment Guide A line that displays when an object is aligned with a document object such as a margin or heading.

Anchor A symbol that displays to the left of a paragraph to indicate which paragraph an object is associated with.

And logical operator A logical comparison of two criteria that is true only when both criteria outcomes are true.

Animation Special visual effect added to an image, chart, or text on a slide.

Animation Painter Tool used to copy animation settings from one object to another.

Annotate Using the Pen tool to write on the slide while the slide show is running.

App A program use to perform a similar set of tasks. For example, Calendar is used to make appointments, and Bing Weather is used to track weather.

App Short for application, often a program purchased through the computer or device application store.

App command A button and command in an application that remains hidden until you need it.

Append row The last row of a datasheet into which a new record is entered.

Application Another word for app or program.

Application software Software used to accomplish specific tasks such as word processing and surfing the Internet.

Area chart A chart type that emphasizes the magnitude of change over time.

Argument The values that a function uses to perform operations or calculations.

Arithmetic operator A symbol that specifies a mathematical operation such as addition or subtraction.

Aspect ratio The width-to-height ratio of a screen.

Asterisk (*) wildcard A wildcard character that matches any combination of characters.

Attachment data type A data type used to store files such as Word documents or digital photo files.

Author-date citation A short citation format that contains the author's last name, the publication year, and the page number if one is available.

AutoComplete A menu of commands that match the characters you type.

AutoCorrect A feature that corrects common spelling errors as you type.

AutoFit A command that automatically changes the column width to accommodate the longest entry.

AutoNumber A field that automatically enters a unique, numeric value when a record is created.

AVERAGE function A function that adds a group of values, and then divides the result by the number of values in the group.

Avg An operator that calculates the average of the values in each group.

Axis A line bordering the chart plot area used as a frame of reference for measurement.

Backstage view A collection of pages on the File tab used to open, save, print, and perform other file management tasks.

Bar chart A chart type that illustrates comparisons among individual items.

Between ... And operator A comparison operator that finds all numbers or dates between and including two values.

Bibliography A compilation of sources referenced in a report and listed on a separate page.

Bing Internet Explorer's default search provider.

Black slide A slide that appears at the end of a presentation in Slide Show view, indicating that the slide show is over.

Block style A business letter format that begins all lines at the left margin except for letterheads, tables, and block quotes. Also known as full-block style.

Bluetooth A wireless technology that connects devices using radio waves over short distances.

Body font Font applied to all text on slide, except for the title.

Browser Software used to view and navigate the Web.

Browsing history The information that Internet Explorer stores as you browse the web.

Bullet Point An individual line of bulleted text on a slide.

Bulleted list A list of items with each item introduced by a symbol—such as a small circle or check mark—in which the list items can be presented in any order.

C drive The internal drive that stores the operating system. It is commonly assigned the letter 'C.'

Calculated column A column in an Excel table that uses a single formula that adjusts for each row.

Calculated field A field in a table or query that derives its values from other fields in the table or query.

Caption A field property that determines what displays in datasheet, form, and report labels.

Card reader A collection of ports designed to accept flash-based memory cards.

Cascading delete A referential integrity option in which you can delete a record on the one side of the relationship and all the related records on the many side will also be deleted.

Cascading update A referential integrity option in which you can edit the primary key values in a table and all the related records in the other table will update accordingly.

Category axis The axis that displays the category labels.

Category label Label that identifies the categories of data in a chart.

Category label Nonnumeric text that identifies the categories of data.

Cell A box formed by the intersection of a row and column into which text, objects, and data can be inserted.

Cell address The column letter and row number that identify a cell; also called the cell reference.

Cell reference The column letter and row number that identify a cell; also called a cell address.

Cell style A prebuilt set of formatting characteristics, such as font, font size, font color, cell borders, and cell shading.

Central Processing Unit The hardware responsible for controlling the computer commands and operations.

Charm A button accessed from the right edge of the screen that can be used to quickly perform common tasks.

Chart A graphical representation of data used to show comparisons, patterns, and trends.

Chart layout A prebuilt set of chart elements that can include a title, legend, or labels.

Chart sheet A workbook sheet that contains only a chart and is useful when you want to view a chart separately from the worksheet data.

Chart style A prebuilt chart format that applies an overall visual look to a chart by modifying its graphic effects, colors, and backgrounds.

Chrome The area of a web browser devoted to toolbars, address boxes, tabs, and menus.

Citation A note in the document that refers the reader to a source in the bibliography.

Click To click the left mouse button.

Clip Art An image, drawing, or photograph accessed from Microsoft Office Online and other online providers.

Clipboard A temporary memory location maintained by the operating system used to copy or move text, objects, files, or folders.

Cloud backup A service that copies your files to a server so that you if you need to, you can recover them.

Cloud computing Services such as file storage, file sharing, and applications provided via the Internet.

Cloud-based service A Cloud-computing resource such as SkyDrive, Facebook, and Flickr.

Clustered bar chart A chart type that is useful when you want to compare values across categories; bar charts organize categories along the vertical axis and the values along the horizontal axis.

Color scales A conditional format that uses color to help the user visualize data distribution and variation.

Column break A nonprinting character that forces the text following the break to flow into the next column.

Column chart A chart type useful for illustrating comparisons among related numbers.

Column chart Used to show comparison among related categories.

Column heading The letter that displays at the top of a column.

Columnar layout A layout that places labels in the first column and data in the second column.

Command An action used to complete a task.

Comment A note that is attached to a cell, separate from other cell content.

Compact and Repair A process that rebuilds database files so that data and database objects are stored more efficiently.

Comparison operator An operator that compares two values, such as > (greater than) or < (less than).

Comparison operator Compares two values and returns either TRUE or FALSE.

Compatibility mode A mode that limits formatting and features to ones that are supported in earlier versions of Office.

Compressed folder A file or group of files compressed into a single file.

Computer A programmable electronic device that can input, process, output, and store data.

Computer window A File Explorer folder window used to access the drives available on your computer.

Conditional formatting A format such as cell shading or font color, which is applied to cells when a specified condition is true.

Content Underlying formulas and data in a cell.

Contextual tab A tab that displays on the Ribbon only when a related object such as a graphic or chart is selected. This tab contains tools used on the object.

Contrast The difference in brightness between two elements on a slide, such as the background and the text or the background and a graphic.

Control An object on a form or in a report such as a label or a text box.

Cookie A small text file written by some websites as you visit them. It is used to add functionality to the page or to analyze the way that you use the website.

Copy A command that places a copy of the selected text or object on the Office Clipboard.

Copyright-free image An image that is not protected by copyright.

Count An operator that calculates the number of records in each group.

COUNT function A function that counts the number of cells that contain numbers.

CPU Central Processing Unit.

CPU cache A storage area dedicated to the processor.

CPU speed A computer specification measured in calculations per second.

Criteria (Access) Conditions in a query used to select the records that answer the query's question.

Criteria (Excel) The condition that is specified in the logical test.

Crosstab query A select query that calculates a sum, an average, or a similar statistic, and then groups the results by two sets of values.

Currency data type A data type that stores numbers formatted as monetary values.

Custom Range A user-determined selection of slides; includes only a selection of the slides in the presentation.

Cut A command that deletes the selected text or object and places a copy in the Office clipboard.

Data bar A format that provides a visual cue to the reader about the value of a cell relative to other cells. The length of the data bar represents the value in the cell.

Data label Text that identifies a data marker in a chart.

Data marker A column, bar, area, dot, pie slice, or other symbol that represents a single data point.

Data point A chart value that originates in an Excel worksheet cell, a Word table cell, or an Access field. Individual data plotted in a chart.

Data series In a chart, data points that are related to one another.

Data series Related data points on a chart; assigned a unique color or pattern represented in the chart legend.

Data source The file that contains the information—such as names and addresses—that changes with each letter or label in the main mail merge document.

Data Type A field property that specifies the type of information that the field will hold; for example, text, number, date, or currency.

Database A collection of structured tables designed to store data.

Database software Software used to store large amounts of data and retrieve that data in useful and meaningful ways.

Database system A program used to both store and manage large amounts data.

Datasheet The presentation of a database table.

Datasheet view An Access view that features the data but also has contextual tabs on the Ribbon so that you can also change the table's design.

Date/Time data type A data type that stores serial numbers that are converted into and formatted as dates or times.

Default home page The page that first displays when you open a web browser.

Default printer The printer that is automatically selected when you do not choose a different printer.

Delay Animation starts after a predetermined amount of time.

Desktop A GUI element that simulates a real desktop in which files are placed. A screen that you use to organize and work with your files and applications.

Desktop app An application that runs from the desktop.

Desktop computer A computer designed to be placed permanently on a desk or at a workstation.

Desktop icon A shortcut to a program, file, or location on your computer.

Desktop publishing software Software designed to produce professional publications such as newsletters, letterheads, business cards, and brochures.

Detail control The area of a report that repeats for each record in the table or query.

Detail sheet A worksheet with cells referred to by summary sheet formulas.

Device A common term for smartphone or tablet.

Displayed value Data displayed in a cell.

Document Information Panel A panel that displays above the worksheet window in which properties or property information is added, viewed, or updated.

Document properties Details about a file that describe or identify the file, such as the title, author name, and keywords.

Document properties Information about a document that can help you identify or organize your files, such as the name of the document author, the file name, and key words.

Domain name A unique name assigned to a website on the World Wide Web.

Dot leader A series of evenly spaced dots that precede a tab stop.

Double-click To click the left mouse button two times quickly without moving the mouse.

Double-spacing The equivalent of a blank line of text displays between each line of text.

Double-tap To tap the screen in the same place two times quickly.

Drag To press and hold the left mouse button while moving the mouse.

Drag and drop A method of moving objects, in which you point to a selection and drag it to a new location.

Drop cap The first letter (or letters) of a paragraph, enlarged and either embedded in the text or placed in the left margin.

DVD A storage device that uses optical laser technology to read and write data.

E-mail attachment A file that is sent with an e-mail message so that the recipient can open and view the file.

E-mail software Software used to receive and send e-mail. Many e-mail programs also include tools for managing appointments, contacts, and tasks.

Edit To insert, delete, or replace text in an Office document, workbook, or presentation.

Edit mode A mode that selects the text inside a control, not the control itself.

Em dash A long dash based on the width of the capital letter M in the current font and font size.

It marks a break in thought, similar to a comma but stronger.

Embedded chart A chart that is placed on the worksheet containing the data.

Embedded computer A small, specialized computer built into a larger component such as an automobile or appliance.

Emphasis effect Animation that emphasizes an object or text that is already displayed.

Endnote A note or comment placed at the end of a section or a document.

Ensure Fit (Slide Size) A setting that scales information down so that it all appears on the slide.

Entrance effect Animation that appears as an object or text is moved onto the screen.

Error indicator A green triangle that indicates a possible error in a formula.

Error value A message that displays whenever a formula or function cannot perform its calculations.

Excel table A series of rows and columns that contains related data that have been formatted as a table.

Exit effect Animation that appears as an object or text is moved off the screen.

Explode To drag a section of a pie chart out to add emphasis.

Expression A combination of fields, mathematical operators, and prebuilt functions that calculates values in tables, forms, queries, and reports.

External drive A solid-state disk drive that attaches to the computer via a USB port.

Eyedropper Tool used to select color from any object or image on a slide and apply the color to another area of the slide; often used to create a cohesive color scheme.

Fair use A rule that allows limited reproduction of images for educational purposes.

Favorite A stored web address that can be clicked to navigate to that page quickly.

Fax service provider A company that receives faxes sent to them from the Internet and then relays the fax to the recipient using phone lines.

Fax service providers typically charge fees for their service.

Field (Access) A common characteristic of the data that the table will describe, such as city, state, or postal code.

Field (Excel) In a PivotTable, a cell that summarizes multiple rows of information from the source data.

Field (Word) A category of data—such as a file name, a page number, or the current date—that can be inserted into a document.

Field size A field property that limits the number of characters that can be typed into a text or number field.

File A collection of data that is saved, opened, and changed by applications.

File Explorer An application that is used to view, find, and organize your files and folders.

File system An organized method to save and retrieve files.

Fill handle The small green square in the lower right corner of the selection.

Filter A command to display only the rows of a table that meet specified criteria. Filtering temporarily hides rows that do not meet the criteria.

Fingerprint scanner An input device that reads fingerprints to authorize computer users.

First line indent The location of the beginning of the first line of a paragraph in relation to the left edge of the remainder of the paragraph.

Flagged error A wavy line indicating a possible spelling, grammar, or style error.

Floating object An object that you can move independently of the surrounding text.

Folder A container in which you store your files.

Folder window A File Explorer window that displays files and folders.

Font A set of characters with the same design and shape; measured in points.

Footer A reserved area for text, graphics, and fields that displays at the bottom of each page in a document.

Footer The text that displays at the bottom of every slide or that prints at the bottom of a sheet of slide handouts.

Footnote A note or comment placed at the bottom of the page.

Foreign key A field that is used to relate records in a second related table. The foreign key field is often the second table's primary key.

Form A database object that is used to find, update, and add table records.

Form data Information that you have typed into forms, such as your sign-in name, e-mail address, and street address.

Format To change the appearance of the text—for example, changing the text color to red.

Format Painter A tool that copies *formatting* from one selection of text to another.

Formatting The process of specifying the appearance of cells or the overall layout of a worksheet.

Formatting mark A character that displays in your document to represent a nonprinting character such as a paragraph, space, or tab.

Formula An equation that performs mathematical calculations on number values in the worksheet.

Formula AutoComplete A feature that suggests values as you type a function.

Formula bar A bar below the Ribbon that displays the value contained in the active cell and is used to enter or edit values or formulas.

Freeze Panes A command used to keep rows or columns visible when scrolling in a large worksheet. The frozen rows and columns become separate panes.

Full Page Slide A printout in which the slide is fit to letter-size paper (8.5 by 11 inches).

Full-block style A business letter format that begins all lines at the left margin except for letterheads, tables, and block quotes. Also known as block style.

Function A prewritten Excel formula that takes a value or values, performs an operation, and returns a value or values.

Future value (Fv) In a loan, the value at the end of the time periods, or the cash balance you want to attain after the last loan payment is made. The future value for a loan is usually zero.

Gallery A visual display of selections from which you can choose.

Gateway A network device that enables communication between networks.

GB The abbreviation for gigabyte.

General format The default number format. It does not display commas or trailing zeros to the right of a decimal point.

Gesture A motion that is performed on a touch display that is interpreted as a command.

Gigabyte A unit of measure for storage devices. One gigabyte can store about one thousand digital photos.

Goal Seek A what-if analysis tool used to find a specific value for a cell by adjusting the value of another cell.

GPU A graphic processing unit.

Gradient fill Gradual progression of colors and shades, usually from one color to another, or from one shade to another shade of the same color, used to add a fill to a shape or placeholder. Gradients come in light and dark variations.

Graphic processing unit A card attached to the computer's main board to improve computer performance.

Graphical user interface A visual system used to interact with the computer.

Group A collection of objects treated as one unit that can be copied, moved, or formatted.

Group By An operator that designates which query column contains the group of values to summarize as a single record, one for each group.

GUI Graphical user interface.

Guide A line that displays on the ruler to give you a visual indication of where the pointer is positioned.

Handout A printout that features multiple slides on a single page; can contain between two and nine slides per page.

Hanging indent An indent where the first line extends to the left of the rest of the paragraph.

Hard disk drive A common storage device in desktop computers that stores data using magnetic charges.

HDD Hard disk drive.

Header A reserved area for text, graphics, and fields that displays at the top of each page in a document.

Header The text that prints at the top of each page of slide handouts.

Headings font Font applied to slide titles.

Home page The starting point for the remainder of the pages at a website.

Homegroup A Windows networking tool that makes it easy to share pictures, videos, music, documents, and devices such as printers.

Hosted e-mail A service used to provide e-mail addresses and related resources.

HTML document A text file with instructions for displaying its content in a web browser. *See also* Hypertext Markup Language document.

Hyperlink (PowerPoint) A connection from one slide to another slide in the same presentation or to a slide in another presentation, an email address, a web page, or a file.

Hyperlink Text or a graphic that you click to go to a file, a location in a file, a web page on the World Wide Web, or a web page on an organization's intranet.

Hyperlink data type A data type that stores links to websites or files located on your computer.

Hypertext Markup Language document A text file that includes instructions for displaying its content in a web browser.

Icon A small button used to represent a file, folder, or command.

IF function A logical function that checks whether criteria is met, and then returns one value when the condition is TRUE, and another value when the condition is FALSE.

Indent The position of paragraph lines in relation to the page margins.

Indeterminate relationship A relationship that does not enforce referential integrity.

Information processing cycle The four basic computer functions that work together in a cycle: input, processing, output, and storage.

InPrivate Browsing An Internet Explorer window that limits the browsing history that is written.

Input The process of gathering information from the user through input devices.

Input device Computer hardware such as keyboards, mice, touch displays, and microphones.

Input mask A set of special characters that control what can and cannot be entered in a field.

Insertion point A flashing vertical line that indicates where text will be inserted when you start typing.

Integrated graphics card A graphics card built into the computer's main board.

IntelliSense A feature that displays Quick Info, ToolTips, and AutoComplete boxes as you type.

Interest The charge for borrowing money; generally a percentage of the amount borrowed.

Internet A global collection of networks that facilitate electronic communication such as e-mail, file sharing, and the World Wide Web.

Internet Explorer A program used to browse the World Wide Web.

Internet service provider An organization that provides Internet connections, typically for a fee.

Internet zone The default security zone applied to all websites.

Intranet A web site that is accessed by only individuals within the organization.

IP address A unique set of numbers assigned to each computer on the Internet.

Is Not Null An operator that tests if a field contains a value (is not empty).

Is Null An operator that tests if a field is empty.

ISP Internet service provider.

Justified text A paragraph alignment that aligns the text with both the left and right margins.

Keep Source Formatting One of the Paste Options, applies the original formatting of the pasted text.

Keep Text Only One of the Paste Options, removes all formatting from the selection.

Keyboard An input device used to type characters and perform common commands.

Keyboard shortcut A combination of CTRL, ALT, WINDOWS, and character keys that perform a command when pressed.

Keyboard shortcut A combination of keys that performs a command.

Label Text data in a cell that identifies a number value.

Label A control on a form or in a report that describes other objects in the report or on the form.

Label report A report formatted so that the data can be printed on a sheet of labels.

Landscape An orientation that is wider than it is tall.

Layout A format that determines how data and labels are arranged in a form or report.

Layout (PowerPoint) The arrangement of the text and graphic elements or placeholders on a slide.

Layout gallery A visual *representation* of several content layouts that you can apply to a slide.

Layout view An Access view used to format a form or report while you are viewing a sample of the data.

Leader A series of characters that form a solid, dashed, or dotted line to fill the space preceding a tab stop.

Leader character The symbol used to fill the space in a leader.

Legend A box that identifies the patterns or colors that are assigned to the data series or categories in the chart.

Legend Identifies the patterns or colors that are assigned to the data in the chart.

Library A collection of folders and files assembled from various locations.

Line chart A chart type that illustrates trends over time, with time displayed along the x-axis and the data point values connected by a line.

Line spacing The vertical distance between lines of text in a paragraph; can be adjusted for each paragraph.

Linked table A table that exists in a file different from the one you are working on; created by an application such as Access or Excel but that can be opened as a table in Access.

List Level A hierarchy of bullets and sub-bullets; each level has its own formatting.

Live Preview A feature that displays what the results of a formatting change will be if you select it.

Local account An account where you can only access one computer and you must create separate accounts for each computer that you use.

Local intranet zone A security zone designed for web content stored on internal networks that is accessed only by those within the organization.

Lock screen A screen that displays shortly after you turn on a computer or device running Windows 8. It also displays when you are not signed in to prevent unauthorized individuals from logging on to your computer.

Logical function A function that applies a logical test to determine if a specific condition is met.

Logical test Any value or expression that can be evaluated as being TRUE or FALSE.

Long Text data type A data type that can store up to 65,535 characters in each record.

Macro A set of saved actions that you can use to automate tasks.

Macro action A prebuilt set of instructions that performs tasks when the macro is run.

Macro Builder An object tab with pre-built commands that you can select and modify to build a macro.

Mail merge A Word feature used to customize letters or labels by combining a main document with a data source.

Main document The mail merge document that contains the text that remains constant.

Malware A type of program designed to harm your computer, control your computer, or discover private information.

Manual page break A document feature that forces a page to end at a location you specify.

Margins The spaces between the text and the top, bottom, left, and right edges of the paper.

Masked character Text that is hidden by displaying characters such as bullets.

MAX function A function that returns the largest value in a range of cells.

Maximize (PowerPoint) A setting that keeps slide content as large as possible and allows some areas to be cropped if needed.

Maximize To size a window to fill the entire screen.

Merge Selected cells are combined into a single cell.

Merge field A field that merges and displays data from a specific column in the data source.

Metadata Information and personal data that is stored with your document.

MHTML file Another name for a web archive.

Microsoft account A single logon used to log on to Windows Cloud-based services such as Hotmail and SkyDrive.

Microsoft Office A suite of productivity programs.

MIN function A function that returns the smallest value in a range of cells.

Mini toolbar A toolbar with common formatting commands that displays near selected text.

Minimize To close a window but leave the application open and its button displayed on the taskbar.

Modal form A form with its Modal property set to Yes so that when the form opens, the Navigation Pane is collapsed, and when the form is closed, the Navigation Pane displays again.

Modem A device that translates signals between a router and an ISP.

Mouse An input device used to point to and click on screen elements.

Name A word that represents a cell or range of cells that can be used as a cell or range reference.

Name Box An area that displays the active cell reference.

Navigation bar A vertical or horizontal bar with hyperlinks to the main pages of a website.

Navigation form A form that contains a Navigation Control with tabs that you can use to quickly open forms and reports.

Navigation toolbar Displays in the lower left corner of the slide in Slide Show view; can be used to move to any slide while the slide show is running.

Network drive A hard drive that is accessed through a network.

Network interface card A card that connects a computer to a network.

NIC Network interface card.

Normal view (Excel) A view that maximizes the number of cells visible on the screen.

Normal View (PowerPoint) A view in which PowerPoint window is divided into two areas— the Slide pane and the left pane, which contains thumbnails of each slide.

Notebook The name given to a OneNote document. It is a loose structure of digital pages.

Notes page Printouts that contain the slide image in the top half of the page and speaker notes in the lower half of the page.

Notes pane The area of the Normal View window used to type notes that can be printed below an image of each slide.

NOW function A function that returns the serial number of the current date and time.

Nudge To move an object in small increments by pressing one of the arrow keys.

Number data type A data type that stores numeric values.

Number format A specific way that Excel displays numbers.

Number value Numeric data in a cell.

Numbered list A list of items with each item introduced by a consecutive number or letter to indicate definite steps, a sequence of actions, or chronological order.

Office 2013 RT A version of Office optimized for working on portable devices with touch screens such as Windows phones and tablets.

Office 365 A Cloud service built around the Office suite of programs.

Office on Demand A streaming version of Office that enables you to work from a computer that does not have Office installed.

Office RT An app version of Office designed to work on tablets with an ARM processor.

Office.com Clip Art A collection of online pictures, provided through Office.com, including pictures, drawings, and graphics.

On Click Animation begins the animation sequence when the mouse button is clicked or the spacebar is pressed.

One-to-many form A two-part form in which the main form displays in Single Form view and the related records display in a subform in Datasheet view.

One-to-many relationship A relationship in which a record in the first table can have many associated records in the second table.

OneDrive (formerly SkyDrive) A Cloud-based service that is used to store and share files.

OneNote A program used to collect notes, drawings, and media from multiple participants.

Online pictures A collection of images stored online and made available for use in presentations.

Onscreen keyboard A virtual keyboard that displays on a touch screen.

Open source software Software that can be sold or given away as long as the source code is provided for free.

OpenDocument Presentation A presentation that can be opened by PowerPoint and other presentation software, including Impress and Google Docs.

Operating system software Software that controls the way the computer works while it is running.

Operator precedence The mathematical rules for performing calculations within a formula.

Or logical operator A logical comparison of two criteria that is true if either of the criteria outcomes is true.

Organization chart A chart that graphically represents the reporting relationships between individuals and groups in an organization.

Orphan The first line of a paragraph that displays as the last line of a page.

Outline A printout that displays the slide text only.

Output The computer process of displaying information through output devices.

Output device Hardware that provides information to the user such as monitors, speakers, and printers.

Page Layout view A view used to adjust how a worksheet will look when it is printed.

Paint A drawing program that is installed with most versions of Windows.

Paragraph spacing The vertical distance above and below each paragraph; can be adjusted for each paragraph.

Password protect To require a password to open a shared file.

Paste A command that inserts a copy of the text or object from the Office Clipboard.

Paste area The target destination for data that has been cut or copied.

PDF document An image of a document that can be viewed using a PDF reader such as Adobe Acrobat Reader instead of the application that created the original document.

.pdf extension The file extension assigned to PDF documents.

PDF file *See* Portable Document Format file.

Peer-to-peer network A small network that connects computers and devices without the need for a server.

Permission level The privilege to read, rename, delete, or change a file.

Phishing website A dishonest website posing as a legitimate site to gain personal information, such as your logon and bank account number.

Photo album A presentation composed primarily of pictures.

Picture An image created with a scanner or digital camera and saved with a graphic file extension such as .jpg, .png, .tif, or .bmp.

Picture One of the Paste Options, pastes the text as a picture.

Picture effect A picture style that includes shadows, reflections, glows, soft edges, bevels, and 3-D rotations.

Picture Style Prebuilt set of formatting borders, effects, and layouts applied to a picture.

Pie chart A chart type that illustrates the relationship of parts to a whole.

Pie chart Used to illustrate percentages or proportions and includes only one data series.

Pinch Slide two fingers closer together to shrink or zoom out.

PivotTable report An interactive, cross-tabulated Excel report used to summarize and analyze data.

Placeholder A box with dotted borders; holds text or objects such as pictures, charts, and tables.

Placeholder A reserved, formatted space into which you enter your own text, pictures, charts, or tables. If nothing is entered, the placeholder text will not print.

Placeholder character A symbol in an input mask that is replaced as you type data into the field.

PMT function A function that calculates the payment for a loan based on constant payments and a constant interest rate.

Point A unit of measure with 72 points per inch typically used for font sizes and character spacing.

Pop-up A small window that displays in addition to the web page you are viewing.

Port The connectors on the outside of the computer to which you connect external devices.

Portable Document Format file A file format that preserves document layout and formatting so that files can be viewed in Word, Windows 8 Reader, or Adobe Acrobat Reader.

Portrait An orientation that is taller than it is wide.

PowerPoint 97-2003 Presentation A presentation which is saved in an older, .ppt format.

PowerPoint Picture Presentation A presentation in which each slide is saved as a picture, rather than a slide with individual components.

PowerPoint Presentation A presentation that can be opened using Microsoft PowerPoint.

PowerPoint Show A PowerPoint presentation which opens automatically as a slide show without the use of presentation software.

Present value (Pv) The total amount that a series of future payments is worth today, often the initial amount of a loan.

Presentation software Software used to arrange information in slides that can be projected on a large screen in front of an audience.

Presenter view A view available in which slides are projected in Slide Show view. Shows notes and slide on computer screen while only the slide is projected to the audience; requires only one monitor.

Primary key A field that uniquely identifies each record in a table.

Principal The initial amount of the loan; the total amount that a series of future payments is worth today. Also called the present value (Pv) of a loan.

Print A command that opens the Print dialog box so that you can select a different printer or different print options.

Print Preview A command that opens a preview of the table with Ribbon commands that enable you to make adjustments to the object you are printing.

Privacy policy A document that explains what types of information are collected and how the information will be used.

Processing The computer process of transforming, managing, and making decisions about the data and information.

Productivity software Software used to accomplish tasks such as reading and composing e-mail, writing documents, and managing tasks.

Program Another word for application or software.

Protected Mode A feature that makes it more difficult for malware to be installed on your computer.

Protected View A view applied to documents downloaded from the Internet that allows you to decide if the content is safe before working with the document.

Public A shared file that does not require a password.

Public computer A computer that is available to others when you are not using it.

Public web site A web site designed for public access.

QAT An acronym for Quick Access Toolbar.

Query A database object that displays a subset of data in response to a question; a database object used to ask questions about—query—the data stored in database tables.

Query design grid The lower half of the Query Design view window that contains the fields the query will display and the query settings that should be applied to each field.

Query design workspace The upper half of the Query Design view window that displays the tables that the query will search.

Question mark (?) wildcard A wildcard character that matches any single character.

Quick Access Toolbar A small toolbar that contains buttons for commonly used commands such as Save and Undo.

Quick Info An IntelliSense box with a message that explains the purpose of the selected AutoComplete command.

Quick Print A command that prints the object directly. You cannot make any adjustments to the object, choose a different printer, or change the printer settings.

Quick Start field A set of fields that can be added with a single click. For example, the Name Quick Start data type inserts the LastName and FirstName fields and assigns the Text data type to each.

Quick Style A style that can be accessed from a Ribbon gallery of thumbnails.

RAM Random access memory; a computer's temporary electronic memory.

Random access memory An electronic chip that provides temporary storage.

Range Two or more cells in a worksheet that are adjacent or nonadjacent.

Range finder An Excel feature that outlines all of the cells referenced in a formula. It is useful for verifying which cells are used in a formula and it can be used to edit formulas.

Rate The percentage that is paid for the use of borrowed money.

Read Mode A view that is used when you need to read, but not edit, electronic documents.

Read privilege A permission level that allows you to open the document, but not change it.

Reader A tablet-like computer designed to bring entertainment features such as books and movies.

Recently Used Fonts Listing of fonts you have selected and applied in the existing presentation.

Record A collection of related data, such as the contact information for a person.

Recycle Bin An area on your drive that stores files you no longer need.

Referential integrity A rule that keeps related values synchronized. For example, the foreign key value must be present in the related table.

Relative cell reference Refers to cells based on their position in relation to (relative to) the cell that contains the formula.

Replace A feature that finds and then replaces a character or string of characters, or in a selected range.

Report A database object that presents tables or query results in a way that is optimized for onscreen viewing or printing.

Report Layout view A view that can be used to format a report while viewing the report's data.

Report view A view optimized for onscreen viewing of reports.

Restricted sites zone A security zone in which you place sites that you explicitly do not trust.

Ribbon An application area that contains commands placed in groups that are organized by tabs.

Rich Text Format file A document file format designed to work with many different types of programs.

Right-click To click one time with the right mouse button.

Router A network device that enables communication between different networks.

Row heading The number that displays at the left of a row.

Royalty-free image An image that can be used in a publication after paying a one-time fee, rather than paying a fee each time the image is printed.

RTF file *See* Rich Text Format file.

Sans serif font A font where the letters do not have serifs.

Scanner An input device that can convert paper images into a digital image.

Screen saver An animation that displays on your screen after a set period of computer inactivity.

Screenshot A snapshot of any window that is open on your desktop.

Script Code downloaded from a web page that provides additional functionality.

SDD Solid-state Disk Drive.

Search provider A website that provides a way for you to search for information on the web.

Search suggestion A word or phrase that displays as you type in a search box.

Section A portion of a document that can be formatted differently from the rest of the document.

Section break A nonprinting character that marks the end of one section and the beginning of another section.

Select query A type of query that selects and displays the records that answer a question without changing the data in the table.

Separator character A character such as a tab or comma designated as the character to separate columns of unformatted text.

Serial number A sequential number.

Series A group of things that come one after another in succession; for example, the months January, February, March.

Serif An extra detail or hook at the end of a character stroke.

Serif font A font where the letters have serifs or extra details or hooks at the end of each stroke.

Server A computer dedicated to providing services to other computers on a network.

Setting A saved preference that changes the way Windows or a program behaves or appears.

SharePoint A web application server designed for organizations to develop an intranet.

Shift-click To click a file while holding down the Shift key. Shift-clicking is often used to select a continuous range of files.

Short Text data type A data type that stores up to 255 characters of text.

Sign in The process of connecting to a computer.

Sign-in screen The screen you use to type your logon information.

Single Form view A view that displays one record at a time with field names in the first column and field values in the second column.

Site index A page of hyperlinks that outline a website.

Site map Another name for site index.

Sizing handle A small square or circle on an object's border that is used to resize the object by dragging.

SkyDrive See OneDrive.

Slide (PowerPoint) An individual page in a presentation that can contain text, pictures, or other objects.

Slide (touch screen) Touch an object and then move the finger across the screen.

Slide handout A printed image of slides on a sheet of paper.

Slide master The highest level slide in a hierarchy of slides, stores theme and slide layout information.

Slide show A series of pictures that change at a set interval.

Slide Sorter view The view that displays all of the slides in your presentation as thumbnails.

Slide transition A motion effect that occurs in a slide show as you move from one slide to another.

Small caps A font effect that displays all characters in uppercase while making any character originally typed as an uppercase letter taller than the ones typed as lowercase letters.

Smart Guide A dashed line that appears on the slide when objects are spaced nearly evenly; indicates when objects are evenly spaced.

Smart phone A cellular phone with an operating system.

SmartArt graphic A visual representation of information that you can use to communicate your message or ideas effectively.

SmartScreen Filter A feature that helps protect you from online threats.

Snap To quickly position a window to either half of the screen by dragging the title bar and the pointer to the screen's edge.

Snip A screenshot created with the Snipping Tool.

Snipping Tool An application used to create screenshots called snips.

Social media A Cloud service where content is shared through the interactions of people connected through social networks.

Software A set of instructions stored on your computer.

Solid-state disk drive A drive that that stores data using electricity and retains the data when the power is turned off.

Source The reference used to find information or data.

Source data The data that is used to create a PivotTable.

Sparkline A chart contained in a single cell that is used to show data trends.

Speech recognition An input technology that performs commands or types text based on words spoken into a microphone.

Split bar A bar that splits a document into two windows.

Spreadsheet The primary document that you use in Excel to store and work with data; also called a worksheet.

Spreadsheet software Software used to organize information in a tabular structure with numeric data, labels, formulas, and charts.

SQL select query A command that selects data from a data source based on the criteria you specify.

Start screen The initial screen that displays when starting PowerPoint 2013, Word 2013, or Excel 2013.

Start screen app An application that runs from the Start screen.

Statistical function A predefined function that describes a collection of data; for example, totals, counts, and averages.

Storage The location where data resides on a computer.

Storage device Computer hardware that stores information after a computer is powered off.

Streaming media A Cloud-based service that provides video and music as you watch or listen to it.

Stretch Slide two fingers apart to enlarge or zoom in.

Student data file A file that you need to complete a project in a textbook.

Style A prebuilt collection of formatting settings that can be assigned to text.

Stylus A pen-like pointing device used with touch screens.

Subdatasheet A datasheet that displays related records from another table by matching the values in the field that relates the two tables. In a datasheet, the subdatasheet displays below each record.

SUM An Excel function that adds all the numbers in a range of cells.

Sum An operator that calculates the total of the values in each group.

Summary sheet A worksheet that displays and summarizes totals from other worksheets.

Summary statistic A calculation for each group of data such as a total, an average, or a count.

Superscript Text that is positioned higher and smaller than the other text.

Swipe Slide in from a screen edge to display app commands, charms, or other temporary areas.

Synonym Words with the same meaning.

Tab scrolling buttons The buttons to the left of the worksheet tabs used to display Excel worksheet tabs that are not in view.

Tab stop A specific location on a line of text marked on the Word ruler to which you can move the insertion point by pressing the Tab key.

Tabbed browsing A feature that you use to open multiple web pages in the same browser window.

Table (Access) A database object that stores the database data so that records are in rows and fields are in columns.

Table The object that stores the data by organizing it into rows and columns. Each column is a field, and each row is a record.

Table Design view An Access view that features table fields and their properties.

Table style Borders and fill colors applied to the entire table in a manner consistent with the presentation theme.

Tablet A portable computer built around a single touch screen.

Tabular layout A layout in which the controls are positioned as table cells in rows and columns.

Tap To touch once with the finger.

Taskbar An area that displays buttons along the bottom of the desktop that represent applications and windows.

TB The abbreviation for terabyte.

Template A pre-built document into which you insert text using the layout and formatting provided in that document.

Template (Excel) A pre-built workbook used as a pattern for creating new workbooks; used to build workbooks without having to start from a blank workbook.

Temporary Internet file A copy of a web page and its images stored in your personal folder. This is used to improve the time that it takes for a frequently visited page to display.

Terabyte A unit of measure for storage devices. One terabyte is approximately a thousand gigabytes.

Text Alignment The placement of text within a placeholder.

Text box (Access) A control on a form or in a report that displays the data from a field in a table or query.

Text box (PowerPoint) An object used to position text anywhere on a slide.

Text box (Word) A movable, resizable container for text or graphics.

Text effect A prebuilt set of decorative formats, such as outlines, shadows, text glow, and colors, that make text stand out in a document.

Text value Character data in a cell that labels number values.

Text wrap A format that displays text on multiple lines within a cell.

The Cloud The collection of services provided by Cloud computing.

Theme A group of pre-built settings, including desktop background, window border color, screen saver, and system sounds.

Theme (PowerPoint) Set of unified, pre-built design elements—colors, fonts, and effects—that provides a unique look for your presentation.

Theme variant Variations of the current theme, with different accent colors.

Thesaurus A reference that lists words that have the same or similar meaning to the word you are looking up.

Three-color scale A conditional format that compares a range of cells and applies a gradation of three colors; the shades represent higher, middle, or lower values.

Three-dimensional Refers to an image that appears to have all three spatial dimensions: length, width, and depth.

Thumb drive Another name for a USB flash drive.

Thumbnail A small graphic representing a larger picture or photo.

Tile A small window that runs an application that presents live, updated information.

TODAY function A function that returns the serial number of the current date.

Toggle button A button used to turn a feature both on and off.

Top-level domain Letters after a domain name that specify the type of organization sponsoring a website—*.gov*, for example.

Top/Bottom Rules A conditional format used to apply formatting to the highest and lowest values in a range of cells.

Total row A row that displays as the last row in an Excel table and provides summary functions in drop-down lists for each column.

Touch display A screen that interprets commands when you touch it with your finger.

Touchpad A flat area on which you can move the finger to position the pointer.

TPL An acronym for Tracking Protection List.

Tracking cookie Gathers information about your web browsing behaviors across multiple websites. They are used to provide ads and services based on your interests.

Tracking Protection List An Internet Explorer add-on that helps prevent websites from collecting information about your visit.

Truncated Cut off.

Trusted sites zone A security zone in which you place sites that you trust not to harm your computer.

Two-color scale A conditional format that compares a range of cells and applies a gradation of two colors; the shade of the color represents higher or lower values.

Underlying formula The formula as displayed in the formula bar.

Underlying value Data displayed in the formula bar.

Unicode (UTF-8) A system for representing a large variety of text characters and symbols. It is used often in HTML documents.

Uniform Resource Locator The unique address of a page on the Internet.

Unsecured network A network that does not require a password to connect to it.

Unzip To decompress a compressed (zipped) folder.

URL Uniform Resource Locator, or web address.

USB flash drive A small, portable solid-state drive about the size of the human thumb.

Use Destination Theme One of the Paste Options, applies the formatting of the slide to which the text is pasted.

Utility program A small program designed to perform a routine task or computer housekeeping task.

Validation rule A field property that requires that specific values be entered into a field.

Value Data in a cell.

Value axis The axis that displays the worksheet's numeric data.

Vertical alignment The space above and below a text or object in relation to the top and bottom of a table cell or top and bottom margins.

Volatile The result of a function that does not remain as entered, but is updated each time the workbook is opened.

Web Another name for World Wide Web.

Web album A Cloud-based service that you use to store, organize, and share photos and video.

Web app An application that runs in a web browser.

Web archive A file that saves web page text and pictures in a single file. These files are typically assigned the *.mht* file extension.

Web browser A program used to navigate the World Wide Web.

Website A collection of connected pages located at a single domain name.

Widow The last line of a paragraph that displays as the first line of a page.

Wildcard A special character, such as an asterisk, used in query criteria to allow matches for any combination of letters or characters.

Windows 8 Store app Software that is downloaded and installed from the Windows 8 Store and run in the Start screen.

Wired network A network that transmits signals through wires.

Wireless network A network that transmits signals via radio waves.

With Previous Animation begins the animation sequence at the same time as any animation preceding it or, if it is the first animation, with the slide transition.

Word processing software Software used to create, edit, format, and print documents containing primarily text and graphics.

Word wrap Words at the right margin automatically move to the next line if they do not fit.

WordArt (PowerPoint) A pre-built set of fills, outlines, and effects used to create decorative effects in your presentation.

WordArt (Word) A set of graphic text styles that can be used to make text look like a graphic.

Workbook A file that you can use to organize various kinds of related information.

Worksheet The primary document that you use in Excel to store and work with data; also called a spreadsheet.

Worksheet tab The labels along the lower border of the workbook window that identify each worksheet or chart sheet.

World Wide Web A collection of linked pages designed to be viewed from any computer connected to the Internet.

WWW An acronym for World Wide Web.

X-axis Another name for the horizontal axis.

XML Paper Specification A file format that preserves formatting and embeds its fonts in such a way that it can be shared on many different devices and programs.

XPS An acronym for XML Paper Specification.

Y-axis Another name for the vertical axis.

Yes/No data type A data type that stores variables that can have one of two possible values—for example, yes or no, or true or false.

Zipped folder Another name for a compressed folder.

Index